Fodor's 2010

NORTHERN CALIFORNIA

Fodor's Travel Publications, New York, Toronto, London, Sydney, Auckland

www.fodors.com

Excerpted from *Fodor's California 2010*

Be a Fodor's Correspondent

Share your trip with Fodor's

Our latest guidebook to Northern California—now in full color—owes its success to travelers like you. Throughout, you'll find photographs submitted by members of Fodors.com to our "Show Us Your . . . California" photo contest. On page 8 you'll find the grand prize-winning photograph by Jay Anderson of a lone hang glider off the coast of Fort Funston.

We are especially proud of this color edition. No other guide to Northern California is as up to date or has as much practical planning information, along with hundreds of color photographs and illustrated maps. We've also included "Word of Mouth" quotes from travelers who shared their experiences with others on our forums. If you're inspired and can plan a better trip because of this guide, we've done our job.

We invite you to join the travel conversation: Your opinion matters to us and to your fellow travelers. Come to Fodors.com to plan your trip, share an experience, ask a question, submit a photograph, post a review, or write a trip report. Tell our editors about your trip. They want to know what went well and how we can make this guide even better. Share your opinions at our feedback center at fodors.com/feedback, or email us at editors@fodors.com with the subject line "Northern California Editor." You might find your comments published in a future Fodor's guide. We look forward to hearing from you.

Happy Traveling!

Tim Jarrell, Publisher

FODOR'S NORTHERN CALIFORNIA 2010

Editors: Michael Nalepa, *lead editor*; Linda Cabasin, Erica Duecy, Paul Eisenberg, Robert I. C. Fisher, Maria Teresa Hart, Rachel Klein, Molly Moker, Jennifer Paull

Editorial Contributors: Cheryl Crabtree, Lisa M. Hamilton, Denise M. Leto, Fiona G. Parrott, Reed Parsell, Natasha Sarkisian, Sharon Silva, Sharron S. Wood, Sura Wood, Christine Vovakes, Bobbi Zane

Production Editor: Carrie Parker
Maps & Illustrations: Mark Stroud, Moon Street Cartography; David Lindroth, Inc., *cartographers*; Bob Blake, Rebecca Baer, *map editors*; William Wu, *information graphics*
Design: Fabrizio La Rocca, *creative director*; Guido Caroti, Siobhan O'Hare, *art directors*; Tina Malaney, Chie Ushio, Ann McBride, Jessica Walsh, *designers*; Melanie Marin, *senior picture editor*
Cover Photo: (Mountain Vineyard, Napa Valley): Martin Sundberg/Uppercut/ Getty Images
Production Manager: Angela L. McLean

COPYRIGHT

ISBN 978-1-4000-0900-8

ISSN 1543-1045

SPECIAL SALES

This book is available at special discounts for bulk purchases for sales promotions or premiums. Special editions, including personalized covers, excerpts of existing books, and corporate imprints, can be created in large quantities for special needs. For more information, write to Special Markets/Premium Sales, 1745 Broadway, MD 6-2, New York, New York 10019, or e-mail specialmarkets@randomhouse.com.

AN IMPORTANT TIP & AN INVITATION

Although all prices, opening times, and other details in this book are based on information supplied to us at press time, changes occur all the time in the travel world, and Fodor's cannot accept responsibility for facts that become outdated or for inadvertent errors or omissions. So **always confirm information when it matters,** especially if you're making a detour to visit a specific place. Your experiences—positive and negative—matter to us. If we have missed or misstated something, **please write to us.** We follow up on all suggestions. Contact the Northern California editor at editors@fodors.com or c/o Fodor's at 1745 Broadway, New York, NY 10019.

PRINTED IN SINGAPORE

10 9 8 7 6 5 4 3 2 1

CONTENTS

Fodor's Features

MAPS

ABOUT THIS BOOK

Our Ratings

Sometimes you find terrific travel experiences, and sometimes they just find you. But usually the burden is on you to select the right combination of experiences. That's where our ratings come in.

As travelers we've all discovered a place so wonderful that its worthiness is obvious, a place is so unique that superlatives don't do it justice. These sights, properties, and experiences get our highest rating, **Fodor's Choice,** indicated by orange stars.

Black stars highlight sights and properties we deem **Highly Recommended,** places that our writers, editors, and readers praise for consistency and excellence.

By default, there's another category: any place we include in this book is by definition worth your time, unless we say otherwise. And we will.

Disagree with any of our choices? Care to nominate a place or suggest that we rate one more highly? Visit our feedback center at www.fodors.com/feedback.

Budget Well

Hotel and restaurant price categories from ¢ to $$$$ are defined in the opening pages of each chapter. For attractions, we always give standard adult admission fees; reductions are usually available for children, students, and senior citizens. Want to pay with plastic? **AE, D, DC, MC, V** following restaurant and hotel listings indicate whether American Express, Discover, Diners Club, MasterCard, and Visa are accepted.

Restaurants

Unless we state otherwise, restaurants are open for lunch and dinner daily. We mention dress only when there's a specific requirement and reservations only when they're essential or not accepted—it's always best to book ahead.

Hotels

Hotels have private bath, phone, TV, and air-conditioning and operate on the European Plan (aka EP, meaning without meals), unless we specify that they use the Continental Plan (CP, with a Continental breakfast), Breakfast Plan (BP, with a full breakfast), or Modified American Plan (MAP, with breakfast and dinner), or are all-inclusive (AI, including all meals and most activities).

We always list facilities but not whether you'll be charged an extra fee to use them.

Listings

- ★ Fodor's Choice
- ★ Highly recommended
- ✉ Physical address
- ✥ Directions or Map Coordinates
- 📫 Mailing address
- ☎ Telephone
- 📠 Fax
- 🌐 On the Web
- ✉ E-mail
- 🎟 Admission fee
- ⏲ Open/closed times
- Ⓜ Metro stations
- 💳 Credit cards

Hotels & Restaurants

- 🏨 Hotel
- 🛏 Number of rooms
- 👍 Facilities
- 🍽 Meal plans
- ✕ Restaurant
- ✍ Reservations
- 🚬 Smoking
- 🍷 BYOB
- ✕🏨 Hotel with restaurant that warrants a visit

Outdoors

- 🏌 Golf
- ⛺ Camping

Other

- 👶 Family-friendly
- ⇨ See also
- ✉ Branch address
- ☞ Take note

Experience Northern California

WHAT'S NEW IN NORTHERN CALIFORNIA

Kitchen Confidential

In Yountville, Thomas Keller, creator of the haute French Laundry, has gone casual offering affordable prix fixes at his new eatery, Ad Hoc. As the name implies, it was supposed to be temporary; now it's open nightly for casual dinners.

Grape Expectations

Oenophiles mourned the death of pioneer winemaker Robert Mondavi in 2008; as honors to the master winemaker continue, so does the crush.

Other familiar names also warrant toasts, though they're not ones you'd necessarily associate with viticulture. Famed film director Francis Ford Coppola acquired Chateau Souverain (now renamed Rosso & Bianco) in Geyserville; and the Jacuzzi family built a new winery in the Carneros region south of Sonoma Valley.

Leave the Driving to Amtrak

Riding the rails can be a very satisfying experience, particularly in California where the distances between destinations can run into the hundreds of miles. You can save money on gas and parking, avoid freeway traffic, and see some of the best the state has to offer.

The best trip is on the new, luxuriously appointed Coast Starlight, a long-distance train with sleeping cars that runs between Seattle and Los Angeles, passing some of California's most beautiful coastline as it hugs the beach. For the best surfside viewing, get a seat or a room on the left side of the train and ride south to north from San Diego to Oakland.

Head for the Hills

Things are looking up for visitors to California's alpine recreation areas, thanks to a host of enhancements. As part of a fittingly gigantic redevelopment project, Mammoth Mountain opened its Top of the Sierra Interpretive Center in spring of 2007 (at an altitude of 11,053 feet, they do mean *top*); and the Westin Monache condominium-hotel, anchor of the Village at Mammoth, is expected to open in time for the upcoming ski season.

Amenities are going upscale around Lake Tahoe, too, with the Ritz-Carlton Highlands breaking ground at Northstar and a ski-in, ski-out complex (Thunder Mountain Lodge) in the works for Kirkwood.

It's Easy Being Green

OK, it isn't *easy,* but San Francisco proves it's viable. The city is in the midst of an environmentally friendly building boom, and you can visit one of the signature structures when the California Academy of Sciences—home of the Natural History Museum, Morrison Planetarium, and Steinhart Aquarium—to see how well sustainable construction can be done.

Homegrown Hospitality

Agritourism in California isn't new (remember, Knott's Berry Farm once *was* a berry farm), but it is on the rise, with farm tours and agricultural festivals sprouting up everywhere.

Wine country is a particularly fertile area—spurred by the success of vineyards, the area's lavender growers and olive-oil producers have started welcoming visitors.

In the Central Valley, America's number-one producer of stone fruit, you can travel themed tourist routes (like Fresno County's Blossom Trail) and tour herb gardens, fruit orchards, organic dairies, and pumpkin patches.

WHEN TO GO

Because it offers activities indoors and out, San Francisco is an all-season destination. Early spring—when the gray whale migration overlaps with the end of the elephant seal breeding season and the start of the bird migration—is the optimal time to visit Point Reyes National Seashore. Yosemite is ideal in the late spring because roads closed in winter are reopened, the summer crowds have yet to arrive, and the park's waterfalls—swollen with melting snow—run fast. Autumn is "crush time" in Napa and Sonoma valleys. Snowfall makes winter peak season for skiers in Mammoth Mountain and Lake Tahoe, where runs typically open around Thanksgiving. (They sometimes remain in operation into June.)

Climate

It's difficult to generalize much about the state's weather beyond saying that precipitation comes in winter and summers are dry in most places. As a rule, inland regions are hotter in summer and colder in winter, compared with coastal areas, which are relatively cool year-round. As you climb into the mountains, seasonal variations are more apparent: winter brings snow (at elevations above 3,000 feet), autumn is crisp, spring can go either way, and summer is sunny and warm (except in San Francisco, where all bets are off).

Microclimates

Mountains separate the California coastline from the state's interior, and the weather can sometimes vary dramatically within a 15-minute drive. On a foggy summer day in San Francisco you'll be grateful for a sweater—but head 50 mi north inland to Napa Valley and you'll likely be content in short sleeves. Day and nighttime temperatures can also vary greatly. Temperature swings elsewhere can be even more extreme. Take Sacramento. On August afternoons the mercury hits the 90s and occasionally exceeds 100°F. Yet as darkness falls, it often plummets to 40°F.

Forecasts

National Weather Service (*www.wrh.noaa.gov*).

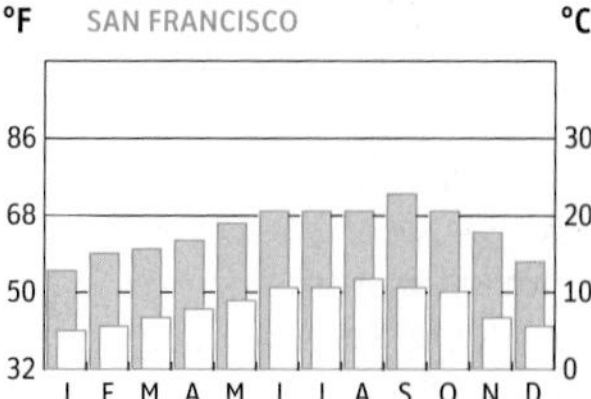

WHAT'S WHERE

The following numbers refer to chapters.

2 The Central Coast. Three of the state's top stops—swanky Santa Barbara, Hearst Castle, and Big Sur—are here.

3 Monterey Bay Area. Postcard-perfect Monterey, surfer's paradise Santa Cruz, Victorian-flavored Pacific Grove, and exclusive Carmel all share this stretch of California coast.

4 San Francisco. To see why so many have left their hearts here, you need to veer off the beaten path and into the city's neighborhoods—posh Pacific Heights, the Hispanic Mission, and gay-friendly Castro.

5 The Bay Area. The area that rings San Francisco is nothing like the city—but you'll find countless cultural and natural draws here.

6 The Wine Country. Napa and Sonoma counties retain their title as *the* California wine country by virtue of award-winning vintages, luxe lodgings, and epicurean eats.

7 The North Coast. The star attractions here are the natural ones, from the secluded beaches and wave-battered bluffs of Point Reyes National Seashore to the towering redwood forests.

8 Redwood National Park. Over 200 mi of trails allow visitors to see these spectacular trees in their primitive environments.

9 The Southern Sierra. In the Mammoth Lakes region sawtooth mountains and deep powdery snowdrifts combine to create the state's premier conditions for skiing and snowboarding.

10 Yosemite National Park. The views immortalized by photographer Ansel Adams—of towering granite monoliths, verdant glacial valleys, and lofty waterfalls—are still camera-ready.

11 Sequoia and Kings Canyon National Parks. The sight of ancient redwoods towering above jagged mountains will take your breath away.

12 Sacramento and the Gold Country. The 1849 gold rush began here, and the former mining camps strung along 185 mi of Highway 49 replay their past to the hilt.

13 Lake Tahoe. With miles of crystalline water reflecting the peaks of the High Sierra, this is the perfect setting for hiking and golfing in summer and skiing in winter.

14 The Far North. California's far northeast corner has a backwoods character that appeals to outdoorsy types.

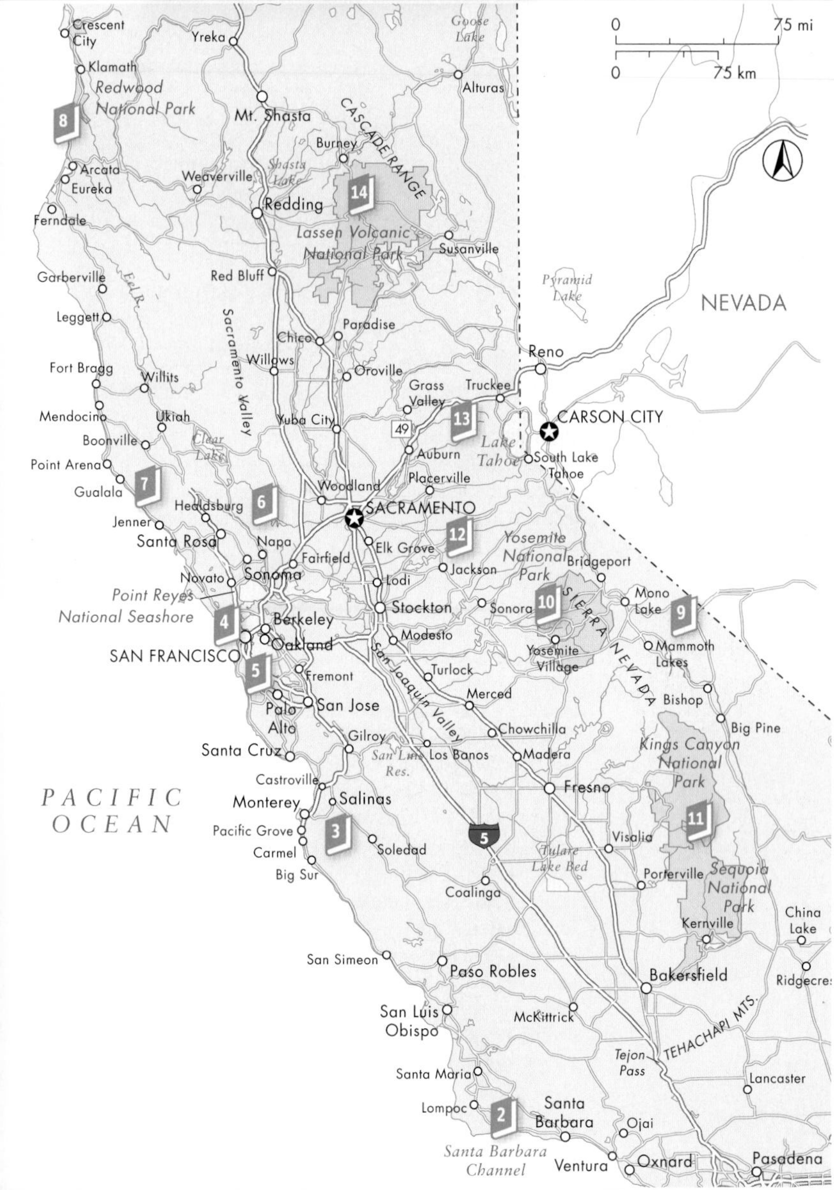

1

Crescent City
Yreka
Goose Lake
0 75 mi
0 75 km
Klamath
Alturas
Redwood National Park
8
Mt. Shasta
CASCADE RANGE
Burney
Arcata
Eureka
Weaverville
Shasta Lake
14
Redding
Ferndale
Lassen Volcanic National Park
Susanville
Garberville
Eel R.
Red Bluff
Pyramid Lake
NEVADA
Leggett
Sacramento Valley
Paradise
Chico
Fort Bragg
Willows
Reno
Oroville
Willits
Grass Valley
Truckee
Mendocino
Ukiah
Yuba City
13
CARSON CITY
49
Boonville
Clear Lake
Lake Tahoe
Auburn
Point Arena
South Lake Tahoe
Gualala
7
Placerville
Woodland
6
Healdsburg
SACRAMENTO
Jenner
12
Santa Rosa
Napa
Elk Grove
Yosemite National Park
Fairfield
Bridgeport
Novato
Sonoma
Jackson
Point Reyes National Seashore
Lodi
SIERRA NEVADA
Mono Lake
9
Stockton
Sonora
10
4
Berkeley
Modesto
Oakland
Mammoth Lakes
Yosemite Village
SAN FRANCISCO
5
Fremont
Turlock
San Joaquin Valley
Merced
Bishop
Palo Alto
San Jose
Big Pine
Chowchilla
Gilroy
Kings Canyon National Park
Santa Cruz
San Luis Res.
Los Banos
Madera
Castroville
Fresno
PACIFIC OCEAN
Monterey
Salinas
Pacific Grove
3
11
Carmel
Soledad
5
Visalia
Big Sur
Tulare Lake Bed
Porterville
Sequoia National Park
Coalinga
China Lake
Kernville
San Simeon
Paso Robles
Ridgecrest
Bakersfield
San Luis Obispo
McKittrick
TEHACHAPI MTS.
Tejon Pass
Santa Maria
Lancaster
Lompoc
2
Santa Barbara
Ojai
Santa Barbara Channel
Ventura
Oxnard
Pasadena

NORTHERN CALIFORNIA PLANNER

Flying In

Air travelers beginning or ending their vacation in San Francisco have two main airports to choose from: San Francisco International (SFO) or Oakland International (OAK) across the Bay. The former lands you closer to the city core (ground transportation will take about 20 minutes versus 35); but the latter is less heavily trafficked and less prone to pesky fog delays. Both airports are served by BART, the Bay Area's affordable rapid-transit system. So your decision will probably rest on which one has the best fares and connections for your particular route.

If your final destination is Monterey or Carmel, San Jose International Airport (SJC), about 40 mi south of San Francisco, is another alternative.

Driving Around

Driving may be a way of life in California, but it isn't cheap (gas prices here are usually among the highest in the nation). It's also not for the fainthearted; you've surely heard horror stories about California's freeways, but even the state's scenic highways and byways have their own hassles. For instance, on the dramatic coastal road between San Simeon and Carmel, twists, turns, and divinely distracting vistas frequently slow traffic; in rainy season mud slides can close the road altogether. **■ TIP→Never cross the double line when driving these roads. If you see that cars are backing up behind you on a long two-lane, no-passing stretch, do everyone (and yourself) a favor and use the first available pullout.**

On California's notorious freeways, other rules apply. Nervous Nellies must resist the urge to stay in the two slow-moving ones on the far right, used primarily by trucks. To drive at least the speed limit, get yourself in the middle lane. If you're ready to bend the rules a bit, the second (lanes are numbered from 1 starting at the center) lane moves about 5 mi faster. But avoid the far-left lane (the one next to the carpool lane), where speeds range from 75 MPH to 90 MPH.

FAQ

I'm not particularly active. Will I still enjoy visiting a national park? Absolutely, the most popular parks really do have something for everyone. Take Yosemite. When the ultrafit embark on 12-hour trail treks, mere mortals can hike Cook's Meadow—an easy 1-mi loop that's also wheelchair accessible. If even that seems too daunting, you can hop on a free shuttle or drive yourself to sites like Glacier Point or the Mariposa Grove of Giant Sequoias.

What's the single best place to take the kids? Well, that depends on your children's ages and interests, but for its sheer smorgasbord of activities, San Francisco is hard to beat. A cable car ride is a no-brainer—but if you have a Thomas the Tank engine fan in tow, be sure to also take a spin on the historic F-line Trolleys. Other classic kid-friendly SF sights include the Exploratorium, the San Francisco Zoo, Alcatraz, the Ferry Building, and the California Academy of Sciences.

But San Francisco is filled with more offbeat activities for adventurous families. Take the kids for dim sum in Chinatown; odds are they'll enjoy picking their dishes from a rolling buffet filled with foods they've likely never seen before. Or head to Musée Mécanique to see what kids played (way) before Nintendo's Wii came out.

Need to blow off some steam? Then head to one of the city's great outdoor venues: Golden Gate Park, the Western Shoreline, the Presidio, or Aquatic Park. If you want to get out of town, take a ferry ride to Sausalito or head to Muir Woods—if you think these massive trees are tall, imagine seeing them from two or three feet lower. Up for a less wild outdoor experience? Then catch a Giants game at beautiful AT&T Park.

California sounds expensive. How can I save on sightseeing? If you're focusing on San Francisco, consider taking a pass—a Go Card Pass (☎*800/887–9103* 🌐*www.gocardusa.com*) that is. Sold in one-day to one-week versions, they're priced from $55 and cover dozens of tours and attractions in the city.

Many museums set aside free-admission days; call ahead to see if any of your planned stops have free days during your trip.

Prefer the great outdoors? An $80 American the Beautiful annual pass (☎*888/275–8747* 🌐*www.nps.gov*) admits you to every site under the National Park Service umbrella. Better yet, depending on the property, passengers in your vehicle get in free, too.

I'm not crazy about spending 14 nights in hotels. Any alternatives? If you want to pretend you're lucky enough to live in California, try a vacation- or time-share rental. Aside from providing privacy (a boon for families and groups), a rental lets you set your own schedule and cook at your leisure (you'll save money, plus it's a great excuse to stock up on that fine California produce!). In terms of coverage, geographically and pricewise, HomeAway (🌐*www.homeaway.com*) is a good place for house hunting. It lists more than 4,000 condos, cottages, beach houses, ski chalets, and villas. *For more information on California trip planning, see the Planning sections at the beginning of each chapter and at the Travel Smart Northern California chapter at the back of the book.*

CALIFORNIA TODAY

The People

California is as much a state of mind as a state in the union—a kind of perpetual Promised Land that has represented many things to many people.

In the 18th century, Spanish missionaries came seeking converts. In the 19th, miners rushed here to search for gold. And, in the years since, a long line of Dust Bowl farmers, land speculators, Haight-Ashbury hippies, migrant workers, dot-commers, real estate speculators, and would-be actors came chasing their own dreams.

The result is a population that leans toward idealism—without necessarily being as liberal as you might think. (Remember, this is Ronald Reagan's old stomping ground.) And despite the stereotype of the blue-eyed, blond surfer, California's population is not homogeneous either. Ten million people who live here (more than 28% of Californians) are foreign born—including Governor Schwarzenegger. Almost half hail from neighboring Mexico; another third emigrated from Asia, following the waves of Chinese workers who arrived in the 1860s to build the railroads and subsequent waves of refugees from the Vietnam War.

The Politics

What's blue and red and green all over? California: a predominantly Democratic state with a red-hot Republican governor and an aggressive "go green" agenda.

When Governor Arnold Schwarzenegger departs from his office in 2010, he'll leave a legacy of introducing several environmental initiatives—most notably placing strict controls on greenhouse gas emissions—that have been lauded in some quarters and decried in others. He also tried to get universal health care reform and stood up for reform of immigration laws, and the debates these issues generate, logically enough, lead to a fair bit of infighting in Sacramento.

But that isn't stopping Californians from taking them to the national level. Residents of this large, rich, heavily populated state—which certainly contributes its fair share to the federal budget—will tell you that's only fair.

The Economy

Leading all other states in terms of the income generated by agriculture, tourism, and industrial activity, California has the country's strongest and most diverse state economy. Moreover, with a gross state product of over $1.6 trillion, California would be one of the top ten economies *in the world* if it were an independent nation.

But the Golden State's economic history is filled with boom and bust cycles—beginning with the mid-19th-century gold rush that started it all—and California (and the rest of the nation) is in the midst of a recession affecting most segments of the economy.

Optimists, however, already have their eyes on the next potential boom: "green companies" focused on alternative energy, renewables, electric cars, and the like.

The Culture

Cultural organizations thrive in California. San Francisco—a city with only about 775,000 residents—has well-regarded ballet, opera, and theater companies, and is home to one of the continent's most noteworthy orchestras. Museums like San Francisco Museum of Modern Art (SFMOMA) and the de Young also represent the city's ongoing commitment to the arts.

The Parks and Preserves

Cloud-spearing redwood groves, snow-tipped mountains, canyon-slashed deserts, primordial lava beds, and a seemingly endless coast: California's natural diversity is staggering—and efforts to protect it started early.

The first national park here was established in 1890, and the National Park Service now oversees 30 sites in California (more than in any other state). When you factor in 278 state parks—which encompass underwater preserves, wildlife reserves, dune systems, and other sensitive habitats—the number of acres involved is almost as impressive as the topography itself.

Due to encroaching development and pollution, keeping these natural treasures in pristine condition is an ongoing challenge. For instance, Sequoia and Kings Canyon (which is plagued by pesticides and other agricultural pollutants blown in from the San Joaquin Valley) has been named America's "smoggiest park" by the National Parks Conservation Association, and the Environmental Protection Agency has designated it as an "ozone non-attainment area with levels of ozone pollution that threaten human health."

The Cuisine

California gave us McDonald's, Denny's, Carl's Jr., Taco Bell, and, of course, In-N-Out Burger. Fortunately for those of us with fast-clogging arteries, the state also kick-started the organic food movement. Back in the 1970s California-based chefs put American cuisine on the culinary map by focusing on freshly prepared seasonal ingredients.

Today this focus has spawned the "locavore" movement—followers try to only consume food produced within a 100-mi radius of where they live, since processing and refining food and transporting goods over long distances is bad for both the body and the environment. This isn't much of a restriction in California, where a huge variety of crops grow year-round. Some 350 cities and towns have certified farmers' markets—and their stalls are filled to overflowing.

California has been America's top agricultural producer for the last 50 years, growing more fruits and vegetables than any other state. Dairies and ranches also thrive here, and fishing fleets harvest fish and shellfish from the rich waters offshore.

QUINTESSENTIAL NORTHERN CALIFORNIA

The Wine

If California were a country, it would rank as the world's fourth-largest wine producer, after Italy, France, and Spain. In those countries, where vino is barely considered an alcoholic beverage, wine drinking has evolved into a relaxing ritual best shared with friends and family. A modern, Americanized version of that mentality integrates wine into daily life in California, and there are many places to sample it. The Napa and Sonoma valleys come to mind first. However, there are other destinations for oenophiles who want a vintage vacation. You can find great wineries around Santa Barbara County, Monterey Bay, and Gold Country's Shenandoah Valley, too. All are respected appellations, and their winery tours and tastings will show you what all the buzz is about.

The Beach

California's beach culture is, in a word, legendary. Of course, it only makes sense that folks living in a state with a 1,264-mi coastline (a hefty portion of which sees the sun upward of 300 days a year) would perfect the art of beach-going. True aficionados begin with a reasonably fit physique, plus a stylish wardrobe consisting of flip-flops, bikinis, wet suits, and such. Mastery of at least one beach skill—surfing, boogie boarding, kayaking, Frisbee tossing, power walking, or soaking up some rays—is also essential. As a visitor, though, you need only a swimsuit and some rented equipment for most sports. You can then hit the beach almost anywhere, thanks to the California belief in coastal access as a birthright. The farther south you go, the wider, sandier, and sunnier the beaches become; moving north they are rockier and foggier, with colder and rougher surf.

Californians live in such a large and splashy state that they sometimes seem to forget about the rest of the country. They've developed a distinctive culture all their own, which you can delve into by doing as the locals do.

The Outdoors

One of California's greatest assets—the mild year-round weather enjoyed by most of the state—inspires residents to spend as much time outside as they possibly can. To be sure, they have a tremendous enthusiasm for every imaginable outdoor sport, and, up north especially, fresh-air adventures are extremely popular (which may explain why everyone there seems to own at least one pair of hiking boots). But, overall, the California-alfresco creed is more broadly interpreted. Indeed, the general rule when planning any activity is "if it can happen outside, it will!" *Plein-air* vacation opportunities include dining on patios, decks, and wharves; shopping in street markets or elaborate open-air malls; hearing almost any kind of music at moonlight concerts; touring the sculpture gardens that grace major art museums; and celebrating everything from gay pride to garlic at outdoor fairs.

The Automobile

Americans may have a love affair with the automobile, but Californians have an out-and-out obsession. Even when gas prices rev up and freeway traffic slows down, their passion burns as hot as ever. You can witness this ardor any summer weekend at huge classic- and custom-car shows held statewide. Even better, you can feel it yourself by taking the wheel. Trace an old stagecoach route through the mountains above Santa Barbara on Highway 154; race migrating whales up the coast to Big Sur; or take 17-Mile Drive along the precipitous edge of the Monterey Peninsula. Glorious for the most part, but authentically congested in some areas down south, Highway 1 runs almost the entire length of the state.

NORTHERN CALIFORNIA'S TOP ATTRACTIONS

A

B

C

Yosemite National Park

(A) Nature looms large here, both literally and figuratively. In addition to hulking Half Dome, the park is home to El Capitan (the world's largest exposed granite monolith, rising 3,593 feet above the glacier-carved valley floor) and Yosemite Falls (North America's tallest cascade). In Yosemite's signature stand of giant sequoias—the Mariposa Grove—even the trees are Bunyanesque. Needless to say, crowds can be super-sized, too, as this is one of America's most popular national parks. But there's plenty of room to roam; almost 95% of the park, which covers almost 1,200 square miles, is undeveloped wilderness. And if you haven't had your fill of natural wonders here, two more parks—Sequoia and Kings Canyon—are due south.

San Francisco

(B) Population-wise, San Francisco is smaller than Indianapolis. But when it comes to sites (and soul), this city is a giant. Start working through the standard travelers' "to do" list by strolling across the Golden Gate Bridge, taking a ferry to Alcatraz, and hopping on the Powell–Hyde cable car. Just leave enough time to explore the diverse neighborhoods where San Francisco's distinctive personality—an amalgam of gold-rush history, immigrant traditions, counterculture proclivities, and millennial materialism—is on display.

Wine Country

(C) Although the vineyard-blanketed hills of California's original Wine Country are undeniably scenic, the wine itself (preferably accompanied by the area's famed cuisine) remains the big draw here. Budding oenophiles can educate their palettes on scores of tours and tasting sessions—provided

they can elbow their way through the high-season hordes.

Point Reyes National Seashore

(D) Aside from the namesake seashore, this Marin County preserve encompasses ecosystems that range from woodlands and marshlands to heathlike grasslands. The range of wildlife here is equally diverse—depending on when you visit, expect to see gray whales, rare tule elk, and almost 500 species of birds. December through March you can also see male elephant seals compete for mates.

Lake Tahoe

(E) Deep, clear, and intensely blue, this forest-rimmed body of water straddling the California–Nevada border is one of the continent's prettiest alpine lakes. That environmental controls can keep it that way is something of a miracle, given Tahoe's popularity. Throngs of outdoor adventurers flock to the California side to ski, hike, bike, and boat. On the Nevada side, where casinos are king, gambling often wins out over fresh-air activities—but natural wonders are never far away.

Gold Country

(F) California's gold rush was one of the most significant events in U.S. history. It saved the Union and helped open the western frontier, when Argonauts flooded a 300-mile-long stretch of the Sierra foothills. Remnants of the gold rush remain to this day in the towns, diggings, trains, museums, and culture that you'll encounter along historic Hwy. 49; it runs north to south from Loyalton near the Nevada border to Oakhurst, just south of Yosemite. Towns along the way, mostly updated and renovated, allow you to dig into the past and discover what the excitement was all about.

NORTHERN CALIFORNIA'S TOP EXPERIENCES

Hit the Road

Kings Canyon Highway, Redwood Highway, Tioga Pass, 17-Mile Drive, the Lake Tahoe loop: California has some splendid and challenging roads. You'll drive through a tunnel formed by towering redwood trees on the Redwood Highway. If you venture over the Sierras by way of Tioga Pass (through Yosemite in summer only), you'll see emerald-green meadows, gray granite monoliths, and pristine blue lakes . . . and very few people.

Go for the Gold

Though California's gold rush ended more than a hundred years ago, you can still feel the forty-niner fever on the western face of the Sierra Nevada in Columbia, a well-preserved town populated by costumed interpreters, where you can pan for gold or tour a mine. Or visit Bodie, an eerie ghost town in the eastern Sierra that remains in a state of "arrested decay."

Think Globally, Eat Locally

Over the years California cuisine has evolved from a mere trend into a respected gastronomic tradition: one that pairs local, often organic or sustainable, ingredients with techniques inspired by European, Asian, and increasingly Indian and Middle Eastern cookery.

Embrace Your Inner Eccentric

Maybe the looming threat of earthquakes makes Californians a little crazy. Maybe they're just quirky. In any case, if you can't beat 'em, join 'em. Begin by touring Hearst Castle—the beautifully bizarre estate William Randolph Hearst built above San Simeon. Lake Tahoe's Vikingsholm (a re-created Viking castle) is equally odd.

Be Transported

San Franciscans take cable cars seriously—and riding on one is a tourist staple. In Sacramento the "iron horses" that opened the American West get their due at the California State Railroad Museum. When you're done looking at the exhibits, head out of town to Jamestown, where you can ride a real locomotive at the museum's Railtown 1897.

Catch the Spirit

You can learn a lot about the Golden State by visiting its places of worship. The venerable Spanish-built missions stretching from San Diego to Sonoma are obvious examples. Yet other sanctuaries—like Tin How Temple in San Francisco's Chinatown—have their own stories to tell. So does Mt. Shasta, which has both a New Age and age-old appeal. Considered sacred by Native Americans, it's also a magnet for shamans, goddess-worshippers, and the occasional alien.

Go Wild

California communities host hundreds of annual events, but some of the best are organized by Mother Nature. The most famous is the "miracle migration" that sees swallows flock back to Mission San Juan Capistrano each March. In Pacific Grove masses of monarch butterflies reliably arrive for their winter vacation every October.

People-Watch

Opportunities for world-class people-watching abound in California. Just saunter the rainbow-flagged streets of San Francisco's Castro neighborhood or the century-old boardwalk in time-warped, resiliently boho Santa Cruz.

GREAT ITINERARIES

SIERRA RICHES: YOSEMITE, GOLD COUNTRY, AND TAHOE

Day 1: Arrival/San Francisco

Straight from the airport, drop your bags at the lighthearted Hotel Monaco near Union Square and request a goldfish for your room. Chinatown, chock-full of dim sum shops, storefront temples, and open-air markets, promises unfamiliar tastes for lunch. Catch a Powell Street cable car to the end of the line and get off to see the bay views and the antique arcade games at Musée Mécanique, the hidden gem of otherwise mindless Fisherman's Wharf. No need to go any farther than cosmopolitan North Beach for cocktail hour, dinner, and live music.

Day 2: San Francisco

A Union Square stroll packs a wallop of people-watching, window-shopping, and architecture-viewing. In Golden Gate Park, linger amid the flora of the conservatory and the arboretum, soak up some art at the de Young Museum, and find serene refreshment at the Japanese Tea Garden. The Pacific surf pounds the cliffs below the Legion of Honor art museum, which has an exquisite view of the Golden Gate Bridge—when the fog stays away. Sunset cocktails at the circa-1909 Cliff House include a prospect over Seal Rock (actually occupied by sea lions). Eat dinner elsewhere: Pacific Heights, the Mission, and SoMa teem with excellent restaurants.

Day 3: Into the High Sierra

First thing in the morning, pick up your rental car and head for the hills. A five-hour drive due east brings you to Yosemite National Park, where Bridalveil Fall and El Capitan, the 350-story granite monolith, greet you on your way to Yosemite Village. Ditch the car and pick up information and refreshment before hopping on the year-round shuttle to explore. Justly famous sights cram Yosemite Valley: massive Half Dome and Sentinel Dome, thundering Yosemite Falls, and wispy Ribbon Fall and Nevada Fall. Invigorating short hikes off the shuttle route lead to numerous vantage points. Celebrate your arrival in one of the world's most sublime spots with dinner in the dramatic Ahwahnee Hotel Dining Room.

Day 4: Yosemite National Park

Ardent hikers consider John Muir Trail a must-do, tackling the rigorous 12-hour round-trip to the top of Half Dome in search of life-changing vistas. The merely mortal hike downhill from Glacier Point on Four-Mile Trail or Panorama Trail, the latter an all-day trek past waterfalls. Less demanding still is a drive to Wawona for a stroll in the Mariposa Grove of Big Trees and lunch at the 19th-century Wawona Hotel. In foul weather, take shelter in the Ansel Adams Gallery and Yosemite Museum; in fair conditions, drive up to Glacier Point for a breathtaking sunset view.

Day 5: Gold Country South

Highway 49 traces the mother lode that yielded many fortunes in gold in the 1850s and 1860s. Step into a living gold-rush town at Columbia State Historic Park, where you can ride a stagecoach and pan for riches. Sutter Creek's well-preserved downtown bursts with shopping opportunities, but the vintage goods displayed at J. Monteverde General Store are not for sale. A different sort of vintage powers the present-day bonanza of Shenandoah Valley, heart of the Sierra Foothills wine country. Taste your way through

zinfandels and Syrahs at boutique wineries such as Domaine de la Terre Rouge, Renwood, and Sobon Estate. Amador City's 1879 Imperial Hotel places you firmly in the past for the night.

Day 6: Gold Country North

In Placerville, a mine shaft invites investigation at Hangtown's Gold Bug Mine, while Marshall Gold Discovery State Historic Park encompasses most of Coloma and preserves the spot where James Marshall's 1849 find set off the California Gold Rush. Old Town Auburn, with its museums and courthouse, makes a good lunch stop, but if you hold out until you reach Grass Valley you can try authentic miners' pasties. A tour of Empire Mine State Historic Park takes you into a mine, and a few miles away horse-drawn carriages ply the narrow, shop-lined streets of downtown Nevada City. Backtrack to Auburn or Placerville to overnight in historic or modern lodgings.

Day 7: To the Lake

Jewel-like Lake Tahoe is a straight shot east of Placerville on Highway 50; stop for picnic provisions in commercial South Lake Tahoe. A stroll past the three magnificent estates in Pope-Baldwin Recreation area hints at the sumptuous lakefront summers once enjoyed by the elite. High above a glittering cove, Emerald Bay State Park offers one of the best lake views as well as a steep hike down to (and pack up from) Vikingsholm, a replica 9th-century Scandinavian castle. Another fine old mansion—plus a nature preserve and many hiking trails—lies in Sugar Pine Point State Park. Tahoe City offers more history and ample dining and lodging choices.

Day 8: Lake Tahoe

With advance reservations you can tour the ultraluxe 1936 Thunderbird Lodge and its grounds. The picture-perfect beaches and bays of Lake Tahoe-Nevada State Park line the Nevada shoreline, a great place to bask in the sun or go mountain biking. For a different perspective of the lake, get out on the azure water aboard the stern-wheeler MS *Dixie II* from Zephyr Cove. In South Lake Tahoe, another view unfurls as the Heavenly Gondola travels 2½ mi up a mountain. Keep your adrenaline pumping into the evening with some action at the massive casinos clustered in Stateline, Nevada.

Day 9: Back to the City

After a morning of driving, return your rental car in San Francisco and soak up some more urban excitement. Good options include lunch at the Ferry Building, followed by a visit to the San Francisco Museum of Modern Art, or lunch in Japantown followed by shopping in Pacific Heights. People-watching excels in the late afternoon bustle of the Castro and the Haight. Say good-bye to Northern California at one of the plush lounges or trendy bars in the downtown hotels.

Day 10: Departure/San Francisco

Check the weather before you start out for the airport: Fog sometimes causes delays at SFO. On a clear day your flight path might give you one last fabulous glimpse of the City by the Bay.

TIPS

❶ Try to time your trip for late spring or early fall to avoid the worst of the crowds and the road-closing snowfalls in Yosemite and around Lake Tahoe. Yosemite's falls peak in spring and early summer, while fall brings the grape harvest in the Sierra Nevada foothills.

❷ Parking in San Francisco is expensive and scarce. When you fly in, take a shuttle or taxi from the airport to the city, then use the excellent public transportation to get around. Car rental from downtown locations costs no more than at the airport.

❸ For a visit in any season, reserve your hotel or campground accommodations in Yosemite as far in advance as possible—up to a year ahead. Staying in the park itself will cost extra, but it will also save you precious time and miles of driving from the gateway communities.

❹ If you can stay longer, extend your Tahoe-area stay with a day in the Nevada mining boom towns around Virginia City and a night amid the bright lights of Reno.

NORCAL'S LOCAVORE FOOD MOVEMENT

Organic, local, and sustainable are buzzwords in Northern California, home to hundreds of small family farmers, sustainable ranchers, and artisan producers in the forefront of the country's back-to-the-earth food movement.

When Alice Waters opened Chez Panisse in Berkeley in 1971 she sparked a culinary revolution that continues today. Initially called California cuisine, the cooking style showcased local, seasonal ingredients in fresh preparations. It also marked a new willingness by American chefs to experiment with international influences. As the movement spread, it became known as New American cooking. This "eat local, think global" ethos has lead to a resurgence of artisanal producers across the country.

The *locavore* (focused on sustainable, local foods) movement's epicenter is still Northern California. At the Ferry Plaza Farmers Market in San Francisco alone, farmers bring over 1,200 varieties of fruits and vegetables to market every year. Chefs proudly call out their purveyors on menus and Web sites, elevating humble vegetable growers to starring culinary roles.

FARMERS' MARKETS

One of the best ways to taste Northern California's bounty is by stopping by the Ferry Plaza Farmers Market, held outside of the Ferry Building on the Embarcadero, at Market Street. Held on Tuesday and Saturday mornings, the market offers produce, meats, fish, and flowers from small regional farmers and ranchers, many of whom are certified organic.

It is also a great place to pick up items for a picnic. Prepared foods, like tamales and pasta are available, as are specialties like jams, breads, and cheeses from local artisan producers.

Check www.cuesa.org for hours.

FRUIT

Northern California's diverse climate makes it an ideal place to grow all types of fruit, from berries to stone fruit. Farmers' markets and restaurants abound with a staggering selection of produce: Blossom Bluff Orchards, south of San Francisco, offers more than 150 varieties of stone fruits, like apricots, nectarines, and peaches. North of the city, The Apple Farm grows 80 varieties of apples, pears, persimmons, quince, and French plums. The Bay Area is also one of the best places in the country to find rare fruit varieties like aprium, cherimoya, cactus pear, jujube, and loquat; California's famous Meyer lemons—sweeter and less acidic than common lemons—are celebrated in restaurant desserts.

VEGETABLES

Some chefs give top billing to their produce purveyors, like a recently observed menu touting a salad of Star Route Farm field greens with Picholine olives, sweet herbs, and goat cheese. Along with these tantalizing items, be on the lookout for locally grown artichokes, Asian vegetables, multi-hued beets and carrots, and heirloom varieties of tomatoes, squash, and beans.

MEAT

Family-owned ranches and farms are prominent in the region, with many raising organic or "humane certified" beef, pork, lamb, and poultry. Upscale

Bay Area restaurants are fervent about recognizing their high-quality protein producers. From recent menus at two well-known San Francisco restaurants: Wolfe Ranch quail and foie gras crostini with Murcott mandarins, smoked bacon and bok choy, and vanilla gastrique; and Prather Ranch lamb with fava greens, cranberry beans, crispy artichokes, and salsa verde.

FISH

Diners and shoppers will find myriad seafood from local waters, from farm-raised scallops to line-caught California salmon. On menus, look for Hog Island Oysters, a local producer that raises more than three million oysters a year in Tomales Bay. Sardines netted in Monterey Bay are popular in preparations like mesquite-grilled sardines with fava beans, French radish and fennel salad, and preserved Meyer lemon.

CHEESE

Restaurant cheese plates, often served before—or in lieu of—dessert, are great way to experience the region's excellent local cheeses. Look for selections from Cypress Grove Chevre, popular for its artisan goat cheeses, and Cowgirl Creamery, a renowned local producer of fresh and aged cow's milk cheeses. Additionally, some shops and bakeries offer fresh local butter and cheeses.

LOS PADRES
National

THE ULTIMATE ROAD TRIP

CALIFORNIA'S LEGENDARY HIGHWAY 1

by Cheryl Crabtree

One of the world's most scenic drives, California's State Route 1 (also known as Highway 1, the Pacific Coast Highway, the PCH) stretches along the edge of the state for nearly 660 miles, from Southern California's Dana Point to its northern terminus near Leggett, about 40 miles north of Fort Bragg. As you travel south to north, the water's edge transitions from long, sandy beaches and low-lying bluffs to towering dunes, craggy cliffs, and ancient redwood groves. The ocean changes as well; the relatively tame and surfable swells lapping the Southern California shore give way to the frigid, powerful waves crashing against weatherbeaten rocks in the north.

HIGHWAY 1 TOP 10

- Santa Monica
- Santa Barbara
- Hearst San Simeon State Historical Monument
- Big Sur
- Carmel
- 17-Mile Drive
- Monterey
- San Francisco
- Marin Headlands
- Point Reyes National Seashore

(opposite) Highway 1 near Mill Creek, Big Sur

Give yourself lots of extra time to pull off the road and enjoy the scenery

STARTING YOUR JOURNEY

You may decide to drive the road's entire 660-mile route, or bite off a smaller piece. In either case, a Highway 1 road trip allows you to experience California at your own pace, stopping when and where you wish. Hike a beachside trail, dig your toes in the sand, and search for creatures in the tidepools. Buy some artichokes and strawberries from a roadside farmstand. Talk to people along the way (you'll run into everyone from soul-searching meditators, farmers, and beatniks to city-slackers and working-class folks), and take lots of pictures. Don't rush—you could easily spend a lifetime discovering secret spots along this route.

To help you plan your trip, we've broken the road into three regions (Santa Monica to Carmel, Carmel to San Francisco, and San Francisco to Fort Bragg); each region is then broken up into smaller segments—many of which are suitable for a day's drive. If you're pressed for time, you can always tackle a section of Highway 1, and then head inland to U.S. 101 or I-5 to reach your next destination more quickly.

For more information, please see our Highway 1 CloseUps in chapter 2 (Central Coast), chapter 3 (Monterey Bay), and chapter 4 (San Francisco).

WHAT'S IN A NAME?

Though it's often referred to as the Pacific Coast Highway (or PCH), sections of Highway 1 actually have different names. The southernmost section (Dana Point to Oxnard) is the Pacific Coast Highway. After that, the road becomes the Cabrillo Highway (Las Cruces to Lompoc), the Big Sur Coast Highway (San Luis Obispo County line to Monterey), the North Coast Scenic Byway (San Luis Obispo city limit to the Monterey County line), the Cabrillo Highway again (Santa Cruz County line to Half Moon Bay), and finally the Shoreline Highway (Marin City to Leggett). To make matters more confusing, smaller chunks of the road have additional honorary monikers.

Just follow the green triangular signs that say "California 1."

HIGHWAY 1 DRIVING

- Rent a convertible. (You will not regret it.)
- Begin the drive north from Santa Monica, where congestion and traffic delays pose less of a problem.
- Mind your manners on the freeway. Don't tailgate or glare at other drivers, and don't fly the finger.
- If you're prone to motion sickness, take the wheel yourself. Focusing on the landscape outside should help you feel less queasy.
- If you're afraid of heights, drive from south to north so you'll be on the mountain rather than the cliff side of the road.

The Central Coast

FROM VENTURA TO BIG SUR

WORD OF MOUTH

"I was blown away by the immense outdoor pool at the Hearst Castle. It is huge, and yet incredibly serene in its surroundings. The Castle is situated on top of the hills in the San Simeon area and allows for massive views of nearly 360 degrees around."
—photo by L Vantreight, Fodors.com member

WELCOME TO THE CENTRAL COAST

TOP REASONS TO GO

★ **Incredible nature:** Much of the Central Coast looks as wild and wonderful as it did centuries ago; the area is home to Channel Islands National Park, two national marine sanctuaries, state parks and beaches, and the vast and rugged Los Padres National Forest.

★ **Edible bounty:** Land and sea provide enough fresh regional foods to satisfy even the savviest of foodies—grapes, strawberries, seafood, olive oil . . . the list goes on and on. Get your fill at countless farmers' markets, wineries, and restaurants.

★ **Outdoor activities:** Kick back and revel in the casual California lifestyle. Surf, golf, kayak, hike, play tennis—or just hang out and enjoy the gorgeous scenery.

★ **Small-town charm, big-city culture:** Small, friendly, uncrowded towns offer an amazing array of cultural amenities. With all the art and history museums, theater, music, and festivals, you might start thinking you're in L.A. or San Francisco.

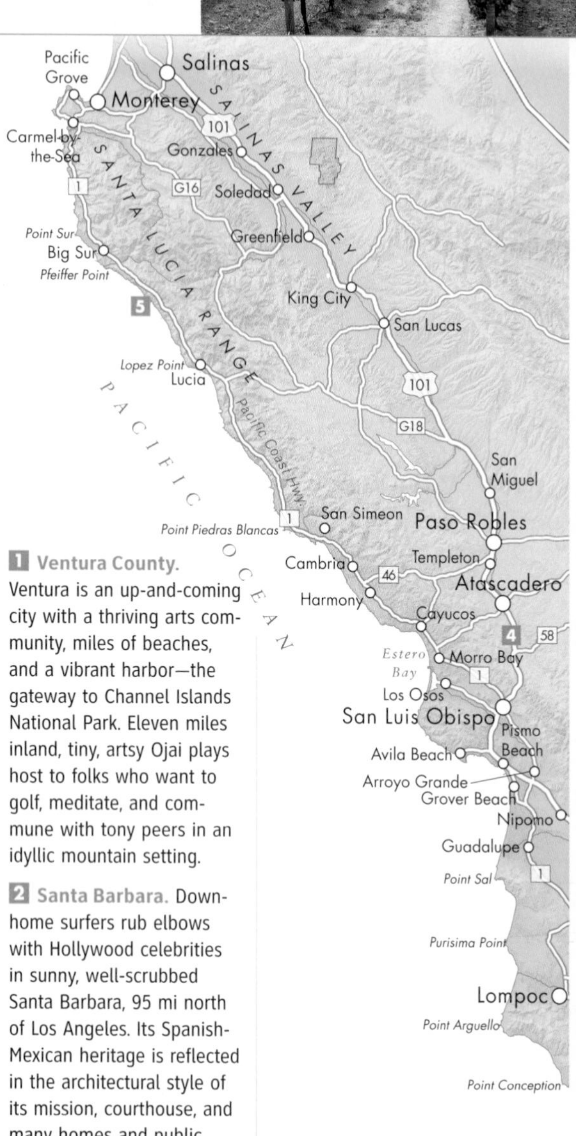

1 Ventura County. Ventura is an up-and-coming city with a thriving arts community, miles of beaches, and a vibrant harbor—the gateway to Channel Islands National Park. Eleven miles inland, tiny, artsy Ojai plays host to folks who want to golf, meditate, and commune with tony peers in an idyllic mountain setting.

2 Santa Barbara. Down-home surfers rub elbows with Hollywood celebrities in sunny, well-scrubbed Santa Barbara, 95 mi north of Los Angeles. Its Spanish-Mexican heritage is reflected in the architectural style of its mission, courthouse, and many homes and public buildings.

3 Santa Barbara County. Wineries, ranches, and small villages dominate the quintessentially Californian landscape here.

4 San Luis Obispo County. Friendly college town San Luis Obispo serves as hub of a burgeoning wine region that stretches nearly 100 mi from Pismo Beach north to Paso Robles; the 230-plus wineries here have earned reputations for high-quality vintages that rival those of northern California.

5 The Big Sur Coastline. Rugged cliffs meet the Pacific for more than 60 mi—one of the most scenic and dramatic drives in the world.

6 Channel Islands National Park. Home to 145 species of plants and animals found nowhere else on Earth, this relatively undiscovered gem of a park encompasses five islands and a mile of surrounding ocean.

GETTING ORIENTED

The Central Coast region begins about 60 mi north of Los Angeles, near the seaside city of Ventura. From there the coastline stretches north about 200 mi, winding through the small cities of Santa Barbara and San Luis Obispo, then north through the small towns of Morro Bay and Cambria to Carmel. The drive through this region, especially the section of Highway 1 from San Simeon to Big Sur, is one of the most scenic in the state.

THE CENTRAL COAST PLANNER

When to Go

The Central Coast climate is usually mild throughout the year. If you like to sunbathe and swim in warmer (though still nippy) ocean waters, July and August are the best months to visit. Be aware that this is also high season. Fog often rolls in all along the coastal areas in early summer; you'll need a jacket, especially after sunset, close to the shore. The rains usually come from December through March. From April to early June and in the early fall the weather is almost as fine as in high season, and the pace is less hectic.

Getting Around

Driving is the easiest way to experience the Central Coast. A car gives you the flexibility to stop at scenic vista points along Highway 1, take detours through wine country, and drive to rural lakes and mountains. Traveling north through Ventura County to San Luis Obispo (note that from just south of Ventura up to San Luis Obispo, U.S. 101 and Highway 1 are the same road), you can take in the rolling hills, peaceful valleys, and rugged mountains that stretch for miles along the shore. Amtrak trains link major cities throughout the region.

About the Hotels

There are plenty of lodging options throughout the Central Coast—but expect to pay top dollar for any rooms along the shore, especially in summer. Moderately priced hotels and motels do exist—most just a short drive inland from their higher-price counterparts. Make your reservations as early as possible and take advantage of midweek specials to get the best rates. It's common for hotels to require minimum stays on holidays and some weekends, especially in summer, and to double their rates during festivals and other events.

About the Restaurants

The cuisine in Ventura and Santa Barbara is every bit as eclectic as it is in California's bigger cities; fresh seafood is a standout. The region from Solvang to Big Sur is far enough off the Interstate to ensure that nearly every restaurant or café has its own personality—from chic to down-home and funky. A foodie renaissance has overtaken the Santa Ynez Valley, San Luis Obispo, Cambria, and Paso Robles, spawning dozens of new restaurants touting nouveau cuisine made with fresh organic produce and meats.

Dining attire on the Central Coast is generally casual, though slightly dressy casual wear is the custom at pricier restaurants.

WHAT IT COSTS

	¢	$	$$	$$$	$$$$
Restaurants	under $10	$10–$15	$16–$22	$23–$30	over $30
Hotels	under $90	$90–$120	$121–$175	$176–$250	over $250

Restaurant prices are for a main course at dinner, excluding sales tax of 7.25%–7.75% (depending on location). Hotel prices are for two people in a standard double room in high season, excluding service charges and 9%–10% tax.

Updated by Cheryl Crabtree

Balmy weather, glorious beaches, crystal clear air, and serene landscapes have lured people to the Central Coast since prehistoric times. It's an ideal place to relax, slow down, and appreciate the good things in life.

Along the Pacific coast, the scenic variety is stunning—everything from dramatic cliffs and grass-tufted bluffs to wildlife estuaries and miles of dunes. Offshore, a pristine national park and a vast marine sanctuary protect the wild, wonderful underwater resources of this incredible corner of the planet. But not all of the Central Coast's top attractions are natural: the small cities of Ventura, Santa Barbara, and San Luis Obispo are filled with sparkling examples of Spanish-Mediterranean architecture, bustling shopping districts, and first-rate restaurants showcasing regional foods and wines.

PLANNING

GETTING HERE AND AROUND

AIR TRAVEL

Alaska Air, Allegiant Air, American, Delta, Horizon Air, United Express, and U.S. Airways fly to Santa Barbara Municipal Airport, 12 mi from downtown. United Express and U.S. Airways provide service to San Luis Obispo County Regional Airport, 3 mi from downtown San Luis Obispo. ⇨ *See Air Travel in Travel Smart Northern California for airline phone numbers.*

Santa Barbara Airbus shuttles travelers between Santa Barbara and Los Angeles for $48 one way and $90 round-trip (slight discount with 24-hour notice, larger discount for groups of six or more). The Santa Barbara Metropolitan Transit District Bus 11 ($1.25) runs every 30 minutes from the airport to the downtown transit center. A taxi between the airport and the hotel district runs $18 to $25.

Airport Contacts San Luis Obispo County Regional Airport (✉ *903-5 Airport Dr., San Luis Obispo* ☎ *805/781-5205* 🌐 *www.sloairport.com*). **Santa Barbara Airport** (✉ *500 Fowler Rd., Santa Barbara* ☎ *805/683-4011* 🌐 *www.flysba.com*).

Continued on page 38

HIGHWAY 1: SANTA MONICA TO BIG SUR

Hearst Castle

THE PLAN

Distance: approx. 335 mi

Time: 3-5 days

Good Overnight Options: Malibu, Santa Barbara, Pismo Beach, San Luis Obispo, Cambria, Carmel

For more information on the sights and attractions along this portion of Highway 1, please see chapters 2 and 3.

SANTA MONICA TO MALIBU (approx. 26 mi)

Highway 1 begins in Dana point, but it seems more appropriate to begin a PCH adventure in **Santa Monica.** Be sure to experience the beach culture, then balance the tacky pleasures of Santa Monica's amusement pier with a stylish dinner in a neighborhood restaurant.

MALIBU TO SANTA BARBARA (approx. 70 mi)

The PCH follows the curve of Santa Monica Bay all the way to **Malibu** and **Point Mugu,** near **Oxnard.** Chances are you'll experience *déjà vu* driving this 27-mile stretch: mountains on one side, ocean on the other, opulent homes perched on hillsides; you've seen this piece of coast countless times on TV and film. Be sure to walk out on the **Malibu Pier** for a great photo opp, then check out **Surfrider Beach,** with three famous points where perfect waves ignited a worldwide surfing rage in the 1960s.

Santa Monica

After Malibu you'll drive through miles of protected, largely unpopulated coastline. Ride a wave at **Zuma Beach**, scout for offshore whales at **Point Dume State Preserve,** or hike the trails at **Point Mugu State Park.** After skirting Point Mugu, Highway 1 merges with U.S. 101 for about 70 mi before reaching **Santa Barbara.** A mini-tour of the city includes a real Mexican lunch at **La Super-Rica,** a visit to the magnificent **Spanish Mission Santa Barbara,** and a walk down hopping **State Street to Stearns Wharf.**

SANTA BARBARA TO SAN SIMEON (approx. 147 mi)

North of Santa Barbara, Highway 1 morphs into the Cabrillo Highway, separating from and then rejoining U.S. 101. The route winds through rolling vineyards and rangeland to **San Luis Obispo,** where any legit road trip includes a photo stop at the wacky, pink **Madonna Inn.** Be sure to also climb the humungous dunes at **Guadalupe-Nipomo Dunes Preserve.**

Santa Barbara

In downtown San Luis Obispo, the **Mission San Luis Obispo de Tolosa** stands by a tree-shaded creek edged with shops and cafés. Highway 1 continues to **Morro Bay** and up the coast. About 15 mi north of Morro Bay, you'll reach the town of **Harmony** (population 18), a tiny burg with artists' studios, a wedding chapel, shops, and a winery. The road continues through **Cambria** to solitary **Hearst San Simeon State Historical Monument**—the art-filled pleasure palace at **San Simeon.** Just four miles north of the castle, elephant seals grunt and cavort at the

Big Sur

TOP 5 PLACES TO LINGER

- Point Dume State Preserve
- Santa Barbara
- Hearst San Simeon State Historical Monument
- Big Sur/Julia Pfeiffer Burns State Park
- Carmel

Piedras Blancas Elephant Seal Rookery, just off the side of the road.

SAN SIMEON TO CARMEL (approx. 92 mi)

Heading north, you'll drive through **Big Sur,** a place of ancient forests and rugged shoreline stretching 90 mi from San Simeon to **Carmel.** Much of Big Sur lies within several state parks and the 165,000-acre **Ventana Wilderness,** itself part of the **Los Padres National Forest.** This famously scenic stretch of the coastal drive, which twists up and down bluffs above the ocean, can last hours. Take your time.

At **Julia Pfeiffer Burns State Park** one easy but rewarding hike leads to an iconic waterfall off a beach-front cliff. When you reach lovely **Carmel,** stroll around the picture-perfect town's mission, galleries, and shops.

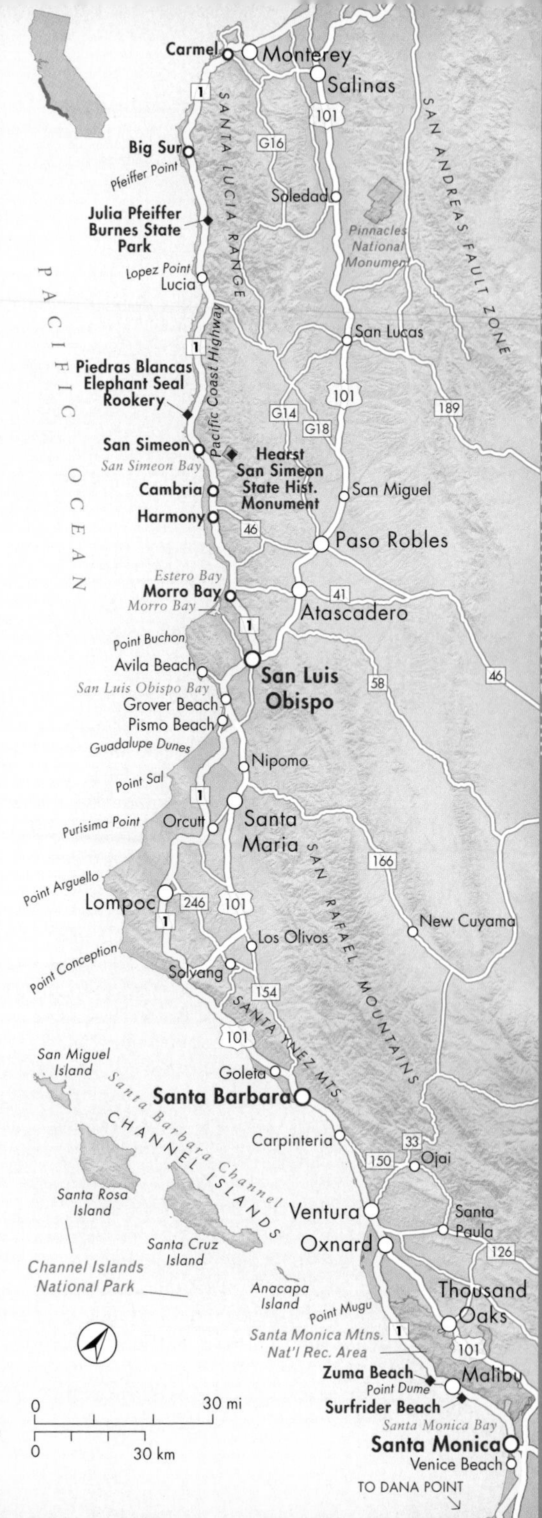

Airport Transfer Contacts **Santa Barbara Airbus** (☎ *805/964–7759, 800/733–6354, 800/423–1618 in CA* 🌐 *www.santabarbaraairbus.com*). **Santa Barbara Metropolitan Transit District** (☎ *805/683–3702 or 805/963–3364* 🌐 *www.sbmtd.gov*).

BUS TRAVEL

Greyhound provides service from San Francisco and Los Angeles to San Luis Obispo, Ventura, and Santa Barbara. From Monterey and Carmel, Monterey-Salinas Transit operates buses to Big Sur between May and mid-October. From San Luis Obispo, Central Coast Transit runs buses around Santa Maria and out to the coast. Santa Barbara Metropolitan Transit District provides local service. The Downtown/State Street and Waterfront shuttles cover their respective sections of Santa Barbara during the day. Gold Coast Transit buses serve the entire Ventura County region.

Bus Contacts **Central Coast Transit** (☎ *805/781–4472* 🌐 *www.slorta.org*). **Gold Coast Transit** (☎ *805/487–4222 or 805/643–3158 for Ojai, Ventura, and Oxnard* 🌐 *www.goldcoasttransit.org*). **Greyhound** (☎ *800/231–2222* 🌐 *www.greyhound.com*). **Monterey-Salinas Transit** (☎ *888/678–2871* 🌐 *www.mst.org*). **San Luis Obispo Transit** (☎ *805/781–4472* 🌐 *www.slorta.org*). **Santa Barbara Metropolitan Transit District** (☎ *805/963–3366* 🌐 *www.sbmtd.gov*).

CAR TRAVEL

Highway 1 and U.S. 101 run north–south and more or less parallel along the Central Coast, with Highway 1 hugging the coast and U.S. 101 running inland. The most dramatic section of the Central Coast is the 70 mi between Big Sur and San Simeon. Don't expect to make good time along here: the road is narrow and twisting with a single lane in each direction, making it difficult to pass the many lumbering RVs. In fog or rain the drive can be downright nerve-racking; in wet seasons mud slides can close portions of the road. Once you start south from Carmel, there is no route east from Highway 1 until Highway 46 heads inland from Cambria to connect with U.S. 101. At Morro Bay Highway 1 turns inland for 13 mi and connects with U.S. 101 at San Luis Obispo. From here south to Pismo Beach the two highways run concurrently. South of Pismo Beach to Las Cruces the roads separate, then run together all the way to Oxnard. Along any stretch where they are separate, U.S. 101 is the quicker route.

U.S. 101 and Highway 1 will get you to the Central Coast from Los Angeles and San Francisco. If you are coming from the east, you can take Highway 46 west from I–5 in the Central Valley (near Bakersfield) to U.S. 101 at Paso Robles, where it continues to the coast, intersecting Highway 1 a few miles south of Cambria. Highway 33 heads south from I–5 at Bakersfield to Ojai. About 60 mi north of Ojai, Highway 166 leaves Highway 33, traveling due west through the Sierra Madre to Santa Maria at U.S. 101 and continuing west to Highway 1 at Guadalupe. South of Carpinteria, Highway 150 winds from Highway 1/U.S. 101 through sparsely populated hills to Ojai. From Highway 1/U.S. 101 at Ventura, Highway 33 leads to Ojai and the Los Padres National Forest. South of Ventura, Highway 126 runs east from Highway 1/U.S. 101 to I–5.

Contacts Caltrans (☎ *800/427–7623* 🌐 *www.dot.ca.gov*).

TRAIN TRAVEL

The Amtrak *Coast Starlight,* which runs between Los Angeles and Seattle via Oakland, stops in Paso Robles, San Luis Obispo, Santa Barbara, and Oxnard. Amtrak runs several *Pacific Surfliner* trains daily between San Luis Obispo, Santa Barbara, Los Angeles, and San Diego. Metrolink Regional Rail Service trains connect Ventura and Oxnard with Los Angeles and points between.

Train Contacts Amtrak (☎ *800/872–7245, 805/963–1015 in Santa Barbara, 805/541–0505 in San Luis Obispo* 🌐 *www.amtrakcalifornia.com*). **Metrolink** (☎ *800/371–5465 within service area, 213/347–2800* 🌐 *www.metrolinktrains.com*).

HEALTH AND SAFETY

In case of emergency, dial 911.

Medical Contacts Big Sur Health Center (✉ *Hwy. 1, ¼ mi south of River Inn, Big Sur* ☎ *831/667–2580*) is open weekdays 10–5 (closed between 1 and 2). **Cottage Hospital** (✉ *Pueblo and Bath Sts., Santa Barbara* ☎ *805/682–7111, 805/569–7210 emergencies*). **Sierra Vista Regional Medical Center** (✉ *1010 Murray Ave., San Luis Obispo* ☎ *805/546–7600*).

TOUR OPTIONS

Cloud Climbers Jeep and Wine Tours offers four types of daily tours: wine-tasting, mountain, sunset, and a discovery tour for families. These trips to the Santa Barbara/Santa Ynez mountains and wine country are conducted in open-air, six-passenger jeeps. Fares range from $89 to $120 per adult. The company also arranges biking, horseback riding, and trap-shooting tours by appointment. Wine Adventures operates customized Santa Barbara County tours and narrated North County wine-country tours in 25-passenger minicoaches. Fares for the wine tours are $110 per person. The Grapeline Wine Country Shuttle leads daily wine and vineyard picnic tours with flexible itineraries in San Luis Obispo County and Santa Barbara County wine country; they stop at many area hotels and can provide private custom tours with advance reservations. Fares range from $42 to $85, depending on pickup location and tour choice.

Spencer's Limousine & Tours offers customized tours of the city of Santa Barbara and wine country via sedan, limousine, van, or minibus. A five-hour basic tour with at least four participants costs about $80 per person. Sultan's Limousine Service has a fleet of super stretches; each can take up to eight passengers on Paso Robles and Edna Valley–Arroyo Grande wine tours and tours of the San Luis Obispo County coast. Hiring a limo for a four-hour wine country tour typically costs $380 to $430 with tip. Sustainable Vine Wine Tours' biodiesel-powered vans can take you on a day of eco-friendly wine touring in the Santa Ynez Valley. Trips include door-to-door transportation from your location in the Santa Barbara or Santa Ynez Valley area, tastings at green-minded wineries, and a gourmet organic picnic lunch.

Tour Contacts Cloud Climbers Jeep and Wine Tours (☎ *805/646–3200* 🌐 *www.ccjeeps.com*). **The Grapeline Wine Country Shuttle** (☎ *805/239–4747 Paso Robles, 805/238–2765 San Luis Obispo, 888/894–6379 Santa Barbara/*

Solvang *www.gogrape.com*). **Spencer's Limousine & Tours** (*805/884-9700* *www.spencerslimo.com*). **Sultan's Limousine Service** (*805/466-3167 North SLO County, 805/544-8320 South SLO County, 805/771-0161 coastal SLO County cities* *www.sultanslimo.com*). **Sustainable Vine Wine Tours** (*805/698-3911* *www.sustainablevine.com*). **Wine Adventures** (*3463 State St., #228, Santa Barbara* *805/965-9463* *www.welovewines.com*).

VISITOR INFORMATION

Contacts **Central Coast Tourism Council** (*Box 3103, Pismo Beach 93446* *www.centralcoast-tourism.com*).

VENTURA COUNTY

Ventura County was first settled by the Chumash Indians. Spanish missionaries were the first Europeans to arrive, followed by Americans and other Europeans, who established bustling towns, transportation networks, and highly productive farms. Since the 1920s, though, agriculture has been steadily replaced as the area's main industry—first by the oil business, and more recently, by tourism.

VENTURA

60 mi north of Los Angeles on U.S. 101.

Like Los Angeles, the city of Ventura enjoys gorgeous weather and sun-kissed beaches—but without the smog and congestion. The city is filled with classic California buildings, farmers' and fish markets, art galleries, and shops. The miles of beautiful beaches attract both athletes—bodysurfers and boogie boarders, runners and bikers—and those who'd rather doze beneath a rented umbrella all day. Ventura Harbor is home to the Channel Islands National Park Visitor Center and myriad fishing boats, restaurants, and water-activity centers where you can rent boats and take harbor cruises. Foodies can get their fix here, too; dozens of upscale cafés and wine and tapas bars have opened in recent years. Ventura is also a magnet for arts and antiques buffs who come to browse the dozens of galleries and shops in the downtown area.

ESSENTIALS

Visitor Information **Ventura Visitors and Convention Bureau** (*101 S. California St.,Ventura* *805/648-2075 or 800/483-6214* *www.ventura-usa.com*).

EXPLORING

You can pick up culinary, antiques, and shopping guides downtown at the **visitor center** (*101 S. California St.* *805/648-2075 or 800/483-6214* *www.ventura-usa.com*) run by the Ventura Visitors and Convention Bureau.

More than three millennia of human history in the Ventura region is charted in the archaeological exhibits at the small **Albinger Archaeological Museum.** Some of the relics on display date back to 1600 BC. *113 E. Main St.* *805/648-5823* *www.albingermuseum.org* *Free* *June–Aug., Wed.–Sun. 10–4; Sept.–May, Wed.–Fri. 10–2, weekends 10–4.*

Lunker largemouth bass, rainbow trout, crappie, redears, and channel catfish live in the waters at **Lake Casitas Recreation Area,** an impoundment of the Ventura River. The lake is one of the country's best bass-fishing areas, and anglers come from all over the United States to test their luck. The park, nestled below the Santa Ynez Mountains' Laguna Ridge, is also a beautiful spot for pitching a tent or having a picnic. The Casitas Water Adventure, which has two water playgrounds and a lazy river for tubing and floating, is a great place to take kids in summer ($12 for an all-day pass; $5 from 5 to 7 PM). The park is 13 mi northwest of Ventura. ✉*11311 Santa Ana Rd., off Hwy. 33* ☎*805/649–2233, 805/649–1122 campground reservations* ⊕*www.lakecasitas.info* *$10 per vehicle, $10 per boat* ⊙*Daily.*

TRAFFIC TIMING

The southbound freeway from Santa Barbara to Ventura and L.A. slows from 4 PM to 6 or 7 PM; the reverse is true heading from Ventura to Santa Barbara in the early morning hours. Traffic in the greater Los Angeles region can clog the roads as early as 2 PM. Traveling south, it's best to depart from Santa Barbara before 1 PM, or after 6 PM. Heading north, you probably won't encounter many traffic problems until you reach the Salinas/San Jose corridor.

The ninth of the 21 California missions, **Mission San Buenaventura** was established in 1782 but burned to the ground in the 1790s. It was rebuilt and rededicated in 1809. A self-guided tour takes you through a small museum, a quiet courtyard, and a chapel with 250-year-old paintings. ✉*211 E. Main St.* ☎*805/643–4318* ⊕*www.sanbuenaventuramission.org* *$2* ⊙*Weekdays 10–5, Sat. 9–5, Sun. 10–4.*

WHERE TO EAT

$$$ AMERICAN ✕**Brooks.** Innovative chef Andy Brooks and his wife Jayme—whose grandfather co-owned the famous Chi Chi supper club in Palm Springs in the 1960s—serve some of the town's finest meals in a slick, contemporary downtown dining room. The ever-changing menu centers around seasonal, mostly local, organic ingredients and features nightly three- and five-course tasting menus, which might include limoncello steamed mussels, cornmeal fried oysters, or prime rib with smoked cheddar grits. Ask for the romaine salad dressed in the legendary Chi Chi creamy garlic dressing. Live music and hip martinis and margaritas attract a loyal following after 9 PM on weekends. ✉*545 E. Thompson Blvd.* ☎*805/652–7070* ▭*AE, D, MC, V* ⊙*Closed Mon. No lunch Sat.–Wed.*

$$ SEAFOOD ✕**Brophy Bros.** The Ventura outpost of this wildly popular Santa Barbara restaurant provides the same fresh seafood-oriented meals in a spacious second-story setting overlooking the harbor. Feast on everything from fish-and-chips and crab cakes to chowder and delectable fish—often straight from the boats moored below. ✉*1559 Spinnaker Dr., in Ventura Harbor Village* ☎*805/639–0865* *Reservations not accepted (except for groups of 10 or more)* ▭*AE, MC, V.*

$ AMERICAN ✕**Busy Bee Cafe.** A local favorite for decades, this classic 1950s diner has a jukebox on every table and serves hearty burgers and American comfort food (think meat loaf and mashed potatoes, pot roast, and Cobb

salad). For breakfast, tuck into a huge breakfast omelet; for a snack or dessert, be sure to order a shake or hot fudge sundae from the soda fountain. ✉*478 E. Main St.* ☎*805/643–4864* ▭*MC, V.*

$$ MEDITERRANEAN ✕**Jonathan's at Peirano's.** The main dining room here has a gazebo where you can eat surrounded by plants and local art. The menu has dishes from Spain, Portugal, France, Italy, Greece, and Morocco. Standouts are the various paellas, the *penne checca* pasta, and the halibut with almonds. The owners also run an evening tapas bar next door, which serves exotic martinis. ✉*204 E. Main St.* ☎*805/648–4853* ▭*AE, D, DC, MC, V* ⊙*Closed Mon.; no lunch Sun.*

WHERE TO STAY

$$–$$$ **Holiday Inn Express Ventura Harbor.** A favorite among travelers to the Channel Islands, this quiet, comfortable lodge sits right at the Ventura Harbor entrance. A major renovation in 2006 transformed the guest quarters into spacious, sophisticated retreats with flat-screen TVs and puffy duvets. The south side of the hotel overlooks the marinas; ask for an upper-floor harborside room or suite for the best views. **Pros:** quiet at night; easy access to harbor restaurants and activities; on shuttle-bus route to city attractions. **Cons:** busy area on weekends; five-minute drive to downtown sights. ✉*1080 Navigator Dr.* ☎*805/856–9533 or 800/315–2621* ⊕*www.hiexpress.com* ⇨*68* *rooms, 23 suites ♿In-room: no a/c, kitchen (some), Internet. In-hotel: pool, gym, laundry service, Wi-Fi, no-smoking rooms ▭AE, D, DC, MC, V 🍴BP.*

$$$ **Pierpont Inn.** Back in 1910, Josephine Pierpont-Ginn built the original Pierpont Inn on a hill overlooking Ventura Beach. Today's renovated complex, which includes an Arts-and-Crafts lobby and English Tudor cottages set amid gardens and gazebos, reflects much of the hotel's original elegance. For a fee you can work out at the neighboring Pierpont Racquet Club, which has indoor and outdoor pools, 15 tennis courts, racquetball courts, spa services, aerobics, and child care. The inn's restaurant has great views of the ocean and harbor. **Pros:** near the beach; lush gardens; Tempur-Pedic mattresses and pillows. **Cons:** near the freeway and train tracks; difficult to walk downtown from here. ✉*550 Sanjon Rd.* ☎*805/643–6144 or 800/285–4667* 🌐*www.pierpontinn.com* *65 rooms, 9 suites, 2 cottages* ♿*In-room: no a/c (some), refrigerator (some), Internet, Wi-Fi. In-hotel: restaurant, bar, no-smoking rooms* ▭*AE, D, DC, MC, V* 🍴*CP.*

HOTEL HELP

Hot Spots (☎*800/793–7666 or 805/564–1637* 🌐*www.hotspotsusa.com*) provides room reservations and tourist information for destinations in Ventura, Santa Barbara, and San Luis Obispo counties.

SPORTS AND THE OUTDOORS

The most popular outdoor activities in Ventura are beach-going and whale-watching. California gray whales migrate offshore through the Santa Barbara Channel from late December through March; giant blue and humpback whales feed here from mid-June through September. In fact, the channel is teeming with marine life year-round, so tours include more than just whale sightings. A cruise through the Santa Barbara Channel with **Island Packers** (✉*1691 Spinnaker Dr., Ventura Harbor* ☎*805/642–1393* 🌐*www.islandpackers.com*) will give you the chance to spot dolphins and seals—and sometimes even whales—throughout the year.

OJAI

15 mi north of Ventura, U.S. 101 to Hwy. 33.

The Ojai Valley, which director Frank Capra used as a backdrop for his 1936 film *Lost Horizon,* sizzles in the summer when temperatures routinely reach 90°F. The acres of orange and avocado groves here evoke postcard images of agricultural Southern California from decades ago. This is a lush, slow-moving place, where many artists and celebrities have sought refuge from life in the fast lane.

ESSENTIALS

Visitor Information Ojai Valley Chamber of Commerce (☎*805/646–8126* 🌐*www.ojaichamber.org*).

EXPLORING

The town can be easily explored on foot; you can also hop on the **Ojai Valley Trolley** (*www.ojaitrolley.com 50¢*), which rides on two routes around Ojai and neighboring Miramonte between 7:15 and 5:40 on weekdays, 9 and 5 on weekends. If you tell the driver you're a visitor, you'll get an informal guided tour.

Maps and tourist information are available at the **Ojai Valley Chamber of Commerce** (*201 S. Signal St. 805/646–8126 www.ojaichamber.org Weekdays 9–4*).

The work of local artists is displayed in the Spanish-style shopping arcade along **Ojai Avenue** *(Hwy. 150)*. Organic and specialty growers sell their produce on Sunday 10–2 (9–1 in summer) at the farmers' market behind the arcade.

The **Ojai Center for the Arts** (*113 S. Montgomery St. 805/646–0117 www.ojaiartcenter.org*) exhibits artwork and presents theater and dance performances.

The **Ojai Valley Museum** (*130 W. Ojai Ave. 805/640–1390 www.ojaivalleymuseum.org*) has exhibits on the valley's history and many Native American artifacts.

The 18-mi **Ojai Valley Trail** (*Parallel to Hwy. 33, from Soule Park in Ojai to ocean in Ventura 805/654–3951 www.ojaichamber.org*) is open to pedestrians, bikers, joggers, equestrians, and nonmotorized vehicles. You can access it anywhere along its route.

WHERE TO EAT

$$ MEDITERRANEAN **Azu.** Delectable tapas, a full bar, slick furnishings, and piped jazz music lure diners to this popular, artsy Mediterranean bistro. You can also order soups, salads, and traditional bistro fare such as veal shanks, paella, and cassoulet. Save room for the homemade gelato. *457 E. Ojai Ave. 805/640–7987 AE, D, MC, V No lunch Mon.*

$ ITALIAN **Boccali's.** Edging a ranch, citrus groves, and a seasonal garden that provides much of the produce for menu items, family-run Boccali's has attracted droves of loyal fans to its modest but cheery restaurant since 1986. In the warmer months, you can dine alfresco in the oak-shaded patio and lawn area and sometimes listen to live music. Best known for their hand-rolled pizzas and homestyle pastas (don't miss the eggplant lasagna), Boccali's also serves a seasonal strawberry shortcake that some patrons drive many miles to savor every year. *3277 Ojai Ave., about 2 mi east of downtown 805/646–6116 No credit cards accepted No lunch Mon. and Tues.*

$$$ AMERICAN ★ **The Ranch House.** This elegant yet laid-back eatery—said to be the best in town—has been around for decades, attracting celebrities like Paul Newman. Main dishes such as rack of lamb in an oyster-and-mushroom cream sauce, and grilled diver scallops with curried sweet-corn sauce are not to be missed. The verdant patio is a wonderful place to have Sunday brunch. *500 S. Lomita Ave. 805/646–2360 AE, D, DC, MC, V Closed Mon. No lunch.*

$$$ CONTINENTAL **Suzanne's Cuisine.** Peppered filet mignon, linguine with steamed clams, and pan-roasted salmon with a roasted mango sauce are among the offerings at this European-style restaurant. Game, seafood, and

vegetarian dishes dominate the dinner menu, and salads and soups star at lunchtime. All the breads and desserts are made on the premises. ✉ *502 W. Ojai Ave.* ☎ *805/640–1961* ▭ *AE, MC, V* ⊙ *Closed Tues. and 1st 2 wks in Jan.*

2

WHERE TO STAY

$–$$ **The Blue Iguana Inn & Cottages.** Artists run this Southwestern-style hotel, and their work (which is for sale) decorates the rooms. The small, cozy main inn is about 2 mi west of downtown. Its sister property, the Emerald Iguana Inn, consists of eight more art-nouveau cottages closer to downtown Ojai. Suites and cottages all have kitchenettes. **Pros:** colorful art everywhere; secluded property; breakfast delivered to each room. **Cons:** two miles from the heart of Ojai; sits on the main highway to Ventura; small. ✉ *11794 N. Ventura Ave., Hwy. 33* ☎ *805/646–5277* 🌐 *www.blueiguanainn.com* *4 rooms, 7 suites, 8 cottages* *In-room: kitchen (some), refrigerator, Wi-Fi. In-hotel: pool, some pets allowed, no-smoking rooms* ▭ *AE, D, DC, MC, V.*

$$$ **Oaks at Ojai.** Rejuvenation is the name of the game at this comfortable spa resort. You can work out all day or just lounge by the pool. The fitness package is a great value and includes lodging; use of the spa facilities; a choice of 16 daily exercise classes, hikes, and fitness activities; and three nutritionally balanced, low-calorie meals a day, plus snacks and beverages. Each of the two courtyard suites has a refrigerator and fireplace; five mini-suites include private patios. Nonguests can eat here, too, but it's mainly for the fitness-conscious. Cell-phone use is not allowed in public areas. Bringing kids under age 16 is discouraged. **Pros:** great place to get fit; peaceful retreat; healthy meals. **Cons:** rooms are basic; sits on the main highway through town. ✉ *122 E. Ojai Ave.* ☎ *805/646–5573 or 800/753–6257* 🌐 *www.oaksspa.com* *44 rooms, 2 suites* *In-hotel: restaurant, pool, gym, spa, Wi-Fi, no-smoking rooms* ▭ *AE, D, MC, V* 🍽 *FAP* ☞ *2-night minimum stay.*

$$$$ ★ **Ojai Valley Inn & Spa.** This outdoorsy, golf-oriented resort and spa is set on beautifully landscaped grounds, with hillside views in nearly all directions. Though many of the rooms have been remodeled in the 21st century, they still reflect the Spanish colonial architecture of the original 1923 resort. If you're a history buff, ask for a room in the original 80-year-old adobe building. The four restaurants tout "Ojai regional cuisine," which incorporates locally grown produce and fresh seasonal meats and seafood. **Pros:** gorgeous grounds; exceptional outdoor activities; romantic yet kid-friendly. **Cons:** expensive; staff isn't always attentive. ✉ *905 Country Club Rd.* ☎ *805/646–1111 or 800/422–6524* 🌐 *www.ojairesort.com* *231 rooms, 77 suites* *In-room: refrigerator, Internet (some), Wi-Fi. In-hotel: 4 restaurants, bar, golf course, tennis courts, pools, spa, bicycles, children's programs (ages 5–12), Wi-Fi, some pets allowed, no-smoking rooms* ▭ *AE, D, DC, MC, V.*

$$$–$$$$ **Su Nido Inn.** Just a short walk from downtown Ojai sights and restaurants, this posh Mission Revival–style inn is nested in a quiet neighborhood a few blocks from Libbey Park. One- and two-bedroom suites, each named after a bird, ring a cobblestone courtyard with fountains and olive trees. All suites have spacious living rooms, private patios, kitchenettes, soaking tubs, fireplaces, and featherbeds. **Pros:** walking

distance from downtown; homey feel. **Cons:** no pool; can get hot during summer. ✉ *301 N. Montgomery St.* ☎ *805/646–7080 or 866/646–7080* 🌐 *www.sunidoinn.com* *3 rooms, 9 suites* *In-room: kitchen (some), refrigerator, DVD, Internet, Wi-Fi. In-hotel: no-smoking rooms* *AE, D, MC, V.*

THE ARTS

On Wednesday evenings in summer, all-American music played by the Ojai Band draws crowds to **Libbey Park** (✉ *Ojai Ave.* ☎ *805/646–8430* *Free*) in downtown Ojai. Since 1947, the **Ojai Music Festival** (☎ *805/646–2094* 🌐 *www.ojaifestival.org*) has attracted internationally known progressive and traditional musicians for outdoor concerts in Libbey Park for a weekend in late May or early June.

SANTA BARBARA

27 mi northwest of Ventura and 29 mi west of Ojai on U.S. 101.

Santa Barbara has long been an oasis for Los Angelenos seeking respite from hectic big-city life. The attractions begin at the ocean and end in the foothills of the Santa Ynez Mountains. A few miles up the coast—but still very much a part of Santa Barbara—is the exclusive residential district of Hope Ranch. Santa Barbara is on a jog in the coastline, so the ocean is actually to the south, instead of the west; for this reason, directions can be confusing. "Up" the coast toward San Francisco is west, "down" toward Los Angeles is east, and the mountains are north.

GETTING HERE AND AROUND

A car is handy but not essential if you're planning to stay in town. The beaches and downtown are easily explored by bicycle or on foot. You can also hop aboard one of the electric shuttles that cruise the downtown and waterfront every 8 to 15 minutes (25¢ each way) and connect with local buses such as Line 22, which goes to major visitor sights (🌐 *www.sbmtd.gov*).

A motorized San Francisco–style cable car operated by **Santa Barbara Trolley Co.** (☎ *805/965–0353* 🌐 *www.sbtrolley.com*) makes 90-minute runs from 10 to 4 past major hotels, shopping areas, and attractions. Get off whenever you like, and pick up another trolley when you're ready to move on (they come every hour). Try to get a seat on the newest vehicle in the fleet, a biodiesel trolley with all seats on the top deck. Trolleys depart from and returns to Stearns Wharf. The fare is $19 for the day.

Visit **Santa Barbara Car Free** (🌐 *www.santabarbaracarfree.org*) for bike-route and walking-tour maps and car-free vacation packages with substantial lodging discounts.

ESSENTIALS

Visitor Information Santa Barbara Conference and Visitors Bureau (✉ *1601 Anacapa St., Santa Barbara* ☎ *805/966–9222* 🌐 *www.santabarbaraca.com*). **Santa Barbara Chamber of Commerce Visitor Information Center** (✉ *1 Garden St., at Cabrillo Blvd.* ☎ *805/965–3021* 🌐 *www.sbchamber.org*).

EXPLORING

Santa Barbara's waterfront is beautiful, with palm-studded promenades and plenty of sand. In the few miles between the beaches and the hills are downtown, the old mission, and the botanic gardens.

WHAT TO SEE

15 **Andree Clark Bird Refuge.** This peaceful lagoon and gardens sits north of East Beach. Bike trails and footpaths, punctuated by signs identifying native and migratory birds, skirt the lagoon. ✉ *1400 E. Cabrillo Blvd.* *Free.*

3 **Carriage and Western Art Museum.** The country's largest collection of old horse-drawn vehicles—painstakingly restored—is exhibited here. Everything from polished hearses to police buggies to old stagecoaches and circus vehicles is on display. In August the Old Spanish Days Fiesta borrows many of the vehicles for a jaunt about town. This is one of the city's true hidden gems, a wonderful place to help history come alive—especially for children. Docents lead tours the third Sunday of every month from 1 to 4 PM. ✉ *129 Castillo St.* ☎ *805/962–2353* *www.carriagemuseum.org* *Free* *Weekdays 9–3.*

6 ★ **El Presidio State Historic Park.** Founded in 1782, El Presidio was one of four military strongholds established by the Spanish along the coast of California. The park encompasses much of the original site in the heart of downtown. El Cuartel, the adobe guardhouse, is the oldest building in Santa Barbara and the second oldest in California. ✉ *123 E. Canon Perdido St.* ☎ *805/965–0093* *www.sbthp.org* *$5* *Daily 10:30–4:30.*

10 **Karpeles Manuscript Library.** Ancient political tracts and old Disney cartoons are among the holdings at this facility, which also houses one of the world's largest privately owned collections of rare manuscripts. Fifty display cases contain a sampling of the archive's million-plus documents. ✉ *21 W. Anapamu St.* ☎ *805/962–5322* *www.karpeles.com* *Free* *Daily 10–4.*

11 Fodor's Choice ★ **Mission Santa Barbara.** Widely referred to as the "Queen of Missions," this is one of the most beautiful and frequently photographed buildings in coastal California. The architecture, which was originally built in 1786, evolved from adobe-brick buildings with thatch roofs to more permanent edifices as its population burgeoned. An earthquake in 1812 destroyed the third church built on the site. Its replacement, the present structure, is still a functioning Catholic church. The building is surrounded by cacti, palms, and other succulents. ✉ *2201 Laguna St.* ☎ *805/682–4149 or 805/682–4713* *www.santabarbaramission.org* *$5* *Daily 9–4:30.*

16 **Montecito.** Since the late 1800s the tree-studded hills and valleys of this town have attracted the rich and famous (Hollywood icons, business tycoons, dot-commers who divested before the crash, and old-money families who installed themselves here years ago). Shady roads wind through the community, which consists mostly of gated estates. Swank boutiques line Coast Village Road, where well-heeled residents such as Oprah Winfrey sometimes browse for truffle oil, picture frames, and designer sweats. Residents also hang out in the Upper Village,

Continued on page 55

DID YOU KNOW?

The mission fathers followed in the footsteps of explorer and navigator Juan Rodriguez Cabrillo, who in 1542 had claimed most of the California coast for Spain.

ON A MISSION

Their soul may belong to Spain, their heart to the New World, but the historic missions of California, with their lovely churches, beckon the traveler on a soulful journey back to the very founding of the American West.

by Cheryl Crabtree and Robert I.C. Fisher

California history changed forever in the 18th century when Spanish explorers founded a series of missions along the Pacific coast. Believing they were following God's will, the Spaniards decided to conquer these beautiful rolling hills with Bibles, not bullets, expanding their great empire while spreading the gospel. The process produced a collision between the Hispanic and *Nativo* cultures, resulting in one of the most striking legacies of Old California: the Spanish mission churches. Rising like mirages in the middle of desert plains and rolling hills, these saintly sites transport you back to the days of the earliest *Californios*.

GOD AND MAN IN CALIFORNIA

Named "Alta California" after an earthly paradise described in a 16th-century Spanish novel, the territory came under pressure around 1750 with the arrival of such interlopers as Russian trappers and English sailors. Unfortunately, Spanish settlers had proved loath to forsake the familiar refinements of Europe for this remote New World. The solution? To build on outsourcing the model that had already worked well in Spain's Mexico colony. The plan involved establishing a series of missions, to be operated by the Catholic Church and protected by four of Spain's *presidios* (military outposts).

In enacting this strategy, ranks of armored conquistadors gave way to a force of Spanish padres. For the most part members of the Franciscan order, the warrior-priests, swiftly succeeded in subjecting the native tribes to peon slavery to create self-governing mission towns.

FATHER OF THE MISSIONS

Father Junípero Serra is an icon of the Spanish colonial period. At the behest of the Spanish government, the tiny, asthmatic padre—then well into his fifties, and despite a chronic leg infection—started out on foot from Baja California to search for suitable mission and presidio sites. He walked northward to San Diego, where in 1769 he helped establish Alta California's first mission and continued his travels until his death, in 1784, by which time he had founded eight more missions. His legacy was threatened in 1833–34, when—after winning independence from Spain—the new government of Mexico claimed large stretches of California and secularized all the missions. But as the *Californios* once took the land from the *Nativos*, so, too, would the *Americanos* ultimately take the land from the *Mexicanos* in 1848. Today, these missions stand as extraordinary monuments to this polyglot past.

MISSION ACCOMPLISHED

California's Mission Trail is the best way to follow in the fathers' footsteps. Here, below, are its 21 settlements, north to south.

Amazingly, all 21 Spanish missions in California are still standing—some in their pristine historic state, others with modifications made over the centuries. Many are found on or near the "King's Road"—El Camino Real—which was constructed to link these mission outposts. At the height of the mission system the trail was approximately 600 miles long, eventually extending from San Diego to Sonoma. You can still see evidence of the road today on portions of routes 101 and 82 in the form of roadside bell markers erected by CalTrans every one to two miles between Orange County and San Francisco.

San Francisco Solano, Sonoma (1823; this was the final California mission constructed.)

San Rafael, San Rafael (1817)

San Francisco de Asís (aka Mission Dolores), San Francisco (1776; see Chapter 4). Situated in the heart of San Francisco, these mission grounds and nearby Arroyo de los Dolores (Creek of Sorrows) are home to the oldest intact building in the city.

Mission San Rafael

Mission Santa Clara de Asís

Santa Clara de Asís, Santa Clara (1777; see Chapter 5). On the campus of Santa Clara University, this beautifully restored mission contains original paintings, statues, a bell, and hundreds of artifacts, as well as a spectacular rose garden.

San José, Fremont (1797)

Santa Cruz, Santa Cruz (1791)

San Juan Bautista, San Juan Bautista (1797; see Chapter 3). Immortalized in Hitchcock's *Vertigo*, this remarkably preserved pueblo contains the largest church of all the California missions, as well as 18th- and 19th-century buildings and a sprawling plaza.

San Carlos Borromeo del Río Carmelo, Carmel (1770; see Chapter 3). Carmel Mission was headquarters for the California mission system under Father Serra; the on-site museum includes Serra's tiny sleeping quarters (where he died in 1784).

Nuestra Señora de la Soledad, Soledad (1791)

San Antonio de Padua, Jolon (1771)

San Miguel Arcángel, San Miguel (1797; see Chapter 2). San Miguel boasts the only intact original interior work of art in any of the missions, painted in 1821 by Native

Mission Santa Inés

American converts under the direction of Spanish artist Esteban Munras. A 2003 earthquake damaged the complex, sections of which are being sequentially reopened.

San Luis Obispo de Tolosa, San Luis Obispo (1772; see Chapter 2). Bear meat from grizzlies captured here saved Spaniards from starving in 1772, convincing Father Serra to establish a mission. Today, traditional ringing patterns are still played on the mission's original bells.

La Purísima Concepción, Lompoc (1787; see Chapter 2). La Purísima is the nation's most completely restored mission complex. It is now a living-history museum with a church and nearly forty craft and residence rooms.

Santa Inés, Solvang (1804; see Chapter 2)

Santa Bárbara, Santa Barbara (1786; see Chapter 2). The "Queen of the Missions" has twin bell towers, gorgeous gardens with heirloom plant varietals, a massive collection of rare

Mission San Fernando Rey de España

artworks and artifacts, and lovely stonework.

San Buenaventura, Ventura (1782; see Chapter 2). This was the last mission founded by Father Serra; it is still an active parish in the Archdiocese of Los Angeles.

San Fernando Rey de España, Mission Hills (1797)

San Gabriel Arcángel, San Gabriel (1771)

San Luis Rey de Francia, Oceanside (1798)

San Juan Capistrano, San Juan Capistrano (1776). This mission is famed for its Saint Joseph's Day (March 19) celebration of the return of swallows in the springtime. The mission's adobe walls enclose acres of lush gardens and historic buildings.

San Diego de Alcalá, San Diego (1769; this was the first California mission constructed.)

Mission San Miguel Arcángel

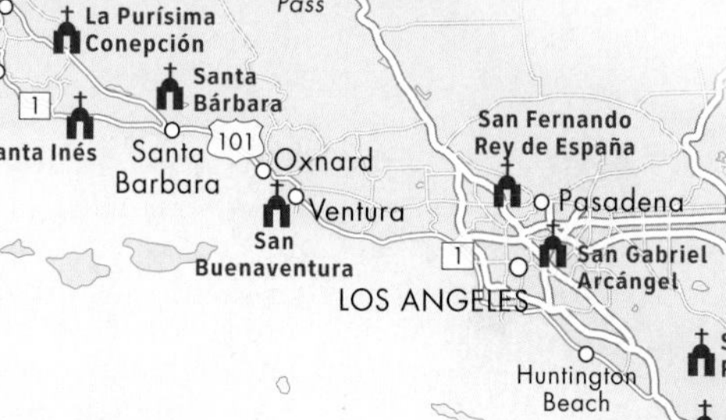

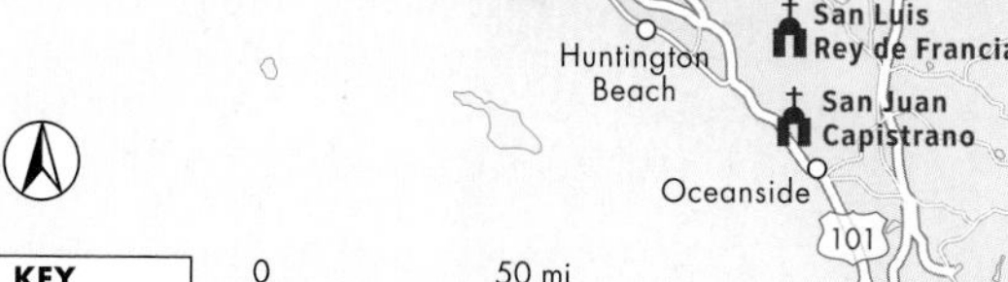

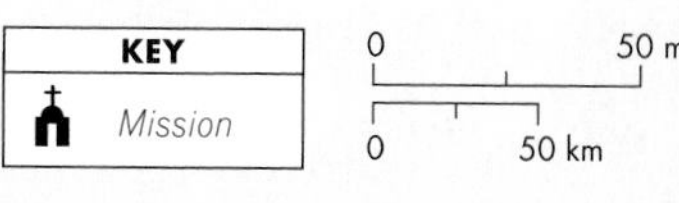

SPANISH MISSION STYLE

(left) Mission San Luis Rey de Francia; (right) Mission San Antonio de Padua

The Spanish mission churches derive much of their strength and enduring power from their extraordinary admixture of styles. As such they became spectacular examples of *mestizaje*, or the mixture of races and cultures that often bloomed along La Frontera, "the Border" between Mexico and California.

SPIRIT OF THE PLACE

Because the overseers were so often of the Franciscan order, these churches became decorative essays in humility and simplicity. In lieu of marble (and wood, which was almost as scarce), whitewashed adobe walls gleamed in the sun. Floors were often composed of packed earth. In place of canvas and costly pigments, elk hides and vegetable hues were used to depict bible stories. Instead of gilded angels, there were *bulto* (devotional) sculptures of the Virgin of Guadalupe (honoring a mystic vision once seen by a Mexican Indian) carved by wandering *santeros*, or saint-makers. And instead of the jeweled splendor of Spain's Churriguerresque-style altar walls, there were simple but colorful wood-carved *retablos* (altar-screens). Straw appliqués took the place of costly tapestries, and pierced-tinwork lamps stood in for chandeliers.

AN ENDURING LEGACY

As for mission architecture, the effects of the new melting- pot rose to high-gear level. While naves followed the simple forms of Franciscan Gothic, cloisters (with beautiful arcades) adopted aspects of the Romanesque style, while ornamental touches of the Spanish Renaissance—including red-tiled *tejas* roofs and wrought-iron grilles—set an elegant note. In the 20th century, the Mission Revival Style had a huge impact on architecture and design in California, as seen in examples ranging from San Diego's Union Station to Stanford University's main quadrangle.

Father Junípero Serra statue at the Mission San Gabriel

FOR WHOM THE BELLS TOLLED

Perhaps the most famous architectural motif of the Spanish Mission churches was the belltower. These took the form of either a campanile—a single tower called a *campanario*—or, more spectacularly, of an open-work *espadana*, a perforated adobe wall housing a series of bells (notable examples of this form are at San Miguel Arcángel and San Diego de Alcalá). Bells were essential to maintaining the routines of daily life at the missions.

MISSION LIFE

Morning bells summoned residents to chapel for services; noontime bells introduced the main meal, while the evening bells sounded the alert to gather around 5 PM for mass and dinner. Many of the natives were happy with their new faith, and even enjoyed putting in 40 hours a week working as farmers, soapmakers, weavers, masons, and herders.

Others, however, were less willing to abandon their traditional culture, but were coerced to abide by the new Spanish laws and mission rules. Gated walls and outlying native sleeping quarters were locked at night to prevent escape. Natives were often mistreated by the friars, who used a system of punishments to enforce submission to their teachings.

NATIVE TRAGEDY

In the end, mission life proved extremely destructive to the Native Californian population. Smallpox and other European diseases caused the death of nearly a third, with some tribes—notably the Chumash—being virtually decimated. One friar was quoted as noting that the Indians "live well free but as soon as we reduce them to a Christian and community life . . . they fatten, sicken, and die."

After the Mexican government secularized the missions in 1833, a majority of the native population, now reduced to poverty, went to live in the new California pueblos—a shameful and tragic end for those whose labor was largely responsible for the magnificent mission churches we see today.

FOR MORE INFORMATION

California Missions Foundation

✉ 4129 Main St., Suite 207
Riverside, CA 92501

☎ 951/369-0440

⊕ www.californiamissionsfoundation.org

Top, Mission San Gabriel Arcángel
Left, Mission San Miguel Arcángel.

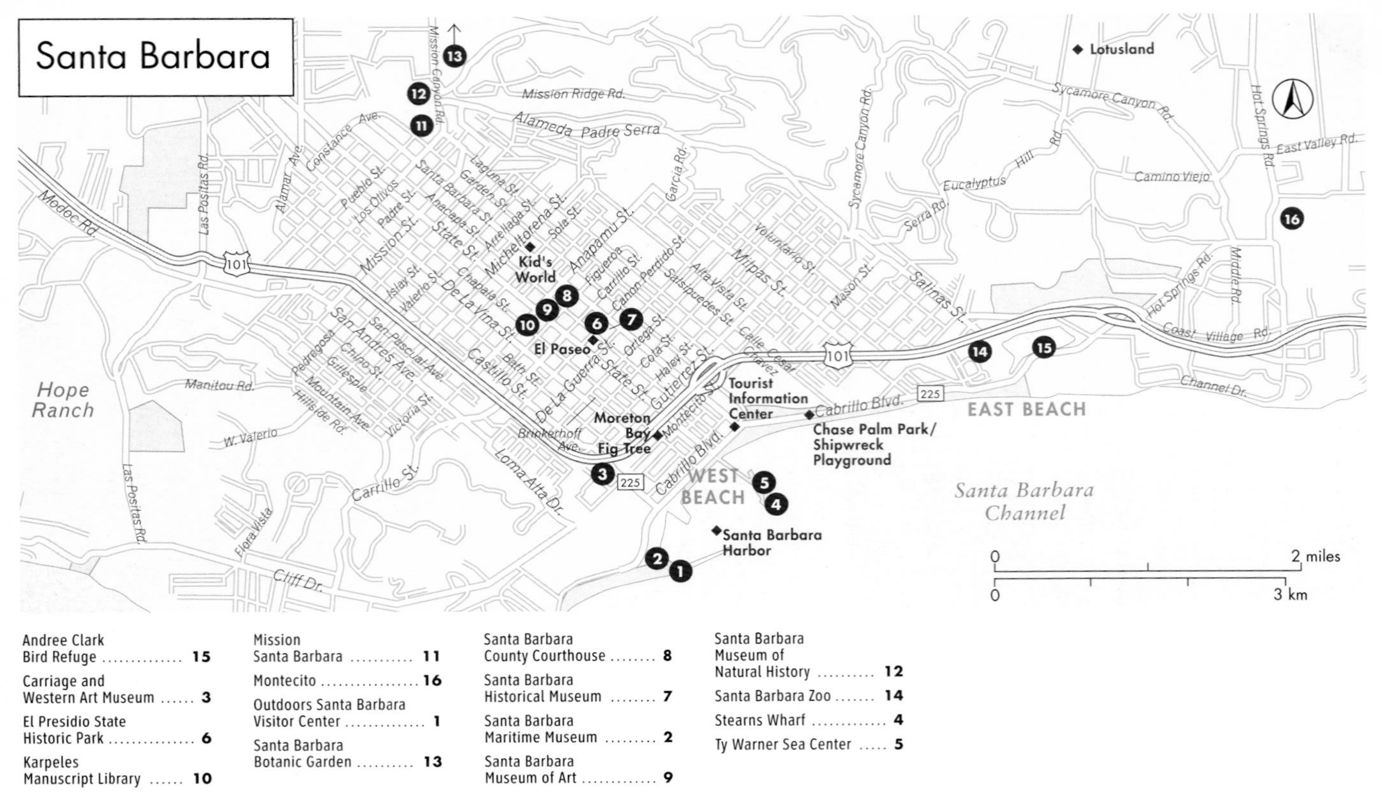
Santa Barbara
Lotusland
Mission Canyon Rd.
Mission Ridge Rd.
Alameda Padre Serra
Sycamore Canyon Rd.
Hot Springs Rd.
East Valley Rd.
Camino Viejo
Eucalyptus Hill Rd.
Serra Rd.
Garcia Rd.
Constance Ave.
Alamar Ave.
Las Positas Rd.
Modoc Rd.
101
Pueblo St.
Los Olivos
Padre St.
Mission St.
Santa Barbara St.
Laguna St.
Garden St.
Anacapa St.
State St.
Arrellaga St.
Micheltorena St.
Sola St.
Anapamu St.
Kid's World
Figueroa
Carrillo St.
Canon Perdido St.
Salsipuedes St.
Alta Vista St.
Milpas St.
Voluntario St.
Mason St.
Salinas St.
Hot Springs Rd.
Middle Rd.
Coast Village Rd.
Channel Dr.
Islay St.
Valerio St.
De La Vina St.
Chapala St.
El Paseo
Ortega St.
Cota St.
Haley St.
Gutierrez St.
Calle Cesar Chavez
Tourist Information Center
Cabrillo Blvd.
225
EAST BEACH
Chase Palm Park/ Shipwreck Playground
Hope Ranch
Manitou Rd.
Pedregosa
San Andres Ave.
San Pascual Ave.
Chino St.
Gillespie
Mountain Ave.
Hillside Rd.
Victoria St.
Castillo St.
Bath St.
De La Guerra St.
State St.
Montecito St.
Moreton Bay Fig Tree
Brinkerhoff Ave.
W. Valerio
Loma Alta Dr.
Carrillo St.
Cabrillo Blvd.
WEST BEACH
Santa Barbara Channel
Las Positas Rd.
Flora Vista
Cliff Dr.
Santa Barbara Harbor
0
2 miles
0
3 km
Andree Clark Bird Refuge 15
Carriage and Western Art Museum 3
El Presidio State Historic Park 6
Karpeles Manuscript Library 10
Mission Santa Barbara 11
Montecito 16
Outdoors Santa Barbara Visitor Center 1
Santa Barbara Botanic Garden 13
Santa Barbara County Courthouse 8
Santa Barbara Historical Museum 7
Santa Barbara Maritime Museum 2
Santa Barbara Museum of Art 9
Santa Barbara Museum of Natural History 12
Santa Barbara Zoo 14
Stearns Wharf 4
Ty Warner Sea Center 5

a chic shopping area with restaurants and cafés at the intersection of San Ysidro and East Valley roads. Montecito is just about 3 mi east of Santa Barbara.

Fodor's Choice ★ The 37-acre Montecito estate called **Lotusland** (☎*805/969–9990* ⊕*www.lotusland.org* ✉*$35*) once belonged to Polish opera singer Ganna Walska. Many of the exotic trees and other subtropical flora were planted in 1882 by horticulturist R. Kinton Stevens. On the two-hour guided tour (the only option for visiting), you'll see an outdoor theater, a topiary garden, a huge collection of rare cycads (an unusual plant genus that has been around since the time of the dinosaurs), and a lotus pond. Tours are conducted mid-February through mid-November, Wednesday through Saturday at 10 and 1:30. Reservations are required. Child-friendly family tours are available for groups with children under the age of 10; contact Lotusland for scheduling.

SANTA BARBARA STYLE

Why does downtown Santa Barbara look so scrubbed and uniform? After a 1925 earthquake, which demolished many buildings, the city seized a golden opportunity to create a Spanish–Mediterranean look. It established an architectural board of review, which, along with city commissions, created strict architectural codes for the downtown district: red tile roofs, earth-tone facades, arches, wrought-iron embellishments, and limited height restrictions (about four stories).

1 **Outdoors Santa Barbara Visitor Center.** The small office provides maps and other information about Channel Islands National Park, Channel Islands National Marine Sanctuary, and the Santa Barbara Maritime Museum, which occupies the same building in the harbor. ✉*113 Harbor Way* ☎*805/884–1475* ⊕*outdoorsb.noaa.gov* ✉*Free* ⏲*Daily 11–5.*

13 **Santa Barbara Botanic Garden.** Scenic trails meander through the garden's 78 acres of native plants. The Mission Dam, built in 1806, stands just beyond the redwood grove and above the restored aqueduct that once carried water to Mission Santa Barbara. An ethnobotanical display demonstrates how Native Americans used plants to create baskets, clothing, and structures. ✉*1212 Mission Canyon Rd.* ☎*805/682–4726* ⊕*www.sbbg.org* ✉*$8* ⏲*Mar.–Oct., daily 9–6; Nov.–Feb., daily 9–5. Guided tours daily at 2, additional tour on weekends at 11.*

8 ★ **Santa Barbara County Courthouse.** Hand-painted tiles and a spiral staircase infuse the courthouse with the grandeur of a Moorish palace. This magnificent building was completed in 1929, part of a rebuilding process after a 1925 earthquake destroyed many downtown structures. At the time, Santa Barbara was also in the midst of a cultural awakening, and the trend was toward an architectural style appropriate to the area's climate and history. The result is the harmonious Mediterranean–Spanish look of much of the downtown area, especially the municipal buildings. An elevator rises to an arched observation area in the courthouse tower that provides a panoramic view of the city. The murals in the ceremonial chambers on the courthouse's second floor were painted by an artist who did backdrops for some of Cecil B. DeMille's films. ✉*1100 block*

of Anacapa St. 805/962–6464 www.santabarbaracourthouse.org Weekdays 8–4:45, weekends 10–4:30. Free guided tours Mon., Tues., and Fri. at 10:30, Mon.–Sat. at 2.

NEED A BREAK?

Both children and adults can enjoy themselves at Kids' World (*Garden St. at Micheltorena St.*), a public playground with a complex, castle-shaped maze of fanciful climbing structures, slides, and tunnels built by Santa Barbara parents.

7 **Santa Barbara Historical Museum.** The historical society's museum exhibits decorative and fine arts, furniture, costumes, and documents from the town's past. Adjacent to it is the Gledhill Library, a collection of books, photographs, maps, and manuscripts. *136 E. De La Guerra St. 805/966–1601 www.santabarbaramuseum.com Museum by donation; library $2–$5 per hr for research Museum Tues.–Sat. 10–5, Sun. noon–5; library Tues.–Fri. 10–4, 1st Sat. of month 10–1.*

8 **Santa Barbara Maritime Museum.** California's seafaring history is the focus at this museum. High-tech, hands-on exhibits, such as a sportfishing activity that lets you catch a "big one" and a local surfing history retrospective, opened in 2008, make this a fun stop for families. *113 Harbor Way 805/962–8404 www.sbmm.org $7 June–Aug., Thurs.–Tues. 10–6; Sept.–May, Thurs.–Tues. 10–5.*

9 **Santa Barbara Museum of Art.** The highlights of this museum's permanent collection include ancient sculpture, Asian art, impressionist paintings, contemporary Latin American art, and American works in several mediums. *1130 State St. 805/963–4364 www.sbma.net $9, free on Sun. Tues.–Sun. 11–5. Free guided tours Tues.–Sun. at noon and 1.*

12 **Santa Barbara Museum of Natural History.** The gigantic skeleton of a blue whale greets you at the entrance of this complex. The major draws include the planetarium, space lab, and a gem and mineral display. A room of dioramas illustrates Chumash Indian history and culture. Startlingly alive-looking stuffed specimens, complete with nests and eggs, roost in the bird diversity room. Many exhibits have interactive components. Outdoors you can stroll on nature trails that wind through the serene oak-studded grounds. Admission is free on the third Sunday of each month. *2559 Puesta del Sol Rd. 805/682–4711 www.sbnature.org $10 Daily 10–5.*

14 **Santa Barbara Zoo.** The grounds of this smallish zoo are so gorgeous people book their weddings here long in advance. The palm-studded lawns on a hilltop overlooking the beach are perfect spots for family picnics. The natural settings of the zoo shelter elephants, gorillas, exotic birds, and big cats such as the rare snow leopard, a thick-furred, high-altitude dweller from Asia. For small children there's a scenic railroad and barnyard petting zoo. *500 Niños Dr. 805/962–5339 main line, 805/962–6310 information www.santabarbarazoo.org Zoo $11, parking $4 Daily 10–5.*

Santa Barbara's downtown is stunning, but be sure to also visit its beautiful—and uncrowded—beaches.

NEED A BREAK?

The antique carousel, large playground with a nautical theme, picnic areas, and snack bar make the scenic waterfront Chase Palm Park and Shipwreck Playground (✉ *Cabrillo Blvd., between Garden St. and Calle Cesar Chavez*) a favorite destination for kids and parents.

4 **Stearns Wharf.** Built in 1872, historic Stearns Wharf is Santa Barbara's most visited landmark. Expansive views of the mountains, cityscape, and harbor unfold from every vantage point on the three-block-long pier. Although it's a nice walk from the Cabrillo Boulevard parking areas, you can also park on the pier and then wander through the shops or stop for a meal at one of the wharf's restaurants. ✉ *Cabrillo Blvd., at foot of State St.* ☎ *805/897–2683 or 805/564–5531.*

5 **Ty Warner Sea Center.** A branch of the Santa Barbara Museum of Natural History, the Sea Center specializes in Santa Barbara Channel marine life and conservation. In 2005 it reopened in a new $6.5 million facility bearing the name of Ty Warner, Beanie Baby mogul and local resident, whose hefty donation helped the center complete the final stages of construction. The new Sea Center is small compared to aquariums in Monterey and Long Beach, but it's a fascinating, hands-on marine science laboratory that lets you participate in experiments, projects, and exhibits, including touch tanks. Haul up and analyze water samples, learn to identify marine mammals, and check out amazing creatures in the tide-pool lab and animal nursery. The two-story glass walls open to stunning ocean, mountain, and city views. ✉ *211 Stearns Wharf* ☎ *805/962–2526* 🌐 *www.sbnature.org* 🎟 *$8* ⏲ *Daily 10–5.*

WHERE TO EAT

$$ JAPANESE ✕**Arigato Sushi.** You might have to wait 45 minutes for a table at this trendy, two-story restaurant and sushi bar—locals line up early for the hip, casual atmosphere and wildly creative combination rolls. Fans of authentic Japanese food sometimes disagree about the quality of the seafood, but all dishes are fresh and artfully presented. The menu includes traditional dishes as well as innovative creations such as sushi pizza on seaweed and Hawaiian sashimi salad. ✉*1225 State St.* ☎*805/965–6074* *Reservations not accepted* ▭*AE, MC, V* ⏲*No lunch.*

LAND SHARK!

Land and Sea Tours (✉State St. at Stearns Wharf ☎*805/683–7600* 🌐*www.out2seesb.com* 🎫*$25* ⏲Tours May–Oct., daily noon, 2, and 4; Nov.–Apr., daily noon and 2) takes visitors on narrated, 90-minute land-and-sea adventures in an amphibious 49-passenger vehicle, nicknamed the Land Shark. Tours begin with a drive through the city and continue with a plunge into the harbor for a cruise along the coast.

$$ SEAFOOD ✕**Brophy Bros.** The outdoor tables at this casual harborside restaurant have perfect views of the marina and mountains. The staff serves enormous, exceptionally fresh fish dishes—don't miss the seafood salad and chowder—and provides you with a pager if there's a long wait for a table. You can stroll along the waterfront until the beep lets you know your table's ready. This place is hugely popular, so it can be crowded and loud, especially on weekend evenings. ✉*119 Harbor Way* ☎*805/966–4418* ▭*AE, MC, V.*

$$$ AMERICAN ✕**Elements.** Different sections within this chic, contemporary, restaurant and bar reflect nature's elements: an outdoor porch overlooking the sunken gardens at the Santa Barbara Courthouse across the street (air); the gold-toned main dining room (earth); an intimate corner with sofas for romantic dining (fire); and an often lively, ocean-hued area where professionals unwind over specialty martinis after work at the slick granite bar. The seasonal world-fusion menu, designed around organic and sustainable foods, might include a grilled ahi tuna wrap with wasabi mayonnaise at lunch, or lemongrass and panko-crusted sea bass with curry-coconut sauce and gingered basmati rice for dinner. ✉*129 E. Anapamu St.* ☎*805/884–9218* ▭*AE, D, MC, V.*

$$$ SEAFOOD ✕**The Hungry Cat.** The hep Santa Barbara sibling of a famed Hollywood eatery, run by famed chefs David Lentz and his wife, Suzanne Goin, dishes up savory seafood in a small but lively nook in the downtown arts district. Feast on sea urchin, addictive peel-and-eat shrimp, and creative cocktails made from farmers' market fruits and veggies. The normally nocturnal Cat awakens for a popular brunch on Sunday. Night or day, come early or be prepared for a wait. ✉*1134 Chapala St.* ☎*805/884–4701* *Reservations not accepted* ▭*AE, D, MC, V* ⏲*Closed Mon. No lunch.*

¢ MEXICAN ★ ✕**La Super-Rica.** Praised by Julia Child, this food stand with a patio on the east side of town serves some of the spiciest and most authentic Mexican dishes between Los Angeles and San Francisco. Fans drive for miles to fill up on the soft tacos served with yummy spicy or mild sauces and legendary beans. Three daily specials are offered each day. Portions are on the small side; order several dishes and share. ✉622 N. Milpas St., at Alphonse St. ☎805/963–4940 ▭No credit cards. ⊙Closed Wed.

BEST VIEWS

Drive along Alameda Padre Serra, a hillside road that begins near the mission and continues to Montecito, to feast your eyes on spectacular views of the city and the Santa Barbara Channel.

2

$$$ ITALIAN ✕**Olio e Limone.** Sophisticated Italian cuisine (with an emphasis on Sicily) is served at this restaurant near the Arlington Center for the Performing Arts. The juicy veal chop is a popular dish, but surprises abound here; be sure to try unusual dishes such as ribbon pasta with quail and sausage in a mushroom ragout, duck ravioli, or swordfish with Sicilian ratatouille. Tables are placed a bit close together, so this may not be the best spot for intimate conversations. *✉17 W. Victoria St. ☎805/899–2699 ▭AE, D, DC, MC, V ⊙No lunch Sun.*

$$$ SOUTHERN ✕**Palace Grill.** Mardi Gras energy, team-style service, lively music, and great food have made the Palace a Santa Barbara icon. Acclaimed for its Cajun and creole dishes such as blackened redfish and jambalaya with dirty rice, the Palace also serves Caribbean fare, including a delicious coconut-shrimp dish. If you're spice-phobic, you can choose pasta, soft-shell crab, or filet mignon. Be prepared to wait as long as 45 minutes for a table on Friday and Saturday night, when reservations are taken for a 5:30 seating only. *✉8 E. Cota St. ☎805/963–5000 ▭AE, MC, V.*

$$$ ECLECTIC ✕**Roy.** Owner-chef Leroy Gandy serves a $25 fixed-price dinner (some selections are $20, some $30)—a real bargain—that includes a small salad, fresh soup, homemade organic bread, and a selection from a rotating list of contemporary American main courses. If you're lucky, the entrée choices might include grilled local fish with a mandarin beurre blanc, or bacon-wrapped filet mignon. You can also choose from an à la carte menu of inexpensive appetizers and entrées, plus local wines. Half a block from State Street in the heart of downtown, Roy is a favorite spot for late-night dining (it's open until midnight and has a full bar). *✉7 W. Carrillo St. ☎805/966–5636 ▭AE, D, DC, MC, V ⊙No lunch.*

$$$$ AMERICAN ★ ✕**The Stonehouse.** Part of the San Ysidro Ranch resort, this elegantly rustic restaurant, which reopened in 2007 following the resort's $150 million remodeling, is housed in a century-old granite farmhouse. Executive chef John Trotta harvests herbs and veggies from the on-site garden, then adds them to an array of top-quality local ingredients to create outstanding regional cuisine. The menu changes constantly, but typically includes favorites such as crab cake with mango relish appetizer and Parmesan-crusted halibut. Dine on the radiant-heated ocean-view deck with stone fireplace, next to a fountain under a canopy of loquat trees, or in the romantic, candlelit dining room overlooking a creek. The Plow & Angel pub, downstairs, offers more casual bistro fare. *✉900 San Ysidro La., Montecito ☎805/969–4100 ✍Reservations essential ▭AE, DC, MC, V ⊙No lunch.*

WHERE TO STAY

$$$$ **Canary Hotel.** The only full-service hotel in the heart of downtown, the Canary blends the feel of a casual beach getaway with tony urban sophistication. It first opened as the Hotel Andalucia in 2004. New owners revamped it in 2008 to match swank sisters Shutters on the Beach and Casa del Mar in Santa Monica. Moroccan rugs, African masks, dark wood floors, and seagrass color schemes create an exotic mood throughout. Homey touches in the light-filled rooms include walnut four-poster beds, yoga mats, candles, and binoculars to take along while touring the town. The Perch, a sixth-floor guests-only rooftop lounge, has a pool and stunning views. The Coast restaurant ($$$) on the lobby floor serves upscale comfort food centered around fresh local ingredients. **Pros:** easy stroll to museums, shopping, dining; friendly, attentive service; adjacent fitness center (fee). **Cons:** across from main bus transit center; some rooms feel cramped. ✉*31 W. Carrillo St.* ☎*805/884–0300 or 877/468–3515* 🌐*www.canarysantabarbara.com* *77 rooms, 20 suites* *In-room: safe, refrigerator, DVD, Internet, Wi-Fi. In-hotel: restaurant, room service, bar, pool, laundry service, Internet terminal, Wi-Fi, parking (paid), some pets allowed, no-smoking rooms* ▭*AE, D, DC, MC, V.*

$$$$ ★ **Four Seasons Resort The Biltmore Santa Barbara.** Surrounded by lush, perfectly manicured gardens and across from the beach, Santa Barbara's grande dame has long been a favorite for quiet, California-style luxury. The sumptuous 10,000-square-foot spa, which includes 11 treatment rooms, near the resort's pool and gardens, is an oasis for rejuvenation. Dining is upscale casual at the ocean-view Bella Vista Restaurant ($$$–$$$$), where the seasonal California-contemporary menu changes monthly. **Pros:** first-class resort; historic Santa Barbara character; personal service; steps from the beach. **Cons:** back rooms are close to train tracks; expensive. ✉*1260 Channel Dr.* ☎*805/969–2261 or 800/332–3442* 🌐*www.fourseasons.com/santabarbara* *181 rooms, 26 suites* *In-room: DVD, Internet, Wi-Fi. In-hotel: restaurant, room service, bar, tennis courts, pool, gym, spa, children's programs (ages 5–12), some pets allowed, no-smoking rooms* ▭*AE, D, DC, MC, V.*

$$$ **Hotel Mar Monte.** A complex of three separate buildings on three landscaped acres, plus a neighboring inn and apartment units, the Mar Monte provides a wide range of value-laden lodging options in a prime location—right across from East Beach and the Cabrillo Pavilion Bathhouse. The lobby and walkways in the historic main building, constructed in 1931, reflect old Santa Barbara: Spanish tiles, wrought-iron chandeliers, and vintage black-and-white photos. All rooms and baths were updated in 2008 and now boast comfy down comforters, flat-screen high-definition TVs, contemporary furnishings, refrigerators, and microwaves; deluxe and ocean view rooms have private balconies or patios. Even if you don't land a room with a view, you can gaze at the ocean and islands from a table in the on-site Bistro 1111 Restaurant or splurge on a treatment in the poolside spa. The Santa Barbara Airbus to LAX stops here six times a day. **Pros:** steps from the beach; many room types and rates; walk to the zoo and waterfront shuttle. **Cons:** motelish vibe; busy area in summer. ✉*1111 E. Cabrillo*

Blvd. ☎*805/963–0744 or 800/643–1994* 🌐*www.hotelmarmonte.com* *218 rooms, 5 apartments* *In-room: kitchen (some), refrigerator, Internet, Wi-Fi. In-hotel: restaurant, room service, bar, pool, gym, spa, Internet terminal, Wi-Fi, parking (free), some pets allowed, no-smoking rooms* ▭*AE, D, MC, V.*

$$$$ **Inn of the Spanish Garden.** A half block from the Presidio in the heart of downtown, this elegant Spanish-Mediterranean retreat celebrates Santa Barbara style, from tile floors, wrought-iron balconies, and exotic plants to original art by famed local plein-air artists. The luxury rooms have private balconies or patios, fireplaces, Frette linens, and deep soaking tubs. In the evening you can order a glass of wine and relax in the candlelighted courtyard. This inn is a good choice if you want to park your car for most of your stay and walk to theaters, restaurants, and shuttle buses. **Pros:** walking distance from downtown; classic Spanish-Mediterranean style; caring staff. **Cons:** far from the beach; not much here for kids. ✉*915 Garden St.* ☎*805/564–4700 or 866/564–4700* 🌐*www.spanishgardeninn.com* *23 rooms* *In-room: Internet, Wi-Fi. In-hotel: bar, pool, gym, laundry service, parking (free), no-smoking rooms* ▭*AE, D, DC, MC, V* *CP.*

$–$$ **Motel 6 Santa Barbara Beach.** A half block from East Beach amid fancier hotels sits this basic but comfortable motel, which was the first Motel 6 in existence. It's an incredible bargain for the location and fills quickly; book months in advance if possible. Kids 17 and under stay free. Sister properties in Goleta and in Carpinteria, 12 mi south of Santa Barbara and 1 mi from the beach, offer equally comfortable rooms at even lower rates. **Pros:** less than a minute's walk from the zoo and beach; friendly staff; clean and comfortable. **Cons:** no frills; motel-style rooms; no breakfast. ✉*443 Corona Del Mar Dr.* ☎*805/564–1392 or 800/466–8356* 🌐*www.motel6.com* *51 rooms* *In-room: refrigerator (some), Wi-Fi. In-hotel: pool, Wi-Fi, some pets allowed, no-smoking rooms* ▭*AE, D, DC, MC, V.*

$$$$ ★ **San Ysidro Ranch.** At this romantic hideaway on a historic property in the Montecito foothills—where John and Jackie Kennedy spent their honeymoon and Oprah sends her out-of-town guests—guest cottages are scattered among groves of orange trees and flower beds. All have down comforters and fireplaces; most have private outdoor spas, and one has its own pool. Seventeen miles of hiking trails crisscross 500 acres of open space surrounding the property. The Stonehouse Restaurant ($$–$$$$; *see above*) and Plow & Angel Bistro ($–$$$) are Santa Barbara institutions. The hotel completed a $150 million restoration in 2007. **Pros:** ultimate privacy; surrounded by nature; celebrity hangout; pet-friendly. **Cons:** very expensive; too remote for some. ✉*900 San Ysidro La., Montecito* ☎*805/565–1700 or 800/368–6788* 🌐*www.sanysidroranch.com* *23 rooms, 4 suites, 14 cottages* *In-room: refrigerator, DVD, Internet, Wi-Fi. In-hotel: 2 restaurants, room service, bar, pool, gym, some pets allowed, no-smoking rooms* ▭*AE, MC, V* ☞*2-day minimum stay on weekends, 3 days on holiday weekends.*

$$$$ ★ **Simpson House Inn.** If you're a fan of traditional B&Bs, this property, with its beautifully appointed Victorian main house and acre of lush gardens, is for you. If privacy and luxury are your priority, choose one of

the elegant cottages or a room in the century-old barn; each has a wood-burning fireplace, luxurious bedding, and state-of-the-art electronics (several even have whirlpool baths). In-room massages and other spa services are available. Room rates include use of a downtown athletic club. **Pros:** impeccable landscaping; walking distance from everything downtown; ranked among the nation's top B&Bs. **Cons:** some rooms in the main building are small; two-night minimum stay on weekends. *⊠121 E. Arrellaga St. ☎805/963–7067 or 800/676–1280 ⊕www.simpsonhouseinn.com ⇨11 rooms, 4 cottages ♢In-room: refrigerator (some), DVD, Wi-Fi. In-hotel: bicycles, no-smoking rooms ▭AE, D, MC, V ♈BP.*

NIGHTLIFE AND THE ARTS

Most major hotels present entertainment nightly during the summer season and on weekends all year. Much of the town's bar, club, and live music scene centers around lower State Street (between the 300 and 800 blocks). The thriving arts district, with theaters, restaurants, and cafés, starts around the 900 block of State Street and continues north to the Arlington Center for the Performing Arts, in the 1300 block. Santa Barbara supports a professional symphony and a chamber orchestra. The proximity to the University of California at Santa Barbara assures an endless stream of visiting artists and performers. To see what's scheduled around town, pick up a copy of the free weekly *Santa Barbara Independent* newspaper or visit their Web site, www.independent.com.

NIGHTLIFE Rich leather couches, a crackling fire in chilly weather, a cigar balcony, and pool tables draw a fancy Gen-X crowd to **Blue Agave** (*⊠20 E. Cota St. ☎805/899–4694*) for good food and designer martinis. All types of people hang out at **Dargan's** (*⊠18 E. Ortega St. ☎805/568–0702*), a lively pub with four pool tables, a great selection of draft beer and Irish whiskeys, and a full menu of traditional Irish dishes. The **James Joyce** (*⊠513 State St. ☎805/962–2688*), which sometimes plays host to folk and rock performers, is a good place to have a few beers and while away an evening.

Joe's Cafe (*⊠536 State St. ☎805/966–4638*), where steins of beer accompany hearty bar food, is a fun, if occasionally rowdy, collegiate scene. A slick sports bar attached to an upscale steak house owned by the maker of Lucky Brand Dungarees, **Lucky's** (*⊠1279 Coast Village Rd., Montecito ☎805/565–7540*) attracts a flock of hip, fashionably dressed patrons hoping to see and be seen.

Swank **Milk & Honey** (*⊠30 W. Anapamu St. ☎805/275–4232*) lures trendy crowds with artfully prepared tapas, coconut-mango mojitos, and exotic cocktails—despite high prices and a reputation for inattentive service.

SOhO (*⊠1221 State St. ☎805/962–7776*)—a hip restaurant, bar, and music club—schedules an eclectic mix of live music groups, from jazz to blues to rock, every night of the week.

THE ARTS **Arlington Center for the Performing Arts** (*⊠1317 State St. ☎805/963–4408*), a Moorish-style auditorium, is the home of the Santa Barbara Symphony. **Center Stage Theatre** (*⊠700 block of State St., 2nd fl. of Paseo Nuevo*

805/963–0408) presents plays, music, dance, and readings. **Ensemble Theatre Company** (*914 Santa Barbara St. 805/962–8606*) stages plays by authors ranging from Henrik Ibsen and David Mamet to rising contemporary dramatists. Originally opened in 1924, the landmark **Granada Theatre** (*1214 State St. 805/899–3000 general info, 805/899–2222 box office*) reopened to great fanfare in 2008 following a $50 million restoration and modernization. The **Lobero Theatre** (*33 E. Canon Perdido St. 805/963–0761*), a state landmark, hosts community theater groups and touring professionals. In Montecito, the **Music Academy of the West** (*1070 Fairway Rd. 805/969–4726, box office 805/969–8787*) showcases orchestral, chamber, and operatic works every summer.

BIRTHPLACE OF THE ENVIRONMENTAL MOVEMENT

In 1969, 200,000 gallons of crude oil spilled into the Santa Barbara Channel, causing an immediate outcry from residents, particularly in the UCSB community. The day after the spill, Get Oil Out (GOO) was established; the group helped lead the successful fight for legislation to limit and regulate offshore drilling in California. The Santa Barbara spill also spawned Earth Day, which is still celebrated in communities across the nation today.

2

SPORTS AND THE OUTDOORS

BEACHES

Santa Barbara's beaches don't have the big surf of the shoreline farther south, but they also don't have the crowds. You can usually find a solitary spot to swim or sunbathe. In June and July, fog often hugs the coast until about noon. The wide swath of sand at the east end of Cabrillo Boulevard on the harbor front is a great spot for people-watching. **East Beach** (*1118 Cabrillo Blvd. 805/897–2680*) has sand volleyball courts, summertime lifeguard and sports competitions, and arts-and-crafts shows on Sunday and holidays. You can use showers, a weight room, and lockers (bring your own towel) and rent umbrellas and boogie boards at the Cabrillo Bathhouse. Next door, there's an elaborate jungle-gym play area for kids. The usually gentle surf at **Arroyo Burro County Beach** (*Cliff Dr., at Las Positas Rd.*) makes it ideal for families with young children.

BICYCLING

The level, two-lane, 3-mi **Cabrillo Bike Lane** passes the Santa Barbara Zoo, the Andree Clark Bird Refuge, beaches, and the harbor. There are restaurants along the way, and you can stop for a picnic along the palm-lined path looking out on the Pacific. **Wheel Fun Rentals** (*23 E. Cabrillo Blvd. 805/966–2282 or 805/962–2585*) has bikes, quadricycles, and skates; a second outlet around the block rents small electric cars and scooters.

BOATS AND CHARTERS

Captain Don's (*Stearns Wharf 805/969–5217*) operates whale-watching and pirate-theme harbor cruises aboard the 40-foot *Harbour Queen*. **Santa Barbara Sailing Center** (*Santa Barbara Harbor launching ramp 805/962–2826 or 800/350–9090*) offers sailing instruction, rents and charters sailboats, and organizes dinner and sunset champagne cruises, island excursions, and whale-watching trips. **Sea Landing** (*Cabrillo Blvd., at Bath St. and the breakwater in the Santa*

Barbara Harbor ☎*805/965–3564*) operates surface and deep-sea fishing charters year-round. From Sea Landing, the *Condor Express* (☎*805/963–3564*), a 75-foot high-speed catamaran, whisks up to 149 passengers toward the Channel Islands on dinner cruises, whale-watching excursions, and pelagic-bird trips. **Truth Aquatics** (☎*805/962–1127*) departs from Sea Landing in the Santa Barbara Harbor to ferry passengers on excursions to the National Marine Sanctuary and Channel Islands National Park. Their three dive boats also take scuba divers on single-day and multiday trips.

GOLF Like Pebble Beach, the 18-hole, par-72 **Sandpiper Golf Club** (✉*7925 Hollister Ave., 14 mi north of downtown on Hwy. 101* ☎*805/968–1541*) sits on the ocean bluffs and combines stunning views with a challenging game. Green fees are $139–$159; a cart (optional) is $16. **Santa Barbara Golf Club** (✉*Las Positas Rd. and McCaw Ave.* ☎*805/687–7087*) has an 18-hole, par-70 course. The green fees are $40–$50; a cart (optional) costs $28 per person.

TENNIS Many hotels in Santa Barbara have courts. The **City of Santa Barbara Parks and Recreation Department** (☎*805/564–5418*) operates public courts with lighted play until 9 PM weekdays. You can purchase day permits ($6) at the courts, or call the department. **Las Positas Municipal Courts** (✉*1002 Las Positas Rd.*) has six lighted hard courts open daily. The 12 hard courts at the **Municipal Tennis Center** (✉*1414 Park Pl., near Salinas St. and U.S. 101*) include an enclosed stadium court and three lighted courts open daily. **Pershing Park** (✉*100 Castillo St., near Cabrillo Blvd.*) has eight lighted courts available for public play after 5 PM weekdays and all day on weekends and Santa Barbara City College holidays.

SHOPPING

SHOPPING AREAS **State Street,** roughly between Cabrillo Boulevard and Sola Street, is the commercial hub of Santa Barbara and a shopper's paradise. Chic malls, quirky storefronts, antiques emporia, elegant boutiques, and funky thrift shops abound here. **Paseo Nuevo** (✉*700 and 800 blocks of State St.*), an open-air mall anchored by chains such as Nordstrom and Macy's, also contains a few local institutions such as the children's clothier This Little Piggy. You can do your shopping on foot or by a battery-powered trolley (25¢) that runs between the waterfront and the 1300 block.

Shops, art galleries, and studios share the courtyard and gardens of **El Paseo** (✉*Canon Perdido St., between State and Anacapa Sts.*), a historic arcade. Antiques and gift shops are clustered in restored Victorian buildings on **Brinkerhoff Avenue** (✉*2 blocks west of State St., at West Cota St.*). Serious antiques hunters can head a few miles south of Santa Barbara to the beach town of **Summerland,** which is full of shops and markets.

CLOTHING **Surf 'N Wear's Beach House** (✉*10 State St.* ☎*805/963–1281*) carries surf clothing, gear, and collectibles; it's also the home of Santa Barbara Surf Shop and the exclusive local dealer of Surfboards by Yater. Established in the early 2000s, the original **Blue Bee** (✉*911½ State St.* ☎805/897–1137) boutique and its chic line of California clothes

WORD OF MOUTH

"California's Central Coast is a popular place for surfers and wind surfers. If you're not up to surfing yourself, spend some time relaxing on the beach and watching the action." —photo by Doreen Miller, Fodors.com member

and accessories quickly morphed into an empire that now includes seven specialty shops peddling designer jeans, shoes, jewelry, and clothing for men, women, and kids; most occupy individual spaces in the La Arcada shopping plaza at State and Figueroa streets, across from the Santa Barbara Museum of Art. **Channel Islands Surfboards** (⊠*36 Anacapa St.* ☎*805/966–7213*) stocks the latest in California beachwear, sandals, and accessories. **Pierre Lafond–Wendy Foster** (⊠*833 State St.* ☎*805/966–2276*) is a casual-chic clothing store for women.**Santa Barbara Outfitters** (⊠*1200 State St.* ☎*805/564–1007* carries stylish, functional clothing, shoes, and accessories for active folks: kayakers, climbers, cyclists, runners, and hikers. **Territory Ahead** (⊠*Main store: 515 State St.* ⊠*Outlet store: 400 State St.* ☎*805/962–5558*), a high-quality outdoorsy catalog company, sells fashionably rugged clothing for men and women.

EN ROUTE

If you choose to drive north via U.S. 101 without detouring to the Solvang/Santa Ynez area, you will drive right past some good beaches. In succession from east to west, **El Capitan, Gaviota, and Refugio state beaches** all have campsites, picnic tables, and fire rings. If you'd like to encounter nature without roughing it, you can try "comfort camping" at **El Capitan Canyon** (⊠*11560 Calle Real, north side of El Capitan State Beach exit* ☎*805/685–3887 or 866/352–2729*). The safari tents and cedar cabins here have fresh linens and creature comforts. There are also spacious sites for tent and RV camping at the adjacent **Ocean Mesa Campground** (☎*805/879–5751 or 866/410–5783*).

SANTA BARBARA COUNTY

Residents refer to the glorious 30-mi stretch of coastline from Carpinteria to Gaviota as the South Coast. The Santa Ynez Mountains divide the county geographically; U.S. 101 passes through a mountain tunnel leading inland. Northern Santa Barbara County used to be known for its sprawling ranches and strawberry and broccoli fields. Today its 100-plus wineries and 22,000 acres of vineyards dominate the landscape from the Santa Ynez Valley in the south to Santa Maria in the north.

The hit film *Sideways* was filmed almost entirely in the North County wine country; when the movie won Golden Globe and Oscar awards in 2005, it sparked national and international interest in visits to the region.

ESSENTIALS

Visitor Information **Santa Barbara County Vintners' Association** (☎*805/688–0881* 🌐*www.sbcountywines.com*).

The Santa Barbara Conference & Visitors Bureau (☎*805/966–9222* 🌐*www.santabarbaraca.com*) created a detailed map highlighting film location spots. Maps can be downloaded from visitor bureau Web sites: www.santaynezvalleyvisit.com or www.santabarbaraca.com.

2

SANTA YNEZ

31 mi north of Goleta via Hwy. 154.

Founded in 1882, the tiny town of Santa Ynez still has many of its original frontier buildings. You can walk through the three-block downtown area in just a few minutes, shop for antiques, and hang around the old-time saloon. At some of the eponymous valley's best restaurants, you just might bump into one of the many celebrities who own nearby ranches.

EXPLORING

Just south of Santa Ynez on the Chumash Indian Reservation lies the sprawling, Las Vegas–style **Chumash Casino Resort** (*3400 E. Hwy. 246* *800/248–6274*). The casino has 2,000 slot machines, and the property includes three restaurants, a spa, and an upscale hotel ($$$–$$$$).

WHERE TO EAT AND STAY

$$ ITALIAN ★ **Trattoria Grappolo.** Authentic Italian fare, an open kitchen, and festive, family-style seating make this trattoria equally popular with celebrities from Hollywood and ranchers from the Santa Ynez Valley. Italian favorites on the extensive menu range from thin-crust pizza to homemade ravioli, risottos, and seafood linguine to grilled lamb chops in red-wine sauce. The noise level tends to rise in the evening, so this isn't the best spot for a romantic getaway. *3687-C Sagunto St.* *805/688–6899* *AE, MC, V* *No lunch Mon.*

$$$$ **Santa Ynez Inn.** This posh two-story Victorian inn in downtown Santa Ynez was built from scratch in 2002. The owners have furnished all the rooms with authentic historical pieces. The inn caters to a discerning crowd with the finest amenities—Frette linens, thermostatically controlled heat and air-conditioning, DVD/CD entertainment systems, and custom-made bathrobes. Most rooms have gas fireplaces, double steam showers, and whirlpool tubs. Rates include a phenomenal evening wine and hors d'oeuvres hour and a full breakfast. **Pros:** near several restaurants; unusual antiques; spacious rooms. **Cons:** high price for location; not in a historic building. *3627 Sagunto St.* *805/688–5588 or 800/643–5774* *www.santaynezinn.com* *20 rooms* *In-room: Internet, Wi-Fi. In-hotel: gym, laundry service, no-smoking rooms* *AE, D, MC, V* *BP.*

SPORTS AND THE OUTDOORS

The scenic rides operated by **Windhaven Glider** (*Santa Ynez Airport, Hwy. 246* *805/688–2517*) cost between $125 and $245 and last up to 30 minutes.

LOS OLIVOS

4 mi north of Santa Ynez on Hwy. 154.

This pretty village in the Santa Ynez Valley was once on Spanish-built El Camino Real (Royal Highway) and later a stop on major stagecoach and rail routes. It's so sleepy today, though, that the movie *Return to Mayberry* was filmed here. A row of tasting rooms, art galleries, antiques stores, and country markets lines Grand Avenue.

EXPLORING

Inside the intimate, 99-square-foot **Carhartt Vineyard Tasting Room** (✉*2990-A Grand Ave.* ☎*805/693–5100* 🌐*www.carharttvineyard.com*), you're likely to meet owners and winemakers Mike and Brooke Carhartt, who pour samples of their small-lot, handcrafted vintages most days.

Historic Heather Cottage, originally an early-1900s doctor's office, houses the **Daniel Gehrs Tasting Room** (✉*2939 Grand Ave.* ☎*800/275–8138* 🌐*www.dgwines.com*). Here you can sample Gehrs's various varietals, produced in limited small-lot quantities.

Firestone Vineyard (✉*5000 Zaca Station Rd.* ☎*805/688–3940* 🌐*www.firestonewine.com*) has been around since 1972. It has daily tours, grassy picnic areas, and hiking trails in the hills overlooking the valley; the views are fantastic.

WHERE TO EAT AND STAY

$$$$ AMERICAN Fodor'sChoice ★ **Brothers Restaurant at Mattei's Tavern.** In the stagecoach days, Mattei's Tavern provided wayfarers with hearty meals and warm beds. Chef-owners and brothers Matt and Jeff Nichols renovated the 1886 building, and while retaining the original character transformed it into one of the best restaurants in the valley. The casual, unpretentious dining rooms with their red-velvet wallpaper and historic photos reflect the rich history of the tavern. The menu changes every few weeks, but often includes house favorites such as spicy fried calamari, prime rib, and salmon, and the locally famous jalapeño corn bread. There's also a full bar and an array of vintages from the custom-built cedar wine cellar. ✉*2350 Railway Ave.* ☎*805/688–4820* *Reservations essential* *AE, MC, V* *No lunch.*

$$ AMERICAN **Los Olivos Cafe.** Site of the scene in *Sideways* where the four main characters dine together and share a few bottles of wine, this down-to-earth restaurant not only provided the setting but served the actors real food from their existing menu during filming. Part wine store and part social hub for locals, the café focuses on wine-friendly fish, pasta, and meat dishes made from local bounty, plus salads, pizzas, and burgers. Don't miss the homemade muffuletta and olive tapenade spreads. Other house favorites include an artisanal cheese plate, baked Brie with honey-roasted hazelnuts, and braised pot roast with whipped potatoes. ✉*2879 Grand Ave.* ☎*805/688–7265* *AE, D, MC, V.*

$$$–$$$$ **The Ballard Inn.** Set among orchards and vineyards in the tiny town of Ballard, 2 mi south of Los Olivos, this inn makes an elegant wine-country escape. Rooms are furnished with antiques and original art. Seven rooms have wood-burning fireplaces; the inn provides room phones and TVs on request. The inn's tasting room serves boutique wines Friday through Sunday. At the Ballard Inn Restaurant ($$$), which serves dinner Wednesday through Sunday, owner-chef Budi Kazali creates sumptuous French–Asian dishes in one of the area's most romantic dining rooms. **Pros:** exceptional food; attentive staff; secluded. **Cons:** some baths could use updating; several miles from Los Olivos and Santa Ynez. ✉*2436 Baseline Ave., Ballard* ☎*805/688–7770 or 800/638–2466* 🌐*www.ballardinn.com* *15 rooms* *In-room: no phone, no TV, Wi-Fi. In-hotel: restaurant, bicycles, Wi-Fi* *AE, MC, V* *BP.*

$$$$ **Fess Parker's Wine Country Inn and Spa.** This luxury inn includes an elegant, tree-shaded French country–style main building and an equally attractive annex across the street with a pool, hot tub, and day spa. The spacious accommodations have fireplaces, seating areas, and wet bars. **Pros:** convenient wine touring base; walking distance from restaurants and galleries; well-appointed rooms. **Cons:** pricey; staff attention is inconsistent. ✉*2860 Grand Ave.* ☎*805/688–7788 or 800/446–2455* 🌐*www.fessparker.com* *20 rooms, 1 suite* *In-room: refrigerator, Internet. In-hotel: restaurant, bar, pool, gym, spa, Wi-Fi, some pets allowed, no-smoking rooms* *AE, DC, MC, V* *BP.*

ON A MISSION

Six important California missions established by Franciscan friars are within the Central Coast region. San Miguel is one of California's best-preserved missions. La Purisima is the most fully restored; Mission Santa Barbara is perhaps the most beautiful in the state; and Mission San Luis Obispo de Tolosa has a fine museum with many Chumash Indian artifacts. Mission Santa Inés is known for its serene gardens and restored artworks, and Mission San Buenaventura has 250-year-old paintings and statuary.

SOLVANG

5 mi south of Los Olivos on Alamo Pintado Rd.; Hwy. 246, 3 mi east of U.S. 101.

You'll know you've reached the town of Solvang when the architecture suddenly changes to half-timber buildings and windmills. This town was settled in 1911 by a group of Danish educators (the flatlands and rolling green hills reminded them of home), and even today more than two-thirds of the residents are of Danish descent. Although it's attracted tourists for decades, in recent years it has become more sophisticated, with galleries, upscale restaurants, and wine-tasting rooms. Most shops are locally owned; the city has an ordinance prohibiting chain stores. A good way to get your bearings is to park your car in one of the many free public lots and stroll around town. Stop in at one of the visitor centers—at 2nd Street and Copenhagen Drive, or Mission Drive (Highway 246) at 5th Street—for maps and helpful advice on what to see and do. Don't forget to stock up on Danish pastries from the town's excellent bakeries before you leave.

ESSENTIALS

Visitor Information **Solvang Conference & Visitors Bureau** (✉*1511 Mission Dr., Solvang 93463* ☎*805/688–6144 or 800/468–6765* 🌐*www.solvangusa.com*).

EXPLORING

Often called the Hidden Gem of the missions, **Mission Santa Inés** (✉*1760 Mission Dr.* ☎*805/688–4815* 🌐*www.missionsantaines.org* *$4* *Daily 9–4:30*) has an impressive collection of paintings, statuary, vestments, and Chumash and Spanish artifacts in a serene bluff-top setting. Take a self-guided tour through the museum, sanctuary, and tranquil gardens.

Housed in an 1884 adobe, the **Rideau Vineyard** (✉*1562 Alamo Pintado Rd.* ☎*805/688–0717* 🌐*www.rideauvineyard.com*) tasting room provides simultaneous blasts from the area's ranching past and from its hand-harvested, Rhône-varietal wine-making present.

Just outside Solvang is the **Alma Rosa Winery** (✉*7250 Santa Rosa Rd.* ☎*805/688–9090* 🌐*www.almarosawinery.com*). Owners Richard and Thekla Sanford helped put Santa Barbara County on the international wine map with a 1989 pinot noir. Recently the Sanfords started a new winery, Alma Rosa, with wines made from grapes grown on their 100-plus-acre certified organic vineyards in the Santa Rita Hills. You can taste the current releases at one of the most environmentally sensitive tasting rooms and picnic areas in the valley. All their vineyards are certified organic, and the pinot noirs and chardonnays are exceptional.

WHERE TO EAT AND STAY

$$ SCANDINAVIAN ✕ **Bit O' Denmark.** Perhaps the most authentic Danish eatery in Solvang, this restaurant (the oldest food establishment in Solvang) occupies an old-beam building that was a church until 1929. Two specialties of the house are the *Frikadeller* (meatballs with pickled red cabbage, potatoes, and thick brown gravy) and the *Medisterpølse* (Danish beef and pork sausage with cabbage). ✉*473 Alisal Rd.* ☎*805/688–5426* ▭*AE, D, MC, V.*

$$$ AMERICAN ✕ **The Hitching Post II.** You'll find everything from grilled artichokes to ostrich at this casual eatery just outside of Solvang, but most people come for what is said to be the best Santa Maria–style barbecue in the state. The oak used in the barbecue imparts a wonderful smoky taste. Be sure to try a glass of owner-chef-winemaker Frank Ostini's signature Highliner pinot noir, a star in the 2004 film *Sideways.* ✉*406 E. Hwy. 246* ☎*805/688–0676* ▭*AE, MC, V* ⊗*No lunch.*

$$$$ ★ **Alisal Guest Ranch and Resort.** Since 1946 this 10,000-acre ranch has been popular with celebrities and plain folk alike. There are lots of activities to choose from here: horseback riding, golf, fishing, sailing in the 100-acre spring-fed lake—although you can also just lounge by the pool or book a treatment at the day spa. The ranch-style rooms and suites come with garden views, covered porches, high-beam ceilings, and wood-burning fireplaces, with touches of Spanish tile and fine Western art. A jacket is required at the nightly dinners (which are included in your room rate). **Pros:** Old West atmosphere; tons of activities; ultra-private. **Cons:** isolated; cut off from the high-tech world; some units are aging. ✉*1054 Alisal Rd.* ☎*805/688–6411 or 800/425–4725* 🌐*www.alisal.com* *36 rooms, 37 suites* *In-room: no a/c, refrigerator, no TV. In-hotel: restaurant, room service, bar, golf courses, tennis courts, pool, gym, spa, bicycles, children's programs (ages 6 and up), Internet terminal* ▭*AE, DC, MC, V* *MAP.*

$ **Best Western King Fredrik Inn.** Rooms at this comfortable and central motel are fairly spacious. If you want to stay right in Solvang and don't want to spend a fortune, this is a good bet. **Pros:** great value; near main square; good choice for families. **Cons:** on main highway; miniature lobby; next to major city parking lot. ✉*1617 Copenhagen Dr.* ☎*805/688–5515 or 800/549–9955* 🌐*www.bwkingfrederik.com*

46 rooms, 1 suite In-room: refrigerator, Internet. In-hotel: pool, Wi-Fi, no-smoking rooms AE, D, DC, MC, V CP.

$$ **Solvang Gardens Lodge.** Lush gardens with fountains and waterfalls, friendly staff, and cheery English-country-theme rooms with antiques make for a peaceful retreat just a few blocks—but worlds away—from Solvang's main tourist area. Rooms range from basic to elegant; each has unique character and furnishings, and many have marble showers and baths. Rates include complimentary access to a gym across the street. **Pros:** homey; family-friendly; colorful gardens. **Cons:** some rooms are tiny; some units need upgrades. *293 Alisal Rd. 805/688–4404 or 888/688–4404 www.solvanggardens.com 16 rooms, 8 suites In-room: no phone, kitchen (some), refrigerator (some), DVD, Wi-Fi. In-hotel: spa, Internet terminal, no-smoking rooms AE, D, MC, V CP.*

LOMPOC

20 mi west of Solvang on Hwy. 246.

Known as the flower-seed capital of the world, Lompoc is blanketed with vast fields of brightly colored flowers that bloom from May through August.

EXPLORING

For five days around the last weekend of June, the **Lompoc Valley Flower Festival** (*805/735–8511 www.flowerfestival.org*) brings a parade, carnival, and crafts show to town.

At **La Purisima Mission State Historic Park** you can see Mission La Purisima Concepción, the most fully restored mission in the state. Founded in 1787, it stands in a stark and still remote location and powerfully evokes the lives of California's Spanish settlers. Docents lead tours every afternoon, and displays illustrate the secular and religious activities that were part of mission life. From March through October the mission holds special events, including crafts demonstrations by costumed docents. *2295 Purisima Rd., off Hwy. 246 805/733–3713 www.lapurisimamission.org $4 per vehicle Daily 9–5; tour daily at 1.*

SAN LUIS OBISPO COUNTY

San Luis Obispo County's pristine landscapes and abundant wildlife areas, especially those around Morro Bay and Montaña de Oro State Park, have long attracted nature lovers. In the south, Pismo Beach and other coastal towns have great sand and surf; inland, a booming wine region stretches from the Edna and Arroyo Grande Valleys in the south to Paso Robles in the north. With historical attractions, a photogenic downtown, and busy shops and restaurants, the college town of San Luis Obispo is at the heart of the county.

ESSENTIALS

Visitor Information **San Luis Obispo County Visitors and Conference Bureau** (*811 El Capitan Way #200, San Luis Obispo 93401 805/541–8000 or 800/634–1414 www.sanluisobispocounty.com*).

PISMO BEACH

U.S. 101/Hwy. 1, about 40 mi north of Lompoc.

VOLCANOES?

Those funny looking, sawed-off peaks along the drive from Pismo Beach to Morro Bay are the Seven Sisters—a series of ancient volcanic plugs. Morro Rock, the northernmost sibling and a state historic monument, is the most famous and photographed of the clan.

About 20 mi of sandy shoreline—nicknamed the Bakersfield Riviera for the throngs of vacationers who come here from the Central Valley—begins at the town of Pismo Beach. The southern end of town runs along sand dunes, some of which are open to cars and off-road vehicles; sheltered by the dunes, a grove of eucalyptus trees attracts thousands of migrating monarch butterflies November through February. A long, broad beach fronts the center of town, where a municipal pier extends into the sea at the foot of shop-lined Pomeroy Street. To the north, hotels and homes perch atop chalky oceanfront cliffs.

Fewer than 10,000 people live in this quintessential surfer haven, but Pismo Beach has a slew of hotels and restaurants with great views of the Pacific Ocean. Still, rooms can sometimes be hard to come by. Each Father's Day weekend the Pismo Beach Classic, one of the West Coast's largest classic-car and street-rod shows, overruns the town. A Dixieland jazz festival in February also draws crowds.

EN ROUTE

The spectacular **Guadalupe-Nipomo Dunes Preserve** stretches 18 mi along the coast south of Pismo Beach. It's the largest and most ecologically diverse dune system in the state, and a habitat for more than 200 species of birds as well as sea otters, black bears, bobcats, coyotes, and deer. The 1,500-foot Mussel Rock is the highest beach dune in the western states. As many as 20 movies have been filmed here, including Cecil B. DeMille's 1923 silent *The Ten Commandments*. The main entrances to the dunes are at Oso Flaco Lake (about 13 mi south of Pismo Beach on U.S. 101/Highway 1, then 3 mi west on Oso Flaco Road) and at the far west end of Highway 166 (Main Street) in Guadalupe. At the **Dunes Center** (✉ *1055 Guadalupe St., 1 mi north of Hwy. 166* ☎ *805/343–2455* 🌐 *www.dunescenter.org* 🕐 *Thurs.–Sun. 10–4*) you can get nature information and view an exhibit about *The Ten Commandments* movie set, which weather and archaeologists are slowly unearthing near Guadalupe Beach. Parking at Oso Flaco Lake is $5 per vehicle.

WHERE TO EAT

$$ SEAFOOD ✕ **Cracked Crab.** This traditional New England–style crab shack imports fresh seafood daily from Australia, Alaska, and the East Coast. Fish is line-caught, much of the produce is organic, and everything is made from scratch. For a real treat, don a bib and chow through a bucket of steamed shellfish with Cajun sausage, potatoes, and corn on the cob, all dumped right onto your table. The menu changes daily. ✉ *751 Price St.* ☎ *805/773–2722* ✍ *Reservations not accepted* 💳 *AE, D, MC, V.*

$$ ITALIAN ✕ **Giuseppe's Cucina Italiana.** The classic flavors of southern Italy are highlighted at this lively, warm downtown spot. Most recipes originate

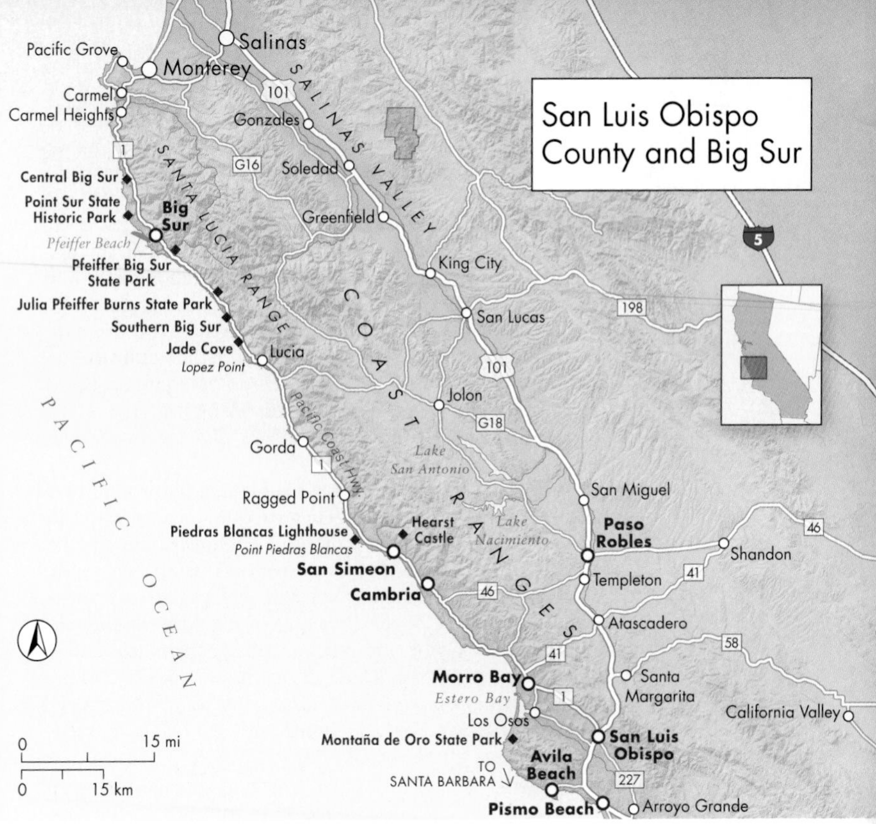

from Bari, a seaport on the Adriatic; the menu includes breads and pizzas baked in the wood-burning oven, hearty dishes such as osso buco and lamb, and homemade pastas. The wait for a table can be long at peak dinner hours, but sometimes an accordion player gets the crowd singing. Next door, their bakery sells take-out selections. ✉ *891 Price St.* ☎ *805/773–2870* *Reservations not accepted* ▭ *AE, D, MC, V* ⏲ *No lunch weekends.*

¢ SEAFOOD ✕ **Splash Café.** Folks line up all the way down the block for clam chowder served in a sourdough bread bowl at this wildly popular seafood stand. You can also order beach food such as fresh steamed clams, burgers, and fried calamari at the counter (no table service)—and many choices on the menu are $7 or less. The grimy, cramped, but cheery hole-in-a-wall, a favorite with locals and savvy visitors, is open daily for lunch and dinner (plus a rock-bottom basic breakfast starting at 8 AM), but closes early on weekday evenings during low season. ✉ *197 Pomeroy St.* ☎ *805/773–4653* ▭ *AE, D, MC, V.*

WHERE TO STAY

$$$$ **Dolphin Bay.** Perched on grass-covered bluffs overlooking Shell Beach, this luxury resort looks and feels like an exclusive condominium community. Choose among sprawling one- or two-bedroom residences, each with a gourmet kitchen, laundry room with washer and dryer,

and contemporary Mission-style furniture. Many have ocean views. Two-bedroom units include either a spa tub or fireplace; penthouse units have both. Rejuvenate at La Bonne Vie day spa, lounge by the infinity pool, or stroll down a short path to the beach to gaze at the sea—this place was made for upscale escape and relaxation. At Lido ($$$–$$$$), the fancy yet casual restaurant (no flip-flops), Chef Evan Treadwell presents an impressive menu of California wine country cuisine with an international flair; favorites include wild salmon medallions with curry sauce, and pulled-pork empanadas. **Pros:** lavish apartment units; as upscale as you can get; killer views; walking distance from the beach. **Cons:** hefty price tag; upper-crust vibe. ✉ *2727 Shell Beach Rd.* ☎ *805/773–4300 or 800/516–0112* 🌐 *www.thedolphinbay.com* *61 residences* *In-room: kitchen, DVD, Internet, Wi-Fi. In-hotel: restaurant, room service, bar, pool, gym, spa, some pets allowed, no-smoking rooms* *AE, D, MC, V.*

$$$$ **Pismo Lighthouse Suites.** Each of the well-appointed two-room, two-bath suites at this oceanfront resort has a private balcony or patio. Some suites are suitable for couples, others for families, and all have crisp nautical-style furnishings. Ask for a corner oceanfront suite for the best views. On the central sport court you can play a variety of games, including chess on a life-size board. **Pros:** lots of space for families and groups; nice pool area. **Cons:** not easy to walk to main attractions; some units are next to busy road. ✉ *2411 Price St.* ☎ *805/773–2411 or 800/245–2411* 🌐 *www.pismolighthousesuites.com* *70 suites* *In-room: refrigerator, Internet, Wi-Fi. In-hotel: pool, gym, laundry facilities, no-smoking rooms* *AE, D, DC, MC, V* *CP.*

$$$ **Sea Venture Resort.** The bright, homey rooms at this hotel all have fireplaces and featherbeds; most have balconies with private hot tubs, and some have beautiful ocean views. A breakfast basket is delivered to your room in the morning, and the elegant Sea Venture Restaurant ($$–$$$, no lunch weekdays)—with sweeping ocean vistas from the third floor—features fresh seafood and local wines. **Pros:** on the beach; excellent food; romantic rooms. **Cons:** touristy area; some rooms and facilities are beginning to age; dark hallways. ✉ *100 Ocean View Ave.* ☎ *805/773–4994 or 800/760–0664* 🌐 *www.seaventure.com* *50 rooms* *In-room: no a/c, refrigerator, Internet, Wi-Fi. In-hotel: restaurant, spa, bicycles, no-smoking rooms* *AE, D, DC, MC, V* *CP.*

$–$$ **Shell Beach Inn.** Just 2½ blocks from the beach, this basic but cozy motor court is a great bargain for the area. Along with a 2005 room remodel, the property upgraded its name from "motel" to "inn." Choose from king, queen, or two-bedded rooms; all have European country-style furnishings and floral details painted on the walls and ceilings. **Pros:** walking distance from the beach; clean rooms; friendly and dependable service. **Cons:** sits on a busy road; small rooms; tiny pool. ✉ *653 Shell Beach Rd.* ☎ *805/773–4373 or 800/549–4727* 🌐 *www.shellbeachinn.com* *10 rooms* *In-room: no a/c, refrigerator. In-hotel: pool, some pets allowed* *AE, D, DC, MC, V.*

2

AVILA BEACH

4 mi north of Pismo Beach on U.S. 101/Hwy. 1.

Because the village of Avila Beach and the sandy, cove-front shoreline for which it's named face south into the Pacific Ocean, they get more sun and less fog than any other stretch of coast in the area. It can be bright and warm here while just beyond the surrounding hills communities shiver under the marine layer. With its fortuitous climate and protected waters, Avila's public beach draws plenty of sunbathers and families; weekends are very busy. Demolished in 1998 to clean up extensive oil seepage from a Unocal tank farm, downtown Avila Beach has sprung back to life. The seaside promenade has been fully restored and shops and hotels have quickly popped up; with mixed results the town has tried to re-create its former offbeat character. For real local color, head to the far end of the cove and watch the commercial fishing boats offload their catch on the old Port San Luis wharf. A few seafood shacks and fish markets do business on the pier while sea lions congregate below. On Fridays from mid-April through mid-September a fish and farmers' market livens up the beach area with music, fresh local produce and seafood, and children's activities.

WHERE TO EAT AND STAY

$$$ SEAFOOD **Olde Port Inn.** Locals swear by this old-fashioned fish house at the end of the Port San Luis Pier. Ask for today's fresh catch, or go for the *cioppino* (spicy tomato-based seafood stew) or fish tacos; simplicity is the key to a decent meal here. You can't beat the views, whether you're looking out over the ocean or through the glass surface of your table into the waters below. *End of 3rd pier* *805/595–2515* *AE, D, MC, V.*

$$$$ **Avila La Fonda.** Modeled after a village in early California's Mexican period, Avila La Fonda surrounds guests with rich jewel tones, fountains, and upscale comfort. The facade of the hotel replicates eight different casitas, including several famous historic homes in Mexico. Inside, stained-glass windows and tiled murals celebrate Mexican art and life in Avila Beach. Guests can choose from two types of rooms: a spa room with a huge tub near the king bed, or a great room with gourmet kitchen, queen Murphy bed, and sofa sleeper. You can also combine adjacent rooms to create your own casita. The lavish Owner's Spa Suite includes a sauna and steam shower—it's available to guests when it's not occupied by the owner or special guests. An added bonus: the beach is just one block away. **Pros:** one-of-a-kind theme and artwork; flexible room combinations; only a block from the beach. **Cons:** pricey; most rooms don't have an ocean view. *101 San Miguel St.* *805/595–1700* *www.avilalafondahotel.com* *32 rooms, 1 suite* *In-room: kitchen (some), refrigerator, DVD, Wi-Fi. In-hotel: laundry service, Wi-Fi, some pets allowed, no-smoking rooms* *AE, D, MC, V.*

$$–$$$ **Sycamore Mineral Springs Resort.** This wellness resort's hot mineral springs bubble up into private outdoor tubs on an oak-and-sycamore-forest hillside. Whether or not you stay here, it's worth coming for a soak—even though the grounds are well within earshot of a busy

road. Each room or suite has its own private balcony with a hot tub; about half have mineral water piped in. The spa offers everything from massages and skin care to yoga classes and a variety of integrative healing arts. Creative spa and California cuisine is served in the romantic Gardens of Avila restaurant ($$–$$$). **Pros:** great place to rejuvenate; nice hiking; incredible spa services. **Cons:** rooms vary in quality; 2½ mi from the beach. ✉ *1215 Avila Beach Dr., San Luis Obispo* ☎ *805/595–7302 or 800/234–5831* 🌐 *www.sycamoresprings.com* *26 rooms, 50 suites* *In-room: refrigerator (some), Internet, Wi-Fi. In-hotel: restaurant, room service, bar, pool, spa, no-smoking rooms* 💳 *AE, D, DC, MC, V.*

SAN LUIS OBISPO

8 mi north of Avila Beach on U.S. 101/Hwy. 1.

About halfway between San Francisco and Los Angeles, San Luis Obispo—nicknamed SLO—spreads out below gentle hills and rocky extinct volcanoes. Its main appeal lies in its architecturally diverse and commercially lively downtown, especially several blocks of Higuera Street. The pedestrian-friendly district bustles with shoppers, restaurant goers, and students from California Polytechnic State University, known as Cal Poly. On Thursday from 6 PM to 9 PM a farmers' market fills Higuera Street with local produce, entertainment, and food stalls. SLO is less a vacation destination than a pleasant stopover along Highway 1; it's a nice place to stay while touring the wine country south of town.

ESSENTIALS

Visitor Information San Luis Obispo Chamber of Commerce (✉ *1039 Chorro St., San Luis Obispo 93401* ☎ *805/781–2777* 🌐 *www.visitslo.com*). **San Luis Obispo Vintners Association** (☎ *805/541–5868* 🌐 *www.slowine.com*).

EXPLORING

Special events often take place on sun-dappled Mission Plaza in front of ★ **Mission San Luis Obispo de Tolosa,** established in 1772. Its small museum exhibits artifacts of the Chumash Indians and early Spanish settlers, and docents sometimes lead tours of the church and grounds. ✉ *751 Palm St.* ☎ *805/543–6850* 🌐 *www.missionsanluisobispo.org* *$3 suggested donation* ⏲ *Apr.–late-Oct., daily 9–5; late Oct.–Mar., daily 9–4.*

The delightful, sparkling new **San Luis Obispo Children's Museum,** reopened in 2008, has 21 indoor and outdoor activities that present a kid-friendly version of the city of San Luis Obispo. Visitors enter through an "imagination-powered" elevator, which transports them to a series of underground caverns beneath the city, while simulated lava and steam sputters from an active volcano. Kids can pick rubber fruit at a farmers' market, clamber up a clockworks tower, race to fight a fire on a fire engine, and learn about solar energy from a 15-foot sunflower. The museum attracts mostly kids under 8; older children may become bored quickly. ✉ *1010 Nipomo St.* ☎ *805/545–5874* 🌐 *www.slocm.org* *$8* ⏲ *Tues.–Fri. 10–4, Sat. 10–5, Sun. and select Mon. holidays 11–5*

Across the street from the old Spanish mission, **San Luis Obispo County Historical Museum** presents rotating exhibits on various aspects of county history—such as Native American life, California ranchos, and the impact of railroads. A separate children's room has theme activities where kids can earn prizes. ✉ *696 Monterey St.* ☎ *805/543–0638* 🌐 *www.slochs.org* *Free* ⏲ *Wed.–Sun. 10–4.*

2

San Luis Obispo is the commercial center of **Edna Valley/Arroyo Grande Valley wine country,** whose appellations stretch east–west from San Luis Obispo toward the coast and toward Lake Lopez in the inland mountains. Many of the 20 or so wineries line Highway 227 and connecting roads. The region is best known for chardonnay and pinot noir, although many wineries experiment with other varietals and blends. Wine-touring maps are readily available around town; note that many wineries charge a small tasting fee and most tasting rooms close at 5.

For sweeping views of the Edna Valley while you sample estate-grown chardonnay, go to the modern tasting bar at **Edna Valley Vineyard** (✉ *2585 Biddle Ranch Rd.* ☎ *805/544–5855* 🌐 *www.ednavalley.com*).

A refurbished 1909 schoolhouse serves as tasting room for **Baileyana Winery** (✉ *5828 Orcutt Rd.* ☎ *805/269–8200* 🌐 *www.baileyana.com*), which produces concentrated chardonnays, pinot noirs, and Syrahs. Its sister winery, Tangent, creates alternative white wines and shares the tasting room.

An ecofriendly winery built from straw bales, **Claiborne & Churchill** (✉ *2649 Carpenter Canyon Rd.* ☎ *805/544–4066* 🌐 *www.claibornechurchill.com*) makes small lots of exceptional Alsatian-style wines such as dry Riesling and Gewürztraminer.

While touring Edna Valley wine country, be sure to stop at **Old Edna** (✉ *Hwy. 227, at Price Canyon Rd.* ☎ *805/544–8062* 🌐 *www.oldedna.com*), a peaceful, 2-acre site that once was the town of Edna. Browse for gifts and antiques, pick up sandwiches at the gourmet deli, and stroll along Old Edna Lane.

A nonprofit entity founded by the San Luis Obispo County Vintners Association, **Taste** (✉ *1003 Osos St.* ☎ *805/269–8278* 🌐 *www.taste-slo.com* ⏲ *Mon.–Sat. 11–9, Sun. 11–5*) pours samples of up to 72 different south county vintages from a nifty dispensing system that keeps oxygen out of the wines. This provides a great downtown wine tasting alternative for those who don't have time to tour outside of town.

WHERE TO EAT

$$ ECLECTIC ★ ✕ **Big Sky Café.** A popular gathering spot three meals a day, this quintessentially Californian, family-friendly (and sometimes noisy) café turns local and organically grown ingredients into global dishes. North African chicken tagine, Thai catfish, New Mexican *pozole* (hominy stew): just pick your continent. Vegetarians have lots to choose from. ✉ *1121 Broad St.* ☎ *805/545–5401* *Reservations not accepted* 💳 *AE, MC, V.*

$$ ITALIAN ✕ **Buona Tavola.** Homemade pasta with river shrimp in a creamy tomato sauce and porcini-mushroom risotto are among the northern Italian dishes served at this casual spot. Daily fresh fish and salad specials and an impressive wine list attract a steady stream of regulars. In good weather you can dine on the flower-filled patio. The Paso Robles branch is equally enjoyable. ✉ *1037 Monterey St.* ☎ *805/545–8000*

DID YOU KNOW?

You can unwind in a private tub fed by hot mineral springs at Avila Beach's Sycamore Mineral Springs Resort. Spaaaaaah.

943 Spring St., Paso Robles *805/237–0600* *AE, D, MC, V* *No lunch weekends.*

¢ SOUTHERN **Mo's Smokehouse BBQ.** Barbecue joints abound on the Central Coast, but this one excels. A variety of Southern-style sauces seasons tender hickory-smoked ribs and shredded meat sandwiches; sides such as baked beans, coleslaw, homemade potato chips, and garlic bread extend the pleasure. *1005 Monterey St.* *805/544–6193* *AE, MC, V.*

DEEP ROOTS

Way back in the 1700s, the Spanish padres who accompanied Father Junípero Serra planted grapevines from Mexico along California's Central Coast, and began using European wine-making techniques to turn the grapes into delectable vintages.

$ ECLECTIC **Novo Restaurant & Lounge.** In the colorful dining room or on the large creek-side deck, this animated downtown eatery will take you on a culinary world tour. The salads, small plates, and entrées come from nearly every continent. The wine and beer list also covers the globe (you can sample various international wines paired with tapas Sunday evenings)—and includes local favorites. Many of the decadent desserts are baked at the restaurant's sister property in Cambria, the French Corner Bakery. *726 Higuera St.* *805/543–3986* *MC, V.*

$$$ AMERICAN ★ **The Park Restaurant.** This is one of the most sophisticated restaurants in the county. Chef-owner Meghan Loring presents food that she describes as "refined rustic." The always-evolving menu relies on seasonal ingredients sourced from local producers. You might find sweet pea–asparagus soup with mint cream, or organic rib eye with panko-fried shiitakes. The well-crafted wine and beer list includes local and international selections. Service is skillful in the spare, white-tablecloth dining room and on the tree-rimmed patio. *1819 Osos St.* *805/545–0000* *AE, MC, V* *Closed Mon. No lunch.*

WHERE TO STAY

$$$–$$$$ **Apple Farm.** Decorated to the hilt with floral bedspreads and watercolors by local artists, this Victorian country-style hotel is one of the most popular places to stay in San Luis Obispo. Each room has a gas fireplace and fresh flowers; some have canopy beds and cozy window seats. There's a working gristmill in the courtyard; within the inn are a restaurant serving American food (the hearty breakfasts are best), a gourmet food and wine shop, a bakery, and a gift shop. **Pros:** flowers everywhere; convenient to Cal Poly and Hwy. 101; creek-side setting. **Cons:** hordes of tourists stop here during the day; too floral for some people's tastes. *2015 Monterey St.* *800/374–3705* *www.applefarm.com* *67 rooms* *In-room: Internet. In-hotel: restaurant, pool, spa, Wi-Fi, no-smoking rooms* *AE, D, MC, V.*

$$–$$$ **Garden Street Inn.** From this fully restored 1887 Italianate Queen Anne, the only lodging in downtown SLO, you can walk to many restaurants and attractions. The individually decorated rooms, each with private bath, are filled with antiques; some have stained-glass windows, fireplaces, and decks. Each evening, wine and hors d'oeuvres are served in the intimate dining room; there's also a lavish homemade breakfast when you rise. **Pros:** classic B&B; walking distance from everywhere

downtown; nice wine-and-cheese reception. **Cons:** city noise filters through some rooms; not a great place for families. ✉*1212 Garden St.* ☎*805/545–9802 or 800/488–2045* 🌐*www.gardenstreetinn.com* *9 rooms, 4 suites* *In-room: no TV (some), Wi-Fi. In-hotel: no-smoking rooms* *AE, D, MC, V* *BP.*

$$–$$$ **Petit Soleil.** A cobblestone courtyard, country-French custom furnishings, and Gallic music piped through the halls evoke a Provençal mood at this cheery inn on upper Monterey Street's motel row. With extensive experience in luxury lodging, the owners are serious about the details: the individually themed rooms, sprinkled with lavender water, have CD players and L'Occitane bath products. Rates include wine and appetizers at cocktail hour and a full homemade breakfast in the sun-filled patio or dining room. **Pros:** French details throughout; scrumptious breakfasts; cozy rooms. **Cons:** sits on a busy avenue; cramped parking. ✉*1473 Monterey St.* ☎*805/549–0321 or 800/676–1588* 🌐*www.psslo.com* *15 rooms, 1 suite* *In-room: no a/c, Internet, Wi-Fi. In-hotel: no-smoking rooms* *AE, MC, V* *BP.*

NIGHTLIFE AND THE ARTS

NIGHTLIFE The club scene in this college town is centered on Higuera Street off Monterey Street. The **Frog and Peach** (✉*728 Higuera St.* ☎*805/595–3764*) is a decent spot to nurse an English beer and listen to live music. A trendy urban crowd hangs out at the slick bar at **Koberl at Blue** (✉*998 Monterey St.* ☎*805/783–1135*), an upscale wine-country restaurant with late-night dining, exotic martinis, and a huge list of local and imported beer and wine. **Linnaea's Cafe** (✉*1110 Garden St.* ☎*805/541–5888*), a mellow java joint, sometimes holds poetry readings, as well as blues, jazz, and folk-music performances. Chicago-style **Mother's Tavern** (✉*725 Higuera St.* ☎*805/541–8733*) draws crowds with good pub food and live entertainment in a turn-of-the-20th-century setting (complete with antique U.S. flags and a wall-mounted moose head).

THE ARTS The **Performing Arts Center** (✉*1 Grand Ave.* ☎*805/756–7222, 805/756–2787 for tickets outside CA, 888/233–2787 for tickets in CA* 🌐*www.pacslo.org*) at Cal Poly hosts live theater, dance, and music performances by artists from around the world. The **San Luis Obispo Mozart Festival** (☎*805/781–3008* 🌐*www.mozartfestival.com*) takes place in late July and early August. Not all the music is Mozart; you'll also hear Haydn and other composers. **San Luis Obispo Art Center** (✉*1010 Broad St., at Mission Plaza* ☎*805/543–8562* 🌐*www.sloartcenter.org* ⏲*Closed Tues. early Sept.–late June*) displays and sells a mix of traditional work and cutting-edge arts and crafts by Central Coast, national, and international artists.

SPORTS AND THE OUTDOORS

A hilly greenbelt with vast amounts of open space and extensive hiking trails surrounds the city of San Luis Obispo. For information on trailheads, call the city **Parks and Recreation Department** (☎*805/781–7300* 🌐*www.slocity.org/parksandrecreation*) or visit its Web site to download a trail map.

EN ROUTE

Instead of continuing north on Highway 1 from San Luis Obispo to Morro Bay, consider taking Los Osos Valley Road (off Madonna Road, south of downtown) past farms and ranches to dramatic **Montaña de Oro State Park** (✉ *7 mi south of Los Osos on Pecho Rd.* ☎ *805/528–0513 or 805/772–7434* 🌐 *www.parks.ca.gov*). The park has miles of nature trails along rocky shoreline, wild beaches, and hills overlooking some of California's most spectacular scenery. Check out the tide pools, watch the waves roll into the bluffs, and picnic in the eucalyptus groves.

MORRO BAY

14 mi north of San Luis Obispo on Hwy. 1.

Commercial fishermen slog around Morro Bay in galoshes, and beat-up fishing boats bob in the bay's protected waters.

EXPLORING

At the mouth of Morro Bay, which is both a state and national estuary, stands 576-foot-high **Morro Rock** (✉ *Northern end of Embarcadero*) one of nine such small volcanic peaks, or morros, in the area. A short walk leads to a breakwater, with the harbor on one side and the crashing waves of the Pacific on the other. You may not climb the rock, where endangered falcons and other birds nest. Sea lions and otters often play in the water at the foot of the peak.

The center of the action on land is the **Embarcadero** (✉ *On waterfront from Beach St. to Tidelands Park*), where vacationers pour in and out of souvenir shops and seafood restaurants and stroll or bike along the scenic half-mile Harborwalk to Morro Rock. From here, you can get out on the bay in a kayak or tour boat.

★ South of downtown Morro Bay, interactive exhibits at the spiffy **Morro Bay State Park Museum of Natural History** teach kids and adults about the natural environment and how to preserve it—both in the Morro Bay estuary and on the rest of the planet. ✉ *State Park Rd.* ☎ *805/772–2694* 🌐 *www.ccnha.org* *$2* *Daily 10–5.*

WHERE TO EAT AND STAY

¢ SOUTHWESTERN ★

✕ **Taco Temple.** The devout stand in line at this family-run diner that serves some of the freshest food around. Seafood anchors a menu of dishes—salmon burritos, superb fish tacos with mango salsa—hailing from somewhere between California and Mexico. Desserts get rave reviews, too. Make an effort to find this gem tucked away in the corner of a supermarket parking lot north of downtown—it's on the frontage road parallel to Highway 1, just north of the Highway 41 junction. A renovation and expansion are planned; call ahead to be sure they're open. ✉ *2680 Main St., at Elena* ☎ *805/772–4965* *Reservations not accepted* *No credit cards* *Closed Tues.*

$$$ SEAFOOD

✕ **Windows on the Water.** From giant picture windows at this second-floor spot, watch the sun set over the water. Fresh fish and other dishes based on local ingredients emerge from the wood-fired oven in the open kitchen; a variety of oysters on the half shell beckon from the raw bar. About 20 of the wines on the extensive, mostly California list are poured by the glass. ✉699 *Embarcadero* ☎*805/772–0677* ▭*AE, D, DC, MC, V* ⊙*No lunch.*

$$$ **Cass House.** The original 1867 home of lumber pioneer Captain James Cass is now a luxurious B&B boasting colorful rose gardens in the heart of Cayucos, a tiny oceanfront enclave about 4 miles north of Morro Bay just west of Highway 1. It reopened in 2007 after a meticulous 14-year restoration that seamlessly blended historic authenticity, eco-friendly operations, and modern conveniences including wireless Internet and high-definition flat-screen TVs with DVD players. Chef Jensen Lorenzen creates sumptuous breakfasts using mostly local, organic ingredients—some of which come from the inn's garden. The intimate dining room ($$$$) also opens to the public for breakfast on weekends and dinner five nights a week. **Pros:** historic property; some ocean views; excellent meals. **Cons:** not near Morro Bay nightlife or tourist attractions; not designed for families. ✉*222 N. Ocean Ave., Cayucos* ☎*805/995–3669* ⊕*www.casshouseinn.com* *5 rooms* *In-room: Wi-Fi. In-hotel: restaurant, Wi-Fi.* ▭*AE, D, DC, MC, V* *CP*

$$–$$$ **The Inn at Morro Bay.** Surrounded by eucalyptus trees on the edge of Morro Bay, the inn abuts a heron rookery and Morro Bay State Park. It's a beautiful setting, even though the birds can cause a din (and make a mess of parked cars). Many of the contemporary French Country-style rooms have fireplaces, private decks with spa tubs, and bay views. The most affordable rooms (petite queens) can seem small and dark, but you'll probably be spending much of your time elsewhere: getting a massage at the on-site wellness center, playing a round (fee) at the golf course across the road, or peddling through the state park on a complimentary bicycle. **Pros:** great for wildlife enthusiasts; stellar bay views from restaurant and some rooms. **Cons:** some rooms are cramped and dark; some sections need updating; birds can wake you early. ✉*60 State Park Rd.* ☎*805/772–5651 or 800/321–9566* ⊕*www.innatmorrobay.com* *97 rooms, 1 cottage* *In-room: refrigerator, Internet. In-hotel: 2 restaurants, room service, bar, pool, spa, bicycles, laundry service, no-smoking rooms* ▭*AE, D, DC, MC, V.*

SPORTS AND THE OUTDOORS

Kayak Horizons (✉*551 Embarcadero* ☎*805/772–6444* ⊕*www.kayakhorizons.com*) rents kayaks and gives lessons and guided tours. **Sub-Sea Tours** (✉*699 Embarcadero* ☎*805/772–9463* ⊕*www.subseatours.com*) operates glass-bottom boat and catamaran cruises, and has kayak and canoe rentals and summer whale-watching cruises. **Virg's Sport Fishing** (✉*1215 Embarcadero* ☎*805/772–1222* ⊕*www.virgs.com*) conducts deep-sea fishing and whale-watching trips.

PASO ROBLES

30 mi north of San Luis Obispo on U.S. 101; 25 mi northeast of Morro Bay via Hwy. 41 and U.S. 101.

In the 1860s tourists began flocking to this dusty ranching outpost to "take the cure" in a luxurious bathhouse fed by underground mineral hot springs. An Old West town, complete with opera house, emerged; grand Victorian homes went up, followed in the 20th century by Craftsman bungalows. A 2003 earthquake demolished or weakened several beloved downtown buildings, but historically faithful reconstruction has proceeded rapidly.

Today the wine industry booms and mile upon mile of vineyards envelop Paso Robles; golfers play the four local courses and spandex-clad bicyclists race along the winding back roads. A mix of down-home and upmarket restaurants, bars, antiques stores, and little shops fills the streets around oak-shaded City Park, where special events of all kinds—custom car shows, an olive festival, Friday night summer concerts—take place on many weekends. Still, Paso (as the locals call it) more or less remains cowboy country: each year in late July and early August the city throws the two-week California Mid-State Fair, complete with livestock auctions, carnival rides, and corn dogs.

LAID-BACK WINE COUNTRY

Hundreds of vineyards and wineries dot the hillsides from Paso Robles to San Luis Obispo, through the scenic Edna Valley and south to northern Santa Barbara County. The wineries offer much of the variety of northern California's Napa and Sonoma valleys—without the glitz and crowds. Since the early 1980s the region has developed an international reputation for high-quality wines, most notably pinot noir, chardonnay, and zinfandel. Wineries here tend to be small, but most have tasting rooms (some have tours), and you'll often meet the winemakers themselves.

ESSENTIALS

Visitor Information Paso Robles Wine Country Alliance (✉ *744 Oak St.* ☎ *805/239–8463* 🌐 *www.pasowine.com*). **Paso Robles Visitors and Conference Bureau** (✉ *1225 Park St., Paso Robles 93446* ☎ *805/238–0506* 🌐 *www.pasoroblleschamber.com*).

EXPLORING

Take a look back at California's rural heritage at the **Paso Robles Pioneer Museum.** Displays of historical ranching paraphernalia, horse-drawn vehicles, hot-springs artifacts, and photos evoke the town's old days; a one-room schoolhouse is part of the complex. ✉ *2010 Riverside Ave.* ☎ *805/239–4556* 🌐 *www.pasoroblespioneermuseum.org* 🎟 *Free* ⏲ *Thurs.–Sun. 1–4.*

The lakeside **River Oaks Hot Springs & Spa,** on 240 hilly acres near the intersection of U.S. 101 and Highway 46E, is a great place to relax before and after wine tasting or festival-going. Soak in a private indoor or outdoor hot tub fed by natural mineral springs, or indulge in a massage or facial. ✉ *800 Clubhouse Dr.* ☎ *805/238–4600* 🌐 *www.riveroakshotsprings.com* 🎟 *Hot tubs $13 to $20 per person per hr* ⏲ *Sun.–Thurs. 9–9, Fri. and Sat. 9–10.*

In **Paso Robles wine country** nearly 200 wineries and more than 26,000 vineyard acres pepper the wooded hills west of U.S. 101 and blanket the flatter, more open land on the east side. The region's brutally hot summer days and cool nights yield stellar grapes that make noteworthy wines, particularly robust reds such as cabernet sauvignon, merlot, zinfandel, and Rhône varietals such as Syrah. An abundance of exquisite whites also comes out of Paso, including chardonnay and Rhône varietals such as Viognier. Small-town friendliness prevails at most wineries, especially smaller ones, which tend to treat visitors like neighbors. Pick up a regional wine-touring map at lodgings, wineries, and attractions around town. Most tasting rooms close at 5 PM; many charge a small fee.

Most of the local wineries pour at the **Paso Robles Wine Festival,** held mid-May in City Park. The outdoor tasting—the largest such California event—includes live bands and diverse food vendors. Winery open houses and winemaker dinners round out the weekend. ✉ *Spring Street, between 10th and 12th Sts., City Park* ☎ *805/239–8463* 🌐 *www.pasowine.com* 🎟 *$55, designated driver $15.*

Small but swank **Justin Vineyards & Winery** (✉ *11680 Chimney Rock Rd.* ☎ *805/238–6932 or 800/726–0049* 🌐 *www.justinwine.com*) makes Bordeaux-style blends at the western end of Paso Robles wine country. This reader favorite offers winery, vineyard, and barrel-tasting tours ($15 to $50). In the tasting room there's a deli bar; a tiny high-end restaurant is also part of the complex.

Tucked in the far-west hills of Paso Robles, **Tablas Creek Vineyard** (✉ *9339 Adelaida Rd.* ☎ *805/237–1231* 🌐 *www.tablascreek.com*) makes some of the area's finest wine by blending organically grown, hand-harvested Rhône varietals such as Syrah, Grenache, Roussanne, and Viognier. Tours include a chance to graft your own grapevine; call to reserve space.

While touring the idyllic west side of Paso Robles, take a break from ★ wine by stopping at **Willow Creek Olive Ranch** (✉ *8530 Vineyard Dr.* ☎ *805/227–0186* 🌐 *www.pasolivo.com*). Find out how they make their Tuscan-style Pasolivo olive oils on a high-tech Italian press, and taste the widely acclaimed results.

In southeastern Paso Robles wine country **Wild Horse Winery & Vineyards** (✉ *1437 Wild Horse Winery Ct., Templeton* ☎ *805/434–2541* 🌐 *www.wildhorsewinery.com*) was a pioneer Central Coast producer. You can try delicious, well-priced pinot noir, chardonnay, and merlot in their simple tasting room.

As they say around Paso Robles, it takes a lot of beer to make good wine, and to meet that need the locals turn to **Firestone Walker Fine Ales** (✉ *1400 Ramada Dr.* ☎ *805/238–2556* 🌐 *www.firestonewalker.com*). In the brewery's taproom, sample medal-winning craft beers such as Double Barrel Ale. They close at 7 PM.

Even if you don't drink wine, stop at **Eberle Winery** (✉ *Hwy. 46E, 3½ mi east of U.S. 101* ☎ *805/238–9607* 🌐 *www.eberlewinery.com*) for a fascinating tour of the huge wine caves beneath the east-side Paso Robles vineyard. Gary Eberle, one of Paso wine's founding fathers, is obsessed with cabernet sauvignon.

For an aerial view of vineyards, ranches, and mountains, make an advance reservation with **Let's Go Ballooning!** Flights carrying up to four passengers launch at sunrise and last about an hour. ✉ *Paso Robles*

Airport, 4912 Wing Way ☎805/458–1530 🌐www.sloballoon.com 🎫$189 per person ⏲Daily.

WHERE TO EAT

$$$ AMERICAN

✕**Artisan.** Innovative renditions of traditional American comfort foods, a well-chosen list of regional wines, a stylish full bar, and a sophisticated urban vibe lure winemakers, locals, and tourists to this small, family-run American bistro in an art-deco building near the town square. Chris Kobayashi (Chef Koby) uses mostly local, organic, wild-caught ingredients to whip up regional favorites, which might include tuna tartare with fried green tomatoes, grilled free-range chicken with white cheddar grits and bourbon gravy, or Colorado lamb shanks with chickpeas and olives. Try to nab a booth facing the open kitchen, and save room for the restaurant's famed homestyle desserts: brownies, peach crumbles, crème brûlée, and the like. ✉ *1401 Park St.* ☎*805/237–8084* ▭*AE, D, MC, V.*

$$$ FRENCH ★

✕**Bistro Laurent.** Owner-chef Laurent Grangien has created a handsome, welcoming French bistro in an 1890s brick building across from City Park. He focuses on traditional dishes such as osso buco, cassoulet, rack of lamb, goat-cheese tart, and onion soup, but always offers a few updated dishes as daily specials. Wines come from around the world. Le Petit Marcel, a tiny nook next door to the main restaurant, is open just for lunch Monday through Saturday. ✉*1202 Pine St.* ☎*805/226–8191* ▭*MC, V* ⏲*Closed Sun. No lunch.*

$$$ AMERICAN

✕**McPhee's Grill.** The grain silos across the street and the floral oilcloths on the tables belie the sophisticated cuisine at this casual chophouse. In an 1860s building in the tiny cow town of Templeton (just south of Paso Robles), the restaurant serves creative, contemporary versions of traditional Western fare—such as oak-grilled filet mignon and cedar-planked salmon. House-label wines, made especially for McPhee's, are quite good. ✉*416 Main St., Templeton* ☎*805/434–3204* ▭*AE, D, MC, V.*

$ FRENCH

✕**Panolivo.** Scrumptious French bistro fare draws a loyal crowd of locals to this cheery downtown café just a block north of the town square. For breakfast, try a fresh pastry or quiche, or build your own omelet. Lunch choices include traditional French dishes like snails baked in garlic-butter sauce or cassoulet as well as sandwiches, salads, and fresh pastas—including the house-made beef cannelloni. ✉*1344 Park St.* ☎*805/239–3366* ▭*AE, D, MC, V* ⏲*No dinner Sun.–Thurs.*

$$$ SOUTHWESTERN

✕**Villa Creek.** With a firm nod to the Southwest, chef Tom Fundero conjures distinctly modern magic with locally and sustainably grown ingredients. The seasonal menu has included butternut-squash enchiladas and braised rabbit with mole negro, but you might also find duck breast with sweet-potato latkes. Central Coast wines dominate the list, with a smattering of Spanish and French selections. All brick and bare wood, the dining room can get loud when winemakers start passing their bottles from table to table, but it's always festive. For lighter appetites or wallets, the bar serves smaller plates—not to mention a killer margarita. ✉*1144 Pine St.* ☎*805/238–3000* ▭*AE, D, MC, V* ⏲*No lunch.*

WHERE TO STAY

¢–$ Fodor's Choice ★ **Adelaide Inn.** Family-owned and -managed, this clean, friendly oasis with meticulous landscaping offers spacious rooms and everything you need: coffeemaker, iron, hair dryer, and peace and quiet. In the lobby complimentary muffins and newspapers are set out in the morning; cookies come out in the afternoon. The motel has been around for decades, but nearly half the rooms were built in 2005. It's a tremendous value, so it books out weeks or even months in advance. A short walk from the fairgrounds, the Adelaide is tucked behind a conglomeration of gas stations and fast-food outlets just west of the U.S. 101 and Highway 46E interchange. **Pros:** great bargain; attractive pool area; ideal for families. **Cons:** not a romantic retreat; near a busy intersection and freeway. ✉ *1215 Ysabel Ave.* ☎ *805/238–2770 or 800/549–7276* 🌐 *www.adelaideinn.com* *109 rooms* *In-room: refrigerator, Internet, Wi-Fi. In-hotel: pool, gym, laundry facilities, laundry service, no-smoking rooms* ▭ *AE, D, DC, MC, V* *CP.*

$$$$ **Hotel Cheval.** Equestrian themes surface throughout this intimate, sophisticated, European-style inn just a half-block from the main square and a short walk from some of Paso's best restaurants. Each of the 16 spacious rooms is named after a famous racehorse (its history and picture hang on the wall) and includes custom European contemporary furnishings, king beds with exquisite linens and comforters, and original works of art. Most rooms have fireplaces and window seats; some have vaulted cedar ceilings. At the on-site Pony Club you can sip local and international wines and champagne at the horseshoe-shaped zinc bar. **Pros:** walking distance from downtown restaurants; European-style facilities; personal service. **Cons:** views aren't great; no pool or hot tub. ✉ *1021 Pine St.* ☎ *805/226–9995 or 866/522–6999* 🌐 *www.hotelcheval.com* *16 rooms* *In-room: DVD (some), Internet, Wi-Fi. In-hotel: bar, Wi-Fi, no-smoking rooms* ▭ *AE, D, MC, V* *CP.*

$$$ **La Bellasera Hotel & Suites.** The swankest full-service hotel for miles around, the La Bellasera, completed in 2008, caters to those looking for luxurious high-tech amenities and close proximity to major Central Coast roadways. The four-story Italianate building rises above vineyards and retail businesses near the intersection of highways 101 and 46 West, just a few miles south of the historic town square. Stone water features, Romanesque columns, marble and granite countertops, and wrought-iron fixtures support an image of elegant opulence throughout the lobby and public areas. Choose among nine different types of oversize (430 square feet and up) rooms and suites, from a deluxe king with a fireplace or whirlpool to a grand three-room suite with kitchen. All rooms include premium linens, baths with walk-in showers, LCD HDTVs, thin client computers, wet bars with refrigerators, and fully stocked minibars. **Pros:** new property; tons of amenities. **Cons:** far from town square; located at major intersection. ✉ *206 Alexa Court* ☎ *805/238–2834 or 866/782–9669* 🌐 *www.labellasera.com* *35 rooms, 25 suites* *In-room: safe, kitchen (some), refrigerator, Internet, Wi-Fi. In-hotel: restaurant, room service, bar, pool, gym, spa, laundry facilities, laundry service, Internet terminal, Wi-Fi, no-smoking rooms.* ▭ *AE, D, DC, MC, V.*

$$ **Paso Robles Inn.** On the site of a luxurious old spa hotel of the same name, the inn is built around a lush, shady garden with a hot mineral pool. The water is still the reason to stay here, and each deluxe room (new and old) has a spring-fed hot tub in its bathroom or on its balcony. Have breakfast in the circular 1940s coffee shop, and on weekends dance with the ranchers in the Cattlemen's Lounge. **Pros:** private spring-fed hot tubs; historic property; across from park and town square. **Cons:** fronts a busy street; rooms vary in size and quality. *1103 Spring St. 805/238–2660 or 800/676–1713 www.pasoroblesinn.com 92 rooms, 6 suites In-room: refrigerator, Internet. In-hotel: restaurant, bar, pool, Wi-Fi, no-smoking rooms AE, D, DC, MC, V.*

CAMBRIA

28 mi west of Paso Robles on Hwy. 46; 20 mi north of Morro Bay on Hwy. 1.

Cambria, set on piney hills above the sea, was settled by Welsh miners in the 1890s. In the 1970s the gorgeous, isolated setting attracted artists and other independent types; the town now caters to tourists, but it still bears the unmistakable imprint of its bohemian past. Both of Cambria's downtowns, the original East Village and the newer West Village, are packed with art and craft galleries, antiques shops, cafés, restaurants, and B&Bs. Late-Victorian homes stand along side streets, and the hills are filled with redwood-and-glass residences.

ESSENTIALS

Visitor Information Cambria Chamber of Commerce (*805/927–3624 www.cambriachamber.org*).

EXPLORING

Lined with low-key motels, **Moonstone Beach Drive** runs along a bluff above the ocean. The boardwalk that winds along the beach side of the drive makes a great walk.

Leffingwell's Landing (*North end of Moonstone Beach Dr. 805/927–2070*), a state picnic ground, is a good place for examining tidal pools and watching otters as they frolic in the surf.

Arthur Beal (aka Captain Nit Wit, Der Tinkerpaw) spent 51 years building **Nit Wit Ridge,** a home with terraced rock gardens. For building materials, he used all kinds of collected junk: beer cans, rocks, abalone shells, car parts, TV antennas—you name it. The site, above Cambria's West Village, is a State Historic Landmark. You can drive by and peek in; better yet, call ahead for a guided tour of the house and grounds. *881 Hillcrest Dr. 805/927–2690 $10 Daily by appointment.*

WHERE TO EAT

$$$ AMERICAN **The Black Cat.** Jazz wafts through the several small rooms of this intimate East Village bistro where leopard-print cushions line the banquettes. Start with an order of the fried olives stuffed with Gorgonzola, accompanied by a glass from the eclectic list of local and imported wines. On the daily-changing, always exciting menu, you might find roasted rack of elk rubbed in cocoa or breast of pheasant stuffed with

caramelized apples. ✉*1602 Main St.* ☎*805/927–1600* *Reservations essential* *AE, D, DC, MC, V* *Closed Tues. and Wed. No lunch.*

¢ CAFÉ ✕ **French Corner Bakery.** Place your order at the counter and then sit outside to watch the passing East Village scene (if the fog has rolled in, take a seat in the tiny deli). The rich aroma of coffee and fresh breakfast pastries makes mouths water in the morning; for lunch, try a quiche with flaky crust or a sandwich on house-baked bread. ✉*2214 Main St.* ☎*805/927–8227* *Reservations not accepted* *No dinner.*

$$ ECLECTIC ✕ **Robin's.** A truly multiethnic and vegetarian-friendly dining experience awaits you at this East Village cottage filled with country antiques. At dinner, choose from lobster enchiladas, pork osso buco, Thai red tofu curry, and more. Lunchtime's extensive salad and sandwich menu embraces burgers and tempeh alike. Unless it's raining, ask for a table on the secluded (and heated) garden patio. ✉*4095 Burton Dr.* ☎*805/927–5007* *MC, V.*

$$$ SEAFOOD ✕ **The Sea Chest.** By far the best seafood place in town—readers give it a big thumbs-up—this Moonstone Beach restaurant fills soon after it opens at 5:30. Those in the know grab seats at the oyster bar, where they can take in spectacular sunsets while watching the chefs broil fresh halibut and steam garlicky clams. If you can't get there early, play some cribbage or checkers while you wait for a table. ✉*6216 Moonstone Beach Dr.* ☎*805/927–4514* *Reservations not accepted* *No credit cards* *Closed Tues. mid-Sept.–May. No lunch.*

WHERE TO STAY

¢–$ **Bluebird Inn.** This sweet motel in Cambria's East Village sits amid beautiful gardens along Santa Rosa Creek. Rooms include simply furnished doubles and nicer creek-side suites with patios, fireplaces, and refrigerators. The Bluebird isn't the fanciest place, but if you don't require beachside accommodations, it's a bargain. **Pros:** excellent value; well-kept gardens; friendly staff. **Cons:** few frills; basic rooms; on Cambria's main drag. ✉*1880 Main St.* ☎*805/927–4634 or 800/552–5434* *www.bluebirdmotel.com* *37 rooms* *In-room: refrigerator (some), Wi-Fi. In-hotel: no-smoking rooms* *D, MC, V.*

$$–$$$ **Cambria Pines Lodge.** With lots of recreational facilities and a range of accommodations—from basic state park–style cabins to motel-style standard rooms to large fireplace suites—this 25-acre retreat up the hill from the East Village is a good choice for families. Walls can be thin in buildings dating as far back as the 1940s; a separate cluster of luxury suites and rooms opened in 2006. The lodge is always busy: its extensive gardens are popular with wedding parties, groups and conferences are big business, and bands play light rock, folk, and jazz in the lounge. **Pros:** short walk from downtown; verdant gardens; spacious grounds. **Cons:** front desk service and housekeeping not always top-quality; some units could use an update. ✉*2905 Burton Dr.* ☎*805/927–4200* *www.cambriapineslodge.com* *72 rooms, 19 cabins, 62 suites* *In-room: refrigerator (some), Internet. In-hotel: restaurant, room service, bar, pool, spa, Wi-Fi, some pets allowed, no-smoking rooms* *AE, D, DC, MC, V.*

$$–$$$ ★ **Moonstone Landing.** Friendly staff, lots of amenities, and reasonable rates make this up-to-date motel a top pick with readers who like to

stay right on Moonstone Beach. All rooms have Mission-style furnishings, DVD players, fireplaces, and Internet access. From their balconies or patios a few of the deluxe rooms, which have marble whirlpool tubs and showers, offer some of the best views in Cambria. **Pros:** sleek furnishings; across from the beach; cheery lounge. **Cons:** narrow property; some rooms overlook a parking lot. ✉*6240 Moonstone Beach Dr.* ☎*805/927–0012 or 800/830–4540* 🌐*www.moonstonelanding.com* *29 rooms* *In-room: refrigerator, DVD, Wi-Fi. In-hotel: no-smoking rooms* *AE, D, MC, V* *CP.*

SAN SIMEON

Hwy. 1, 9 mi north of Cambria and 65 mi south of Big Sur.

Whalers founded San Simeon in the 1850s, but had virtually abandoned the town by the time Senator George Hearst reestablished it 20 years later. Hearst bought up most of the surrounding ranch land, built a 1,000-foot wharf, and turned San Simeon into a bustling port. His son, William Randolph Hearst, further developed the area during the construction of Hearst Castle. Today the town, 4 mi south of the entrance to Hearst San Simeon State Historical Monument, is basically a strip of gift shops and mediocre motels along Highway 1.

EXPLORING

★ **Hearst San Simeon State Historical Monument** sits in solitary splendor atop La Cuesta Encantada (the Enchanted Hill). Its buildings and gardens spread over 127 acres that were the heart of newspaper magnate William Randolph Hearst's 250,000-acre ranch. Hearst devoted nearly 30 years and about $10 million to building this elaborate estate. He commissioned renowned architect Julia Morgan—who also designed buildings at the University of California at Berkeley—but he was very much involved with the final product, a hodgepodge of Italian, Spanish, Moorish, and French styles. The 115-room main building and three huge "cottages" are connected by terraces and staircases and surrounded by pools, gardens, and statuary. In its heyday the castle was a playground for Hearst and his guests, many of whom were Hollywood celebrities. Construction began in 1919 and was never officially completed. Work was halted in 1947 when Hearst had to leave San Simeon because of failing health. The Hearst family presented the property to the State of California in 1958.

Access to the castle is through the large visitor center at the foot of the hill, which contains a collection of Hearst memorabilia and a giant-screen theater that shows a 40-minute film giving a sanitized version of Hearst's life and of the castle's construction. Buses from the visitor center zigzag up the hillside to the neoclassical extravaganza, where guides conduct four different daytime tours of various parts of the main house and grounds. Tour No. 1 (which includes the movie) provides a good overview of the highlights; the others focus on particular parts of the estate. Daytime tours take about two hours. In spring and fall, docents in period costume portray Hearst's guests and staff for the slightly longer evening tour, which begins at sunset. All tours include a ½-mi walk and between 150 and 400 stairs. Reservations for the tours, which can be made up to eight weeks in advance, are necessary. *San Simeon State Park, 750 Hearst Castle Rd. 805/927–2020 or 800/444–4445 www.hearstcastle.com Daytime tours $24, evening tours $30 Tours daily 8:20–3:20, later in summer; additional tours take place most Fri. and Sat. evenings Mar.–May and Sept.–Dec. AE, D, MC, V.*

A large and growing colony (at last count 15,000 members) of elephant seals gathers every year at **Piedras Blancas Elephant Seal Rookery,** on the beaches near Piedras Blancas Lighthouse. The huge males with their pendulous, trunklike noses typically start appearing on shore in late November, and the females begin to arrive in December to give birth—most babies are born in the last two weeks of January. The newborn pups spend about four weeks nursing before their mothers head out to sea, leaving them on their own; the "weaners" leave the rookery when they are about 3½ months old. The seals return once or twice in the spring and summer months to molt or rest, but not en masse as in winter. You can watch them from a boardwalk along the bluffs just a few feet above the beach; do not attempt to approach them, as they are wild animals. Docents are often on hand to give background information and statistics. The rookery is just south of Piedras Blancas Lighthouse (4½ mi north of Hearst San Simeon State Historical Monument); the nonprofit Friends of the Elephant Seal runs a small visitor center and gift shop at their San Simeon office. *Friends of the Elephant Seal, 250 San Simeon Ave., Suite 3 805/924–1628 www.elephantseal.org.*

WHERE TO STAY

$$ **Best Western Cavalier Oceanfront Resort.** Reasonable rates, an oceanfront location, evening bonfires, and well-equipped rooms—some with wood-burning fireplaces and private patios—make this motel one of the best choices in San Simeon. **Pros:** on the bluffs; fantastic views; close to Hearst Castle; bluff bonfires. **Cons:** room amenities and sizes vary; pools are small and sometimes crowded. *9415 Hearst Dr. 805/927–4688 or 800/826–8168 www.cavalierresort.com 90 rooms In-room: refrigerator, DVD, Internet, Wi-Fi (some). In-hotel: 2 restaurants, pools, gym, laundry facilities, some pets allowed, no-smoking rooms AE, D, DC, MC, V.*

$$–$$$ **The Morgan San Simeon.** Conveniently situated on the ocean side of Highway 1, near San Simeon restaurants and shops, the Morgan offers a range of motel-style rooming options while paying tribute to famed Hearst Castle architect Julia Morgan. A 2008 head-to-toe remodel transformed the former Orchid Inn into a stylish Asia-inspired complex in two buildings, encompassing six types of guest rooms, some with fireplaces, soaking tubs, and wet bars. Authentic prints of Julia Morgan's design sketches, juxtaposed with real-life photos, appear in the rooms and throughout the property. **Pros:** fascinating artwork; easy access to Hearst Castle and Highway 1; some ocean views. **Cons:** not right on beach; no fitness room or laundry facilities. *9135 Hearst Dr. 805/927–3878 or 800/451–9900 www.hotel-morgan.com 54 rooms, 1 suite In-room: refrigerator (some), DVD (some), Internet (some), Wi-Fi. In-hotel: bar, pool, spa, Wi-Fi, no-smoking rooms. AE, D, DC, MC, V CP.*

BIG SUR COASTLINE

Long a retreat of artists and writers, Big Sur is a place of ancient forests and rugged shoreline, stretching 90 mi from San Simeon to Carmel. Residents have protected it from overdevelopment, and much of the region lies within several state parks and the more than 165,000-acre Ventana Wilderness, itself part of the Los Padres National Forest.

2

ESSENTIALS

Visitor Information Big Sur Chamber of Commerce (☎*831/667–2100* 🌐*www.bigsurcalifornia.org*).

SOUTHERN BIG SUR

Hwy. 1 from San Simeon to Julia Pfeiffer Burns State Park.

This especially rugged stretch of oceanfront is a rocky world of mountains, cliffs, and beaches.

EXPLORING

Fodor'sChoice ★ One of California's most spectacular drives, **Highway 1** snakes up the coast north of San Simeon. Numerous pullouts along the way offer tremendous views and photo ops. On some of the beaches huge elephant seals lounge nonchalantly, seemingly oblivious to the attention of rubberneckers—but keep your distance. In rainy seasons the southern Big Sur portion of Highway 1 is regularly shut down by mud slides. Contact **CalTrans** (☎*800/427–7623* 🌐*www.dot.ca.gov*) for road conditions.

In Los Padres National Forest just north of the town of Gorda is **Jade Cove** (✉*Hwy. 1, 34 mi north of San Simeon*), a well-known jade-hunting spot. Rock hunting is allowed on the beach, but you may not remove anything from the walls of the cliffs.

Julia Pfeiffer Burns State Park provides some fine hiking, from an easy ½-mi stroll with marvelous coastal views to a strenuous 6-mi trek through the redwoods. The big attraction here, an 80-foot waterfall that drops into the ocean, gets crowded in summer; still, it's an astounding place to sit and contemplate nature. Migrating whales, as well as harbor seals and sea lions, can sometimes be spotted not far from shore. ✉*Hwy. 1, 53 mi north of San Simeon, 15 mi north of Lucia* ☎*831/667–2315* 🌐*www.parks.ca.gov* *$10* *Daily sunrise–sunset.*

WHERE TO STAY

$$–$$$ **Ragged Point Inn.** At this cliff-top resort—the only inn and restaurant for miles around—glass walls in most rooms open to awesome, unobstructed ocean views. Though not especially luxurious, some rooms have spa tubs, kitchenettes, and fireplaces. The restaurant ($$–$$$) is a good place to fill up on standard American fare—sandwiches, salads, pastas, and main courses—before or after the long, winding Highway 1 drive. Even if you're just passing by, stop to stretch your legs on the 14 acres of lush gardens above the sea; you can pick up souvenirs, a burger, or an espresso to go. **Pros:** on the cliffs; great food; idyllic views. **Cons:** busy road stop during the day; often booked for weekend weddings. ✉*19019 Hwy. 1, 20 mi north of San Simeon, Ragged Point* ☎*805/927–4502, 805/927–5708 restaurant* 🌐*www.raggedpointinn.*

WORD OF MOUTH

"The Central Coast in all its glory: I proposed to my fiancé 10 minutes after I took this photo in Julia Pfeiffer Burns State Park." —photo by Valhalla, Fodors.com member

com 30 *rooms* *In-room: no phone, kitchen (some). In-hotel: restaurant, laundry facilities, Wi-Fi, no-smoking rooms* *AE, D, DC, MC, V.*

$$–$$$ **Treebones Resort.** Perched on a hilltop surrounded by national forest and stunning, unobstructed ocean views, this yurt resort opened in 2004. The yurts here—circular structures of heavy-duty fabric, on individual platforms with decks—are designed for upscale camping. Each has one or two queen beds with patchwork quilts, wicker furniture, and pine floors. Electricity and hot and cold running water come to you, but you have to walk to squeaky-clean bathhouse and restroom facilities. The sunny main lodge, where breakfast and dinner (not included) are served, has a big fireplace, games, and a well-stocked sundries and gift shop. Younger children have difficulty on the steep paths between buildings. There is a two-night minimum for stays on weekends and between April and October. **Pros:** 360-degree views; spacious pool area; comfortable beds. **Cons:** steep paths; no private bathrooms; more than a mile from the nearest store; not a good place for families with children under 6. ✉*71895 Hwy. 1, Willow Creek Rd., 32 mi north of San Simeon, 1 mi north of Gorda* ☎*877/424–4787* *www.treebonesresort.com* *16 yurts, 5 campsites* *In-hotel: restaurant, pool, spa, laundry facilities, Internet terminal, some pets allowed* *AE, MC, V* *CP.*

CENTRAL BIG SUR

Hwy. 1, from Partington Cove to Bixby Bridge.

The countercultural spirit of Big Sur—which instead of a conventional town is a loose string of coast-hugging properties along Highway 1—is alive and well today. Its few residents include the very wealthy, the enthusiastically outdoorsy, and the thoroughly evolved: since the 1960s the Esalen Institute, a center for alternative education and East–West philosophical study, has attracted seekers of higher consciousness and devotees of the property's hot springs. Today posh and rustic resorts hidden among the redwoods cater to visitors drawn from near and far by the extraordinary scenery and serene isolation.

EXPLORING

Through a hole in one of the gigantic boulders at secluded **Pfeiffer Beach** you can watch the waves break first on the sea side and then on the beach side. Keep a sharp eye out for the unsigned road to the beach: it is the only ungated paved road branching west of Highway 1 between the post office and Pfeiffer Big Sur State Park. The 2-mi, one-lane road descends sharply. ✉*Off Hwy. 1, 1 mi south of Pfeiffer Big Sur State Park* *$10 per vehicle per day.*

Among the many hiking trails at **Pfeiffer Big Sur State Park** ($10 per vehicle for day use) a short route through a redwood-filled valley leads to a waterfall. You can double back or continue on the more difficult trail along the valley wall for views over miles of treetops to the sea. Stop in at the Big Sur Station visitor center, off Highway 1, less than ½ mi south of the park entrance, for information about the entire area; it's open 8–4:30. ✉*47225 Hwy. 1* ☎*831/667–2315* *www.parks.ca.gov* *$10 per vehicle* *Daily dawn–dusk.*

★ **Point Sur State Historic Park** is the site of an 1889 lighthouse that still stands watch from atop a large volcanic rock. Four lighthouse keepers lived here with their families until 1974, when the light station became automated. Their homes and working spaces are open to the public only on 2½- to 3-hour ranger-led tours. Considerable walking, including up two stairways, is involved. Strollers are not allowed. ✉*Hwy. 1, 7 mi north of Pfeiffer Big Sur State Park* ☎*831/625–4419* 🌐*www.pointsur.org* 🎫*$10* ⏲*Tours generally Nov.–Mar., Sat. and Sun. at 10; Apr.–Oct., Wed. at 1, Sat. at 10 and 2, Sun. at 10; call to confirm.*

The graceful arc of **Bixby Creek Bridge** (✉*Hwy. 1, 6 mi north of Point Sur State Historic Park, 13 mi south of Carmel*) is a photographer's dream. Built in 1932, it spans a deep canyon more than 100 feet wide at the bottom. From the parking area on the north side you can admire the view or walk across the 550-foot span.

WHERE TO EAT

$$ ECLECTIC ✕**Big Sur Roadhouse.** In their colorful, casual bistro Marcus and Heather Foster serve up innovative, well-executed California Latin–fusion fare. Crispy striped bass atop a pillow of carrot-coconut puree, tangy-smoky barbecue chicken breast beneath a julienne of jicama and cilantro: the zesty, balanced flavors wake up your mouth. Emphasizing New World vintages, the wine list is gently priced. The chocolate-caramel layer cake may bring tears to your eyes. ✉*Hwy. 1, 1 mi north of Pfeiffer Big Sur State Park* ☎*831/667–2264* ⏲*Closed Tues. No lunch.*

$$$ AMERICAN ✕**Deetjen's Big Sur Inn.** The candlelighted, creaky-floor restaurant in the main house at the historic inn of the same name is a Big Sur institution. It serves roast duck, steak, and rack of lamb for dinner and wonderfully flavorful eggs Benedict for breakfast. The chef procures much of the fish, meats, and produce from purveyors who practice sustainable farming and fishing practices. ✉ *Hwy. 1, 3½ mi south of Pfeiffer Big Sur State Park* ☎*831/667–2377* 💳*MC, V* ⏲*No lunch.*

$$$ AMERICAN ✕**Nepenthe.** It may be that no other restaurant between San Francisco and Los Angeles has a better coastal view; no wonder Orson Welles and Rita Hayworth once owned the place. The food and drink are overpriced but good; there are burgers, sandwiches, and salads for lunch, and fresh fish and hormone-free steaks for dinner. For the real show, settle on the terraced deck in the late afternoon, order a glass from the extensive wine list, and watch the sun slip into the Pacific Ocean. The less expensive, outdoor Café Kevah serves breakfast and lunch. ✉*Hwy. 1, 2½ mi south of Big Sur Station* ☎*831/667–2345* 💳*AE, MC, V.*

$$$$ AMERICAN ✕**Sierra Mar.** Ocean-view dining doesn't get much better than this. Perched at cliff's edge 1,200 feet above the Pacific at the ultra-chic Post Ranch Inn, Sierra Mar serves cutting-edge American food made from mostly organic, seasonal ingredients, including a stellar four-course prix-fixe menu. The restaurant's wine list is one of the most extensive in the nation. ✉*Hwy. 1, 1½ mi south of Pfeiffer Big Sur State Park* ☎*831/667–2800* ✍*Reservations essential* 💳*AE, MC, V.*

WHERE TO STAY

$–$$$ **Deetjen's Big Sur Inn.** This historic 1930s Norwegian-style property is endearingly rustic and charming, especially if you're willing to go with a camplike flow. The room doors lock only from the inside, and your neighbors can often be heard through the walls—if you plan to bring children, you must reserve an entire building. Still, Deetjen's is a special place. Its village of cabins is nestled in the redwoods, and many of the very individual rooms have their own fireplaces. **Pros:** surrounded by Big Sur history; tons of character; wooded grounds. **Cons:** rustic; thin walls; some rooms don't have private baths. *Hwy. 1, 3½ mi south of Pfeiffer Big Sur State Park 831/667–2377 www.deetjens.com 20 rooms, 15 with bath In-room: no phone, no TV. In-hotel: restaurant, no-smoking rooms MC, V.*

$$$$ Fodor's Choice ★ **Post Ranch Inn.** This luxurious retreat, designed exclusively for adult getaways, has remarkably environmentally conscious architecture. The redwood guesthouses, all of which have views of the sea or the mountains, blend almost invisibly into a wooded cliff 1,200 feet above the ocean. Each unit has its own fireplace, stereo, private deck, and massage table. On-site activities include everything from yoga to stargazing. **Pros:** world-class resort; spectacular views; gorgeous property with hiking trails. **Cons:** expensive; austere design; not a good choice if you're scared of heights. *Hwy. 1, 1½ mi south of Pfeiffer Big Sur State Park Hwy. 1, Box 219, 93920 831/667–2200 or 800/527–2200 www.postranchinn.com 39 units In-room: refrigerator, no TV, Internet (some), Wi-Fi (some). In-hotel: restaurant, bar, pools, gym, spa, Internet terminal, no-smoking rooms AE, MC, V BP.*

$$$$ Fodor's Choice ★ **Ventana Inn & Spa.** Hundreds of celebrities, from Oprah Winfrey to Sir Anthony Hopkins, have escaped to Ventana, a romantic resort on 243 tranquil acres 1,200 feet above the Pacific. The activities here are purposely limited. You can sunbathe (there is a clothing-optional deck and pool), walk or ride horses in the nearby hills, or pamper yourself with mind-and-body treatments at the Allegria Spa or in your own private quarters. All rooms have walls of natural wood and cool tile floors; some have private hot tubs on their patios. The Restaurant at Ventana ($$$–$$$$) showcases fine California cuisine and wine. **Pros:** nature trails everywhere; great food; secluded. **Cons:** simple breakfast; some rooms need updating. *Hwy. 1, almost 1 mi south of Pfeiffer Big Sur State Park 831/667–2331 or 800/628–6500 www.ventanainn.com 25 rooms, 31 suites, 3 houses In-room: DVD, Internet, Wi-Fi (some). In-hotel: restaurant, bar, pools, gym, spa, no-smoking rooms AE, D, DC, MC, V BP.*

¢ **Pfeiffer Big Sur State Park.** Redwood trees tower over this large campground. It's often crowded in summer, so reserve a site or a tent cabin as far ahead as possible. There are no hookups, but the park has Wi-Fi. *Wi-Fi, flush toilets, dump station, drinking water, guest laundry, showers, fire grates, fire pits, picnic tables, food service, public telephone, general store, ranger station 218 sites 47225 Hwy. 1 800/444–7275 reservations www.parks.ca.gov.*

3

The Monterey Bay Area

FROM CARMEL TO SANTA CRUZ

WORD OF MOUTH

"To be able to see, up close, the wonders of the ocean, is an amazing experience at the wonderful Monterey Bay Aquarium."

—photo by mellifluous, Fodors.com member

WELCOME TO THE MONTEREY BAY AREA

TOP REASONS TO GO

★ **Marine life:** Monterey Bay is home to the world's third-largest marine sanctuary, home to whales, otters, and other underwater creatures.

★ **Getaway central:** For more than a century urbanites have come to the Monterey Bay area to unwind, relax, and have fun. It's a great place to browse unique shops and galleries, ride a giant roller coaster, or play a round of golf on a world-class course.

★ **Nature preserves:** More than the sea is protected here—the region boasts nearly 30 state parks, beaches, and preserves, fantastic places for walking, jogging, hiking, and biking.

★ **Wine and dine:** The area's rich agricultural bounty translates to abundant fresh produce, great wines, and fabulous dining. It's no wonder more than 300 culinary events take place here every year.

★ **Small-town vibes:** Even the cities here are friendly, walkable places where you'll feel like a local.

1 Carmel and Pacific Grove. Exclusive Carmel-by-the-Sea and Carmel Valley Village burst with historic charm, fine dining, and unusual boutiques that cater to celebrity residents and well-heeled visitors. Nearby 17-Mile Drive—quite possibly the prettiest stretch of road you'll ever travel—runs between Carmel-by-the-Sea and Victorian-studded Pacific Grove, home to thousands of migrating monarch butterflies between October and February.

2 Monterey. A former Spanish military outpost, Monterey's well-preserved historic district is a hands-on history lesson. Cannery Row, the former center of Monterey's once-thriving sardine industry, has been reborn as a tourist attraction with shops, restaurants, hotels, and the Monterey Bay Aquarium.

3 Around the Bay. Much of California's lettuce, berries, artichokes, and Brussels sprouts come from Salinas and Watsonville. Salinas is also home of the National Steinbeck Center, and Moss Landing and Watsonville encompass pristine wildlife wetlands. Aptos, Capitola, and Soquel are former lumber towns became popular seaside resorts more than a century ago. Today they're filled with antiques shops, restaurants, and wine-tasting rooms; you'll also find some of the bay's best beaches along the shore here.

4 Santa Cruz. Santa Cruz shows its colors along an old-time beach boardwalk and municipal wharf. A University of California campus imbues the town with arts and culture and a liberal mind-set.

The Forest Nisene Marks State Park
Soquel
Aptos
Capitola
Rio del Mar
Soquel Cove
152
1
Freedom
3
Watsonville
129
Pajaro
MONTEREY BAY
Las Lomas
1
Moss Landing
Prunedale
156
Castroville
101
1
Salinas R.
183
SALINAS VALLEY
Marina
Salinas
G17
Point Pinos
Seaside
Spanish Bay
Pacific Grove
Sand City
17-Mile Dr.
Monterey 2
1
Pebble Beach
Del Rey Oaks
Spreckels
68
68
68
Cypress Point
Carmel
SIERRA DE SALINAS
Carmel Bay
G16
Carmel Valley Rd.
G20
1
Carmel River
Point Lobos
Carmel Highlands
G16
Carmel Valley

GETTING ORIENTED

North of Big Sur the coastline softens into lower bluffs, windswept dunes, pristine estuaries, and long, sandy beaches, bordering one of the world's most amazing marine environments—Monterey Bay. On the Monterey Peninsula, at the southern end of the bay, are Carmel-by-the-Sea, Pacific Grove, and Monterey; Santa Cruz sits at the northern tip of the crescent. In between, Highway 1 cruises along the coastline, passing windswept beaches piled high with sand dunes. Along the route are wetlands, artichoke and strawberry fields, and workaday towns such as Castroville and Watsonville.

THE MONTEREY BAY AREA PLANNER

Timing Your Trip

Summer is peak season; mild weather brings in big crowds. In this coastal region a cool breeze generally blows and fog often rolls in from offshore; you will frequently need a sweater or windbreaker. Off-season, from November through April, fewer people visit and the mood is mellower. Rainfall is heaviest in January and February, but autumn through spring days are crystal-clear more often than in summer.

Helpful Contacts

Bed and Breakfast Inns of Santa Cruz County (🌐 *www.santacruzbnb.com*), an association of innkeepers, can help you find a bed-and-breakfast. **Monterey County Convention and Visitors Bureau Visitor Services** (☎ *877/666-8373* 🌐 *www.montereyinfo.org*) operates a lodging referral line and publishes an informational brochure with discount coupons that are good at restaurants, attractions, and shops.

About the Hotels

Monterey-area accommodations range from no-frills motels to luxurious hotels. Pacific Grove, amply endowed with ornate Victorian houses, has quietly turned itself into the region's B&B capital; Carmel also has charming inns in residential areas. Truly lavish resorts, with everything from featherbeds to heated floors, cluster in exclusive Pebble Beach and pastoral Carmel Valley.

High season runs April through October. Rates in winter, especially at the larger hotels, may drop by 50% or more, and B&Bs often offer midweek specials in the off-season. However, special events throughout the year can fill lodgings far in advance. Whatever the month, even the simplest of the area's lodgings are expensive, and most properties require a two-night stay on weekends. ⚠ **Many of the fancier accommodations are not suitable for children, so if you're traveling with kids, be sure to ask before you book.**

About the Restaurants

Between San Francisco and Los Angeles, some of the finest dining to be found is around Monterey Bay. The surrounding waters are full of fish, wild game roams the foothills, and the inland valleys are some of the most fertile in the country—local chefs draw on this bounty for their fresh, truly California cuisine. Except at beachside stands and inexpensive eateries, where anything goes, casual but neat dress is the norm. Only a few places require formal attire.

WHAT IT COSTS

	¢	$	$$	$$$	$$$$
Restaurants	under $10	$10–$15	$16–$22	$23–$30	over $30
Hotels	under $90	$90–$120	$121–$175	$176–$250	over $250

Restaurant prices are for a main course at dinner, excluding sales tax of 7.5%–8.25% (depending on location). Hotel prices are for two people in a standard double room in high season, excluding service charges and 10%–10.5% tax.

3

Updated by Cheryl Crabtree

In the good life of Monterey Bay's coast-side towns, in the pleasures of its luxurious resorts, and in the vitality of its resplendent marine habitat, this piece of California shows off its natural appeal. The abundance is nothing new: an abiding current of plenty runs through the many histories of the region. Military buffs see it in centuries' worth of battles for control of the rich territory. John Steinbeck saw it in the success of a community built on the elbow grease of farm laborers in the Salinas Valley and fishermen along Cannery Row. Biologists see it in the ocean's potential as a more sustainable source of food.

Downtown Carmel-by-the-Sea and Monterey are walks through history. The bay itself is protected by the Monterey Bay National Marine Sanctuary, the nation's largest undersea canyon—bigger and deeper than the Grand Canyon. And of course, the backdrop of natural beauty is still everywhere to be seen.

PLANNING

GETTING HERE AND AROUND

AIR TRAVEL

Monterey Peninsula Airport is 3 mi east of downtown Monterey (take Olmstead Road off Highway 68). It's served by Allegiant Air, American Eagle, United, United Express, and US Airways. ⇨ *See Air Travel in Travel Smart Northern Califoronia for airline phone numbers.* Taxi service to downtown runs about \$12 to \$14; to Carmel the fare is \$20 to \$29. To and from San Jose International Airport and San Francisco International Airport, Monterey Airbus starts at \$35 and the Surf City Shuttle runs \$68 to \$108.

Continued on page 104

HIGHWAY 1: CARMEL TO SAN FRANCISCO

San Francisco

THE PLAN

Distance: approx. 123 mi

Time: 2-4 days

Good Overnight Options: Carmel, Monterey, Santa Cruz, Half Moon Bay, San Francisco

For more information on the sights and attractions along this portion of Highway 1, please see chapters 3, and 4.

CARMEL TO MONTEREY (approx. 4 mi)

Between **Carmel** and **Monterey,** the Highway 1 cuts across the base of the Monterey Peninsula. Pony up the toll and take a brief detour to follow famous **17-Mile Drive,** which traverses a surf-pounded landscape of cypress trees, sea lions, gargantuan estates, and the world famous **Pebble Beach Golf Links.** Take your time here as well, and be sure to allow lots of time for pulling off to enjoy the gorgeous views.

Monterey

If you have the time, spend a day checking out the sights in **Monterey,** especially the kelp forests and bat rays of the **Monterey Bay Aquarium** and the adobes and artifacts of **Monterey State Historic Park.**

MONTEREY TO SANTA CRUZ (approx. 42 mi)

From Monterey the highway rounds the gentle curve of Monterey Bay, passing through sand dunes and artichoke fields on its way to **Moss Landing** and the **Elkhorn Slough National Estuarine Marine Preserve.** Kayak or walk through the protected wetlands here, or board a pontoon safari boat—don't forget your binoculars. The historic seaside villages of **Aptos, Capitola,** and **Soquel,** just off the highway near the bay's midpoint, are ideal stopovers for beachcombing, antiquing, and hiking through redwoods. In boho **Santa Cruz,** just 7 mi north, walk along the **wharf,** ride the historic roller coaster on the **boardwalk,** and perch on the cliffs to watch surfers peel through tubes at **Steamers Lane.**

SANTA CRUZ TO SAN FRANCISCO (approx. 77 mi)

Highway 1 hugs the ocean's edge once again as it departs Santa Cruz and runs

Davenport cliffs, Devenport

northward past a string of secluded beaches and small towns. Stop and stretch your legs in the tiny, artsy town of **Davenport,** where you can wander through several galleries and enjoy sumptuous views from the bluffs. At **Año Nuevo State Reserve,** walk down to the dunes to view gargantuan elephant

FRIGID WATERS

If you're planning to jump in the ocean in Northern California, wear a wetsuit or prepare to shiver. Even in summer, the water temperatures warm up to just barely tolerable. The fog tends to burn off earlier in the day at relatively sheltered beaches near Monterey Bay's midpoint, near Aptos, Capitola and Santa Cruz. These beaches also tend to attract softer waves than those on the bay's outer edges.

Half Moon Bay

TOP 5 PLACES TO LINGER

- 17 Mile Drive
- Monterey
- Santa Cruz
- Año Nuevo State Reserve
- Half Moon Bay

seals lounging on shore, then break for a meal or snack in **Pescadero** or **Half Moon Bay.**

From Half Moon Bay to **Daly City,** the road includes a number of shoulderless twists and turns that demand slower speeds and nerves of steel. Signs of urban development soon appear: mansions holding fast to Pacific cliffs and then, as the road veers slightly inland to merge with Skyline Boulevard, boxlike houses sprawling across **Daly City** and **South San Francisco.**

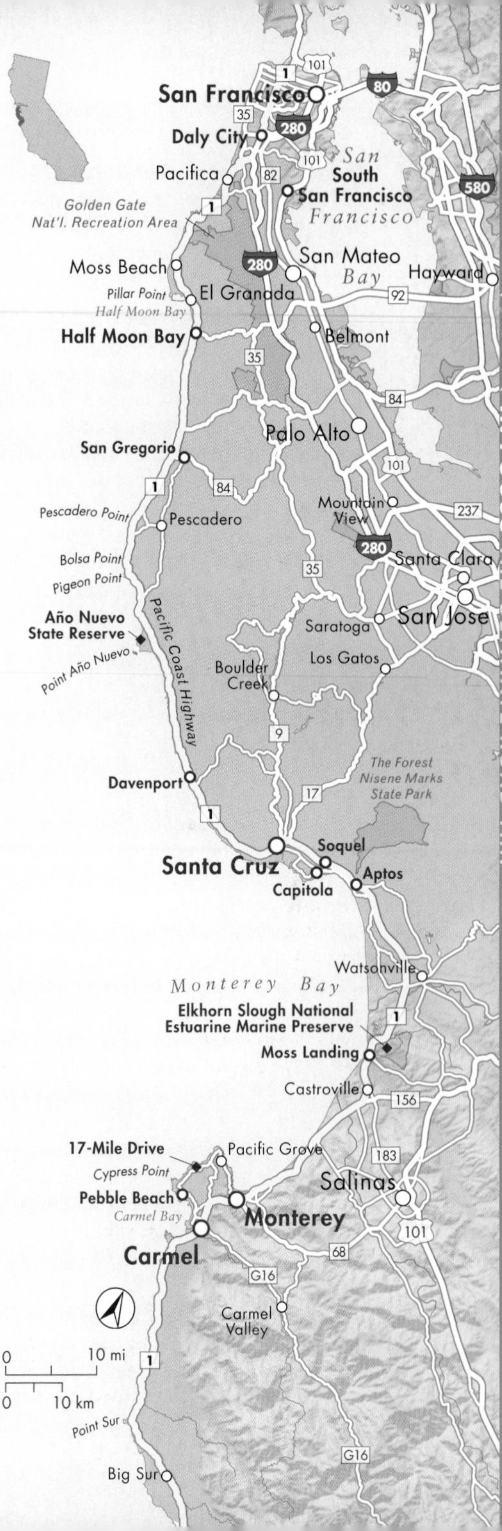

San Francisco
Daly City
Pacifica
South San Francisco
San Francisco Bay
Golden Gate Nat'l. Recreation Area
Moss Beach
Pillar Point
Half Moon Bay
El Granada
San Mateo
Hayward
Half Moon Bay
Belmont
Palo Alto
San Gregorio
Pescadero Point
Pescadero
Mountain View
Bolsa Point
Pigeon Point
Santa Clara
San Jose
Año Nuevo State Reserve
Point Año Nuevo
Pacific Coast Highway
Saratoga
Los Gatos
Boulder Creek
The Forest Nisene Marks State Park
Davenport
Santa Cruz
Soquel
Capitola
Aptos
Watsonville
Monterey Bay
Elkhorn Slough National Estuarine Marine Preserve
Moss Landing
Castroville
17-Mile Drive
Cypress Point
Pacific Grove
Pebble Beach
Carmel Bay
Salinas
Monterey
Carmel
Carmel Valley
0 10 mi
0 10 km
Point Sur
Big Sur

Airport Contact **Monterey Peninsula Airport** (✉ *200 Fred Kane Dr., Monterey* ☎ *831/648–7000* 🌐 *www.montereyairport.com*).

Taxi Contacts **Carmel Taxi** (☎ *831/624–3885*). **Monterey Airbus** (☎ *831/373–7777* 🌐 *www.montereyairbus.com*). **Central Coast Taxi** (☎ *831/626–3333*). **Surf City Shuttle** (☎ *831/419–2642* 🌐 *www.surfcityshuttle.com*). **Yellow Checker Cabs** (☎ *831/646–1234*).

BUS TRAVEL

Greyhound serves Santa Cruz and Monterey from San Francisco three or four times daily. The trips take about 3 and 4½ hours, respectively. Monterey-Salinas Transit provides frequent service between the peninsula's towns and many major sightseeing spots and shopping areas. The base fare is $2.50, with an additional $2.50 for each zone you travel into. A day pass costs $6 to $12, depending on how many zones you'll be traveling through. Monterey-Salinas Transit also runs the MST Trolley, which links major attractions on the Monterey waterfront. The free shuttle operates late May through early September, weekdays from 10 to 7 and weekends and holidays from 10 to 8.

Bus Contacts **Greyhound** (☎ *800/231–2222* 🌐 *www.greyhound.com*). **Monterey-Salinas Transit** (☎ *831/899–2555 or 888/678–2871* 🌐 *www.mst.org*).

CAR TRAVEL

Highway 1 runs south–north along the coast, linking the towns of Carmel-by-the-Sea, Monterey, and Santa Cruz; some sections have only two lanes. The freeway, U.S. 101, lies to the east, roughly parallel to Highway 1. The two roads are connected by Highway 68 from Pacific Grove to Prunedale; Highway 152 from Watsonville to Gilroy; and Highway 17 from Santa Cruz to San Jose. Highway 17 crosses the redwood-filled Santa Cruz Mountains. ⚠ **Traffic near Santa Cruz can crawl to a standstill during commuter hours.**

The drive south from San Francisco to Monterey can be made comfortably in three hours or less. The most scenic way is to follow Highway 1 down the coast past flower, pumpkin, and artichoke fields and small seaside communities. Unless you drive on sunny weekends when locals are heading for the beach, the two-lane coast highway may take no longer than the freeway. A sometimes faster route is I–280 south from San Francisco to Highway 17, north of San Jose. A third option is to follow U.S. 101 south through San Jose to Prunedale and then take Highway 156 west to Highway 1 south into Monterey.

From Los Angeles the drive to Monterey can be made in five to six hours by heading north on U.S. 101 to Salinas and then west on Highway 68. The spectacular but slow alternative is to take U.S. 101 to San Luis Obispo and then follow the hairpin turns of Highway 1 up the coast. Allow about three extra hours if you take this route.

TRAIN TRAVEL

Amtrak's *Coast Starlight* runs between Los Angeles, Oakland, and Seattle. From the train station in Salinas, connecting Amtrak Thruway buses serve Monterey and Carmel-by-the-Sea; from San Jose, connecting buses serve Santa Cruz.

Train Contacts **Amtrak** (☎*800/872-7245* 🌐*www.amtrakcalifornia.com*). **Salinas Amtrak Station** (✉*11 Station Pl., Salinas* ☎*831/422-7458*).

HEALTH AND SAFETY

In the event of an emergency, dial 911. The Monterey Bay Dental Society provides dentist referrals throughout the area. The Monterey County Medical Society and the Santa Cruz County Medical Society can refer you to a doctor in Monterey and Santa Cruz counties, respectively. There are 24-hour Walgreens pharmacies in Seaside, about 4 mi northeast of Monterey via Highway 1, and in Freedom, on the eastern edge of Watsonville.

Hospital and Medical Contacts **Community Hospital of Monterey Peninsula** (✉*23625 Holman Hwy., Monterey* ☎*831/624-5311* 🌐*www.chomp.org*). **Dominican Hospital** (✉*1555 Soquel Dr., Santa Cruz* ☎*831/462-7700* 🌐*www.dominicanhospital.org*). **Monterey Bay Dental Society** (☎*831/658-0168* 🌐*mbdsdentist.com*). **Monterey County Medical Society** (☎*831/455-1008* 🌐*www.montereymedicine.org*). **Santa Cruz County Medical Society** (☎*831/479-7226* 🌐*www.cruzmed.org*). **Watsonville Community Hospital** (✉*75 Nielson St., Watsonville* ☎*831/724-4741* 🌐*www.watsonvillehospital.com*).

Pharmacies **Walgreens** (✉*1055 Fremont Blvd., Seaside* ☎*831/393-9231*). **Walgreens** (✉*1810 Freedom Blvd., Freedom* ☎*831/768-0183*).

TOUR OPTIONS

California Parlor Car Tours operates motor-coach tours from San Francisco that include one or two days in Monterey and Carmel. Ag Venture Tours runs wine-tasting, sightseeing, and agricultural tours in the Monterey, Salinas, Carmel Valley, and Santa Cruz areas.

Tour Contacts **Ag Venture Tours** (☎*831/761-8463* 🌐*www.agventuretours.com*). **California Parlor Car Tours** (☎*415/474-7500 or 800/227-4250* 🌐*www.calpartours.com*).

VISITOR INFORMATION

Contacts **Monterey County Convention & Visitors Bureau** (☎*877/666-8373* 🌐*www.montereyinfo.org*). **Monterey County Vintners and Growers Association** (☎*831/375-9400* 🌐*www.montereywines.org*). **Pajaro Valley Chamber of Commerce & Agriculture** (✉*449 Union St., Watsonville* ☎*831/724-3900* 🌐*www.pajarovalleychamber.com*). **Salinas Valley Chamber of Commerce** (✉*119 E. Alisal St., Salinas* ☎*831/751-7725* 🌐*www.salinaschamber.com*). **San Lorenzo Valley Chamber of Commerce** (✉*Box 661, Ben Lomond* ☎*831/345-2084* 🌐*www.slvchamber.org*). **Santa Cruz County Conference and Visitors Council** (✉*1211 Ocean St., Santa Cruz* ☎*831/425-1234 or 800/833-3494* 🌐*www.santacruz.org*). **Santa Cruz Mountain Winegrowers Association** (✉*7605-A Old Dominion Ct., Aptos* ☎*831/685-8463* 🌐*www.scmwa.com*).

CARMEL AND PACIFIC GROVE

CARMEL-BY-THE-SEA

26 mi north of Big Sur on Hwy. 1.

Although the community has grown quickly through the years and its population quadruples with tourists on weekends and in summer, Carmel-by-the-Sea, commonly referred to as Carmel, retains its identity as a quaint village. Self-consciously charming, the town is populated by many celebrities, major and minor, and has more than its share of quirky ordinances. For instance, women wearing high heels do not have the right to pursue legal action if they trip and fall on the cobblestone streets, and drivers who hit a tree and leave the scene are charged with hit-and-run.

Buildings still have no street numbers (street names are written on discreet white posts) and consequently no mail delivery (if you really want to see the locals, go to the post office). Artists started this community, and their legacy is evident in the numerous galleries. Wandering the side streets off Ocean Avenue, where you can poke into hidden courtyards and stop at cafés for tea and crumpets, is a pleasure.

ESSENTIALS

Visitor Information **Carmel Chamber of Commerce** (✉ *San Carlos, between 5th and 6th, Carmel* ☎ *831/624–2522 or 800/550–4333* 🌐 *www.carmelcalifornia.org*).

Downtown Carmel's chief lure is shopping, especially along its main street, **Ocean Avenue,** between Junipero Avenue and Camino Real; the architecture here is a mishmash of ersatz Tudor, Mediterranean, and other styles.

Carmel Plaza (✉ *Ocean and Junipero Aves.* ☎ *831/624–1385* 🌐 *www.carmelplaza.com*), in the east end of the village proper, holds more than 50 shops and restaurants.

Long before it became a shopping and browsing destination, Carmel was an important religious center during the establishment of Spanish California. That heritage is preserved in the Mission San Carlos Borroméo del Rio Carmelo, more commonly known as the ★ **Carmel Mission.** Founded in 1771, it served as headquarters for the mission system in California under Father Junípero Serra. Adjoining the stone church is a tranquil garden planted with California poppies. Museum rooms at the mission include an early kitchen, Serra's spartan sleeping quarters, and the first college library in California. ✉ *3080 Rio Rd., at Lasuen Dr.* ☎ *831/624–3600* 🌐 *www.carmelmission.org* 💵 *$5* ⏲ *Mon.–Sat. 9:30–5, Sun. 10:30–5.*

Scattered throughout the pines in Carmel-by-the-Sea are houses and cottages originally built for the writers, artists, and photographers who discovered the area decades ago. Among the most impressive dwellings is **Tor House,** a stone cottage built in 1919 by poet Robinson Jeffers on a craggy knoll overlooking the sea. Portraits, books, and unusual art objects fill the low-ceiling rooms. The highlight of the small estate is

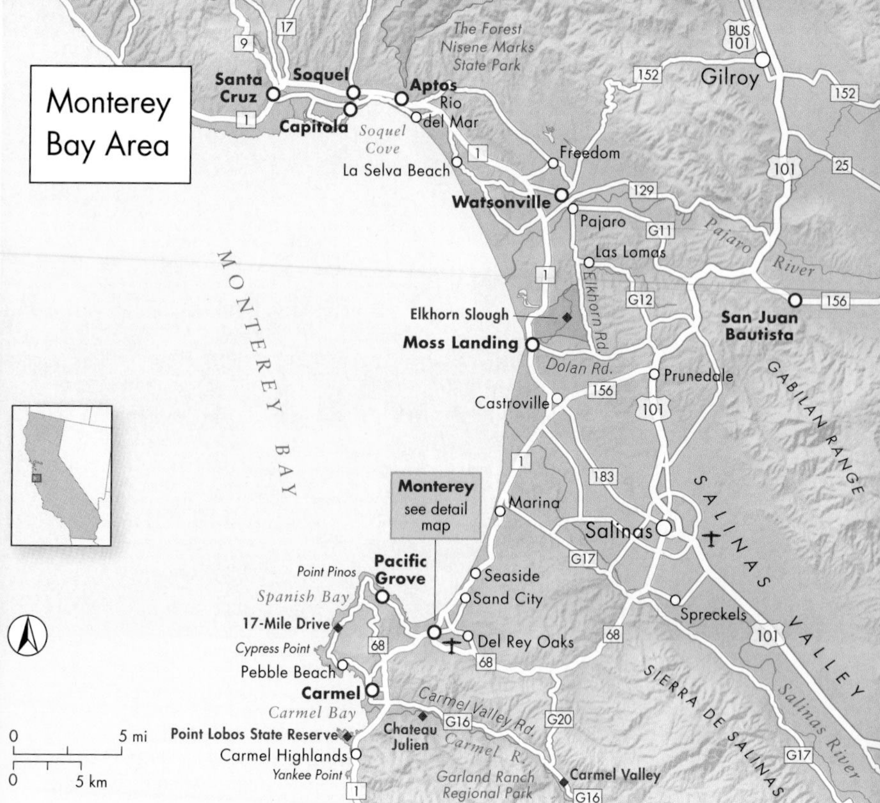

Hawk Tower, a detached edifice set with stones from the Carmel coastline—as well as one from the Great Wall of China. The docents who lead tours (six people maximum) are well informed about the poet's work and life. Reservations for tours are recommended. ✉ *26304 Ocean View Ave.* ☎ *831/624–1813* 🌐 *www.torhouse.org* 🎫 *$7* ⏲ *Tours on the hour Fri. and Sat. 10–3* ☞ *No children under 12.*

Carmel-by-the-Sea's greatest attraction is its rugged coastline, with pine and cypress forests and countless inlets. **Carmel Beach** (✉ *End of Ocean Ave.*), an easy walk from downtown shops, has sparkling white sands and magnificent sunsets.

Carmel River State Beach stretches for 106 acres along Carmel Bay. The sugar-white beach is adjacent to a bird sanctuary, where you might spot pelicans, kingfishers, hawks, and sandpipers. ✉ *Off Scenic Rd. south of Carmel Beach* ☎ *831/624–4909 or 831/649–2836* 🌐 *www.parks.ca.gov* 🎫 *Free* ⏲ *Daily 8 AM–½ hr after sunset.*

★ **Point Lobos State Reserve,** a 350-acre headland harboring a wealth of marine life, lies a few miles south of Carmel. The best way to explore the reserve is to walk along one of its many trails. The Cypress Grove Trail leads through a forest of Monterey cypress (one of only two natural groves remaining), which clings to the rocks above an emerald-green cove. Sea Lion Point Trail is a good place to view sea lions. From those

Point Lobos Reserve State Park is home to one of the only two natural stands of Monterey Cypress in the world.

and other trails you may also spot otters, harbor seals, and (in winter and spring) migrating whales. An additional 750 acres of the reserve is an undersea marine park open to qualified scuba divers. ■ **TIP→ Arrive early (or in late afternoon) to avoid crowds; the parking lots fill up.** No pets are allowed. ✉ *Hwy. 1* ☎ *831/624–4909, 831/624–8413 for scuba-diving reservations* 🌐 *www.pointlobos.org* 🎟 *$10 per vehicle* ⏲ *Daily 8 AM–½ hr after sunset.*

WHERE TO EAT

$$$ CONTINENTAL ✕ **Anton and Michel.** Carefully prepared European cuisine is the draw at this airy restaurant. The rack of lamb is carved at the table, the duck prosciutto is cured in-house, and the desserts are set aflame before your eyes. In summer, you (and your dog!) can have lunch served in the courtyard; inside, the dining room looks onto a lighted fountain. ✉ *Mission St. and 7th Ave.* ☎ *831/624–2406* ✍ *Reservations essential* 💳 *AE, D, DC, MC, V.*

$$$$ AMERICAN ✕ **Aubergine.** To eat and sleep at the luxe L'Auberge Carmel is a weekend in itself, but even those staying elsewhere should consider splurging on the inn's intimate, 12-table restaurant. (This is definitely not a place to bring the kids.) Aubergine epitomizes farm-fresh gourmet dining. Chef Christophe Grosjean grows more than 20 different herbs in his own garden, which he harvests and brings to the restaurant. His menu offers diners various options; you can create your own three-, four-, or five-course menu, for example, wild watercress and oysters, eggplant and lamb, and lemongrass ice cream with peaches. You can also ask the chef to design a surprise gastronomic "journey." There's a 4,500-bottle wine

cellar. ✉ *Monte Verde, at 7th Ave.* ☎ *831/624–8578* ✍ *Reservations essential* ▭ *AE, MC, V* ⊗ *No lunch.*

$$ CARIBBEAN ✕ **Bahama Billy's.** The energy is electric at this always-bustling Caribbean bar and restaurant. An excellent and diverse menu combined with a lively crowd makes it a prime spot for fun and good eating in Carmel. Particularly good is the ahi tuna, which is rolled in Jamaican jerk seasoning, seared, and served with aioli. There's often live music in the bar. ✉ *Barnyard Shopping Center, Hwy. 1 and Carmel Valley Rd.* ☎ *831/626–0430* ✍ *Reservations essential* ▭ *AE, D, MC, V.*

3

$$$ FRENCH ★ ✕ **Bouchée.** The food here presents an innovative bistro-style take on local ingredients. Monterey red abalone is prepared with black truffles, potatoes, and Noilly Prat beurre blanc; smoked California squab breast is served with apricots, heirloom carrots, and kumquats. With its copper bar, the dining room feels more urban than most of Carmel; perhaps this is why Bouchée is the "cool" place in town to dine. The stellar wine list sources the selection at adjoining Bouchée Wine Merchant. ✉ *Mission St., between Ocean and 7th Aves.* ☎ *831/626–7880* ✍ *Reservations essential* ▭ *AE, MC, V* ⊗ *No lunch.*

$$$$ MEDITERRANEAN ★ ✕ **Casanova.** Built in a former home, this cozy restaurant inspires European-style celebration and romance—chairs are painted in all colors, accordions hang from the walls, and tiny party lights dance along the low ceilings. All entrées include antipasti and your choice of appetizers, which all but mandate you to sit back and enjoy a long meal. The food consists of delectable seasonal dishes from southern France and northern Italy. Private dining and a special menu are offered at Van Gogh's Table, a special table imported from France's Auberge Ravoux, the artist's final residence. ✉ *5th Ave., between San Carlos and Mission Sts.* ☎ *831/625–0501* ✍ *Reservations essential* ▭ *AE, MC, V.*

$ AMERICAN ✕ **The Cottage Restaurant.** For the best breakfast in Carmel, look no further: the menu here offers six different preparations of eggs Benedict, and all kinds of sweet and savory crepes. This family-friendly spot serves sandwiches, pizzas, and homemade soups at lunch and simple entreés at dinner, but the best meals appear on the breakfast menu (good thing it's served all day). ✉ *Lincoln St., between Ocean and 7th Aves.* ☎ *831/625–6260* ▭ *MC, V* ⊗ *No dinner Sun.–Wed.*

$$ SEAFOOD ✕ **Flying Fish Grill.** Simple in appearance yet bold with its flavors, this Japanese–California seafood restaurant has quickly established itself as one of Carmel's most inventive eateries. Among the best entrées is the almond-crusted sea bass served with Chinese cabbage and rock shrimp stir-fry. The warm, wood-lined dining room is broken up into very private booths. For the entrance, go down the steps near the gates to Carmel Plaza. ✉ *Mission St., between Ocean and 7th Aves.* ☎ *831/625–1962* ▭ *AE, MC, V* ⊗ *No lunch.*

$ AMERICAN ✕ **Jack London's Grill & Taproom.** If anyone's awake after dinner in Carmel, he's at Jack London's. This publike local hangout is the only Carmel restaurant to serve food until midnight (Sun.–Thurs. until 11). The menu includes everything from nachos to steaks. ✉ *Su Vecino Court on Dolores St., between 5th and 6th Aves.* ☎ *831/624–2336* ▭ *AE, D, DC, MC, V.*

$ AMERICAN **Katy's Place.** Locals flock to Katy's cozy, country-style eatery to fill up on hearty eggs Benedict dishes. (There are 16 types to choose from, each made with three fresh eggs). The huge breakfast menu also includes omelets, pancakes, and eight types of Belgian waffles. An assortment of salads, sandwiches, and burgers is available at lunch—try the grilled calamari burger with melted Monterey Jack cheese. *Mission St., between 5th and 6th Aves. 831/624–0199 No credit cards No dinner.*

$$$ FRENCH **L'Escargot.** Chef-owner Kericos Loutas personally sees to each plate of food served at this romantic and mercifully unpretentious French restaurant (which also has a full bar). Take his recommendation and order the duck confit in puff pastry or the bone-in steak in truffle butter; or, if you can't decide, choose the three-course prix-fixe dinner. Service is warm and attentive. *Mission St., between 4th and 5th Aves. 831/620–1942 Reservations essential AE, DC, MC, V No lunch.*

$$$ SWISS **Lugano Swiss Bistro.** Fondue is the centerpiece here. The house specialty is a version made with Gruyère, Emmentaler, and Appenzeller. Rotisserie-broiled meats are also popular, and include rosemary chicken, plum-basted duck, and fennel pork loin. Ask for a table in the back room, which contains a hand-painted street scene of Lugano, or on the sunny patio. *Barnyard Shopping Center, Hwy. 1 and Carmel Valley Rd. 831/626–3779 AE, DC, MC, V Closed Monday except for private parties and tour buses.*

$ AMERICAN **Tuck Box.** This bright little restaurant is in a cottage right out of a fairy tale, complete with a stone fireplace that's lighted on rainy days. Handmade scones are the house specialty, and are good for breakfast or afternoon tea. *Dolores St., between Ocean and 7th Aves. 831/624–6365 No credit cards No dinner.*

WHERE TO STAY

$$$ ★ **Cobblestone Inn.** Stones from the Carmel River cover the exterior walls of this English-style country inn; inside, the work of local painters is on display. Guest rooms have stone fireplaces, patterned wallpaper and fabrics, and fluffy duvets on the beds. Antiques in the cozy sitting room, and afternoon wine and hors d'oeuvres, contribute to the homey feel. **Pros:** cozy; convenient access to Highway 1; great breakfast. **Cons:** tour buses park nearby; not ideal for families. *Junipero Ave., between 7th and 8th Aves. 831/625–5222 or 800/833–8836 www.cobblestoneinncarmel.com 22 rooms, 2 suites In-room: no a/c, refrigerator, DVD, Wi-Fi. In-hotel: bicycles, no-smoking rooms AE, DC, MC, V BP.*

$$$ **Cypress Inn.** The decorating style here is luxurious but refreshingly simple. Rather than chintz and antiques, there are wrought-iron bed frames, wooden armoires, and rattan armchairs. Some rooms have fireplaces, some hot tubs, and one (Room 215) even has its own sunny veranda that looks out on the ocean. The in-town location makes walking to area attractions easy, and pet owners will be pleased to hear that in the spirit of the dog-loving owner, movie star Doris Day, animal companions are always welcome. **Pros:** luxury without snobbery; popular lounge; traditional British-style afternoon tea. **Cons:** not for the pet-phobic. *Lincoln St. and 7th Ave., Box Y 831/624–3871*

or 800/443–7443 🌐www.cypress-inn.com 39 rooms, 5 suites In-room: no a/c (some). In-hotel: bar, gym, laundry service, Wi-Fi, some pets allowed, no-smoking rooms AE, D, DC, MC, V CP.

$$$$ **Highlands Inn, A Hyatt Hotel.** High on a hill overlooking the Pacific, this place has superb views. Accommodations include king rooms with fireplaces, suites with personal Jacuzzis, and full town houses with all the perks. The excellent menus at the inn's Pacific's Edge restaurant ($$$$; jackets recommended) blend French and California cuisine; the sommelier helps choose the perfect wines. **Pros:** killer views; romantic getaway; great food. **Cons:** thin walls; must drive to Carmel. *✉120 Highlands Dr. ☎831/620–1234, 800/682–4811, 831/622–5445 for restaurant 🌐highlandsinn.hyatt.com 48 rooms, 105 suites In-room: no a/c, safe, kitchen (some), refrigerator, DVD, Internet, Wi-Fi. In-hotel: 2 restaurants, room service, bars, pool, gym, bicycles, laundry service, no-smoking rooms AE, D, DC, MC, V.*

$$$$ Fodor's Choice ★ **L'Auberge Carmel.** Stepping through the doors of this elegant inn is like being transported to a little European village. The rooms are luxurious yet understated, with Italian sheets and huge, classic soaking tubs; sitting in the sun-soaked brick courtyard makes you feel like a movie star. **Pros:** in town but off the main drag; four blocks from the beach; full-service luxury. **Cons:** touristy area; not a good choice for families. *✉Monte Verde, at 7th Ave. ☎831/624–8578 🌐www.laubergecarmel.com 20 rooms In-room: safe, refrigerator, Wi-Fi. In-hotel: restaurant, room service, bar, no-smoking rooms AE, MC, V CP.*

$$ **Mission Ranch.** The property at Mission Ranch is gorgeous and includes a sprawling sheep pasture, bird-filled wetlands, and a sweeping view of the ocean. The ranch is nicely decorated but low-key, with a 19th-century farmhouse as the central building. Other accommodations include rooms in a converted barn, and several cottages, many with fireplaces. Though the ranch belongs to movie star Clint Eastwood, relaxation, not celebrity, is the focus here. **Pros:** farm setting; pastoral views; great for tennis buffs. **Cons:** busy parking lot; must drive to the heart of town. *✉26270 Dolores St. ☎831/624–6436 or 800/538–8221 🌐www.missionranchcarmel.com 31 rooms In-room: no a/c, refrigerator (some). In-hotel: restaurant, bar, tennis courts, gym, no-smoking rooms AE, MC, V CP.*

$$$ **Pine Inn.** A favorite with generations of Carmel-by-the-Sea visitors, the Pine Inn has Victorian-style furnishings, complete with grandfather clock, padded fabric wall panels, antique tapestries, and marble tabletops. Only four blocks from the beach, the property includes a brick courtyard of specialty shops and a modern Italian restaurant. **Pros:** elegant; close to shopping and dining. **Cons:** on the town's busiest street; public areas a bit dark. *✉Ocean Ave. and Monte Verde St. ☎831/624–3851 or 800/228–3851 🌐www.pineinn.com 43 rooms, 6 suites In-room: no a/c, refrigerator (some), Wi-Fi. In-hotel: restaurant, bar, laundry service, Wi-Fi, no-smoking rooms AE, D, DC, MC, V.*

$–$$ **Sea View Inn.** In a residential area a few hundred feet from the beach, this restored 1905 home has a double parlor with two fireplaces, Oriental rugs, canopy beds, and a spacious front porch. Rooms are individually done in cheery colors and country patterns; taller guests might feel cramped in those tucked up under the eaves. Afternoon tea and evening wine and cheese are offered daily. Because of the fragile furnishings and quiet atmosphere, families with kids will likely be more comfortable elsewhere. **Pros:** quiet; private; close to the beach. **Cons:** small building; uphill trek to the heart of town. ✉ *Camino Real, between 11th and 12th Aves.* ☎ *831/624–8778* 🌐 *www.seaviewinncarmel.com* *8 rooms, 6 with private bath* *In-room: no a/c, no phone, no TV, Wi-Fi. In-hotel: no-smoking rooms* *AE, D, MC, V* *CP.*

$$$$ **Tickle Pink Inn.** Atop a towering cliff, this inn has views of the Big Sur coastline, which you can contemplate from your private balcony. After falling asleep to the sound of surf crashing below, you'll wake to a continental breakfast and the morning paper in bed. If you prefer the company of fellow travelers, breakfast is also served buffet-style in the lounge, as are complimentary wine and cheese in the afternoon. Many rooms have wood-burning fireplaces, and there are six luxurious spa suites and a private two-bedroom cottage. **Pros:** close to great hiking; intimate; dramatic views. **Cons:** close to a big hotel; lots of traffic during the day. ✉ *155 Highland Dr.* ☎ *831/624–1244 or 800/635–4774* 🌐 *www.ticklepink.com* *24 rooms, 11 suites, 1 cottage* *In-room: no a/c, refrigerator, DVD, Wi-Fi. In-hotel: room service, Wi-Fi, no-smoking rooms* *AE, DC, MC, V* *CP.*

$$$$ ★ **Tradewinds Inn.** Its sleek decor inspired by the South Seas, this converted motel encircles a courtyard with waterfalls, a meditation garden, and a fire pit. Each room has a tabletop fountain and orchids to complement antique and custom furniture from Bali and China. Some private balconies afford a view of the bay or the mountains. The chic boutique hotel, owned by the same family since it opened in 1959, is on a quiet downtown side street. **Pros:** serene; within walking distance of restaurants; friendly service. **Cons:** no pool; long walk to the beach. ✉ *Mission St. at 3rd Ave.* ☎ *831/624–2776 or 800/624–6665* 🌐 *www.tradewindscarmel.com* *26 rooms, 2 suites* *In-room: no a/c, safe, refrigerator, DVD (some), Wi-Fi. In-hotel: Wi-Fi, some pets allowed, no-smoking rooms* *AE, MC, V* *CP.*

THE ARTS

Carmel Bach Festival (☎ *831/624–2046* 🌐 *www.bachfestival.org*) has presented the works of Johann Sebastian Bach and his contemporaries in concerts and recitals since 1935. The festival runs for three weeks, starting mid-July. **Monterey County Symphony** (☎ *831/646–8511* 🌐 *www.montereysymphony.org*) performs classical concerts from October through May at the Sunset Center.

The **Pacific Repertory Theater** (☎ *831/622–0100 or 866/622–0709* 🌐 *www.pacrep.org*) puts on the Carmel Shakespeare Festival from August through October and performs contemporary dramas and comedies at several area venues from February through July. **Sunset Center** (✉ *San Carlos St., at 9th Ave.* ☎ *831/620–2048* 🌐 *www.sunsetcenter.org*), which presents concerts, lectures, and headline acts, is the Monterey Bay Area's top venue for the performing arts.

SHOPPING

ART GALLERIES **Carmel Art Association** (⊠*Dolores St., between 5th and 6th Aves.* ☎*831/624–6176* 🌐*www.carmelart.org*) exhibits the paintings, sculptures, and prints of local artists. **Galerie Plein Aire** (⊠*Dolores St., between 5th and 6th Aves.* ☎*831/625–5686* 🌐*www.galeriepleinaire.com*) showcases oil paintings by a group of local artists. **Masterpiece Gallery** (⊠*Dolores St. and 6th Ave.* ☎*831/624–2163* 🌐*www.masterpiecegallerycarmel.com*) shows early-California-impressionist art. Run by the family of the late Edward Weston, **Weston Gallery** (⊠*6th Ave., between Dolores and Lincoln Sts.* ☎*831/624–4453* 🌐*www.westongallery.com*) is hands down the best photography gallery around, with contemporary color photography complemented by classic black-and-whites.

SPECIALTY SHOPS **Bittner** (⊠*Ocean Ave., between Mission and San Carlos Sts.* ☎*831/626–8828 or 888/248–8637*) has a fine selection of collectible and vintage pens from around the world. **Intima** (⊠*Mission St., between Ocean and 7th Aves.* ☎*831/625–0599*) is the place to find European lingerie that ranges from lacy to racy. **Jan de Luz** (⊠*Dolores St., between Ocean and 7th Aves.* ☎*831/622–7621*) monograms and embroiders fine linens (including bathrobes) while you wait. **Madrigal** (⊠*Carmel Plaza and Mission St.* ☎*831/624–3477*) carries sportswear, sweaters, and accessories for women.

Mischievous Rabbit (⊠*Lincoln Ave., between 7th and Ocean Aves.* ☎*831/624–6854*) sells toys, nursery accessories, books, music boxes, china, and children's clothing, and specializes in Beatrix Potter items.

CARMEL VALLEY

10 mi east of Carmel, Hwy. 1 to Carmel Valley Rd.

Carmel Valley Road, which heads inland from Highway 1 south of Carmel-by-the-Sea, is the main thoroughfare through this valley, a secluded enclave of horse ranchers and other well-heeled residents who prefer the area's sunny climate to the fog and wind on the coast. Once thick with dairy farms, the valley has recently proved itself as a venerable wine appellation. Tiny Carmel Valley Village, about 13 mi southeast of Carmel-by-the-Sea via Carmel Valley Road, has several crafts shops and art galleries, as well as tasting rooms for numerous local wineries.

At **Bernardus Tasting Room**, you can sample many of the wines—including older vintages and reserves—from the nearby Bernardus Winery and Vineyard. ⊠*5 W. Carmel Valley Rd.* ☎*800/223–2533* 🌐*www.bernardus.com* ⏲*Daily 11–5.*

Pick up fresh veggies, ready-to-eat meals, gourmet groceries, flowers, and gifts at 32-acre **Earthbound Farm** (⊠*7250 Carmel Valley Rd.* ☎*831/625–6219* 🌐*www.ebfarm.com* 🎫*Free* ⏲*Mon.–Sat. 8–6:30, Sun. 9–6*), the world's largest grower of organic produce. You can also take a romp in the kid's garden, cut your own herbs, and stroll through the chamomile aromatherapy labyrinth. On Saturdays from April through December the farm offers special events, from bug walks to garlic-braiding workshops.

Garland Ranch Regional Park (✉*Carmel Valley Rd., 9 mi east of Carmel-by-the-Sea* ☎*831/659–4488*) has hiking trails across nearly 4,500 acres of property that includes meadows, forested hillsides, and creeks.

The extensive **Château Julien** winery, recognized internationally for its chardonnays and merlots, gives weekday tours at 10:30 and 2:30 and weekends at 12:30 and 2:30, all by appointment. The tasting room is open daily. ✉*8940 Carmel Valley Rd.* ☎*831/624–2600* 🌐*www.chateaujulien.com* ⏲*Weekdays 8–5, weekends 11–5.*

WINE TOURING WITH THE MST

Why risk driving while wine tasting when you can hop aboard the Carmel Valley Grapevine Express? This Monterey-Salinas Transit bus travels between downtown Monterey and Carmel Valley Village, with stops near wineries, restaurants, and shopping centers. Buses depart daily every hour from 11 to 6. At $6 for a ride-all-day pass, it's an incredible bargain. For more information, call 888/678–2871 or visit www.mst.org.

WHERE TO EAT AND STAY

$ ITALIAN **Café Rustica.** Italian-inspired country cooking is the focus at this lively roadhouse. Specialties include roasted meats, pastas, and thin-crust pizzas from the wood-fired oven. Because of the tile floors, it can get quite noisy inside; opt for a table outside if you want a quieter meal. ✉*10 Delfino Pl.* ☎*831/659–4444* *Reservations essential* *MC, V* ⏲*Closed Mon.*

¢ AMERICAN **Wagon Wheel Coffee Shop.** This local hangout decorated with wagon wheels, cowboy hats, and lassos serves up terrific hearty breakfasts, including date-walnut-cinnamon French toast and a plate of trout and eggs. The lunch menu includes a dozen different burgers and other sandwiches. ✉*Valley Hill Center, Carmel Valley Rd., next to Quail Lodge* ☎*831/624–8878* *No credit cards* ⏲*No dinner.*

$$$ AMERICAN **Will's Fargo.** On the main street of Carmel Valley Village since the 1920s, this restaurant calls itself a "dressed-up saloon." Steer horns and gilt-frame paintings adorn the walls of the Victorian-style dining room; you can also eat on the patios. The menu is mainly seafood and steaks, including a 20-ounce porterhouse. ✉*16 E. Carmel Valley Rd.* ☎*831/659–2774* *AE, DC, MC, V* ⏲*No lunch.*

$$$$ Fodor'sChoice ★ **Bernardus Lodge.** Even before you check in at this luxury spa resort, the valet hands you a glass of chardonnay. Spacious guest rooms have vaulted ceilings, featherbeds, fireplaces, patios, and bathtubs for two. The restaurant, Marinus ($$$$; jacket recommended), is perhaps the best in the Monterey Bay area, with a menu that changes daily to highlight local meats and produce. Reserve the chef's table in the main kitchen and you can talk to the chef as he prepares your meal. **Pros:** exceptional personal service; outstanding food and wine. **Cons:** some guests can seem snooty; pricey. ✉*415 Carmel Valley Rd.* ☎*831/658–3400 or 888/648–9463* 🌐*www.bernardus.com* *54 rooms, 3 suites* *In-room: safe, refrigerator, DVD, Wi-Fi. In-hotel: 2 restaurants, room service, bar, tennis courts, pool, gym, spa, laundry service, Internet terminal, no-smoking rooms* *AE, DC, MC, V.*

$$$$ ★ **Quail Lodge.** What began as the Carmel Valley Country Club—a hangout for Frank Sinatra, among others—is now a semiprivate golf club and resort in the valley's west side. Winding around swimming pools and putting greens, the buildings' exteriors recall the old days, but indoors the luxury is totally updated with a cool, modern feel: plasma TVs swing out from the walls, the toiletries include giant tea bags to infuse your bath with herbs, and each room has a window seat overlooking a private patio. The Covey at Quail Lodge ($$$–$$$$; jacket recommended) serves contemporary California cuisine in a romantic lakeside dining room. **Pros:** on the golf course; on-site Land Rover Driving School; pastoral views. **Cons:** some rooms need updating; 5 mi from the beach and Carmel Valley Village. ✉ *8205 Valley Greens Dr.* ☎ *831/624–2888 or 888/828–8787* 🌐 *www.quaillodge.com* *83 rooms, 14 suites* *In-room: safe, refrigerator, DVD, Internet, Wi-Fi. In-hotel: 2 restaurants, room service, bars, golf course, tennis courts, pools, gym, spa, bicycles, laundry service, Wi-Fi, some pets allowed, no-smoking rooms* *AE, DC, MC, V.*

$$$$ Fodor's Choice ★ **Stonepine Estate Resort.** Set on 330 pastoral acres, this former estate of the Crocker banking family has been converted to a luxurious inn. The oak-paneled main château holds eight elegantly furnished rooms and suites, and a dining room for guests (although with advance reservations it's also possible for nonguests to dine here). The property's "cottages" are equally opulent, each with its own luxurious identity (the Hermes House has four fireplaces and a 27-foot-high living-room ceiling). Fresh flowers, afternoon tea, and evening champagne are offered daily. This is a quiet property, best suited to couples traveling without children. **Pros:** supremely exclusive. **Cons:** difficult to get a reservation; far from the coast. ✉ *150 E. Carmel Valley Rd.* ☎ *831/659–2245* 🌐 *www.stonepinecalifornia.com* *3 rooms, 9 suites, 3 cottages* *In-room: no a/c, safe (some), DVD (some), Wi-Fi. In-hotel: restaurant, room service, tennis courts, pools, gym, bicycles, laundry service, Wi-Fi, no-smoking rooms* *AE, MC, V* *BP.*

THE ARTS

Hidden Valley Performing Arts Institute (✉ *Carmel Valley Road, at Ford Rd.* ☎ *831/659–3115* 🌐 *www.hiddenvalleymusic.org*) gives classes for promising young musicians and holds a year-round series of classical and jazz concerts by students, masters, and the Monterey Peninsula Choral Society.

SPORTS AND THE OUTDOORS

The **Golf Club at Quail Lodge** (✉ *8000 Valley Greens Dr.* ☎ *831/624–2770*) incorporates several lakes into its course. Depending on the season and day of the week, greens fees range from $150 to $185 for guests and $185 to $210 for nonguests, including cart rental. **Rancho Cañada Golf Club** (✉ *4860 Carmel Valley Rd., 1 mi east of Hwy. 1* ☎ *831/624–0111 or 800/536–9459*) is a public course with 36 holes, some of them overlooking the Carmel River. Fees range from $35 to $80, plus $36 for cart rental, depending on course and tee time.

17-MILE DRIVE

Fodor'sChoice ★ *Off North San Antonio Rd. in Carmel-by-the-Sea or off Sunset Dr. in Pacific Grove.*

Primordial nature resides in quiet harmony with palatial late-20th-century estates along 17-Mile Drive, which winds through an 8,400-acre microcosm of the Monterey coastal landscape. Dotting the drive are rare Monterey cypress, trees so gnarled and twisted that Robert Louis Stevenson described them as "ghosts fleeing before the wind." Some sightseers balk at the $9.25-per-car fee collected at the gates—this is the only private toll road west of the Mississippi—but most find the drive well worth the price. An alternative is to grab a bike: **■TIP→ cyclists tour for free, as do those with confirmed lunch or dinner reservations at one of the hotels.**

You can take in views of the impeccable greens at **Pebble Beach Golf Links** (⊠ *17-Mile Dr., near Lodge at Pebble Beach* ☎ *800/654–9300* 🌐 *www.pebblebeach.com*) over a drink or lunch at the Lodge at Pebble Beach. The ocean plays a major role in the 18th hole of the famed links. Each winter the course is the main site of the AT&T Pebble Beach Pro-Am (formerly the Bing Crosby Pro-Am), where show-business celebrities and golf pros team up for one of the nation's most glamorous tournaments.

Many of the stately homes along 17-Mile Drive reflect the classic Monterey or Spanish Mission style typical of the region. A standout is the **Crocker Marble Palace,** about a mile south of the Lone Cypress (⇨ *below*). It's a private waterfront estate inspired by a Byzantine castle, easily identifiable by its dozens of marble arches.

The most-photographed tree along 17-Mile Drive is the weather-sculpted **Lone Cypress,** which grows out of a precipitous outcropping above the waves about 1½ mi up the road from Pebble Beach Golf Links. You can stop for a view of the Lone Cypress at a parking area, but you can't walk out to the tree.

Sea creatures and birds—as well as some very friendly ground squirrels—make use of **Seal Rock,** the largest of a group of islands about 2 mi north of Lone Cypress.

Bird Rock, the largest of several islands at the southern end of the Monterey Country Club's golf course, teems with harbor seals, sea lions, cormorants, and pelicans.

WHERE TO STAY

$$$$ ★ **Casa Palmero.** This exclusive spa resort evokes a stately Mediterranean villa. Rooms are decorated with sumptuous fabrics and fine art; each has a wood-burning fireplace and heated floor, and some have private outdoor patios with in-ground Jacuzzis. Complimentary cocktail service is offered each evening in the main hall and library. The spa is state-of-the-art, and you have use of all facilities at the Lodge at Pebble Beach and the Inn at Spanish Bay. **Pros:** ultimate in pampering; more private than sister resorts; right on the golf course. **Cons:** pricey; may be *too* posh for some. ⊠ *1518 Cypress Dr., Pebble Beach* ☎ *831/622–6650 or 800/654–9300* 🌐 *www.pebblebeach.com* ⇁ *21*

rooms, 3 suites ♿*In-room: no a/c, refrigerator, Wi-Fi. In-hotel: room service, bar, golf course, pool, spa, bicycles, laundry service, no-smoking rooms* 💳*AE, D, DC, MC, V.*

$$$$ **Inn at Spanish Bay.** This resort sprawls across a breathtaking stretch of shoreline, and has lush, 600-square-foot rooms. Peppoli's restaurant ($$–$$$), which serves Tuscan cuisine, overlooks the coast and the golf links; Roy's Restaurant ($$$–$$$$) serves more casual and innovative Euro-Asian fare. When you stay here, you're also allowed privileges at the Lodge at Pebble Beach, which is under the same management. **Pros:** attentive service; tons of amenities; spectacular views. **Cons:** huge hotel; far from other Pebble Beach resorts' facilities. ✉*2700 17-Mile Dr., Pebble Beach* ☎*831/647–7500 or 800/654–9300* 🌐*www.pebblebeach.com* *252 rooms, 17 suites* ♿*In-room: no a/c, refrigerator, Internet, Wi-Fi. In-hotel: 3 restaurants, room service, bar, golf course, tennis courts, pool, gym, beachfront, bicycles, laundry service, Internet terminal, no-smoking rooms* 💳*AE, D, DC, MC, V.*

$$$$ ★ **Lodge at Pebble Beach.** All rooms have fireplaces and many have wonderful ocean views at this circa 1919 resort. The golf course, tennis club, and equestrian center are posh. Overlooking the 18th green, the intimate Club XIX restaurant ($$$$; jackets recommended) serves expertly prepared French cuisine. When staying here, you also have privileges at the Inn at Spanish Bay. **Pros:** world-class golf; borders the ocean and fairways; fabulous facilities. **Cons:** some rooms are on the small side; very pricey. ✉*1700 17-Mile Dr., Pebble Beach* ☎*831/624–3811 or 800/654–9300* 🌐*www.pebblebeach.com* *142 rooms, 19 suites* ♿*In-room: no a/c, refrigerator, DVD (some), Internet, Wi-Fi. In-hotel: 3 restaurants, bars, golf course, tennis courts, pool, gym, spa, beachfront, bicycles, laundry service, Internet terminal, some pets allowed, no-smoking rooms* 💳*AE, D, DC, MC, V.*

SPORTS AND THE OUTDOORS

GOLF The **Links at Spanish Bay** (✉*17-Mile Dr., north end* ☎*831/624–3811, 831/624–6611, or 800/654–9300*), which hugs a choice stretch of shoreline, is designed in the rugged manner of a traditional Scottish course, with sand dunes and coastal marshes interspersed among the greens. The greens fee is $260, plus $35 per person for cart rental (cart is included for resort guests); nonguests can reserve tee times up to two months in advance.

Pebble Beach Golf Links (✉*17-Mile Dr., near Lodge at Pebble Beach* ☎*831/624–3811, 831/624–6611, or 800/654–9300*) attracts golfers from around the world, despite a greens fee of $495, plus $35 per person for an optional cart (complimentary cart for guests of the Pebble Beach and Spanish Bay resorts). Nonguests can reserve a tee time only one day in advance on a space-available basis (up to a year for groups); resort guests can reserve up to 18 months in advance.

Peter Hay (✉*17-Mile Dr.* ☎*831/622–8723*), a 9-hole, par-3 course, charges $25 per person, no reservations necessary. **Poppy Hills** (✉*3200 Lopez Rd., at 17-Mile Dr.* ☎*831/625–2035*), a splendid 18-hole course designed in 1986 by Robert Trent Jones Jr., has a greens fee of $200; an optional cart costs $36. Individuals may reserve up to one month in advance, groups up to a year.

Spyglass Hill (✉ *Stevenson Dr. and Spyglass Hill Rd.* ☎ *831/624–3811, 831/624–6611, or 800/654–9300*) is among the most challenging Pebble Beach courses. With the first five holes bordering on the Pacific and the other 18 reaching deep into the Del Monte Forest, the views offer some consolation. The greens fee is $340, and an optional cart costs $35 (the cart is complimentary for resort guests). Reservations are essential and may be made up to one month in advance (18 months for guests).

HORSEBACK RIDING The **Pebble Beach Equestrian Center** (✉ *Portola Rd. and Alva La.* ☎ *831/624–2756*) offers guided trail rides along the beach and through 26 mi of bridle trails in the Del Monte Forest. Rates are $60–$115 per rider.

PACIFIC GROVE

3 mi north of Carmel-by-the-Sea on Hwy. 68.

This picturesque town, which began as a summer retreat for church groups more than a century ago, recalls its prim and proper Victorian heritage in its host of tiny board-and-batten cottages and stately mansions. However, long before the church groups flocked here the area received thousands of annual pilgrims—in the form of bright orange-and-black monarch butterflies. They still come, migrating south from Canada and the Pacific Northwest to take residence in pine and eucalyptus groves from October through March. In Butterfly Town USA, as Pacific Grove is known, the sight of a mass of butterflies hanging from the branches like a long, fluttering veil is unforgettable.

A prime way to enjoy Pacific Grove is to walk or bicycle the 3 mi of city-owned shoreline along Ocean View Boulevard, a cliff-top area landscaped with native plants and dotted with benches meant for sitting and gazing at the sea. You can spot many types of birds here, including colonies of web-foot cormorants crowding the massive rocks rising out of the surf.

Among the Victorians of note is the **Pryor House** (✉ *429 Ocean View Blvd.*), a massive, shingled, private residence with a leaded- and beveled-glass doorway.

Green Gables (✉ *5th St. and Ocean View Blvd.* ☎ *831/375–2095* 🌐 *www.greengablesinnpg.com*), a romantic Swiss Gothic–style mansion with peaked gables and stained-glass windows, is a B&B.

The view of the coast is gorgeous from **Lovers Point Park** (☎ *831/648–5730*), on Ocean View Boulevard midway along the waterfront. The park's sheltered beach has a children's pool and picnic area, and the main lawn has a sandy volleyball court and snack bar.

BUTTERFLY SPOTTING

The **Monarch Grove Sanctuary** (✉ *1073 Lighthouse Ave., at Ridge Rd.* 🌐 *www.pgmuseum.org*) is a fairly reliable spot for viewing the butterflies between October and February. Contact Friends of the Monarchs (☎ *831/375–0982* 🌐 *www.pgmuseum.org*) for the latest information. If you're in Pacific Grove when the monarch butterflies aren't, you can view the well-crafted butterfly tree exhibit at the **Pacific Grove Museum of Natural History.** ✉ *165 Forest Ave.* ☎ *831/648–5716* 🌐 *www.pgmuseum.org* *$2 suggested donation* *Tues.–Sat. 10–5.*

DID YOU KNOW?

The Lone Cypress has stood on this rock for over 250 years. The tree is the official symbol of Pebble Beach.

At the 1855-vintage **Point Pinos Lighthouse,** the oldest continuously operating lighthouse on the West Coast, you can learn about the lighting and foghorn operations and wander through a small museum containing U.S. Coast Guard memorabilia. *Lighthouse Ave., off Asilomar Blvd. 831/648–5716 www.pgmuseum.org $2 Thurs.–Mon. 1–4.*

Asilomar State Beach (*831/646–6440 www.parks.ca.gov*), a beautiful coastal area, is on Sunset Drive between Point Pinos and the Del Monte Forest in Pacific Grove. The 100 acres of dunes, tidal pools, and pocket-size beaches form one of the region's richest areas for marine life—including surfers, who migrate here most winter mornings.

WHERE TO EAT

$$ MEDITERRANEAN **Fandango.** The menu here is mostly Mediterranean and southern French, with such dishes as calves' liver and onions and paella served in a skillet. The decor follows suit: stone walls and country furniture give the restaurant the earthy feel of a European farmhouse. This is where locals come when they want to have a big dinner with friends, drink wine, have fun, and generally feel at home. *223 17th St. 831/372–3456 AE, D, DC, MC, V.*

$$ FRENCH **Fifi's Bistro Café.** Candlelight and music fill this small bistro known for its generous wine pours and French cuisine. The menu ranges from escargots to petrale sole *piccata* (sautéed and served with a sauce made from lemon juice, parsley, and pan dripping sauce) to steak *frites* (french fries); lunch and the early-bird dinner (until 6 PM) are an exceptional value. *1188 Forest Ave. 831/372–5325 Reservations essential AE, D, DC, MC, V.*

$$ SEAFOOD **Fishwife.** Fresh fish with a Latin accent makes this a favorite of locals for lunch or a casual dinner. Standards are the sea garden salads topped with your choice of fish and the fried seafood plates with fresh veggies. Large appetites appreciate the fisherman's bowls, which feature fresh fish served with rice, black beans, spicy cabbage, salsa, vegetables, and crispy tortilla strips. *1996½ Sunset Dr., at Asilomar Blvd. 831/375–7107 AE, D, MC, V.*

$$ ITALIAN **Joe Rombi's.** Pastas, fish, and veal are the specialties at this modern trattoria, which is the best in town for Italian food. The look is spare and clean, with colorful antique wine posters decorating the white walls. Next door, Joe Rombi's La Piccola Casa serves lunch and early dinner Wednesday through Sunday. *208 17th St. 831/373–2416 AE, MC, V Closed Mon. and Tues. No lunch.*

$$ AMERICAN ★ **Passionfish.** South American artwork and artifacts decorate the room, and Latin and Asian flavors infuse the dishes at Passionfish. Chef Ted Walter—lauded for his commitment to using eco-friendly, sustainable ingredients—shops at local farmers' markets several times a week to find the best produce, fish, and meat available, then pairs it with creative sauces. The ever-changing menu might include crispy squid with spicy orange-cilantro vinaigrette. *701 Lighthouse Ave. 831/655–3311 AE, D, MC, V No lunch.*

$ MEXICAN **Peppers Mexicali Cafe.** A local favorite, this cheerful white-walled storefront serves traditional dishes from Mexico and Latin America, with an emphasis on fresh seafood. Excellent red and green salsas are made throughout the day, and there's a large selection of beers. *170*

Forest Ave. ☎*831/373–6892* ▭*AE, D, DC, MC, V* ⊗*Closed Tues. No lunch Sun.*

$$ AMERICAN ✕**Red House Café.** When it's nice out, sun pours through the big windows of this cozy restaurant and across tables on the porch; when fog rolls in, the fireplace is lighted. The American menu is simple but selective, including grilled lamb fillets atop mashed potatoes for dinner and a huge Dungeness crab cake over salad for lunch. Breakfast on weekends is a local favorite. ✉*662 Lighthouse Ave.* ☎*831/643–1060* ▭*AE, D, DC, MC, V* ⊗*Closed Mon.*

$$ AMERICAN ✕**Taste Café and Bistro.** A favorite of locals, Taste serves hearty European-inspired food in a casual, airy room with high ceilings and an open kitchen. Meats, such as grilled marinated rabbit, roasted half chicken, and filet mignon, are the focus. ✉*1199 Forest Ave.* ☎*831/655–0324* ▭*AE, MC, V.*

WHERE TO STAY

$$$ ★ **Green Gables Inn.** Stained-glass windows and ornate interior details compete with spectacular ocean views at this Queen Anne–style mansion, built by a businessman for his mistress in 1888. Rooms in a carriage house perched on a hill out back are larger, have more modern amenities, and afford more privacy, but rooms in the main house have more charm. Afternoon wine and cheese are served in the parlor. **Pros:** exceptional views; impeccable attention to historic detail. **Cons:** some rooms are small; thin walls. ✉*301 Ocean View Blvd.* ☎*831/375–2095 or 800/722–1774* ⊕*www.greengablesinnpg.com* *7 rooms, 4 with bath; 4 suites* *In-room: no a/c, DVD (some), Wi-Fi. In-hotel: bicycles, no-smoking rooms* ▭*AE, D, DC, MC, V* *BP.*

$$–$$$ **The Inn at 213 Seventeen Mile Drive.** Set in a residential area just past town, this carefully restored 1920s Craftsman-style home and cottage are surrounded by gardens and redwood, cypress, and eucalyptus trees. Spacious, well-appointed rooms have simple, homey furnishings. The innkeepers offer complimentary wine and hors d'oeuvres in the evening and tea and snacks throughout the day. **Pros:** off the beaten path; historic charm; verdant gardens. **Cons:** far from restaurants and shops; few extra amenities. ✉*213 17-Mile Dr.* ☎*831/642–9514 or 800/526–5666* ⊕*www.innat17.com* *14 rooms* *In-room: no a/c, Wi-Fi. In-hotel: no-smoking rooms* ▭*AE, MC, V* *BP.*

$$–$$$ **Lighthouse Lodge and Resort.** Near the tip of the peninsula, this complex straddles Lighthouse Avenue—the lodge is on one side, the all-suites Lighthouse Resort facility on the other. Suites have fireplaces and whirlpool tubs. Standard rooms are simple, but they're decently sized and much less expensive. ■**TIP→ With daily afternoon barbecues at the lodge, this is a woodsy alternative to downtown Pacific Grove's B&B scene.** (The suites do not have a daily barbecue, but instead feature a wine-and-cheese spread.) **Pros:** near lighthouse and 17-Mile Drive; friendly reception; upgraded beds and linens in 2006. **Cons:** next to a cemetery; lodge rooms are basic. ✉*1150 and 1249 Lighthouse Ave.* ☎*831/655–2111 or 800/858–1249* ⊕*www.lhls.com* *64 rooms, 31 suites* *In-room: no a/c, refrigerator, Wi-Fi. In-hotel: room service, pool, spa, some pets allowed, no-smoking rooms* ▭*AE, D, DC, MC, V* *BP.*

$$$–$$$$ **Martine Inn.** The glassed-in parlor and many guest rooms at this 1899 Mediterranean-style villa have stunning ocean views. The inn is furnished with exquisite antiques, and the owner's collection of classic race cars is on display in the patio area. In the rooms, thoughtful details such as robes, rocking chairs, and nightly turndown combine in luxuriant comfort. Lavish breakfasts—and winemaker dinners of up to 12 courses—are served on lace-clad tables set with china, crystal, and silver. Because of the fragility of the antiques, the inn is not suitable for children, except in the two-bedroom family suite. **Pros:** romantic; fancy breakfast; ocean views. **Cons:** not child-friendly; sits on a busy thoroughfare. ⊠*255 Ocean View Blvd.* ☎*831/373–3388 or 800/852–5588* ⊕*www.martineinn.com* *24 rooms* *In-room: no a/c, refrigerator, no TV, Internet, Wi-Fi. In-hotel: Internet terminal, Wi-Fi, no-smoking rooms* *AE, D, MC, V* *BP.*

SPORTS AND THE OUTDOORS

GOLF Greens fees at the 18-hole **Pacific Grove Municipal Golf Links** (⊠*77 Asilomar Blvd.* ☎*831/648–5777* ⊕*www.ci.pg.ca.us/golf*) run between $40 and $45 (you can play 9 holes for $20–$25), with an after-2 PM twilight rate of $20. Optional carts cost $34 ($20 for 9 holes). The course has spectacular ocean views on its back 9. Tee times may be reserved up to seven days in advance.

TENNIS The municipal **Morris Dill Tennis Courts** (⊠*515 Junipero St.* ☎*831/648–5729*) are available for public play for a small hourly fee. The pro shop here rents rackets and offers lessons.

MONTEREY

Early in the 20th century Carmel Martin, the first mayor of the city of Monterey, saw a bright future for his town: "Monterey Bay is the one place where people can live without being disturbed by manufacturing and big factories. I am certain that the day is coming when this will be the most desirable place in the whole state of California." It seems that Mayor Martin was not far off the mark.

ESSENTIALS

Visitor Information Monterey County Convention & Visitors Bureau (☎*877/666-8373* ⊕*www.montereyinfo.org*).

HISTORIC MONTEREY

2 mi southeast of Pacific Grove via Lighthouse Ave.; 2 mi north of Carmel-by-the-Sea via Hwy. 1.

WHAT TO SEE

15 **A Taste of Monterey.** Without driving the back roads, you can taste the wines of up to 70 area vintners while taking in fantastic bay views. Purchase a few bottles and pick up a map and guide to the county's wineries and vineyards. ⊠*700 Cannery Row, Suite KK* ☎*831/646–5446 or 888/646–5446* ⊕*www.tastemonterey.com* *Wine tastings $10–$15* *Daily 11–6.*

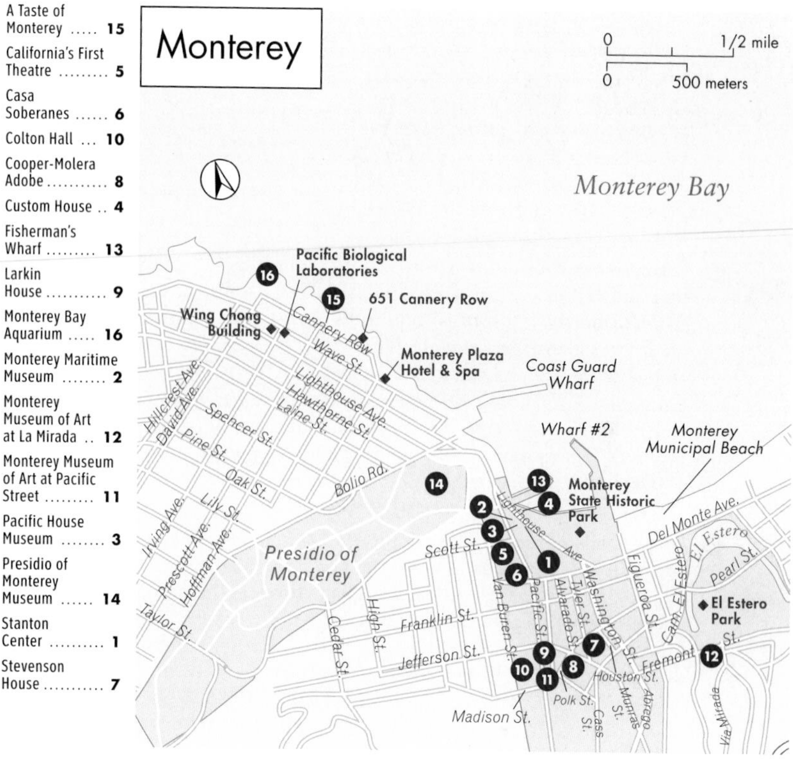

❺ **California's First Theatre.** This adobe began its life in 1846 as a saloon and lodging house for sailors. Four years later stage curtains were fashioned from army blankets, and some U.S. officers staged plays to the light of whale oil lamps. As of this writing, the building is undergoing restoration and is rarely open. ✉*Monterey State Historic Park, Scott and Pacific Sts.* ☎*831/649–7118* 🌐*www.parks.ca.gov/mshp* *Free* ⏲*Call for hrs.*

Cannery Row. When John Steinbeck published the novel *Cannery Row* in 1945, he immortalized a place of rough-edged working people. The waterfront street once was crowded with sardine canneries processing, at their peak, nearly 200,000 tons of the smelly silver fish a year. During the mid-1940s, however, the sardines disappeared from the bay, causing the canneries to close. Through the years the old tin-roof canneries have been converted into restaurants, art galleries, and malls with shops selling T-shirts, fudge, and plastic sea otters. Recent tourist development along the row has been more tasteful, however, and includes several stylish inns and hotels. ✉*Cannery Row, between Prescott and David Aves.* 🌐*www.canneryrow.com.*

❻ **Casa Soberanes.** A classic low-ceiling adobe structure built in 1842, this was once a Custom House guard's residence. Exhibits at the house survey life in Monterey from the era of Mexican rule to the present.

The building is open only during the free 45-minute tours, but feel free to stop at the peaceful rear garden, which has a lovely rose-covered arbor and sitting benches. ✉ *Monterey State Historic Park, 336 Pacific St.* ☎ *831/649–7118* 🌐 *www.parks.ca.gov/mshp* 🎫 *Free* 🕒 *Tours Fri.–Wed. at 11:30 and 3.*

MONTEREY: FORMER CAPITAL OF CALIFORNIA

In 1602 Spanish explorer Sebastian Vizcaino stepped ashore on a remote California peninsula. He named it after the viceroy of New Spain—Count de Monte Rey. Soon the Spanish built a military outpost, and the site was the capital of California until the state came under American rule.

10 **Colton Hall.** A convention of delegates met in 1849 to draft the first state constitution at California's equivalent of Independence Hall. The stone building, which has served as a school, a courthouse, and the county seat, is a city-run museum furnished as it was during the constitutional convention. The extensive grounds outside the hall surround the Old Monterey Jail. ✉ *500 block of Pacific St., between Madison and Jefferson Sts.* ☎ *831/646–5640* 🌐 *www.monterey.org/museum* 🎫 *Free* 🕒 *Daily 10–4.*

8 **Cooper-Molera Adobe.** The restored 2-acre complex includes a house dating from the 1820s, a visitor center, a bookstore, and a large garden enclosed by a high adobe wall. The mostly Victorian-era antiques and memorabilia that fill the house provide a glimpse into the life of a prosperous early sea merchant's family. The building is open only during organized 45-minute tours, which leave from the Cooper Museum Store. ✉ *Monterey State Historic Park, Polk and Munras Sts.* ☎ *831/649–7118 or 831/649–7111* 🌐 *www.parks.ca.gov/mshp* 🎫 *Free* 🕒 *Tours Fri.–Wed. at noon and 3.*

4 **Custom House.** This adobe structure built by the Mexican government in 1827—now California's oldest standing public building—was the first stop for sea traders whose goods were subject to duties. At the beginning of the Mexican-American War, in 1846, Commodore John Sloat raised the American flag over the building and claimed California for the United States. The house's lower floor displays cargo from a 19th-century trading ship. ✉ *Monterey State Historic Park, 1 Custom House Plaza, across from Fisherman's Wharf* ☎ *831/649–7118* 🌐 *www.parks.ca.gov/mshp* 🎫 *Free* 🕒 *Daily 10–4.*

13 **Fisherman's Wharf.** The mournful barking of sea lions provides a steady sound track all along Monterey's waterfront, but the best way to actually view the whiskered marine mammals is to walk along one of the two piers across from Custom House Plaza. Fisherman's Wharf is lined with souvenir shops, seafood restaurants, and whale-watching tour boats. It's undeniably touristy, but still a lively and entertaining place. Up the harbor to the right is Wharf No. 2, a working municipal pier where you can see fishing boats unloading their catches to one side, and fishermen casting their lines into the water on the other. The pier has a couple of low-key restaurants, from whose seats lucky customers may spot otters and harbor seals. ✉ *At end of Calle Principal* ☎ *831/649–6544* 🌐 *www.montereywharf.com.*

Trained "seals" that perform in circuses are actually California sea lions, intelligent, social animals that live (and sleep) close together in groups.

9 **Larkin House.** A veranda encircles the second floor of this architecturally significant two-story adobe built in 1835, whose design bears witness to the Mexican and New England influences on the Monterey style. The rooms are furnished with period antiques, many of them brought from New Hampshire by the building's namesake, Thomas O. Larkin, an early California statesman. The building is open only during organized 45-minute tours. ✉ *Monterey State Historic Park, 464 Calle Principal, between Jefferson and Pacific Sts.* ☎ *831/649–7118* 🌐 *www.parks.ca.gov/mshp* 🎫 *Free* 🕒 *Tours Fri.–Wed. at 10 and noon.*

16 **Monterey Bay Aquarium.** The minute you hand over your ticket at this extraordinary aquarium you're surrounded by sea creatures; right at the entrance, you can see dozens of them swimming in a three-story-tall, sunlit kelp forest tank. The beauty of the exhibits here is that they are all designed to give a sense of what it's like to be in the water with the animals—sardines swim around your head in a circular tank, and jellyfish drift in and out of view in dramatically lighted spaces that suggest the ocean depths. A petting pool gives you a hands-on experience with bat rays, and the million-gallon Outer Bay tank shows the vast variety of creatures (from sharks to placid-looking turtles) that live in the eastern Pacific. A Splash Zone with 45 interactive bilingual exhibits opened in 2008: here, kids (and kids-at-heart) can commune with sea dragons, potbellied seahorses, and other fascinating creatures. The only drawback to the experience is that it must be shared with the throngs of people that crowd the place daily; most think it's worth it. To avoid the crowds, arrive as soon as the aquarium opens or visit in mid-afternoon, after the field trip groups depart and youngsters head home for their

Fodor's Choice ★

naps. ⊠*886 Cannery Row* ☎*831/648–4888, 800/756–3737 in CA for advance tickets* ⊕*www.montereybayaquarium.org* 🎟*$25* ⊙*Late May–June and early Sept., daily 9:30–6; July–Aug., weekdays 9:30–6, weekends 9:30–8; early Sept.–late May, daily 10–6.*

2 **Monterey Maritime Museum.** Maintained by the Monterey History and Art Association, this collection of maritime artifacts belonged to Allen Knight, who was Carmel-by-the-Sea's mayor from 1950 to 1952. Highlights are a collection of outstanding scrimshaw, including fully jointed pocketknives and a toy guillotine, and a lively movie from 1943 chronicling a day in the life of the cannery that used to stand where the aquarium is. The jewel in the museum's crown is the enormous, multifaceted Fresnel lens from the lighthouse at Point Sur Light Station. ⊠*Stanton Center, 5 Custom House Plaza* ☎*831/372–2608* ⊕*www.montereyhistory.org* 🎟*Free* ⊙*Tues.–Sun. 10–5.*

12 **Monterey Museum of Art at La Mirada.** Asian and European antiques fill this 19th-century adobe house. A newer 10,000-square-foot gallery space, designed by Charles Moore, houses Asian and California regional art. Outdoors are magnificent rose and rhododendron gardens. A single fee covers admission to the La Mirada and Pacific Street facilities of the Monterey Museum of Art. ⊠*720 Via Mirada, at Fremont St.* ☎*831/372–3689* ⊕*www.montereyart.org* 🎟*$5* ⊙*Wed.–Sat. 11–5, Sun. 1–4.*

11 **Monterey Museum of Art at Pacific Street.** Photographs by Ansel Adams and Edward Weston, as well as works by other artists who have spent time on the peninsula, are on display here. There's also a colorful collection of international folk art; the pieces range from Kentucky hearth brooms to Tibetan prayer wheels. A single fee covers admission to the Pacific Street and La Mirada facilities of the Monterey Museum of Art. ⊠*559 Pacific St., across from Colton Hall* ☎*831/372–5477* ⊕*www.montereyart.org* 🎟*$5* ⊙*Wed.–Sat. 11–5, Sun. 1–4.*

Monterey State Historic Park. You can glimpse Monterey's early history in the well-preserved adobe buildings scattered along several city blocks. Far from being a hermetic period museum, the park facilities are an integral part of the day-to-day business life of the town—within some of the buildings are a store, a theater, and government offices. At some of the historic houses the gardens (open daily 10 to 4) are worthy sights themselves. Departing from the Pacific House Museum, guided 45-minute walking tours of Old Monterey take place Friday through Wednesday at 10:30 AM. ⊠*20 Custom House Plaza* ☎*831/649–7118* ⊕*www.parks.ca.gov/mshp* 🎟*Free* ⊙*Call for hrs.*

3 **Pacific House Museum.** Once a hotel and saloon, this visitor center and museum now commemorates early-California life with gold-rush relics and photographs of Old Monterey. The upper floor displays Native American artifacts, including gorgeous baskets and pottery. ⊠*Monterey State Historic Park, 10 Custom House Plaza* ☎*831/649–7118* ⊕*www.parks.ca.gov/mshp* 🎟*Free* ⊙*Daily 10–4.*

14 **Presidio of Monterey Museum.** This spot has been significant for centuries as a town, a fort, and the site of several battles, including the skirmish in which the pirate Hipoleto Bruchard conquered the Spanish garrison that stood here. Its first incarnation was as a Native American village

for the Rumsien tribe; then it became known as the landing site for explorer Sebastien Vizcaíno in 1602, and father of the California missions, Father Serra, in 1770. The indoor museum tells the stories; the outdoor sites are marked with plaques. ✉ *Corporal Ewing Rd., Presidio of Monterey* ☎ *831/646–3456* 🌐 *www.monterey.org/museum/pom* 🎟 *Free* ⏲ *Mon. 10–1, Thurs.–Sat. 10–4, Sun. 1–4.*

1 **Stanton Center.** This is the place to go to load up on maps and area information. Especially worthwhile are the brochures on self-guided walking tours of historic Monterey and Cannery Row; admission to most sites along the walks is free, and most are open daily. The Maritime Museum of Monterey is in the Stanton Center; you can also view a free 20-minute film about Old Monterey. ✉ *5 Custom House Plaza* ☎ *831/372–2608* 🌐 *www.montereyhistory.org* 🎟 *Free* ⏲ *Tues.–Sun. 10–5.*

7 **Stevenson House.** This house was named in honor of author Robert Louis Stevenson, who boarded here briefly in a tiny upstairs room. Items from his family's estate furnish Stevenson's room; period-decorated chambers elsewhere in the house include a gallery of the author's memorabilia and a children's nursery stocked with Victorian toys and games. ✉ *Monterey State Historic Park, 530 Houston St.* ☎ *831/649–7118* 🌐 *www.parks.ca.gov/mshp* 🎟 *Free* ⏲ *Sun.–Wed. 1:30–4, Fri.–Sat. 1–4; tours Fri.–Wed at 2.*

WHERE TO EAT

$$$$ FRENCH ✕ **Fresh Cream.** For years this dining room with a view of glittering Heritage Harbor has provided one of the most refined dining experiences in Monterey. The wine list is carefully chosen, the service is attentive yet restrained, and everything carries an air of luxury. The menu centers around imaginative variations on classic French cuisine, such as lobster and prawns with white-corn bisque. Though there's no requirement for dress, men will feel more comfortable in a jacket. ✉ *99 Pacific St., Suite 100C* ☎ *831/375–9798* ✍ *Reservations essential* 💳 *AE, D, DC, MC, V* ⏲ *No lunch.*

$$ SEAFOOD ✕ **Monterey's Fish House.** Casual yet stylish, and removed from the hubbub of the wharf, this always-packed seafood restaurant attracts locals and frequent visitors to the city. If the dining room is full, you can wait at the bar and savor deliciously plump oysters on the half shell. The bartenders and waitstaff will gladly advise you on the perfect wine to go with your poached, blackened, or oak-grilled seafood. ✉ *2114 Del Monte Ave.* ☎ *831/373–4647* 💳 *AE, D, DC, MC, V* ⏲ *No lunch weekends.*

$$ AMERICAN Fodor's Choice ★ ✕ **Montrio Bistro.** This quirky, converted firehouse, with its rawhide walls and iron indoor trellises, has a wonderfully sophisticated menu. Chef Tony Baker uses organic produce and meats to create imaginative dishes that reflect local agriculture, such as baby artichoke risotto and whole stuffed quail with savory French toast and apple-blackberry reduction. Likewise, the wine list draws primarily on California, and many come from the Monterey area. ✉ *414 Calle Principal* ☎ *831/648–8880* ✍ *Reservations essential* 💳 *AE, D, DC, MC, V* ⏲ *No lunch.*

¢ AMERICAN ✕ **Old Monterey Café.** Breakfast here gets constant local raves. Its fame rests on familiar favorites in many incarnations: a dozen kinds of omelets, and pancakes from blueberry to cinnamon-raisin-pecan. The lunch and dinner menus have good soups, salads, and sandwiches, and this is a great place to relax with an afternoon cappuccino. ⊠*489 Alvarado St.* ☎*831/646–1021* *Reservations not accepted* ▭*AE, D, MC, V.*

$$$ ECLECTIC ✕ **Stokes Restaurant & Bar.** This 1833 adobe building glows with well-being, its many fireplaces, booths, and banquettes bringing coziness to the numerous intimate dining rooms. Regional ingredients handled with Mediterranean techniques combine in dishes such as Monterey Bay sardines *escabèche* (a spicy marinade) and pork shoulder with celery-root gratin. Small plates are a specialty, and wines come from all over the world. ⊠*500 Hartnell St.* ☎*831/373–1110* ▭*AE, D, DC, MC, V* ⏲*No lunch.*

$$ AMERICAN ✕ **Tarpy's Roadhouse.** Fun, dressed-up American favorites—a little something for everyone—are served in this renovated early-1900s stone farmhouse several miles outside town. The kitchen cranks out everything from Cajun-spiced prawns to meat loaf with marsala-mushroom gravy to grilled ribs and steaks. Eat indoors by a fireplace or outdoors in the courtyard. ⊠*2999 Monterey–Salinas Hwy., Hwy. 68* ☎*831/647–1444* ▭*AE, D, DC, MC, V.*

WHERE TO STAY

$$–$$$ **Best Western Beach Resort Monterey.** With a great waterfront location about 2 mi north of town—with views of the bay and the city skyline—and a surprising array of amenities, this hotel is one of the best values in town. A $5 million renovation transformed the nondescript rooms into modern getaways with platform beds and puffy duvets, flat-screen TVs, and fine linens. The grounds are pleasantly landscaped, and there's a large pool with a sunbathing area. **Pros:** on the beach; great value; family-friendly. **Cons:** several miles from major attractions; big-box mall neighborhood. ⊠*2600 Sand Dunes Dr.* ☎*831/394–3321 or 800/242–8627* 🌐*www.montereybeachresort.com* *196 rooms* *In-room: safe, refrigerator, Wi-Fi. In-hotel: restaurant, room service, bar, pool, gym, beachfront, laundry service, Internet terminal, Wi-Fi, parking (paid), some pets allowed, no-smoking rooms* ▭*AE, D, DC, MC, V.*

$–$$ ★ **Monterey Bay Lodge.** Location (on the edge of Monterey's El Estero Park) and superior amenities give this cheerful facility an edge over other motels in town. Lots of greenery, indoors and out, views over El Estero Lake, and a secluded courtyard with a heated pool are other pluses. **Pros:** within walking distance of beach and playground; quiet at night; good family choice. **Cons:** near busy boulevard. ⊠*55 Camino Aguajito* ☎*831/372–8057 or 800/558–1900* 🌐*www.montereybaylodge.com* *45 rooms, 2 suites* *In-room: safe, refrigerator, Internet, Wi-Fi. In-hotel: restaurant, pool, some pets allowed, no-smoking rooms* ▭*AE, D, DC, MC, V.*

$$$–$$$$ ★ **Monterey Plaza Hotel and Spa.** This full-service hotel commands a waterfront location on Cannery Row, where you can see frolicking sea otters from the wide outdoor patio and many room balconies. The architecture blends early California and Mediterranean styles, and also echoes elements of the old cannery design. Meticulously maintained, the property offers both simple and luxurious accommodations. On

the top floor, the spa offers a full array of treatments, perfect after a workout in the penthouse fitness center. **Pros:** on the ocean, lots of amenities, attentive service. **Cons:** touristy area; heavy traffic. ✉ *400 Cannery Row* ☎ *831/646–1700 or 800/334–3999* 🌐 *www.montereyplazahotel.com* *280 rooms, 10 suites* *In-room: DVD, Internet, Wi-Fi. In-hotel: 2 restaurants, room service, gym, spa, laundry service, no-smoking rooms* 💳 *AE, D, DC, MC, V.*

THE FIRST ARTICHOKE QUEEN

Castroville, a tiny town off Highway 1 between Monterey and Watsonville, produces about 95% of U.S. artichokes. Back in 1948, the town chose its first queen to preside during its Artichoke Festival—a beautiful young woman named Norma Jean Mortenson, who later changed her name to Marilyn Monroe.

$$$$ Fodor's Choice ★ **Old Monterey Inn.** This three-story manor house was the home of Monterey's first mayor, and today it remains a private enclave within walking distance of downtown. Lush gardens are shaded by huge old trees and bordered by a creek. Rooms are individually decorated with tasteful antiques; many have fireplaces, and all have featherbeds. Those with private entrances have split doors; you can open the top half to let in cool air and the sound of birds. In the spa room, indulge in a massage or wrap in front of the fireplace. The extensive breakfast is delivered to the rooms, and wine, cheese, and cookies are served each afternoon in the parlor. **Pros:** gorgeous gardens; refined luxury; serene. **Cons:** must drive to attractions and sights; fills quickly. ✉ *500 Martin St.* ☎ *831/375–8284 or 800/350–2344* 🌐 *www.oldmontereyinn.com* *6 rooms, 3 suites, 1 cottage* *In-room: no a/c, DVD (some), Internet, Wi-Fi. In-hotel: spa, no-smoking rooms* 💳 *MC, V* 🍽 *BP.*

$–$$ **Quality Inn Monterey.** This attractive motel has a friendly, country-inn feeling. Rooms are light and airy, some have fireplaces—and the price is right. **Pros:** indoor pool; bargain rates; cheerful innkeepers. **Cons:** street is busy during the day; some rooms are dark. ✉ *1058 Munras Ave.* ☎ *831/372–3381 or 800/361–3835* 🌐 *www.qualityinnmonterey.com* *55 rooms* *In-room: refrigerator, Internet, Wi-Fi. In-hotel: pool, no-smoking rooms* 💳 *AE, D, DC, MC, V* 🍽 *CP.*

NIGHTLIFE AND THE ARTS

NIGHTLIFE **Planet Ultralounge and Restaurant** (✉ *2110 N. Fremont St.* ☎ *831/373–1449* 🌐 *www.theplanetmonterey.com*) presents comedy shows on weekends and dancing to a DJ or live music most nights. An Italian restaurant with a big bar area, **Cibo** (✉ *301 Alvarado St.* ☎ *831/649–8151* 🌐 *www.cibo.com*) brings live jazz, Latin, soul, and more to downtown Tuesday through Sunday. Loungey **Monterey Live** (✉ *414 Alvarado St.* ☎ *831/373–5483* 🌐 *www.montereylive.org*), in the heart of downtown, presents jazz, rock, and comedy acts, including some big names, nightly.

THE ARTS ★ **Dixieland Monterey** (☎ *831/675–0298 or 888/349–6879* 🌐 *www.dixieland-monterey.com*), held on the first full weekend of March, presents traditional jazz bands at waterfront venues on the harbor. The **Monterey Bay Blues Festival** (☎ *831/394–2652* 🌐 *www.montereyblues.*

com) draws blues fans to the Monterey Fairgrounds the last weekend in June. The **Monterey Jazz Festival** (☎*831/373–3366* 🌐*www.montereyjazzfestival.org*), the world's oldest, attracts jazz and blues greats from around the world to the Monterey Fairgrounds on the third full weekend of September.

Monterey Bay Theatrefest (☎*831/622–0100*) presents free outdoor performances at Custom House Plaza on weekend afternoons and evenings from late June to mid-July. The **Bruce Ariss Wharf Theater** (✉*One Fisherman's Wharf* ☎*831/649–2332*) focuses on American musicals past and present.

WHALE-WATCHING

Thousands of gray whales pass close by the Monterey Coast on their annual migration between the Bering Sea and Baja California. The gigantic creatures are sometimes visible through binoculars from shore, but a whale-watching cruise is the best way to get a close look at these magnificent mammals. The migration south takes place from December through March; January is prime viewing time. The whales migrate north from March through June. In addition, some 2,000 blue whales and 600 humpbacks pass the coast and are easily spotted in late summer and early fall.

SPORTS AND THE OUTDOORS

Throughout most of the year, the Monterey Bay area is a haven for those who love tennis, golf, surfing, fishing, biking, hiking, scuba diving, and kayaking. In the rainy winter months, when the waves grow larger, adventurous surfers flock to the water. The **Monterey Bay National Marine Sanctuary** (☎*831/647–4201* 🌐*montereybay.noaa.gov*), home to mammals, seabirds, fishes, invertebrates, and plants, encompasses a 276-mi shoreline and 5,322 square mi of ocean. Ringed by beaches and campgrounds, it's a place for kayaking, whale-watching, scuba diving, and other water sports.

BICYCLING For bicycle and surrey rentals, visit **Bay Bikes** (✉*585 Cannery Row* ☎*831/655–2453* 🌐*www.baybikes.com*). **Adventures by the Sea, Inc.** (✉*299 Cannery Row* ☎*831/372–1807 or 831/648–7236* 🌐*www.adventuresbythesea.com*) rents tandem and standard bicycles.

FISHING **Randy's Fishing and Whale Watching Trips** (✉*66 Fisherman's Wharf* ☎*831/372–7440 or 800/251–7440* 🌐*www.randysfishingtrips.com*), a small family-run business, has been operating since 1949.

KAYAKING **Monterey Bay Kayaks** (✉*693 Del Monte Ave.* ☎*831/373–5357, 800/649–5357* 🌐*www.montereybaykayaks.com*) rents equipment and conducts classes and natural-history tours.

SCUBA DIVING Monterey Bay waters never warm to the temperatures of their Southern California counterparts (the warmest they get is low 60s), but that's one reason why the marine life here is among the world's most diverse. The staff at **Aquarius Dive Shop** (✉*2040 Del Monte Ave.* ☎*831/375–1933, 831/657–1020 diving conditions* 🌐*www.aquariusdivers.com*) gives diving lessons and tours, and rents equipment. Their scuba-conditions information line is updated daily.

WALKING From Custom House Plaza, you can walk along the coast in either direction on the 29-mi-long **Monterey Bay Coastal Trail** (☎*831/372–3196* *www.mtycounty.com/pgs-parks/bike-path.html*) for spectacular views of the sea. It runs all the way from north of Monterey to Pacific Grove, with sections continuing around Pebble Beach.

WHALE-WATCHING ★ **Monterey Bay Whale Watch** (*84 Fisherman's Wharf* *831/375–4658* *www.montereybaywhalewatch.com*), which operates out of the Monterey Bay Whale Watch Center at Fisherman's Wharf, gives three- to five-hour tours led by marine biologists. **Monterey Whale Watching** (*96 Fisherman's Wharf #1* *831/372–2203 or 800/979–3370* *www.montereywhalewatching.com*) provides three tours a day on a 150-passenger high-speed cruiser and a large 75-foot boat.

SHOPPING

Bargain hunters can sometimes find little treasures at the **Cannery Row Antique Mall** (*471 Wave St.* *831/655–0264*), which houses 150 local vendors under one roof. Historical society–operated, **The Pickett Fence** (*Monterey State Historic Park, 1 Custom House Plaza, across from Fisherman's Wharf* *831/649–3364*) sells high-end garden accessories and furnishings.

AROUND THE BAY

As Highway 1 follows the curve of the bay between Monterey and Santa Cruz it passes through a rich agricultural zone. Opening right onto the bay, where the Salinas and Pajaro rivers drain into the Pacific, a broad valley brings together fertile soil, an ideal climate, and a good water supply to create optimum growing conditions for crops such as strawberries, artichokes, Brussels sprouts, and broccoli. Several beautiful beaches line this part of the coast.

MOSS LANDING

17 mi north of Monterey on Hwy. 1.

Moss Landing is not much more than a couple of blocks of cafés and antiques shops plus a busy fishing port, but therein lies its charm. It's a fine place to stop for lunch and get a dose of nature.

ESSENTIALS

Visitor Information **Moss Landing Chamber of Commerce** (*Box 41, Moss Landing 95039* *831/633–4501* *www.mosslandingchamber.com*).

★ In the **Elkhorn Slough National Estuarine Research Reserve** (*1700 Elkhorn Rd., Watsonville* *831/728–2822* *www.elkhornslough.org* *$2.50* *Wed.–Sun. 9–5*) 1,400 acres of tidal flats and salt marshes form a complex environment that supports some 300 species of birds. On a walk or a kayak trip along the meandering waterways and wetlands you can see hawks, white-tailed kites, owls, herons, and egrets. Sea otters, sharks, rays, and many other animals also live or visit here. On weekends guided walks from the visitor center to the heron rookery begin at 10 and 1. Although the reserve lies across the town line in Watsonville, you reach its entrance through Moss Landing.

Aboard a 27-foot pontoon boat operated by **Elkhorn Slough Safari** (*Moss Landing Harbor* *831/633–5555* *www.elkhornslough.*

SALINAS AND JOHN STEINBECK'S LEGACY

Salinas (17 mi east of Monterey), a hard-working city surrounded by vegetable fields, honors the memory and literary legacy of John Steinbeck, its most well-known native, at the modern **National Steinbeck Center** (✉*1 Main St., 17 mi east of Monterey via Hwy. 68, Salinas* ☎*831/796–3833, 831/775–4721 museum store* 🌐*www.steinbeck.org* 🎫*$11* ⏲*Daily 10–5; closed Sun.–Mon. from Jan.–Mar.*). Exhibits document the life of the Pulitzer- and Nobel-prize winner and the history of the local communities that inspired Steinbeck novels such as *The Grapes of Wrath.* Highlights include reproductions of the green pickup-camper from *Travels with Charley* and of the bunkroom from *Of Mice and Men*; you can watch actors read from Steinbeck's books on video screens throughout the museum. The museum is the centerpiece of the revival of Old Town Salinas, where handsome turn-of-the-20th-century stone buildings have been renovated and filled with shops and restaurants. Two blocks from the National Steinbeck Center is the author's Victorian birthplace, **Steinbeck House** (✉*132 Central Ave.* ☎*831/424–2735*). It operates as a lunch spot Tuesday through Saturday and displays some Steinbeck memorabilia.

com) a naturalist leads an up-close look at wetlands denizens. Advance reservations are required for the two-hour tours ($32).

Tom's Sportfishing (✉*Moss Landing Harbor* ☎*831/633–2564* 🌐*www.tomssportfishing.com*) takes anglers out onto Monterey Bay ($65 to $70). Depending on the season, king salmon, albacore, or halibut may be the quarry.

WHERE TO EAT

$ SEAFOOD ✕**Phil's Fish Market & Eatery.** Exquisitely fresh, simply prepared seafood (try the cioppino) is on the menu at this warehouselike restaurant on the harbor; all kinds of glistening fish are on offer at the market in the front. ■ **TIP→ Phil's Snack Shack, a tiny sandwich-and-smoothie joint, serves quicker meals at the north end of town.** ✉*7600 Sandholdt Rd.* ☎*831/633–2152* ▭*AE, D, DC, MC, V.*

WATSONVILLE

7 mi north of Moss Landing on Hwy. 1.

If ever a city was built on strawberries, Watsonville is it. Produce has long driven the economy here, and this is where the county fair takes place each September.

One feature of the Santa Cruz County Fairgrounds is the **Agricultural History Project,** which preserves the history of farming in the Pajaro Valley. In the Codiga Center and Museum you can examine antique tractors and milking machines, enjoy an exhibit on the era when Watsonville was the "frozen food capitol of the West," and watch experts restore farm implements and vehicles. ✉*2601 E. Lake Ave.* ☎*831/724–5898* 🌐*www.aghistoryproject.org* 🎫*$2 suggested donation* ⏲*Thurs.–Sun. noon–4.*

SAN JUAN BAUTISTA

About as close to early-19th-century California as you can get, San Juan Bautista (15 mi east of Watsonville on Hwy. 156) has been protected from development since 1933, when much of it became a state park. Small antiques shops and restaurants occupy the Old West and art-deco buildings that line 3rd Street.

The wide green plaza of San Juan Bautista State Historic Park is ringed by 18th- and 19th-century buildings, many of them open to the public. The cemetery of the long, low, colonnaded mission church contains the unmarked graves of more than 4,300 Native American converts. Nearby is an adobe home furnished with Spanish-colonial antiques, a hotel frozen in the 1860s, a blacksmith shop, a stable, a pioneer cabin, and a jailhouse.

The first Saturday of each month costumed volunteers engage in quilting bees, tortilla making, and other frontier activities. *www.san-juan-bautista.ca.us.*

Every Memorial Day weekend, aerial performers execute elaborate aerobatics at the **Watsonville Fly-in & Air Show.** More than 300 classic, experimental, and military aircraft are on display; concerts and other events fill three days. *Watsonville Municipal Airport, 100 Aviation Way 831/763–5600 www.watsonvilleflyin.org $15.*

APTOS

7 mi north of Watsonville on Hwy. 1.

Backed by a redwood forest and facing the sea, downtown Aptos—known as Aptos Village—is a place of wooden walkways and false-fronted shops. Antiques dealers cluster along Trout Gulch Road, off Soquel Drive east of Highway 1.

ESSENTIALS

Visitor Information **Aptos Chamber of Commerce** (*7605-A Old Dominion Ct., Aptos 831/688–1467 www.aptoschamber.com*).

Sandstone bluffs tower above **Seacliff State Beach** (*201 State Park Dr. 831/685–6442 www.parks.ca.gov $8 per vehicle*), a favorite of locals. You can fish off the pier, which leads out to a sunken World War I tanker ship built of concrete.

WHERE TO EAT AND STAY

$$$ MEDITERRANEAN ★ **Bittersweet Bistro.** A large old tavern with cathedral ceilings houses this popular bistro, where chef-owner Thomas Vinolus draws culinary inspiration from the Mediterranean. The menu changes seasonally, but regular highlights include pan-seared Monterey Bay petrale sole, seafood putanesca (pasta with a spicy sauce of garlic, tomatoes, anchovies, and olives), and grilled pork tenderloin. The decadent chocolate desserts are not to be missed. You can order many of the entrées in small or regular portions. Lunch is available to go from the express counter. *787 Rio Del Mar Blvd. 831/662–9799 AE, MC, V.*

$$$ **Best Western Seacliff Inn.** A favorite lair of families and business travelers, this 6-acre Best Western near Seacliff State Beach is more resort than motel. Six two-story lodge buildings encircle a large pool and lush gardens with a koi pond and waterfall—ask for a room in a building away from the busy restaurant and bar, which can get noisy at night. The decent-size rooms, totally redecorated in 2006, have a fresh—if somewhat generic—contemporary look. **Pros:** walking distance from the beach; family-friendly; includes full breakfast. **Cons:** close to the freeway; occasional nighttime bar noise. ✉*7500 Old Dominion Ct.* ☎*831/688–7300 or 800/367–2003* 🌐*www.seacliffinn.com* *139 rooms, 10 suites* *In-room: refrigerator, Internet. In-hotel: restaurant, room service, bar, pool, gym, laundry facilities, laundry service, Wi-Fi, no-smoking rooms* *AE, D, MC, V* *BP.*

$$$ **Flora Vista.** Multicolored fields of flowers, strawberries, and fresh veggies unfold in every direction at this luxury neo-Georgian inn set on two serene acres in a rural community just south of Aptos; Sand Dollar Beach is just a short walk away. Innkeepers Deanna and Ed Boos transformed the 1867 home, a replica of Abe Lincoln's Springfield farmhouse, adding modern conveniences like Wi-Fi and spa tubs while retaining the house's original redwood floors and country charm. Guests wake to a full breakfast—which might include the neighbor's strawberries—and enjoy a wine and cheese spread in the late afternoon. Each room has its own sparkling bathroom and gas fireplace; three have a spa tub with shower. Stroll through the eclectic gardens (something's always in bloom) or play tennis on the two tournament-quality Har-Tru tennis courts. The inn is on the Pacific Coast Bike Route and welcomes cyclists for stopovers. **Pros:** super-private; near the beach; flowers everywhere. **Cons:** no restaurants or nightlife within walking distance; not a good place for kids. ✉*1258 San Andreas Rd., La Selva Beach* ☎*831/724–8663 or 877/753–5672* 🌐*www.floravistainn.com* *5 rooms* *In-room: no a/c, Wi-Fi. In-hotel: tennis courts, no-smoking rooms* *AE, MC, V* *BP.*

$$$$ **Seascape Beach Resort.** On a bluff overlooking Monterey Bay, Seascape is a full-fledged resort that makes it easy to unwind. The spacious suites sleep from two to six people; each has a kitchenette and fireplace, and many have ocean-view patios with barbecue grills. Treat yourself to an in-room manicure, facial, or massage, or a bonfire with s'mores on the beach. **Pros:** time-share-style apartments; access to miles of beachfront; superb views. **Cons:** far from city life; most bathrooms are small. ✉*1 Seascape Resort Dr.* ☎*831/688–6800 or 800/929–7727* 🌐*www.seascaperesort.com* *285 suites* *In-room: no a/c, kitchen (some), DVD, Internet, Wi-Fi. In-hotel: restaurant, room service, pools, gym, spa, beachfront, children's programs (ages 5–10), laundry service, Internet terminal, no-smoking rooms* *AE, D, DC, MC, V.*

CAPITOLA AND SOQUEL

4 mi northwest of Aptos on Hwy. 1.

On the National Register of Historic places as California's first seaside resort town, the village of Capitola has been in a holiday mood since the late 1800s. Its walkable downtown is jam-packed with casual eateries, surf shops, and ice-cream parlors. Inland, across Highway 1, antiques shops line Soquel Drive in the town of Soquel. Wineries dot the Santa Cruz Mountains beyond.

CALIFORNIA'S OLDEST RESORT TOWN

As far as anyone knows for certain, Capitola is the oldest seaside resort town on the Pacific Coast. In 1856 a pioneer acquired Soquel Landing, the picturesque lagoon and beach where Soquel Creek empties into the bay, and built a wharf. Another man opened a campground along the shore, and his daughter named it Capitola after a heroine in a novel series. After the train came to town in the 1870s, thousands of vacationers began arriving to bask in the sun on the glorious beach.

ESSENTIALS

Visitor Information Capitola-Soquel Chamber of Commerce (✉ *716-G Capitola Ave., Capitola* ☎ *831/475-6522* 🌐 *www.capitolachamber.com*).

New Brighton State Beach (✉ *1500 State Park Dr.* ☎ *831/464-6330* 🌐 *www.parks.ca.gov* 🎫 *$8 per vehicle*), once the site of a Chinese fishing village, is now a popular surfing and camping spot. Its Pacific Migrations Visitor Center, opened in 2006, traces the history of the Chinese and other peoples who settled around Monterey Bay, as well as the migratory patterns of the area's wildlife, such as monarch butterflies and gray whales. **■TIP→ New Brighton Beach connects with Seacliff Beach, and at low tide you can walk or run along this scenic stretch of sand for nearly 16 mi south (you might have to wade through a few creeks). The 1½-mile stroll from New Brighton to Seacliff's cement ship is a local favorite.**

WHERE TO EAT AND STAY

¢ SEAFOOD ✕ **Carpo's.** Locals line up in droves at Carpo's counter, hankering for mouthwatering, casual family meals. The menu leans heavily toward seafood, but also includes burgers, salads, and steaks. Favorites include the fishermen's baskets of fresh battered snapper, calamari and prawns, seafood kabobs, and homemade olallieberry pie. Nearly everything here costs less than $10. Go early to beat the crowds, or be prepared to wait for a table. ✉ *2400 Porter St.* ☎ *831/476-6260* 💳 *D, MC, V.*

¢ CAFÉ ✕ **Gayle's Bakery & Rosticceria.** Whether you're in the mood for an orange-olallieberry muffin, a chicken-*satay* (marinated and served with spicy peanut sauce) salad, or tri-tip on garlic toast, this bakery-cum-deli's varied menu is likely to satisfy. Munch your chocolate macaroon on the shady patio or dig into the daily blue-plate dinner amid the whirl inside. ✉ *504 Bay Ave.* ☎ *831/462-1200* 💳 *AE, MC, V.*

$$ AMERICAN ✕ **Michael's on Main.** Classic comfort food with a creative gourmet twist, reasonable prices, and attentive service draw a lively crowd of locals to this upscale-but-casual creek-side eatery. Chef Michael Clark's commitment to locally sustainable fisheries and farmers has earned him community accolades and infuses dishes with the inimitable taste that comes from using fresh local ingredients. The menu changes seasonally, but you can always count on finding such home-style dishes as Yankee-style pot roast and mashed potatoes as well as unusual entrées like pistachio-crusted salmon with mint vinaigrette. For a quiet conversation

3

spot, ask for a table on the romantic patio overlooking the creek. The busy bar area hosts Wednesday karaoke nights and live music Thursday through Saturday. ✉ *2591 Main St.* ☎ *831/479–9777* ▭ *AE, D, MC, V* ⊙ *Closed Mon.*

$$$ CONTINENTAL ✕ **Shadowbrook.** To get to this romantic spot overlooking Soquel Creek you can take a cable car or walk the stairs down a steep, fern-lined bank beside a running waterfall. Dining room options include the rooftop Redwood Room, the wood-paneled Wine Cellar, and the airy, glass-enclosed Garden Room. Prime rib and grilled seafood are the stars of the simple menu. A cheaper menu of light entrées is available in the lounge. Champagne brunch is served on Sunday. ✉ *1750 Wharf Rd.* ☎ *831/475–1511 or 800/975–1511* ▭ *AE, D, DC, MC, V* ⊙ *No lunch.*

$$$ AMERICAN ★ ✕ **Theo's.** Theo's is on a quiet side street in a residential neighborhood. It serves mainly five- and seven-course prix-fixe dinners; seasonal standouts include duck with garden vegetables and currants, as well as rack of lamb with ratatouille. Much of the produce comes from the ¾-acre organic garden behind the restaurant (where you can stroll between courses); the rest comes from area farmers and ranchers. Service is gracious and attentive, and the wine list has won awards from *Wine Spectator* 15 years in a row. ✉ *3101 N. Main St., Soquel* ☎ *831/462–3657* ✍ *Reservations essential* ▭ *AE, MC, V* ⊙ *Closed Sun. and Mon. No lunch.*

$$$$ **Inn at Depot Hill.** This inventively designed B&B in a former rail depot sees itself as a link to the era of luxury train travel. Each double room or suite, complete with fireplace and featherbeds, is inspired by a different destination—Italy's Portofino, France's Côte d'Azur, Japan's Kyoto. One suite is decorated like a Pullman car for a railroad baron. Some accommodations have private patios with hot tubs. This is a great place for an adults-only weekend. **Pros:** short walk to beach and village; historic charm; excellent service. **Cons:** fills quickly; hot-tub conversation on the patio may irk second-floor guests. ✉ *250 Monterey Ave. 95010* ☎ *831/462–3376 or 800/572–2632* 🌐 *www.innsbythesea.com/depot-hill* *8 rooms, 4 suites* *In-room: no a/c, Wi-Fi. In-hotel: Wi-Fi, no-smoking rooms* ▭ *AE, D, MC, V.*

SANTA CRUZ

5 mi west of Capitola on Hwy. 1; 48 mi north of Monterey on Hwy. 1.

The big city on this stretch of the California coast, Santa Cruz (pop. 57,500) is less manicured than Carmel or Monterey. Long known for its surfing and its amusement-filled beach boardwalk, the town is a mix of grand Victorian-era homes and rinky-dink motels. The opening of the University of California campus in the 1960s swung the town sharply to the left, and the counterculture more or less lives on here. At the same time, the revitalized downtown and an insane real-estate market reflect the city's proximity to Silicon Valley and to a growing wine country in the surrounding mountains.

ESSENTIALS

Visitor Information **Santa Cruz Chamber of Commerce** (✉611 Ocean St., Ste. 1, Santa Cruz ☎831/457–3713 🌐www.santacruzchamber.org).

WHAT TO SEE

Santa Cruz has been a seaside resort since the late 19th century. Along one end of the broad, south-facing beach, the **Santa Cruz Beach Boardwalk** has entertained holidaymakers for almost as long—it celebrated its 100th anniversary in 2007. Its Looff carousel and classic wooden Giant Dipper roller coaster, both dating from the early 1900s, are surrounded by high-tech thrill rides and easygoing kiddie rides with ocean views. Video and arcade games, a mini-golf course, and a laser-tag arena pack one gigantic building. You have to pay to play, but you can wander the entire boardwalk for free while sampling delicacies such as corn dogs and chowder fries. ✉*Along Beach St.* ☎*831/423–5590 or 831/426–7433* 🌐*www.beachboardwalk.com* *$30 day pass for unlimited rides* *Late May–early Sept., daily; early Sept.–late May, weekends, weather permitting; call for hrs.*

Jutting half a mile into the ocean near one end of the Santa Cruz Beach Boardwalk, the **Santa Cruz Municipal Wharf** (✉*Beach St., at Pacific Ave.* ☎*831/420–6025* 🌐*www.santacruzwharf.com*) is topped with seafood restaurants, souvenir shops, and outfitters offering bay cruises, fishing trips, and boat rentals. A salty sound track drifts up from under the wharf, where barking sea lions lounge in heaps on crossbeams.

West Cliff Drive winds along the top of an oceanfront bluff from the municipal wharf to Natural Bridges State Beach. It's a spectacular drive, but it's much more fun to walk, blade, or bike the paved path that parallels the road. Groups of surfers bob and swoosh in Monterey Bay at several points near the foot of the bluff, especially at a break known as Steamer Lane. Named for a surfer who died here in 1965, nearby Mark Abbott Memorial Lighthouse stands at Point Santa Cruz, the cliff's major promontory. From here you can watch pinnipeds hang out, sunbathe, and frolic on Seal Rock.

★ The **Santa Cruz Surfing Museum,** inside the Mark Abbott Memorial Lighthouse, traces local surfing history back to the early 20th century. Historical photographs show old-time surfers, and a display of boards includes rarities such as a heavy redwood plank predating the fiberglass era and the remains of a modern board chomped by a great white shark. Surfer-docents are on site to talk about the old days. ✉*701 W. Cliff Dr.* ☎*831/420–6289* 🌐*www.santacruzsurfingmuseum.org* *$2 suggested donation* *Sept.–June, Thurs.–Mon. noon–4; July–Aug. Weds.–Mon. 10–5*

At the end of West Cliff Drive lies **Natural Bridges State Beach,** a stretch of soft sand edged with tide pools and sea-sculpted rock bridges. **TIP→ From October to early March a colony of monarch butterflies roosts in a eucalyptus grove.** ✉*2531 W. Cliff Dr.* ☎*831/423–4609* 🌐*www.parks.ca.gov* *Beach free, parking $8* *Daily 8 AM–sunset. Visitor center Oct.–Feb., daily 10–4; Mar.–Sept., weekends 10–4.*

Seymour Marine Discovery Center, part of Long Marine Laboratory at UCSC's Institute of Marine Sciences, looks more like a research facility than a slick aquarium. Interactive exhibits demonstrate how scientists study the ocean, and the aquarium displays creatures of particular interest to marine biologists. The 87-foot blue whale skeleton is the world's largest. ✉*100 Shaffer Rd., off Delaware St. west of Natural Bridges State Beach* ☎*831/459–3800* 🌐*seymourcenter.ucsc.edu* 🎫*$6* ⏲*Tues.–Sat. 10–5, Sun. noon–5.*

HAWAIIAN ROYALTY SURFS THE BAY

In 1885 relatives of Hawaiian Queen Kapiolani reputedly visited Santa Cruz and surfed near the mouth of the San Lorenzo River. Nearly 20 years later, legendary Hawaiian surfer Duke Kahanamoku also surfed the Santa Cruz swells.

In the Cultural Preserve of **Wilder Ranch State Park** you can visit the homes, barns, workshops, and bunkhouse of a 19th-century dairy farm. Nature has reclaimed most of the ranch land, and native plants and wildlife have returned to the 7,000 acres of forest, grassland, canyons, estuaries, and beaches. Hike, bike, or ride horseback on miles of ocean-view trails. ✉*Hwy. 1, 1 mi north of Santa Cruz* ☎*831/426–0505 Interpretive Center, 831/423–9703 trail information* 🌐*www.parks.ca.gov* 🎫*Parking $8* ⏲*Daily 8 AM–sunset.*

When you've had your fill of the city's beaches and waters, take a stroll in downtown Santa Cruz, especially on **Pacific Avenue** between Laurel and Water streets. Vintage boutiques and mountain-sports stores, sushi bars and Mexican restaurants, day spas and nightclubs keep the main drag and the surrounding streets hopping midmorning until late evening.

Pop into **Vinocruz** (✉*725 Front St., #101* ☎*831/426–8466* 🌐*www.vinocruz.com* ⏲*Mon.–Thurs. 11–7, Fri. and Sat. 11–8, Sun. noon–6*) for one-stop tasting of Santa Cruz Mountain wines. They pour vintages from more than 60 local wineries, including small operations that don't have their own tasting rooms. The slick, contemporary space in Abbott Square off Cooper Street in historic downtown was once part of an old jail.

On the northern fringes of downtown, **Santa Cruz Mission State Historic Park** preserves the site of California's 12th Spanish mission, built in the 1790s and destroyed by an earthquake in 1857. A museum in a restored 1791 adobe and a half-scale replica of the mission church are part of the complex. ✉*144 School St.* ☎*831/425–5849* 🌐*www.parks.ca.gov* 🎫*Free* ⏲*Thurs.–Sun. 10–4.*

Hokey tourist trap or genuine scientific enigma? Since 1940 curious throngs baffled by the **Mystery Spot** have made it one of the most visited attractions in Santa Cruz. The laws of gravity and physics don't appear to apply in this tiny patch of redwood forest, where balls roll uphill and people stand on a slant. ✉*465 Mystery Spot Rd.* ☎*831/423–8897* 🌐*www.mysteryspot.com* 🎫*Mystery Spot $5, parking $5* ⏲*Late May–early Sept., daily 9–7, early Sept.–late May, daily 9–5.*

The modern 2,000-acre campus of the **University of California at Santa Cruz** nestles in the forested hills above town. Its sylvan setting, sweeping ocean vistas, and redwood architecture make the university worth visit. Campus tours, offered several times daily (reserve in advance), offer a glimpse of college life and campus highlights. They run about an hour and 45 minutes and combine moderate walking with shuttle transport. Half a mile beyond the main campus entrance, the **UCSC Arboretum** (*1156 High St. 831/427–2998 www2.ucsc.edu/arboretum $5 Daily 9–5, guided tours Sat. at 11*) is a stellar collection of gardens arranged by geography. A path leads through areas dedicated to the plants of California, Australia, New Zealand, and South Africa. *Main entrance at Bay and High Sts. 831/459–0111 www.ucsc.edu.*

OFF THE BEATEN PATH

★ **Santa Cruz Mountains.** Highway 9 heads northeast from Santa Cruz into hills densely timbered with massive coastal redwoods. The road winds through the lush San Lorenzo Valley, past hamlets consisting of a few cafés, antiques shops, and old-style tourist cabins. Here residents of the hunting-and-fishing persuasion coexist with hardcore flower-power survivors and wannabes. Along Highway 9 and its side roads are about a dozen **wineries,** most notably Bonny Doon Vineyard, Organic Wineworks, and David Bruce Winery. **TIP→ The Santa Cruz Mountains Winegrowers Association (www.scmwa.com) distributes a wine-touring map at many lodgings and attractions around Santa Cruz.**

WHERE TO EAT

$$ ITALIAN

Gabriella Café. The work of local artists hangs on the walls of this petite, romantic café in a tile-roof cottage. Featuring organic produce from area farms, the seasonal Italian menu has offered steamed mussels, braised lamb shank, and grilled portobello mushrooms. *910 Cedar St. 831/457–1677 AE, D, MC, V.*

¢ AMERICAN

Seabright Brewery. Great burgers, big salads, and stellar house-made microbrews make this a favorite hangout in the youthful Seabright neighborhood east of downtown. Sit outside on the large patio or inside at a comfortable, spacious booth; both are popular with families. *519 Seabright Ave. 831/426–2739 AE, MC, V.*

$$ MEDITERRANEAN

Soif. Wine reigns at this sleek bistro and wine shop that takes its name from the French word for thirst. The lengthy list includes selections from near and far, dozens of which you can order by the taste or glass. Infused with the tastes of the Mediterranean, small plates and mains are served at the copper-top bar, the big communal table, and private tables. A jazz combo or solo pianist plays some evenings. *105 Walnut Ave. 831/423–2020 AE, MC, V No lunch Sun.–Tues.*

¢ AMERICAN

Zachary's. This noisy café filled with students and families defines the funky essence of Santa Cruz. It also dishes up great breakfasts: stay simple with sourdough pancakes, or go for Mike's Mess—eggs scrambled with bacon, mushrooms, and home fries, then topped with sour cream, melted cheese, and fresh tomatoes. **⚠ If you arrive after 9 AM, expect a long wait for a table; lunch is a shade calmer, but closing time is 2:30 PM.** *819 Pacific Ave. 831/427–0646 Reservations not accepted D, MC, V Closed Mon. No dinner.*

WHERE TO STAY

$$$–$$$$

Babbling Brook Inn. Though it's smack in the middle of Santa Cruz, this B&B has lush gardens, a running stream, and tall trees that make you feel like you're in a secluded wood. All rooms have fireplaces (though a few are electric) and featherbeds; most have private patios.

Complimentary wine, cheese, and fresh-baked cookies are available in the afternoon. **Pros:** close to UCSC; walking distance from downtown shops; woodsy feel. **Cons:** near a high school; some rooms are close to a busy street. ✉ *1025 Laurel St.* ☎ *831/427–2437 or 800/866–1131* 🌐 *www.innsbythesea.com/babbling-brook* *11 rooms, 2 suites* *In-room: no a/c. In-hotel: no-smoking rooms* *AE, D, DC, MC, V* *BP.*

$$$–$$$$ **Chaminade.** A full-on renovation in 2005 sharpened this hilltop resort's look and enhanced its amenities. Secluded on 300 acres of redwood and eucalyptus forest, the mission-style complex commands expansive views of Monterey Bay. Guest rooms are furnished in a modern Spanish style, with dark wood, deep colors, and patterned fabrics; some have private patios or decks. The spa employs all-natural products in its complete menu of body and beauty treatments. **Pros:** far from city life; spectacular property; ideal spot for romance and rejuvenation. **Cons:** must drive to attractions and sights; near major hospital. ✉ *1 Chaminade La.* ☎ *800/283–6569* 🌐 *www.chaminade.com* *112 rooms, 44 suites* *In-room: safe, refrigerator (some), Internet, Wi-Fi. In-hotel: 3 restaurants, bar, tennis courts, pool, gym, spa, laundry service, Wi-Fi, no-smoking rooms* *AE, D, DC, MC, V.*

$$$$ **Pleasure Point Inn.** Tucked in a residential neighborhood at the east end of town, this modern Mediterranean-style B&B sits right across the street from the ocean and a popular surfing beach (where surfing lessons are available). The rooms are handsomely furnished and include such deluxe amenities as fireplaces and private patios. You have use of the large rooftop sundeck and hot tub, which overlook the Pacific. Because this is a popular romantic getaway spot, it's best not to bring kids. **Pros:** fantastic views; ideal for checking the swells; quirky neighborhood. **Cons:** few rooms; several miles from major attractions. ✉ *2–3665 E. Cliff Dr.* ☎ *831/475–4657* 🌐 *www.pleasurepointinn.com* *4 rooms* *In-room: no a/c, safe, refrigerator, DVD, Wi-Fi. In-hotel: beachfront, no-smoking rooms* *MC, V* *CP.*

$$$$ **Santa Cruz Dream Inn.** Just a short stroll from the boardwalk and wharf, this full-service luxury hotel is the only lodging in Santa Cruz directly on the beach. All rooms have private balconies or patios overlooking Monterey Bay. New owners completed a top-to-bottom remodel of the hotel in summer 2008; rooms now sparkle with contemporary furnishings, bold colors, and upscale linens—but the main draw here is having the ocean at your doorstep. Have the valet store your surf board or bike for free, then take in the Pacific sunset from the poolside bar. **Pros:** directly on the beach. **Cons:** expensive. ✉ *175 W. Cliff Dr.* ☎ *831/426–4330 or 800/663–1144* *831/427–2025* 🌐 *www.jdvhotels.com* *149 rooms, 16 suites* *In-room: safe, refrigerator, Wi-Fi. In-hotel: restaurant, room service, bars, pool, laundry service, Internet terminal, no-smoking rooms* *AE, D, DC, MC, V.*

$$$–$$$$ **West Cliff Inn.** Perched on the bluffs across from Cowell's Beach, this posh nautical-theme inn commands sweeping views of the boardwalk and Monterey Bay. Built in 1877, the Italianate three-story Victorian emerged from a top-to-bottom renovation in 2007 in classic California-

beach style with color schemes that hint of ocean, sky, and reflecting light. All rooms have a comfy king bed, fireplace, and fancy marble tile bathroom, many with spa tubs and some with sitting areas; rooms facing the bay have the best views. For the ultimate in privacy, ask for the room that has a private patio and hot tub. In the morning, enjoy a lavish breakfast in the elegant dining room and watch the surfers and seals catching the waves below. **Pros:** killer views; walking distance from the beach; close to downtown. **Cons:** boardwalk noise; street traffic. ✉*174 West Cliff Dr.* ☎*800/979–0910* 🌐*www.westcliffinn.com* *7 rooms, 2 suites* *In-room: DVD, Wi-Fi. In-hotel: no-smoking rooms* *AE, D, MC, V* *BP.*

NIGHTLIFE AND THE ARTS

NIGHTLIFE ★ Dance with the crowds at **The Catalyst** (✉*1011 Pacific Ave.* ☎*831/423–1338* 🌐*www.catalystclub.com*), a huge, grimy downtown club that has regularly featured big names, from Neil Young to Nirvana to Ice T. Renowned in the international jazz community, and drawing performers such as Herbie Hancock, Pat Metheny, and Charlie Hunter, the nonprofit **Kuumbwa Jazz Center** (✉*320–2 Cedar St.* ☎*831/427–2227* 🌐*www.kuumbwajazz.org*) bops with live music most nights; "Jazz and Dinner" Thursday includes a meal with the show. Blues, salsa, reggae, funk: you name it, **Moe's Alley** (✉*1535 Commercial Way* ☎*831/479–1854* 🌐*www.moesalley.com*) has it all, six nights a week.

THE ARTS Each August, the **Cabrillo Festival of Contemporary Music** (☎*831/426–6966, 831/420–5260 box office* 🌐*www.cabrillomusic.org*) brings some of the world's finest artists to the Santa Cruz Civic Auditorium to play groundbreaking symphonic music, including major world premieres. Using period and reproduction instruments, the **Santa Cruz Baroque Festival** (☎*831/457–9693* 🌐*www.scbaroque.org*) presents a wide range of classical music at various venues throughout the year. As the name suggests, the focus is on 17th- and 18th-century composers such as Bach and Handel.

Shakespeare Santa Cruz (✉*SSC/UCSC Theater Arts Center, 1156 High St.* ☎ *831/459–2121, 831/459–2159 tickets* 🌐*www.shakespearesantacruz.org*) stages a six-week Shakespeare festival in July and August that may also include the occasional modern dramatic performance. Most performances are outdoors under the redwoods. A holiday program is also performed in December.

SPORTS AND THE OUTDOORS

BICYCLING Park the car and rent a beach cruiser at **Bicycle Shop Santa Cruz** (✉*1325 Mission St.* ☎*831/454–0909* 🌐*www.thebicycleshopsantacruz.com*). Mountain bikers should head to **Another Bike Shop** (✉*2361 Mission St.* ☎*831/427–2232* 🌐*www.anotherbikeshop.com*) for tips on the best trails around and a look at cutting-edge gear made and tested locally.

BOATS AND CHARTERS **Chardonnay Sailing Charters** (☎*831/423–1213* 🌐*www.chardonnay.com*) cruises Monterey Bay year-round on a variety of trips, such as whale-watching, astronomy, and winemaker sails. The 70-foot *Chardonnay II* leaves from the yacht harbor in Santa Cruz. Food and drink are served on many of their cruises. Reservations are essential. **Stagnaro Sport Fishing** (✉ *June–Aug., Santa Cruz Municipal Wharf; Sept.–May, Santa Cruz West Harbor* ☎ *831/427–2334* 🌐 *www.stagnaros.com*) operates salmon, albacore, and rock-cod fishing expeditions; the fees ($49 to $75) include bait. The company also runs whale-watching cruises ($41) year-round.

Designed by famed golf architect Dr. Alister MacKenzie in 1929, semi-private **Pasatiempo Golf Club** (✉ *20 Clubhouse Rd.* ☎ *831/459–9155* 🌐 *www.pasatiempo.com*), set amid undulating hills just above the city, often ranks among the nation's top championship courses in annual polls. Golfers rave about the spectacular views and challenging terrain. The greens fee is $220; an electric cart is $30 per player.

KAYAKING Explore hidden coves and kelp forests with **Venture Quest Kayaking** (✉ *#2 Santa Cruz Wharf* ☎ *831/427–2267 or 831/425–8445* 🌐 *www.kayaksantacruz.com*). The company's guided nature tours depart from Santa Cruz Wharf or Harbor, depending on the season. A two-hour kayak nature tour and introductory lesson costs $55. A three-hour kayak rental is $30 and includes wet suit and gear. Venture Quest also arranges tours at other Monterey Bay destinations, including Capitola and Elkhorn Slough.

SURFING Surfers gather for spectacular waves and sunsets at **Pleasure Point** (✉ *E. Cliff and Pleasure Point Drs.*). **Steamer Lane,** near the lighthouse on West Cliff Drive, has a decent break. The area plays host to several competitions in summer.

Find out what all the fun is about at **Club-Ed Surf School and Camps** (✉ *Cowell Beach, at Coast Santa Cruz Hotel* ☎ *831/464–0177 or 800/287–7873* 🌐 *www.club-ed.com*). Your first private or group lesson ($85 and up) includes all equipment. The most welcoming place in town to buy or rent surf gear is **Paradise Surf Shop** (✉ *3961 Portola Dr.* ☎ *831/462–3880* 🌐 *www.paradisesurf.com*). The shop is owned and run by women who aim to help everyone feel comfortable on the water. **Cowell's Beach Surf Shop** (✉ *30 Front St.* ☎ *831/427–2355* 🌐 *www.cowellssurfshop.com*) sells bikinis, rents surfboards and wet suits, and offers lessons.

San Francisco

WORD OF MOUTH

"Rode the cable cars and what fun that is! . . . And a little scary when you are standing on the side that must squeeze past the cable car passing by in the opposite direction! Just couldn't believe the HILLS! Whose idea was it to build a city on all these hills? It's magnificent!"

—mwessel

WELCOME TO SAN FRANCISCO

TOP REASONS TO GO

★ **The bay:** It's hard not to gasp as you catch sight of sunlight dancing on the water when you crest a hill, or watch the Golden Gate Bridge vanish and reemerge in the summer fog.

★ **The food:** San Franciscans are serious about what they eat, and with good reason. Home to some of the nation's best chefs, top restaurants, and finest local produce, it's hard not to eat well here.

★ **The shopping:** Shopaholics visiting the city will not be disappointed: San Francisco is packed with browsing destinations, everything from quirky boutiques to massive malls.

★ **The good life:** A laid-back atmosphere, beautiful surroundings, and oodles of cultural, culinary, and aesthetic pleasures . . . if you spend too much time here, you might not leave!

★ **The great outdoors:** From Golden Gate Park to sidewalk cafés in North Beach, San Franciscans relish their outdoor spaces.

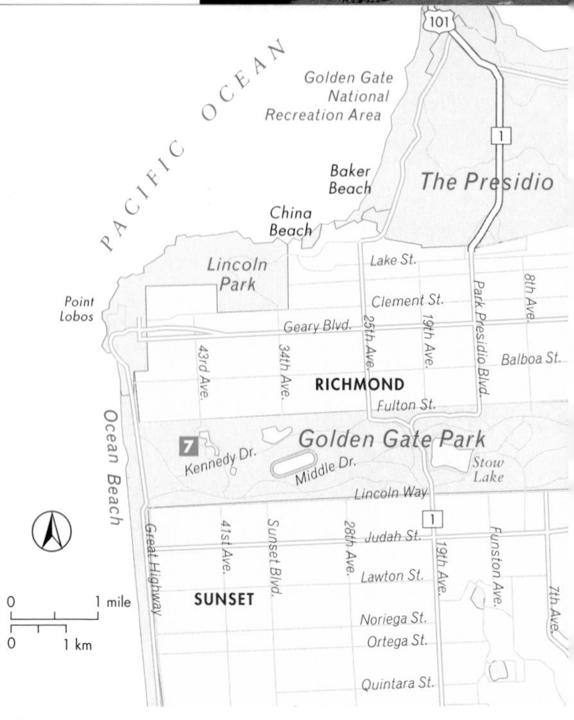

1 Union Square and Chinatown. Union Square has hotels, public transportation, and shopping; walking through Chinatown is like visiting another country.

2 SoMa and Civic Center. SoMa is anchored by SFMOMA and Yerba Buena Gardens; the city's performing arts venues are in Civic Center.

3 Nob Hill and Russian Hill. Nob Hill is old money San Francisco; Russian Hill's steep streets have excellent eateries and shopping.

4 North Beach. This small Italian neighborhood is a great place to enjoy an espresso.

5 On the Waterfront. Head here to visit the exquisitely restored Ferry Building, Fisherman's Wharf, Pier 39, and Ghirardelli Square.

6 The Marina and the Presidio. The Marina has trendy boutiques, restaurants, and cafés; the wooded Presidio offers great views of the Golden Gate Bridge.

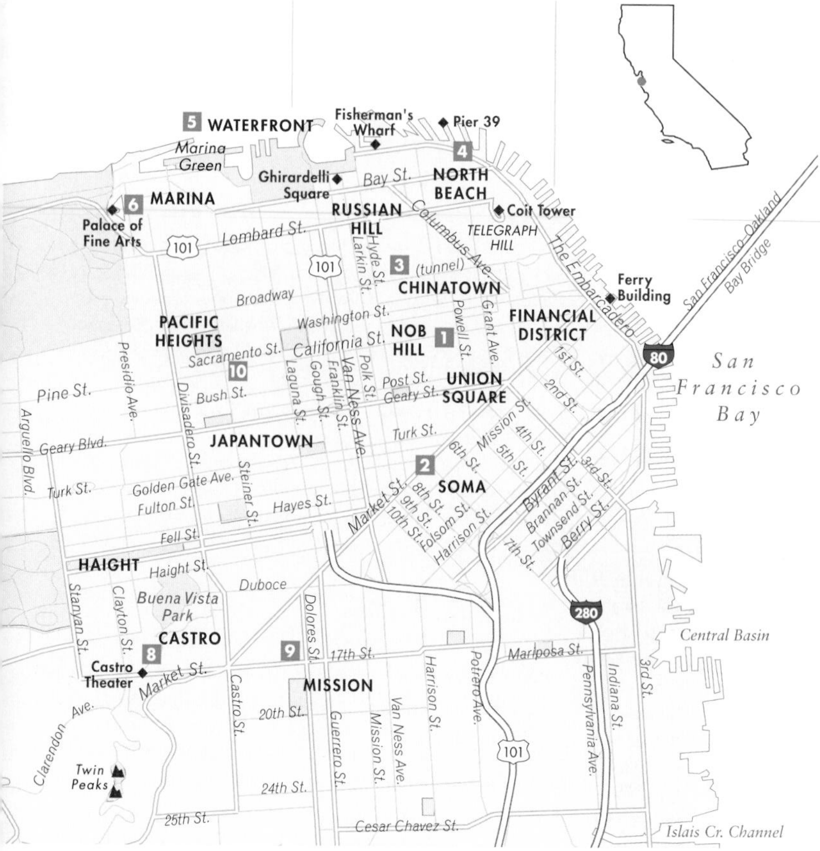

7 Golden Gate Park and the Western Shoreline. San Francisco's 1,000-acre backyard has sports fields, windmills, museums, and gardens; the windswept Western Shoreline stretches for miles.

8 The Haight, the Castro, and Noe Valley. After you've seen the blockbuster sights, come to these neighborhoods to see where the city's heart beats.

9 The Mission. This Latino neighborhood has destination restaurants, bargain ethnic eateries, and a hip bar scene.

10 Pacific Heights and Japantown. Pacific Heights has some of the city's most opulent real estate; Japantown is packed with authentic Japanese shops and restaurants.

GETTING ORIENTED

San Francisco is a compact city; just 46½ square mi. Essentially a tightly packed cluster of extremely diverse neighborhoods, the city dearly rewards walking. The areas that most visitors cover are easy (and safe) to reach on foot, but many have steep—make that *steep*—hills.

SAN FRANCISCO PLANNER

Wacky Weather

San Francisco's unique weather can be a blessing and a curse. On the positive side, there's hardly any rain between June and October, and there are warm days even in the rainy winter months. But although daytime temperatures rarely drop below 50°F, they seldom get *above* 70°F—and the famous fog often makes the "real feel" even colder.

At any time of year you may need to bundle up in a hat and wool coat in the morning, then strip down to a T-shirt and don your sunglasses in the afternoon. Layering is important. If you intend to be near the water or on a boat, bring a jacket and a hat—yes, even in summer! For biking, hiking, and boating, windbreakers are ideal.

Beaches can be extremely cold, and surfers and kite boarders wear full wet suits year-round.

About the Restaurants

San Francisco is a vital culinary crossroads, with nearly every ethnic cuisine represented. Although locals have long headed to the Mission District for Latin food, Chinatown for Asian food, and North Beach for Italian food, they also know that every part of the city offers dining experiences beyond the neighborhood tradition.

Some renowned restaurants are booked weeks or even months in advance. But you can get lucky at the last minute if you're flexible—and friendly. Most restaurants keep a few tables open for walk-ins and VIPs. Show up for dinner early (5:30 PM) or late (after 9 PM) and politely inquire about any last-minute vacancies or cancellations.

About the Hotels

San Francisco is one of the country's best hotel towns, offering a rich selection of properties that satisfy most tastes and budgets. Whether you're seeking a cozy inn, a kitschy motel, a chic boutique, or a grande-dame hotel, this city has got the perfect room for you.

San Francisco hotel prices, among the highest in the United States, may come as an unpleasant surprise. Weekend rates for double rooms in high season average about $132 a night citywide. Rates may vary according to room availability; always inquire about special rates and packages when making reservations; call the property directly, but also check its Web site and try Internet booking agencies.

WHAT IT COSTS

	¢	$	$$	$$$	$$$$
Restaurants	under $10	$10–$14	$15–$22	$23–$30	over $30
Hotels	under $90	$90–$149	$150–$199	$200–$250	over $250

Dining prices are per person for a typical main course. Note: if a restaurant offers only prix-fixe (set-price) meals, it has been given the price category that reflects the full prix-fixe price. Lodging prices are for two people in a standard double room in high season, excluding 14% tax.

4

Updated by Denise M. Leto, Fiona G. Parrott, Natasha Sarkisian, Sharon Silva, Sharron S. Wood, Sura Wood

"You could live in San Francisco a month and ask no greater entertainment than walking through it," wrote Inez Hayes Irwin, author of *The Californiacs*, an effusive 1921 homage to the Golden State and the City by the Bay. Follow in her footsteps, and you'll find that her claim still rings true today: simply wandering around this beautiful metropolis on foot is the best way to experience all of its diverse wonders.

Snuggling on a 46½-square-mi strip of land between San Francisco Bay and the Pacific Ocean, San Francisco is a relatively small city of about 750,000 residents. San Franciscans cherish their city for the same reasons visitors do: the proximity to the Bay and its pleasures, rows of Victorian homes clinging precariously to the hillsides, the sun setting behind the Golden Gate Bridge. But the city's attraction goes much deeper, from the diversity of its neighborhoods to the progressive free spirit here. Take all these things together, and you'll begin to understand why many San Franciscans can't imagine calling anyplace else home—despite the dizzying cost of living.

San Francisco's charms are great and small. You won't want to miss Golden Gate Park, the Palace of Fine Arts, The Golden Gate Bridge, or a cable-car ride over Nob Hill. But a walk down the Filbert Street Steps or through Macondray Lane or an hour gazing at murals in the Mission or the thundering Pacific from the cliffs of Lincoln Park can be equally inspiring.

PLANNING

GETTING HERE AND AROUND

AIR TRAVEL

The major gateway to San Francisco is San Francisco International Airport (SFO), 15 mi south of the city. It's off U.S. 101 near Millbrae and San Bruno. Oakland International Airport (OAK) is across the bay, not much farther away from downtown San Francisco (via I–80 east and I–880 south), but rush-hour traffic on the Bay Bridge may lengthen

Continued on page 150

HIGHWAY 1: SAN FRANCISCO TO FORT BRAGG

Mendocino Coast Botanical Garden

THE PLAN

Distance: 177 mi

Time: 2-4 days

Good Overnight Options: San Francisco, Olema, Bodega Bay, Gualala, Mendocino, Fort Bragg

For more information on the sights and attractions along this portion of Highway 1, please see chapters 4, 5, and 7.

SAN FRANCISCO

The official Highway 1 heads straight through **San Francisco** along 19th Avenue through **Golden Gate Park** and the **Presidio** toward the **Golden Gate Bridge.** For a more scenic tour, watch for signs announcing exits for 35 North/Skyline Boulevard, then Ocean Beach/The Great Highway (past Lake Merced). The Great Highway follows the coast along the western border of San Francisco; you'll cruise past entrances to the **San Francisco Zoo, Golden Gate Park,** and the **Cliff House.** Hike out to **Point Lobos** or **Land's End** for awesome vistas, then drive through **Lincoln Park** and the **Palace of the Legion of Honor** and follow El Camino de Mar/Lincoln Boulevard all the way to the Golden Gate Bridge.

Golden Gate Bridge

The best way to see San Francisco is on foot and public transportation. A **Union Square** stroll—complete with people-watching, window-shopping, and architecture-viewing—is a good first stop. In **Chinatown,** department stores give way to storefront temples, open-air markets, and delightful dim-sum shops. After lunch in one, catch a **Powell Street cable car** to the end of the line and get off to see the bay views and the antique arcade games at **Musée Mécanique** (the gem of otherwise mindless **Fisherman's Wharf**). For dinner and live music, try cosmopolitan **North Beach.**

SAN FRANCISCO TO OLEMA (approx. 37 mi)

Leaving the city the next day, your drive across the Golden Gate Bridge and a stop at a **Marin Headlands** overlook will yield memorable views (if fog hasn't socked in the bay). So will a hike in **Point Reyes National Seashore,** farther up Highway 1 (now called Shoreline Highway). On this wild swath of coast you'll likely be able to claim an unspoiled beach for yourself. You should expect company, however, around the lighthouse at the tip of Point Reyes because year-round views—and seasonal elephant seal- and whale-watching—draw crowds. If you have time, poke around tiny **Olema,** which has some excellent restaurants, and **Inverness,** home to the famous Manka's Inverness Lodge.

Point Reyes National Seashore

OLEMA TO MENDOCINO (approx. 131 mi)

Passing only a few minuscule towns, this next stretch of Highway 1 showcases the northern coast in all its rugged glory. The reconstructed compound of eerily foreign buildings at **Fort Ross State Historic Park** recalls the era of Russian fur trading in California. Pull into **Gualala** for an espresso, a sandwich, and a little human contact before rolling onward. After

Point Reyes National Seashore

TOP 5 PLACES TO LINGER

- San Francisco
- Marin Headlands
- Point Reyes National Seashore
- Fort Ross State Historic Park
- Mendocino

another 50 mi of tranquil state beaches and parks you'll return to civilization in **Mendocino.**

MENDOCINO TO FORT BRAGG (approx. 9 mi)

Exploring Mendocino you may feel like you've fallen through a rabbit hole: the weather screams Northern California, but the 19th-century buildings—erected by homesick Yankee loggers—definitely say New England. Once you've browsed around the artsy shops, continue on to the **Mendocino Coast Botanical Gardens;** then travel back in time on the **Skunk Train,** which follows an old logging route from **Fort Bragg** deep into the redwood forest.

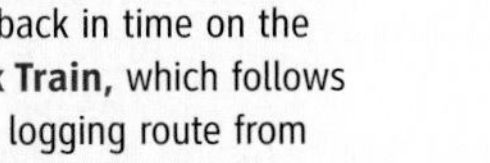

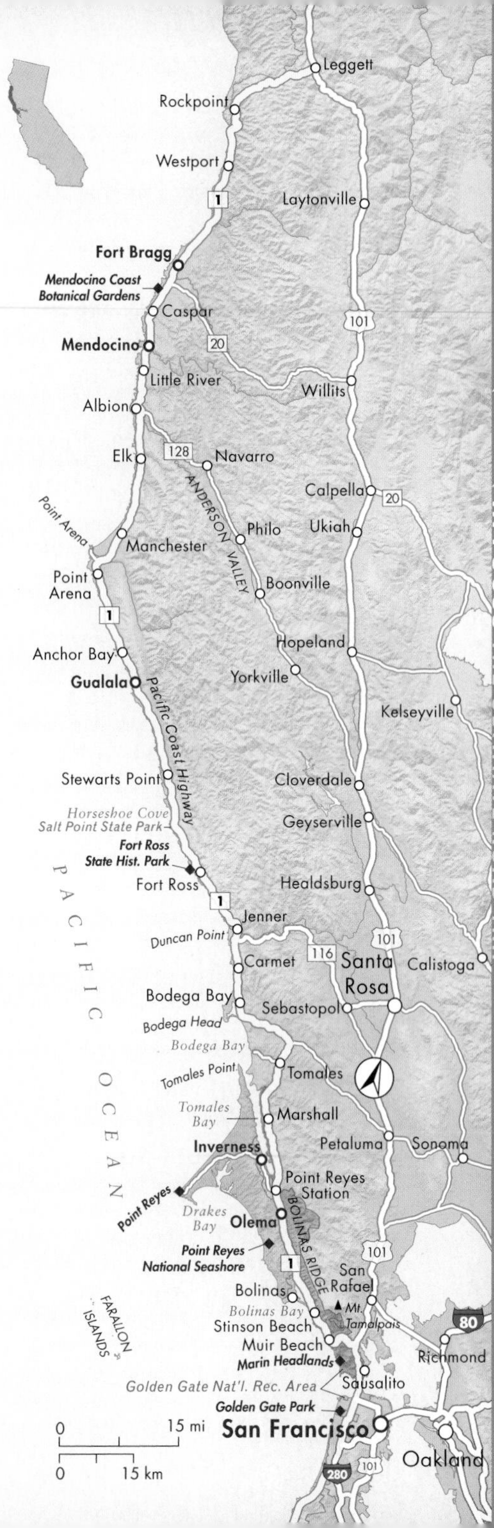

Leggett
Rockpoint
Westport
Laytonville
Fort Bragg
Mendocino Coast Botanical Gardens
Caspar
101
20
Mendocino
Little River
Willits
Albion
Elk
128
Navarro
Anderson Valley
Calpella
Point Arena
Philo
Ukiah
Manchester
Point Arena
Boonville
1
Hopeland
Anchor Bay
Gualala
Yorkville
Pacific Coast Highway
Kelseyville
Stewarts Point
Cloverdale
Horseshoe Cove
Salt Point State Park
Geyserville
Fort Ross State Hist. Park
Fort Ross
Healdsburg
Pacific Ocean
Jenner
Duncan Point
116
Carmet
Santa Rosa
Calistoga
Bodega Bay
Sebastopol
Bodega Head
Bodega Bay
Tomales Point
Tomales
Tomales Bay
Marshall
Petaluma
Sonoma
Inverness
Point Reyes Station
Point Reyes
Drakes Bay
Olema
Bolinas Ridge
Point Reyes National Seashore
San Rafael
Bolinas
Bolinas Bay
Mt. Tamalpais
Farallon Islands
Stinson Beach
80
Muir Beach
Richmond
Marin Headlands
Sausalito
Golden Gate Nat'l. Rec. Area
Golden Gate Park
San Francisco
Oakland
280
0 15 mi
0 15 km

travel times considerably. San Jose International Airport (SJC) is about 40 mi south of San Francisco; travel time depends largely on traffic flow, but plan on an hour and a half with moderate traffic.

Airports **San Francisco International Airport** (*SFO* ☎ *800/435–9736* 🌐 *www.flysfo.com*). **Oakland International Airport** (*OAK* ☎ *510/563–3300* 🌐 *www.flyoakland.com*). **San Jose International Airport** (*SJC* ☎ *408/277–4759* 🌐 *www.sjc.org*).

Airport Transfers **American Airporter** (☎ *415/202–0733* 🌐 *www.americanairporter.com*). **BayPorter Express** (☎ *415/467–1800* 🌐 *www.bayporter.com*). **Caltrain** (☎ *800/660–4287* 🌐 *www.caltrain.com*). **East Bay Express Airporter** (☎ *877/526–0304* 🌐 *www.eastbaytransportation.com*). **Lorrie's Airport Service** (☎ *415/334–9000* 🌐 *www.gosfovan.com*). **Marin Airporter** (☎ *415/461–4222* 🌐 *www.marinairporter.com*). **Marin Door to Door** (☎ *415/457–2717* 🌐 *www.marindoortodoor.com*). **SamTrans** (☎ *800/660–4287* 🌐 *www.samtrans.com*). **South & East Bay Airport Shuttle** (☎ *800/548–4664* 🌐 *www.southandeastbayairportshuttle.com*). **SuperShuttle** (☎ *415/558–8500 or 800/258–3826* 🌐 *www.supershuttle.com*). **VIP Airport Shuttle** (☎ *408/986–6000* or *800/235–8847* 🌐 *www.yourairportride.com*).

BART TRAVEL

Bay Area Rapid Transit (BART) trains, which run until midnight, travel under the bay via tunnel to connect San Francisco with Oakland, Berkeley, Pittsburgh/Bay Point, Richmond, Fremont, Dublin/Pleasanton, and other small cities and towns in between. Within San Francisco, stations are limited to downtown, the Mission, and a couple of outlying neighborhoods.

Trains travel frequently from early morning until evening on weekdays. After 8 PM weekdays and on weekends there's often a 20-minute wait between trains on the same line. Trains also travel south from San Francisco as far as Millbrae. BART trains connect downtown San Francisco to San Francisco International Airport; a ride is $5.35.

Intracity San Francisco fares are $1.50; intercity fares are $2.65 to $5.60. BART bases its ticket prices on miles traveled and does not offer price breaks by zone. A monthly ticket, called a Fast Pass, is available for $48 and can be used on BART and on all Muni lines (including cable cars) within city limits.

Contact **Bay Area Rapid Transit** (*BART* ☎ *415/989–2278 or 650/992–2278* 🌐 *www.bart.gov*).

BOAT AND FERRY TRAVEL

Several ferry lines run out of San Francisco. Blue & Gold Fleet operates a number of routes, including service to Sausalito ($11 one-way) and Tiburon ($11 one-way). Tickets are sold at Pier 41 (between Fisherman's Wharf and Pier 39), where the boats depart. There are also weekday Blue & Gold commuter ferries to Tiburon ($11) and Vallejo ($13) from the San Francisco Ferry Building. Alcatraz Cruises, owned by Hornblower Yachts, operates the ferries to Alcatraz Island ($26 including audio tour and National Park Service ranger-led programs) from Pier 33, about a half-mile east of Fisherman's Wharf ($3 shuttle buses serve several area hotels and other locations). Boats leave 10 times a day (14 times a day in summer) and the journey itself is 30 minutes. Allow roughly 3 hours for a round-trip jaunt. Golden Gate Ferry runs daily to and from Sausalito and Larkspur (each costs $7.45 one-way), leaving from Pier 1, behind the San Francisco Ferry Building. The Alameda/Oakland Ferry operates daily between Alameda's Main Street Ferry Building, Oakland's Jack London Square, and San Francisco's Pier 41 and the Ferry Building ($6.25 one-way); some ferries go only to Pier 41 or the Ferry Building, so ask when you board. Purchase tickets onboard.

Ferry Lines Alameda/Oakland Ferry (☎ *510/522-3300* ⊕ *www.eastbayferry.com*). **Alcatraz Cruises** (☎ *415/981-7625* ⊕ *www.alcatrazcruises.com*). **Blue & Gold Fleet** (☎ *415/705-5555 or 415/705-8200* ⊕ *www.blueandgoldfleet.com*). **Golden Gate Ferry** (☎ *415/923-2000* ⊕ *www.goldengateferry.org*).

Ferry Terminal San Francisco Ferry Building (✉ *1 Ferry Bldg., at foot of Market St. on Embarcadero*).

CABLE CAR TRAVEL

The fare (for one direction) is $5 (Muni Passport holders pay a $1 supplement). You can buy tickets onboard (exact change isn't necessary) or at the kiosks at the cable car turnarounds at Hyde and Beach streets and at Powell and Market streets.

The heavily traveled Powell–Mason and Powell–Hyde lines begin at Powell and Market streets near Union Square and terminate at Fisherman's Wharf; lines for these routes can be long, especially in summer. The California Street line runs east and west from Market and California streets to Van Ness Avenue; there is often no wait to board this route.

CAR TRAVEL

Driving in San Francisco can be a challenge because of the one-way streets, snarly traffic, and steep hills. The first two elements can be frustrating enough, but those hills are tough for unfamiliar drivers. **■ TIP→ Remember to curb your wheels when parking on hills—turn wheels away from the curb when facing uphill, toward the curb when facing downhill. You can get a ticket if you don't do this.**

MUNI TRAVEL

The San Francisco Municipal Railway, or Muni, operates light-rail vehicles, the historic F-line streetcars along Fisherman's Wharf and Market Street, trolley buses, and the world-famous cable cars. Light rail travels along Market Street to the Mission District and Noe Valley (J line), the Ingleside District (K line), and the Sunset District (L, M, and N lines); during peak hours (Mon.–Fri., 6 AM–9 AM and 3 PM–7 PM) the J line continues around the Embarcadero to the Caltrain station at 4th and King streets. The new T line light rail runs from the Castro, down Market Street, around the Embarcadero, and south past Hunters Point and Monster Park to Sunnydale Avenue and Bayshore Boulevard. Muni provides 24-hour service on select lines to all areas of the city.

On buses and streetcars the fare is $1.50. Exact change is required, and dollar bills are accepted in the fare boxes. For all Muni vehicles other than cable cars, 90-minute transfers are issued free upon request at the time the fare is paid. These are valid for two additional transfers in any direction. Cable cars cost $5 and include no transfers (⇨*see By Cable Car, above*).

One-day ($11), three-day ($18), and seven-day ($24) Passports valid on the entire Muni system can be purchased at several outlets, including the cable-car ticket booth at Powell and Market streets and the visitor information center downstairs in Hallidie Plaza. A monthly ticket, called a Fast Pass, is available for $45 and can be used on all Muni lines (including cable cars) and on BART within city limits. The San Francisco CityPass, a discount ticket booklet to several major city attractions, also covers all Muni travel for seven consecutive days.

The San Francisco Municipal Transit and Street Map ($3) is a useful guide to the extensive transportation system. You can buy the map at most bookstores and at the San Francisco Visitor Information Center, on the lower level of Hallidie Plaza at Powell and Market streets.

Outside the city, AC Transit serves the East Bay, and Golden Gate Transit serves Marin and Sonoma counties.

Bus Lines **AC Transit** (☎ *510/839–2882* 🌐 *www.actransit.org*). **Golden Gate Transit** (☎ *415/923–2000* 🌐 *www.goldengate.org*). **San Francisco Municipal Railway System** (*Muni* ☎ *415/673–6864* 🌐 *www.sfmuni.com*).

TAXI TRAVEL

Taxi service is notoriously bad in San Francisco, and hailing a cab can be frustratingly difficult in some parts of the city, especially on weekends. Popular nightspots such as the Mission, SoMa, North Beach, the Haight, and the Castro have a lot of cabs but a lot of people looking for taxis, too. Midweek, and during the day, you shouldn't have much of a problem—unless it's raining. In a pinch, hotel taxi stands are an option, as is calling for a pickup. But be forewarned: taxi companies frequently don't answer the phone in peak periods. The absolute worst time to find a taxi is Friday afternoon and evening; plan well ahead, and if you're going to the airport, make a reservation or book a shuttle instead. Most taxi companies take advance reservations for airport and out-of-town runs but not in-town transfers.

Taxis in San Francisco charge $2.50 for the first ⅙ mi (one of the highest base rates in the U.S.), 40¢ for each additional ⅕ mi, and 40¢ per minute in stalled traffic. There is no charge for additional passengers; there is no surcharge for luggage. For trips outside city limits, multiply the metered rate by 1.5.

Taxi Companies **City Wide Cab** (☎ *415/920–0700*). **DeSoto Cab** (☎ *415/970–1300*). **Luxor Cab** (☎ *415/282–4141*). **Veteran's Taxicab** (☎ *415/648–1313*). **Yellow Cab** (☎ *415/626–2345*).

Taxi Complaints **San Francisco Police Department Taxi Detail** (☎ *415/553–1447*).

TRAIN TRAVEL

Amtrak trains travel to the Bay Area from some cities in California and the United States. The *Coast Starlight* travels north from Los Angeles to Seattle, passing the Bay Area along the way, but contrary to its name, the train runs inland through the Central Valley for much of its route through Northern California; the most scenic stretch is in Southern California, between San Luis Obispo and Los Angeles. Amtrak also has several routes between San Jose, Oakland, and Sacramento. The *California Zephyr* travels from Chicago to the Bay Area and has spectacular alpine vistas as it crosses the Sierra Nevada mountains. San Francisco doesn't have an Amtrak train station but does have an Amtrak bus station, at the Ferry Building, which provides service to trains in Emeryville, just over the Bay Bridge. Shuttle buses also connect the Emeryville train station with downtown Oakland, the Caltrain station, and other points in downtown San Francisco.

Caltrain connects San Francisco to Palo Alto, San Jose, Santa Clara, and many smaller cities en route. In San Francisco, trains leave from the main depot, at 4th and Townsend streets, and a rail-side stop at 22nd and Pennsylvania streets. One-way fares are $2.25 to $11, depending on the number of zones through which you travel. Tickets are valid for four hours after purchase time. A ticket is $5.75 from San Francisco to Palo Alto, at least $7.50 to San Jose. You can also buy a day pass ($4.50–$22) for unlimited travel in a 24-hour period. Trips last 1 to 1¾ hours; it's worth waiting for an express train. On weekdays, trains depart three or four times per hour during the morning and evening, twice per hour during daytime non-commute hours, and as infrequently as once per hour in the evening. Weekend trains run once per hour. The system shuts down at midnight. There are no onboard ticket sales. You must buy tickets before boarding the train or risk paying a $250 fine for fare evasion.

Train Lines **Amtrak** (☎ *800/872–7245* 🌐 *www.amtrak.com*). **Caltrain** (☎ *800/660–4287* 🌐 *www.caltrain.com*).

Train Depot **San Francisco Caltrain station** (✉ *700 4th St., at King St.* ☎ *800/660–4287*).

VISITOR INFORMATION

The San Francisco Convention and Visitors Bureau can mail you brochures, maps, and festivals and events listings. Once you're in town, you can stop by their info center near Union Square. Information about the Wine Country, redwood groves, and northwestern California is available at the California Welcome Center on Pier 39.

Contacts **San Francisco Convention and Visitors Bureau** (✉ *201 3rd St., Suite 900, San Francisco* ☎ *415/391–2000, 415/392–0328 TDD* 🌐 *www.onlyinsanfrancisco.com*). **San Francisco Visitor Information Center** (✉ *Hallidie Plaza, lower level, 900 Market St., Union Sq.* ☎ *415/391–2000, 415/392–0328 TDD* 🌐 *www.onlyinsanfrancisco.com*).

EXPLORING SAN FRANCISCO

UNION SQUARE AND CHINATOWN

The Union Square area bristles with big-city bravado, while just a stone's throw away is a place that feels like a city unto itself, Chinatown. The two areas share a strong commercial streak, although manifested very

4

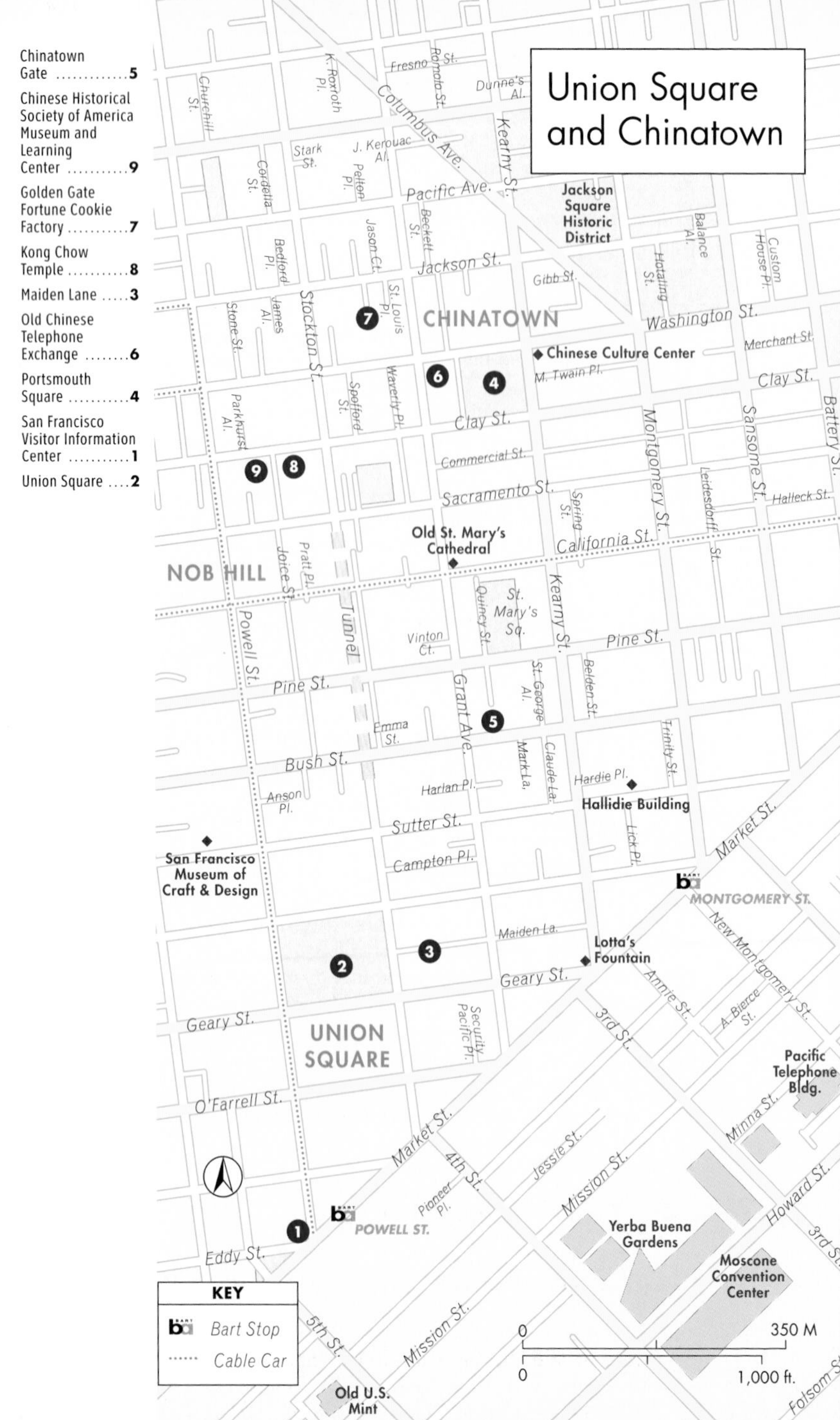

Union Square and Chinatown
Chinatown Gate 5
Chinese Historical Society of America Museum and Learning Center 9
Golden Gate Fortune Cookie Factory 7
Kong Chow Temple 8
Maiden Lane 3
Old Chinese Telephone Exchange 6
Portsmouth Square 4
San Francisco Visitor Information Center 1
Union Square 2
CHINATOWN
NOB HILL
UNION SQUARE
Jackson Square Historic District
Chinese Culture Center
Old St. Mary's Cathedral
St. Mary's Sq.
Hallidie Building
San Francisco Museum of Craft & Design
Lotta's Fountain
Pacific Telephone Bldg.
Yerba Buena Gardens
Moscone Convention Center
Old U.S. Mint
MONTGOMERY ST.
POWELL ST.
Tunnel
Columbus Ave.
Pacific Ave.
Jackson St.
Washington St.
Clay St.
Sacramento St.
California St.
Pine St.
Bush St.
Sutter St.
Geary St.
O'Farrell St.
Eddy St.
Market St.
Mission St.
Howard St.
Folsom St.
Stockton St.
Powell St.
Grant Ave.
Kearny St.
Montgomery St.
Sansome St.
Battery St.
KEY
Bart Stop
Cable Car
0 350 M
0 1,000 ft.

differently. In Union Square the crowds zigzag among international brands, trailing glossy shopping bags. A few blocks north people dash between small neighborhood stores, their arms draped with plastic totes filled with groceries or souvenirs.

CABLE CAR TERMINUS

Two of the three cable-car lines begin and end their runs at Powell and Market streets, a couple of blocks south of Union Square. These two lines are the most scenic, and both pass near Fisherman's Wharf, so they're usually clogged with first-time sightseers. The wait to board a cable car at this intersection is longer than at any other stop in the system. If you'd rather avoid the mob, board the less-touristy California line at the bottom of Market Street, at Drumm Street.

WHAT TO SEE IN UNION SQUARE

3 **Maiden Lane.** Known as Morton Street in the raffish Barbary Coast era, this former red-light district reported at least one murder a week during the late 19th century. Things cooled down after the 1906 fire destroyed the brothels, and these days Maiden Lane is a chic, boutique-lined pedestrian mall stretching two blocks, between Stockton and Kearny streets. Wrought-iron gates close the street to traffic most days between 11 and 5, when the lane becomes a patchwork of umbrella-shaded tables.

At **140 Maiden Lane** you can see the only Frank Lloyd Wright building in San Francisco. Walking through the brick archway and recessed entry feels a bit like entering a glowing cave. The interior's graceful, curving ramp and skylights are said to have been his model for the Guggenheim Museum in New York. Xanadu Tribal Arts, a gallery showcasing Baltic, Latin-American, and African folk art, now occupies the space. ⊠*Between Stockton and Kearny Sts., Union Square.*

1 **San Francisco Visitor Information Center.** A multilingual staff operates this facility below the cable car terminus. Staffers answer questions and provide maps and pamphlets. You can also pick up discount coupons—the savings can be significant, especially for families—and hotel brochures here. If you're planning to hit the big-ticket stops like the California Academy of Sciences, the Exploratorium, and SFMOMA, and ride the cable cars, consider picking up a CityPass here (or at any of the attractions it covers). ■ **TIP→The CityPass ($59, $44 ages 5–17), good for nine days including seven days of transit, will save you about 50%.** Also buy your Muni Passport here. ⊠*Hallidie Plaza, lower level, Powell and Market Sts., Union Square* ☎*415/391–2000 or 415/283–0177* 🌐*www.onlyinsanfrancisco.com* ⏲*Weekdays 9–5, Sat. 9–3; also Sun. 9–3 in May–Oct.*

2 **Union Square.** The heart of San Francisco's downtown since 1850, a 2½-acre square surrounded by department stores and the St. Francis Hotel, is about the only place you can sit for free in this part of town. The public responded to Union Square's 2002 redesign with a resounding shrug. With its pretty landscaping, easier street access, and the addition of a café (welcome, but nothing special), it's certainly an improvement over the old concrete wasteland, but no one's beating a

path downtown to hang out here. Four globular lamp sculptures by the artist R. M. Fischer preside over the space; there's also an open-air stage, a visitor information booth, and a front-row seat to the cable-car tracks. And there's a familiar kaleidoscope of characters: office workers sunning and brown-bagging, street musicians, shoppers taking a rest, kids chasing pigeons, and a fair number of homeless people.

The square takes its name from the violent pro-union demonstrations staged here before the Civil War. At center stage, Robert Ingersoll Aitken's *Victory Monument* commemorates Commodore George Dewey's victory over the Spanish fleet at Manila in 1898. The 97-foot Corinthian column, topped by a bronze figure symbolizing naval conquest, was dedicated by Theodore Roosevelt in 1903 and withstood the 1906 earthquake. After the earthquake and fire of 1906, the square was dubbed Little St. Francis because of the temporary shelter erected for residents of the St. Francis Hotel. Actor John Barrymore (grandfather of actress Drew Barrymore and a notorious carouser) was among the guests pressed into volunteering to stack bricks in the square. His uncle, thespian John Drew, remarked, "It took an act of God to get John out of bed and the United States Army to get him to work."

On the eastern edge of Union Square, **TIX Bay Area** (☎ *415/433–7827 info only* 🌐 *www.theatrebayarea.org*) provides half-price day-of-performance tickets to all types of performing-arts events, as well as regular full-price box-office services. Union Square covers a convenient four-level garage, allegedly the first underground garage in the world. ✉ *Bordered by Powell, Stockton, Post, and Geary Sts., Union Square.*

WHAT TO SEE IN CHINATOWN

5 **Chinatown Gate.** This is the official entrance to Chinatown. Stone lions flank the base of the pagoda-topped gate; the lions, dragons, and fish up top symbolize wealth, prosperity, and other good things. The four Chinese characters immediately beneath the pagoda represent the philosophy of Sun Yat-sen (1866–1925), the leader who unified China in the early 20th century. Sun Yat-sen, who lived in exile in San Francisco for a few years, promoted the notion of friendship and peace among all nations based on equality, justice, and goodwill. The vertical characters under the left pagoda read "peace" and "trust," the ones under the right pagoda "respect" and "love." The whole shebang usually telegraphs the internationally understood message of "photo op." ✉ *Grant Ave. at Bush St., Chinatown.*

9 **Chinese Historical Society of America Museum and Learning Center.** This airy, light-filled gallery has displays about the Chinese-American experience from 19th-century agriculture to 21st-century food and fashion trends, including a poignant collection of racist games and toys. A separate room hosts rotating exhibits by contemporary Chinese-American artists. ✉ *965 Clay St., Chinatown* ☎ *415/391–1188* 🌐 *www.chsa.org* 🎟 *$3, free 1st Thurs. of month* ⏲ *Tues.–Fri. noon–5, Sat. 11–4.*

7 **Golden Gate Fortune Cookie Factory.** Follow your nose down Ross Alley to this tiny but fragrant cookie factory. Workers sit at circular motorized griddles and wait for dollops of batter to drop onto a tiny metal plate, which rotates into an oven. A few moments later out comes a cookie

Chinatown bursts into color and light on Chinese New Year.

that's pliable and ready for folding. It's easy to peek in for a moment, and hard to leave without a few free samples. A bagful of cookies—with mildly racy "adult" fortunes or more-benign ones—costs about $3. You can also purchase the cookies "fortuneless" in their waferlike unfolded state, which makes snacking that much more efficient. Being allowed to photograph the cookie makers at work will set you back 50¢. ✉*56 Ross Alley, west of and parallel to Grant Ave., between Washington and Jackson Sts., Chinatown* ☎*415/781–3956* *Free* *Daily 9–8.*

8 **Kong Chow Temple.** This ornate temple sets a somber, spiritual tone right away with a sign warning visitors not to touch *anything*. The god to whom the members of this temple pray represents honesty and trust. Chinese stores and restaurants often display his image because he's thought to bring good luck in business. Chinese immigrants established the temple in 1851; its congregation moved to this building in 1977. Take the elevator up to the fourth floor, where incense fills the air. You can show respect by placing a dollar or two in the donation box and by leaving your camera in its case. Amid the statuary, flowers, and richly colored altars (red wards off evil spirits and signifies virility, green symbolizes longevity, and gold connotes majesty), a couple of plaques announce that MRS. HARRY S. TRUMAN CAME TO THIS TEMPLE IN JUNE 1948 FOR A PREDICTION ON THE OUTCOME OF THE ELECTION . . . THIS FORTUNE CAME TRUE. The temple's balcony has a good view of Chinatown. ✉*855 Stockton St., Chinatown* ☎*No phone* *Free* *Mon.–Sat. 9–4.*

6 **Old Chinese Telephone Exchange.** After the 1906 earthquake many Chinatown buildings were rebuilt in western style with pagoda roof and fancy balconies slapped on. This building—today the Bank of Canton—is

the exception, an example of top-to-bottom Chinese architecture. The intricate three-tier pagoda was built in 1909. The exchange's operators were renowned for their prodigious memories, about which the San Francisco Chamber of Commerce boasted in 1914: "These girls respond all day with hardly a mistake to calls that are given (in English or one of five Chinese dialects) by the name of the subscriber instead of by his number—a mental feat that would be practically impossible to most high-schooled American misses." ✉*Bank of Canton, 743 Washington St., Chinatown.*

4 **Portsmouth Square.** Chinatown's living room buzzes with activity. The square, with its pagoda-shaped structures, is a favorite spot for morning tai chi; by noon dozens of men huddle around Chinese chess tables, engaged in not-always-legal competition. Kids scamper about the square's two grungy playgrounds (warning: the bathrooms are sketchy). Back in the late 19th century this land was near the waterfront and Robert Louis Stevenson, the author of *Treasure Island,* often dropped by, chatting up the sailors who hung out here. Some of the information he gleaned about life at sea found its way into his fiction. A bronze galleon sculpture, a tribute to Stevenson, is anchored in a corner of the square. ✉*Bordered by Walter Lum Pl. and Kearny, Washington, and Clay Sts., Chinatown.*

SOMA AND CIVIC CENTER

To a newcomer, SoMa (short for "south of Market") and Civic Center may look like cheek-by-jowl neighbors—they're divided by Market Street. To locals, though, these areas are firmly separate entities, especially since Market Street itself is considered such a strong demarcation line. SoMa is less a neighborhood than it is a sprawling area of wide, traffic-heavy boulevards lined with office high-rises and pricey live-work lofts. Across Market Street from the western edge of SoMa is Civic Center, with San Francisco's eye-catching, gold-domed City Hall. Tickets to a show at one of the neighborhood's grand performance halls are the main reason to venture here.

WHAT TO SEE IN SOMA

4 **Cartoon Art Museum.** Krazy Kat, Zippy the Pinhead, Batman, and other colorful cartoon icons greet you at the Cartoon Art Museum, established with an endowment from cartoonist-icon Charles M. Schulz. The museum's strength is its changing exhibits, which explore such topics as America from the perspective of international political cartoons, and the output of women and African-American cartoonists. Serious fans of cartoons—especially those on the quirky underground side—will likely enjoy the exhibits; those with a casual interest may be disappointed. The museum store carries lots of cool books. ✉*655 Mission St., SoMa* ☎*415/227–8666* 🌐*www.cartoonart.org* 🎫*$6, pay what you wish 1st Tues. of month* 🕒*Tues.–Sun. 11–5.*

1 **Metreon.** Child's play meets the 21st century at this high-tech mall, adored by gearheads and teenage boys obsessed with tabletop games. At Kamikaze Pop, pick up anime and manga DVDs and cute gear, or head to Things From Another World for a huge selection of comic

Continued on page 165

CHINATOWN

Chinatown's streets flood the senses. Incense and cigarette smoke mingle with the scents of briny fish and sweet vanilla. Rooflines flare outward, pagoda-style. Loud Cantonese bargaining and honking car horns rise above the sharp clack of mah-jongg tiles and the eternally humming cables beneath the street.

Most Chinatown visitors march down Grant Avenue, buy a few trinkets, and call it a day. Do yourself a favor and dig deeper. This is one of the largest Chinese communities outside Asia, and there is far more to it than buying a back-scratcher near Chinatown Gate. To get a real feel for the neighborhood, wander off the main drag. Step into a temple or an herb shop and wander down a flag-draped alley. And don't be shy: residents welcome guests warmly, though rarely in English.

Whatever you do, don't leave without eating something. Noodle houses, bakeries, tea houses, and dim sum shops seem to occupy every other storefront. There's a feast for your eyes as well: in the market windows on Stockton and Grant, you'll see hanging whole roast ducks, fish, and shellfish swimming in tanks, and strips of shiny, pink-glazed Chinese-style barbecued pork. (For the scoop on dim sum, *see* the Union Square and Chinatown spotlight in the Where to Eat chapter.)

CHINATOWN'S HISTORY

Sam Brannan's 1848 cry of "Gold!" didn't take long to reach across the world to China. Struggling with famine, drought, and political upheaval at home, thousands of Chinese jumped at the chance to try their luck in California. Most came from the Pearl River Delta region, in the Guangdong province, and spoke Cantonese dialects. From the start, Chinese businesses circled around Portsmouth Square, which was conveniently central. Bachelor rooming houses sprang up, since the vast majority of new arrivals were men. By 1853, the area was called Chinatown.

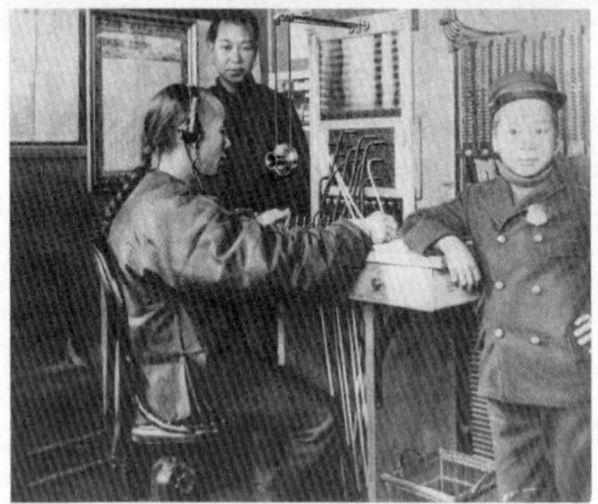

The Street of Gamblers (Ross Alley), 1898 (top). The first Chinese telephone operator in Chinatown (bottom).

COLD WELCOME

The Chinese faced discrimination from the get-go. Harrassment became outright hostility as first the gold rush, then the work on the Transcontinental Railroad petered out. Special taxes were imposed to shoulder aside competing "coolie labor." Laws forbidding the Chinese from moving outside Chinatown kept the residents packed in like sardines, with nowhere to go but up and down—thus the many basement establishments in the neighborhood. State and federal laws passed in the 1870s deterred Chinese women from immigrating, deeming them prostitutes. In the late 1870s, looting and arson attacks on Chinatown businesses soared.

The coup de grace, though, was the Chinese Exclusion Act, passed by the U.S.

Chinatown's Grant Avenue.

Women and children flooded into the neighborhood after the Great Quake.

Congress in 1882, which slammed the doors to America for "Asiatics." This was the country's first significant restriction on immigration. The law also prevented the existing Chinese residents, including American-born children, from becoming naturalized citizens. With a society of mostly men (forbidden, of course, from marrying white women), San Francisco hoped that Chinatown would simply die out.

OUT OF THE ASHES

When the devastating 1906 earthquake and fire hit, city fathers thought they'd seize the opportunity to kick the Chinese out of Chinatown and get their hands on that desirable piece of downtown real estate. Then Chinatown businessman Look Tin Eli had a brainstorm of Disneyesque proportions.

He proposed that Chinatown be rebuilt, but in a tourist-friendly, stylized, "Oriental" way. Anglo-American architects would design new buildings with pagoda roofs and dragon-covered columns. Chinatown would attract more tourists—the curious had been visiting on the sly for decades—and add more tax money to the city's coffers. Ka-ching: the sales pitch worked.

PAPER SONS

For the Chinese, the 1906 earthquake turned the virtual "no entry" sign into a flashing neon "welcome!" All the city's immigration records went up in smoke, and the Chinese quickly began to apply for passports as U.S. citizens, claiming their old ones were lost in the fire. Not only did thousands of Chinese become legal overnight, but so did their sons in China, or "sons," if they weren't really related. Whole families in Chinatown had passports in names that weren't their own; these "paper sons" were not only a windfall but also an uncomfortable neighborhood conspiracy. The city caught on eventually and set up an immigration center on Angel Island in 1910. Immigrants spent weeks or months being inspected and interrogated while their papers were checked. Roughly 250,000 people made it through. With this influx, including women and children, Chinatown finally became a more complete community.

A GREAT WALK THROUGH CHINATOWN

■ Start at the Chinatown Gate and walk ahead on Grant Avenue, entering the souvenir gauntlet. (You'll also pass Old St. Mary's Cathedral.)

■ Make a right on Clay Street and walk to Portsmouth Square. Sometimes it feels like the whole neighborhood's here, playing chess and exercising.

■ Head up Washington Street to the elaborately pagodaed Old Chinese Telephone Exchange building, now the Bank of Canton. Across Grant, look left for Waverly Place. Here Republic of China flags flap over some of the neighborhood's most striking buildings, including Tin How Temple.

■ At the Sacramento Street end of Waverly Place stands the oddly beautiful brick First Chinese Baptist Church of 1908. Just across the way, the Clarion Music Center is chock-full of unusual instruments, as well as exquisite lion-dance sets.

■ Head back to Washington Street and check out the herb shops, like the Superior Trading Company (No. 839) and the Great China Herb Co. (No. 857).

■ Follow the scent of vanilla from Washington Street down Ross Alley (entrance across from Superior Trading Company) to the Golden Gate Fortune Cookie Factory. Then head across the alley to Sam Bo Trading Co., where religious items are stacked chockablock in the narrow space. Tell the friendly owners your troubles and they'll prepare a package of joss papers, joss sticks, and candles, and tell you how and when to offer them up.

■ Turn left on Jackson Street; ahead is the real Chinatown's main artery, Stockton Street. This is where most residents do their grocery shopping; if it's Saturday, get ready for throngs (and their elbows). Look toward the back of stores for Buddhist altars with offerings of oranges and grapefruit. From here you can loop one block east back to Grant.

ALL THE TEA IN CHINATOWN

Preparing a perfect brew at Red Blossom Tea.

San Francisco's close ties to Asia have always made it more tea-conscious than other American burgs, but these days the city is in the throes of a tea renaissance, with new tasting rooms popping up in every neighborhood. Below are our favorite Chinatown spots for every tea under the sun.

Red Blossom Tea. A light and modern shop—the staff really know their stuff. It's a favorite among younger tea enthusiasts, who swear by its excellent bang-for-the-buck value. While Red Blossom doesn't do formal tastings or sell tea by the cup, they'll gladly brew up perfect samples of the teas you're interested in. ✉ *831 Grant Ave.* ☎ *415/395–0868*

Vital Tea Leaf. Tastings here work like those for wine—one of the gregarious, knowledgeable servers chooses the teas and describes them as you sample. It's a great spot for tea newbies to get their feet wet without a hard sell, but local connoisseurs grumble about the high prices and the self-promotion. ✉ *1044 Grant Ave.* ☎ *415/981–2388.*

Imperial Tea Court. If you want to visit the most respected of traditional tea purveyors, you'll need to venture outside of Chinatown. Imperial Tea Court's serene Powell Street oasis closed unexpectedly in 2007, but you'll find the same great selection and expertise at their fancy new digs in the Ferry Building. ☎ *415/544–9830.*

WAITING FOR CUSTARD

As you're strolling down Grant Avenue, past the plastic Buddhas and yin/yang balls, be sure to stop at the **Golden Gate Bakery** (No. 1029) for some delicious eggy *dan tat* (custard tarts). These flaky-crusted treats are heaven for just a buck. There's often a line, but it's worth the wait.

DON'T-MISS SHOPS

Locals snap up flowers from an outdoor vendor.

If you're in the market for a pair of chirping metal crickets (oh you'll hear them, trust us), you can duck into any of the obvious souvenir-stuffed storefronts. But if you're looking for something special, head for these tempting sources. **■ TIP→ Fierce neighborhood competition keeps prices within reason, but for popular wares like jade, it pays to shop around before making a serious investment. Many stores accept cash only.**

Chinatown Kite Shop. Family-run shop selling bright, fun-shaped kites —dragons, butterflies, sharks—since the 1960s. ✉ *717 Grant Ave.* ☎ *415/989–5182.*

Dragon House. A veritable museum: the store sells authentic, centuries-old antiques like ivory carvings. ✉ *455 Grant Ave.* ☎ *415/421–3693.*

Jade Galore. Not the cheapest place to pick up jade figures and jewelry, but locals trust its quality and adore its wide selection of Chinese bling. ✉ *1000 Stockton St.* ☎ *415/982–4863.*

Old Shanghai. One of the largest selections of hand-painted robes, formal dresses, and jackets in Chinatown, plus chic Asian-inspired pieces. ✉ *645 Grant Ave.* ☎ *415/986–1222.*

CHINATOWN WITH KIDS

It can be tough for the little ones to keep their hands to themselves, especially when all sorts of curios spill out onto the sidewalk at just the right height. To burn off some steam (in them) and relieve some stress (in you), take them to the small but spruce playground directly behind Old St. Mary's at Grant Avenue and California Street. If that setting's too tranquil, head to the more boisterous Willie Wong Playground, on Sacramento Street at Waverly Place.

books, graphic novels, and related novelties. Or play at Tilt, a high-tech interactive arcade. A 15-screen multiplex and IMAX theater, retail shops—including local specialty publisher Chronicle Books—and outposts of some of the city's favorite restaurants—including a new Tavern on the Green—are all part of the complex. It's a good place to pick up lunch for a picnic in the Yerba Buena Gardens, right outside; if you forgot your blanket, head to the patio tables outside Metreon's second floor. ✉ *101 4th St., between Mission and Howard Sts., SoMa* ☎ *800/638–7366* 🌐 *www.metreon.com* ⏲ *Sun.–Thur. 10–9, Fri.–Sat. 10–10.*

LOOK UP!

When wandering around Chinatown, don't forget to look up! Above the chintziest souvenir shop might loom an ornate balcony or a curly pagoda roof. The best examples are on the 900 block of Grant Avenue (at Washington St.) and at Waverly Place.

4

5 **San Francisco Museum of Modern Art** *(SFMOMA)*. With its brick facade
Fodor's Choice ★ and a striped central tower lopped at a lipstick-like angle, architect Mario Botta's SFMOMA building fairly screams "modern-art museum." Indeed it is. The stripes continue inside, from the black marble and gray granite of the floors right up the imposing staircase to the wooden slats on the ceiling.

■ **TIP→ Taking in all of SFMOMA's four exhibit floors can be overwhelming, so having a plan is helpful. Keep in mind that the museum's heavy hitters are on floors 2 and 3.** Floor 2 gets the big-name traveling exhibits and collection highlights such as Matisse's *Woman with the Hat,* Diego Rivera's *The Flower Carrier,* and Georgia O'Keeffe's *Black Place 1.* Photography buffs should hustle up to floor 3, with its works by Ansel Adams and Alfred Stieglitz. The large-scale contemporary exhibits on floors 4 and 5 can usually be seen quickly (or skipped). If it's on display, don't miss sculptor Jeff Koons' memorably creepy, life-size gilded porcelain *Michael Jackson and Bubbles,* on the fifth floor at the end of the Turret Bridge, a vertiginous catwalk dangling under the central tower. The window at the bridge's other end offers a great view over the Yerba Buena Gardens below.

Seating in the museum can be scarce, so luckily Caffè Museo, accessible from the street, provides a refuge for quite good, reasonably priced drinks and light meals. It's easy to drop a fortune at the museum's large store, chockablock with fun gadgets, artsy doodads of all kinds, very modern furniture, and possibly the best selection of kids' books in town. ■ **TIP→ No ticket is required to visit the lobby, so if it's the architecture you're interested in, save yourself the admission and have a gander for free.** ✉ *151 3rd St., SoMa* ☎ *415/357–4000* 🌐 *www.sfmoma.org* 🎟 *$12.50, free 1st Tues. of month, ½ price Thurs. 6–9* ⏲ *Labor Day–Memorial Day, Fri.–Tues. 11–5:45, Thurs. 11–8:45; Memorial Day–Labor Day, Fri.–Tues. 10–5:45, Thurs. 10–8:45.*

3 **Yerba Buena Center for the Arts.** If MOMA's for your parents, the Center is for you. You never know what's going to be on at this facility in the Yerba Buena Gardens, but whether it's an exhibit of Mexican street

graphics (graffiti to laypeople), innovative modern dance, or baffling video installations, it's likely to be memorable. The productions here tend to draw a young, energetic crowd and lean hard toward the cutting edge. ✉ *701 Mission St., SoMa* ☎ *415/978–2787* 🌐 *www.ybca.org* 🎫 *Galleries $7, free 1st Tues. of month* ⏲ *Galleries and box office Tues., Wed., and Fri.–Sun. noon–5, Thurs. noon–8.*

2 ★ **Yerba Buena Gardens.** There's not much south of Market that encourages lingering outdoors, or indeed walking at all, with this notable exception. These two blocks encompass the **Center for the Arts, Metreon, Moscone Convention Center,** and the convention center's rooftop **Zeum,** but the gardens themselves are the everyday draw. Office workers escape to the green swath of the East Garden. The memorial to Martin Luther King Jr. is the focal point here. Powerful streams of water surge over large, jagged stone columns, mirroring the enduring force of King's words that are carved on the stone walls and on glass blocks behind the waterfall. Moscone North is behind the memorial, and an overhead walkway leads to Moscone South and its rooftop attractions. ■ TIP→ The gardens are liveliest during the week and especially during the **Yerba Buena Gardens Festival** (May–October, www.ybgf.org), when free performances run from Latin music to Balinese dance.

Atop the Moscone Convention Center perch a few lures for kids. The historic **Looff carousel** ($3 for two rides) twirls daily 11 to 6. South of the carousel is **Zeum** (☎ *415/820–3320* 🌐 *www.zeum.org*), a high-tech, interactive arts-and-technology center (adults, $10; kids 3–18, $8) geared to children ages eight and over. Kids can make Claymation videos, work in a computer lab, and view exhibits and performances. Zeum is open 1 to 5 Wednesday through Friday and 11 to 5 weekends during the school year and Tuesday through Sunday 11 to 5 when school's out. Also part of the rooftop complex are gardens, an ice-skating rink, and a bowling alley. ✉ *Bordered by 3rd, 4th, Mission, and Folsom Sts., SoMa* ☎ *No phone* 🌐 *www.yerbabuena.org* 🎫 *Free* ⏲ *Daily sunrise–10* PM.

WHAT TO SEE IN CIVIC CENTER

7 ★ **Asian Art Museum.** Expecting a building full of Buddhas and jade? Well, yeah, you can find plenty of that here. Happily, though, you don't have to be a connoisseur of Asian art to appreciate a visit to this splendidly renovated museum, whose monumental exterior conceals a light, open, and welcoming space. The fraction of the museum's items on display (about 2,500 pieces from a 15,000-plus-piece collection) is laid out thematically and by region, making it easy to follow developments.

Begin on the third floor, where highlights of Buddhist art in Southeast Asia and early China include a large, jewel-encrusted, exquisitely painted 19th-century Burmese Buddha and clothed rod puppets from Java. On the second floor you can find later Chinese works, as well as pieces from Korea and Japan. Look for a cobalt tiger jauntily smoking a pipe on a whimsical Korean jar and delicate Japanese tea implements. The ground floor displays rotating exhibits, including contemporary and traveling shows. ■ TIP→ If you'd like to attend one of the occasional tea ceremonies and tastings at the Japanese Teahouse, call ahead, since

Light streams in through the skylight atop the bold striped cylinder of the San Francisco Museum of Modern Art (SFMOMA)

preregistration is required. ✉ *200 Larkin St., between McAllister and Fulton Sts., Civic Center* ☎ *415/581–3500* 🌐 *www.asianart.org* 🎟 *$12, free 1st Sun. of month; $5 Thurs. 5–9; tea ceremony $20, includes museum* ⏲ *Tues., Wed., and Fri.–Sun. 10–5, Thurs. 10–9.*

6 **City Hall.** This imposing 1915 structure with its massive gold-leaf dome—higher than the U.S. Capitol's—is about as close to a palace as you're going to get in San Francisco. (The metal detectors take something away from the grandeur, though.) The classic granite-and-marble behemoth was modeled after St. Peter's Cathedral in Rome. Architect Arthur Brown Jr., who also designed Coit Tower and the War Memorial Opera House, designed an interior with grand columns and a sweeping central staircase. San Franciscans were thrilled, and probably a bit surprised, when his firm built City Hall in just a few years. The building it replaced, dubbed "the new City Hall ruin," had lined the pockets of corrupt builders and politicians during its 27 years of construction. That 1899 structure collapsed in about 27 seconds in the 1906 earthquake, revealing trash and newspapers mixed into the building materials.

City Hall was spruced up and seismically retrofitted in the late 1990s, but the sense of history remains palpable. Some noteworthy events that have taken place here include the marriage of Marilyn Monroe and Joe DiMaggio (1954); the hosing—down the central staircase—of civil-rights and freedom-of-speech

WORD OF MOUTH

"City Hall is one of the most beautiful public buildings I have ever seen. Open to the public, and the free tour is worth an hour of your time." –QC

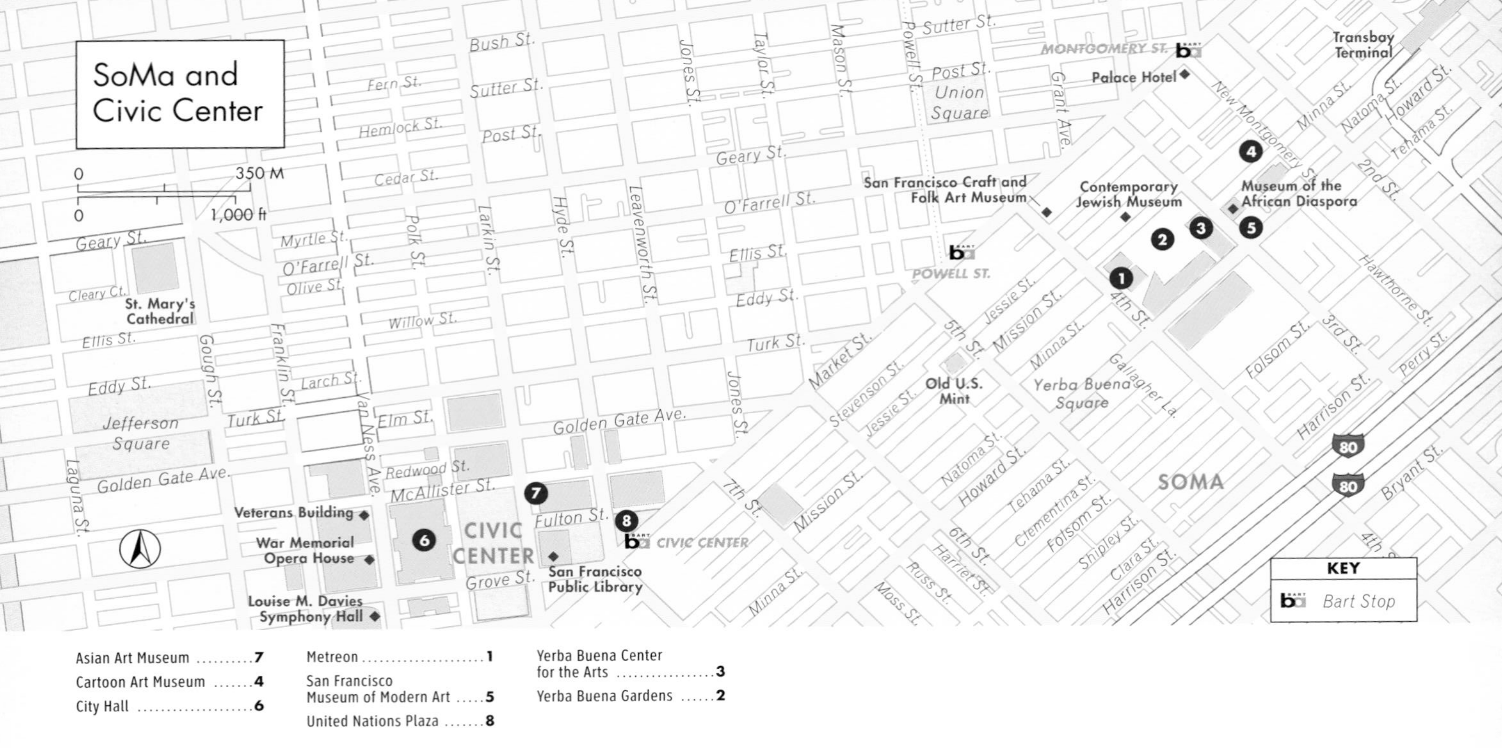
SoMa and
Civic Center
0 350 M
0 1,000 ft
KEY
Bart Stop
Bush St.
Sutter St.
Post St.
Geary St.
O'Farrell St.
Ellis St.
Eddy St.
Turk St.
Golden Gate Ave.
McAllister St.
Fulton St.
Grove St.
Fern St.
Hemlock St.
Cedar St.
Myrtle St.
Olive St.
Willow St.
Larch St.
Elm St.
Redwood St.
Cleary Ct.
Laguna St.
Gough St.
Franklin St.
Van Ness Ave.
Polk St.
Larkin St.
Hyde St.
Leavenworth St.
Jones St.
Taylor St.
Mason St.
Powell St.
Grant Ave.
Market St.
Stevenson St.
Jessie St.
Mission St.
Minna St.
Natoma St.
Howard St.
Tehama St.
Clementina St.
Folsom St.
Shipley St.
Clara St.
Harrison St.
Bryant St.
Perry St.
Hawthorne St.
New Montgomery St.
Gallagher La.
Russ St.
Moss St.
Harriet St.
2nd St.
3rd St.
4th St.
5th St.
6th St.
7th St.
80
St. Mary's Cathedral
Jefferson Square
Veterans Building
War Memorial Opera House
Louise M. Davies Symphony Hall
CIVIC CENTER
San Francisco Public Library
Union Square
MONTGOMERY ST.
Palace Hotel
Transbay Terminal
San Francisco Craft and Folk Art Museum
Contemporary Jewish Museum
Museum of the African Diaspora
POWELL ST.
Old U.S. Mint
Yerba Buena Square
SOMA
Asian Art Museum 7
Cartoon Art Museum 4
City Hall 6
Metreon 1
San Francisco Museum of Modern Art 5
United Nations Plaza 8
Yerba Buena Center for the Arts 3
Yerba Buena Gardens 2

protesters (1960); the murders of Mayor George Moscone and openly gay supervisor Harvey Milk (1978); the torching of the lobby by angry members of the gay community in response to the light sentence given to the former supervisor who killed both men (1979); and the registrations of scores of gay couples in celebration of the passage of San Francisco's Domestic Partners Act (1991). February 2004 has come to be known as the Winter of Love: thousands of gay and lesbian couples responded to Mayor Gavin Newsom's decision to issue marriage licenses to same-sex partners, turning City Hall into the site of raucous celebration and joyful nuptials for a month before the state Supreme Court ordered the practice stopped. That celebratory scene replayed during 2008, when scores of couples were wed between the court's June ruling that everyone enjoys the civil right to marry and the November passage of California's ballot proposition banning same-sex marriage. (Stay tuned . . .) Free tours are offered weekdays at 10, noon, and 2.

HAYES VALLEY

Hayes Valley, right next door to the Civic Center, is an offbeat neighborhood with terrific eateries, cool watering holes, and great browsing in its funky clothing and home decor boutiques. Swing down main drag Hayes Street, between Franklin and Laguna, and you can hit the highlights, including two very popular restaurants, Absinthe and Suppenküche. Comfy Place Pigalle (at Hayes and Octavia streets) is also a favorite for its living-room atmosphere, wines, and microbrews. Locals love this quarter, but without any big-name draws it remains off the radar for most visitors.

The South Light Court houses a modest, rotating display from the collection of the **Museum of the City of San Francisco** (*www.sfmuseum.org*), including historical items, maps, and photographs. That enormous, 700-pound iron head once crowned the *Goddess of Progress* statue, which topped the old City Hall building when it crumbled during the 1906 earthquake. Unlike the building, the statue survived the earthquake in one piece, but the subsequent removal proved too much for it.

Across Polk Street is **Civic Center Plaza,** with lawns, walkways, seasonal flower beds, a playground, and an underground parking garage. This sprawling space is generally clean but somewhat grim. A large part of the city's homeless population hangs out here, despite frequently being shunted away, so the plaza can feel dodgy. *Bordered by Van Ness Ave. and Polk, Grove, and McAllister Sts., Civic Center 415/554–6023 www.sfgov.org/site/cityhall Free Weekdays 8–8.*

8 **United Nations Plaza.** Locals know this plaza for two things: its Wednesday and Sunday farmers' market—cheap and earthy to the Ferry Building's pricey and beautiful—and its homeless population, which seems to return no matter how many times the city tries to shunt them aside. Brick pillars listing various nations and the dates of their admittance into the United Nations line the plaza, and its floor is inscribed with the goals and philosophy of the United Nations charter, which was signed at the War Memorial Opera House in 1945. *Fulton St. between Hyde and Market Sts., Civic Center.*

NOB HILL AND RUSSIAN HILL

In place of the quirky charm and cultural diversity that mark other San Francisco neighborhoods, Nob Hill exudes history and good breeding. Topped with some of the city's most elegant hotels, Gothic Grace Cathedral, and private blue-blood clubs, it's the pinnacle of privilege. One hill over, across Pacific Avenue, is another old-family bastion, Russian Hill. It may not be quite as wealthy as Nob Hill, but it's no slouch—and it's known for its jaw-dropping views.

Nob Hill was officially dubbed during the 1870s when "the Big Four"—Charles Crocker, Leland Stanford, Mark Hopkins, and Collis Huntington, who were involved in the construction of the transcontinental railroad—built their hilltop estates. The lingo is thick from this era: those on the hilltop were referred to as "nabobs" (originally meaning a provincial governor from India) and "swells," and the hill itself was called Snob Hill, a term that survives to this day. By 1882 so many estates had sprung up on Nob Hill that Robert Louis Stevenson called it "the hill of palaces." But the 1906 earthquake and fire destroyed all the palatial mansions, except for portions of the Flood brownstone. History buffs may choose to linger here, but for most visitors a casual glimpse from a cable car will be enough.

Essentially a tony residential neighborhood of spiffy pieds-à-terre, Victorian flats, Edwardian cottages, and boxlike condos, Russian Hill also has some of the city's loveliest stairway walks, hidden garden ways, and steepest streets—brave drivers can really have some fun here—not to mention those bay views. Several stories explain the origin of Russian Hill's name. One legend has it that Russian farmers raised vegetables here for Farallon Islands seal hunters; another attributes the name to a Russian sailor of prodigious drinking habits who drowned when he fell into a well on the hill. A plaque at the top of the Vallejo Steps gives credence to the version that says sailors of the Russian-American company were buried here in the 1840s. Be sure to visit the sign for yourself—its location offers perhaps the finest vantage point on the hill.

WHAT TO SEE IN NOB HILL

❷ **Grace Cathedral.** Not many churches can boast a Keith Haring sculpture and not one but two labyrinths. The seat of the Episcopal Church in San Francisco, this soaring Gothic-style structure, erected on the site of Charles Crocker's mansion, took 53 years to build, wrapping up in 1964. The gilded bronze doors at the east entrance were taken from casts of Lorenzo Ghiberti's incredible Gates of Paradise, which are on the baptistery in Florence, Italy. A black-and-bronze stone sculpture of St. Francis by Beniamino Bufano greets you as you enter.

The 35-foot-wide labyrinth, a large, purplish rug, is a replica of the 13th-century stone maze on the floor of Chartres cathedral. All are encouraged to walk the ¼-mi-long labyrinth, a ritual based on the tradition of meditative walking. There's also a terrazzo outdoor labyrinth on the church's north side. The AIDS Interfaith Chapel, to the right as you enter Grace, contains a metal tryptich sculpture by the late artist Keith Haring and panels from the AIDS Memorial Quilt. ■ **TIP→ Especially dramatic times to view the cathedral are during Thursday-night evensong**

Grace Cathedral 2
Ina Coolbrith Park 3
Lombard Street 5
Macondray Lane 4
Pacific Union Club 1
San Francisco Art Institute 6

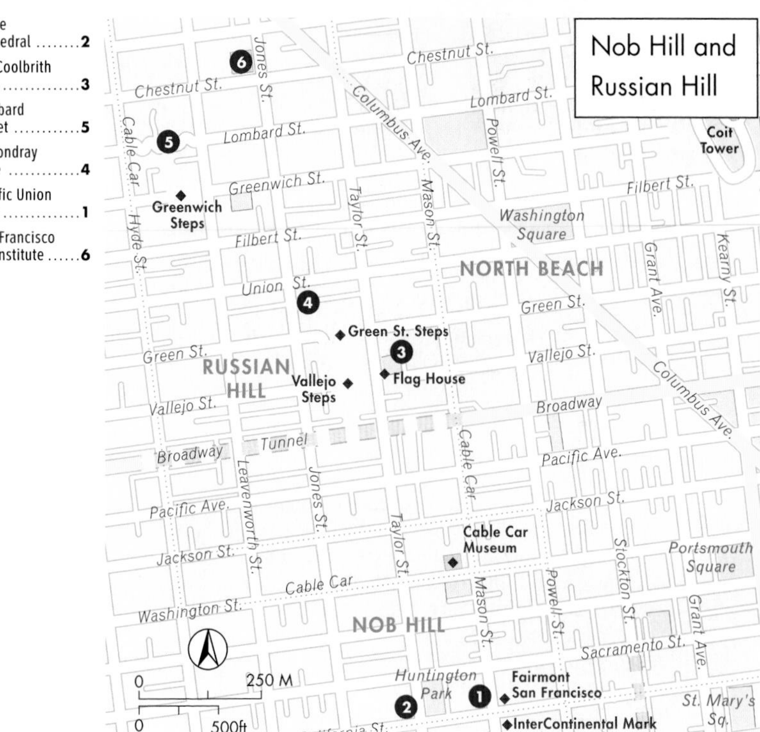

(5:15) and during special holiday programs. ✉ *1100 California St., at Taylor St., Nob Hill* ☎ *415/749–6300* 🌐 *www.gracecathedral.org* ⏲ *Weekdays 7–6, Sat. 8–6, Sun. 7–7.*

❶ **Pacific Union Club.** The former home of silver baron James Flood cost a whopping $1.5 million in 1886, when even a stylish Victorian like the Haas-Lilienthal House cost less than $20,000. All that cash did buy some structural stability. The Flood residence (to be precise, its shell) was the only Nob Hill mansion to survive the 1906 earthquake and fire. The Pacific Union Club, a bastion of the wealthy and powerful, purchased the house in 1907 and commissioned Willis Polk to redesign it; the architect added the semicircular wings and third floor. (The ornate fence design dates from the mansion's construction.) West of the house, Huntington Park is the site of the Huntington mansion, destroyed in 1906. Mrs. Huntington donated the land to the city for use as a park; the Crockers purchased the Fountain of the Tortoises, based on the original in Rome. ■ **TIP→ The benches around the fountain offer a welcome break after climbing Nob Hill.**

It's hard to get the skinny on the club itself; its 700 or so members allegedly follow the directive "no women, no Democrats, no reporters." Those who join usually spend decades on the waiting list and undergo a stringent vetting process, the rigors of which might embarrass the

NSA. Needless to say, the club is closed to the public. ✉ *1000 California St., Nob Hill.*

WHAT TO SEE IN RUSSIAN HILL

3 ★ **Ina Coolbrith Park.** If you make it all the way up here, you may have the place all to yourself, or at least feel like you do. The park's terraces are carved from a hill so steep that it's difficult to see if anyone else is there or not. Locals love this park because it feels like a secret no one else knows about—one of the city's magic hidden gardens, with a meditative setting and spectacular views of the bay peeking out from among the trees. A poet, Oakland librarian, and niece of Mormon prophet Joseph Smith, Ina Coolbrith (1842–1928) introduced Jack London and Isadora Duncan to the world of books. For years she entertained literary greats in her Macondray Lane home near the park. In 1915 she was named poet laureate of California. ✉ *Vallejo St. between Mason and Taylor Sts., Russian Hill.*

5 **Lombard Street.** The block-long "Crookedest Street in the World" makes eight switchbacks down the east face of Russian Hill between Hyde and Leavenworth streets. Residents bemoan the traffic jam outside their front doors, and occasionally the city attempts to discourage drivers by posting a traffic cop near the top of the hill, but the determined can find a way around. If no one is standing guard, join the line of cars waiting to drive down the steep hill, or avoid the whole mess and walk down the steps on either side of Lombard. You take in super views of North Beach and Coit Tower whether you walk or drive—though if you're the one behind the wheel, you'd better keep your eye on the road lest you become yet another of the many folks who ram the garden barriers. **■ TIP→ Can't stand the throngs? Thrill seekers of a different stripe may want to head two blocks south of Lombard to Filbert Street. At a gradient of 31.5%, the hair-raising descent between Hyde and Leavenworth streets is the city's steepest. Go slowly!** ✉ *Lombard St. between Hyde and Leavenworth Sts., Russian Hill.*

4 Fodor's Choice ★ **Macondray Lane.** San Francisco has no shortage of impressive, grand homes, but it's the tiny fairy-tale lanes that make most folks want to move here, and Macondray Lane is the quintessential hidden garden. Enter under a lovely wooden trellis and proceed down a quiet, cobbled pedestrian lane lined with Edwardian cottages and flowering plants and trees. **■ TIP→ Watch your step—the cobblestones are quite uneven in spots.** A flight of steep wooden stairs at the end of the lane leads to Taylor Street—on the way down you can't miss the bay views. If you've read any of Armistead Maupin's *Tales of the City* books, you may find the lane vaguely familiar. It's the thinly disguised setting for part of the series' action. ✉ *Between Jones and Taylor Sts., and Union and Green Sts., Russian Hill.*

6 ★ **San Francisco Art Institute.** A Moorish-tile fountain in a tree-shaded courtyard draws the eye as soon as you enter the institute. The number-one reason for a visit is Mexican master Diego Rivera's *Making of a Fresco Showing the Building of a City* (1931), in the student gallery to your immediate left inside the entrance. Rivera himself is in the fresco—his broad behind is to the viewer—and he's surrounded by his assistants.

Continued on page 177

CABLE CARS

The moment it dawns on you that you severely underestimated the steepness of the San Francisco hills will likely be the same moment you look down and realize those tracks aren't just for show—or just for tourists.

Sure, locals rarely use the cable cars for commuting these days. (That's partially due to the recent fare hikes—hear that, Muni?) So you'll likely be packed in with plenty of fellow sightseers. You may even be approaching cable-car fatigue after seeing its image on so many souvenirs. But if you fear the magic is gone, simply climb on board, and those jaded thoughts will dissolve. Grab the pole and gawk at the view as the car clanks down an insanely steep grade toward the bay. Listen to the humming cable, the clang of the bell, and the occasional quip from the gripman. It's an experience you shouldn't pass up, whether on your first trip or your fiftieth.

HOW CABLE CARS WORK

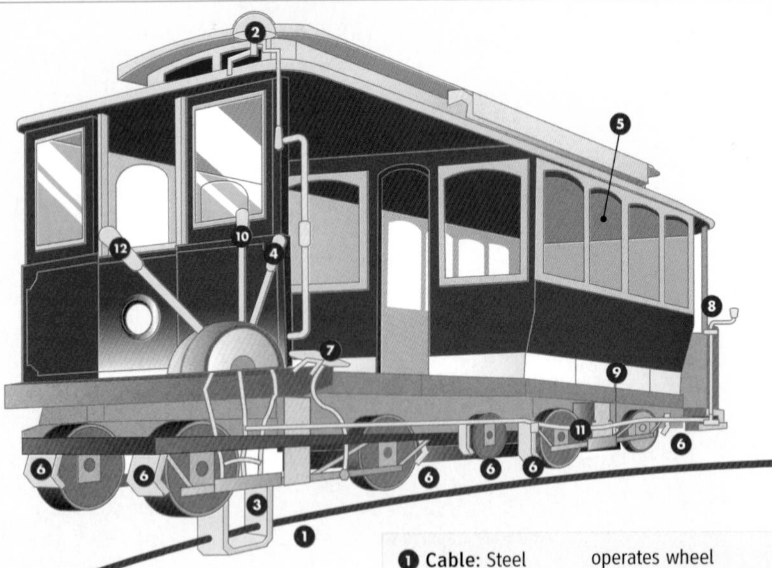

The mechanics are pretty simple: cable cars grab a moving subterranean cable with a "grip" to go. To stop, they release the grip and apply one or more types of brakes. Four cables, totaling 9 miles, power the city's three lines. If the gripman doesn't adjust the grip just right when going up a steep hill, the cable will start to slip and the car will have to back down the hill and try again. This is an extremely rare occurrence—imagine the ribbing the gripman gets back at the cable car barn!

Gripman: Stands in front and operates the grip, brakes, and bell. Favorite joke, especially at the peak of a steep hill: "This is my first day on the job folks . . ."

Conductor: Moves around the car, deals with tickets, alerts the grip about what's coming up, and operates the rear wheel brakes.

1. **Cable:** Steel wrapped around flexible sisal core; 2 inches thick; runs at a constant 9½ mph.
2. **Bells:** Used for crew communication; alerts other drivers and pedestrians.
3. **Grip:** Vice-like lever extends through the center slot in the track to grab or release the cable.
4. **Grip Lever:** Left-hand lever; operates grip.
5. **Car:** Entire car weighs 8 tons.
6. **Wheel Brake:** Steel brake pads on each wheel.
7. **Wheel Brake Lever:** Foot pedal; operates wheel brakes.
8. **Rear Wheel Brake Lever:** Applied for extra traction on hills.
9. **Track Brake:** 2-foot long sections of Monterey pine push down against the track to help stop the car.
10. **Track Brake Lever:** Middle lever; operates track brakes.
11. **Emergency Brake:** 18-inch steel wedge, jams into street slot to bring car to an immediate stop.
12. **Emergency Brake Lever:** Right-hand lever, red; operates emergency brake.

ROUTES

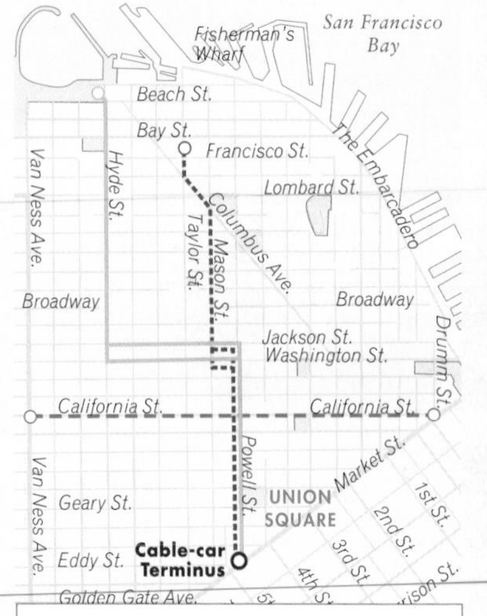

Cars run at least every 15 minutes, from around 6 AM to about 1 AM.

Powell–Hyde line: Most scenic, with classic Bay views. Begins at Powell and Market streets, then crosses Nob Hill and Russian Hill before a white-knuckle descent down Hyde Street, ending near the Hyde Street Pier.

Powell–Mason line: Also begins at Powell and Market streets, but winds through North Beach to Bay and Taylor streets, a few blocks from Fisherman's Wharf.

California line: Runs from the foot of Market Street, at Drumm Street, up Nob Hill and back. Great views (and aromas and sounds) of Chinatown on the way up. Sit in back to catch glimpses of the Bay. **■TIP→ Take the California line if it's just the cable-car experience you're after—the lines are shorter, and the grips and conductors say it's friendlier and has a slower pace.**

RULES OF THE RIDE

Tickets. A whopping $5 each way. There are ticket booths at all three turnarounds, or you can pay the conductor after you board (they can make change). Try not to grumble about the price—they're embarrassed enough as it is.

■TIP→ If you're planning to use public transit a few times, or if you'd like to ride back and forth on the cable car without worrying about the price, consider a one-day Muni passport ($11). You can get passports online, at the Powell Street turnaround, the TIX booth on Union Square, or the Fisherman's Wharf cable-car ticket booth at Beach and Hyde streets.

All Aboard. You can board on either side of the cable car. It's legal to stand on the running boards and hang on to the pole, but keep your ears open for the gripman's warnings. **■TIP→ Grab a seat on the outside bench for the best views.**

Most people wait (and wait) in line at one of the cable car turnarounds, but you can also hop on along the route. Board wherever you see a white sign showing a figure climbing aboard a brown cable car; wave to the approaching driver, and wait until the car stops.

Riding on the running boards can be part of the thrill.

CABLE CAR HISTORY

HALLIDIE FREES THE HORSES

In the 1850s and '60s, San Francisco's streetcars were drawn by horses. Legend has it that the horrible sight of a car dragging a team of horses downhill to their deaths roused Andrew Smith Hallidie to action. The English immigrant had invented the "Hallidie Ropeway," essentially a cable car for mined ore, and he was convinced that his invention could also move people. In 1873, Hallidie and his intrepid crew prepared to test the first cable car high on Russian Hill. The anxious engineer peered down into the foggy darkness, failed to see the bottom of the hill, and promptly turned the controls over to Hallidie. Needless to say, the thing worked . . . but rides were free for the first two days because people were afraid to get on.

SEE IT FOR YOURSELF

The **Cable Car Museum** is one of the city's best free offerings and an absolute must for kids. (You can even ride a cable car there, since all three lines stop between Russian Hill and Nob Hill.) The museum, which is inside the city's last cable-car barn, takes the top off the system to let you see how it all works. Eternally humming and squealing, the massive powerhouse cable wheels steal the show. You can also climb aboard a vintage car and take the grip, let the kids ring a cable-car bell (briefly), and check out vintage gear dating from 1873.

✉ 1201 Mason St., at Washington St., Nob Hill ☎ 415/474–1887 🌐 www.cablecarmuseum.com 🎫 Free 🕒 Oct.–Mar., daily 10–5; Apr.–Sept., daily 10–6

■ TIP→ The gift shop sells cable car paraphernalia, including an authentic gripman's bell for $600 (it'll sound like Powell Street in your house every day). For significantly less, you can pick up a key chain made from a piece of worn-out cable.

CHAMPION OF THE CABLE CAR BELL

Each July the city's best and brightest come together to crown a bell-ringing champion at Union Square. The crowd cheers gripmen and conductors as they stomp, shake, and riff with the rope. But it's not a popularity contest; the ringers are judged by former bell-ringing champions who take each ping and gong very seriously.

They in turn are surrounded by a construction scene, laborers, and city notables such as sculptor Robert Stackpole and architect Timothy Pfleuger. *The Making of a Fresco* is one of three San Francisco murals painted by Rivera. The number-two reason to come here is the café, or more precisely the eye-popping, panoramic view from the café, which serves surprisingly decent food for a song.

The older portions of the Art Institute, including the lovely Mission-style bell tower, were erected in 1926. To this day, otherwise pragmatic people claim that ghostly footsteps can be heard in the tower at night. Ansel Adams created the school's fine-arts photography department in 1946, and school directors established the country's first fine-arts film program. Notable faculty and alumni have included painter Richard Diebenkorn and photographers Dorothea Lange, Edward Weston, and Annie Leibovitz. The **Walter & McBean Galleries** (☎*415/749–4563* ⏲*Tues.–Sat. 11–6*) exhibit the often provocative works of established artists. ✉*800 Chestnut St., North Beach* ☎*415/771–7020* 🌐*www.sfai.edu* 🎫*Galleries free* ⏲*Student gallery daily 8:30–8:30.*

4

NORTH BEACH

San Francisco novelist Herbert Gold calls North Beach "the longest-running, most glorious American bohemian operetta outside Greenwich Village." Indeed, to anyone who's spent some time in its eccentric old bars and cafés, North Beach evokes everything from the Barbary Coast days to the no-less-rowdy beatnik era. Italian bakeries appear frozen in time, homages to Jack Kerouac and Allen Ginsberg pop up everywhere, and the modern equivalent of the Barbary Coast's "houses of ill repute," strip joints, do business on Broadway. With its outdoor café tables, throngs of tourists, and holiday vibe, this is probably the part of town Europeans are thinking of when they say San Francisco is the most European city in America.

WHAT TO SEE IN NORTH BEACH

6 ★ **City Lights Bookstore.** Take a look at the exterior of the store: the replica of a revolutionary mural destroyed in Chiapas, Mexico, by military forces; the poetry in the windows; and the sign that says TURN YOUR SELL [sic] PHONE OFF. BE HERE NOW. This place isn't just doling out best sellers. Designated a city landmark, the hangout of Beat-era writers—Allen Ginsberg and store founder Lawrence Ferlinghetti among them—remains a vital part of San Francisco's literary scene. Browse the three levels of sometimes haphazardly arranged poetry, philosophy, politics, fiction, history, and local 'zines, to the tune of creaking wood floors. ■ **TIP→ Be sure to check their calendar of literary events.**

Back in the day, the basement was a kind of literary living room, where writers like Ginsberg and Kerouac would read and even receive mail. Ferlinghetti cemented City Lights' place in history by publishing Ginsberg's *Howl and Other Poems* in 1956. The small volume was ignored in the mainstream . . . until Ferlinghetti and the bookstore manager were arrested for corruption of youth and obscenity. In the landmark First Amendment trial that followed the judge exonerated both, saying a work that has "redeeming social significance" can't be obscene. *Howl* went on to become a classic.

Kerouac Alley, branching off Columbus Avenue next to City Lights, was rehabbed in 2007. Embedded in the pavement are quotes from Lawrence Ferlinghetti, Maya Angelou, Confucius, John Steinbeck, and of course, the namesake himself. ✉ *261 Columbus Ave., North Beach* ☎ *415/362–8193* 🌐 *www.citylights.com* ⏲ *Daily 10* AM*–midnight.*

8 ★ **Coit Tower.** Whether you think it resembles a fire hose or something more, ahem, adult, this 210-foot tower is among San Francisco's most distinctive skyline sights. Although the monument wasn't intended as a tribute to firemen, it's often considered as such because of the donor's special attachment to the local fire company. As the story goes, a young gold rush–era girl, Lillie Hitchcock Coit (known as Miss Lil), was a fervent admirer of her local fire company—so much so that she once deserted a wedding party and chased down the street after her favorite engine, Knickerbocker No. 5, while clad in her bridesmaid finery. She became the Knickerbocker Company's mascot and always signed her name "Lillie Coit 5." When Lillie died in 1929 she left the city $125,000 to "expend in an appropriate manner...to the beauty of San Francisco."

You can ride the elevator to the top of the tower—the only thing you have to pay for here—to enjoy the view of the Bay Bridge and the Golden Gate Bridge; due north is Alcatraz Island. ■ **TIP→ The views from the base of the tower are also expansive—and free. Parking at Coit Tower is limited; in fact, you may have to wait (and wait) for a space. Save yourself some frustration and take the 39 bus which goes all the way up to the tower's base or, if you're in good shape, hike up.** *For more details on the lovely stairway walk, see Telegraph Hill, below.*

Inside the tower, 19 Depression-era murals depict California's economic and political life. The federal government commissioned the paintings from 25 local artists, and ended up funding quite a controversy. The radical Mexican painter Diego Rivera inspired the murals' socialist-realist style, with its biting cultural commentary, particularly about the exploitation of workers. At the time the murals were painted, clashes between management and labor along the waterfront and elsewhere in San Francisco were widespread. ✉ *Telegraph Hill Blvd. at Greenwich St. or Lombard St., North Beach* ☎ *415/362–0808* 🎫 *Free; elevator to top $5* ⏲ *Daily 10–6.*

7 Fodor's Choice ★ **Telegraph Hill.** Hill residents have some of the best views in the city, as well as the most difficult ascents to their aeries. The hill rises from the east end of Lombard Street to a height of 284 feet and is capped by Coit Tower (*see above*). Imagine lugging your groceries up that! If you brave the slope, though, you can be rewarded with a "secret treasure" SF moment. Filbert Street starts up the hill, then becomes the Filbert Steps when the going gets too steep. You can cut between the Filbert Steps and another flight, the Greenwich Steps, on up to the hilltop. As you climb, you can pass some of the city's oldest houses and be surrounded by beautiful, flowering private gardens. In some places the trees grow over the stairs so they feel like a green tunnel; elsewhere, you'll have wide-open views of the bay. And the telegraphic name? It

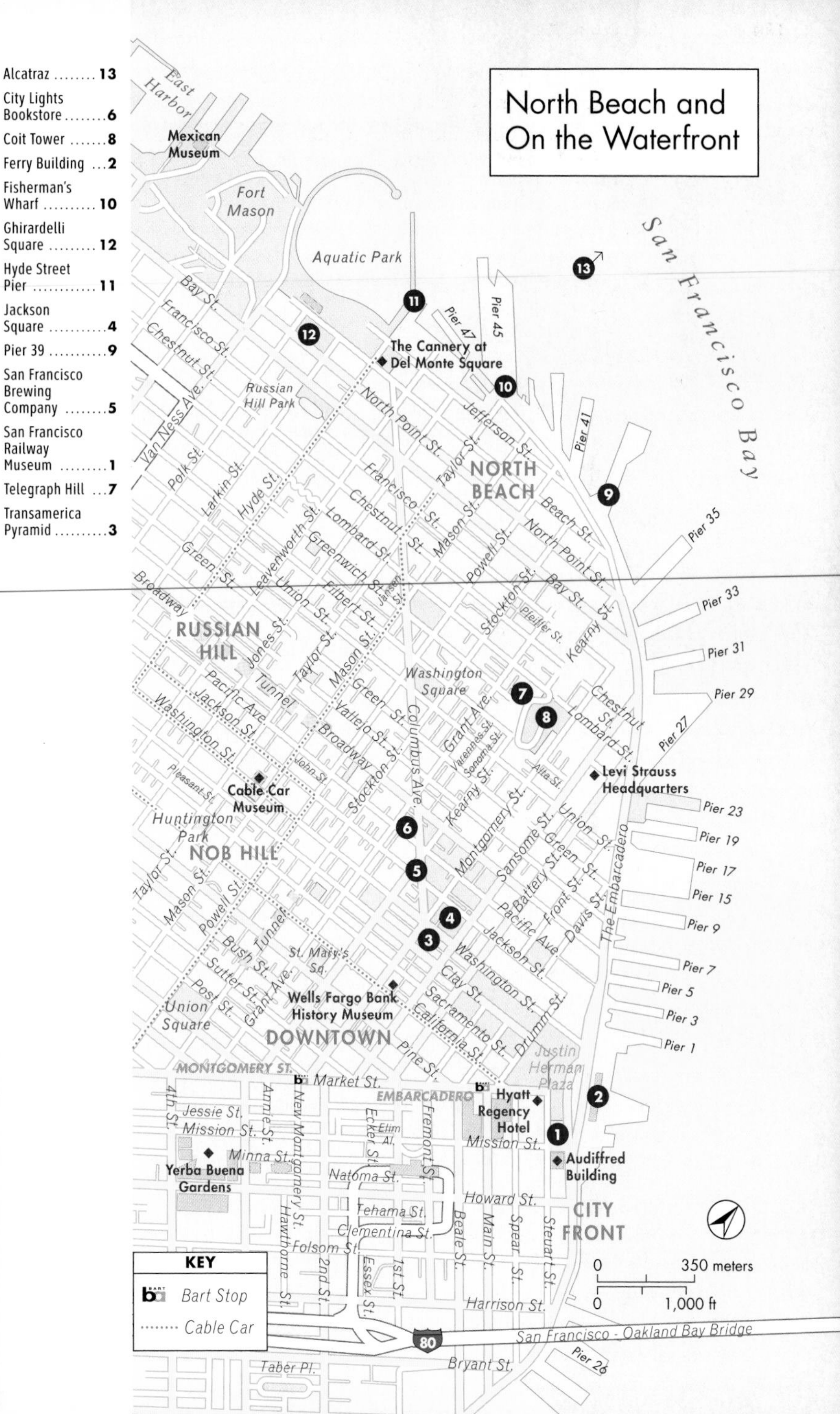

North Beach and On the Waterfront
Alcatraz 13
City Lights Bookstore 6
Coit Tower 8
Ferry Building ... 2
Fisherman's Wharf 10
Ghirardelli Square 12
Hyde Street Pier 11
Jackson Square 4
Pier 39 9
San Francisco Brewing Company 5
San Francisco Railway Museum 1
Telegraph Hill ... 7
Transamerica Pyramid 3
East Harbor
Mexican Museum
Fort Mason
Aquatic Park
San Francisco Bay
The Cannery at Del Monte Square
Russian Hill Park
NORTH BEACH
RUSSIAN HILL
Washington Square
Levi Strauss Headquarters
Cable Car Museum
Huntington Park
NOB HILL
St. Mary's Sq.
Wells Fargo Bank History Museum
Union Square
DOWNTOWN
Justin Herman Plaza
MONTGOMERY ST.
EMBARCADERO
Hyatt Regency Hotel
Audiffred Building
Yerba Buena Gardens
CITY FRONT
Pier 47
Pier 45
Pier 41
Pier 35
Pier 33
Pier 31
Pier 29
Pier 27
Pier 23
Pier 19
Pier 17
Pier 15
Pier 9
Pier 7
Pier 5
Pier 3
Pier 1
Pier 26
The Embarcadero
San Francisco - Oakland Bay Bridge
80
KEY
Bart Stop
Cable Car
0 350 meters
0 1,000 ft

CLOSE UP

The Birds

While on Telegraph Hill, you might be startled by a chorus of piercing squawks and a rushing sound of wings. No, you're not about to have a Hitchcock bird-attack moment. These small, vivid green parrots with cherry-red heads number in the hundreds; they're descendants of former pets that escaped or were released by their owners. (The birds dislike cages and they bite if bothered . . . must've been some disillusioned owners along the way.)

The parrots like to roost high in the aging cypress trees on the hill, chattering and fluttering, sometimes taking wing en masse. They're not popular with most residents, but they did find a champion in local bohemian Mark Bittner, a former street musician. Bittner began chronicling their habits, publishing a book and battling the homeowners who wanted to cut down the cypresses. A documentary, *The Wild Parrots of Telegraph Hill*, made the issue a cause célèbre. In 2007 City Hall, which recognizes a golden goose when it sees one, stepped in and brokered a solution to keep the celebrity birds in town. The city will cover the homeowners' insurance worries and plant new trees for the next generation of wild parrots.

–Denise M. Leto

comes from the hill's status as the first Morse code signal station back in 1853. ✉ *Bordered by Lombard, Filbert, Kearny, and Sansome Sts., North Beach.*

ON THE WATERFRONT

San Francisco's waterfront neighborhoods have fabulous views and utterly different personalities. Kitschy, overpriced Fisherman's Wharf struggles to maintain the last shreds of its existence as a working wharf, while Pier 39 is a full-fledged consumer circus. The Ferry Building draws well-heeled locals with its culinary pleasures, firmly reconnecting the Embarcadero to downtown. Between the Ferry Building and Pier 39, a former maritime no-man's land is filling in a bit—especially near Pier 33, where the perpetually booked Alcatraz cruises depart—with a waterfront restaurant here and a restored pedestrian-friendly pier there.

Today's shoreline was once Yerba Buena Cove, filled in during the latter half of the 19th century when San Francisco was a brawling, extravagant gold-rush town. Jackson Square, now a genteel and upscale corner of the inland Financial District, was the heart of the Barbary Coast, bordering some of the roughest wharves in the world. Below Montgomery Street (in today's Financial District), between California Street and Broadway, lies a remnant of these wild days: more than 100 ships abandoned by frantic crews and passengers caught up in gold fever lie under the foundations of buildings here.

WHAT TO SEE ON THE WATERFRONT

13 Fodor's Choice ★ **Alcatraz.** The boat ride to the island is brief (15–30 minutes) but affords beautiful views of the city, Marin County, and the East Bay. The audio tour, highly recommended, includes observations by guards

Thousands of visitors take ferries to Alcatraz each day to walk in the footsteps of the notorious criminals who were held on "The Rock."

and prisoners about life in one of America's most notorious penal colonies. Plan your schedule to allow at least three hours for the visit and boat rides combined. Buying your tickets in advance, even in the off-season, is strongly recommended. ✉ *Pier 33, Fisherman's Wharf* ☎ *415/981–7625* 🌐 *www.nps.gov/alca, www.parkconservancy.org/visit/alcatraz, www.alcatrazcruises.com* 🎫 *$24.50, including audio tour; $31.05 evening tour, including audio* ⏲ *Ferry departs every 30–45 mins Sept.–late May, daily 9:30–2:15, 4:20 for evening tour Thurs.–Mon. only; late May–Aug., daily 9–4, 6:10 and 6:50 for evening tour.*

2 Fodor's Choice ★ **Ferry Building.** Renovated in 2003, the Ferry Building is the jewel of the Embarcadero. The beacon of the port area, erected in 1896, has a 230-foot clock tower modeled after the campanile of the cathedral in Seville, Spain. On the morning of April 18, 1906, the tower's four clock faces, powered by the swinging of a 14-foot pendulum, stopped at 5:17—the moment the great earthquake struck—and stayed still for 12 months.

Today San Franciscans flock to the street-level Market Hall, stocking up on supplies from local favorites such as Acme Bread, Scharffen Berger Chocolate, and Cowgirl Creamery. Lucky diners claim a coveted table at Slanted Door, the city's beloved high-end Vietnamese restaurant. The seafood bars at Hog Island Oyster Company and Ferry Plaza Seafood have fantastic city panoramas—or you can take your purchases around to the building's bay side, where benches face views of the Bay Bridge. Saturday mornings the plaza in front of the building buzzes with an upscale, celebrity-chef-studded farmers' market. Extending from the piers on the north side of the building south to the Bay Bridge, the waterfront promenade is a favorite among joggers and picnickers, with a front-row view of the sailboats slipping by. The Ferry Building also serves actual ferries: from behind the building they sail to Sausalito, Larkspur, Tiburon, and the East Bay. ✉ *Embarcadero at foot of Market St., Embarcadero* 🌐 *www.ferrybuildingmarketplace.com.*

NEED A BREAK?

Even locals love the cheery Buena Vista Café (✉ *2765 Hyde St., Fisherman's Wharf* ☎ *415/474–5044*), which claims to be the first place in the United States to have served Irish coffee. The café opens at 9 AM weekdays (8 AM weekends) and dishes up a great breakfast. They serve about 2,000 Irish coffees a day, so it's always crowded; try for a table overlooking nostalgic Victorian Park and its cable-car turntable.

10 **Fisherman's Wharf.** It may be one of the city's best-known attractions, but the wharf is a no-go zone for most locals, who shy away from the difficult parking, overpriced food, and cheesy shops at third-rate shopping centers like the Cannery at Del Monte Square. If you just can't resist a visit here, come early to avoid the crowds and get a sense of the wharf's functional role—it's not just an amusement park replica.

Most of the entertainment at the wharf is schlocky and overpriced, with one notable exception: the splendid **Musée Mécanique** (☎ *415/346–2000* ⏲ *Weekdays 10–7, weekends 10–8*), a time-warped arcade with antique mechanical contrivances, including peep shows and nickelodeons. Some favorites are the giant and rather creepy "Laffing Sal" (you enter the museum through his gaping mouth), an arm-wrestling machine, the world's only steam-powered motorcycle, and mechanical fortune-telling figures that speak from their curtained boxes. Note the depictions of race that betray the prejudices of the time: stoned Chinese figures in the "Opium-Den" and clown-faced African-Americans eating watermelon in the "Mechanical Farm." Admission is free, but you'll need quarters to bring the machines to life.

Among the two floors of exhibits at **Ripley's Believe It or Not! Museum** (✉ *175 Jefferson St., Fisherman's Wharf* ☎ *415/771–6188* 🌐 *www.ripleysf.com* 🎫 *$14.99* ⏲ *Late June–Labor Day, Sun.–Thurs. 9–6, Fri. and Sat. 9–12; Labor Day–early June, Sun.–Thurs. 10–10, Fri. and Sat. 10–12*) is a tribute to San Francisco—an 8-foot-long scale model of a cable car, made entirely of matchsticks. Notables from local boy Robin Williams to Jesus await at the **Wax Museum** (✉ *145 Jefferson St., Fisherman's Wharf* ☎ *415/439–4305* 🌐 *www.waxmuseum.com*), open weekdays 10 to 9, weekends 9 AM to 11 PM. Admission is $12.95.

The **USS Pampanito** (✉ *Pier 45, Fisherman's Wharf* ☎ *415/775–1943* 🌐 *www.maritime.org/pamphome.htm* ⏲ *Oct.–Memorial Day, Sun.–Thurs. 9–6, Fri. and Sat. 9–8; Memorial Day–Sept., Thurs.–Tues. 9–8, Wed. 9–6*) provides an intriguing if mildly claustrophobic glimpse into life on a submarine during World War II. The sub sank six Japanese warships and damaged four others. Admission is $9; the family pass is a great deal at $20 for two adults and up to four kids. ✉ *Jefferson St. between Leavenworth St. and Pier 39, Fisherman's Wharf.*

12 **Ghirardelli Square.** Most of the redbrick buildings in this early-20th-century complex were once part of the Ghirardelli factory. Now tourists

come here to pick up the famous chocolate, but you can purchase it all over town and save yourself a trip to what is essentially a mall. (If you're a shopaholic, though, it definitely beats the Cannery.) There are three Ghirardelli stores here, as well as gift shops and a couple of restaurants—including Ana Mandara—that even locals love. Fairmont recently opened an upscale urban time-share directly on the square. Placards throughout the square describe the factory's history. ⊠ *900 North Point St. , Fisherman's Wharf* ☎ *415/775–5500* 🌐 *www.ghirardellisq.com.*

11 **Hyde Street Pier.** Cotton candy and souvenirs are all well and good, but if you want to get to the heart of the Wharf—boats—there's no better place to do it than at this pier, by far one of the Wharf area's best bargains. Depending on the time of day, you might see boat builders at work or children pretending to man an early-1900s ship.

Don't pass up the centerpiece collection of historic vessels, part of the **San Francisco Maritime National Historic Park,** almost all of which can be boarded. The newly restored *Balclutha,* an 1886 full-rigged three-masted sailing vessel that's more than 250 feet long, sailed around Cape Horn 17 times; kids especially love the *Eureka,* a side-wheel passenger and car ferry, for her onboard collection of vintage cars; the *Hercules* is a steam-powered tugboat. The *C. A. Thayer,* a three-masted schooner, recently underwent a painstaking restoration and is back on display. Across the street from the pier and almost a museum in itself is the San Francisco Maritime National Historic Park's **Visitor Center** (⊠ *499 Jefferson St., at Hyde St., Fisherman's Wharf* ☎ *415/447–5000* ⏲ *Memorial Day–Sept., daily 9:30–7; Oct.–Memorial Day, daily 9:30–5*), happily free of mind-numbing, text-heavy displays. Instead, fun, large-scale exhibits, such as a huge First Order Fresnel lighthouse lens and a shipwrecked boat, make this an engaging and relatively quick stop. ⊠ *Hyde and Jefferson Sts., Fisherman's Wharf* ☎ *415/561–7100* 🌐 *www.nps.gov/safr* 🎫 *Ships $5* ⏲ *Memorial Day–Sept., daily 9:30–5:30; Oct.–Memorial Day, daily 9:30–5.*

4 **Jackson Square.** This was the heart of the Barbary Coast of the Gay '90s (the 1890s, that is). Although most of the red-light district was destroyed in the fire that followed the 1906 earthquake, old redbrick buildings and narrow alleys recall the romance and rowdiness of San Francisco's early days. The days of brothels and bar fights are long gone—now Jackson Square is a genteel, quiet corner of the Financial

F-LINE TROLLEYS

The F-line, the city's system of vintage electric trolleys, gives the cable cars a run for their money as San Francisco's best-loved mode of transportation. These beautifully restored streetcars—some dating from the 19th century—run from the Castro all the way down Market Street to the Embarcadero, then north to Fisherman's Wharf. Each car is unique, restored to the colors of its city of origin, from New Orleans and Philadelphia to Moscow and Milan. The trolleys are so popular that would-be riders sometimes have to wait as car after car pass the stop too packed to admit one more. Purchase tickets on board; exact change is required. 🌐 *www.streetcar.org* 🎫 *$1.50.*

District. It's of interest to the historically inclined and antiques-shop browsers, but otherwise safely skipped.

Some of the city's first business buildings, survivors of the 1906 quake, still stand between Montgomery and Sansome streets. After a few decades of neglect, these old-timers were adopted by preservation-minded interior designers and wholesale-furniture dealers for use as showrooms. In 1972 the city officially designated the area—bordered by Columbus Avenue on the west, Broadway and Pacific Avenue on the north, Washington Street on the south, and Sansome Street on the east—San Francisco's first historic district. When property values soared, many of the fabric and furniture outlets fled to Potrero Hill. Advertising agencies, attorneys, and antiques dealers now occupy the Jackson Square–area structures. Restored 19th-century brick buildings line Hotaling Place, which connects Washington and Jackson streets. The lane is named for the head of the **A. P. Hotaling Company whiskey distillery** (✉ *451 Jackson St., at Hotaling Pl.*), which was the largest liquor repository on the West Coast in its day. (Hotaling whiskey is still made in the city, by the way; look for their single malts for a sip of truly local flavor.)

It takes a bit of conjuring to evoke the wild Barbary Coast days when checking out the now-gentrified gold rush–era buildings in the 700 block of **Montgomery Street.** But this was an especially colorful block. Author Mark Twain was a reporter for the spunky *Golden Era* newspaper, which occupied No. 732 (now part of the building at No. 744). From 1959 to 1996 the late ambulance-chaser extraordinaire, lawyer Melvin Belli, had his headquarters there. There was never a dull moment in Belli's world; he represented clients from Mae West to Gloria Sykes (who in 1964 claimed that a cable-car accident turned her into a nymphomaniac) to Jim and Tammy Faye Bakker. Whenever he won a case, he fired a cannon and raised the Jolly Roger. Belli was also known for receiving a letter from the never-caught Zodiac killer. It seems fitting that the building sat for years, deteriorating and moldering, while the late attorney's sons fought wife number five (joined with Belli in holy matrimony just three months before his death). She eventually won, and the building may finally be renovated. ✉ *Jackson Sq. district bordered by Broadway and Washington, Kearny, and Sansome Sts., Financial District.*

9 **Pier 39.** The city's most popular waterfront attraction draws millions of visitors each year who come to browse through its vertiginous array of shops and concessions hawking every conceivable form of souvenir. The pier can be quite crowded, and the numerous street performers may leave you feeling more harassed than entertained. Arriving early in the morning ensures you a front-row view of the sea lions, but if you're here to shop—and make no mistake about it, Pier 39 wants your money—be aware that most stores don't open until 9:30 or 10 (later in winter).

Pick up a buckwheat hull–filled otter neck wrap or a plush sea lion to snuggle at the **Marine Mammal Store** (☎ *415/289–7373*), whose proceeds benefit Sausalito's respected wild-animal hospital, the Marine Mammal Center. Sales of the excellent books, maps, and collectibles—including a series of gorgeous, distinctive art-deco posters for Alcatraz, the Presidio, Fort Point, and the other members of the Golden Gate National Recreation Area—at the **National Park Store** (☎*415/433–7221*) help to support the National Park Service. Brilliant colors enliven the double-decker **San Francisco Carousel** (*$3 per ride*), decorated with images of such city landmarks as the Golden Gate Bridge and Lombard Street.Follow the sound of barking to the northwest side of the pier to view the hundreds of sea lions that bask and play on the docks. At **Aquarium of the Bay** (☎*415/623–5300 or 888/732–3483* *www.aquariumofthebay.com* *$14.95*) moving walkways transport you through a space surrounded on three sides by water filled with indigenous San Francisco Bay marine life, from fish and plankton to sharks. Many find the aquarium overpriced; if you can, take advantage of the family rate ($37.95 for two adults and two kids under 12). The aquarium is open June through September daily 9–8; during the rest of the year it's open Monday through Thursday 10–6 and Friday through Sunday 10–7.

WHISKEY RHYME

The Italianate Hotaling building survived the disastrous 1906 quake and fire—a miracle considering the thousands of barrels of inflammable liquid inside. A plaque on the side of the structure repeats a famous query: IF, AS THEY SAY, GOD SPANKED THE TOWN FOR BEING OVER FRISKY, WHY DID HE BURN THE CHURCHES DOWN AND SAVE HOTALING'S WHISKEY?

The **California Welcome Center** (☎*415/981–1280* *Daily 10–5* *www.visitcwc.com*), on Pier 39's second level, includes an Internet café. Parking (free with validation from a Pier 39 restaurant) is at the Pier 39 Garage, off Powell Street at the Embarcadero. ✉*Beach St. at Embarcadero, Fisherman's Wharf* *www.pier39.com.*

5 **San Francisco Brewing Company.** Built in 1907, this pub looks like a museum piece from San Francisco's Barbary Coast days. An old upright piano sits in the corner under the original stained-glass windows. Take a seat at the mahogany bar, where you can look down at the white-tile spittoon. An adjacent room holds the handmade copper brewing kettle used to produce a dozen beers—with names such as Pony Express—by means of old-fashioned gravity-flow methods. ✉*155 Columbus Ave., North Beach* ☎*415/434–3344* *www.sfbrewing.com* *Mon.–Sat. 11:30–1* AM, *Sun. noon–1* AM.

1 **San Francisco Railway Museum.** A labor of love brought to you by the same vintage-transit enthusiasts responsible for the F-line's revival, this one-room museum and store celebrates the city's storied streetcars and cable cars with photographs, models, and artifacts. The permanent exhibit will eventually include the (replicated) end of a streetcar with a working cab for kids to explore. In the meantime, little ones will have to content themselves with operating the cool, antique Wiley birdcage traffic signal and viewing (but not touching) models and display cases. Right on the F-line track, just across from the Ferry Building, this is a great quick stop. ✉*77 Steuart St., Embarcadero* ☎*415/974–1948* *www.streetcar.org* *Free* *Wed.–Sun. 10–6.*

3 **Transamerica Pyramid.** It's neither owned by Transamerica nor is it a pyramid, but this 853-foot-tall obelisk *is* the most photographed of the city's high-rises. Excoriated in the design stages as "the world's largest architectural folly," the icon was quickly hailed as a masterpiece when it opened in 1972. Today it's probably the city's most recognized structure after the Golden Gate Bridge. A fragrant redwood grove along the east side of the building, replete with benches and a cheerful fountain, is a placid patch in which to unwind. ✉ *600 Montgomery St., Financial District* 🌐 *www.transamerica.com.*

THE MARINA AND THE PRESIDIO

Yachts bob at their moorings, satisfied-looking folks jog along the Marina Green, and multimillion-dollar homes overlook the bay in this picturesque, if somewhat sterile, neighborhood. Does it all seem a bit too perfect? Well, it got this way after the hard knock of Loma Prieta—the current pretty face was put on after hundreds of homes collapsed in the 1989 earthquake. Just west of this waterfront area is a more natural beauty: the Presidio. Once a military base, this beautiful, sprawling park is mostly green space, with hills, woods, and the marshlands of Crissy Field.

WHAT TO SEE IN THE MARINA

2 ★ **Exploratorium.** Walking into this fascinating "museum of science, art, and human perception" is like visiting a mad scientist's laboratory. Most of the exhibits are supersize, and you can play with everything. You can feel like Alice in Wonderland in the distortion room, where you seem to shrink and grow as you walk across the slanted, checkered floor. In the shadow room, a powerful flash freezes an image of your shadow on the wall; jumping is a favorite pose. "Pushover" demonstrates cow-tipping, but for people: stand on one foot and try to keep your balance while a friend swings a striped panel in front of you (trust us, you're going to fall).

More than 650 other exhibits focus on sea and insect life, computers, electricity, patterns and light, language, the weather, and much more. "Explainers"—usually high-school students on their days off—demonstrate cool scientific tools and procedures, like DNA sample-collection and cow-eye dissection. One surefire hit is the pitch-black, touchy-feely Tactile Dome. In this geodesic dome strewn with textured objects, you crawl through a course of ladders, slides, and tunnels, relying solely on your sense of touch. Not surprisingly, lovey-dovey couples sometimes linger in the "grope dome," but be forewarned: the staff will turn on the lights if they have to. ■ **TIP→ Reservations are required for the Tactile Dome and will get you 75 minutes of access. You have to be at least seven years old to go through the dome, and the space is not for the claustrophobic.** ✉ *3601 Lyon St., at Marina Blvd., Marina* ☎ *415/561–0360 general information, 415/561–0362 Tactile Dome reservations* 🌐 *www.exploratorium.edu* 🎫 *$14, free 1st Wed. of month; Tactile Dome $3 extra* ⏲ *Tues.–Sun. 10–5.*

1 Fodor's Choice ★ **Palace of Fine Arts.** At first glance this stunning, rosy rococo palace seems to be from another world, and indeed, it's the sole survivor of the many tinted-plaster structures (a temporary classical city of sorts) built for

The Marina and the Presidio

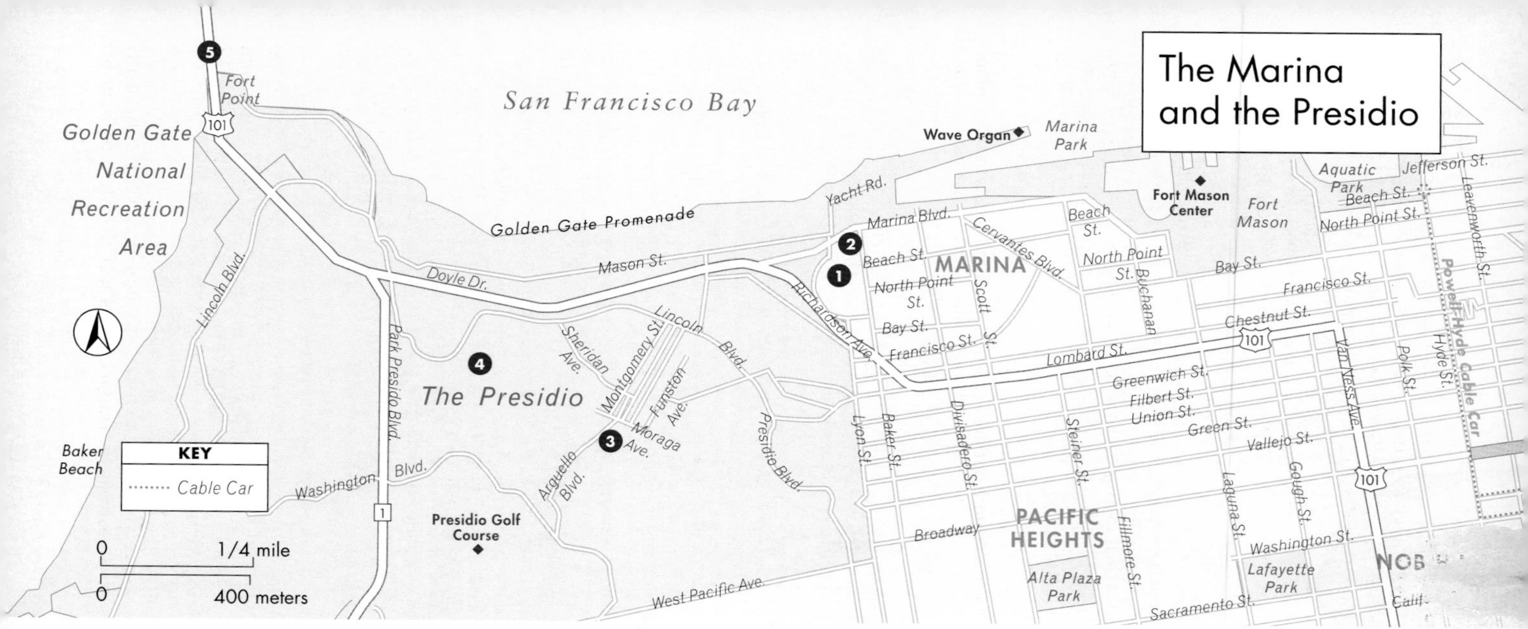

KEY

.... Cable Car

0 — 1/4 mile

0 — 400 meters

Exploratorium **2**

Golden Gate Bridge **5**

Palace of Fine Arts **1**

Presidio **4**

Presidio Officers' Club and Visitor Center **3**

4

the 1915 Panama-Pacific International Exposition, the world's fair that celebrated San Francisco's recovery from the 1906 earthquake and fire. The expo buildings originally extended about a mile along the shore. Bernard Maybeck designed this faux–Roman Classic beauty, which was reconstructed in concrete and reopened in 1967.

A victim of the elements, the Palace completed a piece-by-piece renovation. The massive columns (each topped with four "weeping maidens"), great rotunda, and swan-filled lagoon have been used in countless fashion layouts, films, and wedding photo shoots. After admiring the lagoon, look across the street to the house at 3460 Baker Street. If the maidens out front look familiar, they should—they're original casts of the lovely "garland ladies" you can see in the Palace's colonnade. The house was on the market in 2007; if you'd had a cool $8 million, it could've been yours. ✉ *Baker and Beach Sts., Marina* ☎ *415/561–0364 Palace history tours* 🌐 *www.exploratorium.edu/palace* 🎟 *Free* 🕑 *Daily 24 hrs.*

WHAT TO SEE IN THE PRESIDIO

5 Fodor'sChoice ★ **Golden Gate Bridge.** The suspension bridge that connects San Francisco with Marin County has long wowed sightseers with its simple but powerful art-deco design. Completed in 1937 after four years of construction, the 2-mi span and its 750-foot towers were built to withstand winds of more than 100 MPH. It's also not a bad place to be in an earthquake: designed to sway up to 27.7 feet, the Golden Gate Bridge, unlike the Bay Bridge, was undamaged by the 1989 Loma Prieta quake. (If you're on the bridge when it's windy, stand still and you can feel it swaying a bit.) Though it's frequently gusty and misty—always bring a jacket, no matter what the weather's like—the bridge provides unparalleled views of the Bay Area. Muni buses 28 and 29 make stops at the Golden Gate Bridge toll plaza, on the San Francisco side. However, drive to fully appreciate the bridge from multiple vantage points in and around the Presidio; you'll be able to park at designated areas.

From the bridge's eastern-side walkway—the only side pedestrians are allowed on—you can take in the San Francisco skyline and the bay islands; look west for the wild hills of the Marin Headlands, the curving coast south to Land's End, and the Pacific Ocean. On sunny days, sailboats dot the water, and brave windsurfers test the often-treacherous tides beneath the bridge. ■ **TIP→ A vista point on the Marin side gives you a spectacular city panorama.**

But there's a well-known, darker side to the bridge's story, too. The bridge is perhaps the world's most popular suicide platform, with an average of about 20 jumpers per year. (The first leaped just three months after the bridge's completion, and the official count was stopped in 1995 as the 1,000th jump approached.) Signs along the bridge read "There is hope. Make the call," referring the disconsolate to the special telephones on the bridge. Bridge officers, who patrol the walkway and watch by security camera to spot potential jumpers, successfully talk down two-thirds to three-quarters of them each year. Documentary filmmaker Eric Steel's controversial 2006 movie *The Bridge* once again put pressure on the Golden Gate Bridge Highway and Transportation District to install a suicide barrier; various options are being considered, with most

Armed with only helmets, safety harnesses, and painting equipment, a full-time crew of 38 painters keeps the Golden Gate Bridge clad in International Orange.

locals supporting an unobtrusive net. ✉ *Lincoln Blvd. near Doyle Dr. and Fort Point, Presidio* ☎ *415/921–5858* 🌐 *www.goldengatebridge.org* ⏲ *Pedestrians Mar.–Oct., daily 5 AM–9 PM; Nov.–Feb., daily 5 AM–6 PM; hrs change with daylight saving time. Bicyclists daily 24 hrs.*

4 ★ **Presidio.** When San Franciscans want to spend a day in the woods, they head here. The Presidio has 1,400 acres of hills and majestic woods, two small beaches, and—the one thing Golden Gate Park doesn't have—stunning views of the bay, the Golden Gate Bridge, and Marin County. Famed environmental artist Andy Goldsworthy's new sculpture greets visitors at the Arguello Gate entrance. Erected at the end of 2008, the 100-plus-foot *Spire*, made of 37 cypress logs reclaimed from the Presidio, looks like a rough, natural version of a church spire. ■ **TIP→The best lookout points lie along Washington Boulevard, which meanders through the park.**

Part of the **Golden Gate National Recreation Area,** the Presidio was a military post for more than 200 years. Don Juan Bautista de Anza and a band of Spanish settlers first claimed the area in 1776. It became a Mexican garrison in 1822, when Mexico gained its independence from Spain; U.S. troops forcibly occupied the Presidio in 1846. The U.S. Sixth Army was stationed here until October 1994, when the coveted space was transferred into civilian hands.

Today the area is being transformed into a self-sustaining national park with a combination of public, commercial, and residential projects. In 2005 Bay Area filmmaker George Lucas opened the **Letterman Digital Arts Center,** his 23-acre digital studio "campus," along the eastern edge of the land. Seventeen of those acres are exquisitely landscaped and open to the public, but not even landscaping this perfect can compete with the wilds of the Presidio. A lodge at the Main Post is in the planning stages.

The battle over the fate of the rest of the Presidio is ongoing. Many older buildings have been reconstructed; the issue now is how to fill them. The original plan described a nexus for arts, education, and environmental groups. Since the Presidio's overseeing trust must make the park financially self-sufficient by 2013, which means generating enough revenue to keep afloat without the federal government's monthly $20 million checks, many fear that money will trump culture. The Asian-theme SenSpa has opened, a Walt Disney museum is on the way, and Donald Fisher—founder of the Gap clothing chain—wants to build a home for his huge modern-art collection near the parade ground (this has become a compelling and controversial proposal). With old military housing now repurposed as apartments and homes with rents up to $10,000 a month, there's some concern that the Presidio will become an incoherent mix of pricey real estate. Still, the $6 million that Lucas shells out annually for rent does plant a lot of saplings....

The Presidio also has two beaches, a golf course, a visitor center, and picnic sites; the views from the many overlooks are sublime.

★ Especially popular is **Crissy Field,** a stretch of restored marshlands along the sand of the bay. Kids on bikes, folks walking dogs, and joggers share the paved path along the shore, often winding up at the Warming Hut, a combination café and store at the end of the path, for a hot chocolate in the shadow of the Golden Gate Bridge. Midway along the Golden Gate Promenade that winds along the shore is the Gulf of the Farallones National Marine Sanctuary Visitor Center, where kids can get a close-up view of small sea creatures and learn about the rich ecosystem offshore. Toward the promenade's eastern end, Crissy Field Center offers great children's programs and has cool science displays. West of the Golden Gate Bridge is sandy **Baker Beach,** beloved for its spectacular views and laid-back vibe (read: you'll see naked people here). This is one of those places locals like to show off to visitors. ✉ *Between Marina and Lincoln Park, Presidio* 🌐 *www.presidio.gov.*

3 **Presidio Officers' Club and Visitor Center.** A remnant of the days when the Presidio was an army base, this Mission-style clubhouse now doubles as a temporary visitor center and exhibit space. Hit the visitor center for maps, schedules of the walking and biking tours, recaps of the Presidio's history, and a good selection of Bay Area books and souvenirs.

The club's temporary art exhibitions explore the unique cultural identity of the American West and the Pan-Pacific, such as Japanese wood-block prints. The space also sometimes offers dance performances, lectures, and theater. And a bonus that's rare in San Francisco: ample free parking. In one of the Presidio's most exciting projects, the parade ground parking lot (on what's known as the Main Post) is slated to become a lodge—most likely a swank and green one—and a swath of restored habitat that will stretch all the way to Crissy Field. ✉ *50 Moraga Ave., Presidio* ☎ *415/561–4323 visitor center, 415/561–5500 for exhibits www.presidiotrust.gov Visitor center daily 9–5; exhibit space Wed.–Sun. 11–5.*

GOLDEN GATE PARK AND THE WESTERN SHORELINE

More than 1,000 acres, stretching from the Haight all the way to the windy Pacific coast, Golden Gate Park is a vast patchwork of woods, trails, lakes, lush gardens, sports facilities, museums—even a herd of buffalo. There's more natural beauty beyond the park's borders, along San Francisco's wild Western Shoreline.

WHAT TO SEE IN GOLDEN GATE PARK

5 **Botanical Garden at Strybing Arboretum.** One of the best picnic spots in a very picnic-friendly park, this 55-acre arboretum specializes in plants from areas with climates similar to that of the Bay Area. Walk the newly updated Eastern Australian garden to see tough, pokey shrubs and plants with cartoon-like names, such as the hilly-pilly tree. Kids gravitate toward the large shallow fountain and the pond with ducks, turtles, and egrets. Another favorite is an area devoted to aromatic plants; take a deep sniff of lemon verbena or lavender. The bookstore is also a great resource. Maps are available at the main and Eugene L. Friend entrances. *Enter the park at 9th Ave. at Lincoln Way, Golden Gate Park 415/661–1316 www.sfbotanicalgarden.org Free Weekdays 8–4:30, weekends 10–5.*

1 **Conservatory of Flowers.** Whatever you do, be sure to at least drive by the Conservatory of Flowers—it's just too darn pretty to miss. The gorgeous, white-framed 1878 glass structure is topped with a 14-ton glass dome. Stepping inside the giant greenhouse is like taking a quick trip to the rain forest; it's humid, warm, and smells earthy. The undeniable highlight is the Aquatic Plants section, where lily pads float and carnivorous plants dine on bugs to the sounds of rushing water. On the east side of the conservatory (to the right as you face the building), cypress, pine, and redwood trees surround the Dahlia Garden, which blooms in summer and fall. To the west is the Rhododendron Dell, which contains 850 varieties, more than any other garden in the country. It's a favorite local Mother's Day picnic spot. *John F. Kennedy Dr. at Conservatory Dr., Golden Gate Park 415/666–7001 www.conservatoryofflowers.org $5, free 1st Tues. of month Tues.–Sun. 9–5, last entry at 4:30.*

3 **de Young Museum.** It seems that everyone in town has a strong opinion about the new museum, unveiled in 2005. Some adore the striking copper facade, while others grimace and hope that the green patina of age will mellow the effect. Most maligned is the 144-foot tower, but the view from its ninth-story observation room, ringed by floor-to-ceiling windows, is worth the price of admission alone. The building almost overshadows the de Young's respected collection of American, African, and Oceanic art. Works by Wayne Thiebaud, John Singer Sargent, Winslow Homer, and Richard Diebenkorn are the painting collection's highlights. Your ticket here is also good for same-day admission to the Legion of Honor. *50 Hagiwara Tea Garden Dr., Golden Gate Park*

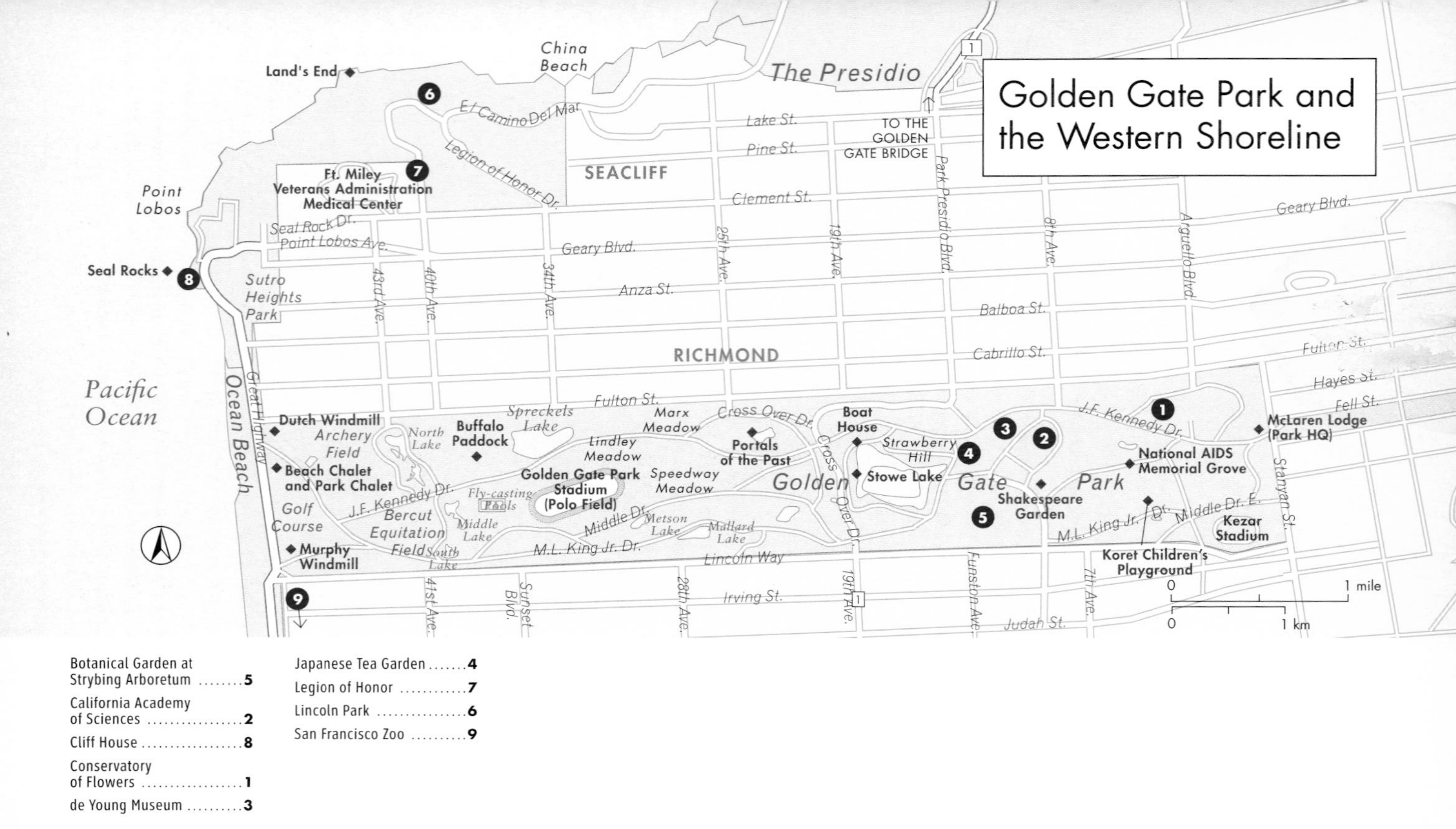
Golden Gate Park and the Western Shoreline
The Presidio
China Beach
Land's End
Point Lobos
Seal Rocks
Pacific Ocean
Ocean Beach
Great Highway
Sutro Heights Park
Ft. Miley Veterans Administration Medical Center
Seal Rock Dr.
Point Lobos Ave.
El Camino Del Mar
Legion of Honor Dr.
SEACLIFF
RICHMOND
TO THE GOLDEN GATE BRIDGE
Lake St.
Pine St.
Clement St.
Geary Blvd.
Anza St.
Balboa St.
Cabrillo St.
Fulton St.
Hayes St.
Fell St.
43rd Ave.
40th Ave.
34th Ave.
25th Ave.
19th Ave.
Park Presidio Blvd.
8th Ave.
Arguello Blvd.
Stanyan St.
41st Ave.
Sunset Blvd.
28th Ave.
Funston Ave.
7th Ave.
Irving St.
Judah St.
Lincoln Way
Dutch Windmill
Archery Field
North Lake
Buffalo Paddock
Spreckels Lake
Beach Chalet and Park Chalet
Golf Course
Murphy Windmill
J.F. Kennedy Dr.
Bercut Equitation Field
South Lake
Fly-casting Pools
Middle Lake
Golden Gate Park Stadium (Polo Field)
Lindley Meadow
Marx Meadow
Speedway Meadow
Middle Dr.
Metson Lake
Mallard Lake
M.L. King Jr. Dr.
Cross Over Dr.
Portals of the Past
Boat House
Strawberry Hill
Stowe Lake
Golden Gate Park
Shakespeare Garden
National AIDS Memorial Grove
McLaren Lodge (Park HQ)
Middle Dr. E.
Kezar Stadium
Koret Children's Playground
0
1 mile
0
1 km
Botanical Garden at Strybing Arboretum 5
California Academy of Sciences 2
Cliff House 8
Conservatory of Flowers 1
de Young Museum 3
Japanese Tea Garden 4
Legion of Honor 7
Lincoln Park 6
San Francisco Zoo 9

415/863–3330 www.deyoungmuseum.org $10, free 1st Tues. of month Tues.–Sun. 9:30–5:15, Fri. until 8:45.

4 **Japanese Tea Garden.** As you amble through the manicured landscape, past Japanese sculptures and perfect miniature pagodas, over ponds of carp that have been here since before the 1906 quake, you may be transported to a more peaceful plane. Or maybe the shrieks of kids clambering over the almost vertical "humpback" bridges will keep you firmly in the here and now. Either way, this garden is one of those tourist spots that are truly worth a stop (a half-hour will do). And at 5 acres, it's large enough that you'll always be able to find a bit of serenity, even when the tour buses drop by. The garden is especially lovely in April, when the cherry blossoms are in bloom. *Hagiwara Tea Garden Dr., off John F. Kennedy Dr., Golden Gate Park 415/752–4227 $4, free Mon., Wed., and Fri. 9 AM–10 AM Mar.–Sept., daily 9–6; Oct.–Feb., daily 9–4:45.*

2 **California Academy of Sciences.** Renzo Piano's audacious, prescient design for this natural history museum—which opened in September 2008—complements the dramatic transformation of Golden Gate Park's Music Concourse. An eco-friendly, energy-efficient adventure in biodiversity and green architecture, the museum is equipped with a rain forest, a planetarium, and a retractable ceiling over the central courtyard—but its most dramatic feature is a "living roof" that's covered with native plants. *55 Music Concourse Dr., Golden Gate Park 415/379–8000 www.calacademy.org $24.95 Mon.–Sat. 9:30–5, Sun. 11–5.*

WHAT TO SEE ON THE WESTERN SHORELINE

8 **Cliff House.** A meal at the Cliff House isn't about the food—the spectacular ocean view is what brings folks here. The vistas, which include offshore Seal Rock (the barking marine mammals who reside there are actually sea lions), can be 30 mi or more on a clear day—or less than a mile on foggy days. ■ **TIP→ Come for drinks just before sunset; then head back into town for dinner.**

Three buildings have occupied this site since 1863. The current building dates from 1909; a 2004 renovation has left a strikingly attractive restaurant and a squat concrete viewing platform out back. The complex, owned by the National Park Service, includes a gift shop.

Sitting on the observation deck is the **Giant Camera,** a cute yellow-painted wooden model of an old-fashioned camera with its lens pointing skyward. Built in the 1940s and threatened many times with demolition, it's now on the National Register of Historic Places. Step into the dark, tiny room inside (for a rather steep $5 fee); a fascinating 360-degree image of the surrounding area—which rotates as the "lens" on the roof rotates—is projected on a large, circular table. ■ **TIP→ In winter and spring, you may also glimpse migrating gray whales from the observation deck.**

To the north of the Cliff House are the ruins of the once-grand glass-roof **Sutro Baths,** which you can explore on your own (they look a bit like water-storage receptacles). Adolf Sutro, eccentric onetime San Francisco mayor and Cliff House owner, built the bath complex, including a train out to the site, in 1896, so that everyday folks could enjoy the benefits of swimming. Six enormous baths (some freshwater and some seawater), more than 500 dressing rooms, and several restaurants covered 3 acres north of the Cliff House and accommodated 25,000 bathers. Likened to Roman baths in a European glass palace, the baths were for decades the favorite destination of San Franciscans in search of entertainment. The complex fell into disuse after World War II, was closed in 1952, and burned down (under officially questionable circumstances, wink wink) during demolition in 1966. ✉ *1090 Point Lobos Ave., Outer Richmond* ☎ *415/386–3330* 🌐 *www.cliffhouse.com* 🎟 *Free* 🕒 *Weekdays 9* AM*–9:30* PM*, weekends 9* AM*–10* PM.

7 ★ **Legion of Honor.** The old adage of real estate—location, location, location—is at full force here. You can't beat the spot of this museum of European art—situated on cliffs overlooking the ocean, the Golden Gate Bridge, and the Marin Headlands. A pyramidal glass skylight in the entrance court illuminates the lower-level galleries, which exhibit prints and drawings, English and European porcelain, and ancient Assyrian, Greek, Roman, and Egyptian art. The 20-plus galleries on the upper level display the permanent collection of European art (paintings, sculpture, decorative arts, and tapestries) from the 14th century to the present day.

The noteworthy Auguste Rodin collection includes two galleries devoted to the master and a third with works by Rodin and other 19th-century sculptors. An original cast of Rodin's *The Thinker* welcomes you as you walk through the courtyard. As fine as the museum is, the setting and view outshine the collection and make a trip here worthwhile.

The **Legion Café,** on the lower level, serves tasty light meals (soups, sandwiches, grilled chicken) inside and on a garden terrace. (Unfortunately, there's no view.) Just north of the museum's parking lot is George Segal's *The Holocaust,* a stark white installation that evokes life in concentration camps during World War II. It's haunting at night, when backlighted by lights in the Legion's parking lot. ■ **TIP→ Admission to the Legion also counts as same-day admission to the de Young Museum.** ✉ *34th Ave. at Clement St., Outer Richmond* ☎ *415/750–3600* 🌐 *www.thinker.org* 🎟 *$10, $2 off with Muni transfer, free 1st Tues. of month* 🕒 *Tues.–Sun. 9:30–5:15.*

6 ★ **Lincoln Park.** Although many of the city's green spaces are gentle and welcoming, Lincoln Park is a wild 275-acre park with windswept cliffs and panoramic views. The newly renovated Coastal Trail, the park's most dramatic, leads out to **Lands End**; pick it up west of the Legion of Honor (at the end of El Camino del Mar) or from the parking lot at Point Lobos and El Camino del Mar. Time your hike to hit Mile Rock at low tide, and you might catch a glimpse of two wrecked ships peeking up from their watery graves. ■ **TIP→ Do be careful if you hike here; landslides are frequent, and many people have fallen into the sea by standing too close to the edge of a crumbling bluff top.**

On the tamer side, large Monterey cypresses line the fairways at Lincoln Park's 18-hole golf course, near the Legion of Honor. At one time this land was the Golden Gate Cemetery, where the dead were segregated by nationality; most were indigent and interred without ceremony in the potter's field. In 1900, the Board of Supervisors voted to ban burials within city limits, and all but two city cemeteries (at Mission Dolores and the Presidio) were moved to Colma, a small town just south of San Francisco. When digging has to be done in the park, bones occasionally surface again. ✉*Entrance at 34th Ave. at Clement St., Outer Richmond.*

Ocean Beach. Stretching 3 mi along the western side of the city from the Richmond to the Sunset, this sandy swath of the Pacific coast is good for jogging or walking the dog—but not for swimming. The water is so cold that surfers wear wet suits year-round, and riptides are strong. As for sunbathing, it's rarely warm enough here; think meditative walking instead of sun worshipping.

4

Paths on both sides of the Great Highway lead from Lincoln Way to Sloat Boulevard (near the zoo); the beachside path winds through landscaped sand dunes, and the paved path across the highway is good for biking and in-line skating. (Though you have to rent bikes elsewhere.) The **Beach Chalet** restaurant and brewpub is across the Great Highway from Ocean Beach, about five blocks south of the Cliff House. ✉*Along Great Hwy. from Cliff House to Sloat Blvd. and beyond.*

9 **San Francisco Zoo.** Awash in bad press since one of its tigers escaped its enclosure and killed a visitor on Christmas day 2007, the city's zoo is struggling to polish its image, raise its attendance numbers, scrounge up funds to update its habitats, and restore its reputation with animal welfare organizations. Nestled onto prime oceanfront property, the zoo—which some have accused of caring more about human entertainment than the welfare of its wards—is touting its metamorphosis into the "New Zoo," a wildlife-focused recreation center that inspires visitors to become conservationists. Integrated exhibits group different species of animals from the same geographic areas together in enclosures that don't look like cages. More than 250 species reside here, including endangered species such as the snow leopard, Sumatran tiger, and grizzly bear. ✉*Sloat Blvd. and 47th Ave., Sunset* ✣*Muni L–Taraval streetcar from downtown* ☎*415/753–7080* 🌐*www.sfzoo.org* *$15, $1 off with Muni transfer* ⏲*Daily 10–5. Children's zoo 10–4:30.*

THE HAIGHT, THE CASTRO, AND NOE VALLEY

Once you've seen the blockbuster sights and you're getting curious about the neighborhoods where the city's soul resides, come out to these three areas. They wear their personalities large and proud, and all are perfect for just strolling around. You can move from the Haight's residue of 1960s counterculture to the Castro's connection to 1970s and '80s gay life to 1990s gentrification in Noe Valley. Although history thrust the Haight and the Castro onto the international stage, both are anything but stagnant—they're still dynamic areas well worth exploring. Noe Valley may lack the headlines, but a mellow morning walk here will make you feel like a local.

WHAT TO SEE IN THE HAIGHT

3 **Haight-Ashbury intersection.** On October 6, 1967, hippies took over the intersection of Haight and Ashbury streets to proclaim the "Death of Hip." If they thought hip was dead then, they'd find absolute confirmation of it today, what with the only tie-dye in sight on the Ben & Jerry's storefront on the famed corner.

Everyone knows the Summer of Love had something to do with free love and LSD, but the drugs and other excesses of that period have tended to obscure the residents' serious attempts to create an America that was more spiritually oriented, more environmentally aware, and less caught up in commercialism. The Diggers, a radical group of actors and populist agitators, for example, operated a free shop a few blocks off Haight Street. Everything really was free at the free shop; people brought in things they didn't need and took things they did. (The group also coined immortal phrases like "Do your own thing.")

Among the folks who hung out in or near the Haight during the late 1960s were writers Richard Brautigan, Allen Ginsberg, Ken Kesey, and Gary Snyder; anarchist Abbie Hoffman; rock performers Marty Balin, Jerry Garcia, Janis Joplin, and Grace Slick; LSD champion Timothy Leary; and filmmaker Kenneth Anger. If you're keen to feel something resembling the hippie spirit these days, there's always Hippie Hill, just inside the Haight Street entrance of Golden Gate Park. Think drum circles, guitar players, and whiffs of pot smoke.

WHAT TO SEE IN THE CASTRO

2 ★ **Castro Theatre.** Here's a classic way to join in the Castro community: grab some popcorn and catch a flick at this gorgeous, 1,500-seat art-deco theater; opened in 1922, it's the grandest of San Francisco's few remaining movie palaces. The neon marquee, which stands at the top of the Castro strip, is the neighborhood's great landmark. The Castro was the fitting host of 2008's red-carpet preview of Gus Van Sant's film *Milk,* starring Sean Penn as openly gay San Francisco supervisor Harvey Milk. The theater's elaborate Spanish baroque interior is fairly well preserved. Before many shows the theater's pipe organ rises from the orchestra pit and an organist plays pop and movie tunes, usually ending with the Jeanette McDonald standard "San Francisco" (go ahead, sing along). The crowd can be enthusiastic and vocal, talking back to the screen as loudly as it talks to them. Classics such as *Who's Afraid of Virginia Woolf?* take on a whole new life, with the assembled beating the actors to the punch and fashioning even snappier comebacks for Elizabeth Taylor. Head here to catch classics, a Fellini film retrospective, or the latest take on same-sex love. ✉*429 Castro St., Castro* ☎*415/621–6120.*

1 **Harvey Milk Plaza.** An 18-foot-long rainbow flag, the symbol of gay pride, flies above this plaza named for the man who electrified the city in 1977 by being elected to its Board of Supervisors as an openly gay candidate. In the early 1970s Milk had opened a camera store on the block of Castro Street between 18th and 19th streets. The store became the center for his campaign to open San Francisco's social and political life to gays and lesbians.

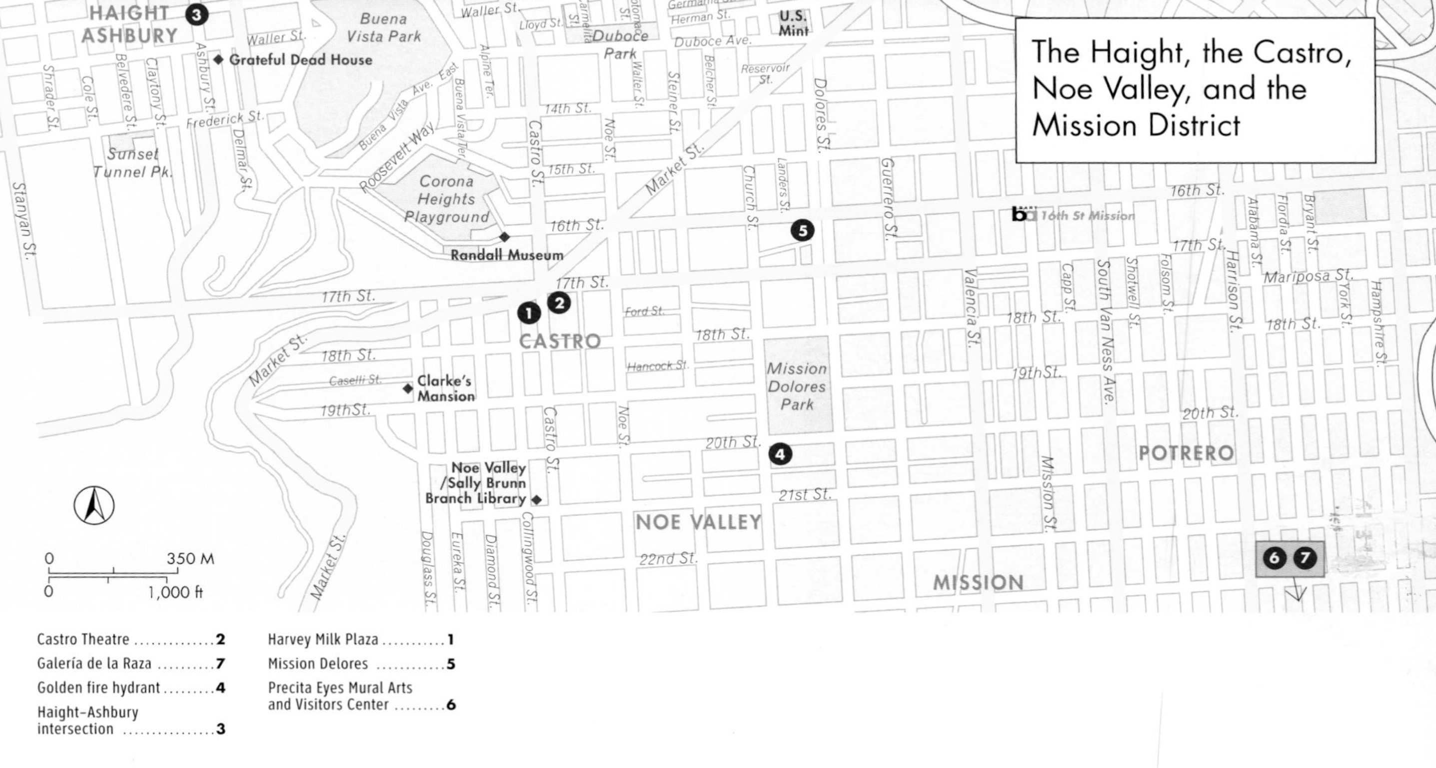
The Haight, the Castro, Noe Valley, and the Mission District
HAIGHT ASHBURY
Buena Vista Park
Grateful Dead House
Waller St.
Lloyd St.
Carmelita St.
Potomac St.
Duboce Park
Germania St.
Herman St.
Duboce Ave.
U.S. Mint
Reservoir St.
Shrader St.
Cole St.
Belvedere St.
Claytony St.
Ashbury St.
Frederick St.
Delmar St.
Buena Vista Ave. East
Buena Vista Ter.
Alpine Ter.
Walter St.
Steiner St.
Belcher St.
Dolores St.
Sunset Tunnel Pk.
Stanyan St.
Roosevelt Way
Corona Heights Playground
Randall Museum
Castro St.
14th St.
Noe St.
15th St.
16th St.
17th St.
Market St.
Church St.
Landers St.
Guerrero St.
16th St Mission
Alabama St.
Flordia St.
Bryant St.
Mariposa St.
Harrison St.
Folsom St.
Shotwell St.
South Van Ness Ave.
Capp St.
Valencia St.
18th St.
York St.
Hampshire St.
Ford St.
CASTRO
Hancock St.
Caselli St.
Clarke's Mansion
19thSt.
Mission Dolores Park
20th St.
POTRERO
Mission St.
Noe Valley /Sally Brunn Branch Library
21st St.
NOE VALLEY
22nd St.
MISSION
Douglass St.
Eureka St.
Diamond St.
Collingwood St.
0 350 M
0 1,000 ft
Castro Theatre 2
Galería de la Raza 7
Golden fire hydrant 4
Haight-Ashbury intersection 3
Harvey Milk Plaza 1
Mission Delores 5
Precita Eyes Mural Arts and Visitors Center 6
4

Punchy street art is a hallmark of the Haight.

The liberal Milk hadn't served a full year of his term before he and Mayor George Moscone, also a liberal, were shot in November 1978 at City Hall. The murderer was a conservative ex-supervisor named Dan White, who had recently resigned his post and then became enraged when Moscone wouldn't reinstate him. Milk and White had often been at odds on the board, and White thought Milk had been part of a cabal to keep him from returning to his post. Milk's assassination shocked the gay community, which became infuriated when the infamous "Twinkie defense"—that junk food had led to diminished mental capacity—resulted in a manslaughter verdict for White. During the so-called White Night Riot of May 21, 1979, gays and their sympathizers stormed City Hall, torching its lobby and several police cars.

Milk, who had feared assassination, left behind a tape recording in which he urged the community to continue the work he had begun. His legacy is the high visibility of gay people throughout city government; a bust of him was unveiled at City Hall on his birthday in 2008; and the 2008 film *Milk* gives insight into his life. A plaque at the base of the flagpole lists the names of past and present openly gay and lesbian state and local officials. ✉*Southwest corner of Castro and Market Sts., Castro.*

WHAT TO SEE IN NOE VALLEY

❹ **Golden fire hydrant.** When all the other fire hydrants went dry during the fire that followed the 1906 earthquake, this one kept pumping. Noe Valley and the Mission District were thus spared the devastation wrought elsewhere in the city, which explains the large number of pre-quake homes here. Every year on April 18 (the anniversary of the quake), the famous hydrant gets a fresh coat of gold paint. ✉ *Church and 20th Sts., southeast corner, across from Dolores Park, Noe Valley.*

CASTRO AND NOE WALK

The Castro and Noe Valley are both neighborhoods that beg to be walked—or ambled through, really, without time pressure or an absolute destination. Hit the Castro first, beginning at Harvey Milk Plaza under the gigantic rainbow flag. If you're going on to Noe Valley, first head east down Market Street for the cafés, bistros, and shops, then go back to Castro Street and head south, past the glorious art-deco Castro Theatre, checking out boutiques and cafés along the way. To tour Noe Valley, go east down 18th Street to Church (at Dolores Park), and then either strap on your hiking boots and head south over the hill or hop the J-Church to 24th Street, the center of this rambling neighborhood.

4

MISSION DISTRICT

The Mission has a number of distinct personalities: it's the Latino neighborhood, where working-class folks raise their families and where gangs occasionally clash; it's the hipster hood, where tattooed and pierced twenty- and thirtysomethings hold court in the coolest cafés and bars in town; it's a culinary epicenter, with the strongest concentration of destination restaurants and affordable ethnic cuisine; and it's the artists' quarter, where murals adorn literally blocks of walls. It's also the city's equivalent of the Sunshine State—this neighborhood's always the last to succumb to fog.

WHAT TO SEE IN THE MISSION DISTRICT

7 **Galería de la Raza.** San Francisco's premier showcase for contemporary Latino art, the gallery exhibits the works of mostly local artists. Events include readings and spoken word by local poets and writers, screenings of Latin American and Spanish films, and theater works by local minority theater troupes. Just across the street, amazing art festoons the 24th Street/York Street Minipark, a tiny urban playground. A mosaic-covered Quetzalcoatl serpent plunges into the ground and rises, creating hills for little ones to clamber over, and mural-covered walls surround the space. ✉ *2857 24th St., at Bryant St., Mission* ☎ *415/826–8009* 🌐 *www.galeriadelaraza.org* ⏲ *Gallery Tues. 1–7, Wed.–Sat. noon–6.*

5 ★ **Mission Dolores.** Two churches stand side by side at this mission, including the small adobe **Mission San Francisco de Asís,** the oldest standing structure in San Francisco. Completed in 1791, it's the sixth of the 21 California missions founded by Father Junípero Serra in the 18th and early 19th centuries. Its ceiling depicts original Ohlone Indian basket designs, executed in vegetable dyes. The tiny chapel includes frescoes and a hand-painted wooden altar. There's a hidden treasure here, too. In 2004 an archaeologist and an artist crawling along the ceiling's rafters opened a trap door behind the altar and rediscovered the mission's original mural, painted with natural dyes by Native Americans in 1791. The centuries have taken their toll, so the team photographed the 20- by 22-foot mural and began digitally restoring the photographic version. Among the images is a dagger-pierced Sacred Heart of Jesus.

There's a small museum covering the mission's founding and history, and the pretty little mission cemetery (made famous by a scene in Alfred Hitchcock's *Vertigo*) maintains the graves of mid-19th-century European immigrants. (The remains of an estimated 5,000 Native Americans lie in unmarked graves.) Services are held in both the Mission San Francisco de Asís and next door in the handsome multi-dome basilica. ✉*Dolores and 16th Sts., Mission* ☎*415/621–8203* 🌐*www.missiondolores.org* 🎟*$5 donation, audio tour $7* ⏲*Nov.–Apr., daily 9–4; May–Oct., daily 9–4:30.*

6 **Precita Eyes Mural Arts and Visitors Center.** Founded by muralists, this nonprofit arts organization designs and creates murals. The artists themselves lead informative guided walks of murals in the area. Most tours start with a 45-minute slide presentation. The bike and walking trips, which take between one and three hours, pass several dozen murals. May is Mural Awareness Month, with visits to murals-in-progress and presentations by artists. You can pick up a map of 24th Street's murals at the center and buy art supplies, T-shirts, postcards, and other mural-related items. Bike tours are available by appointment; Saturday's 11 AM walking tour meets at Cafe Venice, at 24th and Mission streets. (All other tours meet at the center.) ✉*2981 24th St., Mission* ☎*415/285–2287* 🌐*www.precitaeyes.org* 🎟*Center free, tours $10–$12* ⏲*Center weekdays 10–5, Sat. 10–4, Sun. noon–4; walks weekends at 11 and 1:30 or by appointment.*

PACIFIC HEIGHTS AND JAPANTOWN

Pacific Heights and Japantown are something of an odd couple: privileged, old-school San Francisco and the workaday commercial center of Japanese-American life in the city, stacked virtually on top of each other. The sprawling, extravagant mansions of Pacific Heights gradually give way to the more modest Victorians and unassuming housing tracts of Japantown. The cool boutiques and cafés of northern Fillmore Street fade into salons and pizzerias farther south. The most interesting spots in Japantown huddle in the Japan Center, the neighborhood's two-block centerpiece, and along Post Street. You can find plenty of authentic Japanese treats in the shops and restaurants, but unless you have a special interest in these, the area likely won't make it onto your must-see list.

■ TIP→ Japantown is a relatively safe area, but the Western Addition, south of Geary Boulevard, can be dangerous even during the daytime. Avoid going too far west of Fillmore Street on either side of Geary.

WHAT TO SEE IN PACIFIC HEIGHTS

5 **Franklin Street buildings.** What at first looks like a stone facade on the **Golden Gate Church** (✉*1901 Franklin St., Pacific Heights*) is actually redwood painted white. A Georgian-style residence built in the early 1900s for a coffee merchant sits at 1735 Franklin. On the northeast corner of Franklin and California streets is a **Christian Science church**; built in the Tuscan Revival style, it's noteworthy for its terra-cotta detailing. The **Coleman House** (✉*1701 Franklin St., Pacific Heights*) is an impressive twin-turret Queen Anne mansion that was built for

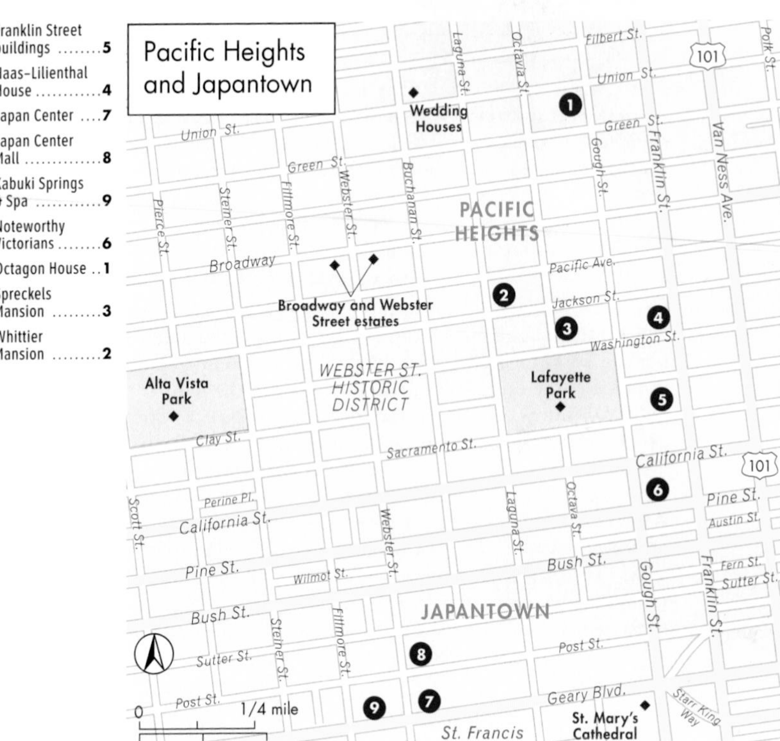

4

a gold-rush mining and lumber baron. Don't miss the large, brilliant-purple stained-glass window on the house's north side. ✉*Franklin St. between Washington and California Sts., Pacific Heights.*

❹ **Haas-Lilienthal House.** A small display of photographs on the bottom floor of this elaborate, gray 1886 Queen Anne house makes clear that despite its lofty stature and striking, round third-story tower, the house was modest compared with some of the giants that fell victim to the 1906 earthquake and fire. The Foundation for San Francisco's Architectural Heritage operates the home, whose carefully kept rooms provide an intriguing glimpse into late-19th-century life through period furniture, authentic details (antique dishes in the kitchen built-in), and photos of the family who occupied the house until 1972. Volunteers conduct one-hour house tours three days a week and informative two-hour walking tours ($8) of the Civic Center, Broadway, and Union Street areas on Saturday afternoon, and of the eastern portion of Pacific Heights on Sunday afternoon (call or check Web site for schedule). ✉*2007 Franklin St., between Washington and Jackson Sts., Pacific Heights* ☎*415/441–3004* 🌐*www.sfheritage.org* 🎟*Entry $8* ⏲*1-hr tour Wed. and Sat. noon–3, Sun. 11–4; 2-hr tour Sun. at 12:30.*

❻ **Noteworthy Victorians.** Two **Italianate Victorians** (✉*1818 and 1834 California St., Pacific Heights*) stand out on the 1800 block of California. A block farther is the Victorian-era **Atherton House** (✉*1990 California St., Pacific Heights*), whose mildly daffy design incorporates Queen Anne, Stick-Eastlake, and other architectural elements. Many claim the house—now apartments—is haunted by the ghosts of its 19th-century residents, who regularly whisper, glow, and generally cause a mild fuss. The oft-photographed **Laguna Street Victorians,** on the west side of the 1800 block of Laguna Street, cost between $2,000 and $2,600 when they were built in the 1870s. No bright colors here though—most of the paint jobs are in soft beiges or pastels. ✉*California St. between Franklin and Octavia Sts., and Laguna St. between Pine and Bush Sts., Pacific Heights.*

❶ **Octagon House.** This eight-sided home sits across the street from its original site on Gough Street; it's one of two remaining octagonal houses in the city (the other is on Russian Hill), and the only one open to the public. White quoins accent each of the eight corners of the pretty blue-gray exterior, and a colonial-style garden completes the picture. Inside, it's full of antique American furniture, decorative arts (paintings, silver, rugs), and documents from the 18th and 19th centuries. A deck of Revolutionary-era hand-painted playing cards takes an antimonarchist position: in place of kings, queens, and jacks, the American upstarts substituted American statesmen, Roman goddesses, and Indian chiefs. ✉*2645 Gough St., Pacific Heights* ☎*415/441–7512* *Free, donations encouraged* ⏲*Feb.–Dec., 2nd Sun. and 2nd and 4th Thurs. of month noon–3; group tours weekdays by appointment.*

❸ **Spreckels Mansion.** Shrouded behind tall juniper hedges at the corner of lovely winding, brick Octavia Street, overlooking Lafayette Park, the estate was built for sugar heir Adolph Spreckels and his wife Alma. Mrs. Spreckels was so pleased with her house that she commissioned George Applegarth to design another building in a similar vein: the Legion of Honor. One of the city's great iconoclasts, Alma Spreckels was the model for the bronze figure atop the Victory Monument in Union Square. Today this house belongs to prolific romance novelist Danielle Steel. ✉*2080 Washington St., at Octavia St., Pacific Heights.*

❷ **Whittier Mansion.** With a Spanish-tile roof and scrolled bay windows on all four sides, this is one of the most elegant 19th-century houses in the state. An anomaly in a town that lost most of its grand mansions to the 1906 quake, the Whittier Mansion was built so solidly that only a chimney toppled over during the disaster. ✉*2090 Jackson St., Pacific Heights.*

WHAT TO SEE IN JAPANTOWN

❼ **Japan Center.** Intriguing browsing, noodle houses and sushi joints, a destination bookstore, and a peek at Japanese culture high and low await at this 5-acre complex, designed in 1968 by noted American architect Minoru Yamasaki. Architecturally, the development hasn't aged well, and its Peace Plaza, where seasonal festivals are held, is an unwelcoming sea of cement. The Japan Center includes the shop- and restaurant-filled Kintetsu and Kinokuniya buildings; the excellent Kabuki Springs & Spa; the Hotel Kabuki; and the Sundance Kabuki, Robert Redford's fancy, reserved-seating cinema/restaurant complex.

DID YOU KNOW?

These soft-colored Victorian homes in Pacific Heights are closer to the original hues sported back in the 1900s. It wasn't until the 1960s that the bold, electric colors now seen around SF gained popularity. Before that, the most typical house paint color was a standard gray.

The Kinokuniya Bookstores, in the Kinokuniya Building, have an extensive selection of Japanese-language books, *manga* (graphic novels), books on design, and English-language translations and books on Japanese topics. Just outside, follow the Japanese teenagers to Pika Pika, where you and your friends can step into a photo booth and then use special effects and stickers to decorate your creation. On the bridge connecting the center's two buildings, check out Shige Antiques for *yukata* (lightweight cotton kimonos) for kids and lovely silk kimonos, and Asakichi and its tiny incense shop for tinkling wind chimes and display-worthy teakettles. Continue into the Kintetsu Building for a selection of Japanese restaurants.

Between the Miyako Mall and Kintetsu Building are the five-tier, 100-foot-tall **Peace Pagoda** and the Peace Plaza. The pagoda, which draws on the 1,200-year-old tradition of miniature round pagodas dedicated to eternal peace, was designed in the late 1960s by Yoshiro Taniguchi to convey the "friendship and goodwill" of the Japanese people to the people of the United States. The plaza itself is a shadeless, unwelcoming stretch of cement with little seating. Continue into the Miyako Mall to Ichiban Kan, a Japanese dollar store where you can pick up fun Japanese kitchenware, tote bags decorated with hedgehogs, and erasers shaped like food. ⊠*Bordered by Geary Blvd. and Fillmore, Post, and Laguna Sts., Japantown* ☎*No phone.*

8 **Japan Center Mall.** The buildings lining this open-air mall are of the shoji school of architecture. The mall's many good restaurants draw a lively crowd of nearby workers for lunch, but the atmosphere remains weirdly hushed. The shops are geared more toward locals—travel agencies, electronics shops—but there are some fun Japanese goods stores. Arrive early in the day and you may score some fabulous *mochi* (a soft, sweet Japanese rice treat) at **Benkyodo** (⊠*1747 Buchanan St., Japantown* ☎*415/922–1244*). It's easy to spend hours among the fabulous origami and craft papers at **Paper Tree** (⊠*1743 Buchanan St., Japantown* ☎*415/921–7100*), open since the 1960s. Be sure to swing around the corner, just off the mall, to **Super 7** (⊠*1628 Post St., Japantown* ☎*415/409–4700*), home of many large plastic Godzillas, glow-in-the-dark robots, and cool graphic tees. You can have a seat on local artist Ruth Asawa's twin origami-style fountains, which sit in the middle of the mall; they're squat circular structures made of fieldstone, with three levels for sitting and a brick floor. ⊠*Buchanan St. between Post and Sutter Sts., Japantown* ☎*No phone.*

9 ★ **Kabuki Springs & Spa.** This serene spa is one Japantown destination that draws locals from all over town, from hipster to grandma, Japanese-American or not. Balinese urns decorate the communal bath area of this house of tranquillity, and you're just as likely to hear soothing flute or classical music as you are Kitaro.

The massage palette has also expanded well beyond traditional Shiatsu technique. The experience is no less relaxing, however, and the treatment regimen includes facials, salt scrubs, and mud and seaweed wraps. You can take your massage in a private room with a bath or in a curtained-off area. The communal baths ($20 weekdays, $25 weekends) contain hot and cold tubs, a large Japanese-style bath, a sauna, a steam room, and showers. Bang the gong for quiet if your fellow bathers are speaking too loudly.

The clothing-optional baths are open for men only on Monday, Thursday, and Saturday; women bathe on Wednesday, Friday, and Sunday. Bathing suits are required on Tuesday, when the baths are coed. Men and women can reserve private rooms daily. An 80-minute massage-and-bath package with a private room costs $130; a package that includes a 50-minute massage and the use of the communal baths costs $95. *✉1750 Geary Blvd.,Japantown ☎415/922–6000 🌐www.kabukisprings.com ⏲Daily 10–10.*

WHERE TO EAT

You can find just about any food in San Francisco, a place where trends are set and culinary diversity rules. Since the 1849 gold rush flooded the city with foreign flavors, residents' appetites for exotic eats haven't diminished by even one bite.

UNION SQUARE

$$$ MEDITERRANEAN

✕**Cortez.** Young, well-dressed hipsters with just-cashed paychecks clog this bright, modern space in the Hotel Adagio. In the past, Cortez was one of the town's premier destinations for small plates, but nowadays the menu is a healthy mix of small and large, and folks don't seem to mind the change. The menu is always in flux—and in recent years, the chef's toque has been, too—but under Jenn Puccio, whose reign dates from spring 2008, you can find such superb dishes as seared padrón peppers with olive oil and sea salt and pork short ribs with roasted grapes under small plates, and grilled lamb chops with eggplant purée under big plates. Cap off the meal with sugar and spice beignets with chocolate fondue and you'll go home happy. If you're in a rush, enjoy crispy fries with *harissa*-spiked aioli chased by a martini in the bar. *✉Hotel Adagio, 550 Geary St., Union Sq. ☎415/292–6360 ▭AE, MC, V ⏲No lunch ✥E4.*

$$$$ AMERICAN Fodor'sChoice ★

✕**Michael Mina.** Decorated in celadon and ivory with stately columns and a vaulted ceiling, this elegant space, inside the Westin St. Francis Hotel, is a match for chef Michael Mina's highly refined fare. His three-course prix-fixe (multiple choices for each course) includes a trio of tastes on each plate—for example, three preparations of pork for a first (terrine with foie gras, belly pork with frisée and quail egg, short ribs bourguignon with forest mushrooms), or of chocolate for a dessert (white chocolate and rose panna cotta, s'mores, chocolate ice cream with lavender and shortbread). Folks who prefer one taste rather than triple bites can opt for one of Mina's signature dishes, such as black mussel soufflé or lobster potpie. Deep-pocketed diners can splurge on a six-course tasting menu. Diners who want to taste Mina's food but not squander next month's rent can stop in at the swanky Clock Bar, across the lobby, where the same kitchen turns out lobster corn dogs, lamb panini, and black-truffle popcorn, all nicely partnered with some

BEST BETS FOR SAN FRANCISCO DINING

With thousands of restaurants to choose from, how will you decide where to eat? Fodor's writers and editors have selected their favorite restaurants by price, cuisine, and experience in the Best Bets lists below. In the first column, Fodor's Choice designations represent the "best of the best" in every price category. You can also search by neighborhood for excellent eats—just peruse the following pages.

Fodor's Choice ★

A16, $$$ p. 217
Boulevard, $$$$ p. 209
Coi, $$$$ p. 212
Delfina, $$$ p. 217
Gary Danko, $$$$ p. 215
Jardinière, $$$$ p. 214
L'Osteria del Forno, $ p. 213
Michael Mina, $$$$ p. 205
Swan Oyster Depot, $ p. 214
Zuni Café, $$$ p. 215

By Price

$

L'Osteria del Forno, p. 213
Swan Oyster Depot, p. 214

$$

Nopa, p. 219

$$$

A16, p. 217
Delfina, p. 217
Zuni Café, p. 215

$$$$

Boulevard, p. 209
Gary Danko, p. 215
Jardinière, p. 214
Michael Mina, p. 205

By Cuisine

AMERICAN

Nopa, p. 219

CHINESE

R&G Lounge, p. 212
Yank Sing, p. 207

FRENCH

Chez Papa, p. 208

INDIAN

Indian Oven, p. 218

ITALIAN

A16, p. 217
Delfina, p. 217

JAPANESE

Mifune, p. 214

LATIN AMERICAN

La Mar Cebicheria, p. 209

MEDITERRANEAN

Cortez, p. 205

MEXICAN

Los Jarritos, p. 218

SEAFOOD

Hog Island Oyster Company, p. 209
Plouf, p. 207
Swan Oyster Depot, p. 214

STEAK HOUSE

Acme Chophouse, p. 208

VIETNAMESE

Slanted Door, p. 209

By Experience

BAY VIEWS

Slanted Door, p. 209

BRUNCH

Rose's Café, p. 217

BUSINESS DINING

Boulevard, p. 209

CHILD-FRIENDLY

Yank Sing, p. 207

COMMUNAL TABLE

Bocadillos, p. 207
Nopa, p. 219

HISTORIC INTEREST

Boulevard, p. 209
Swan Oyster Depot, p. 214

HOT SPOTS

A16, p. 217
Nopa, p. 219
Spruce, p. 214

SMALL PLATES

Bocadillos, p. 207
Laïola, p. 217

SPECIAL OCCASION

Boulevard, p. 209
Gary Danko, p. 215
Jardinière, p. 214
Michael Mina, p. 205

of the best cocktails in town. ✉ *Westin St. Francis Hotel, 335 Powell St., Union Sq.* ☎ *415/397–9222* ✍ *Reservations essential* ▭ *AE, D, DC, MC, V* ⏲ *Closed Sun. and Mon. No lunch* ✥ *E4.*

4

FINANCIAL DISTRICT

$$ SPANISH ✕ **Bocadillos.** The name means "sandwiches," but that's only half the story here. You'll find 11 bocadillos at lunchtime: plump rolls filled with everything from serrano ham to Catalan sausage with arugula to a memorable lamb burger. But at night chef-owner Gerald Hirigoyen, who also owns the high-profile Piperade, focuses on tapas, offering some two dozen choices, including a delicious grilled quail, an equally superb pig's trotters with herbs, and calamari with *romesco* (a thick combination of red pepper, tomato, almonds, and garlic) sauce. His wine list is well matched to the food. A youngish crowd typically piles into the modern, red-brick-wall dining space, so be prepared to wait for a seat. A large communal table is a good perch for singles. If you're in the neighborhood at breakfast time, there is plenty here to keep you happy, including a scrambled eggs and cheese bocadillo or house-made chorizo and eggs. ✉ *710 Montgomery St., Financial District* ☎ *415/982–2622* ✍ *Reservations not accepted* ▭ *AE, MC, V* ⏲ *Closed Sun. No lunch Sat.* ✥ *F3.*

$$ SEAFOOD ✕ **Plouf.** This French-friendly spot is a gold mine for mussel lovers, with six preparations to choose from, plus a mussels and clams combo, all at a modest price. Among the best are *marinière* (white wine, garlic, and parsley) and one combining coconut milk, lime juice, and chili. Add a side of the skinny fries and that's all most appetites need. The menu changes seasonally and includes grilled rack of lamb and roasted duck to satisfy any unrepentant carnivores. Many of the appetizers—oysters on the half shell, calamari with fennel tempura, tuna tartare—stick to seafood, as well. The tables are squeezed together in the bright, lively dining room, so you might overhear neighboring conversations. On temperate days and nights, try for one of the outdoor tables. ✉ *40 Belden Pl., Financial District* ☎ *415/986–6491* ▭ *AE, MC, V* ⏲ *Closed Sun. No lunch Sat.* ✥ *F3.*

$$ CHINESE ✕ **Yank Sing.** This is the granddaddy of the city's dim sum teahouses. It opened in a plain-Jane storefront in Chinatown in 1959 but left its Cantonese neighbors behind for the high-rises of downtown by the 1970s. This brightly decorated location on quiet Stevenson Street (there's also a big, brassy branch in the Rincon Center) serves some of San Francisco's best dim sum to office workers—bosses and clerks alike—on weekdays and to big, boisterous families on weekends. The kitchen cooks up some 100 varieties of dim sum on a rotating basis, offering 60 different types daily. These include both the classic (steamed pork buns, shrimp dumplings, egg custard tartlets) and the creative (scallion-skewered prawns tied with bacon, lobster and tobiko roe dumplings, basil seafood dumplings). A take-out counter makes a meal on the run a satisfying and penny-wise compromise when office duties—or touring—won't wait. ✉ *49 Stevenson St., Financial District* ☎ *415/541–4949* ▭ *AE, DC, MC, V* ⏲ *No dinner* ✉ *1 Rincon Center, 101 Spear St., Embarcadero* ☎ *415/957–9300* ▭ *AE, DC, MC, V* ⏲ *No dinner* ✥ *F4/G4.*

SOMA

$$$ STEAKHOUSE ✕ **Acme Chophouse.** Dine here and you'll agree that cows shouldn't eat corn. Grass-fed beef, served up as a filet mignon and tartare, is the specialty at this old-style chophouse next door to the Giants baseball park. The kitchen stocks only naturally raised local meats and poultry, including a 22-ounce rib eye that's sized to satisfy a sumo wrestler and priced for an emperor. All the familiar chophouse sides—creamed spinach, crisp onion rings, creamy mac-and-cheese—will keep traditionalists smiling. The setting is suitably casual, with lots of wood; TV monitors in the bar area mean no inning is missed. The lunch menu is more casual, with burgers, a crab-and-shrimp salad, pastrami on rye, and a flatiron steak that won't break the bank. Open hours vary on game days, so check before the first pitch. ✉ *24 Willie Mays Plaza, SoMa* ☎ *415/644–0242* ▭ *AE, DC, MC, V* ⊙ *Closed Sun. and Mon. No lunch Sat.* ✣ *G6.*

$$$ ITALIAN ✕ **Ducca.** Nowadays some of the city's best restaurants are in hotel dining rooms, and Ducca, resting smartly in a busy neighborhood of museums, movie houses, and theater spaces, is part of that welcome trend. Start off right with an aperitif and little fried rice balls concealing truffled cheese, or a handful of fried green olives stuffed with Gorgonzola. Follow that up with chef Richard Corbo's dreamy lobster *sformato* (a custardy soufflé) or rustic—and delicious—whole-wheat pasta tossed with sardines and caramelized fennel. Mains are split nearly evenly between meats and fish, including chicken riding alongside polenta flecked with chanterelles and peas. Alas, service is unforgivably ragged at times. Just looking to rest your feet? Join the after-work crowd in the handsome alfresco bar (wisely heated) for a drink and a snack. ✉ *Westin San Francisco Market Street, 50 3rd St., SoMa* ☎ *415/977–0271* ▭ *AE, D, DC, MC, V* ✣ *F5.*

POTRERO HILL

$$ FRENCH ✕ **Chez Papa.** France arrived on Potrero Hill with Chez Papa, which delivers food, waiters, and charm that would be right at home in Provence. The modest corner restaurant, with a Mediterranean blue awning, big windows overlooking the street, and a small heated patio, caters to a lively crowd that makes conversation difficult. Small plates include mussels in wine, *brandade de morue* (salt-cod gratin), and caramelized onion tart with anchovies. Big plates range from rack of lamb and salmon with braised endives to homey lamb daube. Leave space for a typically Gallic crème brûlée or wedge of lemon tart. If you're pennywise, sit down before 6:30 PM Monday through Thursday for a three-course prix-fixe supper priced at $25. To accommodate the overflow of Hill residents who have packed this place since Day One, the owners opened the tiny (and more casual) Chez Maman (crepes, burgers with blue cheese, salads) halfway down the block. ✉ *1401 18th St., Potrero Hill* ☎ *415/255–0387* ▭ *AE, DC, MC, V* ⊙ *No lunch Sun.* ✣ *G6.*

EMBARCADERO

$$$$ AMERICAN Fodor'sChoice ★ **Boulevard.** Two of San Francisco's top restaurant celebrities—chef Nancy Oakes and designer Pat Kuleto—are responsible for this high-profile, high-priced eatery in the magnificent 1889 Audiffred Building, a Parisian look-alike and one of the few downtown structures to survive the 1906 earthquake. Kuleto's Belle Époque interior and Oakes's sophisticated American food with a French accent attract well-dressed locals and flush out-of-towners. The menu changes seasonally, but count on generous portions of dishes like roasted quail stuffed with sweetbreads, chanterelle bisque with pan-seared ricotta gnocchi, and wood-grilled extra-thick pork chop with roasted Lady apples. Save room (and calories) for one of the dynamite desserts, such as butterscotch-almond apple tart Tatin with cinnamon ice cream. There's counter seating for folks too hungry to wait for a table, and a Kobe beef burger at lunchtime that lets you eat with the swells without raiding your piggy bank. *1 Mission St., Embarcadero 415/543–6084 Reservations essential AE, D, DC, MC, V No lunch weekends H4.*

$$ SEAFOOD **Hog Island Oyster Company.** Hog Island, a thriving oyster farm in Tomales Bay, north of San Francisco, serves up its harvest at this attractive raw bar and retail shop in the busy Ferry Building. The U-shaped counter and a handful of tables seat no more than three dozen diners, who come here for impeccably fresh oysters (from Hog Island and elsewhere) or clams (from Hog Island) on the half shell. Other mollusk-centered options include a first-rate oyster stew, clam chowder, and Manila clams with white beans. The bar also turns out what is arguably the best grilled-cheese sandwich (with three artisanal cheeses on artisanal bread) this side of Wisconsin. You need to eat early, however, as the bar closes at 8 on weekdays and 6 on weekends. Happy hour, 5 to 7 on Monday and Thursday, is an oyster lover's dream and jam-packed: sweetwaters for a buck apiece and beer for $3.50. *Ferry Bldg., Embarcadero at Market St., Embarcadero 415/391–7177 AE, MC, V Closed Sun. H3.*

$$ LATIN AMERICAN **La Mar Cebicheria.** This big, casually swanky restaurant, plunked right down on the water's edge, is divided into three areas: a lounge with a long, lively ceviche bar where diners perch and watch chefs put together their plates; the savvy Pisco Bar facing the Embarcadero, where mixologists make a dozen different cocktails based on Peru's famed Pisco brandy; and a bright blue and whitewashed dining room overlooking an outdoor patio and the bay. The waiter starts you out with a pile of potato and plantain chips and three dipping sauces, and then you're on your own, choosing from a long list of ceviches, *causas* (cubed potatoes topped with choices of fish, shellfish, or vegetable salads), and everything from grilled octopus and a tangle of crisp, light deep-fried fish and shellfish to shellfish soups and stews and rice dishes. The original La Mar is in Lima, Peru. San Francisco is the first stop in its campaign to open a string of *cebicherias* across the United States and Latin America. *Pier 1½ between Washington and Jackson Sts., Embarcadero 415/397–8880 AE, D, MC, V G3.*

$$$ VIETNAMESE **Slanted Door.** If you're looking for homey Vietnamese food served in a down-to-earth dining room at a decent price, *don't* stop here. Celebrated

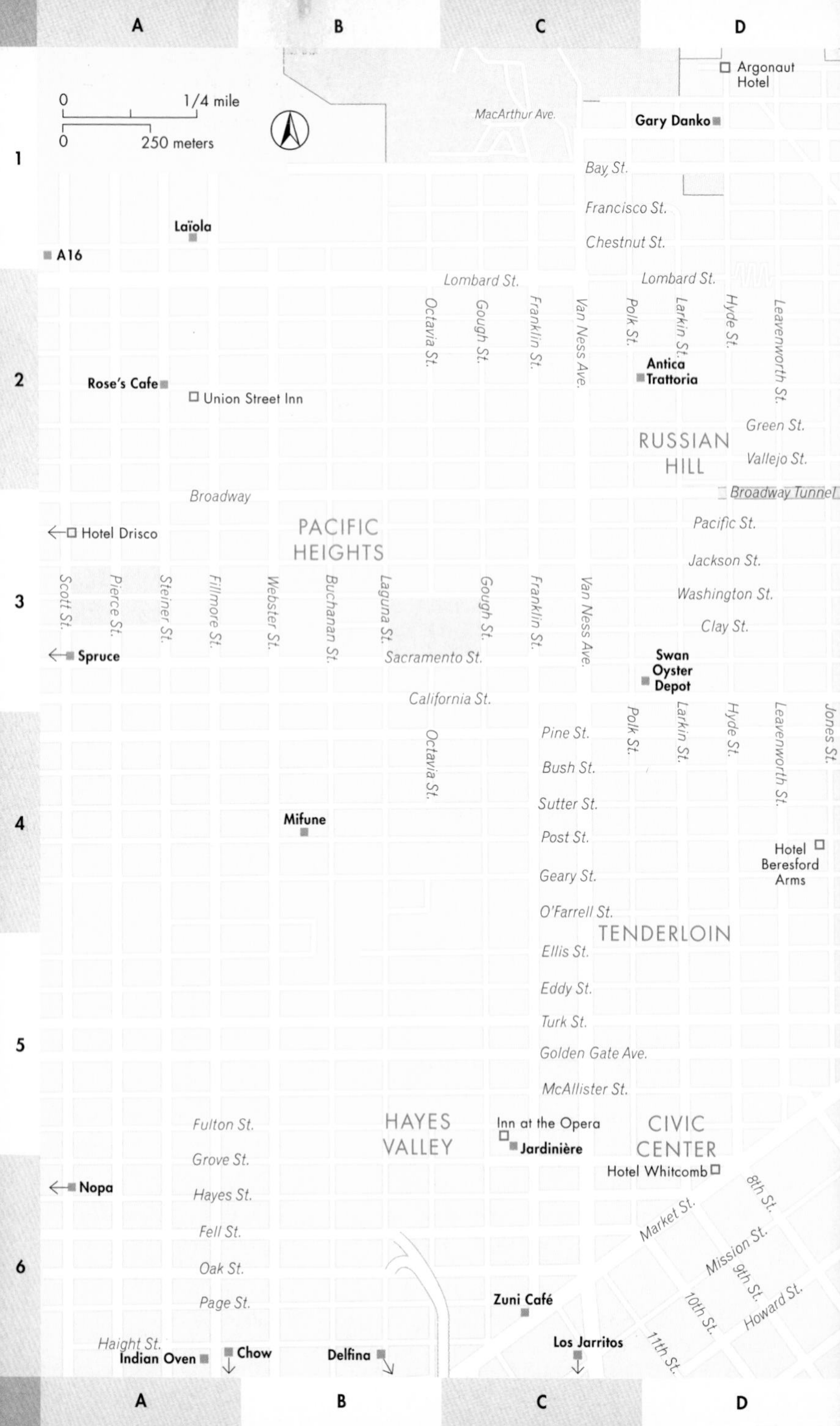
A
B
C
D
1
2
3
4
5
6
0
1/4 mile
0
250 meters
Argonaut Hotel
MacArthur Ave.
Gary Danko
Bay St.
Francisco St.
Chestnut St.
Laïola
A16
Lombard St.
Lombard St.
Octavia St.
Gough St.
Franklin St.
Van Ness Ave.
Polk St.
Larkin St.
Hyde St.
Leavenworth St.
Antica Trattoria
Rose's Cafe
Union Street Inn
Green St.
RUSSIAN HILL
Vallejo St.
Broadway
Broadway Tunnel
Hotel Drisco
PACIFIC HEIGHTS
Pacific St.
Jackson St.
Washington St.
Clay St.
Scott St.
Pierce St.
Steiner St.
Fillmore St.
Webster St.
Buchanan St.
Laguna St.
Gough St.
Franklin St.
Van Ness Ave.
Spruce
Sacramento St.
Swan Oyster Depot
California St.
Pine St.
Bush St.
Octavia St.
Polk St.
Larkin St.
Hyde St.
Leavenworth St.
Jones St.
Sutter St.
Mifune
Post St.
Hotel Beresford Arms
Geary St.
O'Farrell St.
TENDERLOIN
Ellis St.
Eddy St.
Turk St.
Golden Gate Ave.
McAllister St.
Fulton St.
HAYES VALLEY
Inn at the Opera
Jardinière
CIVIC CENTER
Grove St.
Hotel Whitcomb
Nopa
Hayes St.
8th St.
Market St.
Fell St.
Mission St.
Oak St.
9th St.
Zuni Café
10th St.
Howard St.
Page St.
Haight St.
Indian Oven
Chow
Delfina
Los Jarritos
11th St.
A
B
C
D

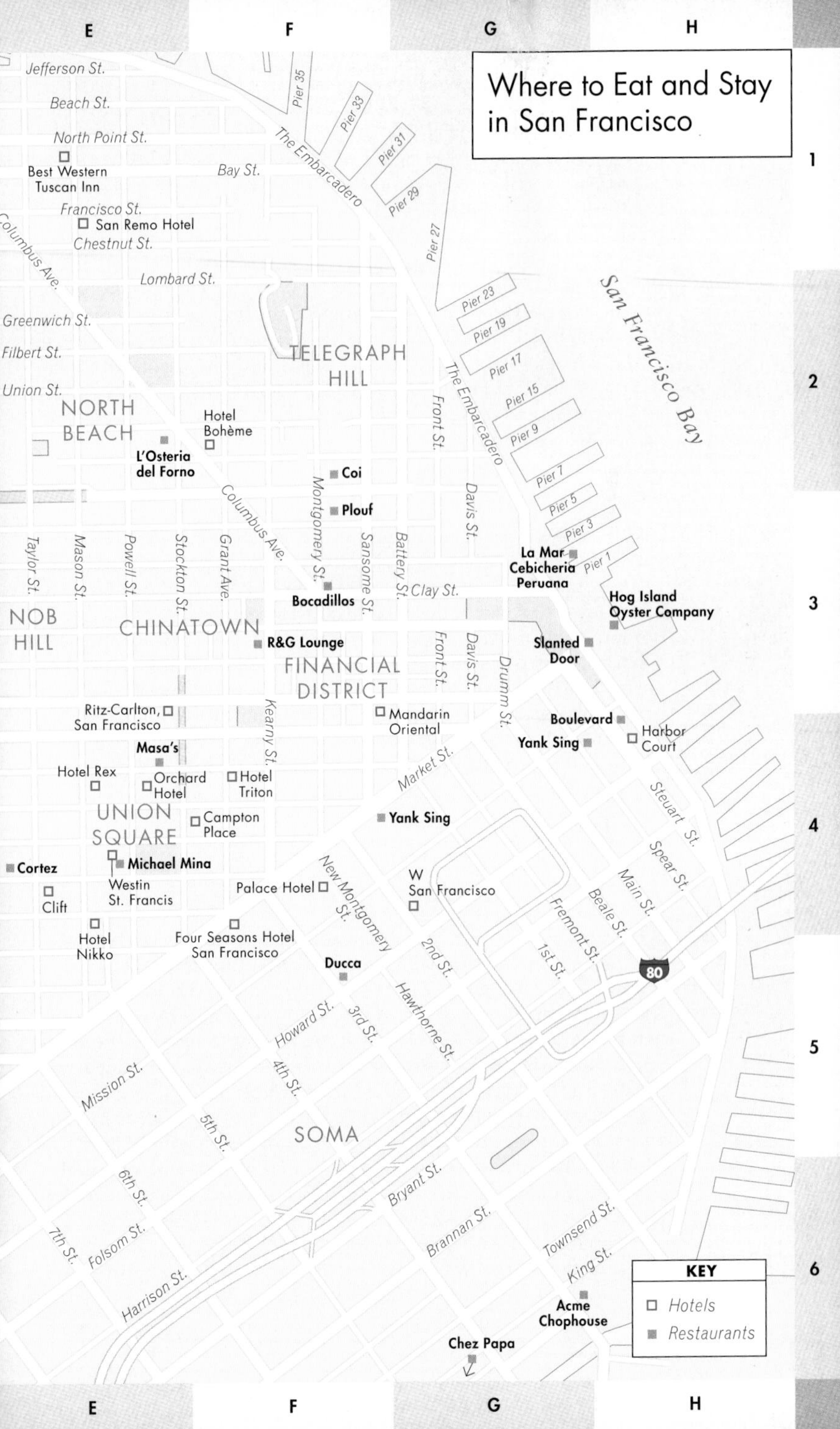
E
F
G
H
Where to Eat and Stay in San Francisco
1
2
3
4
5
6
Jefferson St.
Beach St.
North Point St.
Best Western Tuscan Inn
Bay St.
Francisco St.
San Remo Hotel
Chestnut St.
Columbus Ave.
Lombard St.
Greenwich St.
Filbert St.
Union St.
Pier 35
Pier 33
Pier 31
Pier 29
Pier 27
Pier 23
Pier 19
Pier 17
Pier 15
Pier 9
Pier 7
Pier 5
Pier 3
Pier 1
The Embarcadero
San Francisco Bay
TELEGRAPH HILL
NORTH BEACH
Hotel Bohème
L'Osteria del Forno
Coi
Plouf
Front St.
Davis St.
Columbus Ave.
Montgomery St.
Sansome St.
Battery St.
Clay St.
Taylor St.
Mason St.
Powell St.
Stockton St.
Grant Ave.
La Mar Cebicheria Peruana
Hog Island Oyster Company
Bocadillos
NOB HILL
CHINATOWN
R&G Lounge
FINANCIAL DISTRICT
Slanted Door
Drumm St.
Ritz-Carlton, San Francisco
Kearny St.
Mandarin Oriental
Boulevard
Yank Sing
Harbor Court
Masa's
Hotel Rex
Orchard Hotel
Hotel Triton
Market St.
Steuart St.
UNION SQUARE
Campton Place
Yank Sing
Spear St.
Cortez
Michael Mina
Westin St. Francis
New Montgomery St.
W San Francisco
Main St.
Beale St.
Fremont St.
Clift
Palace Hotel
Hotel Nikko
Four Seasons Hotel San Francisco
Ducca
2nd St.
1st St.
80
Howard St.
3rd St.
Hawthorne St.
4th St.
Mission St.
5th St.
SOMA
6th St.
Bryant St.
7th St.
Folsom St.
Brannan St.
Townsend St.
King St.
Harrison St.
Acme Chophouse
Chez Papa
KEY
Hotels
Restaurants

chef-owner Charles Phan has mastered the upmarket, Western-accented Vietnamese menu. To showcase his cuisine, he chose a big space with sleek wooden tables and chairs, white marble floors, a cocktail lounge, a bar, and an enviable bay view. Among his popular dishes are green papaya salad, cellophane crab noodles, chicken clay pot, and shaking beef (tender beef cubes with garlic and onion). Alas, the crush of fame means that no one speaking in a normal voice can be heard. To avoid the midday and evening crowds (and to save some bucks), stop in for the afternoon-tea menu (spring rolls, grilled pork over rice noodles), or visit Out the Door, Phan's take-out counter around the corner from the restaurant. A second Out the Door, complete with table service, is in the Westfield Centre downtown, and a third one, again with table service, is slated for Lower Pacific Heights. ✉ *Ferry Bldg., Embarcadero at Market St., Embarcadero* ☎ *415/861–8032* ✍ *Reservations essential* ▭ *AE, MC, V* ✣ *G3.*

CHINATOWN

$$
CHINESE
✕ **R&G Lounge.** The name conjures up an image of a dark, smoky bar with a piano player, but this Cantonese restaurant is actually as bright as a new penny. On the lower level (entrance on Kearny Street) is a no-tablecloth dining room that's packed at lunch and dinner. The classy upstairs space (entrance on Commercial Street) is a favorite stop for Chinese businessmen on expense accounts and special-occasion banquets. The street-level room on Kearny is a comfortable spot to wait for a table to open. A menu with photographs helps you pick from the many wonderful, sometimes pricey, always authentic dishes, such as salt-and-pepper Dungeness crab, roast squab, and shrimp-stuffed tofu. You can sip a lychee- or watermelon-flavor martini while waiting for your table. ✉ *631 Kearny St., Chinatown* ☎ *415/982–7877 or 415/982–3811* ▭ *AE, D, DC, MC, V* ✣ *F3.*

NORTH BEACH

$$$$
AMERICAN
Fodor's Choice ★
✕ **Coi.** Daniel Patterson, who has made a name for himself both as a chef and as a pundit on contemporary restaurant trends, has had a restless career, but seems to have settled in at this intriguing 50-seat spot on the gritty end of Broadway. Coi (pronounced *kwa*) is really two restaurants. One is a 30-seat formal dining room—ascetic gold-taupe banquettes on two walls—that offers an 11-course tasting menu ($120). The food matches the space in sophistication, with such inspired dishes as chilled piquillo pepper soup, smoked and seared bone marrow with pomegranate and Asian pear, seared bison with gold turnips, and Monterey Bay abalone with escarole. The menu in the more casual—and more casually priced—lounge is à la carte, with less than a dozen items, including a crisp-skinned roast chicken, a bowl of udon noodles, and a grilled Gruyère cheese sandwich. ✉ *373 Broadway, North Beach* ☎ *415/393–9000* ✍ *Reservations not accepted for lounge* ▭ *AE, MC, V* ⏲ *Closed Sun. and Mon. No lunch* ✣ *F2.*

$ ITALIAN Fodor'sChoice ★ **L'Osteria del Forno.** A staff chattering in Italian and seductive aromas drifting from the open kitchen make customers who pass through the door of this modest storefront, with its sunny yellow walls and friendly waitstaff, feel as if they've stumbled into a homey trattoria in Italy. Each day the kitchen produces small plates of simply cooked vegetables (grilled radicchio, roasted carrots and fennel), a few pastas, a daily special or two, milk-braised pork, a roast of the day, creamy polenta, and thin-crust pizzas—including a memorable "white" pie topped with porcini mushrooms and mozzarella. Wine drinkers will find a good match for any dish they order on the all-Italian list, which showcases gems from limited-production vineyards. At lunch try one of North Beach's best focaccia sandwiches. *519 Columbus Ave., North Beach 415/982–1124 No credit cards Closed Tues. E2.*

4

NOB HILL

$$$$ FRENCH **Masa's.** Although the toque has been passed to several chefs since the death of founding chef Masataka Kobayashi, this 25-year-old restaurant, with its chocolate-brown walls, white fabric ceiling, and red-silk-shaded lanterns, is still one of the country's most celebrated food temples. Chef Gregory Short, who worked alongside Thomas Keller at the famed French Laundry for seven years, is at the helm these days, and his tasting menus of six and nine courses, including a vegetarian option, are pleasing both diners and critics. The fare is dubbed New French, and all the dishes are laced with fancy ingredients, leaving diners struggling to choose between foie gras *au torchon* with poached Seckel pears and foie gras *en sous vide* with Agen prunes. In fall, when northern Italy's exquisite white truffles are in season, Short typically puts together a tasting menu that tucks them into every course, including dessert, which in a past season featured white truffle ice cream perched next to an apple tartlet. Wine drinkers are bound to find something that suits them, with 900 bottles on the list. Be prepared for a decidedly stuffy, though not suffocating, atmosphere (a jacket is preferred for gentlemen). *Hotel Vintage Court, 648 Bush St., Nob Hill 415/989–7154 Reservations essential AE, D, DC, MC, V Closed Sun. and Mon. No lunch E4.*

RUSSIAN HILL

$$ ITALIAN **Antica Trattoria.** The dining room—pale walls, dark-wood floors, a partial view of the kitchen—reflects a strong sense of restraint. The same no-nonsense quality characterizes the authentic Italian food of owner-chef Ruggero Gadaldi, who also operates the flashier Beretta in the Mission. A small, regularly shifting, honestly priced menu delivers archetypal dishes such as carpaccio with capers and Parmesan, pappardelle with wild boar, *tagliata di manzo* (beef fillet slices) with arugula, and tiramisu. The wine list is fairly priced, and the genial service is polished but not stiff. *2400 Polk St., Russian Hill 415/928–5797 DC, MC, V Closed Mon. No lunch C2.*

VAN NESS/POLK

$ SEAFOOD Fodor'sChoice ★ ✕**Swan Oyster Depot.** Here is old San Francisco at its best. Half fish market and half diner, this small, slim seafood operation, open since 1912, has no tables, only a narrow marble counter with about a dozen and a half stools. Most people come in to buy perfectly fresh salmon, halibut, crabs, and other seafood to take home. Everyone else—locals and out-of-towners—hops onto one of the rickety stools to enjoy a bowl of clam chowder—the only hot food served—a dozen oysters, half a cracked crab, a big shrimp salad, or a smaller shrimp cocktail. Come early or late to avoid a long wait. ✉*1517 Polk St., Van Ness/ Polk* ☎*415/673–1101* *Reservations not accepted* *No credit cards* *Closed Sun. No dinner* ✢*D3.*

PACIFIC HEIGHTS

$$$$ AMERICAN ✕**Spruce.** One of the hottest reservations in town from the day it opened, Spruce caters to the city's social set, with the older crowd sliding into the mohair banquettes in the early hours and the younger set taking their places after eight. The large space, a former 1930s auto barn, shelters a high-style dining room and a more casual bar-cum-library lounge, and the menu, which boasts burgers and foie gras, beer and Champagne, is served in both. Charcuterie, bavette steak with bordelaise sauce and duck-fat fries, and sweetbreads and chanterelles reflect the French slant of the modern American menu. If you can't wrangle a table, stop in at the take-out café next door, which carries not only sandwiches, salads, and pastries but also anything from the dining room menu to go. And if you are watching your pocketbook, you can graze off the bar menu and watch the swells come and go. ✉*3640 Sacramento St., Pacific Heights* ☎*415/931–5100* *Reservations essential* *AE, D, DC, MC, V* *No lunch weekends* ✢*A3.*

JAPANTOWN

$ JAPANESE ✕**Mifune.** Thin brown soba and thick white udon are the stars at this long-popular North American outpost of an Osaka-based noodle empire. A line regularly snakes out the door, but the house-made noodles, served both hot and cold and with a score of toppings, are worth the wait. Seating is at wooden tables, where diners of every age can be heard slurping down big bowls of such traditional Japanese combinations as *nabeyaki udon,* wheat noodles topped with tempura, chicken, and fish cake; and *tenzaru,* cold noodles and hot tempura with gingery dipping sauce served on lacquered trays. The noodle-phobic can choose from a few rice dishes. ✉*Japan Center, Kintetsu Bldg., 1737 Post St., Japantown* ☎*415/922–0337* *AE, MC, V* ✢*B4.*

HAYES VALLEY

$$$$ AMERICAN Fodor'sChoice ★ ✕**Jardinière.** A special anniversary? An important business dinner? A fat tax refund? These are the reasons you book a table at Jardinière. The restaurant takes its name from its chef-owner, Traci Des Jardins, and the sophisticated interior, with its eye-catching oval atrium and

curving staircase, fills nightly with locals and out-of-towners alike. The equally sophisticated French-cum-Californian dining-room menu, served upstairs in the atrium, changes daily but regularly includes such high-priced adornments as caviar, foie gras, and truffles. Downstairs, the lounge menu, with smaller plates and smaller prices ($8 to $25), is ideal for when you want to eat light while visiting with friends or tame your hunger before or after the nearby opera or symphony. Cheese lovers will appreciate the wide variety of choices—both Old World and New—housed in the glassed-in cheese-aging chamber in the rear of the restaurant. ✉ *300 Grove St., Hayes Valley* ☎ *415/861–5555* ✍ *Reservations essential* ▭ *AE, DC, MC, V* ⊗ *No lunch* ✥ *C5.*

$$$ MEDITERRANEAN Fodor's Choice ★

✕ **Zuni Café.** After one bite of chef Judy Rodgers' succulent brick-oven-roasted whole chicken with Tuscan bread salad, you'll understand why she's a national star. Food is served here on two floors; the rabbit warren of rooms on the second level includes a balcony overlooking the main dining room. The crowd is a disparate mix that reflects the makeup of the city: casual and dressy, young and old, hip and staid. At the long copper bar trays of briny-fresh oysters on the half shell are dispensed along with cocktails and wine. The southern French–Italian menu changes daily (though the signature chicken, prepared for two, is a fixture). Rotating dishes include house-cured anchovies with Parmigiano-Reggiano, deep-fried squid and lemons, nettle and onion soup with a poached egg, and brick-oven squab with polenta. Desserts are simple and satisfying and include crumbly crusted tarts and an addictive cream-laced coffee granita. The lunchtime burger on rosemary focaccia with a side of shoestring potatoes is a favorite with locals. ✉ *1658 Market St., Hayes Valley* ☎ *415/552–2522* ▭ *AE, MC, V* ⊗ *Closed Mon.* ✥ *C6.*

FISHERMAN'S WHARF

$$$$ AMERICAN Fodor's Choice ★

✕ **Gary Danko.** Be prepared to wait your turn for a table behind chef Gary Danko's legion of loyal fans, who typically keep the reservation book chock-full here (plan on reserving two months in advance). The cost of a meal ($66–$98) is pegged to the number of courses, from three to five. The menu, which changes seasonally, may include pancetta-wrapped frogs' legs, seared foie gras with Fuji apples, shellfish with Thai red curry, and quail stuffed with foie gras and pine nuts. A diet-destroying chocolate soufflé with two sauces is usually among the desserts. So, too, is a "no-cholesterol" Grand Marnier soufflé with raspberry sorbet, perfect for diners with a conscience or a heart problem. The wine list is the size of a small-town phone book, and the banquette-lined room, with beautiful wood floors and stunning (but restrained) floral arrangements, is as memorable as the food. ✉ *800 North Point St., Fisherman's Wharf* ☎ *415/749–2060* ✍ *Reservations essential* ▭ *D, DC, MC, V* ⊗ *No lunch* ✥ *D1.*

CLOSE UP

Eating with Kids

Kids can be fussy eaters, but parents can be, too, so picking places that will satisfy both is important. Fortunately, there are plenty of excellent possibilities all over town.

If you're downtown for breakfast, stop at the venerable **Sears Fine Foods** (✉ *439 Powell St., near Post St.* ☎ *415/986–0700*), home of "the world-famous Swedish pancakes." Eighteen of the silver-dollar-size beauties cost less than a movie ticket. Nearby in Chinatown, **City View Restaurant** (✉ *662 Commercial St., near Kearny St.* ☎ *415/398–2838*) serves a varied selection of dim sum, with tasty pork buns for kids and more exotic fare for adults.

If you found yourself dragging the kids through SFMOMA, you can win them back with lunch at the nearby **Crêpe O Chocolate** (✉ *75 O'Farrell St., between Stockton St. and Grant Ave.* ☎ *415/362–0255*), where they can fill up on a turkey and cheese sandwich and a crepe filled with peanut butter and chocolate—and you can, too. Try **Pluto's** (✉ *627 Irving St., between 7th and 8th Sts.* ☎ *415/753–8867*) after a visit to Golden Gate Park. Small kids love the chicken nuggets, which arrive with good-for-you carrot and celery sticks, whereas bigger kids will likely opt for one of the two-fisted sandwiches. Everyone will want a double fudge brownie for dessert. **Barney's Gourmet Burgers** (✉ *3344 Steiner St., near Union St.* ☎ *415/563–0307*), not far from Fort Mason and the Exploratorium, caters to older kids and their parents with mile-high burgers and giant salads. But Barney's doesn't forget "kids under 8," who have their own menu featuring a burger, an all-beef frank, chicken strips with ranch dressing, and more.

Nearly everybody loves pasta, and **Pasta Pomodoro** (✉ *655 Union St., near Powell St.* ☎ *415/399–0300*) in North Beach provides plenty of plates to choose from, including a kids'-only menu that lets youngsters match up any one of three pasta shapes with five different sauces.

The Mission has dozens of no-frills taco-and-burrito parlors; especially worthy is the bustling, friendly **La Corneta** (✉ *2731 Mission St., between 23rd and 24th Sts.* ☎ *415/252–9560*), which has a baby burrito. Banana splits and hot fudge sundaes are what **St. Francis Fountain** (✉ *2801 24th St., at York St.* ☎ *415/826–4200*) is known for, along with its vintage decor. Opened in 1918, it recalls the early 1950s, and the menu, with its burgers, BLT, grilled cheese sandwich, and chili with corn bread, is timeless. In Lower Haight the small **Rosamunde Sausage Grill** (✉ *545 Haight St., between Steiner and Fillmore Sts.* ☎ *415/437–6851*) serves just that—a slew of different sausages, from Polish to duck to *Weisswurst* (Bavarian veal). Grilled onions, sauerkraut, and chili are extra, and since there are only six stools, plan on takeout. Carry your meal to nearby Duboce Park, with its charming playground.

Finally, both kids and adults love to be by the ocean, and the **Park Chalet** (✉ *1000 Great Hwy., at Fulton St.* ☎ *415/386–8439*), hidden behind the two-story Beach Chalet, offers pizza, a juicy burger, sticky ribs, a big banana split, and, on sunny days, outdoor tables and a wide expanse of lawn where kids can play while parents relax.

—Sharon Silva

COW HOLLOW

$$ ITALIAN

Rose's Café. Sleepy-headed locals turn up at Rose's for the breakfast pizza of ham, eggs, and fontina; house-baked pastries and breads; poached eggs with Yukon gold potatoes and chanterelles, or soft polenta with mascarpone and jam. Midday is time for a roasted chicken and fontina sandwich; pizza with mushrooms, feta, and thyme; or pasta with clams. Evening hours find customers eating their way through more pizza and pasta if they are on a budget, and sirloin steak and roasted sea bass if they aren't. The ingredients are top-notch, the service is friendly, and the seating is in comfortable booths, at tables, and at a counter. At the outside tables, overhead heaters keep you toasty when the temperature dips. Expect long lines for Sunday brunch. ⊠*2298 Union St., Cow Hollow* ☎*415/775-2200* ▭*AE, D, DC, MC, V* ✥*A2.*

MARINA

$$$ ITALIAN Fodor's Choice ★

A16. Marina residents—and, judging from the crowds, everybody else—gravitate to this lively trattoria named for the autostrada that winds through Italy's sunny south. The kitchen serves the food of Naples and surrounding Campania, such as *burrata* (cream-filled mozzarella) with olive oil and crostini and crisp-crust pizzas, including a classic Neapolitan Margherita (mozzarella, tomato, and basil). Among the regularly changing mains are chicken meatballs with fennel and *salsa verde* (green sauce), and rock cod, scallops, and clams in *acqua pazza* (literally, "crazy water"). A big wine list of primarily southern Italian with some California wines suits the fare perfectly. The long space includes an animated bar scene near the door; ask for a table in the quieter alcove at the far end. Reservations are easier to snag midweek. ⊠*2355 Chestnut St., Marina* ☎*415/771-2216* ▭*AE, MC, V* ⊙*No lunch Sat.–Tues* ✥*A1.*

$$ SPANISH

Laïola. San Franciscans never seem to tire of tapas, as the crowds—mostly young—at this smart, compact Marina outpost of Spanish small plates prove. Try for a seat at the long copper-top bar or at a window table, and then contemplate the seasonally shifting menu that boasts some two dozen tempting tapas, such as braised pork meatballs, Brussels sprouts flecked with bacon, potatoes with pepper-spiked aioli, chickpea croquettes, and slow-roasted piglet. Most regulars seem to skip the four large plates but save room for a creamy chocolate pudding sprinkled with sea salt and olive oil. On Monday nights you can fill up on a big plate of chicken and seafood paella, churros and hot chocolate, and a glass of wine for just $30. If you are hard of hearing or don't want to speak in a raised voice, this is not the restaurant for you, unless you go on a very slow weeknight. ⊠*2031 Chestnut St., Marina* ☎*415/346-5641* ▭*AE, D, MC, V* ⊙*No lunch* ✥*A1.*

THE MISSION

$$$ ITALIAN Fodor's Choice ★

Delfina. "Irresistible." That's how countless die-hard fans describe Craig and Anne Stoll's Delfina. Such wild enthusiasm has made patience the critical virtue for anyone wanting a reservation here. The interior is comfortable, with hardwood floors, aluminum-top tables, a tile bar, and a casual, friendly atmosphere. The menu changes daily, and among the usual offerings are salt cod *mantecato* (whipped with olive oil) with fennel flatbread and grilled squid with warm white-bean salad. If Piedmontese fresh white truffles have made their way to San Francisco, you are likely to find hand-cut *tagliarini* dressed with butter, cream, and the pricey aromatic fungus on the menu alongside dishes built on more prosaic ingredients. On warm nights, try for a table on the outdoor heated patio. The storefront next door is home to pint-size Pizzeria Delfina. And for folks who can't get to the Mission, the Stolls have opened a second pizzeria on California Street in lively Lower Pacific Heights. ✉ *3621 18th St., Mission* ☎ *415/552–4055* ✍ *Reservations essential* ▭ *MC, V* ⏲ *No lunch* ✥ *B6.*

$ MEXICAN ✕ **Los Jarritos.** A *jarrito* is an earthenware cup used for drinking tequila and other beverages in Mexico. You'll see plenty of these small traditional mugs hanging from the ceiling and decorating the walls in this old-time, sun-filled, family-run restaurant. At brunch, try the hearty *chilaquiles,* made from day-old tortillas cut into strips and cooked with cheese, eggs, chilies, and sauce. Or order eggs scrambled with cactus or with *chicharrones* (crisp pork skins) and served with freshly made tortillas. Soup offerings change daily, with Tuesday's *albondigás* (meatballs) comfort food at its best. On weekend evenings adventurous eaters may opt for *birria,* a spicy goat stew, or *menudo,* a tongue-searing soup made from tripe, calf's foot, and hominy. The latter is a time-honored hangover cure. Bring plenty of change for the jukebox loaded with Latin hits. ✉ *901 Van Ness Ave., Mission* ☎ *415/648–8383* ▭ *MC, V* ✥ *C6.*

THE CASTRO

$ AMERICAN ✕ **Chow.** Wildly popular and consciously unpretentious, Chow is a funky yet savvy diner where soporific standards like hamburgers, pizzas, and spaghetti and meatballs are treated with culinary respect. A magnet for penny-pinchers, the restaurant has built its top-notch reputation on honest fare made with fresh local ingredients priced to sell. Salads, pastas, and mains come in two sizes to accommodate big and small appetites, there's a daily sandwich special, and kids can peruse their mini-menu. Because reservations are restricted to large parties, folks hoping to snag seats usually surround the doorway. Come early (before 6:30) or late (after 10) to reduce the wait, and don't even think about leaving without trying the ginger cake with caramel sauce. ✉ *215 Church St., Castro* ☎ *415/552–2469* ▭ *MC, V* ✥ *A6.*

THE HAIGHT

$$ INDIAN ✕ **Indian Oven.** This Victorian storefront draws diners from all over the city who come for the tandoori specialties—chicken, lamb, breads. The *saag paneer* (spinach with Indian cheese), *aloo gobi* (potato, cauliflower, and spices), and *bengan bartha* (roasted eggplant with onions and spices) are also excellent. The chef wants to keep his clientele around for the long haul, too, and puts a little "heart healthy" icon next to some of the menu items. On Friday and Saturday nights famished patrons overflow onto the sidewalk as they wait for open tables. If you try to linger over

a mango *lassi* or an order of the excellent *kheer* (rice pudding) on one of these nights, you'll probably be hurried along by a waiter. For better service, come on a slower weeknight. ✉*233 Fillmore St., Lower Haight* ☎*415/626–1628* ▭*AE, D, DC, MC, V* ⊙*No lunch* ✣*A6.*

$$ AMERICAN ✕**Nopa.** In the mid-2000s North of the Panhandle became the city's newest talked-about neighborhood, in part because of the big, bustling Nopa, which is cleverly named after it. This casual space, with its high ceilings, concrete floor, long bar, and sea of tables, suits the high-energy crowd of young suits and neighborhood residents that fills it every night. They come primarily for the rustic fare, like an irresistible flatbread topped with fennel sausage and chanterelles; creamy cauliflower soup with almonds and mint; smoky, crisp-skinned rotisserie chicken; a juicy grass-fed hamburger with thick-cut fries; and dark ginger cake with caramelized pears and cream. But they also love the lively spirit of the place. Unfortunately, that buzz sometimes means that raised voices are the only way to communicate with fellow diners. A big community table eases the way for anyone dining out on his or her own. ✉*560 Divisadero St., Haight* ☎*415/864–8643* ▭*MC, V* ⊙*No lunch* ✣*A6.*

4

WHERE TO STAY

San Francisco is one of the country's best hotel towns, offering a rich selection of properties that satisfy most tastes and budgets. Whether you're seeking a cozy inn, a kitschy motel, a chic boutique, or a grande-dame hotel, this city has got the perfect room for you.

CIVIC CENTER/VAN NESS

$–$$ **Hotel Whitcomb.** Built in 1910, this historic hotel (formerly the Ramada Plaza) was the temporary seat of city government from 1912 to 1915 before becoming a hotel in 1916. (What was once the mayor's office now serves as the hotel's administrative offices, and the jail cells are still intact in the hotel basement.) The expansive, well-appointed lobby boasts marble balustrades and columns, carved wooden ceilings, rare Janesero paneling, Austrian crystal chandeliers, Tiffany stained glass, and a ballroom with one of the largest parquet dance floors in the city. Broad halls lead to spacious, newly refurbished rooms with flat-screen TVs and baths. Northeast corner suites offer views of Market Street and the gold-encrusted dome of City Hall. Stroll out the front door to find the Civic Center Muni and BART stations and the main public library; the Asian Art Museum, Opera House, Davies Symphony Hall, and Westfield Centre are close by. **Pros:** good location; rich architectural and historical legacy; opulent lobby; spacious rooms; airport shuttle. **Cons:** difficult to find street parking; area can be dodgy at night. ✉*1231 Market St., Civic Center* ☎*415/626–8000 or 800/227–4747* ⎙*415/861–1435* 🌐*www.hotelwhitcomb.com* *486 rooms, 12 suites* *In room: Wi-Fi. In hotel: restaurant, room service, bar, gym, laundry facilities, laundry service, Wi-Fi, parking (paid), no-smoking rooms* ▭*AE, D, DC, MC, V* ✣*D6.*

BEST BETS FOR SAN FRANCISCO LODGING

Fodor's offers a selective listing of quality lodging experiences at every price range, from the city's best budget motel to its most sophisticated luxury hotel. Here we've compiled our top recommendations by price and experience. The very best properties—in other words, those that provide a particularly remarkable experience in their price range—are designated in the listings with the Fodor's Choice logo.

Fodor'sChoice★

Argonaut Hotel, $$$$ p. 221

Four Seasons Hotel San Francisco, $$$$ p. 223

Hotel Drisco, $$$ p. 223

Hotel Nikko, $$$$ p. 228

Mandarin Oriental, $$$$ p. 221

Orchard Hotel, $$$ p. 229

Palace Hotel, $$$$ p. 224

Ritz-Carlton, $$$$ p. 222

San Remo Hotel, ¢ p. 222

Union Street Inn, $$$ p. 223

By Price

$$

Hotel Beresford Arms, p. 228

Harbor Court, p. 224

$$$

Hotel Drisco, p. 223

Orchard Hotel, p. 229

$$$$

Campton Place, p. 225

Hotel Nikko, p. 228

Mandarin Oriental, p. 221

Ritz-Carlton, p. 222

By Experience

BUSINESS TRAVELERS

Four Seasons Hotel San Francisco, $$$$ p. 223

Hotel Nikko, $$$$ p. 228

GREAT CONCIERGE

Hotel Triton, $$$ p. 229

Ritz-Carlton, $$$$ p. 222

HISTORICAL FLAVOR

Hotel Whitcomb, $ p. 219

Westin St. Francis, $$$ p. 230

JET-SETTING CLIENTELE

Clift, $$$$ p. 228

Hotel Triton, $$$ p. 229

W San Francisco, $$$ p. 225

MOST ROMANTIC

Hotel Drisco, $$$ p. 223

TOP B&BS

Hotel Drisco, $$$ p. 223

TOP SPAS

Mandarin Oriental, $$$$ p. 221

FINANCIAL DISTRICT

$$$$ Fodor'sChoice ★ **Mandarin Oriental, San Francisco.** Two towers connected by glass-enclosed sky bridges compose the top 11 floors of one of San Francisco's tallest buildings. Spectacular panoramas grace every room, and windows open so you can hear that trademark San Francisco sound: the "ding ding" of the cable cars some 40 floors below. The rooms, corridors, and lobby areas are decorated in rich hues of red, gold, and chocolate brown. The Mandarin Rooms have extra-deep tubs next to picture windows, enabling guests to literally and figuratively soak up what one reader called "unbelievable views from the Golden Gate to the Bay Bridge and everything in between." Pamper yourself with luxurious Egyptian-cotton sheets, two kinds of robes (terry and waffle-weave), and cozy slippers. A lovely complimentary tea-and-cookie tray delivered to your room upon your arrival is one among many illustrations of the hotel's commitment to service. The pricey mezzanine-level restaurant, Silks, earns rave reviews for innovative American cuisine with an Asian flair. Special rate plans for families are available. Several top-floor suites have been recently revamped, as has the Mandarin Lounge. **Pros:** spectacular "bridge-to-bridge" views; attentive service. **Cons:** located in a business area that's quiet on weekends; restaurant is excellent but expensive (as is the hotel). ✉ *222 Sansome St., Financial District* ☎ *415/276–9600 or 800/622–0404* 📠 *415/276–9304* 🌐 *www.mandarinoriental.com/sanfrancisco* *151 rooms, 7 suites* *In-room: safe, DVD, Internet, Wi-Fi. In-hotel: restaurant, room service, bar, gym, laundry service, Internet terminal, Wi-Fi, parking (paid), some pets allowed, no-smoking rooms* 💳 *AE, D, DC, MC, V* ✣ *F3.*

FISHERMAN'S WHARF/NORTH BEACH

$$$–$$$$ Fodor'sChoice ★ **Argonaut Hotel.** When the four-story Haslett Warehouse was a fruit-and-vegetable canning complex in 1907, boats docked right up against the building. Today it's a hotel with a nautical decor—think anchors, ropes, compasses, and a row of cruise-ship deck chairs in the lobby—that reflects its unique partnership with the San Francisco Maritime National Historical Park. Spacious rooms, many with a sofa bed in the sitting area, have exposed-brick walls, wood-beam ceilings, and whitewashed wooden furniture reminiscent of a summer beach house. Windows open to the sea air and the sounds of the waterfront, and many rooms have views of Alcatraz and the Golden Gate Bridge. Suites come with extra-deep whirlpool tubs and telescopes for close-up views of passing ships. **Pros:** bay views; clean rooms; near Hyde Street cable car; sofa beds; toys for the kids. **Cons:** nautical theme isn't for everyone; cramped public areas; service can be hit or miss; location is a bit of a hike from other parts of town. ✉ *495 Jefferson St., at Hyde St., Fisherman's Wharf* ☎ *415/563–0800 or 866/415–0704* 📠 *415/563–2800* 🌐 *www.argonauthotel.com* *239 rooms, 13 suites* *In-room: safe, refrigerator, Internet. In-hotel: restaurant, room service, bar, gym, laundry service, Wi-Fi, parking (paid), some pets allowed, no-smoking rooms* 💳 *AE, D, DC, MC, V* ✣ *D1.*

4

$$–$$$ **Best Western Tuscan Inn.** Described by some Fodors.com users as a "hidden treasure," this hotel's redbrick facade barely hints at the Tuscan country villa that lies within. Each small, Italianate room has white-pine furniture, floral bedspreads and curtains, a completely mirrored wall, and a refurbished bathroom. Complimentary beverages and biscotti are laid out mornings near the fireplace in the oak-panel lobby, where a convivial wine hour is held nightly. There's free morning limousine service to the Financial District. Café Pescatore, the Italian seafood restaurant off the lobby, provides room service for breakfast. **Pros:** wine/beer hour; down-home feeling. **Cons:** congested touristy area; small rooms. ✉ *425 N. Point St., at Mason St., Fisherman's Wharf* ☎ *415/561–1100 or 800/648–4626* 📠 *415/561–1199* 🌐 *www.tuscaninn.com* *209 rooms, 12 suites* *In-room: Wi-Fi. In-hotel: restaurant, room service, bar, laundry service, Internet terminal, parking (paid), some pets allowed, no-smoking rooms* ▭ *AE, D, DC, MC, V* ✣ *E1.*

¢ **San Remo Hotel.** A few blocks from Fisherman's Wharf, this three-story 1906 Italianate Victorian—once home to longshoremen and Beat poets—has a narrow stairway from the street leading to the front desk and labyrinthine hallways. Rooms are small but charming, with lace curtains, forest green-painted wood floors, brass beds, and other antique furnishings. The top floor is brighter, because it's closer to the skylights that provide sunshine to the thriving population of potted plants that line the brass-banistered hallways. About a third of the rooms have sinks, and all share spotless black-and-white-tile bathroom facilities with pull-chain toilets. A rooftop suite must be reserved three to six months in advance. Fior D'Italia, "America's Oldest Italian Restaurant," occupies the building's entire first floor. **Pros:** inexpensive. **Cons:** some rooms are dark; no private bath; spartan amenities. ✉ *2237 Mason St., North Beach* ☎ *415/776–8688 or 800/352–7366* 📠 *415/776–2811* 🌐 *www.sanremohotel.com* *62 rooms with shared baths, 1 suite* *In-room: no a/c, no phone, no TV, Wi-Fi. In-hotel: laundry facilities, Internet terminal, Wi-Fi, parking (paid), no-smoking rooms* ▭ *AE, MC, V* ✣ *E1.*

Fodor's Choice ★

NOB HILL

$$$$ **Ritz-Carlton, San Francisco.** A preferred destination for travel-industry honchos, movie stars, and visitors alike, this hotel—a stunning tribute to beauty and attentive, professional service—completed a $12.5-million renovation of its guest rooms and meeting spaces in 2006. Ionic columns grace the neoclassical facade; crystal chandeliers illuminate Georgian antiques and museum-quality 18th- and 19th-century paintings in the lobby. All rooms have flat-screen TVs, featherbeds with 300-thread-count Egyptian-cotton Frette sheets, and down comforters. Club Level rooms include use of the upgraded Club Lounge, which has a dedicated concierge and several elaborate complimentary food presentations daily. The Dining Room has a seasonal menu with modern French accents. The delightful afternoon tea service in the Lobby Lounge, which overlooks the beautifully landscaped Terrace courtyard, is a San Francisco institution. **Pros:** terrific service; all-day food service on Club level; beautiful surroundings. **Cons:** expensive; hilly location. ✉ *600 Stockton St.,*

Fodor's Choice ★

at California St., Nob Hill ☎415/296–7465 ⎙415/291–0288 ⊕www.ritzcarlton.com ⇨276 rooms, 60 suites ♁In-room: safe, refrigerator, DVD, Wi-Fi. In-hotel: 2 restaurants, room service, bars, pool, gym, laundry service, Internet terminal, parking (paid), some pets allowed, no-smoking rooms ▭AE, D, DC, MC, V ✥E3.

PACIFIC HEIGHTS/COW HOLLOW/THE MARINA

$$–$$$$ Fodor'sChoice ★ **Hotel Drisco.** Pretend you're a resident of one of the wealthiest and most beautiful residential neighborhoods in San Francisco at this understated, elegant 1903 Edwardian hotel. The quiet haven, which feels like a secluded B&B, serves as a celebrity hideaway for the likes of Ethan Hawke and Ashley Judd. Genteel furnishings and luxurious amenities like flat-screen TVs grace pale yellow-and-white rooms, some of which have sweeping city views. Morning newspaper, plush robes, slippers, and nightly turndown service are included. A free breakfast is offered in a sunny, spacious room; wine is set out each evening in a lovely area off the lobby. Guests have commented on the helpful and incredibly friendly staff. Recent renovations added flat-screen TVs and new carpeting, furnishings, and bedding to the guest rooms. **Pros:** great service; comfortable rooms; quiet residential retreat. **Cons:** small rooms; far from downtown. ✉*2901 Pacific Ave., Pacific Heights ☎415/346–2880 or 800/634–7277 ⎙415/567–5537 ⊕www.hoteldrisco.com ⇨29 rooms, 19 suites ♁In-room: no a/c, safe, refrigerator, DVD. In-hotel: laundry service, Internet terminal, no-smoking rooms ▭AE, D, DC, MC, V* 🍽*CP ✥A3.*

$$$–$$$$ Fodor'sChoice ★ **Union Street Inn.** Precious family antiques and unique artwork helped British innkeepers Jane Bertorelli and David Coyle (former chef for the Duke and Duchess of Bedford) transform this green-and-cream 1902 Edwardian into a delightful B&B. Equipped with candles, fresh flowers, wineglasses, and fine linens, rooms are popular with honeymooners and couples looking for a romantic getaway. The newly renovated Carriage House, separated from the main house by an old-fashioned English garden planted with lemon trees, is equipped with a double Jacuzzi, refinished hardwood floors, and upgraded bathrooms. An elaborate breakfast, which many guests rave about, is included, as are afternoon tea and evening hors d'oeuvres. **Pros:** personal service; excellent full breakfast; romantic setting. **Cons:** congested neighborhood; no a/c; no elevator. ✉*2229 Union St., Cow Hollow ☎415/346–0424 ⎙415/922–8046 ⊕www.unionstreetinn.com ⇨6 rooms ♁In-room: no a/c, Wi-Fi. In-hotel: parking (paid), no-smoking rooms ▭AE, D, MC, V* 🍽*BP ✥A2.*

SOMA

$$$$ Fodor'sChoice ★ **Four Seasons Hotel San Francisco.** Occupying floors 5 through 17 of a skyscraper, this luxurious hotel, designated as the "heart of the city," is sandwiched between multimillion-dollar condos, elite shops, and a premier sports-and-fitness complex. Elegant rooms with contemporary artwork and fine linens have floor-to-ceiling windows overlooking either Yerba Buena Gardens or the historic downtown. All have

deep soaking tubs, glass-enclosed showers, and flat-screen TVs. From the contemporary street-level lobby, take the elevator to the vast Sports Club/LA, where you have free access to the junior Olympic pool, full-size indoor basketball court, and the rest of the magnificent facilities, classes, and spa services. Seasons restaurant serves high-end California cuisine, with a strong focus on seasonal and local ingredients. Various packages offer focuses on art, shopping, and cooking. **Pros:** near museums, galleries, restaurants, and clubs; terrific fitness facilities. **Cons:** pricey. ✉ *757 Market St., SoMa* ☎ *415/633–3000, 800/332–3442, or 800/819–5053* 📠 *415/633–3001* 🌐 *www.fourseasons.com/sanfrancisco* *231 rooms, 46 suites* *In-room: safe, DVD, Internet, Wi-Fi. In-hotel: 2 restaurants, room service, bar, pool, gym, spa, laundry service, Internet terminal, parking (paid), some pets allowed, no-smoking rooms* 💳 *AE, D, DC, MC, V* ✣ *F4.*

$$–$$$ **Harbor Court.** Exemplary service and a friendly staff earn high marks for this cozy hotel, which overlooks the Embarcadero and is within shouting distance of the Bay Bridge. Guest rooms are on the small side, but have double sets of soundproof windows and include nice touches such as wall-mounted 27-inch flat-screen TVs. Brightly colored throw pillows adorn beds with 320-thread-count sheets, and tub-showers have curved shower-curtain rods for more elbow room. Some rooms have views of the Bay Bridge and the Ferry Building. Complimentary evening wine and late-night cookies and milk are served in the lounge, where coffee and tea are available mornings. The hotel provides free use of the adjacent YMCA. **Pros:** convenient location; quiet; friendly service; cozy. **Cons:** small rooms. ✉ *165 Steuart St., SoMa* ☎ *415/882–1300 or 866/792–6283* 📠 *415/882–1313* 🌐 *www.harborcourthotel.com* *130 rooms, 1 suite* *In-room: Wi-Fi. In-hotel: bar, laundry service, Internet terminal, Wi-Fi, parking (paid), some pets allowed, no-smoking rooms* 💳 *AE, D, DC, MC, V* ✣ *H4.*

$$$$ Fodor's Choice ★ **Palace Hotel.** "Majestic" is the word that best sums up this landmark hotel, which was the world's largest and most luxurious when it opened in 1875. It was completely rebuilt after the 1906 earthquake and fire, and the carriage entrance reemerged as the grand Garden Court restaurant. Today the hotel is still graced with architectural details that recall a bygone era, like chandeliers; tall, mirrored glass doors; and eight pairs of turn-of-the-century, bronze-filigreed marble columns supporting a magnificent dome ceiling filtering natural light; it's a refined environment ideally suited for the high tea served on weekends and daily during holiday periods. Rooms, with twice-daily maid service and nightly turndown, have soaring 14-foot ceilings, traditional mahogany furnishings, flat-screen TVs, and marble bathrooms. The wood-panel Pied Piper Bar is named after the delightful 1909 Maxfield Parrish mural behind the bar. **Pros:** gracious service; close to Union Square; near BART. **Cons:** older design; small rooms with even smaller baths; many nearby establishments closed on weekends; west-facing rooms can be warm and stuffy. ✉ *2 New Montgomery St., SoMa* ☎ *415/512–1111 or 888/627–7196* 📠 *415/243–8062* 🌐 *www.sfpalace.com* *518 rooms, 34 suites* *In-room: safe, refrigerator, Internet. In-hotel: 3 restaurants, room service, bar, pool, gym, spa, laundry service, Wi-Fi, parking (paid), no-smoking rooms* 💳 *AE, D, DC, MC, V* ✣ *F4.*

$$$–$$$$ **W San Francisco.** The epitome of cool urban chic and fashion forward in design and clientele, this swanky 31-story Starwood hotel owes some of its cachet to a prime location next door to the San Francisco Museum of Modern Art. The hotel is infused with hip energy: techno-pop pulses in the lobby and café, and otherworldly mobiles (which change with the seasons) hang overhead; add the mauve leather ottomans and blue velvet sofas to the mix, and you have a cross between a fashion-show runway and a stage set. Compact guest rooms, some of which have upholstered window seats, come with flat-screen TVs, luxurious beds, comfy pillow-top mattresses, and goose-down comforters and pillows. Sleek baths have green glass countertops and shiny steel sinks. The glass-roof pool and hot-tub area, next to Bliss Spa, is open 24/7, as is the Whatever/Whenever concierge desk in the lobby. In the evening there's a lively bar scene, and the lobby, lit by candlelight, sets the mood for XYZ, the hotel's signature restaurant, an "in spot" that attracts celebs like Sharon Stone and Kanye West. Upper floors boast excellent views of the Museum of Modern Art, Yerba Buena Gardens, and/or the Bay Bridge. During the week the majority of the clientele are businesspeople, but on weekends the hotel is kid-friendly, and pets are always welcome. The accommodating staff will help parents arrange for babysitting and will take your pup for a walk. Fragrances waft throughout the hotel and guest rooms, so sensitive noses should call ahead to request special preparations. **Pros:** hip energy; mod, sophisticated digs; in the heart of the cultural district. **Cons:** three blocks from BART; hotel's signature scents could pose a problem for sensitive noses. ✉ *181 3rd St., SoMa* ☎ *415/777–5300* 🖷 *415/817–7823* 🌐 *www.whotels.com/sanfrancisco* *404 rooms, 9 suites* *In-room: safe, refrigerator, DVD, Internet, Wi-Fi. In-hotel: restaurant, room service, bar, pool, gym, spa, laundry service, Internet terminal, Wi-Fi, parking (paid), some pets allowed, no-smoking rooms* 💳 *AE, D, DC, MC, V* ✣ *G4.*

UNION SQUARE/DOWNTOWN

$$$$ **Campton Place.** Beauty and highly attentive service remain the hallmarks of this exquisite jewel-like, top-tier hotel. Fresh-cut orchids and Japanese floral arrangements bring natural beauty inside, where you'll feel sheltered from the teeming crowds on the street. Rooms can be small, but are well laid-out and elegantly decorated in a contemporary Italian style, with sandy earth tones and handsome pearwood paneling and cabinetry. Limestone baths have deep soaking tubs; double-pane windows keep city noises at bay, a plus in this active neighborhood. The Campton Place Restaurant, whose new East Indian chef serves French-infused contemporary cuisine at dinner, is famed for its lavish breakfasts. The lounge is a popular cocktail-hour hangout for the downtown crowd. **Pros:** attentive service; first-class restaurant; abundant natural light. **Cons:** smallish rooms; pricey (but worth it). ✉ *340 Stockton St., Union Square* ☎ *415/781–5555 or 866/332–1670* 🖷 *415/955–5585* 🌐 *www.camptonplace.com* *101 rooms, 9 suites* *In-room: safe, DVD, Wi-Fi. In-hotel: restaurant, room service, bar, gym, laundry service, Wi-Fi, parking (paid), some pets allowed, no-smoking rooms* 💳 *AE, DC, MC, V* ✣ *F4.*

Mandarin Oriental

Argonaut Hotel

Hotel Drisco

Palace Hotel

Union Stree Inn

Four Seasons Hotel

Orchard Hotel

Hotel Nikko

The Ritz-Calton

$$$$ **Clift.** A favorite for hipsters, music industry types, and celebrities fleeing the media onslaught—security discreetly keeps photographers and other heat-seekers away—this sexy hotel, whose entrance is so nondescript you can walk right past it without a hint of what's inside, is the brainchild of entrepreneur Ian Schrager and artist-designer Philippe Starck, known for his collection of eccentric chairs. The moody, dramatically illuminated lobby is dominated by a gigantic Napoleonic chair that could accommodate Shrek, with room to spare. This theatrical staging is enhanced by surreal seating options like a leather love seat with buffalo tusks and a miniature "drink me" chair, all surrounding a floor-to-ceiling, pitch-black fireplace. Spacious rooms—as light as the lobby is darkly intriguing—have translucent orange Plexiglas tables, high ceilings, flat-screen TVs, and two huge "infinity" wall mirrors. Some visitors have remarked on the thin walls and advise booking a room on an upper-level floor to avoid street noise. The art-deco Redwood Room bar, paneled with wood from a 2,000-year-old tree, is known for its "beautiful people." Asia de Cuba restaurant prepares an artful fusion of Asian and Latino cuisines. **Pros:** good rates compared to similar top-tier hotels in SF; surreal moody interior design; ideal location for shopping and theaters; close to public transportation; discreet and helpful staff. **Cons:** some guests note thin walls; street noise. *495 Geary St., Union Square 415/775–4700 or 800/606–6090 415/441–4621 www.clifthotel.com 337 rooms, 26 suites In-room: safe, Internet, Wi-Fi. In-hotel: restaurant, room service, bar, gym, laundry service, Internet terminal, parking (paid), some pets allowed, no-smoking rooms AE, D, DC, MC, V E4.*

$–$$ **Hotel Beresford Arms.** Surrounded by fancy molding and 10-foot-tall windows, the red-carpet lobby of this ornate brick Victorian explains why the building is on the National Register of Historic Places. Rooms with dark-wood antique-reproduction furniture vary in size and setup: junior suites have sitting areas and either a wet bar or kitchenette; full suites have two queen beds, a Murphy bed, and a kitchen. All suites have a bidet in the bathroom. Continental breakfast, afternoon tea, and wine are served beneath a crystal chandelier in the lobby. **Pros:** moderately priced; suites with kitchenettes and Murphy beds are a plus for families with kids. **Cons:** no a/c. *701 Post St., Union Square 415/673–2600 or 800/533–6533 415/929–1535 www.beresford.com 83 rooms, 12 suites In-room: no a/c, kitchen (some), refrigerator, Internet, Wi-Fi. In-hotel: laundry service, Internet terminal, Wi-Fi, parking (paid), some pets allowed, no-smoking rooms AE, D, DC, MC, V CP D4.*

$$$$ Fodor's Choice ★ **Hotel Nikko.** The vast gray-flecked white marble and gurgling fountains in the neoclassical lobby of this business traveler hotel has the sterility of an airport. Crisply designed rooms in muted tones have flat-screen TVs, modern bathrooms with sinks that sit on top of black vanities, and "in-vogue" separate showers and tubs. Some higher-end rooms come with complimentary breakfast. The excellent, 10,000-square-foot Club Nikko fitness facility has traditional *ofuros* (Japanese soaking tubs), his-and-her *kamaburso* (Japanese meditation rooms), and a glass-enclosed 16-meter rooftop pool and a whirlpool. The Rrazz

Room, San Francisco's only cabaret theater, located on the lobby level, is a venue for national talent and nostalgia acts most evenings. **Pros:** friendly multilingual staff; some rooms have ultramodern baths; very clean. **Cons:** rooms and antiseptic lobby lack color; some may find the atmosphere cold; expensive parking. ✉*222 Mason St., Union Square* ☎*415/394–1111 or 800/248–3308* 📠*415/394–1106* 🌐*www.hotelnikkosf.com* *510 rooms, 22 suites* *In-room: refrigerator, Internet, Wi-Fi. In-hotel: restaurant, room service, bar, pool, gym, laundry service, Internet terminal, Wi-Fi, parking (paid), some pets allowed, no-smoking rooms* *AE, D, DC, MC, V* ✥*E4.*

4

$$–$$$$ **Hotel Triton.** The spirit of fun has taken up full-time residence in this Kimpton property, which has a youngish, super-friendly staff; pink and blue neon elevators; and a colorful psychedelic lobby mural depicting the San Francisco art and music scene—think flower power mixed with Andy Warhol. Playful furniture includes a green-and-gold metallic couch and striped carpeting, a whimsical and far-out setting for free morning coffee and tea, fresh afternoon cookies, evening wine events, and the on-call tarot reader. Smallish rooms are painted silver-gray and tomato-soup red, and come with ergonomic desk chairs, flat-screen TVs, and oddball light fixtures; sinks are positioned outside the bathrooms, European style. Twenty-four "environmentally sensitive" rooms have water- and air-filtration systems and biodegradable soap. A 24-hour yoga channel will help you find that elusive path to inner peace. **Pros:** attentive service; refreshingly funky atmosphere; hip arty environs; good location. **Cons:** rooms and baths are on the small side. ✉*342 Grant Ave., Union Square* ☎*415/394–0500 or 800/433–6611* 📠*415/394–0555* 🌐*www.hoteltriton.com* *133 rooms, 7 suites* *In-room: refrigerator, DVD, Wi-Fi. In-hotel: restaurant, bar, gym, laundry service, parking (paid), some pets allowed, no-smoking rooms* *AE, D, DC, MC, V* ✥*F4.*

$$$–$$$$ Fodor's Choice ★ **Orchard Hotel.** Unlike most other boutique hotels in the area, which sometimes occupy century-old buildings, the strictly-21st-century Orchard was built in 2000. The 104-room hotel embraces state-of-the-art technology—from CD and DVD players in each room to Wi-Fi access throughout the building—mixing cutting-edge Silicon Valley chic with classic European touches. The hotel's marble lobby, where the bronze statue *Spring Awakening* greets visitors, previews the dramatic architectural embellishments, like arched openings, vaulted ceilings, and stone floors that are found throughout the hotel. With just 12 rooms per floor, the hotel feels quite intimate; some guests have compared it to a cozy (decidedly upscale) mountain inn. Rooms, sizable by boutique hotel standards, are done in a soft palette of relaxing colors, a balm for harried shoppers returning from a busy day of retail therapy in Union Square. The hotel's restaurant, Daffodil, serves seasonal California fare for breakfast and dinner. Like its "green sister," the Orchard Garden, this hotel is also going for its LEED certification, giving SF visitors yet another eco-friendly option. **Pros:** cutting-edge technology. **Cons:** can be a bit pricey. ✉*665 Bush St., Union Square* ☎*415/362–8878 or 888/717–2881* 📠*415/362–8088* 🌐*www.theorchardhotel.com* *104 rooms, 9 suites* *In-room: safe, DVD, Wi-Fi. In-hotel: restaurant,*

room service, laundry service, parking (paid), some pets allowed, no-smoking rooms ▭*AE, D, DC, MC, V* ⊕*E4.*

$$$–$$$$ **Westin St. Francis.** Since its 1904 opening, this historic hotel has hosted the likes of Hirohito, Queen Elizabeth II, several U.S. presidents, and a roster of international luminaries. The site of sensational, banner headline scandals, the hotel's past is shrouded in as much infamy as stardust. This is the place where Sara Jane Moore tried to assassinate Gerald Ford, where Al Jolson died playing poker; Suite 1219–1221 was the scene of a massive scandal, which erupted when a 30-year-old aspiring actress died after a night of heavy boozing in the close company of silent film comedian Fatty Arbuckle. (The incident destroyed his career.) The hotel is comprised of the original building (Empire-style furnishings, Victorian moldings) and a modern 32-story tower (Asian-inspired lacquered furniture, glass elevators); guests are divided when it comes to the virtues of the modern addition vs. the historic building. At this writing, the hotel was undergoing a $40 million renovation—the most extensive in its history—of all guest rooms and common areas. The imposing facade, black-marble lobby, and gold-top columns form an impressive public space that was restored to its original grandeur in July 2008. Adding to the air of upscale sophistication is the cool chic of Michael Mina's classy restaurant and his new cocktail lounge, the Clock Bar, as well as the venerable Oak Room Restaurant and Lounge. **Pros:** fantastic beds; prime location; spacious rooms, some with great views. **Cons:** some guests comment on the long wait at check-in; rooms in original building can be small; glass elevators are not for the faint of heart. ✉*335 Powell St., Union Square* ☎*415/397–7000 or 800/917–7458* ℻*415/774–0124* 🌐*www.westinstfrancis.com* *1,155 rooms, 40 suites* *In-room: safe, refrigerator (some), Internet, Wi-Fi. In-hotel: 3 restaurants, room service, bars, spa, laundry service, Internet, parking (paid), some pets allowed, no-smoking rooms* ▭*AE, D, DC, MC, V* ⊕*E4.*

NIGHTLIFE

This small city packs the punch of a much larger metropolis after dark. Sophisticated, trendy, relaxed, quirky, and downright outrageous could all be used to describe San Francisco's diverse and vibrant collection of bars, clubs, and performance venues.

THE 4-1-1

Entertainment information is printed in the pink Sunday "Datebook" section (🌐*www.sfgate.com/datebook*) and the more-calendar-based Thursday "96 Hours" section (🌐*www.sfgate.com/96hours*) in the *San Francisco Chronicle*. Also consult any of the free alternative weeklies, notably the *SF Weekly* (🌐*www.sfweekly.com*), which blurbs nightclubs and music, and the *San Francisco Bay Guardian* (🌐*www.sfbg.com*), which lists neighborhood, avant-garde, and budget events. SF Station (🌐*www.sfstation.com; online only*) has an up-to-date calendar of entertainment goings-on.

BARS AND LOUNGES

Cliff House. A bit classier than the Beach Chalet, with a more impressive, sweeping view of Ocean Beach, the Cliff House is our pick if you must choose just one oceanfront restaurant/bar. Sure, it's the site of many high-school prom dates, and you could argue that the food and drinks are overpriced, and some say the sleek facade looks like a mausoleum—but the views are terrific. The best window seats are reserved for diners, but there's a small upstairs lounge where you can watch gulls sail high above the vast blue Pacific. Come before sunset. ✉*1090 Point Lobos, at Great Hwy., Lincoln Park* ☎*415/386–3330* 🌐*www.cliffhouse.com.*

Eos Restaurant and Wine Bar. Though it's just a few blocks away, Cole Valley is a world apart from funky, grungy Haight Street. Eos, along with the handful of restaurants and bars that line this part of Cole Street, manages to be both sophisticated and unpretentious—and truly fantastic. This narrow and romantically lighted space, with more than 400 wines by the bottle and 40-plus by the glass, offers two different wine flights—one red and one white—every month. The adjoining restaurant's excellent East-meets-West cuisine is available at the bar. ✉*901 Cole St., at Carl St., Haight* ☎*415/566–3063* 🌐*www.eossf.com.*

Hôtel Biron. Sharing an alleylike block with the backs of Market Street restaurants, this tiny, cavelike (in a good way) spot displays rotating artwork of the Mission School aesthetic on its brick walls. The clientele is well-behaved twenty- to thirtysomethings who enjoy the cramped quarters, good range of wines and prices, off-the-beaten-path location, soft lighting, and hip music. If it's too crowded, CAV is just around the corner. ✉*45 Rose St., off Market St., Hayes Valley* ☎*415/703–0403* 🌐*www.hotelbiron.com.*

MatrixFillmore. Don a pair of Diesel jeans and a Michael Kors sweater and sip cosmos or Cabernet with the Marina's bon vivants. This is the premier spot in the "Triangle" (short for Bermuda Triangle, named for all of the singles who disappear in the bars clustered at Greenwich and Fillmore streets). Although there's a small dance floor where some folks bump and grind to high-energy DJ-spun dance tracks, the majority of the clientele usually vie for the plush seats near the central open fireplace, flirt at the bar, or huddle for romantic tête-à-têtes in the back. The singles scene can be overwhelming on weekends. ✉*3138 Fillmore St., between Greenwich and Filbert Sts., Marina* ☎*415/563–4180* 🌐*www.matrixfillmore.com.*

Park Chalet. You'll feel like you're in a cabin in the woods as you relax in an Adirondack chair under a heat lamp, enclosed by the greenery of Golden Gate Park. In addition to serving pub food such as burgers, salads, steaks, and fish-and-chips, the brewery churns out its own beer. The Park Chalet shares a building with the Beach Chalet—but it isn't waterside, so you won't freeze if it's overcast. ✉*1000 Great Hwy., near Martin Luther King Jr. Dr., Golden Gate Park* ☎*415/386–8439* 🌐*www.beachchalet.com.*

Redwood Room. Opened in 1933 and updated by über-hip designer Philippe Starck in 2001, the Redwood Room at the Clift Hotel is a San Francisco icon. The entire room, floor to ceiling, is paneled with the wood from a single redwood tree, giving the place a rich, monochromatic look. The gorgeous original art-deco sconces and chandeliers still hang, but bizarre video installations on plasma screens also adorn the walls. It's packed on weekend evenings after 10, when young scenesters swarm the hotel; for maximum glamour, visit on a weeknight. ✉*Clift Hotel, 495 Geary St., at Taylor St., Union Square* ☎*415/929–2300 for table reservations, 415/775–4700.*

Tonga Room. Since 1947 the Tonga Room has given San Francisco a taste of high Polynesian kitsch. Fake palm trees, grass huts, a lagoon (three-piece combos play pop standards on a floating barge), and faux monsoons—courtesy of sprinkler-system rain and simulated thunder and lightning—grow more surreal as you quaff fruity cocktails. ✉*Fairmont San Francisco, 950 Mason St., at California St., Nob Hill* ☎*415/772–5278.*

Vesuvio Café. If you're only hitting one bar in North Beach, it should be this one. The low-ceiling second floor of this raucous boho hangout, little altered since its 1960s heyday (when Jack Kerouac frequented the place), is a fine vantage point for watching the colorful Broadway and Columbus Avenue intersection. Another part of Vesuvio's appeal is its diverse, always-mixed clientele (20s to 60s), from neighborhood regulars and young couples to Bacchanalian posses of friends. ✉*255 Columbus Ave., at Broadway, North Beach* ☎*415/362–3370* 🌐*www.vesuvio.com.*

GAY AND LESBIAN NIGHTLIFE

The *Bay Area Reporter* (☎*415/861–5019* 🌐*www.ebar.com*), a biweekly newspaper, lists gay and lesbian events in its calendar. The biweekly *San Francisco Bay Times* (☎*415/626–0260* 🌐*www.sfbaytimes.com*) is aimed at gay and lesbian readers.

GAY MALE BARS

Eagle Tavern. Bikers are courted with endless drink specials and, increasingly, live rock music at this humongous indoor-outdoor leather bar, one of the few SoMa bars remaining from the days before AIDS and gentrification. The Sunday-afternoon "Beer Busts" (3–6 PM) are a social high point and benefit charitable organizations. It's a surprisingly welcoming place for people from all walks of life. ✉*398 12th St., at Harrison St., SoMa* ☎*415/626–0880* 🌐*www.sfeagle.com.*

Martuni's. A mixed crowd enjoys cocktails in the semi-refined environment of this elegant bar at the intersection of the Castro, the Mission, and Hayes Valley; variations on the martini are a specialty. In the intimate back room a pianist plays nightly, and patrons take turns singing show tunes. It's a favorite post-theater spot—especially after the symphony or opera, which are within walking distance. ✉*4 Valencia St., at Market St., Mission* ☎*415/241–0205.*

The Stud. Mingle with glam trannies, tight-teed pretty boys, ladies and their ladies, and a handful of straight onlookers who dance to the live DJ and watch world-class drag performers on the small stage. The entertainment is often campy, pee-your-pants funny, and downright talented. Each night's music is different—from funk, soul, and hip-hop to '80s tunes and disco favorites. The club is closed on Monday. ✉*399 9th St., at Harrison St., SoMa* ☎*415/863–6623* 🌐*www.studsf.com.*

LESBIAN BARS

Lexington Club. According to its slogan, "every night is ladies' night" at this all-girl club geared to urban alterna-dykes in their 20s and 30s (think piercings and tattoos, not lipstick). Catfights are not uncommon. ■ **TIP→The women's room has awesome graffiti.** ✉*3464 19th St., at Lexington St., Mission* ☎*415/863–2052* 🌐*www.lexingtonclub.com.*

JAZZ CLUBS

★ **Yoshi's.** The legendary Oakland club that has pulled in some of the world's best jazz musicians—Pat Martino, Branford Marsalis, Betty Carter, and Dizzy Gillespie, to name just a few—opened a San Francisco location in late 2007. The new club has terrific acoustics, a 9-foot Steinway grand piano (broken in by Chick Corea), and seating for 411; it's been hailed as "simply the best jazz club in the city." Yoshi's also serves Japanese food in an adjoining restaurant set in a soaring two-story space, decorated with blond wood and hanging paper lanterns (you can also order food at café tables in the club). And yes, the coupling of sushi and jazz *is* as elegant as it sounds. ✉*1330 Fillmore St., at Eddy St., Japantown* ☎*415/655–5600* 🌐*www.yoshis.com.*

ROCK, POP, HIP-HOP, FOLK, AND BLUES CLUBS

Bimbo's 365 Club. The plush main room and adjacent lounge of this club, here since 1951, retain a retro vibe perfect for the "Cocktail Nation" programming that keeps the crowds entertained. For a taste of the old-school San Francisco nightclub scene, you can't beat this place. Indie low-fi and pop bands like Stephen Malkmus and the Jicks and Camera Obscura fill the bill. ✉*1025 Columbus Ave., at Chestnut St., North Beach* ☎*415/474–0365* 🌐*www.bimbos365club.com.*

BooM BooM RooM. John Lee Hooker's old haunt has been an old-school blues haven for years, attracting top-notch acts from all around the country. Luck out with legendary masters like James "Super Chikan" Johnson, or discover new blues and funk artists. ✉*1601 Fillmore St., at Geary Blvd., Japantown* ☎*415/673–8000* 🌐*www.boomboomblues.com.*

Bottom of the Hill. This is a great live-music dive—in the best sense of the word—and truly the epicenter for independent rock in the Bay Area. The club has hosted some great acts over the years, including the Strokes and the Throwing Muses. Rap and hip-hop acts occasionally make it to the stage. ✉*1233 17th St., at Texas St., Potrero Hill* ☎*415/621–4455* 🌐*www.bottomofthehill.com.*

The Fillmore. This is *the* club that all the big names, from Coldplay to Clapton, want to play. San Francisco's most famous rock-music hall serves up a varied menu of national and local acts: rock, reggae, grunge, jazz, folk, acid house, and more. Most tickets cost $20–$30, and some shows are open to all ages. ■ **TIP→Avoid steep service charges by buying tickets at the Fillmore box office on Sunday (10–4).** ✉*1805 Geary Blvd., at Fillmore St., Western Addition* ☎*415/346–6000* 🌐*www.thefillmore.com.*

Built as a bordello in 1907, the Great American Music Hall now pulls in top-tier performers.

Great American Music Hall. You can find top-drawer entertainment at this great, eclectic nightclub. Acts range from the best in blues, folk, and jazz to up-and-coming college-radio and American-roots artists to of-the-moment indie rock stars (OK Go, Mates of State) and the establishment (Cowboy Junkies). The colorful marble-pillared emporium (built in 1907 as a bordello) also accommodates dancing at some shows. Pub grub is available most nights. ☒ *859 O'Farrell St., between Polk and Larkin Sts., Tenderloin* ☎ *415/885–0750* 🌐 *www.musichallsf.com.*

THE ARTS

San Francisco's symphony, opera, and ballet all perform in the Civic Center area, also home to the 928-seat Herbst Theatre, which hosts many fine soloists and ensembles. **San Francisco Performances** (☒ *500 Sutter St., Suite 710* ☎ *415/398–6449* 🌐 *www.performances.org*) brings an eclectic array of topflight global music and dance talents to various venues—mostly the Yerba Buena Center for the Arts, Davies Symphony Hall, and Herbst Theatre. Artists have included the Los Angeles Guitar Quartet, Edgar Meyer, the Paul Taylor Dance Company, and Midori.

TICKETS

City Box Office (☒ *180 Redwood St., Suite 100, off Van Ness Ave. between Golden Gate Ave. and McAllister St., Civic Center* ☎ *415/392–4400* 🌐 *www.cityboxoffice.com*), a charge-by-phone service, offers tickets for many performances and lectures. You can buy tickets in person at its downtown location weekdays 9:30–5:30. You can charge tickets for everything from jazz concerts to Giants games by phone or online through **Tickets.com** (☎ *800/955–5566* 🌐 *www.tickets.com*). Half-price, same-day tickets for many local and touring stage shows go on sale (cash only) at 11 AM Tuesday through Saturday at the **TIX Bay Area** (✉ *Powell St. between Geary and Post Sts., Union Square* ☎ *415/433–7827* 🌐 *www.theatrebayarea.org*) booth on Union Square. TIX is also a full-service ticket agency for theater and music events around the Bay Area, open Tuesday through Thursday 11 to 6, Friday 11 to 7, Saturday 10 to 7, and Sunday 10 to 3.

THE 4-1-1

The best guide to the arts is the Sunday "Datebook" section (🌐 *www.sfgate.com/datebook)*, printed on pink paper, in the *San Francisco Chronicle*. The four-day entertainment supplement "96 Hours" (🌐 *www.sfgate.com/96hours*) is in the Thursday *Chronicle*. Also be sure to check out the city's free alternative weeklies, including *SF Weekly* (🌐 *www.sfweekly.com*) and the more avant-garde *San Francisco Bay Guardian* (🌐 *www.sfbg.com*).

Online, SF Station (🌐 *www.sfstation.com*) has a frequently updated arts and nightlife calendar. San Francisco Arts Monthly (🌐 *www.sfarts.org*), which is published at the end of the month, has arts features and events, plus a helpful "Visiting San Francisco?" section. For offbeat, emerging artist performances, consult CounterPULSE (🌐 *www.counterpulse.org*).

4

DANCE

San Francisco Ballet. Under artistic director Helgi Tomasson, the San Francisco Ballet's works—both classical and contemporary—have won admiring reviews. The primary season runs from February through May. Its repertoire includes full-length ballets such as *Don Quixote* and *Sleeping Beauty;* the December presentation of the *Nutcracker* is one of the most spectacular in the nation. The company also performs bold new dances from star choreographers such as William Forsythe and Mark Morris, alongside modern classics by George Balanchine and Jerome Robbins. Tickets and information are available at the **War Memorial Opera House.** ✉ *War Memorial Opera House, 301 Van Ness Ave., Civic Center* ☎ *415/865–2000* 🌐 *www.sfballet.org* ⏲ *Weekdays 10–4.*

MUSIC

San Francisco Symphony. One of America's top orchestras, the San Francisco Symphony performs from September through May, with additional summer performances of light classical music and show tunes; visiting artists perform here the rest of the year. Michael Tilson Thomas, who is known for his innovative programming of 20th-century American works (most notably his Grammy Award–winning Mahler cycle), is the music director, and he and his orchestra often perform with soloists of the caliber of Andre Watts, Gil Shaham, and Renée Fleming. Just to illustrate the more adventuresome side of the organization, this symphony once collaborated with the heavy-metal group Metallica. David Byrne has performed here, as well. Tickets run about $15 to

$100. ✉ *Davies Symphony Hall, 201 Van Ness Ave., at Grove St., Civic Center* ☎ *415/864–6000* 🌐 *www.sfsymphony.org.*

MUSIC FESTIVALS

Stern Grove Festival. The nation's oldest continuous free summer music festival hosts Sunday-afternoon performances of symphony, opera, jazz, pop music, and dance. The amphitheater is in a beautiful eucalyptus grove below street level, perfect for picnicking before the show. (Dress for cool weather.) ✉ *Sloat Blvd. at 19th Ave., Sunset* ☎ *415/252–6252* 🌐 *www.sterngrove.org.*

OPERA

San Francisco Opera. Founded in 1923, this world-renowned company has resided in the Civic Center's War Memorial Opera House since the building's completion in 1932. Over its split season—September through January and June through July—the opera presents about 70 performances of 10 to 12 operas. Translations are projected above the stage during almost all non-English operas. Long considered a major international company and the most important operatic organization in the United States outside New York, the opera frequently embarks on productions with European opera companies. Ticket prices can range from $25 to $195. The full-time box office (Monday 10–5, Tuesday–Friday 10–6) is at 199 Grove Street, at Van Ness Avenue. ✉ *War Memorial Opera House, 301 Van Ness Ave., at Grove St., Civic Center* ☎ *415/864–3330 tickets* 🌐 *www.sfopera.com.*

THEATER

American Conservatory Theater. Not long after its founding in the mid-1960s, the city's major nonprofit theater company became one of the nation's leading regional theaters. During its season, which runs from early fall to late spring, ACT presents approximately eight plays, from classics to contemporary works, often in rotating repertory. In December ACT stages a much-loved version of Charles Dickens's *A Christmas Carol*. The **ACT ticket office** (✉ *405 Geary St., Union Square* ☎ *415/749–2228*) is next door to Geary Theater, the company's home. ✉ *Geary Theater, 425 Geary St., Union Square* 🌐 *www.act-sf.org.*

Teatro ZinZanni. Contortionists, chanteuses, jugglers, illusionists, and circus performers ply the audience as you're served a surprisingly good five-course dinner in a fabulous antique Belgian traveling-dance-hall tent. Be ready to laugh, and arrive early for a front-and-center table. Reservations are essential; tickets are $125 to $150. Dress fancy. ✉ *Pier 29, Embarcadero at Battery St., Embarcadero* ☎ *415/438–2668* 🌐 *www.zinzanni.org.*

SPORTS AND THE OUTDOORS

BASEBALL

Fodor'sChoice ★ The **San Francisco Giants** (⊠*AT&T Park, 24 Willie Mays Plaza, between 2nd and 3rd Sts., SoMa* ☎*415/972–2000 or 800/734–4268* ⊕*sanfrancisco.giants.mlb.com*) play in beautiful, classic AT&T Park. **Tickets.com** (☎*877/473–4849* ⊕*www.tickets.com*) sells game tickets over the phone and charges a per-ticket fee of $2–$10, plus a per-call processing fee of up to $5. The **Giants Dugout** (⊠*AT&T Park, 24 Willie Mays Plaza, SoMa* ☎*415/972–2000 or 800/734–4268* ⊠*4 Embarcadero Center, Embarcadero* ☎*415/951–8888*) sells tickets in any of its stores (check the Web site, ⊕*sanfrancisco.giants.mlb.com/sf/ballpark/dugout_stores.jsp*, for all locations); a surcharge is added at all but the ballpark store.

BICYCLING

The **San Francisco Bicycle Coalition** (☎*415/431–2453* ⊕*www.sfbike.org*) has extensive information about the policies and politics of riding a bicycle in the city, and lists local events for cyclists on its Web site. You can also download (but not print) a PDF version of the *San Francisco Bike Map and Walking Guide.*

NO UPHILL BATTLE

Don't want to get stuck slogging up 30-degree inclines? Then be sure to pick up a copy of the foldout *San Francisco Bike Map and Walking Guide* ($3), which indicates street grades by color and delineates bike routes that avoid major hills and heavy traffic. You can pick up a copy in bicycle shops, select bookstores, or at the San Francisco Bicycle Coalition's Web site *(see above).*

WHERE TO RENT

Bike and Roll. You can rent bikes here for $7 per hour or $27 per day; discounted weekly rates are available. They have three locations and also have complimentary maps. ⊠*899 Columbus Ave., North Beach* ⊠*353 Jefferson St. between Jones and Leavenworth Sts., Fisherman's Wharf* ⊠*Leavenworth St. between Jefferson and Beach Sts., Fisherman's Wharf* ☎*415/229–2000 or 888/245–3929* ⊕*www.bicyclerental.com.*

Bike Hut. Known for its mom-and-pop–style service, the Hut is a small rental, repair, and used-bike shop. Hourly rentals go for $5, daily rentals for $20. ⊠*Pier 40, SoMa* ☎*415/543–4335* ⊕*www.thebikehut.com.*

Blazing Saddles. This outfitter rents bikes for $7 to $11 an hour, depending on the type of bike, or $28 to $68 a day, and shares tips on sights to see along the paths. ⊠*2715 Hyde St., Fisherman's Wharf* ⊠*465 Jefferson St., at Hyde St., Fisherman's Wharf* ⊠*Pier 43½ near Taylor St., Fisherman's Wharf* ⊠*Pier 41 at Powell St., Fisherman's Wharf* ⊠*1095 Columbus, North Beach* ☎*415/202–8888* ⊕*www.blazingsaddles.com.*

San Francisco Cyclery. Rent a bike for $15 for one to two hours, $20 for two to four hours, or $30 for eight hours. ⊠*672 Stanyan St., between Page and Haight Sts., Haight* ☎*415/379–3870* ⊕*www.sanfranciscocyclery.com* ⏲*Wed.–Mon. 10–6.*

SHOPPING

MAJOR SHOPPING DISTRICTS

THE CASTRO AND NOE VALLEY

The Castro, often called the gay capital of the world, is also a major shopping destination for all travelers. It's filled with men's clothing boutiques and home-accessories stores geared to the neighborhood's fairly wealthy demographic. Of course, there are plenty of places hawking kitsch, too, and if you're looking for something to shock your Aunt Martha back home, you've come to the right place. Just south of the Castro on 24th Street, largely residential Noe Valley is an enclave of fancy-food stores, bookshops, women's clothing boutiques, and specialty gift stores.

CHINATOWN

The intersection of Grant Avenue and Bush Street marks the gateway to Chinatown. The area's 24 blocks of shops, restaurants, and markets are a nonstop tide of activity. Dominating the exotic cityscape are the sights and smells of food: crates of bok choy, tanks of live crabs, cages of live partridges, and hanging whole chickens. Racks of Chinese silks, colorful pottery, baskets, and carved figurines are displayed chockablock on the sidewalks, alongside fragrant herb shops where your bill might be tallied on an abacus. And if you need to knock off souvenir shopping for the kids and office-mates in your life, the dense and multiple selections of toys, T-shirts, mugs, magnets, decorative boxes, and countless other trinkets make it a quick, easy, and inexpensive proposition.

FISHERMAN'S WHARF

A constant throng of sightseers crowds Fisherman's Wharf, and with good reason: Pier 39, the Anchorage, Ghirardelli Square, and the Cannery are all here, each with shops and restaurants, as well as outdoor entertainment—musicians, mimes, and magicians. Best of all are the Wharf's view of the bay and its proximity to cable-car lines, which can shuttle shoppers directly to Union Square. Many of the tourist-oriented shops border on tacky, peddling the requisite Golden Gate tees, taffy, and baskets of shells, but tucked into the mix are a few fine galleries, clothing shops, and groceries that even locals will deign to visit.

THE HAIGHT

Haight Street is a perennial attraction for visitors, if only to see the sign at Haight and Ashbury streets—the geographic center of the Flower Power movement during the 1960s, so it can be a bummer to find this famous intersection is now the turf for Gap and Ben & Jerry's. Don't be discouraged; it's still possible to find high-quality vintage clothing, funky shoes, folk art from around the world, and used records and CDs galore in this always-busy neighborhood.

HAYES VALLEY

A community park called Hayes Green breaks up a crowd of cool shops just west of the Civic Center. Here you can find everything from hip housewares to art galleries to handcrafted jewelry. The density of

The beat movement of the 1950s was born in San Francisco's most famous bookstore, City Lights.

unique stores—as well as the lack of chains anywhere in sight—makes it a favorite destination for many San Francisco shoppers.

JAPANTOWN

Unlike the ethnic enclaves of Chinatown, North Beach, and the Mission, the 5-acre **Japan Center** (✉*Bordered by Laguna, Fillmore, and Post Sts. and Geary Blvd.* ☎*No phone*) is under one roof. The three-block complex includes a reasonably priced public garage and three shop-filled buildings. Especially worthwhile are the Kintetsu and Kinokuniya buildings, where shops sell things like bonsai trees, tapes and records, jewelry, antique kimonos, *tansu* (Japanese chests), electronics, and colorful glazed dinnerware and teapots.

THE MARINA DISTRICT

With the city's highest density of (mostly) non-chain stores, the Marina is an outstanding shopping nexus. But it's nobody's secret—those with plenty of cash and style to burn flood the boutiques to snap up luxe accessories and housewares. Union Street and Chestnut Street in particular cater to the shopping whims of the grown-up sorority sisters and frat boys who live in the surrounding pastel Victorians.

THE MISSION

The aesthetic of the resident Pabst Blue Ribbon–downing hipsters and starving-artist types contributes to the affordability and individuality of shopping here. These night owls keep the city's best thrift stores, vintage-furniture shops, alternative bookstores, and, increasingly, small clothing boutiques afloat. As the Mission gentrifies, though, bargain hunters find themselves trekking the long blocks in search of truly local flavor. Thankfully, many of the city's best bakeries and cafés are sprinkled throughout the area.

NORTH BEACH

Although it's sometimes compared to New York City's Greenwich Village, North Beach is only a fraction of the size, clustered tightly around Washington Square and Columbus Avenue. Most of its businesses are small eateries, cafés, and shops selling clothing, antiques, and vintage wares. Once the center of the Beat movement, North Beach still has a bohemian spirit that's especially apparent at the rambling City Lights Bookstore, where Beat poetry lives on.

PACIFIC HEIGHTS

The rest of the city likes to deprecate its wealthiest neighborhood, but no one has any qualms about weaving through the mansions to come to Fillmore and Sacramento streets to shop. With grocery and hardware stores sitting alongside local clothing ateliers and international designer outposts, these streets manage to mix small-town America with big-city glitz. After you've splurged on a cashmere sweater or a handblown glass vase, snag an outdoor seat at Peet's or Coffee Bean; it's the perfect way to pass an afternoon watching the parade of old money, dogs, and strollers.

UNION SQUARE

Serious shoppers head straight to Union Square, San Francisco's main shopping area and the site of most of its department stores, including Macy's, Neiman Marcus, Barneys, and Saks Fifth Avenue. Also here are the Virgin Megastore, the Disney Store, and Borders Books, Music & Cafe. Nearby are such platinum-card international boutiques as Yves Saint Laurent, Cartier, Emporio Armani, Gucci, Hermès of Paris, Louis Vuitton, and Gianni Versace.

The latest major arrival is the **Westfield San Francisco Shopping Centre** (✉ *865 Market St., between 4th and 5th Sts., Union Square* ☎ *415/495–5656*), anchored by Bloomingdale's and Nordstrom. Besides the sheer scale of this mammoth mall, it's notable for its gorgeous atriums and its top-notch dining options (no typical food courts here—instead you'll find branches of a few top local restaurants). The area is also home to the new Barneys CO-OP; the New York institution's SF outpost has high, urban fashion on seven exquisitely appointed floors.

5

The Bay Area

WITH MARIN COUNTY, BERKELEY, OAKLAND, AND THE COASTAL PENINSULA

WORD OF MOUTH

"It was quite easy to get to Muir Woods. You have to go over the Golden Gate Bridge. After you get over the bridge, there are signs. I would suggest getting there as soon as it opens—it is so peaceful!"

—Kerry392

WELCOME TO THE BAY AREA

TOP REASONS TO GO

★ **Great outdoors:** A wealth of wild land lies right outside San Francisco's borders, including the beaches, forests, and meadows of the Golden Gate National Recreation Area; Point Reyes National Seashore; Big Basin Redwoods State Park; and numerous state beaches.

★ **Wining and dining:** Some of the best restaurants and markets in California (and in the country) are in the greater Bay Area, most notably Chez Panisse in Berkeley.

★ **Two-wheeling:** Whether you're cycling through the countryside or bombing down a mountainside single track, great cycling opportunities are everywhere here in the birthplace of mountain biking.

★ **Café culture:** While away your day over a latte. Coffeehouses, tearooms, and bookstore cafés abound, especially in the East Bay.

★ **On the water:** The Bay itself is a place to explore, by sailboat, kayak, or ferry.

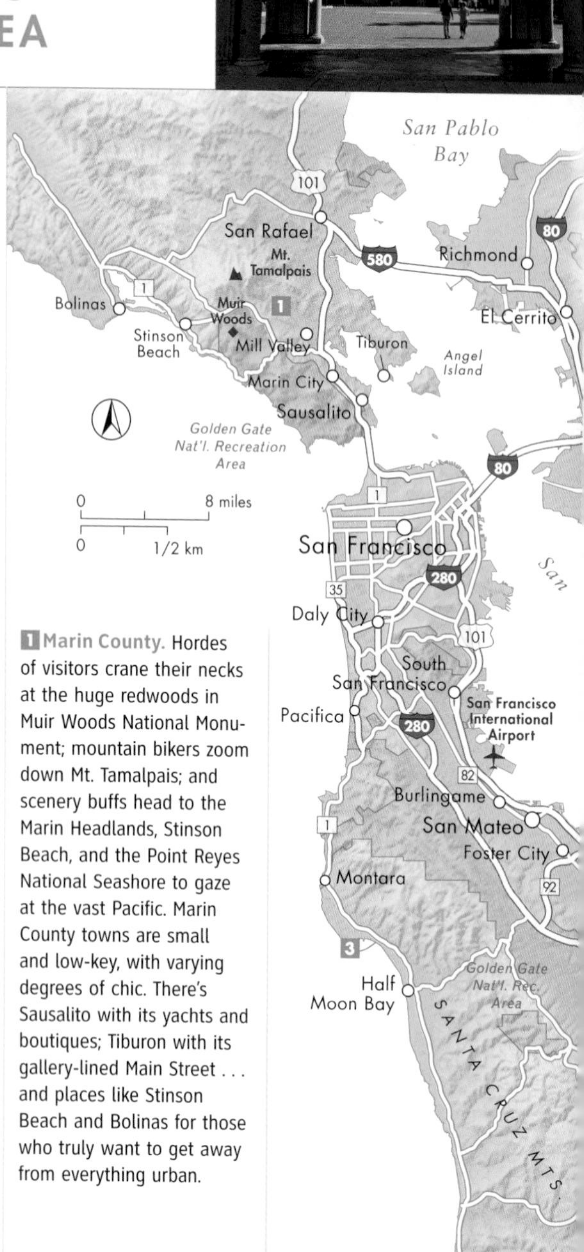

1 Marin County. Hordes of visitors crane their necks at the huge redwoods in Muir Woods National Monument; mountain bikers zoom down Mt. Tamalpais; and scenery buffs head to the Marin Headlands, Stinson Beach, and the Point Reyes National Seashore to gaze at the vast Pacific. Marin County towns are small and low-key, with varying degrees of chic. There's Sausalito with its yachts and boutiques; Tiburon with its gallery-lined Main Street . . . and places like Stinson Beach and Bolinas for those who truly want to get away from everything urban.

2 The East Bay. When San Franciscans refer to it, the East Bay often means nothing more than what you can see across the bay from the city—mainly Oakland and Berkeley. Oakland is gritty and diverse, home to a buzzing arts scene, Jack London Square, and famous jazz joint Yoshi's. Berkeley, defined by its University of California campus and liberal-to-radical politics, is a place of renegade spirits, bursting bookstores, and creature comforts like Alice Waters's Chez Panisse.

3 The Coastal Peninsula. The coastal towns between Santa Cruz and San Francisco have long been agricultural outposts, supplying food for the missions and the towns that succeeded them. Today artichokes and other cool-weather crops still grow in coastal fields, but the big attraction here is the beaches. The shoreline is nearly all public and varies widely from long, sandy stretches to tide pool–covered flats.

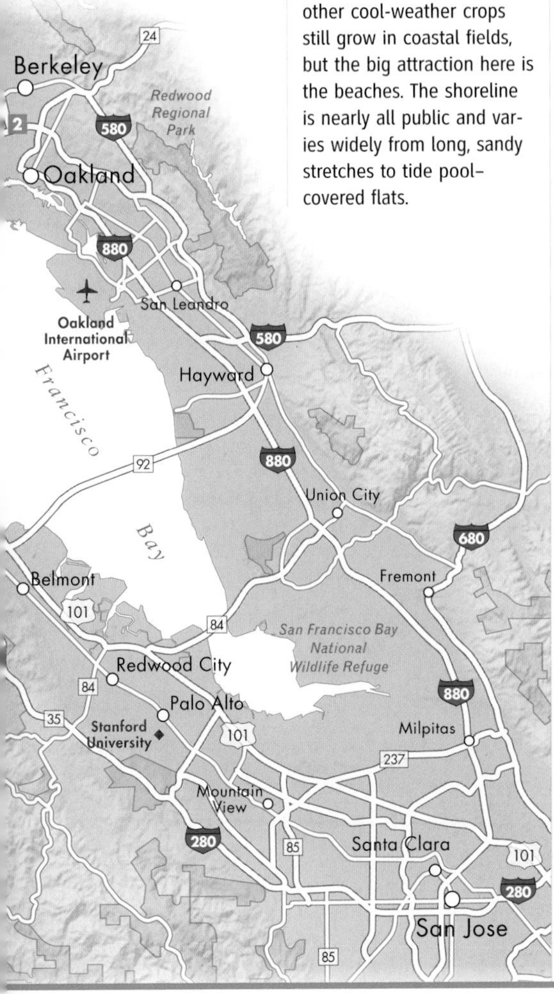

GETTING ORIENTED

Cross the Golden Gate Bridge and head north to reach Marin County's rolling hills and green expanses, where residents enjoy an haute-suburban lifestyle. East of the city, across the San Francisco Bay, are Berkeley and Oakland, which most Bay Area residents refer to as the East Bay. Life here feels more relaxed than in the city—but every bit as vibrant. To the south of San Francisco lies the peninsula; which part you see depends on your route: Highway 1 passes through a sparsely populated landscape along the coast, while inland a tangle of freeways leads to bustling Silicon Valley.

THE BAY AREA PLANNER

When to Go

For such a small place, the Bay Area has a surprisingly varied climate. The rainy season runs from about November through March, and temperatures in the 50s and 60s are generally constant across the region. But on any given day between April and November 10 different local cities can have 10 different forecasts. Some things hold constant: protected from the fog, inland areas stay warm and dry, while coastal areas see-saw between sun and fog (and rarely get truly hot). The East Bay is usually warmer and sunnier than points west, though when the fog rolls in hard it can hit here, too.

Getting Around

Getting around the Bay Area can be challenging. Rush hour on the highways is maddening, and in some neighborhoods looking for a parking space can feel like punishment. Public transit options—trains, subways, buses, and ferries—are abundant, but this is only a good option if you're traveling between the city and major destinations like Oakland, Berkeley, Sausalito, Tiburon, and Palo Alto.

About the Restaurants

The Bay Area is home to some of the most popular and innovative restaurants in the country, including Berkeley's famous Chez Panisse Café & Restaurant. Expect an emphasis on locally grown produce, hormone-free meats, and California wine—and not just in the finest dining rooms. Even casual spots like Fish, in Sausalito, serve memorable meals.

About the Hotels

There aren't many hotels in Berkeley or Oakland, but Marin is a destination where hotels package themselves as cozy retreats. Summer is often booked well in advance, despite weather that is often mercurial and sometimes downright chilly. Along the coastal peninsula accommodations tend to have homegrown character and cater to San Franciscans and weekend visitors here for a romantic getaway. Because of the weekend demand on the coast you'd be wise to make reservations as far in advance as possible. Inland Peninsula and South Bay lodgings generally attract business travelers—most are chain motels and hotels, though a handful of B&Bs have popped up in recent years. During the week, when business conventions are in full swing, many of these hotels are fully booked up two weeks in advance. However, some are nearly empty on weekends—this is when rates plummet and package deals abound.

WHAT IT COSTS

	¢	$	$$	$$$	$$$$
Restaurants	under $10	$10–$14	$15–$22	$23–$30	over $30
Hotels	under $90	$90–$149	$150–$199	$200–$250	over $250

Restaurant prices are for a main course at dinner, excluding sales tax of 8.25% (depending on location). Hotel prices are for two people in a standard double room in high season, excluding service charges and 10% tax.

Updated by Lisa M. Hamilton and Fiona G. Parrott

5

It's rare for a metropolis to compete with its suburbs for visitors, but the view from any of San Francisco's hilltops shows that the Bay Area's temptations extend far beyond the city limits.

To the north is Marin County, the beauty queen: small but chic villages like Tiburon and Mill Valley plus dramatic coastal scenery. East of town are two energetic urban centers, Berkeley and Oakland. Formerly radical Berkeley is getting more glam, while Oakland is slowly shaking off its image as San Francisco's ugly stepsister. Along the peninsula south of San Francisco you'll find a largely undeveloped coastline dotted with small towns and wild beaches—a place so peaceful it's hard to believe that behind the rolling green hills lies Silicon Valley.

MARIN COUNTY

Marin is quite simply a knockout—some go so far as to call it spectacular and wild. This isn't an extravagant claim, since more than 40% of the county (180,000 acres), including the majority of the coastline, is parkland. The territory ranges from chaparral, grassland, and coastal scrub to broadleaf and evergreen forest, redwood, salt marsh, and rocky shoreline.

Adrenaline junkies mountain bike down Mt. Tamalpais, and those who want solitude take a walk on one of Point Reyes's many empty beaches. Cosmopolitan Sausalito is just over the Golden Gate Bridge from San Francisco; across an inlet are Tiburon and Belvedere, lined with grand homes that regularly appear on fund-raising circuits.

West Marin is about as far as you can get from the big city, both physically and ideologically. Separated from the inland county by the slopes and ridges of giant Mt. Tamalpais, this territory beckons to mavericks, artists, ocean lovers, and other free spirits. Stinson Beach has tempered its isolationist attitude to accommodate out-of-towners, as have Inverness and Point Reyes Station. Bolinas, on the other hand, would prefer you not know its location.

PLANNING

GETTING HERE AND AROUND

BOAT AND FERRY TRAVEL

The Golden Gate Ferry crosses the bay to Sausalito from the south wing of San Francisco's Ferry Building (at Market Street and the Embarcadero). Blue & Gold Fleet ferries depart daily for Sausalito and Tiburon from Pier 41 at Fisherman's Wharf; weekday commuter ferries leave from the Ferry Building for Tiburon. The trip to Sausalito takes 30 minutes; to Tiburon, it takes 20 minutes. Seas can be choppy, but the ride is not long. Expect more crowds on weekends and during peak commute times.

The Angel Island–Tiburon Ferry sails across the strait to the island daily April through September and weekends the rest of the year.

Boat and Ferry Lines **Angel Island–Tiburon Ferry** (☎ *415/435–2131* 🌐 *www.angelislandferry.com*). **Blue & Gold Fleet** (☎ *415/705–8200* 🌐 *www.blueandgoldfleet.com*). **Golden Gate Ferry** (☎ *415/455–2000* 🌐 *www.goldengateferry.org*).

BUS TRAVEL

Golden Gate Transit buses travel to Sausalito, Tiburon, and Mill Valley from 1st and Mission streets as well as from other points in San Francisco. For Mt. Tamalpais State Park, take Bus 10, 70, or 80 to Marin City; in Marin City transfer to Golden Gate Transit Bus 63 (weekends and holidays, mid-March through early December only). To reach points in West Marin (e.g., Bolinas, Point Reyes Station, and the edge of Mt. Tamalpais State Park) on weekdays only, take West Marin Stagecoach vans from Marin City; call for routes and schedules. San Francisco MuniBus 76 runs hourly from 4th and Townsend streets to the Marin Headlands Visitor Center on Sunday and major holidays only. The trip takes roughly 45 minutes.

Bus Lines **Golden Gate Transit** (☎ *415/455–2000* 🌐 *www.goldengate.org*). **San Francisco Muni** (☎ *415/701–2311* 🌐 *www.sfmuni.com*). **West Marin Stagecoach** (☎ *415/526–3239* 🌐 *www.marin-stagecoach.org*).

CAR TRAVEL

To cross the Golden Gate Bridge, take U.S. 101 north. For Sausalito, take the first exit, Alexander Avenue, just past Vista Point; after winding all the way down the hill to the water, the road becomes Bridgeway. Continue north on Bridgeway to the municipal parking lot near the center of town—but expect the lot to be full on weekends, in which case you should continue north and hunt for street spots. For Tiburon, exit at Tiburon Boulevard.

The Marin Headlands are a logical stop en route to Sausalito, but reaching them can be tricky. After exiting on Alexander Avenue, take the first left (signs read SAN FRANCISCO/U.S. 101 SOUTH), pass through a tunnel under the freeway, and make a hard right up the steep hill just before the road merges back onto the bridge toward San Francisco. You should see a small sign that says FORTS BARRY AND CRONKHITE. Conzelman Road follows the cliffs that face the ocean and becomes one-way

before a spectacular drop toward Point Bonita; Bunker Road is a less spectacular inland route through Rodeo to the forts.

For Muir Woods and Mt. Tamalpais, take the Route 1–Stinson Beach exit off U.S. 101 and follow Route 1 west and then north. Both trips may take from 30 minutes to more than an hour, depending on traffic; allow plenty of extra time on summer weekends.

SIGHTSEEING GUIDES

Super Sightseeing offers a four-hour bus tour of Muir Woods. The tour, which stops in Sausalito en route, leaves at 9 AM and 2 PM daily from North Point and Taylor Street at Fisherman's Wharf and costs $46 ($45 senior citizens, $24 ages 5–11); 24-hour advance reservations are recommended. Great Pacific Tour Co. runs four-hour morning and afternoon tours of Muir Woods and Sausalito for $49 ($47 senior citizens, $39 ages 5–11), with hotel pickup in 14-passenger vans with excellent interpretation.

By Bus and Van **Great Pacific Tour Co.** (☎ *415/626–4499* 🌐 *www.greatpacifictour.com*). **Super Sightseeing** (☎ *415/777–2288* 🌐 *www.supersightseeing.com*).

VISITOR INFORMATION

Contact **Marin County Visitors Bureau** (✉ *1013 Larkspur Landing Circle, Larkspur* ☎ *866/925–2060* 🌐 *www.visitmarin.org*).

SAUSALITO

2 mi north of Golden Gate Bridge.

Bougainvillea-covered hillsides and an expansive yacht harbor give Sausalito the feel of an Adriatic resort. The town sits on the northwestern edge of San Francisco Bay, where it's sheltered from the ocean by the Marin Headlands; the mostly mild weather here is perfect for strolling and outdoor dining. Nevertheless, morning fog and afternoon winds can roll over the hills without warning, funneling through the central part of Sausalito once known as Hurricane Gulch.

WORD OF MOUTH

"Be sure to get out onto the water. A ferry ride to Sausalito, Tiburon, or Larkspur will reward you with wonderful views and there are things to be seen in each of those places."

—Grasshopper

South on **Bridgeway** (toward San Francisco), which snakes between the bay and the hills, a waterside esplanade is lined with restaurants on piers that lure diners with good seafood and even better views. Stairs along the west side of Bridgeway climb the hill to wooded neighborhoods filled with both rustic and opulent homes. As you amble along Bridgeway past boutiques, gift shops, and galleries, you'll notice the absence of basic services. If you need an aspirin or some groceries (or if you want to see the locals), you'll have to head to Caledonia Street, which runs parallel to Bridgeway, north of the ferry terminus and inland a couple of blocks. The streets closest to the ferry landing flaunt their fair share of shops selling T-shirts and kitschy souvenirs. Venture into some of the side streets or narrow alleyways to catch a bit more of the town's taste for eccentric jewelry and handmade crafts.

■ TIP→ The ferry is the best way to get to Sausalito from San Francisco; you get more romance (and less traffic) and disembark in the heart of downtown.

ESSENTIALS

Visitor Information Sausalito Chamber of Commerce (✉ *780 Bridgeway* ☎ *415/332–0505 or 415/331–7262* 🌐 *www.sausalito.org*).

Get your bearings and find out what's happening in town at the **Sausalito Visitors Center & Historical Exhibit** (✉ *780 Bridgeway* ☎ *415/332–0505*), operated by the town's historical society. It's closed Monday.

EXPLORING

The landmark **Plaza Viña del Mar** (✉ *Bridgeway and Park St.*), named for Sausalito's sister city in Chile, marks the center of town. Flanked by two 14-foot-tall elephant statues (created in 1915 for the Panama-Pacific International Exposition), the fountain is a great setting for snapshots and people-watching.

On the waterfront between the Hotel Sausalito and the Sausalito Yacht Club is an unusual historic landmark—a **drinking fountain.** It's inscribed with HAVE A DRINK ON SALLY in remembrance of Sally Stanford, the former San Francisco madam who later became the town's mayor in the 1970s. Sassy Sally, as they called her, would have appreciated the

The rolling hills of Marin County are a serene backdrop for the crowded piers of the Sausalito waterfront.

fountain's eccentric custom attachment: a knee-level basin that reads HAVE A DRINK ON LELAND, in memory of her beloved dog.

NEED A BREAK?

Judging by the crowds gathered outside Hamburgers (✉ *737 Bridgeway 94965* ☎ *415/332–9471*), you'd think someone was juggling flaming torches out front. They're really gaping at the juicy hand-formed beef patties sizzling on a rotating grill. Brave the line (it moves fast), get your food to go, and head for the esplanade to enjoy the sweeping views. Hours are 11 AM to 5 PM.

An anonymous-looking World War II shipyard building holds one of Sausalito's great treasures: the sprawling (more than 1½ acres) **Bay Model** of the entire San Francisco Bay and the San Joaquin–Sacramento River delta, complete with flowing water. The U.S. Army Corps of Engineers uses the model to reproduce the rise and fall of tides, the flow of currents, and the other physical forces at work on the bay. ✉ *2100 Bridgeway, at Marinship Way* ☎ *415/332–3870 recorded information, 415/332–3871 operator assistance* 🌐 *www.spn.usace.army.mil/bmvc* *Free* ⏲ *Memorial Day–Labor Day, Tues.–Fri. 9–4, weekends 10–5; Labor Day–Memorial Day, Tues.–Sat. 9–4.*

The **Bay Area Discovery Museum** fills five former military buildings with entertaining and enlightening hands-on exhibits related to science and the arts. Kids and their families can fish from a boat at the indoor wharf, imagine themselves as marine biologists in the Wave Workshop, and play outdoors at Lookout Cove, a 2½-acre bay-in-miniature made up of scaled-down sea caves, tidal pools, and even a re-created shipwreck. At Tot Zone, toddlers and preschoolers can play in an indoor-outdoor interactive area. From San Francisco, take the Alexander Avenue exit from U.S. 101 and follow signs to East Fort Baker. ✉ *557 McReynolds Rd., at East Fort Baker* ☎ *415/339–3900* ⊕ *www.baykidsmuseum.org* *$10; children under 1 free* ⊙ *Tues.–Fri. 9–4, weekends 10–5.*

WHERE TO EAT

$–$$$ SEAFOOD Fodor's Choice ★ ✕ **Fish.** If you're wondering where the locals go, this is the place. For fresh seafood, you can't beat this gleaming dockside fish house a mile north of downtown. Order at the counter, and then grab a seat by the floor-to-ceiling windows or at a picnic table on the pier, overlooking the yachts and fishing boats. Most of the sustainably caught fish is hauled in from the owner's boats, right at the dock outside. Try the ceviche, crab Louis, cioppino, barbecue oysters, or anything fresh that day that's being grilled over the oak-wood fire. Outside, kids can doodle with sidewalk chalk on the pier. ✉ *350 Harbor Dr.* ☎ *415/331–3474* *Reservations not accepted* ▭ *No credit cards.*

$$ FRENCH ✕ **Le Garage.** When Sausalito executives and entrepreneurs want a stylish lunch with a bayside setting, they head to Chef Olivier Souvestre's local lunch hot spot. Brittany born Souvestre serves traditional French bistro fare in a relaxed, sidewalk café–style setting. The menu is small, but the dishes are substantial in flavor and presentation. Standouts include frisée salad with poached egg, bacon, croutons, and pancetta vinaigrette; steak *frites* with a shallot confit and crispy fries; and a chef's selection of cheese or charcuterie with soup and mixed greens. The restaurant only seats 35 inside and 15 outside, so to avoid a long wait for lunch, arrive before 11:30 or after 1:30 PM. ✉ *85 Liberty Ship Way #109, Sausalito* ☎ *415/332–5625* ▭ *MC, V.*

$$–$$$ ITALIAN ★ ✕ **Poggio.** One of the few restaurants in Sausalito to attract both food-savvy locals and tourists, Poggio serves modern Tuscan cuisine in a handsome, open-wall space that spills onto the street. Expect dishes such as grilled lamb chops with roasted eggplant, braised artichokes with polenta, feather-light gnocchi, and pizzas from the open kitchen's wood-fired oven. ✉ *777 Bridgeway* ☎ *415/332–7771* *Reservations essential* ▭ *AE, D, MC, V.*

$$–$$$ JAPANESE ★ ✕ **Sushi Ran.** Sushi aficionados swear this is the Bay Area's best for raw fish, but don't overlook the excellent Pacific Rim fusions, a result of Japanese ingredients and French cooking techniques, served up in unusual presentations. Because Sushi Ran is so highly ranked among area foodies, book two to seven days in advance for dinner. Otherwise, expect a long wait, which you can soften by sipping one of the 45 by-the-glass sakes from the outstanding wine-and-sake bar. **■ TIP→ If you wander in after a day of sightseeing and can't get a table, you can sup in the noisy bar.** ✉ *107 Caledonia St.* ☎ *415/332–3620* ▭ *AE, D, MC, V* ⊙ *No lunch weekends.*

WHERE TO STAY

$$$$ **Cavallo Point.** Set in the Golden Gate National Park, this luxury hotel and resort's location is truly one of a kind. A former Army post, it features turn-of-the-20th-century buildings converted into well-appointed yet eco-friendly rooms. Both historic and contemporary guest rooms are scattered around the property, most overlooking a massive lawn with stunning views of the Golden Gate Bridge and San Francisco Bay. The

staff is accommodating and helpful. Murray Circle, the notable on-site restaurant with a Michelin-starred chef, serves top-notch California ingredients and features an impressive wine cellar. The neighboring casual bar offers food and drink on a large porch. **Pros:** numerous activities: a cooking school, yoga classes, and nature walks; spa with a tea bar; art gallery. **Cons:** landscaping feels incomplete; some staff act a bit informal. ✉ *601 Murray Circle, Fort Baker, Sausalito* ☎ *415/339–4700* 📠 *415/339–4792* 🌐 *www.cavallopoint.com* *68 historic and 74 contemporary guest rooms* *In-room: no a/c (some), safe, refrigerator, Internet, Wi-Fi. In-hotel: 2 restaurants, room service, bar, pool, gym, spa, water sports, laundry service, parking (paid), some pets allowed, no-smoking rooms* 💳 *AE, D, DC, MC, V.*

$$$$ **The Inn Above Tide.** The only hotel in the Bay Area with balconies literally hanging over the water, each of its rooms has a perfect-10 view that takes in wild Angel Island as well as the city lights across the bay. In the corner Vista Suite (the most expensive room here, at nearly triple the standard-room rate), you can even watch San Francisco twinkle from the king-size bed. Lovely touches—gardenias by the sink, large tubs, binoculars in every room, complimentary California wine and imported cheese—abound, and most rooms have wood-burning or gas fireplaces. Although it's set in the middle of town, this place is tranquil. **Pros:** great complimentary breakfast; minutes from restaurants/attractions; free in-room binoculars let you indulge in the incredible views. **Cons:** costly parking; some rooms are on the small side; no room service. ✉ *30 El Portal* ☎ *415/332–9535 or 800/893–8433* 📠 *415/332–6714* 🌐 *www.innabovetide.com* *29 rooms, 2 suites* *In-room: DVD, Wi-Fi. In-hotel: laundry service* 💳 *AE, DC, MC, V* *CP.*

5

SPORTS AND THE OUTDOORS

Specializing in sea kayaking, **Sea Trek Ocean Kayaking Center** (✉ *Schoonmaker Point Marina, off Libertyship Way* ☎ *415/488–1000* 🌐 *www.seatrekkayak.com*) offers guided half-day trips underneath the Golden Gate Bridge and full- and half-day trips to Angel Island, both for beginners. Starlight and full-moon paddles are particularly popular. Trips for experienced kayakers, classes, and rentals also are available. Prices start at $20 per hour for rentals; $65 for a three-hour guided trip.

SHOPPING

Edith Caldwell Gallery. Elegant, spare, and inviting, this gallery draws passersby with its intriguing shows. You'll find a mix of figurative and still-life paintings, unique objets d'art, and stunning tapestries. ✉ *819 Broadway, Sausalito* ☎ *415/331–5003.*

Something/Anything Gallery. Tucked away where Broadway ends and curves toward the dock, this gallery has a huge array of jewelry and gifts, from unique watches to humorous pendants. With friendly service and carefully crafted mementos of Sausalito, it's easy to find an inexpensive souvenir. ✉ *20 Princess St., Sausalito* ☎ *415/339–8831.*

TIBURON

2 mi north of Sausalito, 7 mi north of Golden Gate Bridge.

On a peninsula that was called Punta de Tiburon (Shark Point) by the Spanish explorers, this beautiful Marin County community retains the feel of a village, despite the encroachment of commercial establishments from the downtown area. The harbor faces Angel Island across Raccoon Strait, and San Francisco is directly south across the bay—which makes the views from the decks of harbor restaurants a major attraction. Tiburon is slightly more low-key than Sausalito, and the community favors Sunday brunch and cocktail hour. Since its incarnation, in 1884, when ferries from San Francisco connected the point with a railroad to San Rafael, the town has centered on the waterfront. ■ **TIP→The ferry is the most relaxing (and fastest) way to get here whenever the weather is pleasant, particularly in summer, allowing you to skip traffic and parking problems. Think about avoiding a midweek visit to Tiburon. Although there will be fewer strollers on the street, most shops close either Tuesday or Wednesday, or both.**

WORD OF MOUTH

"Sausalito is nice, if you want to say you've been there, but has become very touristy. They do have lots of small art galleries. I recommend Tiburon if you want to head in that direction; you'll get an amazing view, and it's got little shops." —andiamo

ESSENTIALS

Visitor Information Tiburon Peninsula Chamber of Commerce (✉ *96-B Main St. 94920* ☎ *415/435–5633* 🌐 *www.tiburonchamber.org*).

EXPLORING

Tiburon's narrow **Main Street** is on the bay side; you can browse the shops and galleries or relax on a restaurant's deck jutting out over the harbor.

Past the pink-brick bank building, Main Street is known as **Ark Row** (🌐 *www.landmarks-society.org*) and has a tree-shaded walk lined with antiques and specialty stores. Look closely and you can see that some of the buildings are actually old houseboats. They floated in Belvedere Cove before being beached and transformed into stores. If you're curious about architectural history, the Tiburon Heritage & Arts Commission prints a self-guided walking-tour map, which you can pick up at local businesses.

The stark-white **Old St. Hilary's Landmark and Wildflower Preserve,** an 1886 Carpenter Gothic church barged over from Strawberry Point in 1957, overlooks the town and the bay from its hillside perch. ■ **TIP→The church is surrounded by a wildflower preserve that is spectacular in May and June, when the rare black jewel flower blooms.** Expect a steep walk uphill to reach the preserve. ✉ *201 Esperanza St., off Mar West St.* ☎ *415/435–1853* 🌐 *www.landmarks-society.org* 🎟 *$2 suggested donation* ⏲ *Apr.–Oct., Wed. and Sun. 1–4 and by appointment.*

WHERE TO EAT

$$–$$$ AMERICAN **Rooney's.** Beloved by locals, this is a Tiburon favorite. A friendly greeting will make you feel as if you're at home, as will the lanterns and polished wood floors (head inside over dining dockside). Comfort food anchors the lunch menu with choices like "New York–style" sandwiches, salads, and a few surprises such as African chicken. For dinner, choose from fresh Dungeness crab, rib-eye steak, or seasonal specials. Last orders are taken at 9 PM except on Friday and Saturday, when you have an extra half hour. *38 Main St. 415/435–1911 MC, V No dinner Mon. or Tues.*

$$–$$$ AMERICAN **Sam's Anchor Cafe.** Open since 1921, this casual dockside restaurant with mahogany wainscoting is the town's most famous eatery. Today, most people flock here for the deck, where out-of-towners and old salts sit shoulder to shoulder for bay views, beer, seafood, and Ramos fizzes. The lunch menu is nothing special—burgers, sandwiches, salads, fried fish with tartar sauce—and you'll sit on plastic chairs at tables covered with blue-and-white-checked oilcloths. At night you can find standard seafood dishes with vegetarian and meat options. Expect a wait for outside tables on weekends (there are no reservations for deck seating or weekend lunch). Mind the seagulls; they know no restraint. *27 Main St. 415/435–4527 AE, D, DC, MC, V.*

WHERE TO STAY

$$–$$$$ ★ **Waters Edge Hotel.** Checking into this spacious and elegant hotel in downtown Tiburon feels like tucking away into a cozy retreat by the water. The views are stunning, the lighting perfect. Most rooms have a gas fireplace, and many have balconies with bay views. Furnishings are chic and modern in cocoa and cream colors; down comforters and high-thread-count linens make the beds deliciously comfortable. High-vaulted ceilings show off the carefully placed, Asian-influenced objects, which line the hallways and front living room area. **TIP→In the morning, breakfast is delivered to your door, but take your coffee outside to the giant communal sundeck over the water; the south-facing views of San Francisco Bay are incredible.** **Pros:** complimentary wine and cheese for guests every evening, restaurants/sights are minutes away. **Cons:** no room service; some rooms need to be updated; not a great place to bring small children. *25 Main St. 415/789–5999 or 877/789–5999 415/789–5888 www.marinhotels.com 23 rooms In-room: DVD, Wi-Fi. In-hotel: laundry service AE, D, DC, MC, V CP.*

THE MARIN HEADLANDS

★ The term "Golden Gate" may now be synonymous with the world-famous bridge, but it originally referred to the grassy, poppy-strewn hills flanking the passageway into San Francisco Bay. To the north of the gate lie the **Marin Headlands,** part of the Golden Gate National Recreation Area (GGNRA) and the most dramatic scenery in these parts. The raw beauty of the headlands, which consist of several small but steep bluffs, is particularly striking if you've just come from the enclosed silence of the nearby redwood groves. Windswept hills plunge down to the ocean, and creek-fed thickets shelter swaying wildflowers.

5

Shutterbugs rejoice in catching a scenic Muir Beach sunset.

The headlands stretch from the Golden Gate Bridge to Muir Beach. Photographers flock to the southern headlands for shots of the city, with the Golden Gate Bridge in the foreground and the skyline on the horizon. Equally remarkable are the views north along the coast and out to sea, where the Farallon Islands are visible on clear days. ■ **TIP→Almost any of the roads, all very windy, offer great coast views, especially as you drive at higher elevations. You'll see copious markers for scenic spots.**

The headlands' strategic position at the mouth of San Francisco Bay made them a logical site for World War II military installations. Today you can explore the crumbling concrete batteries where naval guns protected the approaches from the sea; kids especially love climbing on these structures. The headlands' main attractions are centered on Forts Barry and Cronkhite, which lie just across Rodeo Lagoon from each other. Fronting the lagoon is Rodeo Beach, a dark stretch of sand that attracts sand-castle builders and dog owners.

⚠ **Note: The beaches at the Marin Headlands are not safe for swimming. The giant cliffs are steep and unstable, so hiking down them can be dangerous. Stay on trails. Head farther north, to Muir Beach and beyond, for better ocean access.**

EXPLORING

The **Marin Headlands Visitor Center** (✉ *Fort Barry, Field and Bunker Rds., Bldg. 948* ☎ *415/331–1540* 🌐 *www.nps.gov/goga/marin-headlands.htm*), open daily 9:30 to 4:30, sells a useful guide to historic sites and wildlife and has exhibits on the area's history and ecology. Pick up the park newspaper, which lists a calendar of events, including a schedule of guided walks. Kids will enjoy the "please touch" educational sites and small play area inside.

★ At the end of Conzelman Road, in the southern headlands, is the **Point Bonita Lighthouse**, a restored beauty that still guides ships to safety with its original 1855 refractory lens. Half the fun of a visit is the steep ½-mi walk from the parking area down to the lighthouse, which takes you through a rock tunnel and across a suspension bridge. Signposts along the way detail the bravado of surfmen, as the early lifeguards were called, and the tenacity of the "wickies," the first keepers of the light. ✉ *End of Conzelman Rd.* *Free* *Sat.–Mon. 12:30–3:30.*

If you're an art lover, stop by the **Headlands Center for the Arts** (✉ *944 Fort Barry* ☎ *415/331–2787* *www.headlands.org* *Weekdays 10–5, Sun. noon–5*), where you can see contemporary art in a rustic natural setting. All but one of the center's nine converted military buildings are usually closed to the public, but you can visit the main building (the former barracks) to see several changing installations. The downstairs "archive room" features an odd assortment of objects found and created by residents, such as natural rocks, interesting glass bottles filled with collected items, and unusual masks. Stop by the industrial gallery space, two flights up, to see what the resident visual artists are up to—most of the work is quite contemporary. The center also hosts biweekly public programs, from artist talks to open studios. Call for current schedules.

5

Small but scenic, **Muir Beach**, a rocky patch of shoreline off Route 1 in the northern headlands, is a good place to stretch your legs and gaze out at the Pacific. Locals often walk their dogs here, and anglers and boogie boarders share the gentle surf. Families and cuddling couples come for picnicking and sunbathing. At one end of the sand is a cluster of waterfront homes, and at the other are the bluffs of Golden Gate National Recreation Area.

WHERE TO STAY

¢ **Marin Headlands Hostel.** As hostels go, it's hard to beat this beautifully located, well-maintained property in a valley on the north side of the headlands. This is also the only lodging in the GGNRA that isn't a campsite. Accommodations, inside the old military infirmary, consist of private rooms with space for up to five, or shared dorm-style rooms that sleep six to 22 people in bunk beds. Cook your own food in the communal kitchen and eat at a table in the giant common area near the woodstove; big windows look out onto stands of pine and eucalyptus. Couples can share rooms in a separate two-story house made cozy with couches in some rooms, comfortable wooden tables, and forest views. Don't miss the map of the world, which reaches over a corner and across two walls in the main house. **Pros:** plenty of peace and quiet; great prices; lovely setting. **Cons:** no Wi-Fi; difficult to get to without a car or bike; far from restaurants and shops. ✉ *941 Fort Barry* ☎ *415/331–2777* *www.norcalhostels.org/marin* *7 private rooms, 8 dormitory rooms; all with shared bath* *In-room: no a/c, no phone, no TV. In-hotel: laundry facilities* *D, MC, V.*

$$$–$$$$ ★ **Pelican Inn** [illegible]s slate roof to its whitewashed plaster walls, this inn looks so Tu[illegible]hat it's hard to believe it was built in the 1970s. The Pelican is English to the core, with its smallish guest rooms upstairs (no elevator), high half-tester beds draped in heavy fabrics, and bangers and grilled tomatoes for breakfast. Downstairs, the little pub pours ales and ports, and "the snug" is a private fireplace lounge for overnight guests. At dinner in the tavernlike or solarium dining rooms ($$–$$$), keep it simple with fish-and-chips, roasted hen, or prime rib, and focus on the well-crafted wine list. Lunch is served, too . . . a good thing, since your nearest alternatives are miles away via slow, winding roads. **Pros:** five-minute walk to beach; great bar and restaurant; peaceful setting. **Cons:** 20-minute drive to nearby attractions; no Wi-Fi or wheelchair access to bedrooms. ✉ *10 Pacific Way, off Rte. 1, Muir Beach* ☎ *415/383–6000* 📠 *415/383–3424* 🌐 *www.pelicaninn.com* *7 rooms* *In-room: no a/c, no phone, no TV. In-hotel: restaurant, bar* *MC, V* *BP.*

MUIR WOODS NATIONAL MONUMENT

Fodor's Choice ★ *12 mi northwest of the Golden Gate Bridge.*

One hundred fifty million years ago, ancestors of redwood and sequoia trees grew throughout the United States. Today the *Sequoia sempervirens* can be found only in a narrow, cool coastal belt from Monterey to Oregon. The 550 acres of Muir Woods National Monument contain some of the most majestic redwoods in the world—some nearly 250 feet tall and 1,000 years old. The stand was saved from destruction in 1905, when it was purchased by a couple who donated it to the federal government. Three years later it was named after naturalist John Muir, whose environmental campaigns helped to establish the national park system. His response: "This is the best tree lover's monument that could be found in all of the forests of the world. Saving these woods from the ax and saw is in many ways the most notable service to God and man I have heard of since my forest wandering began."

Muir Woods, part of the Golden Gate National Recreation Area, is a pedestrian's park. The trails vary in difficulty and distance. Beginning from the park headquarters, a 2-mi, wheelchair-accessible **loop trail** crosses streams and passes ferns and azaleas, as well as magnificent redwood groves. Among the most famous are **Bohemian Grove** and the circular formation called **Cathedral Grove.** On summer weekends visitors oohing and aahing in a dozen languages line the trail. If you prefer a little more serenity, consider the challenging **Dipsea Trail,** which climbs west from the forest floor to soothing views of the ocean and the Golden Gate Bridge. For a complete list of trails, check with rangers, who can also help you pick the best one for your ability level.

■ TIP→ The weather in Muir Woods is usually cool and often wet, so wear warm clothes and shoes appropriate for damp trails. Picnicking and camping aren't allowed, and pets aren't permitted. Parking can be difficult here—the lots are small and the crowds are large—so try to come early in the morning or late in the afternoon. The **Muir Woods Visitor Center** has a wide selection of books and exhibits on redwood trees and the history of Muir Woods.

DID YOU KNOW?

The gorgeous old-growth redwood trees in Muir Woods are often enveloped in fog, a useful dampness for the trees, especially to counteract the dry summers.

To get here from San Francisco, take U.S. 101 north across the Golden Gate Bridge to the Mill Valley/Stinson Beach exit and then follow signs to Highway 1 north. On weekends, Memorial Day through Labor Day, Golden Gate Transit operates a free shuttle from Mill Valley every half hour. Park in Marin City at the Gateway Shopping Center (look for lighted signs directing you from U.S. 101) or at the Manzanita Park-and-Ride, at the Highway 1 exit off U.S. 101 (look for the lot under the elevated freeway), or take connecting bus service from San Francisco with Golden Gate Transit. At this writing, there were plans to expand the service to year-round operation; call ahead. ☒*Panoramic Hwy. off Hwy. 1, approximately 12 mi north of Golden Gate Bridge* ☎*415/388–2595 park information, 415/921–5858 shuttle information* ⊕*www.nps.gov/muwo* *$5* ⊙*Daily 8 AM–sunset.*

WORD OF MOUTH

"One word of advice about Muir Woods: The parking lots are very small and when they fill, people start parking along the road. . . . Granted we went on a Saturday, but I was still surprised at such a crowd (or such small parking lots?)." —polly229

MT. TAMALPAIS STATE PARK

16 mi northwest of Golden Gate Bridge.

Although the summit of Mt. Tamalpais is only 2,571 feet high, the mountain rises practically from sea level, dominating the topography of Marin County. Adjacent to Muir Woods National Monument, Mt. Tamalpais State Park affords views of the entire Bay Area and the Pacific Ocean to the west. The mountain was sacred to Native Americans, who saw in its profile—as you can see today—the silhouette of a sleeping Indian maiden. Locals fondly refer to it as the "Sleeping Lady." For years the 6,300-acre park has been a favorite destination for hikers. There are more than 200 mi of trails, some rugged but many developed for easy walking through meadows, grasslands, and forests and along creeks. Mt. Tam, as it's called by locals, is also the birthplace (in the 1970s) of mountain biking, and today many spandex-clad bikers whiz down the park's winding roads.

The park's major thoroughfare, the Panoramic Highway, snakes its way up from U.S. 101 to the **Pantoll Ranger Station** (☒*3801 Panoramic Hwy., at Pantoll Rd.* ☎*415/388–2070* ⊕*www.parks.ca.gov*). The office is staffed sporadically, depending on funding, but if you leave a phone message, a ranger will call you back (within several days) during business hours. From the ranger station, the Panoramic Highway drops down to the town of Stinson Beach. Pantoll Road branches off the highway at the station, connecting up with Ridgecrest Boulevard. Along these roads are numerous parking areas, picnic spots, scenic overlooks, and trailheads. Parking is free along the roadside, but there's a fee at the ranger station and at some of the other parking lots.

STINSON BEACH

20 mi northwest of Golden Gate Bridge.

Stinson Beach is the most expansive stretch of sand in Marin County. It's as close (when the fog hasn't rolled in) as you can get to the stereotypical feel of a Southern California beach. ⚠ **Swimming here is recommended only from early May through September, when lifeguards are on duty, because the undertow can be strong and shark sightings, although infrequent, aren't unusual.** There are several clothing-optional areas (such as Red Rock Beach). On any hot summer weekend every road to Stinson Beach is jam-packed, so factor this into your plans. The town itself is very down to earth—like tonier Mill Valley, but more relaxed.

WHERE TO EAT AND STAY

$$–$$$ AMERICAN **Parkside Cafe.** Most people know the Parkside for its beachfront snack bar (cash only), but inside is the best restaurant in Stinson Beach. The food is classic Cal cuisine, with appetizers such as day-boat scallops, ceviche, and mains such as lamb with goat-cheese-stuffed red peppers. Breakfast, a favorite among locals, is served until 2 PM. Eat on the sunny patio, which is sheltered from the wind by creeping vines, or by the fire in the contemporary dining room. ✉ *43 Arenal Ave.* ☎ *415/868–1272* ▭ *MC, V.*

$$–$$$ AMERICAN **Sand Dollar.** The town's oldest restaurant still attracts all the old salts from Muir Beach to Bolinas, but these days they sip whisky over an up-to-date bar or beneath market umbrellas on the spiffy deck. The food is good—try the panfried sand dabs (small flatfish) and pear salad with blue cheese—but the big draw is the lively atmosphere. Musicians play weekends in summer, and on sunny afternoons the deck gets so packed that people sit on the fence rails, sipping beer. ✉ *3458 Rte. 1* ☎ *415/868–0434* ▭ *AE, MC, V* ⊗ *No lunch Tues. Nov.–Mar.*

$–$$$ **Stinson Beach Motel.** Built in the 1930s, this motel surrounds three courtyards that burst with flowering greenery. Rooms are immaculate, simple, and summery, with freshly painted walls, good mattresses, and some kitchenettes. The motel is on the main drag, so it's convenient to everything in town, but it can get loud on busy summer weekend days. ■ **TIP→Room 3 has the most privacy, though all rooms face a central courtyard, not the street.** Weekday room rates ($90–$150) are a bargain for the north coast. **Pros:** minutes from the beach; cozy, unpretentious rooms. **Cons:** no Wi-Fi; not much to do once the sun sets. ✉ *3416 Hwy. 1* ☎ *415/868–1712* 🖷 *415/868–1790* 🌐 *www.stinsonbeachmotel.com* *7 rooms* *In-room: no a/c, no phone, kitchen (some)* ▭ *D, MC, V.*

BOLINAS

7 mi north of Stinson Beach.

The tiny town of Bolinas wears its 1960s idealism on its sleeve, attracting potters, poets, and peace lovers to its quiet streets. With a funky gallery, a general store selling organic produce, a café, and an offbeat saloon, the main thoroughfare, Wharf Road, looks like a hippie-fied version of Main Street USA. Although privacy-seeking locals openly dislike tourism and have torn down signs to the town, Bolinas isn't difficult to find: heading north from Stinson Beach on Route 1, make a left at the first road just past the Bolinas Lagoon (Bolinas-Olema Road), and then turn left at the stop sign. **■ TIP→The road dead-ends smack-dab in the middle of the tiny town, so drive slowly lest you find yourself in a confrontation with an angry local.**

POINT REYES NATIONAL SEASHORE

Fodor'sChoice ★ *15 mi north of Stinson Beach on Hwy. 1.*

One of the Bay Area's most spectacular treasures and the only national seashore on the West Coast, the 66,500-acre Point Reyes National Seashore (*www.nps.gov/pore*) encompasses secluded beaches, rugged chaparral, and grasslands. The hills and dramatic cliffs afford hikers, whale-watchers, and solitude seekers magnificent views of the sea.

A few tiny towns along its eastern boundary serve as gateways to the national seashore. **Olema,** a crossroads with a couple of fine restaurants and small inns, is where you'll find the main visitor center. Two miles north on Highway 1 is **Point Reyes Station,** the biggest burg in the area. A mix of upscale, counterculture, and mom-and-pop shops and eateries lines several blocks, and numerous B&Bs lie north of town. On Sir Francis Drake Boulevard, which parallels Highway 1 up the opposite shore of Tomales Bay, **Inverness** overlooks the water from a forested hillside. There are also several lodgings here, where you sleep humbly or extravagantly.

ESSENTIALS

Visitor Information West Marin Chamber of Commerce (*415/663–9232 www.pointreyes.org*).

EXPLORING

The **Bear Valley Visitor Center** (*Bear Valley Rd., west of Hwy. 1 in Olema 415/464–5100 Weekdays 9–5, weekends 8–5*) has exhibits about park history and wildlife. Rangers here dispense information about beaches, whale watching, and hiking trails. The infamous San Andreas Fault runs along the eastern edge of the park and up the center of Tomales Bay; take the short **Earthquake Trail** from the visitor center to see the impact near the epicenter of the 1906 earthquake that devastated San Francisco.

Drive past Inverness on Sir Francis Drake Boulevard to reach the heart of the park: a 20-mi-long road through rolling hills spotted with cattle ranches and dairy farms. There are turnoffs to several beaches along the way; those on the western side compose a 10-mi-long beach that has reliably dramatic surf and gorgeous dunes. At **Drakes Beach** the water is usually calmer (often even swimmable), and there's a visitor center. Drakes also has an excellent café (*415/669–1297 Closed Tues. and Wed., no lunch weekdays*) that serves hamburgers from beef raised on the surrounding ranches; on Friday and Saturday nights it transforms into the most romantic restaurant on the coast, serving a four-course, prix-fixe dinner (reservations required). In late winter and spring, wildlife enthusiasts should make a stop at **Chimney Rock,** just

DID YOU KNOW?

Majestic Point Reyes National Seashore offers a variety of attractions for nature-lovers: hiking, bird watching, camping, or whale watching depending on the season. But flower picking isn't an approved activity; the wild flowers here are protected.

before the lighthouse, and take the short walk to the Elephant Seal Overlook. Even from up on the cliff, the males look enormous as they spar for the resident females.

★ At the very end of Sir Francis Drake Boulevard (22 mi from the Bear Valley Visitor Center) is the **Point Reyes Lighthouse** (☎*415/669–1534* ⏲*Thurs.–Mon. 10–4:30, except in very windy weather*), which has been in operation since December 1, 1870. Half a mile from the parking lot, 308 steps—the equivalent of 30 stories—lead down to (and back up from) the lighthouse: the view is worth it. On busy whale-watching weekends (late December through mid-April), parking may be restricted and shuttle buses ($5, children free) put in service from Drakes Beach. You don't have to walk down the stairs to have a view of the whales. Along the park's northernmost finger of land, the 4.7-mi (one way) **Tomales Point Trail** follows the spine of a ridge through Tule Elk Preserve, providing spectacular ocean views from high bluffs. Expect to see lots of elk, even very close to the trail, but keep your distance from the animals. To reach the fairly easy hiking trail, head north out of Inverness on Sir Francis Drake Boulevard and turn right on Pierce Point Road. Park at the end of the road by the old ranch buildings.

WHERE TO EAT

¢ CAFÉ ✕**Bovine Bakery.** You can spot this tiny bakery from all the way down Main Street—just look for the line of people streaming out the door. Cyclists get their sugar fix here courtesy of the delectable pastries; locals come for the excellent coffee (but, as a sign inside states emphatically, NO ESPRESSO). ✉*11315 Hwy. 1, Point Reyes Station* ☎*415/663–9420* ▭*No credit cards* ⏲*No dinner.*

$$$–$$$$ AMERICAN ✕**Olema Inn.** West Marin County is a locus for small-scale, organic farming, and that is the backbone of the cuisine here. Steak from Point Reyes is paired with potatoes from Bolinas; Dungeness crab might come with fiddlehead ferns, fava beans, and wild mushrooms. The food is elegant, the dining room ($$$$; no lunch weekdays) is spare and sophisticated, though casual, and the staff is unpretentious. Come on Monday, locals' night, when there's live music and you can browse a delectable small-plates menu. ✉*10000 Sir Francis Drake Blvd.* ☎*415/663–9559* ▭*AE, MC, V* ⏲*No lunch weekdays.*

¢–$ CAFÉ ✕**Tomales Bay Foods.** A renovated hay barn houses this collection of food shops. Watch workers making Cowgirl Creamery cheese, then buy some at a counter that sells exquisite artisanal cheeses from around the world. Little Shorty's Golden Point Produce showcases local organic fruits and vegetables and premium packaged foods, and the Cantina deli turns the best ingredients into creative sandwiches, salads, and soups. The shops are open until 6 PM. ✉*80 4th St., Point Reyes Station* ☎*415/663–9335* ▭*AE, D, MC, V* ⏲*Closed Mon. and Tues.*

WHERE TO STAY

$$$$ Fodor'sChoice ★ **Manka's Inverness Lodge.** Chef-owner Margaret Grade realizes a rustic fantasy in her 1917 hunting lodge and cabins, where mica-shaded lamps cast an amber glow and bearskin rugs warm wide-plank floors. Each detail—featherbeds, deep leather armchairs, huge soaking tubs—bespeaks sensuous indulgence, but this is a private hideout, not a swanky

resort. All rooms have fireplaces. **Pros:** total rustic luxury; serene; close to the park. **Cons:** hard to get a reservation. ✉*30 Callendar Way, at Argyll Way, Inverness* ☎*415/669–1034* 🌐*www.mankas.com* *4 rooms, 1 suite, 3 cabins* *In-room: no a/c, no phone (some), kitchen (some), no TV, Wi-Fi. In-hotel: some pets allowed, no-smoking rooms* *AE, MC, V* *BP.*

$$–$$$$ ★ **Olema Druids Hall.** Built in 1885 as the meeting place for a men's social club called the Druids, this gorgeous, rambling building has been renovated into a place where everything is deluxe. In winter, rooms are warmed by radiant heat that comes up through the original hardwood floors (marble floors in the bathrooms). The suite has a gourmet kitchen (complete with Viking range and dishwasher), a real wood-burning fireplace, and a private deck that leads into the garden's gazebo. The Japanese-influenced cottage has a bedroom made private by shoji screens and a Jacuzzi bath with double showerheads above. All rooms have down bedding and an emphasis on privacy. **Pros:** luxurious; private. **Cons:** not much is within walking distance. ✉*9870 Hwy. 1, Olema* ☎*415/663–8727 or 866/554–4255* 🌐*www.olemadruidshall.com* *2 rooms, 1 suite, 1 cottage* *In-room: no a/c, kitchen (some), DVD, Wi-Fi. In-hotel: Wi-Fi, no-smoking rooms* *AE, MC, V* *BP.*

CAMPING Within the Point Reyes National Seashore are four hike-in campgrounds in isolated wilderness areas 3–6½ mi from trailheads. All sites have barbecue pits, picnic tables, pit toilets, and food-storage lockers; the water isn't potable and dogs are not allowed. The fee is $15 per night for up to six people. Reservations are essential spring through fall and can be booked up to three months in advance; to reserve call ☎*415/663–8054* weekdays between 9 and 2 or inquire in person at the Bear Valley Visitor Center. For detailed information about camping, call the park at ☎*415/464–5100* or visit 🌐*www.nps.gov/pore.*

MARSHALL

13 mi north of Point Reyes National Seashore on Hwy. 1.

The northern side of Point Reyes National Seashore is divided from the mainland by Tomales Bay, a finger of water 15 mi long and only 1 mi wide at most points. Heading north from Point Reyes Station, Highway 1 follows the eastern edge of the bay through the tiny town of Marshall. Nearly every building here hugs the strip of land between the highway and the bay, which means pretty much anywhere you go there's a great view of the water and the park beyond.

EXPLORING

In the past Marshall was known for its dairy farming, but these days it's famous for oysters, which you can buy throughout town. **Tomales Bay Oyster Company** (✉*15479 Hwy. 1, Marshall* ☎*415/663–1242* ⏲*Daily 8–6*) has farmed oysters since 1909. Today visitors buy them by the dozen and eat at the picnic tables, usually barbecuing the bivalves on the grills. Bring your shucking knife, fixings, and charcoal. Known as the growers of the Bay Area's most gourmet bivalves, **Hog Island Oyster Company** (✉*20215 Hwy. 1, Marshall* ☎*415/663–9218* ⏲*Daily 9–5*) is so popular it must charge for picnicking. On weekends reservations are required, and there's a fee of $8 per person for a table on the water (oysters not included); during the week it's first come first served, fee $5. Most people supplement by bringing drinks and (often elaborate) picnics. **The Marshall Store** (✉ *19225 Hwy. 1, Marshall* ☎ *415/663–1339* ⏲ *Daily 10–5:30, Closed Tues.*) offers oysters raw, grilled and Rockefeller-style, along with food from a full deli and wine market. Seats and tables line the waterfront.

WHERE TO EAT AND STAY

¢–$ SEAFOOD ✕ **Tony's Seafood.** Giant barbecued and fried oysters are the specialty at this friendly joint, family-owned and -operated since it opened in 1948. For those who think bivalves are slimy, there are good, cheap hamburgers as well. ✉ *18663 Hwy. 1, Marshall* ☎ *415/663–1107* ▭ *No credit cards* ⏲ *Fri.–Sun. noon–8.*

$$$–$$$$ **Nick's Cove.** Long famous as a settlement of funky cabins surrounding a greasy-spoon restaurant, Nick's Cove has been transformed into the area's premier "rustic chic" spot. The unique cottages are like deluxe hunting cabins, with cushy king-size beds, wood-burning stoves, and minibars stocked with top-shelf tequila and gin. As the fog sets in the five cabins with decks over the water become particularly sublime. The wood-paneled restaurant ($–$$$$) tips its hat to a former life with deer trophies and a long bar decorated with fishing rope, but the food is decidedly 21st-century California: mostly organic, with excellent local seafood and meats. **Pros:** cozy; quiet; a place to indulge. **Cons:** noise from the road can break the quiet. ✉ *23240 Hwy. 1* ☎ *415/663–1033* 🌐 *www.nickscove.com* *12 cottages* *In-room: no a/c, refrigerator, Wi-Fi. In-hotel: restaurant, room service, some pets allowed, no-smoking rooms* ▭ *AE, D, MC, V.*

SPORTS AND THE OUTDOORS

Blue Waters Kayaking (✉ *19225 Highway 1* ☎ *415/669–2600* 🌐 *www.bwkayak.com*) provides guided morning, full-day, sunset, full-moon, and overnight camping paddles out of their launches in Marshall and Inverness. They also rent out kayaks and offer beginner through advanced lessons. Best to make a reservation in summer, especially on weekends.

THE EAST BAY

To San Franciscans, the East Bay is shorthand for Berkeley and Oakland, both across the Bay Bridge from the city. Berkeley is defined by its University of California campus and its liberal-to-radical politics. Ever since the Free Speech Movement ignited at the Cal campus in the 1960s, Berkeley has been the place for renegade spirits, bursting bookstores, and caffeine-fueled debates. It's not all intellectual-politico jargon, though; there are plenty of creature comforts too. Most famously, there's Chez Panisse, the restaurant that embodies seasonal, simple, local cooking—but there are countless tasty treasures to be sampled in Berkeley's Gourmet Ghetto. Or you could shop for indie tracks at Amoeba Music, obscure tomes at Moe's Books, or the perfect bottle of Sancerre at Kermit Lynch Wine Merchant.

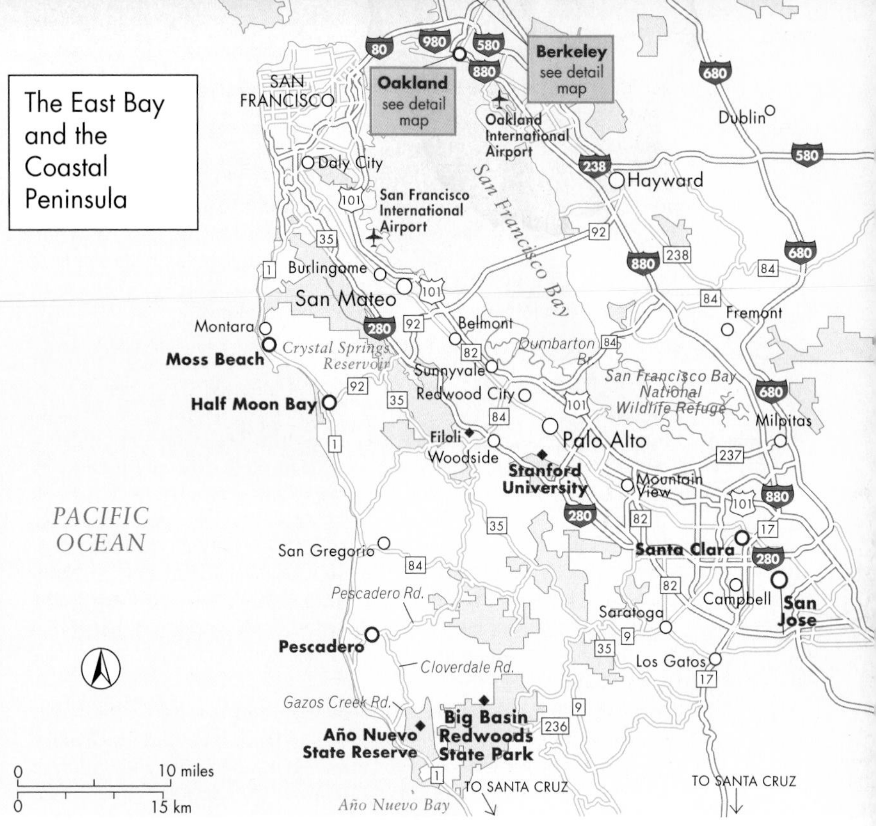

Oakland is grittier and even more diverse, with a buzzing arts scene. Small pockets of the city are pretty dodgy, so it's important to know where you're going. Old Oakland has a concentration of evocative Victorian buildings, now full of cafés and shops; the Rockridge neighborhood is home to lovely Market Hall, a European-style market. Jack London Square may be the best place to get a sense of Oakland's role as a major port, but it feels pretty sterile. Head to a jazz joint like Yoshi's or a gallery-bar like Café van Kleef, though, and you'll feel the city's indomitable energy.

PLANNING

GETTING HERE AND AROUND

BOAT AND FERRY TRAVEL

The Alameda/Oakland Ferry runs several times daily between San Francisco's Ferry Building or Pier 39, Alameda, and the Clay Street dock near Oakland's Jack London Square; one-way tickets are $6.25. The trip lasts 30 to 45 minutes, depending on your departure point, and leads to the heart of Oakland's gentrified shopping and restaurant district. Arriving in Oakland by boat conveys a historic sense of the city's heyday as a World War II–era shipbuilding center. Purchase tickets on board.

Boat and Ferry Contacts **Alameda/Oakland Ferry** (☎ *510/522–3300* 🌐 *www.eastbayferry.com*).

BUS TRAVEL

Although Bay Area Rapid Transit (BART) travel is often cheaper and more convenient, buses run frequently between San Francisco's Trans-Bay Terminal (at 1st and Mission streets) and the East Bay. AC Transit's F and FS lines stop near the university and 4th Street shopping in Berkeley. Lines C and P travel to Piedmont in Oakland. The O bus stops at the edge of Chinatown near downtown Oakland.

Bus Contacts **AC Transit** (☎ *817–1717 after any Bay Area area code* 🌐 *www.actransit.org*).

CAR TRAVEL

From San Francisco, take I–80 east across the Bay Bridge. For most of Berkeley, take the University Avenue exit through downtown Berkeley to the campus or take the Ashby Avenue exit and turn left on Telegraph Avenue to the traditional campus entrance; there's a parking garage on Channing Way. For Oakland, take I–580 off the Bay Bridge to the Grand Avenue exit for Lake Merritt. To reach downtown and the waterfront, take I–980 from I–580 and exit at 12th Street. Both trips take about 30 minutes, unless it's rush hour or a weekend afternoon, when you should count on an hour.

TRAIN TRAVEL

BART (Bay Area Rapid Transit, formally) trains make stops in downtown Berkeley and in several parts of Oakland, including Rockridge. Use the Lake Merritt Station for the Oakland Museum and southern Lake Merritt; the Oakland City Center–12th Street Station for downtown, Chinatown, and Old Oakland; and the 19th Street Station for the Paramount Theatre and the north side of Lake Merritt. From the Berkeley (not North Berkeley) Station, walk a block up Center Street to get to the western edge of campus. Both trips take 30 to 45 minutes one way from the center of San Francisco.

Train Contacts **BART** (☎ *510/465–2278* 🌐 *www.bart.gov*).

OAKLAND

Directly east of Bay Bridge.

Often overshadowed by San Francisco's beauty and Berkeley's offbeat antics, Oakland's allure lies in its amazing diversity. Here you can find a Nigerian clothing store, a beautifully renovated Victorian home, a Buddhist meditation center, and a lively salsa club, all within the same block.

Everyday life here revolves around the neighborhood, with a main business strip attracting both shoppers and strollers. In some areas, such as high-end Piedmont and Rockridge, you'd swear you were in Berkeley or San Francisco's Noe Valley or Cow Hollow. These are perfect places for browsing, eating, or just relaxing between sightseeing trips to Oakland's architectural gems, rejuvenated waterfront, and numerous green spaces. Between Rockridge and Piedmont and to the west, you can find

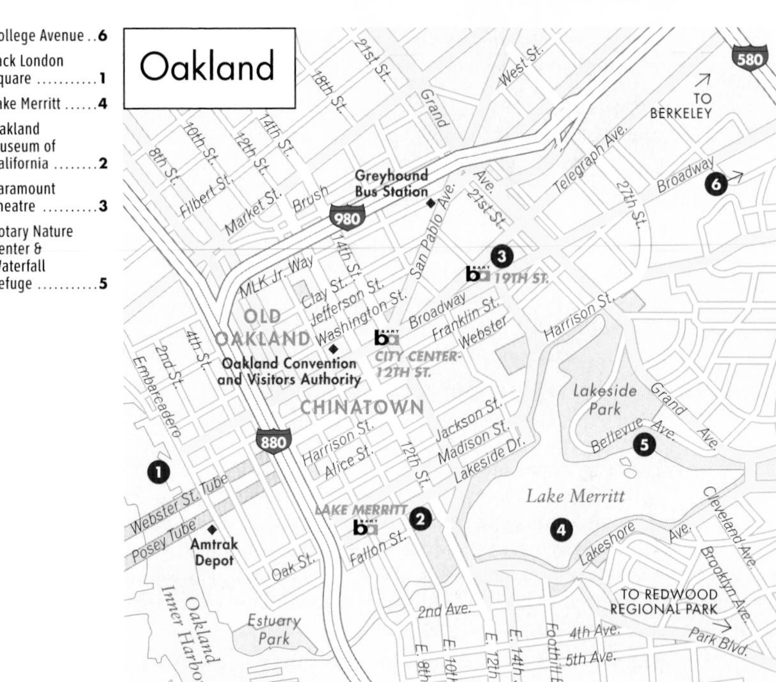

the Temescal District, along Telegraph Avenue just south of 51st Street, which is beginning to attract a small collection of eateries and shops.

ESSENTIALS

Visitor Information **Oakland Convention and Visitors Bureau** (*463 11th St. 510/839–9000 www.oaklandcvb.com*).

EXPLORING

2 One of Oakland's top attractions, the **Oakland Museum of California** is an excellent introduction to a tour of California, and its detailed exhibits on the state's art, history, and natural wonders can help fill the gaps on a brief visit. You can travel through the state's myriad ecosystems in the Natural Sciences Gallery, from the sand dunes of the Pacific to the coyotes and brush of the Nevada border. Kids love the lifelike wild-animal exhibits, especially the snarling wolverine, big-eyed harbor seal, and trove of hidden creatures. The rambling Cowell Hall of California History includes everything from Spanish-era armor to a small but impressive collection of vintage vehicles, including a gorgeous, candy-apple-red "Mystery" car from the 1960s and a gleaming red, gold, and silver fire engine that battled the flames in San Francisco in 1906. The Gallery of California Art holds an eclectic collection of modern works and early landscapes. Of particular interest are paintings by Richard Diebenkorn, Joan Brown, Elmer Bischoff, and David Park, all

members of the Bay Area Figurative School, which flourished here after World War II. Fans of Dorothea Lange won't want to miss the gallery's comprehensive collection of her work. The museum also has a sculpture garden with a view of the Oakland and Berkeley hills in the distance. ✉*1000 Oak St., at 10th St.* ☎*510/238–2200* 🌐*www.museumca.org* 🎫*$8, free 2nd Sun. of month* 🕓*Wed.–Sat. 10–5, until 9 1st Fri. of month, Sun. noon–5.*

WORD OF MOUTH

"I believe the downtown/historic area of Oakland is undergoing/has undergone a bit of a renaissance—galleries, restaurants, etc . . . I'm not referring to Jack London Square, which does have the dubious honor of being home to the oldest bar in California. Anyone know if that's true? That tiny old place that slants?" —Leely

4 The 155-acre **Lake Merritt** (✉*Bordered by Lakeshore Ave. on the south, Lakeside Dr. on the west, Harrison St. on the north, and Bellevue Ave. on the east*), a natural saltwater lake, sits in the middle of downtown Oakland. Joggers and power-walkers charge along the 3-mi path that encircles the lake, crew teams often glide across the water, and boatmen guide snuggling couples in authentic Venetian gondolas. **California gondoliers** (✉*568 Bellevue Ave., Lake Merritt* ☎*866/737–8494* 🌐*www.gondolaservizio.com*) is by the sign that says "Sailboat House, Gondola Servizio." Fares start at $45 per couple for 30 minutes.

Lakeside Park, which surrounds the north side of Lake Merritt, has
5 several outdoor attractions, including a children's park. The **Rotary Nature Center and Waterfowl Refuge** is the nesting site of herons, egrets, geese, and ducks in spring and summer. Migrating birds pass through from September through February, and you can watch the birds being fed daily at 3:30 (year-round). ✉*600 Bellevue Ave.* ☎*510/238–7275* 🌐*www.oaklandnet.com/parks/facilities/points_lakeside_park.asp* 🎫*Free* 🕓*Daily 10–5.*

Given Oakland's reputation for Victorian and Craftsman homes, newcomers are generally surprised by the profusion of art-deco architecture in the downtown neighborhood around the 19th Street BART station.
3 Some of these buildings have fallen into disrepair, but the **Paramount**
★ **Theatre,** perhaps the most glorious example of art-deco architecture in the city, if not the entire Bay Area, still operates as a venue for concerts and performances of all kinds, from the Oakland Ballet to Tom Waits and Elvis Costello. You can take a two-hour tour of the building, which starts near the box office on 21st Street at 10 AM on the first and third Saturday of each month. Just behind the Paramount on Telegraph Avenue, the Fox Theater, another art-deco landmark, was saved from the wrecking ball and is being lovingly restored. ✉*2025 Broadway* ☎*510/465–6400* 🌐*www.paramounttheatre.com* 🎫*Tour $5.*

1 Shops, restaurants, small museums, and historic sites line **Jack London Square,** which is named after one of California's best-known authors; London wrote *The Call of the Wild* and *The Sea Wolf,* among many other books. When he lived in Oakland, he spent many a day boozing and brawling in the waterfront area. The tiny, wonderful **Heinold's First**

Heinold's First and Last Chance Saloon is a fun place to wet your whistle.

and Last Chance Saloon (✉ *48 Webster St. 94607* ☎ *510/839–6761*) was one of London's old haunts. It has been serving since 1883, although it's a little worse for the wear since the 1906 earthquake. The Klondike cabin in which London spent a summer in the late 1890s was moved from Alaska and reassembled here, next door to Heinold's saloon, in 1970. The square also contains a bronze bust of London. **■ TIP→ Since it's on the waterfront, the square is an obvious spot for tourists to visit and is worth a peek if you take a ferry that docks here; to really get a feel for Oakland, though, you're better off browsing downtown, or at least in Rockridge.** ✉ *Embarcadero at Broadway* ☎ *866/295–9853* 🌐 *www.jacklondonsquare.com*.

Bordered by 7th, 10th, Clay, and Washington streets in the shadow of the convention center and towering downtown hotels, **Old Oakland** was once a booming business district. Today the restored Victorian storefronts lining these four blocks house restaurants, cafés, shops, galleries, and a lively three-block farmers' market, which takes place Friday morning. Architectural consistency distinguishes the area from surrounding streets and lends it a distinct neighborhood feel. **Ratto's International Market** (✉ *827 Washington St.* ☎ *510/832–6503*), the Italian grocer that's been dishing up meat, cheese, imported sweets, and liquor to the neighborhood since 1897, has fresh deli sandwiches. **Pacific Coast Brewing Company** (✉ *906 Washington St.* ☎ *510/836–2739*) is a homey place for some pub grub and a microbrew. The block-long Swan's Marketplace houses shops and the **Housewives Market** (✉ *907 Washington St.*), an old-fashioned market with stalls for meat, seafood, and even a sausage maker.

Across Broadway from Old Oakland but worlds apart, **Chinatown** is a densely packed, bustling neighborhood. Unlike its San Francisco counterpart, Oakland's Chinatown makes no concessions to tourists; you won't find baskets of trinkets lining the sidewalk and souvenir displays in the shop windows. Supermarkets such as **Yuen Hop Noodle Company and Asian Food Products** (⊠*824 Webster St.*), open since 1931, overflow with goodies. The line for sweets, breads, and towering cakes snakes out the door of **Napoleon Super Bakery** (⊠*810 Franklin St.*).

The upscale neighborhood of **Rockridge** is one of Oakland's most desirable places to live. Explore the tree-lined streets that radiate out from College Avenue just north and south of the Rockridge BART station for a look at California bungalow architecture at its finest.

6 **College Avenue** is the main shopping drag in Rockridge. By day it's crowded with shoppers buying fresh flowers, used books, and clothing; by night the same folks are back for dinner and locally brewed ales in the numerous restaurants and pubs. The hub of College Avenue life in Rockridge is **Market Hall** (⊠*5655 College Ave.* ☎*510/250–6000* 🌐*www.rockridgemarkethall.com*), an airy European-style marketplace with pricey specialty-food shops. The avenue ends at the California College of the Arts campus.

WHERE TO EAT

¢–$$ MEDITERRANEAN ✕**À Côté.** This is *the* place for Mediterranean food in the East Bay. It's all about small plates, cozy tables, and family-style eating here—and truly excellent food. The butternut-squash ravioli, Alsatian goose sausage, and pear-and-walnut flatbread are all lovely choices. And you won't find a better plate of *pommes frites* anywhere. The restaurant offers more than 40 wines by the glass from an extensive, ever-changing wine list. Desserts here are tempting: try the warm crème-fraîche pound cake with apple confit, vanilla ice cream, and huckleberry sauce or a tangy pomegranate sorbet. The heavy wooden tables, cool tiles, and natural light make this a coveted destination for students, families, couples, and after-work crowds. ⊠*5478 College Ave., Rockridge* ☎*510/655–6469* ✍*Reservations not accepted* ▭*AE, MC, V* ⏲*No lunch.*

$$ AMERICAN ✕**Camino.** This first solo venture from chef-owner Russell Moore (a Chez Panisse alum of 21 years) and co-owner Allison Hopelain was quite the labor of love. Many of the menu's simple, seasonal, and straightforward dishes emerge from the enormous crackling *camino* (Italian for "fireplace"). Everything is made with top-notch ingredients, including local sardines; grilled lamb and sausage with shell beans; and grilled white sea bass with green beans and new potatoes. The menu of approximately eight dishes rotates nightly, with vegetarian options such as eggplant gratin available as well. The restaurant is decorated in a Craftsman-meets-refectory style, with brick walls and two long redwood communal tables filled with East Bay couples and friends. Seasonally inspired cocktails from the small bar are not to be missed; the gin-based drink with house-made cherry and hibiscus bitters is notably delicious. ⊠*3917 Grand Ave., Oakland* ☎*510/547–5035* ▭*AE, MC, V* ⏲*Closed Tues. No lunch.*

$$ MEXICAN ✕ **Doña Tomás.** A neighborhood favorite, this spot in Oakland's up-and-coming Temescal District serves seasonal Mexican fare to a hip but low-key crowd. Mexican textiles and art adorn walls in two long rooms; there's also a vine-covered patio. Banish all images of taquería grub and tuck into starters such as quesadillas filled with butternut squash and goat cheese and entrées such as *albondigas en sopa de zanahoria* (pork-and-beef meatballs in carrot puree). A fine selection of tequilas rounds out the offerings. ✉*5004 Telegraph Ave.* ☎*510/450–0522* ▭*AE, MC, V* ⏲*Closed Sun. and Mon. No lunch.*

WORD OF MOUTH

"Oakland has one of the most beautiful urban drives in the USA: Skyline Drive/Boulevard. It's a winding drive, bordering the Oakland/Berkeley Hills. From it, you have absolutely stunning views of the entire Bay. One advantage of a view from Oakland is that you are looking at San Francisco's famous landmarks." —CaliNurse

5

$–$$$ FRENCH ✕ **Luka's Taproom & Lounge.** Luka's is a real taste of downtown Oakland: hip and urban, with an unpretentious vibe. Diners nibble on *frites* any Belgian would be proud of and entrées like *choucroute garni* (sauerkraut with duck confit, ham hock, and pork shoulder). The brews draw 'em in, too—you'd be hard pressed to find a larger selection of Belgian beer this side of the pond—and the DJs in the adjacent lounge keep the scene going late. ✉*2221 Broadway, at West Grand Ave.* ☎*510/451–4677* ▭*AE, MC, V* ⏲*No lunch Sat.*

WHERE TO STAY

$–$$ **Washington Inn Hotel.** This stylish four-story brick hotel sits across the street from the convention center, in the heart of Old Oakland. In operation since 1905, the hotel has up-to-the-minute decor. Red couches brighten the spacious lobby, which has Wi-Fi access. Elegant touches include intricately molded ceiling tiles and a wrought-iron elevator, a relic of the building's early days. Guest rooms are chic but on the small side. Rooms overlooking the atrium lobby are the quietest (and smallest); corner rooms get the most sunlight. **Pros:** central location; good restaurant. **Cons:** rooms are small; parking is pricey. ✉*495 10th St., at Washington St.,* ☎*510/452–1776* 📠*510/452–4436* 🌐*www.thewashingtoninn.com* *47 rooms, 6 suites* *In-room: safe, DVDs, Wi-Fi. In-hotel: restaurant, bar, gym, laundry service, Wi-Fi, parking (paid)* ▭*AE, D, DC, MC, V* *CP.*

$$–$$$ **Waterfront Plaza Hotel.** One of Oakland's more appealing neighborhoods is home to this thoroughly modern waterfront hotel. Rooms in the hotel's five-story section overlook Jack London Square and have shared balconies; those in the three-story building each have a private balcony facing the water. Some rooms have fireplaces. **Pros:** great location; dog-friendly ($35 per day); newly remodeled rooms. **Cons:** pricey; service can be spotty. ✉*10 Washington St., Jack London Sq.* ☎*510/836–3800 or 800/729–3638* 📠*510/832–5695* 🌐*www.watervfrontplaza.com* *143 rooms* *In-room: safe, Wi-Fi. In-hotel: restaurant, room service, bar, pool, gym, laundry service, Wi-Fi, parking (paid)* ▭*AE, D, DC, MC, V.*

NIGHTLIFE AND THE ARTS

Oakland is where practicing artists have landed, drawn by cheaper rent and loft spaces. Oakland's underground arts scene—visual arts, indie music, spoken word, film—is definitely buzzing.

> **WORD OF MOUTH**
>
> "The weather is nicer [in Oakland] than San Francisco, because we have the same breeze without so much fog." —oaklander

Fodor'sChoice ★ **Café van Kleef.** When Dutch artist Peter van Kleef first opened his gallery in this downtown space, the booze flowed freely—and free, for lack of a liquor license. That gallery has morphed into this candle-strewn, funky café-bar that crackles with creative energy. Van Kleef has a lot to do with the convivial atmosphere; the garrulous owner loves sharing tales about his quirky, floor-to-ceiling collection of mementos, including what he claims are Cassius Clay's boxing gloves and Dorothy's ruby slippers. The café also has a consistently solid calendar of live music, heavy on the jazz side. And the drinks may not be free anymore, but they're quite possibly the stiffest in town. ✉*1621 Telegraph Ave., between 16th and 17th Sts.* ☎*510/763–7711* 🌐*www.cafevankleef.com.*

Mama Buzz Café. At this well-worn café-gallery, a kind of living room for the indie arts crowd, you can get the lowdown on one of the most diverse arts communities around. In addition to coffee and light fare, the calendar includes poetry readings, live-music events, art exhibits, and hard-to-categorize events such as Punk Rock Haircut Night (get a new 'do, cheap), the Knitty Gritty knitting circle, and the Left-Wing Letter Bee. The owners publish the 'zine *Kitchen Sink.* ✉*2318 Telegraph Ave.* ☎*510/465–4073* 🌐*www.mamabuzzcafe.com.*

The Parkway Speakeasy Theater. Billing itself as the "anti-multiplex," this movie theater feels like a college experience, when everyone crowded into a dorm lounge for communal watching. Pick up a beer or glass of wine, served alongside pizza and snacks, and then sprawl on a love seat or cozy recliner as you settle in for a first-run or indie film or any of the eclectic series that the Parkway dreams up. ✉*1834 Park Blvd.* ☎*510/848–1994* 🌐*www.parkway-speakeasy.com.*

Fodor'sChoice ★ **Yoshi's.** Oma Sosa and Charlie Hunter are among the musicians who play at Yoshi's, one of the area's best jazz venues. Monday through Saturday, shows start at 8 PM and 10 PM; Sunday shows usually start at 2 PM and 8 PM. The cover runs from $10 to $30. ✉*510 Embarcadero St., between Washington and Clay Sts.* ☎*510/238–9200* 🌐*www.yoshis.com.*

SPORTS AND THE OUTDOORS

BASEBALL The American League's **Oakland A's** (✉*McAfee Coliseum, 7000 Coliseum Way, off I–880, north of Hegenberger Rd.* ☎*510/638–4900* 🌐*oakland.athletics.mlb.com*), formally the Oakland Athletics, play at the **McAfee Coliseum.** Same-day tickets usually can be purchased at the stadium box office (Gate D), but advance purchase is recommended. On Wednesday entry is a bargain at $2 and you can buy a hot dog for a dollar. To get to the game, take a BART train to the Coliseum/Oakland Airport Station.

SHOPPING

College Avenue is great for upscale strolling, shopping, and people-watching. The streets around Lake Merritt and the Grand Lake have more casual fare and smaller boutiques.

Diesel. Wandering bibliophiles collect armfuls of the latest fiction and nonfiction here. The loftlike space, with its high ceilings and spare design, encourages airy contemplation, and on chilly days (a rarity) there's a fire going in the hearth. Keep an eye out for their excellent reading series. ✉ *5433 College Ave., Oakland* ☎ *510/653–9965.*

Maison d'Etre. Close to the Rockridge BART station, this store crystallizes the funky-chic shopping scene of Rockridge. Look for impulse buys like whimsical watches, imported fruit tea blends, and a basket of funky slippers near the back. ✉ *5640 College Ave., Oakland* ☎ *510/658–2801.*

BERKELEY

5

2 mi northeast of Bay Bridge.

The birthplace of the Free Speech Movement, the radical hub of the 1960s, the home of arguably the nation's top public university, and the city whose government condemned the bombing of Afghanistan—Berkeley is all of those things. The city of 100,000 facing San Francisco across the bay is also culturally diverse, a breeding ground for social trends, a bastion of the counterculture, and an important center for Bay Area writers, artists, and musicians. Berkeley residents, students, and faculty spend hours nursing various coffee concoctions while they read, discuss, and debate at any of the dozens of cafés that surround the campus. Oakland may have Berkeley beat when it comes to cutting-edge arts, and the city may have forfeited some of its renegade 1960s spirit, as some residents say, but unless a guy in a hot-pink satin body suit, skull cap, and cape rides a unicycle around *your* town, you'll likely find that Berkeley remains plenty offbeat.

It's the quintessential university town, and many who graduated years ago still bask in daily intellectual conversation, great weather, and good food. Residents will walk out of their way to go to the perfect bread shop or consult with their favorite wine merchant. And every September residents gently lampoon themselves during the annual "How Berkeley Can You Be?" parade and festival where they celebrate their tie-dyed past and consider its new incarnations.

ESSENTIALS

Visitor Information Berkeley Convention and Visitors Bureau (✉ *2015 Center St.* ☎ *510/549–7040* 🌐 *www.visitberkeley.com*).

The state legislature chartered the **University of California** (🌐 *www.berkeley.edu*) in 1868 as the founding campus of the state university system, and established it five years later on a rising plain of oak trees split by Strawberry Creek. Frederick Law Olmsted, who designed New York City's Central Park, proposed the first campus plan. University architects over the years have included Bernard Maybeck as well as Julia Morgan, who designed Hearst Castle at San Simeon. The central campus occupies 178

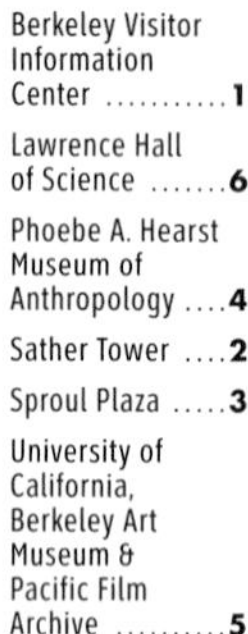

acres, bound by Bancroft Way to the south, Hearst Avenue to the north, Oxford Street to the west, and Gayley Road to the east. With more than 30,000 students and a full-time faculty of 1,400, the university, known simply as "Cal," is one of the leading intellectual centers in the United States and a major site for scientific research.

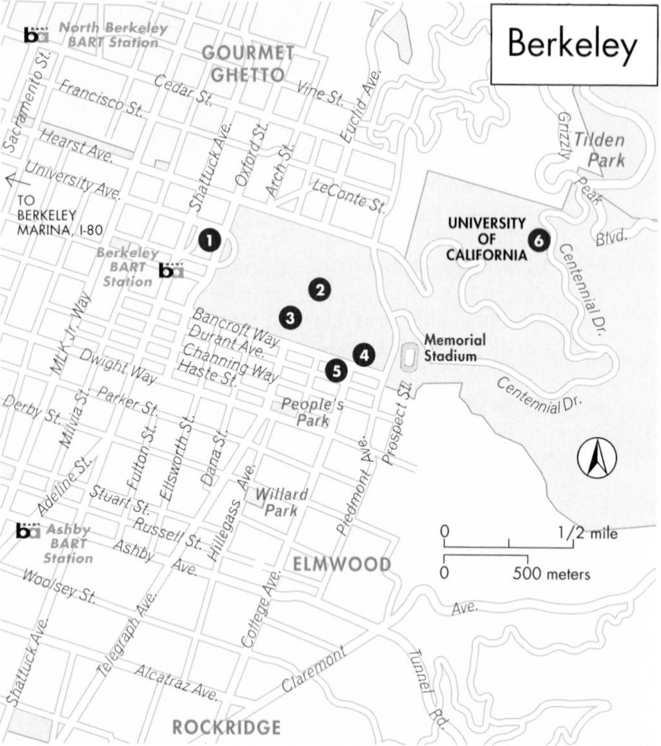

❶ The **Berkeley Visitor Information Center** (✉ *University Hall, Room 101, 2200 University Ave., at Oxford St.* ☎ *510/642–5215* ⏲ *Weekdays 8:30–4:30*) is the starting point for the free, student-guided tours of the campus, which last 1½ hours and start at 10 on weekdays. (*Weekend tours depart from Sather Tower, see below.*)

❷ Student-guided campus tours leave from **Sather Tower,** the campus landmark popularly known as the Campanile, at 10 on Saturday and 1 on Sunday. The 307-foot structure, modeled on St. Mark's Tower in Venice and completed in 1914, can be seen for miles. The carillon is played daily at 7:50 AM, noon, and 6 PM and for an extended 45-minute concert Sunday at 2. Take the elevator up 175 feet; then walk another 38 steps to the observation deck for a view of the campus and a close-up look at the iron bells, each of which weighs up to 10,500 pounds. ✉ *South of University Dr.* 🎫 *$2* ⏲ *Weekdays 10–4, Sat. 10–5, Sun. 10–1:30 and 3–5.*

3 **Sproul Plaza** (✉ *Telegraph Ave. and Bancroft Way*), just inside the U.C. Berkeley campus border on Bancroft Way, was the site of several free-speech and civil-rights protests in the 1960s. Today a lively panorama of political and social activists, musicians, and students shows off Berkeley's flair for the bizarre. Preachers orate atop milk crates, amateur entertainers bang on makeshift drum sets, and protesters distribute leaflets about everything from marijuana to the Middle East. No matter what the combination, on weekdays when school is in swing it always feels like a carnival. ■ **TIP→Walk through at noon for the liveliest show of student spirit.**

4 The collection of the **Phoebe A. Hearst Museum of Anthropology** counts almost 4 million artifacts, of which fewer than 1% are on display at any time. The Native Californian Cultures gallery showcases items related to the native peoples of California. Changing exhibits may cover the archaeology of ancient America or spotlight the museum's especially strong ancient Egyptian holdings. Mood music enhances the experience. ✉ *Kroeber Hall, Bancroft Way, at end of College Ave.* ☎ *510/642–3682* ⊕ *hearstmuseum.berkeley.edu* *Free; guided tour $5* ⊙ *Wed.–Sat. 10–4:30, Sun. noon–4.*

5 The **University of California, Berkeley Art Museum & Pacific Film Archive** has an interesting collection of works that spans five centuries, with an emphasis on contemporary art. Changing exhibits line the spiral ramps and balcony galleries. Look for the museum's enormous orange-red statue of a man hammering, which can be seen from the outside when strolling by its floor-to-ceiling windows. Don't miss the museum's series of vibrant paintings by abstract expressionist Hans Hofmann in the main gallery. On the ground floor the Pacific Film Archive has a library and hosts discussions and programs about historic and contemporary films, but the exhibition theater is across the street at 2575 Bancroft Way, near Bowditch Street. The downstairs galleries, which house rotating exhibits, are always free. The museum's raw foods café is famous, and you can also find some cooked options, too. ✉ *2626 Bancroft Way, entrance to theater at 2575 Bancroft Way between College and Telegraph* ☎ *510/642–0808, 510/642–1124 film-program information* ⊕ *www.bampfa.berkeley.edu* *$8* ⊙ *Wed. and Fri.–Sun. 11–5, Thurs. 11–7.*

6 At the fortresslike **Lawrence Hall of Science**, a dazzling hands-on science center, kids can look at insects under microscopes, solve crimes using chemical forensics, and explore the physics of baseball. On weekends there are special lectures, demonstrations, and planetarium shows. The museum runs a popular (and free) stargazing program, which is held on the first and third Saturday of each month, weather permitting. (Call for times.) ✉ *Centennial Dr. near Grizzly Peak Blvd.* ☎ *510/642–5132* ⊕ *www.lawrencehallofscience.org* *$11* ⊙ *Daily 10–5.*

South of campus, along College Avenue between Ashby Avenue and Claremont, shops and cafés pack the area known as **Elmwood**, a local favorite for browsing. Generations of Berkeleyites have enjoyed BLTs and sundaes at the counter of **Ozzie's Soda Fountain** (✉ *2900 College Ave.* ☎ *510/841–0989*), the last pharmacy soda fountain in the Bay Area, open since 1921 inside the Elmwood Pharmacy. The menu tops out at $6. **Nabolom Bakery** (✉ *2708 Russell St.* ☎ *510/845–2253*), which has been around since 1976, is a workers' collective where politics and delicious pastries collide. Shingled houses line tree-shaded streets nearby.

Telegraph Avenue is Berkeley's student-oriented thoroughfare and the best place to get a dose of the city's famed counterculture. On any given day you might encounter a troop of chanting Hare Krishnas or a drumming band of Rastafarians. First and foremost, however, Telegraph is a place for socializing and shopping, the only uniquely Berkeley shopping experience in town and a definite don't-miss. **■ TIP→ Take care when wandering the street at night, things can feel a bit edgy. Nearby People's Park, mostly harmless by day, is best avoided at night.** Cafés, bookstores, poster shops, and street vendors line the avenue. T-shirt vendors and tarot-card readers come and go on a whim, but a few establishments—**Rasputin Music** (No. 2401), **Amoeba Music** (No. 2455), and **Moe's Books** (No. 2476)—are neighborhood landmarks. Allen Ginsberg wrote his acclaimed poem "Howl" at **Caffe Mediterraneum** (No. 2475), a relic of 1960s-era café culture.

An industrial area on **4th Street** north of University Avenue has been converted into a pleasant shopping stretch with popular eateries and shops selling handcrafted and eco-conscious goods. About six blocks long, this compact area is busiest on bright weekend afternoons. Popular destinations are the Stained Glass Garden, Hear Music, and the Crate and Barrel Outlet along with a mini-slew of upscale boutiques and wonderful paper stores.

Northwest of the U.C. Berkeley campus, **Walnut Square,** at Walnut and Vine streets, has coffee shops and an eclectic assortment of boutiques proffering such goodies as holistic products for your pet, African masks, and French children's clothing. Around the corner on Shattuck Avenue is Chez Panisse Café & Restaurant, at the heart of what is locally known as the **Gourmet Ghetto,** a three-block stretch of specialty shops and eateries. Your senses will immediately perk up as you enter the upscale market **Epicurious Garden** (✉ *1509–1513 Shattuck Ave.*), which has everything from impeccable sushi to gelato. Outside, you can find a terraced garden—the only place to sit—that winds up four levels and ends at the Imperial Tea Court. The restaurant Taste anchors this zone; it offers a rechargeable wine-tasting card that guests use to help themselves to 1-ounce automated pours from new wine selections.

NEED A BREAK?

With a jazz combo playing in the storefront and a long line snaking down the block, Cheeseboard Pizza (✉ *151 Shattuck Ave.* ☎ *510/549–3055* ⏲ *Tues.–Fri. 11:30–2 [until 3 on Sat.], and 4:30–7*) counts out the pulse of the Gourmet Ghetto. This cooperatively owned take-out spot (if you're lucky, you can grab one of the few inside tables) is an institution, drawing devoted customers with the smell of just-baked garlic, fresh vegetables,

The trailblazing restaurant Chez Panisse focuses on seasonal local ingredients.

and perfect sauces. The jovial worker-owners serve up just one freshly baked pizza daily—always vegetarian—and you can find surprises such as fresh corn, zucchini, or a small lime wedge to squeeze over your slice. Next door at the bakery-cheese shop, customers take a playing card instead of a number and are served in suites. It can get crowded, and jokers are wild.

Vine Street is another culinary destination. In a historic building **Vintage Berkeley** (✉*2113 Vine St.* ☎*510/665–8600*) gathers locals in its large front garden for nightly wine-tastings of California wines from smaller vineyards. Take the stairs up to the top floor of Walnut Square to find **Love at First Bite** (✉*1510 Walnut St., Suite G* ☎*510/848–5727*) a cupcakery showcasing scrumptious confections. **Twig & Fig** (✉*210 Vine St., Suite B,* ☎*510/848–5599*) invites you in for a peek at its three rhythmically clacking letterpresses. Stop in for one-of-a-kind papery gifts and publications such as *Inside the Brambles*, a local's guide to Tilden Park. Of all the coffeehouses in caffeine-crazed Berkeley, the one that deserves a pilgrimage is **Peet's** (✉*2124 Vine St.* ☎*510/841–0564*). When this, the original, opened at Vine and Walnut streets in 1966, the unparalleled coffee was roasted in the store and brewed by the cup. Named after the Dutch last name of the founder, Peet's has since expanded, but this isn't a café where you can sit on sofas or order quiche. It's strictly coffee, tea, and sweets to go.

WHERE TO E[illegible]

Dining in Berkeley is a low-key affair; even in the finest restaurants—and some are quite fine—most folks dress casually. Late diners be forewarned: Berkeley is an "early to bed" kind of town. For inexpensive lodging, investigate University Avenue, west of campus. The area is noisy, congested, and somewhat dilapidated, but does include a few decent motels and chain properties. All Berkeley lodgings, except for the swanky Claremont, are strictly mid-range.

$$$–$$$$ AMERICAN Fodor'sChoice ★

Chez Panisse Café & Restaurant. At Chez Panisse, even humble pizza is reincarnated in new ways, with innovative toppings of the freshest local ingredients. The downstairs portion of Alice Waters's legendary eatery is noted for its formality and personal service. Here, the daily-changing multicourse dinners are prix-fixe ($$$$), with the cost slightly lower on weekdays. Upstairs, in the informal café, the crowd is livelier, the prices are lower ($$–$$$$), and the ever-changing menu is à la carte. The food is simpler, too: penne with new potatoes, arugula, and sheep's-milk cheese; fresh figs with Parmigiano-Reggiano cheese and arugula; and grilled tuna with Savoy cabbage, for example. Legions of loyal fans insist Chez Panisse lives up to its reputation and delivers a dining experience well worth the price. Visiting foodies won't want to miss a meal here, upstairs or down; be sure to make reservations a few weeks ahead of time to avoid disappointment. And, yes, it's that good. *1517 Shattuck Ave., north of University Ave., 510/548–5525 restaurant, 510/548–5049 café Reservations essential AE, D, DC, MC, V Closed Sun. No lunch in restaurant.*

$$–$$$ MEDITERRANEAN ★

Lalime's. The food served in this charming, flower-covered house reflects the entire Mediterranean region. The menu, constantly changing and unfailingly great, depends on the availability of fresh seasonal ingredients. Choices might include grilled ahi tuna or creamy Italian risotto. The light colors of the dining room, which has two levels, help to create a cheerful mood. A star in its own right, Lalime's is a good second choice if Chez Panisse is booked. *1329 Gilman St. 510/527–9838 Reservations essential AE, DC, MC, V No lunch.*

¢–$ MEXICAN

Picante Cocina Mexicana. A barnlike space full of cheerful Mexican tiles and folk-art masks, Picante is a find for anyone seeking good Mexican food for a song. The *masa* (flour) is freshly ground for the tortillas and tamales, the salsas are complex, and the combinations are inventive. Try tamales filled with butternut squash and chilies or a simple taco of roasted poblanos and sautéed onions; we challenge you to finish a plate of super nachos. Order at the counter and grab a table inside or on the back patio. *1328 6th St. 510/525–3121 Reservations not accepted MC, V.*

WHERE TO STAY

$$$$ Fodor'sChoice ★

Claremont Resort and Spa. Straddling the Oakland–Berkeley border, the hotel beckons like a gleaming white castle in the hills. Traveling executives come for the business amenities, including T-1 Internet connections, guest e-mail addresses, and oversize desks. The Claremont also draws

WORD OF MOUTH

"There are great art movie houses in Berkeley. There is also very good theater. You might check out either Berkeley Rep Theatre or Aurora Theatre to see what they are playing." —PamSF

honeymooners and leisure travelers with its luxurious suites, therapeutic massages, and personalized yoga workouts at the on-site spa. The rooms on the spa side of the hotel glow with new fixtures and furniture. Some offer spa tubs and, if you're high enough up, spectacular bay views. ■TIP→**Another advantage: the scents wafting upward from the spa treatment rooms.** **Pros:** amazing spa; supervised child care; some rooms have great views of the bay. **Cons:** parking is pricey; the hotel can be busy with weddings; so-so lobby. ✉*41 Tunnel Rd., at Ashby and Domingo Aves.,* ☎*510/843–3000 or 800/551–7266* 🖷*510/843–6629* 🌐*www.claremontresort.com* *249 rooms, 30 suites* *In-room: safe, refrigerator (some), Wi-Fi. In-hotel: 2 restaurants, bars, tennis courts, pools, gym, spa, children's programs (ages 6 wks–10 yrs), laundry service, Wi-Fi, parking (paid)* *AE, D, DC, MC, V.*

$$ **Hotel Durant.** This newly renovated boutique hotel has long been the mainstay of parents visiting their children at U.C. Berkeley; it's also a good option for those who want to be a short walk from campus and the restaurants and shops of Telegraph Avenue. The rooms, updated in 2006 with new bathrooms and dark wood set against deep jewel tones, are small without feeling cramped. The historic photos of Berkeley highlight the hotel's storied past, and the central location is perfect for the car-less. This hotel is also eco-conscious, using nonchemical, all-natural cleaning products. The flat-screen TVs, iPod docks, ceiling fans, and pillow selection in the rooms are impressive. ■TIP→**Guests receive free passes to the extensive Cal Recreational Sports Facility, known as RSF.** **Pros:** blackout shades; organic bathrobes; fantastic attention to detail. **Cons:** downstairs bar can get a little noisy during Cal games; pricey parking. ✉*2600 Durant Ave.* ☎*510/845–8981* 🖷*510/486–8336* 🌐*www.hoteldurant.com* *139 rooms, 5 suites* *In-room: no a/c, safe, refrigerator. In-hotel: restaurant, room service, bar, laundry service, Wi-Fi, parking (paid)* *AE, D, DC, MC, V.*

NIGHTLIFE AND THE ARTS

Berkeley Repertory Theatre. One of the region's highly respected resident professional companies and a Tony Award winner for Outstanding Regional Theatre (in 1997), the theater performs classic and contemporary plays from autumn to spring. Well-known pieces such as *Mother Courage* and *Oliver Twist* mix with edgier fare. The theater's complex is near BART's Downtown Berkeley Station. ✉*2025 Addison St.* ☎*510/845–4700* 🌐*www.berkeleyrep.org.*

Berkeley Symphony Orchestra. The ensemble has risen to considerable prominence under artistic director Kent Nagano. The works of 20th-century composers, from Messiaen to Zappa, are a focus, but more traditional pieces are also performed. The orchestra plays a handful of concerts each year in Zellerbach Hall and other locations around Berkeley. ✉*1942 University Avenue, Suite 207* ☎*510/841–2800* 🌐*www.berkeleysymphony.org.*

★ **Cal Performances.** The series, running from September through May at various U.C. Berkeley venues, offers the Bay Area's most varied bill of internationally acclaimed artists in all disciplines, from classical soloists to the latest jazz, world-music, theater, and dance ensembles. Look for frequent campus colloquia or preshow talks featuring Berkeley's professors. ✉ *University of California, Zellerbach Hall, Telegraph Ave. and Bancroft Way* ☎ *510/642–9988* 🌐 *www.calperfs.berkeley.edu.*

Fodor's Choice ★ **Freight & Salvage Coffee House.** Some of the most talented practitioners of folk, blues, Cajun, and bluegrass perform in this alcohol-free space, one of the finest folk houses in the country. Most tickets are less than $20. ✉ *1111 Addison St.* ☎ *510/548–1761* 🌐 *www.thefreight.org.*

SHOPPING

Fodor's Choice ★ **Amoeba Music.** Heaven for audiophiles, this legendary Berkeley favorite is *the* place to go for new and used CDs, records, cassettes, and DVDs. The dazzling stock includes thousands of titles for all music tastes—no matter what you're looking for, you can probably find it here. The store even has its own record label. There are now branches in San Francisco and Hollywood, but this is the original. ✉ *2455 Telegraph Ave., at Haste St.,* ☎ *510/549–1125.*

Black Oak Books. This has long been one of Berkeley's beloved new- and used-book stores. The shop hosts frequent author events, which often function like a public intellectual salon, with old Berkeleyites sparking debate. The renowned Poetry Flash series relocated here for their Sunday night readings after Cody's on Telegraph closed. ✉ *1491 Shattuck Ave., at Vine St.,* ☎ *510/486–0698.*

Body Time. The local chain, founded in Berkeley in 1970, emphasizes the premium-quality ingredients it uses in its natural perfumes and skin-care and aromatherapy products. Sustainably harvested essential oils that you can combine and dilute to create your own personal fragrances are the specialty. Its distinct Citrus, Lavender-Mint, and China Rain scents are all popular Berkeley favorites. ✉ *1942 Shattuck Ave.* ☎ *510/841–5818.*

Kermit Lynch Wine Merchant. A Berkeley institution, Kermit Lynch has friendly salespeople who can direct you to the latest bargains from France. Lynch's newsletters describing his finds are legendary, as is his friendship with Alice Waters of Chez Panisse. Responsible for taking American appreciation of French wine to another level, the shop is a great place to explore as you educate your palate. ✉ *1605 San Pablo Ave., at Dwight Way* ☎ *510/524–1524.*

Moe's Books. The spirit of Moe—the cantankerous, cigar-smoking late proprietor—lives on in this four-story house of books. Students and professors come here for used books, including large sections of literary and cultural criticism, art books, and literature in foreign languages. ■ **TIP→** Wear good shoes and eat lunch first; you won't want to come out for hours. ✉ *2476 Telegraph Ave., near Haste St.,* ☎ *510/849–2087.*

THE COASTAL PENINSULA

Bookended by San Francisco and Silicon Valley are some surprisingly low-key and unspoiled natural treasures. The vistas here are the Pacific and rolling hills, making it easy to forget the hustle and bustle that's just out of sight.

PLANNING

GETTING HERE AND AROUND

AIR TRAVEL

All the major airlines serve San Francisco International Airport, and most of them fly to San Jose International Airport. *See Air Travel in Travel Smart Northern California for airline and airport phone numbers.*

BUS TRAVEL

SamTrans buses travel to Moss Beach and Half Moon Bay from the Daly City BART (Bay Area Rapid Transit) station. Another bus connects Half Moon Bay with Pescadero. Each trip takes approximately one hour. Call for schedules, because departures are infrequent.

Contacts SamTrans (☎ *800/660–4287* ⊕ *www.samtrans.org*).

CAR TRAVEL

Public transportation to coastal areas is limited (and you'll likely want a car to get around once you arrive), so it's probably best to drive. To get to Moss Beach or Half Moon Bay, take Highway 1, also known as the Coast Highway, south along the length of the San Mateo coast. When coastal traffic is heavy, you can also reach Half Moon Bay via I–280, the Junipero Serra Freeway; follow it south as far as Route 92, where you can turn west toward the coast. To get to Pescadero, drive south 16 mi on Highway 1 from Half Moon Bay. For Año Nuevo continue south on Highway 1 another 12 mi.

HEALTH AND SAFETY

In an emergency dial 911.

Hospitals Seton Coastside Medical Center (✉ *600 Marine Blvd., Moss Beach* ☎ *650/563–7100*).

VISITOR INFORMATION

Contact California State Parks (☎ *800/777–0369* ⊕ *www.parks.ca.gov*).
Half Moon Bay Chamber of Commerce (✉ *235 Main St., Half Moon Bay* ☎ *650/726–8380* ⊕ *www.halfmoonbaychamber.org*).

BIG BASIN REDWOODS STATE PARK

17 mi north of Santa Cruz on Hwy. 1.

California's oldest state park is the best place to see old-growth redwoods without going north of San Francisco (and it's far less crowded than Muir Woods and other famous spots). The parkland ranges from sea level up to 2,000 feet in elevation, which means the landscape changes often, from dark redwood groves to oak pastures that are deep green in winter and bleached nearly white in summer. The mountain setting also makes for countless waterfalls, most visible during the winter rains. The visitor center is inland, at park headquarters in Boulder Creek. Staffing is spotty, but park information and camping check-in are always available at a self-service kiosk.

Coming from the coast, you'll access the park at Waddell Creek (Highway 1, 17 mi north of Santa Cruz), where a confluence of waterways pours out of the redwoods and into the ocean. A short walk on the Marsh Trail leads to the **Rancho Del Oso Nature Center** (☎*831/427–2288* ⏲*Weekends noon–4*), which has natural-history exhibits and is the starting point for several self-guided nature walks. Mountain bikers, horseback riders, and hikers can take the nearly level Canyon Road (a dirt fire road) back up the creek and into the woods. Hikers looking for solitude might consider a more strenuous, uphill climb on Clark Connection to Westridge Trail, which rewards hard work with spectacular views of the ocean. Those who don't want to go anywhere can just stay on the windswept beach, where the main attraction is watching kite surfers get huge air on the windy shoreline waves. ✉*21600 Big Basin Way, Boulder Creek* ☎*831/338–8860* 🎫*$6 parking fee.*

AÑO NUEVO STATE RESERVE

21 mi north of Santa Cruz on Hwy. 1.

★ At the height of mating season, upward of 4,000 elephant seals congregate at Año Nuevo, the world's only approachable mainland rookery. The seals are both vocal and spectacularly big (especially the males, which can weigh up to 2½ tons), and some are in residence year-round. An easy, 1½-hour round-trip walk takes you to the dunes, from which you can look down onto the animals lounging on the shoreline. Note that during mating season (mid-December through March) visitors may do the hike only as part of a 2½-hour guided tour, for which reservations must be made well in advance. The area's visitor center has a fascinating film about the seals and some natural-history exhibits (including a sea otter's pelt that you can touch). Dogs are not allowed, even in cars in the parking lot. ✉*Hwy. 1, 13 mi south of Pescadero* ☎*650/879–2025, 800/444–4445 for tour reservations* 🎫*Tour $7, parking $7* ⏲*Guided tours leave every 15 min, mid-Dec.–Mar., daily 8:45–3.*

PESCADERO

12 mi north of Año Nuevo State Reserve on Hwy. 1.

As you walk down Stage Road, Pescadero's main street, it's hard to believe you're only 30 minutes from Silicon Valley. If you could block out the throngs of weekend cyclists, the downtown area could almost serve as the backdrop for a Western movie. (In fact, with few changes, Duarte's Tavern could fill in as the requisite saloon.) This is a good place to stop for a bite or to browse for antiques. The real attractions, though, are the spectacular beaches and hiking in the area.

If a quarantine is not in effect (watch for signs), from November through April you can look for mussels amid tidal pools and rocky outcroppings at **Pescadero State Beach,** then roast them at the barbecue pits. Any time of year is good for exploring the beach, the north side of which has several secluded spots along sandstone cliffs. Across U.S. 101, the **Pescadero Marsh Natural Preserve** has hiking trails that cover 600 acres of marshland. Early spring and fall are the best times to come, when there are lots of migrating birds and other wildlife to see. ⊠*14½ mi south of Half Moon Bay on Hwy. 1* ☎*650/879–2170* *Free, parking $6* ⏲*Daily 8 AM–sunset.*

WHERE TO EAT

$–$$$ AMERICAN ✕**Duarte's Tavern.** Though it has been noted by the national press, this 19th-century roadhouse continues to serve simple American fare with a modest, hometown attitude. The restaurant's bar, for instance, is a great place to sip a whisky; but it's also the town's liquor store, which means that some locals take their orders to go. The no-frills dining room offers a solid menu based on locally grown vegetables and fresh fish. House specialties include abalone ($40), artichoke soup, and old-fashioned olallieberry pie à la mode (which *Life* magazine once named best in the United States). ⊠*202 Stage Rd.* ☎*650/879–0464* 🌐*www.duartestavern.com* 💳*AE, MC, V.*

5

HALF MOON BAY

16 mi north of Pescadero on Hwy. 1.

It may be the largest and most visited of the coastal communities, but Half Moon Bay is still by all measures a small town. Looking from the highway, you'd hardly even know it was there. Turn onto Main Street, though, and you'll find five blocks of galleries, shops, and cafés, many of which occupy renovated 19th-century buildings. While traditionally this was an agricultural center for local growers of artichokes and other coastal crops, in recent years it has also come to be a haven for Bay Area retirees.

ESSENTIALS

Visitor Information **Half Moon Bay Chamber of Commerce** (⊠*235 Main St., Half Moon Bay* ☎*650/726–8380* 🌐*www.halfmoonbaychamber.org*).

The town comes to life on the third weekend in October, when 250,000 people gather for the **Half Moon Bay Art and Pumpkin Festival** (☎*650/726–9652*). Highlights include a parade, pie-eating contests, street performers and a "weigh-off" of giant pumpkins, some as big as 1,200 pounds.

The 4-mi stretch of **Half Moon Bay State Beach** (⊠*Hwy. 1, west of Main St.* ☎*650/726–8819*) is perfect for long walks, kite flying, and picnic lunches, though the 50°F water and dangerous currents make swimming inadvisable. There are three access points, one in Half Moon Bay and two south of town off the highway. To find them, look for road signs that have a picture of footsteps.

WHERE TO EAT

$$–$$$$ MEDITERRANEAN ★ ✕**Cetrella.** This is the coast at its most dressed up. The restaurant is all polished wood and pressed tablecloths, and hits every gourmet mark—adventurous wine list, sumptuous cheese course, and live jazz on Friday

CLOSE UP

The Inland Peninsula

Driving south of San Francisco along the San Mateo coast, it's hard to believe that inland, behind the rolling hills, is Silicon Valley. And while the high-tech hub is known more for its semiconductors and Fortune 500 companies than its sightseeing, it does have a few highlights worth stopping for—especially if you're already driving through on I–280.

Adorable Palo Alto and it's intellectual neighbor, **Stanford University** (*450 Serra Mall, Stanford 650/723–2300 www.stanford.edu*), are about 35 mi south of San Francisco. Stanford's gorgeous grounds are home to a primordial-looking cactus garden, a stone sculpture by Scottish artist Andy Goldsworthy, aboriginal artworks from Papua New Guinea, and an excellent art museum—The Iris and B. Gerald Cantor Center for Visual Arts—whose lawn is planted with bronzes by Rodin. Free one-hour walking tours of the campus leave daily at 11 and 3:15 from the visitor center in the front hall of Memorial Auditorium.

In the center of Santa Clara University's campus is the **Mission Santa Clara de Asis.** Roof tiles of the current building, a reproduction of the original, were salvaged from earlier structures, which dated from the 1790s and 1820s. Early adobe walls and a spectacular garden with 4,500 roses remain intact as well. *500 El Camino Real 408/554–4023 www.scu.edu/visitors/mission Free Self-guided tours daily 1–sundown.*

At the southern end of Silicon Valley, San Jose is home to several good museums. The permanent collection at the **San Jose Museum of Art** (*110 S. Market St., San Jose 408/294–2787 www.sjmusart.org $8 Tues.–Sun. 11–5*) focuses on cutting-edge California and Latino artists. The**Tech Museum of Innovation** (*201 S. Market St., San Jose 408/294–8324 www.thetech.org $8 Daily 10–5*) is a hands-on, high-tech children's museum. The **Rosicrucian Egyptian Museum** (*1342 Naglee Ave., San Jose 408/947–3635 www.egyptianmuseum.org $9 Mon., Wed., and Fri. 10–5, Thurs. 10–8, weekends 11–6*) showcases an exquisite collection of Egyptian and Babylonian antiquities.

Southwest of San Jose are the pretty village of Saratoga and the ritzy town of Los Gatos, nestled in the foothills of the Coastal Range. Los Gatos is also home to one of the finest restaurants in the country, **Manresa** (*320 Village La., Los Gatos 408/354–4330 www.manresarestaurant.com AE, MC, V Closed Mon. and Tues. No lunch*), which runs its own farm to produce ingredients for its French-Catalan cuisine.

and Saturday nights. The creative menu (which changes daily) pairs regional produce and fish with choice imported ingredients, like tangy Italian *Burrata di Bufala* cheese. What results is sophisticated but not stuffy, for instance the Catalonian shellfish stew, which has a tomato, almond, and saffron broth and comes with a lobster cracker and extra napkins. The café has a smaller and cheaper but no less delectable menu. *845 Main St. 650/726–4090 www.cetrella.com AE, D, DC, MC, V No lunch.*

$$–$$$$ ITALIAN ★ **Pasta Moon.** As one of the best restaurants on the coast between San Francisco and Monterey, Pasta Moon boasts a friendly, laid-back staff and fun, jovial crowd. Local produce flavors the seasonal menu, which includes such highlights as wood-fired pizzas and grilled quail. Beware that the dining room can get slightly noisy on weekend nights. *315 Main St. 650/726–5125 www.pastamoon.com AE, D, DC, MC, V.*

WHERE TO STAY

$$–$$$$ ★ **Old Thyme Inn.** The owners of this 1898 Princess Anne Victorian love herbs and flowers. If you have a green thumb of your own, this is the place for you. The gardens alongside the house burst with blossoms year-round, guest rooms are filled with fragrant bouquets, and each room is named after an herb and decorated in its colors. Down comforters and luxury linens make the beds here especially wonderful. **Pros:** pretty; laid-back; comfortable. **Cons:** close quarters when the inn is full. *779 Main St. 650/726–1616 or 800/720–4277 www.oldthymeinn.com 7 rooms In-room: no a/c, Internet, Wi-Fi. In-hotel: Wi-Fi, no-smoking rooms AE, D, MC, V BP.*

$$$$ ★ **The Ritz-Carlton.** With its enormous and elegantly decorated rooms, secluded oceanfront property, and a staff that waits on guests hand and foot, this golf and spa resort defines opulence. Attention to detail is remarkable, right down to the silver service, china, and 300-thread-count Egyptian cotton sheets. During cocktail hour, view the ocean from the plush Conservatory bar, or from under a heavy blanket on an Adirondack chair on the lawn. The main restaurant, Navio ($$$–$$$$), is suitably decadent, with a kitchen that turns local fish and produce into dishes like squid tagliatelle with arugula and Meyer lemon, and carrot cake with carrot sorbet and cream-cheese ice cream. **Pros:** four-star service; total luxury; ocean views. **Cons:** formal; not within walking distance of anything. *1 Miramontes Point Rd. 650/712–7000 or 800/241–3333 www.ritzcarlton.com 239 rooms, 22 suites In-room: safe, DVD, Internet, Wi-Fi. In-hotel: 2 restaurants, room service, bars, golf courses, tennis courts, gym, spa, bicycles, children's programs, laundry service, Internet terminal, Wi-Fi, some pets allowed, no-smoking rooms AE, D, DC, MC, V.*

SPORTS

The Bike Works (*520 Kelly St. 650/726–6708*) rents bikes and can provide information on organized rides up and down the coast. If you prefer to go it alone, try the 3-mi bike trail that leads from Kelly Avenue in Half Moon Bay to Mirada Road in Miramar.

MOSS BEACH

7 mi north of Half Moon Bay on Hwy. 1; 20 mi south of San Francisco on Hwy. 1.

Moss Beach was a busy outpost during Prohibition, when regular shipments of liquid contraband from Canada were unloaded at the secluded beach and hauled off to San Francisco. The town stayed under the radar out of necessity, with only one local hotel and bar (now the Distillery) where Bay Area politicians and gangsters could go for a drink while waiting for their shipments. Today, although it has grown into a cheerful surfing town with charming inns and restaurants, it is still all but invisible from the highway—a good hideaway for those allergic to crowds.

The biggest Moss Beach attraction is the **Fitzgerald Marine Reserve** (✉ *California and North Lake Sts.* ☎ *650/728–3584*), a 3-mi stretch of bluffs and tide pools. Since the reserve was protected in 1969, scientists have discovered 25 new aquatic species here; depending on the tide, you'll most likely find shells, anemones, or starfish.

Just off the coast at Moss Beach is **Mavericks.** When there's a big swell, it's one of the biggest surfing breaks in the world. Waves here have reportedly reached 60 feet in height, and surfers get towed out to them by Jet Skis. The break is a mile offshore, so seeing it from the coast can be tough and requires a challenging hike.

The intrepid can get photocopied directions at the Distillery restaurant, then drive 3 mi south for the trail out of **Pillar Point Harbor.** Even if you're not hunting for waves, the harbor is a nice place to wander, with its laid-back restaurants and waters full of fishing boats and sea lions.

Built in 1928 after two horrible shipwrecks on the point, the **Point Montara Lighthouse** still has its original light keeper's quarters from the late 1800s. Gray whales pass this point during their migration from November through April, so bring your binoculars. Visiting hours coincide with morning and afternoon check-in and check-out times at the adjoining youth hostel ($22 to $25 dorm beds, $62 to $90 private room). ✉ *16th St., at Hwy. 1, Montara* ☎ *650/728–7177* ⏲ *Daily 8 AM–sunset.*

WHERE TO EAT

$$–$$$ MEDITERRANEAN ★ ✕ **Cafe Gibraltar.** While the cuisine here is broadly called Mediterranean, in the kitchen of chef-owner Jose Luiz Ugalde that term can mean sweet crab dumplings with sumac butter and Turkish spices, or Sardinian shellfish cassoula with garlic aioli. The imaginative food here is served in a warm, pretty dining room; peach walls are lighted by flickering candles, and the booths are adorned with curtains and pillows. Two miles south of Moss Beach on the east side of the highway, the restaurant is a bit hard to find—but definitely worth the hunt. At signs for Pillar Point Harbor, turn inland onto Capistrano, then right onto Alhambra. ✉ *425 Ave. Alhambra, at Palma Ave., El Granada* ☎ *650/560–9039* 🌐 *www.cafegibraltar.com* ▭ *AE, D, DC, MC, V* ⏲ *Closed Mon. No lunch.*

$$ SEAFOOD ✕ **Sam's Chowder House.** An East Coast–style seafood joint in the Bay Area? This waterfront restaurant isn't textbook Cape Cod, but that's OK—dine here, and you'll get the best of both coasts: true New England–style clam chowder and lump crab cakes and ahi tuna poke with sesame oil and scallions or local halibut with mango salsa. Indoor seats are in one of several long dining rooms; outdoor seats are warmed by gas fire pits and heaters on chilly days; and every seat in the house looks out to the water. The attached market sells fresh fish and picnic food. ✉ *4210 N. Hwy. 1* ☎ *650/712–0245* ▭ *AE, D, DC, MC, V.*

6

The Wine Country

WORD OF MOUTH

"We went to Cline Cellars on Route 121, which makes some French style wines with Rhone varietals. The tasting was free, and we really enjoyed the wines—the best part, though, was that they had "wooly weeders" at work in the vineyards, which means sheep grazing between the vines. My wife thought this was endlessly cute."

—smetz

WELCOME TO THE WINE COUNTRY

TOP REASONS TO GO

★ **Biking:** Cycling is one of the best ways to see the Wine Country—the Russian River and Dry Creek valleys are particularly beautiful.

★ **Browsing the farmers' markets:** Almost every town in Napa and Sonoma has a seasonal farmers' market, each rounding up an amazing variety of local produce.

★ **Touring the di Rosa Preserve:** Though this art and nature preserve is just off the busy Carneros Highway, it's a relatively unknown treasure.

★ **Canoeing on the Russian River:** Trade in your car keys for a paddle and glide down the Russian River. May through October is the best time to be on the water.

★ **Cocktails at Cyrus:** Think it's virtually sacrilege to drink anything other than wine in this neck of the woods? At the bar of Healdsburg's hottest restaurant, the bartenders mix superb, inventive drinks.

1 Napa Valley. Big names abound here, from high-profile wineries to world-renowned chefs. Napa, the valley's oldest town, sweet-life St. Helena, and down-to-earth Calistoga all make good home bases here. (Calistoga has the extra draw of local thermal springs.) Yountville has become a culinary boomtown, while the tiny communities of Oakville and Rutherford are surrounded by major vintners like Robert Mondavi and Francis Ford Coppola.

2 Sonoma Valley. Historic attractions and an unpretentious attitude. The town of Sonoma, with its atmospheric central plaza, is rich with 19th-century buildings. Glen Ellen, meanwhile, has a special connection with author Jack London.

GETTING ORIENTED

The Napa and Sonoma valleys run roughly parallel, northwest to southeast, and are separated by the Mayacamas Mountains. Northwest of the Sonoma Valley are several more important viticultural areas in Sonoma County, including Dry Creek, Alexander Valley, and the Russian River Valley. The Carneros region, which spans southern Sonoma and Napa counties, is just north of San Pablo Bay, and the closest of all these wine regions to San Francisco.

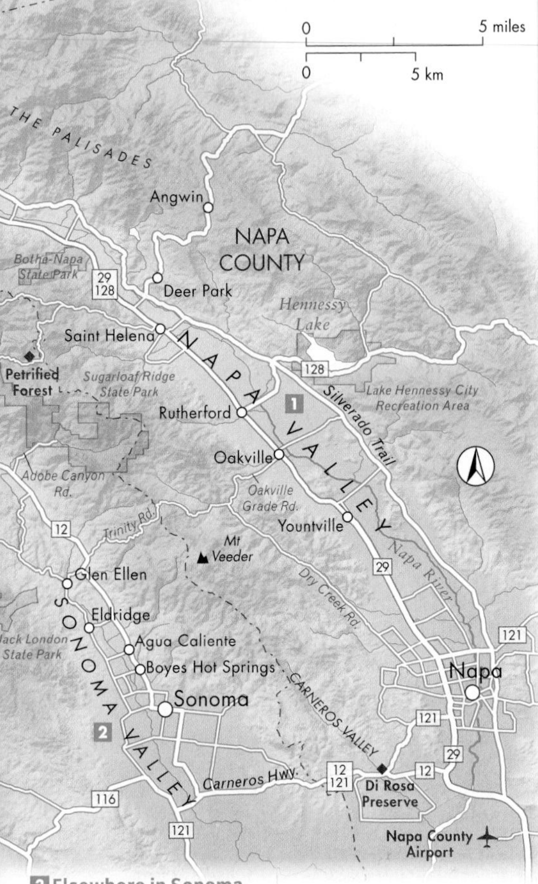

3 Elsewhere in Sonoma. The lovely Russian River, Dry Creek, and Alexander valleys are all excellent places to seek out pinot noir, zinfandel, and chardonnay. The small town of Healdsburg is getting lots of attention lately, thanks to its terrific restaurants, B&Bs, and chic boutiques.

6

WINE COUNTRY PLANNER

Getting Around

Driving your own car is by far the best way to explore the Wine Country. Well-maintained roads zip through the centers of the Napa and Sonoma valleys, while scenic routes thread through the backcountry. Distances between towns are fairly short, and you can sometimes drive from one end of the Napa or Sonoma Valley to the other in less than an hour—if there's no significant traffic. (However, it's not quite as easy as you might think to get between the two valleys, since they're divided by the Mayacamas Mountains.) This may be a relatively rural area, but the usual rush hours still apply, and high-season weekend traffic can be excruciatingly slow, especially on Route 29. ■ **TIP→If you're wine-tasting, either select a designated driver or be very careful of your wine intake. Those sips add up.** Local cops are quick with DUIs.

Timing

"Crush," the term used to indicate the season when grapes are picked and crushed, usually takes place in September or October, depending on the weather. From September until November the entire Wine Country celebrates its bounty with street fairs and festivals. The Sonoma County Harvest Fair, with its famous grape stomp, is held the first weekend in October. Golf tournaments, wine auctions, and art and food fairs occur throughout the fall.

In season (April through October), Napa Valley draws crowds of tourists, and traffic along Route 29 from St. Helena to Calistoga is often backed up on weekends. The Sonoma Valley, Santa Rosa, and Healdsburg are less crowded. In season and over holiday weekends it's best to book lodging, restaurant, and winery reservations at least a month in advance. Many wineries give tours at specified times and require appointments.

To avoid crowds, visit the Wine Country during the week and get an early start (most wineries open around 10). Because many wineries close as early as 4 or 4:30—and almost none are open past 5—you'll need to get a reasonably early start if you want to fit in more than one or two, especially if you're going to enjoy the leisurely lunch customary in the Wine Country. Summer is usually hot and dry, and autumn can be even hotter, so dress appropriately if you go during these times.

About the Hotels

Napa and Sonoma know the tourism ropes well; their inns and hotels range from low-key to utterly luxurious, and generally maintain high standards. Most of the bed-and-breakfasts are in historic Victorian and Spanish buildings, and the breakfast part of the equation often involves fresh local produce. The newer hotels tend to have a more modern, streamlined aesthetic and decadent, spa-like bathrooms. Many hotels and B&Bs have excellent restaurants on their grounds, and all that don't are still just a short car ride away from gastronomic bliss.

However, all of this comes with a hefty price tag. As the cost of vineyards and grapes has risen, so have lodging rates. Santa Rosa, the largest population center in the area, has the widest selection of moderately priced rooms. Try there if you've failed to reserve in advance or have a limited budget. In general, all accommodations in the area often have lower rates on weeknights, and prices are about 20% lower in winter.

On weekends, two- or even three-night minimum stays are commonly required, especially at smaller inns and B&Bs. If you'd prefer to stay a single night, though, innkeepers are usually more flexible in winter. Many B&Bs book up long in advance of the summer and fall seasons, and they're often not suitable for children.

WINE COUNTRY COSTS

	¢	$	$$	$$$	$$$$
Restaurants	under $10	$10–$14	$15–$22	$23–$30	over $30
Hotels	under $200	$200–$250	$251–$300	$301–$400	over $400

Restaurant prices are per person for a main course at dinner, or for a prix-fixe if a set menu is the only option. Hotel prices are for two people in a standard double room in high season.

About the Restaurants

Star chefs from around the world have come into the Wine Country's orbit, drawn by the area's phenomenal produce, artisanal foods, and wines. These days, some visitors come to Napa and Sonoma as much for the restaurants' tasting menus as for the wineries' tasting rooms.

Although excellent meals can be found virtually everywhere in the region, the small town of Yountville has become a culinary crossroads under the influence of chef Thomas Keller. If a table at Keller's famed French Laundry is out of reach, keep in mind that he's also behind a number of more modest restaurants in town. And the buzzed-about restaurants in Sonoma County, including Cyrus and Farmhouse Inn, offer plenty of mouthwatering options.

Such high quality often means high prices, but you can also find appealing, inexpensive eateries. High-end delis serve superb picnic fare, and brunch is a cost-effective strategy at pricey restaurants, as is sitting at the bar and ordering a few appetizers instead of sitting down to a full-blown meal. Increasingly, wineries are starting to serve cheese or other pairings with their wine tastings. Sometimes these can serve as a light lunch, especially if you've eaten a big breakfast at your B&B and have extravagant dinner plans for the evening.

Updated by Sharron Wood

Life is good in the California Wine Country. Eating and, above all, drinking are cultivated as high arts. Have you been daydreaming about driving through vineyards, stopping here and there for a wine tasting or a picnic? Well, that fantasy is a common reality here.

It's little wonder that so many visitors to San Francisco take a day or two—or five or six—to unwind in the Napa and Sonoma valleys. They join the locals in the tasting rooms, from serious wine collectors making their annual pilgrimages to wine newbies who don't know the difference between a merlot and Mourvèdre but are eager to learn.

The state's wine industry is booming, and the Napa and Sonoma valleys have long led the field. For instance, in 1975 Napa Valley had no more than 20 wineries; today there are more than 250. A recent up-and-comer is the Carneros region, which overlaps Napa and Sonoma counties at the head of the San Francisco Bay. (As it turns out, chardonnay and pinot noir grapes thrive on its cool, windy hillsides.)

In the past decade, many individual grape growers have started producing their own wines instead of selling their crops to larger wineries. These small "boutique" wineries are turning out excellent, reasonably priced wines that have caught the attention of connoisseurs and critics. Meanwhile, the larger wineries continue to consolidate land and expand their grape varietals.

Great dining and wine go hand in hand, and the local viticulture has naturally encouraged a robust passion for food. Several outstanding chefs have taken root here, sealing the area's reputation as one of the best restaurant destinations in the country. The lust for fine food doesn't stop at the doors of the bistros, either. Whether you visit an artisanal olive-oil producer, nibble locally made cheese, or browse the fresh vegetables in the farmers' markets, you'll soon see why Napa and Sonoma are considered a foodie paradise.

Napa and Sonoma counties are also rich in history. In the town of Sonoma, for example, you can explore buildings from California's Spanish and Mexican past. Some wineries, such as Napa Valley's Beringer, have cellars or tasting rooms dating back to the late 1800s. The town of Calistoga is a flurry of Steamboat Gothic architecture, gussied up with the fretwork favored by late-19th-century spa goers. Modern architecture is the exception rather than the rule, but one standout example is the postmodern extravaganza of Clos Pegase winery.

Binding all these temptations together is the sheer scenic beauty of the place. Much of Napa Valley's landscape unspools in orderly, densely planted rows of vines. Sonoma's vistas are broken by rolling hills or stands of ancient oak and madrone trees.

PLANNING

GETTING HERE AND AROUND

AIR TRAVEL

If you'd like to bypass San Francisco or Oakland, you can fly directly to the small Charles M. Schulz Sonoma County Airport (STS) in Santa Rosa on Horizon Air, which has direct flights from Los Angeles, Portland, Las Vegas, and Seattle. Rental cars are available from Avis, Enterprise, and Hertz at the airport.

BUS TRAVEL

Bus travel is an inconvenient way to explore Wine Country. Service is infrequent and the buses can only get you to Santa Rosa or the town of Vallejo, south of Napa—neither of which is close to the vineyards. Sonoma County Transit offers daily bus service to points all over the county. VINE (Valley Intracity Neighborhood Express) provides bus service within the city of Napa and between other Napa Valley towns.

Bus Contacts **Greyhound** (☎ *800/231–2222*). **Sonoma County Transit** (☎ *707/576–7433 or 800/345–7433*). **VINE** (☎ *707/251–2800*).

CAR TRAVEL

Five major roads cut through the Napa and Sonoma valleys. U.S. 101 and routes 12 and 121 travel through Sonoma County. Route 29 heads north from Napa. The 25-mi Silverado Trail, which runs parallel to Route 29 north from Napa to Calistoga, is Napa Valley's more scenic, less-crowded alternative to Route 29.

■ **TIP→ Remember, if you're wine-tasting, either select a designated driver or be very careful of your wine intake. (When you're taking just a sip or two of any given wine, it can be hard to keep track of how much you're drinking.)** Also, keep in mind that you'll likely be sharing the road with cyclists; keep a close eye on the shoulder.

When calculating the time it will take you to drive between Napa and Sonoma valleys, remember that the Mayacamas Mountains are between the two. If it's not too far out of your way, you might want to travel between the two valleys along Highway 12/121 to the south, or along Highway 128 to the north, to avoid the slow, winding drive on the Oakville Grade, which connects Oakville, in Napa, and Glen Ellen, in Sonoma.

From San Francisco to Napa: Cross the Golden Gate Bridge, then go north on U.S. 101. Next go east on Route 37 toward Vallejo, then north on Route 121, also called the Carneros Highway. Turn left (north) when

Route 121 runs into Route 29. This should take about 1½ hours when traffic is light.

From San Francisco to Sonoma: Cross the Golden Gate Bridge, then go north on U.S. 101, east on Route 37 toward Vallejo, and north on Route 121, aka the Carneros Highway. When you reach Route 12, take it north. If you're going to any of the Sonoma County destinations north of the valley, take the U.S. 101 all the way north through Santa Rosa to Healdsburg. This should take about an hour, not counting substantial traffic.

From Berkeley and other East Bay towns: Take Interstate 80 north to Route 37 west, then on to Route 29 north. To head up the Napa Valley, continue on Route 29; to reach Sonoma County, turn off Route 29 onto Route 121 heading north. Getting from Berkeley to Napa will take at least 45 minutes, from Berkeley to Sonoma at least an hour.

BED AND BREAKFAST ASSOCIATIONS

Bed & Breakfast Association of Sonoma Valley (*✉ 214 Napa St. E., Sonoma ☎ 707/938-9513 or 800/969-4667 🌐 www.sonomabb.com*). **The Wine Country Inns of Sonoma County** (*☎ 800/946-3268 🌐 www.winecountryinns.com*).

HEALTH AND SAFETY

The best-equipped emergency room and trauma center in the Wine Country is at **Santa Rosa Memorial Hospital** (*✉ 1165 Montgomery Dr., Santa Rosa ☎ 707/546-3210*). **Walgreens** (*✉ 4610 Sonoma Hwy., Santa Rosa ☎ 707/538-0964*) pharmacy is open 24 hours a day.

TOURS

Full-day guided tours of the Wine Country usually include lunch and cost about $60–$90 per person. Reservations are usually required.

Beau Wine Tours (*✉ 21707 8th St. E, Sonoma ☎ 707/938-8001 🌐 www.beauwinetours.com*) organizes personalized tours of Napa and Sonoma in their limos, vans, and shuttle buses. **Gray Line** (*✉ Pier 43½ Embarcadero, San Francisco ☎ 415/434-8687 or 800/966-8125 🌐 www.grayline.com*) has a tour that covers both southern Napa and Sonoma valleys in a single day, with a stop for lunch in Yountville. **Great Pacific Tour Co.** (*✉ 518 Octavia St., Hayes Valley, San Francisco ☎ 415/626-4499 🌐 www.greatpacifictour.com*) operates full-day tours of Napa and Sonoma, including a restaurant or picnic lunch, in passenger vans that seat 14. In addition to renting bikes by the day, **Wine Country Bikes** (*✉ 61 Front St., Healdsburg ☎ 707/473-0610 🌐 www.winecountrybikes.com*) organizes both one-day and multiday trips throughout Sonoma County.

THE NAPA VALLEY

Napa Valley rules the roost of American wine production. With more than 250 wineries and many of the biggest brands in the business, there are more high-profile places here than anywhere else in the state. Vastly diverse soils and microclimates give Napa vintners the chance to make a tremendous variety of wines.

Beyond the glossy advertising and well-known names, most communities here are small, quirky towns with restored, gingerbread-frilled

Victorian buildings. Napa itself, at the bottom of the valley, has been sprucing up its historic downtown. Compact Yountville, in the lower Napa Valley, is a culinary boomtown, while St. Helena, in the middle of the valley, attracts big spenders with elegant shops and restaurants. Calistoga, near the north border of Napa County, feels a bit like an Old West frontier town, with wooden-plank storefronts and a more casual feel than many other Wine Country towns.

ESSENTIALS

Contacts Napa Valley Conference and Visitors Bureau (✉ *1310 Napa Town Center, Napa* ☎ *707/226–7459* 🌐 *www.napavalley.com*).

NAPA

46 mi from San Francisco via I–80 east and north, Rte. 37 west, and Rte. 29 north.

The town of Napa is the valley's largest, and many visitors who get a glimpse of the strip malls and big-box stores from Highway 29 speed right past on the way to the smaller and more seductive Yountville or Calistoga. But if you take the time to explore, you might discover that Napa no longer entirely merits its dowdy reputation. Though the tourists have yet to arrive in droves, Napa's top-notch restaurants attract food-savvy valley residents, and the shops in the pedestrian-friendly downtown area are more down-to-earth than the pricey boutiques of, say, St. Helena. The recent renovations of historic buildings such as the glamorous 1880 Napa Valley Opera House and the ongoing construction of new hotels and restaurants mean that Napa is a town on the upswing. Nevertheless, you'll still see some empty storefronts as you stroll around town, and the shuttering in 2008 of the financially beleaguered Copia was another sign that the town of Napa hasn't entirely taken off.

Many visitors choose to stay in Napa after experiencing hotel sticker shock; prices in Napa are marginally more reasonable than elsewhere. If you set up your home base here, you'll undoubtedly want to spend most of your time getting out into the beautiful countryside, but you could easily spend a few hours browsing the Napa's Oxbow Public Market or relaxing at one of the town's several wine bars.

★ The majestic château of **Domaine Carneros** looks for all the world like it belongs in France, and in fact it does: it's modeled after Champagne Taittinger's Château de la Marquetterie, an 18th-century castle near Epernay, France. Carved into the hillside beneath the winery, Domaine Carneros's cellars produce delicate sparkling wines reminiscent of those made by Taittinger and use only grapes grown locally in the Carneros wine district. They sell full glasses, flights, and bottles—their offerings also include still wines, including a handful of pinot noirs and a merlot—and serve them with cheese plates or caviar to those seated in the Louis XV–inspired salon or on the terrace overlooking the vineyards. Though this makes a visit here a tad more expensive than most stops on a winery tour, it's also one of the most opulent ways to enjoy the Carneros district. ✉ *1240 Duhig Rd.* ☎ *707/257–0101* 🌐 *www.domainecarneros.com* 🎫 *Tasting $6.75–$15, tour $25* ⏲ *Daily 10–6; tour daily at 11, 1, and 3.*

Continued on page 304

WINE
TASTING *in*
NAPA *and*
SONOMA

The tantalizing pop of a cork. Roads unspooling through hypnotically even rows of vines. Sun glinting through a glass of sparkling wine or ruby colored cabernet. If these are your daydreams, you won't be disappointed when you get to Napa and Sonoma. The vineyard-blanketed hills, shady town squares, and ivy-draped wineries—not to mention the luxurious restaurants, hotels, and spas—really *are* that captivating.

(opposite page) Carneros vineyards in autumn, Napa Valley. (top) Pinot Gris grapes (bottom) Bottles from Far Niente winery.

VISITING WINERIES

Napa and Sonoma are outstanding destinations for both wine newcomers and serious wine buffs. Tasting rooms range from modest to swanky, offering everything from a casual conversation over a few sips of wine to in-depth tours of winemaking facilities and vineyards. And there's a tremendous variety of wines to taste. The one constant is a deep, shared pleasure in the experience of wine tasting.

Wineries in Napa and Sonoma range from faux châteaux with vast gift shops to rustic converted barns where you might have to step over the vintner's dog in the doorway. Many are regularly open to the public, usually daily from around 10 AM to 5 PM. Others require advance reservations to visit, and still others are closed to the public entirely. When in doubt, call ahead.

There are many, many more wineries in Napa and Sonoma than we could possibly include here. Free maps pinpointing most of them are widely available, though; ask the staff at the tasting rooms you visit or look for the ubiquitous free tourist magazines.

Pick a designated driver before setting out for the day. Although wineries rarely advertise it, many will provide a free nonalcoholic drink for the designated driver; it never hurts to ask.

Fees. In the past few years, tasting fees have skyrocketed. Most Napa wineries charge $10 to $20 to taste four or so wines, though $30 or even $40 fees aren't unheard of. Sonoma wineries are often a bit cheaper, in the $5 to $15 range, and you'll still find the occasional freebie.

Some winery tours are free, in which case you're usually required to pay a separate fee if you want to taste the wine. If you've paid a fee for the tour—often $10 to $30—your wine tasting is usually included in that price.

MAKING THE MOST OF YOUR TIME

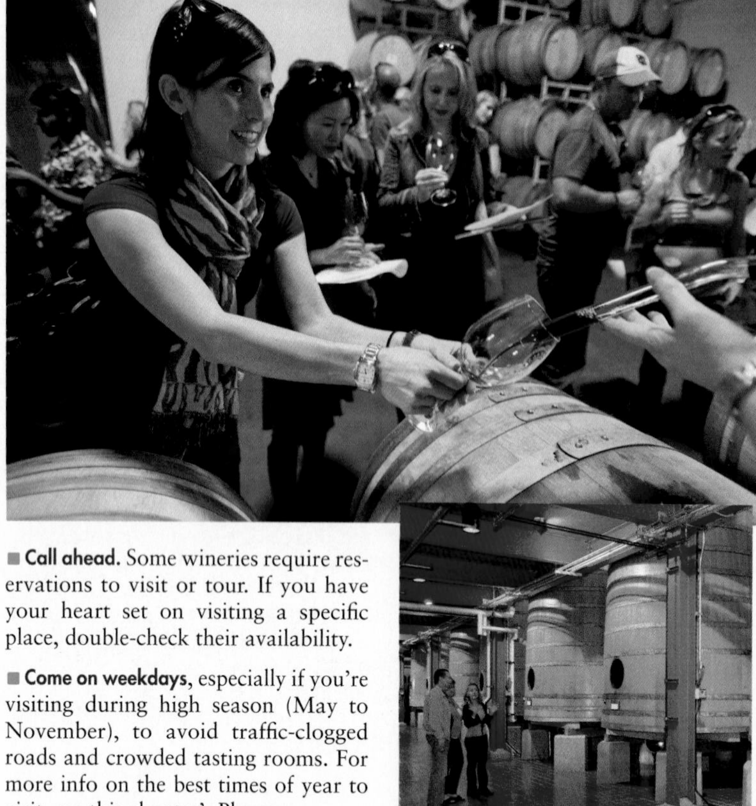

(top) Sipping and swirling in the De Loach tasting room. (bottom) Learning about barrel aging at Robert Mondavi Winery.

■ **Call ahead.** Some wineries require reservations to visit or tour. If you have your heart set on visiting a specific place, double-check their availability.

■ **Come on weekdays,** especially if you're visiting during high season (May to November), to avoid traffic-clogged roads and crowded tasting rooms. For more info on the best times of year to visit, see this chapter's Planner.

■ **Get an early start.** Tasting rooms are often deserted before 11 AM or so, when most visitors are still lingering over a second cup of coffee. If you come early, you'll have the staff's undivided attention. You'll usually encounter the largest crowds between 3 and 5 PM.

■ **Consider skipping Napa.** If you've got less than two days to spend in the Wine Country, dip into the Carneros area or the Sonoma Valley rather than Napa Valley or northern Sonoma County. Though you might find fewer big-name wineries and critically acclaimed restaurants, these regions are only about an hour and half away from the city . . . if you don't hit traffic.

■ **Divide your attention.** If you're lucky enough to have three nights or more here, split your overnights between Napa and Sonoma to easily see the best that both counties have to offer.

A tasting at Heitz Cellar.

AT THE BAR

In most tasting rooms, you'll be handed a list of the wines available that day. The wines will be listed in a suggested tasting order, starting with the lightest-bodied whites, progressing to the most intense reds, and ending with dessert wines. If you can't decide which wines to choose, tell the server what types of wines you usually like and ask for a recommendation.

The server will pour you an ounce or so of each wine you select. As you taste it, feel free to take notes or ask questions. Don't be shy—the staff are there to educate you about their wine. If you don't like a wine, or you've simply tasted enough, feel free to pour the rest into one of the dump buckets on the bar.

TOURS

Tours tend to be the most exciting (and the most crowded) in September and October, when the harvest and crushing are underway. Tours typically last from 30 minutes to an hour and give you a brief overview of the winemaking process. At some of the older wineries, the tour guide might focus on the history of the property.

■ TIP→ **If you plan to take any tours, wear comfortable shoes, since you might be walking on wet floors or stepping over hoses or other equipment.**

MONEY-SAVING TIPS

■ Many hotels distribute coupons for free or discounted tastings to their guests—don't forget to ask.

■ If you and your travel partner don't mind sharing a glass, servers are happy to let you split a tasting.

■ Some wineries will refund all or part of the tasting fee if you buy a bottle, making it so much easier to rationalize buying that $80 bottle of cabernet.

■ Almost all wineries will also waive the fee if you join their wine club program. However, this typically commits you to buying a certain number of bottles of their wine for a period of time, so be sure you really like their wines before signing up.

Preston Vineyards bottles only estate-grown grapes.

TOP 2-DAY ITINERARIES

First-Timer's Napa Tour

Start: **Oxbow Public market, Napa.** Get underway by browsing the shops selling wines, spices, locally grown produce, and other fine foods, for a taste of what the Wine Country has to offer.

Rubicon Estate, Rutherford.
The tour here is a particularly fun way to learn about the history of Napa winemaking—and you can see the old, atmospheric, ivy-covered château.

Frog's Leap, Rutherford.
Friendly, unpretentious, and knowledgeable staff makes this place great for wine newbies. (Make sure you get that advance reservation lined up.)

Dinner and Overnight: **St. Helena.**
Spluge at Meadowood Resort with dinner at

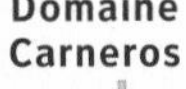

Wine Buff's Tour

Start: **Stag's Leap Wine Cellars, Yountville.**
Famed for its cabernet sauvignon and Bordeaux blends.

Beaulieu Vineyard, Rutherford.
Pony up the extra fee to visit the reserve tasting room to try their flagship cabernet sauvignon.

Caymus Vineyards, Rutherford.
The low-key tasting room is a great place to learn more about Rutherford and Napa cabernet artistry. Reserve in advance.

Dinner and Overnight: **Yountville.**
Have dinner at one of the Thomas Keller restaurants. Splurge at the Villagio Inn & Spa; save at Maison Fleurie.

Next Day: **Robert Mondavi, Oakville.**
Spring for the reserve room tasting so you can sip the top-of-the-line wines, especially the stellar cabernet. Head across Highway 29 to the Oakville Grocery to pick up a picnic lunch.

Terra. Save at El Bonita Motel with dinner at Taylor's.

Next Day: Poke around St. Helena's shops, then drive to Yountville for lunch.

di Rosa Preserve, Napa.
Call ahead to book a one- or two-hour tour of the acres of gardens and galleries, which are chock-full of thousands of works of art.

Domaine Carneros, Napa.
Toast your trip with a glass of outstanding bubbly.

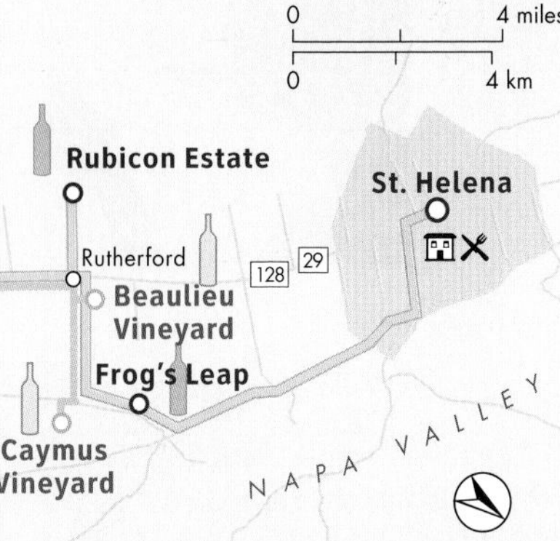

Far Niente, Oakville. You have to reserve in advance and the fee for the tasting and tour is steep, but the payoff is an especially intimate winery experience. You'll taste excellent cabernet and chardonnay, then end your trip on a sweet note with a dessert wine.

Sonoma Backroads

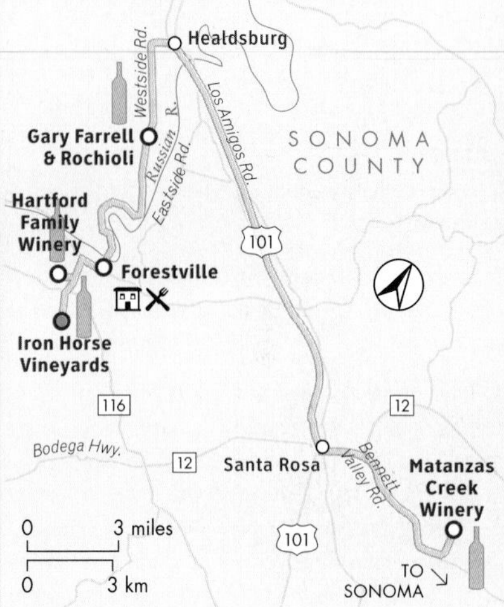

Start: Iron Horse Vineyards, Russian River Valley.
Soak up a view of vine-covered hills and Mount St. Helena while sipping a sparkling wine or pinot noir at this beautifully rustic spot.

Hartford Family Winery, Russian River Valley.
A terrific source for pinot noir and chardonnay, the stars of this valley.

Dinner and Overnight: Forestville. Splurge at either the Farmhouse or Applewood Inn, each of which has a top-notch restaurant (save with Applewood's decadent breakfast included in the room rate).

Next Day: Westside Road, Russian River Valley.
This scenic route, which follows the river, is crowded with worthwhile wineries like Gary Farrell and Rochioli—but it's not crowded with visitors. Pinot fans will find a lot to love. Picnic at Rochioli: it has the best views.

Matanzas Creek Winery, near Santa Rosa.
End on an especially relaxed note with a walk through their lavender fields (best in June).

WINE TASTING 101

Swirl

Sniff

Sip

TAKE A GOOD LOOK.

Hold your glass by the stem, raise it to the light, and take a close look at the wine. Check for clarity and color. (This is easiest to do if you can hold the glass in front of a white background.) Any tinge of brown usually means that the wine is over the hill or has gone bad.

BREATHE DEEP.

1. Sniff the wine once or twice to see if you can identify any smells.

2. Swirl the wine gently in the glass. Aerating the wine this way releases more of its aromas. (It's called "volatilizing the esters," if you're trying to impress someone.)

3. Take another long sniff. You might notice that experienced wine tasters spend more time sniffing the wine than drinking it. This is because this step is where the magic happens. The number of scents you might detect is almost endless, from berries, apricots, honey, and wildflowers to leather, cedar, or even tar. Does the wine smell good to you? Do you detect any "off" flavors, like wet dog or sulfur?

AT LAST! TAKE A SIP.

1. Swirl the wine around your mouth so that it makes contact with all your taste buds and releases more of its aromas. Think about the way the wine feels in your mouth. Is it watery or rich? Is it crisp or silky? Does it have a bold flavor, or is it subtle? The weight and intensity of a wine are called its body.

2. Hold the wine in your mouth for a few seconds and see if you can identify any developing flavors. More complex wines will reveal many different flavors as you drink them.

SPIT OR SWALLOW.

The pros typically spit, since they want to preserve their palate (and sobriety!) for the wines to come, but you'll find that swallowers far outnumber the spitters in the winery tasting rooms. Whether you spit or swallow, notice the flavor that remains after the wine is gone (the finish).

DODGE THE CROWDS

To avoid bumping elbows in the tasting rooms, look for wineries off the main drags of Highway 29 in Napa and Highway 12 in Sonoma. The back roads of the Russian River, Dry Creek, and Alexander valleys, all in Sonoma, are excellent places to explore. In Napa, try the northern end. Also look for wineries that are open by appointment only; they tend to schedule visitors carefully to avoid a big crush at any one time.

HOW WINE IS MADE

1. CRUSHING
Harvested grapes go into a stemmer-crusher, which separates stems from fruit and crushes the grapes to release "free-run" juice.

2. PRESSING
Remaining juice is gently extracted from grapes. Usually done by pressing grapes against the walls of a tank with an inflatable bladder.

3. FERMENTING
Extracted juice (and also grape skins and pulp, when making red wine) goes into stainless-steel tanks or oak barrels to ferment. During fermentation, sugars convert to alcohol.

4. AGING
Wine is stored in stainless-steel or oak casks or barrels to develop flavors.

5. RACKING
Wine is transferred to clean barrels; sediment is removed. Wine may be filtered and fined (clarified) to improve its clarity, color, and sometimes flavor.

6. BOTTLING
Wine is bottled either at the winery or at a special facility, then stored again for bottle-aging.

WHAT'S AN APPELLATION?

A specific region with a particular set of grape-growing conditions, such as soil type, climate, and elevation, is called an appellation. What makes things a little confusing is that appellations, which are defined by the Alcohol and Tobacco Tax and Trade Bureau, often overlap. California is an appellation, for example, but so is the Napa Valley. Napa and Sonoma counties are each county appellations, but they, too, are divided into even smaller regions, usually called subappellations or AVAs (American Viticultural Areas). You'll hear a lot about these AVAs from the staff in the tasting rooms; they might explain, for example, why the Russian River Valley AVA is such an excellent place to grow pinot noir grapes. By law, if the label on a bottle of wine lists the name of an appellation, then at least 85% of the grapes in that wine must come from that appellation.

Wine and contemporary art find a home at the di Rosa Preserve.

Fodor's Choice ★

When you're driving along the Carneros Highway on your way to Napa from San Francisco, it would be easy to zip by one of the region's best-kept secrets: the **di Rosa Preserve.** Metal sculptures of sheep grazing in the grass mark the entrance to this sprawling, art-stuffed property. Thousands of 20th-century artworks by hundreds of Northern California artists crop up everywhere—in galleries, in the former di Rosa residence, on every lawn, in every courtyard, and even on the lake. If you stop by without a reservation, you can only gain access to the Gatehouse Gallery, where there's a small collection of riotously colorful figurative and abstract sculpture and painting. **■ TIP→For the full effect, reserve ahead for a one-hour tour of the grounds, or opt for the two-hour tour, which allows more time to browse the main gallery.** ✉ *5200 Carneros Hwy.* ☎ *707/226–5991* ⊕ *www.dirosapreserve.org* 🎫 *$3, tours $10–$15 (free Wed.)* ⏲ *Tues.–Fri. 9:30–3, Sat. by reservation; call for tour times.*

With its modern, minimalist look in the tasting room, which is dug into a Carneros hilltop, and contemporary sculptures and fountains on the property, **Artesa Vineyards & Winery** is a far cry from the many faux French châteaus and rustic Italian-style villas in the region. Although the Spanish owners once made sparkling wines exclusively, they now produce still wines—mostly chardonnay and pinot noir, but also cabernet sauvignon and a smattering of other limited-release wines such as Syrah and Albariño. Call ahead to reserve a spot on one of the specialty tours, such as the guided tasting in the barrel room or the walk through the vineyard ($40–$50). ✉ *1345 Henry Rd., north of Old Sonoma Rd. and Dealy La.* ☎ *707/224–1668* ⊕ *www.artesawinery.com* 🎫 *Tasting $10–$15, tour $15* ⏲ *Daily 10–5; tour daily at 11 and 2.*

Though it's not terribly large, **Oxbow Public Market,** a collection of about 20 small shops, wine bars, and artisanal food producers, is a fun place to begin your introduction to the wealth of food and wine available in the Napa Valley. Swoon over the decadent charcuterie at the Fatted Calf, slurp down some oysters on the half shell at Hog Island Oyster Company, or get a whiff of the hard-to-find seasonings at the Whole Spice Company before sitting down to a glass of wine at one of the two wine bars. A branch of the retro fast-food joint Taylor's Automatic Refresher tempts those who prefer hamburgers to duck-liver mousse. ✉ *610 and 644 1st St.* ☎ *No phone* 🌐 *www.oxbowpublicmarket.com* 🎫 *Free* ⏲ *Generally Mon.–Sat. 9–7, Sun. 10–5, though hrs of some merchants vary.*

Luna Vineyards was established in 1995 by veterans of the Napa wine industry intent on making less-conventional wines, particularly Italian varieties such as Sangiovese and pinot grigio. Though these days you're just as likely to taste a merlot or a cabernet blend in their cozy Tuscan-style tasting room with a coffered ceiling, it's worth a stop, especially for a nip of late-harvest dessert wine of pinot grigio called Mille Baci ("a thousand kisses" in Italian). ✉ *2921 Silverado Trail* ☎ *707/255–5862* 🌐 *www.lunavineyards.com* 🎫 *Tasting $15–$25* ⏲ *Daily 10–5.*

6

Austere **Clos du Val** doesn't seduce you with dramatic architecture or lush grounds, but it doesn't have to: the wines, crafted by winemaker John Clews, have a wide following, especially among those who are patient enough to cellar the wines for a number of years. Though Clews's team makes great pinot noir and chardonnay, the real claim to fame is the reserve cabernet. Library wines are poured on weekends, as well as on weekdays during the high season. Anyone is welcome to try a hand at the boccie-style game of pétanque. ✉ *5330 Silverado Trail* ☎ *707/259–2200* 🌐 *www.closduval.com* 🎫 *Tasting $10–$20* ⏲ *Daily 10–5; tour by appointment.*

Fodor's Choice ★ The **Hess Collection Winery and Vineyards** is a delightful discovery on Mt. Veeder 9 mi northwest of the city of Napa. (Don't give up; the road leading to the winery is long and winding.) The simple limestone structure, rustic from the outside but fairly modern and airy within, contains Swiss owner Donald Hess's personal art collection, including mostly large-scale works by such contemporary European and American artists as Robert Motherwell, Andy Goldsworthy, and Frank Stella. Cabernet sauvignon is the real strength here, though Hess also produces some fine chardonnays. Self-guided tours of the art collection and guided tours of the winery's production facilities are both free. ✉ *4411 Redwood Rd., west of Rte. 29* ☎ *707/255–1144* 🌐 *www.hesscollection.com* 🎫 *Tasting $10–$20* ⏲ *Daily 10–5, tasting until 4; guided tours daily, hourly 10:30–3:30.*

WHERE TO EAT

$$$ FRENCH ✕ **Angèle.** An 1890s boathouse with a vaulted wood-beam ceiling sets the scene for romance at this cozy French bistro. Though the style is casual—tables are fairly close together and the warm, crusty bread is plunked right down on the paper-topped tables—the food is always well executed. Look for classic French dishes like beef bourguignonne,

Napa Valley
LAKE COUNTY
Mount St Helena
Robert Louis Stevenson State Park
THE PALISADES
Aetna Springs
POPE VALLEY
Pope Valley
Pope Canyon Rd.
Lake Berryessa
Knoxville Rd.
Howell Mtn Rd.
Lake Berryessa Recreation Area
Calistoga
Tubbs Ln.
Dunaweal Ln.
Larkmead Ln.
Angwin
Angwin Airport
Petrified Forest Rd.
Chiles Pope Valley Rd.
Bothe-Napa State Park
Diamond Mountain
NAPA COUNTY
Deer Park
Sanitarium Rd.
Bale Grist Mill State Historic Park
Hennessy Lake
SONOMA COUNTY
Silverado Trail
Saint Helena
Pope
Sage Canyon Rd.
NAPA
Sugarloaf Ridge State Park
Lake Hennessy City Recreation Area
Hood Mountain Regional Park
Rutherford
Atlas Peak
Sonoma Hwy.
Adobe Canyon Rd.
Bald Mountain
Oakville Cross Rd.
Mt St. John
Oakville
FOSS VALLEY
Annadel State Park
Oakville Grade Rd.
Yontville Hills
Yountville Cross Rd.
Kenwood
Napa River
VALLEY
Yountville
Trinity Rd.
Silverado Trail
Bennett Valley Rd.
Mt Veeder
SONOMA
Oak Knoll
Big Ranch Rd.
Glen Ellen
Dry Creek Rd.
Sonoma Mountain
REDWOOD CANYON
Monticello Rd.
Eldridge
VALLEY OF THE MOON
Jack London State Park
Agua Caliente
CARNEROS VALLEY
Trancas St.
Pueblo
Lincoln
Arnold Dr.
Boyes Hot Springs
Redwood Rd.
Browns Valley Rd.
1st
SONOMA MOUNTAINS
El Verano
Napa
Sonoma
Henry Rd.
Imola Ave.
Old Sonoma Rd.
Napa Rd.
Dealy La.
Washington
Adobe Rd.
Temelec
Petaluma
Carneros Hwy.
Lakeville Hwy.
Bonness Rd.
0 4 mi
0 4 km
Napa County Airport
Artesa Vineyards & Winery . 3
Beaulieu Vineyard 19
Beringer Vineyards 27
Castello di Amorosa 28
Caymus Vineyards 21
Charles Krug Winery 26
Château Montelena 33
Clos du Val 7
Clos Pegase 32
Culinary Institute of America 23
di Rosa Preserve 2
Domaine Carneros 1
Domaine Chandon 8
Dutch Henry Winery 30
Far Niente 13
Frog's Leap 20
Hess Collection Winery and Vineyards 5
Luna Vineyards 6
Mumm Napa Valley 23
Napa Valley Museum 12
Oakville Grocery 14
Oxbow Public Market 4
Opus One 16
Robert Louis Stevenson State Park 34
Robert Mondavi 15
Robert Sinskey 10
Round Pond 22
Rubicon Estate 17
Rutherford Hill Winery 24
Schramsberg 29
St. Supéry 18
Stag's Leap Wine Cellars ... 9
Sterling Vineyards 31
V Marketplace 11

Climbing ivy and lily pads decorate the Hess Collection's rustic exterior.

a rib-eye steak with red wine sauce and french fries, or a starter of *ris de veau* (veal sweetbreads). In fair weather, the outdoor tables are as charming as those inside. ✉*540 Main St.* ☎*707/252–8115* ▭*AE, D, DC, MC, V.*

$$ ITALIAN ★ ✕**Bistro Don Giovanni.** Dramatic flower arrangements and a roaring fire in cool weather brighten this lively bistro. The Cal-Italian food is simultaneously inventive and comforting: risotto with chanterelles, artichokes, and pancetta; pizza with caramelized onions and Gorgonzola; and rabbit braised in cabernet. Dishes roasted in the wood-burning oven are a specialty. Fodors.com Forum users suggest snagging a table on the covered patio near the fireplace for a "more intimate and quiet" experience. ✉*4110 Howard La./Rte. 29* ☎*707/224–3300* ▭*AE, D, DC, MC, V.*

$$ AMERICAN ✕**Boon Fly Cafe.** Part of the Carneros Inn complex, west of downtown Napa, this small spot has a rural charm–meets–industrial chic theme. Outside, rocking chairs and swings occupy the porch of a modern red barn; inside, things get sleek with high ceilings and galvanized steel tabletops. The small menu of modernized American classics includes dishes such as braised short ribs with mashed potatoes and roasted *cipollini* onions and flatbread topped with bacon, Point Reyes blue cheese, and sautéed mushrooms. If there's a wait for a table, never fear: belly up to the wine bar, where you can find a good selection of reasonably priced glasses. ✉*4048 Sonoma Hwy.* ☎*707/299–4872* *Reservations not accepted* ▭*AE, D, MC, V.*

$$ AMERICAN ★ ✕**Bounty Hunter.** A triple threat, Bounty Hunter is a wine store, wine bar, and restaurant in one. You can stop by for just a glass of wine from their impressive list—a frequently changing list of 40 available

Where to Eat and Stay in Napa Valley
LAKE COUNTY
Mount St Helena
Robert Louis Stevenson State Park
THE PALISADES
Aetna Springs
Pope Valley
POPE VALLEY
Howell Mtn Rd.
Angwin
Angwin Airport
Lake Berryessa Recreation Area
Knoxville Rd.
Chiles Pope Valley Rd.
Tubbs Ln.
Calistoga
Petrified Forest Rd.
Petrified Forest
Dunaweal Ln.
Larkmead Ln.
Diamond Mountain
Bothe-Napa State Park
NAPA COUNTY
Deer Park
Sanitarium Rd.
Bale Grist Mill State Historic Park
Silverado Trail
Lake Hennessy
Sage Canyon Rd.
SONOMA COUNTY
Saint Helena
Pope
NAPA
Lake Hennessy City Recreation Area
Sugarloaf Ridge State Park
Hood Mountain Regional Park
Bald Mountain
Rutherford
Sonoma Hwy.
Adobe Canyon Rd.
Mt St. John
Oakville
Oakville Cross Rd.
Yountville Hills
Atlas Peak
FOSS VALLEY
Annadel State Park
Kenwood
Oakville Grade Rd.
Yountville Cross Rd.
Stag's Leap Hills
Yountville
Napa River
VALLEY
Trinity Rd.
Mt Veeder
Bennett Valley Rd.
SONOMA VALLEY
Glen Ellen
Dry Creek Rd.
Oak Knoll
Big Ranch Rd.
Sonoma Mountain
REDWOOD CANYON
VALLEY OF THE MOON
Eldridge
Jack London State Park
Agua Caliente
Trancas St.
Monticello Rd.
Pueblo
Lincoln
Redwood Rd.
Arnold Dr.
Boyes Hot Springs
CARNEROS VALLEY
Browns Valley Rd.
1st
El Verano
Napa
Sonoma
Henry Rd.
Old Sonoma Rd.
Imola Ave.
SONOMA MOUNTAINS
Napa Rd.
Dealy La.
Washington
Adobe Rd.
Temelec
Petaluma
Lakeville Hwy.
Carneros Hwy.
Bonness Rd.
0 4 mi
0 4 km
Napa County Airport
Restaurants
Ad Hoc 16
All Seasons Bistro 32
Angèle 3
Auberge du Soleil 21
Bar Vino 36
Bistro Don Giovanni 10
Bistro Jeanty 13
Boon Fly Cafe 1
Bounty Hunter 4
Bouchon 14
Calistoga Inn Restaurant and Brewery 31
French Laundry 15
Go Fish 24
Market 26
Martini House 23
Mustards Grill 12
Taylor's Automatic Refresher 25
Terra 27
Ubuntu 9
Wine Spectator Greystone Restaurant 29
ZuZu 8
Hotels
Auberge du Soleil 21
Blackbird Inn 5
Brannan Cottage Inn 33
Calistoga Ranch 30
Carneros Inn 2
Cottage Grove Inn 34
El Bonita Motel 20
Indian Springs 37
Maison Fleurie 17
Meadowlark Country House 35
Meadowood Resort 22
Milliken Creek Inn 11
Napa River Inn 6
Solage 38
Villagio Inn & Spa 18
Vintage Inn 19
Westin Verasa 7
Wine Country Inn 28

by the glass in both 2- and 5-ounce pours, 400 by the bottle—but it's best to come with an appetite. Their minuscule kitchen means the menu is similarly small, but every dish is a standout, from the pulled pork and beef brisket sandwiches served with three types of barbecue sauce to the signature beer-can chicken and meltingly tender St. Louis–style ribs. The space is whimsically rustic, with taxidermied game trophies on the wall and leather saddles standing in for seats at a couple of tables, but the pressed-tin ceilings and granite-topped café tables also give it a casually chic vibe. ■ **TIP→It's open until midnight on Friday and Saturday, making it a popular spot among locals for a late-night bite.** ✉ *975 1st St.* ☎ *707/226–3976* ✍ *Reservations not accepted* ▭ *AE, MC, V.*

$$$ VEGETARIAN Fodor's Choice ★ ✕ **Ubuntu.** Wine Country foodies are abuzz over this Napa newcomer, a "vegetable restaurant" that draws heavily on local farms and its own biodynamic gardens. Though vegetarian restaurants can sometimes seem ascetic—this one is even attached to a yoga studio, whose students can be faintly seen through translucent windows—the experience here is anything but. Each of chef Jeremy Fox's gorgeously composed plates reveals a unique combination of flavors, from the marcona almonds generously dusted with lavender sugar and sea salt, to the grits served with barbecued Brussels sprouts and a celery-root salad. Innovative desserts, like the "Bowl of Frosted Feuilletine," which mimics a tiny bowl of cereal topped with caramelized bananas and warm malted milk, prove that the restaurant doesn't take itself too seriously. The dining room strikes a New-Age-chic-meets-Wine-Country-rustic pose, with extremely high ceilings, parchment-colored lamps, fieldstone walls, and a long communal table. ✉ *1140 Main St.* ☎ *707/251–5656* ▭ *AE, D, MC, V.*

$$ SPANISH ✕ **ZuZu.** Ocher-color walls, a weathered wood bar, a faded tile floor, and hammered-tin ceiling panels set the scene for a menu composed almost entirely of tapas. These little dishes, so perfect for sharing, and Latin jazz on the stereo help make this place a popular spot for festive get-togethers. Diners down *cava* (Spanish sparkling wine) or sangria with dishes such as white anchovies with endive, ratatouille, and salt cod with garlic croutons. Reservations aren't accepted, so expect a wait on weekends, when local twentysomethings flood the zone. Bocadillos (Spanish-style sandwiches) and empanadas available at lunch make it an inexpensive stop for a midday stop. ✉ *829 Main St.* ☎ *707/224–8555* ✍ *Reservations not accepted* ▭ *AE, MC, V* ⊙ *No lunch weekends.*

WHERE TO STAY

$–$$ **Blackbird Inn.** Arts and Crafts style infuses this 1905 building, from the lobby's enormous fieldstone fireplace to the lamps that cast a warm glow over the impressive wooden staircase. The style is continued in the attractive guest rooms, with sturdy turn-of-the-20th-century oak beds and matching night tables, which nonetheless are updated with spacious, modern bathrooms, most with spa bathtubs. The inn is within walking distance of Napa's historic, restaurant-rich downtown area. It tends to book up quickly, so reserve well in advance. **Pros:** gorgeous architecture and period furnishings; convenient to downtown Napa; free DVD library. **Cons:** must be booked well in advance; some rooms are on the small side. ✉ *1755 1st St.* ☎ *707/226–2450 or 888/567–9811* *www.blackbirdinnnapa.com* *8 rooms* *In-room: DVD, Wi-Fi. In-hotel: no-smoking rooms* *AE, D, DC, MC, V* *CP.*

$$$$ Fodor's Choice ★ **Carneros Inn.** Freestanding board-and-batten cottages with rocking chairs on each porch are simultaneously rustic and chic at this luxurious property. Inside, each cottage is flooded with natural light but still manages to maintain privacy worthy of a paparazzi-ducking celebrity, with windows and French doors leading to a private garden. Wood-burning fireplaces, ethereal beds topped with Italian linens and pristine white down comforters, and spacious bathrooms with heated slate floors and large indoor-outdoor showers may make it difficult to summon the will to leave the cottage and enjoy the hilltop infinity swimming pool and hot tub. The Hilltop Dining Room, with views of the neighboring vineyards, is open to guests only for breakfast and lunch, but Boon Fly Cafe (⇨ *see above*) and FARM, their public restaurants, are popular with visitors throughout the Wine Country. **Pros:** cottages afford lots of privacy; beautiful views from the hilltop pool and hot tub; heaters on each private patio encourage lounging outside in the evening. **Cons:** a long drive from destinations up-valley; smallish rooms with limited seating options. *4048 Sonoma Hwy.* *707/299–4900* *www.thecarnerosinn.com* *76 rooms, 10 suites* *In-room: safe, refrigerator, DVD, Wi-Fi. In-hotel: 3 restaurants, room service, bar, pool, gym, spa, bicycles, laundry service, Wi-Fi, some pets allowed, no-smoking rooms* *AE, D, DC, MC, V.*

$$$$ **Milliken Creek Inn.** Soft jazz and sunset wine and cheese set a romantic mood in the intimate lobby, with its terrace overlooking the Napa River and a lush lawn. The chic rooms take a page from the style book of British-colonial Asia with a khaki-and-cream color scheme alongside hydrotherapy spa tubs and some of the fluffiest beds in the Wine Country. A tiny deck overlooking the river is the spot for massages and private yoga classes. All of the treatment rooms at the serene spa, including one used for popular couple's treatments, have river views. **Pros:** cloudlike beds; serene hotel-guests-only spa; breakfast delivered to your room (or wherever you'd like to eat on the grounds). **Cons:** expensive; late (4 PM) check-in and early (11 AM) checkout; some rooms have small bathrooms. *1815 Silverado Trail* *707/255–1197 or 800/835–6112* *www.millikencreekinn.com* *12 rooms* *In-room: refrigerator, DVD, Wi-Fi. In-hotel: room service, spa, no kids under 18, no-smoking rooms* *AE, D, DC, MC, V* *CP.*

$–$$ **Napa River Inn.** Almost everything's close at hand here: this waterfront inn is part of a complex of restaurants, shops, a gallery, and a spa, all within easy walking distance of downtown Napa. Guest rooms spread through three neighboring buildings. Those in the 1884 Hatt Building, in Victorian style, are arguably the most romantic, with deep red walls, original architectural details such as maple hardwood floors, and old-fashioned slipper tubs. Brighter colors dominate in the rooms of the Plaza and Embarcadero buildings, many of which have river views. Baked goods from the neighboring bakery are delivered to your door for breakfast. **Pros:** new pedestrian walkway connects the hotel to downtown Napa; unusual pet-friendly policy; wide range of room sizes and prices. **Cons:** river views could be more scenic (there's a major road across the river); some rooms get noise from nearby restaurants or construction projects. ✉*500 Main St.* ☎*707/251–8500 or 877/251–8500* 🌐*www.napariverinn.com* *65 rooms, 1 suite* *In-room: safe, refrigerator, DVD (some), Wi-Fi. In-hotel: 4 restaurants, room service, bar, gym, spa, bicycles, laundry service, Internet terminal, some pets allowed, no-smoking rooms* *AE, D, DC, MC, V* *CP.*

NIGHTLIFE AND THE ARTS

The interior of the 1879 Italianate Victorian **Napa Valley Opera House,** which had its grand reopening in 2003, isn't quite as majestic as the facade, but the intimate 500-seat venue is still an excellent place to see all sorts of performances, from Pat Metheny and Mandy Patinkin to various dance companies and, yes, even the occasional opera. ✉*1030 Main St.* ☎*707/226–7372* 🌐*www.napavalleyoperahouse.org.*

MAKING TRACKS IN NAPA

Turn the driving over to someone else—a train conductor. The **Napa Valley Wine Train** (✉*1275 McKinstry St., Napa* ☎*707/253–2111 or 800/427–4124* 🌐*www.winetrain.com*) runs a scenic route between Napa and St. Helena with several restored 1915–17 Pullman railroad cars. The ride often includes a meal, such as brunch or dinner. While it's no bargain (starting at around $90 for lunch, $100 for dinner) and can feel a bit hokey, the train gives you a chance to enjoy the vineyard views without any driving worries.

SPORTS AND THE OUTDOORS

BICYCLING Thanks to the long country roads that wind through the region, bicycling is a popular pastime. The Silverado Trail, with its gently rolling hills, is more scenic than Route 29, which nevertheless tempts some bikers with its pancake-flat aspect. ■TIP→**There are almost no designated bike lanes in Wine Country, though, so when cycling on the shoulders of the roads be sure to pay attention to traffic.**

Napa Valley Bike Tours (✉*6488 Washington St., Yountville* ☎*707/944–2953 or 800/707–2453*) rents bikes (with helmets), including tandem bikes, for $30–$65 per day and will deliver bikes to many hotels in the Napa Valley if you're renting at least two bikes for a full day. Most one-day winery biking tours are $139, including lunch and van support.

YOUNTVILLE

13 mi north of the town of Napa on Rte. 29.

These days Yountville is something like Disneyland for the foodie set. It all started with Thomas Keller's French Laundry, long regarded as one of the best restaurants in the United States. Now Keller is also behind two more casual restaurants just a few blocks away from his mothership—and that's only the beginning. You could stay here for a week and barely have time to exhaust all the options in this tiny town with a big culinary reputation.

Yountville is full of small inns and high-end hotels that cater to those who prefer to walk—not drive—after an extravagant meal. It's also

CLOSE UP

Winespeak

You might hear wine connoisseurs tossing around terms like "Brett effect" and "*botrytis*," but don't let that turn you off. Like any activity, wine making and wine tasting have specialized vocabularies, and most of the terms are actually quite helpful, once you have them down. Here's a handful of core terms to know:

Aroma and bouquet. Aroma is the fruit-derived scent of young wine. It diminishes with fermentation and becomes a more complex **bouquet** as the wine ages.

Body. The wine's density as experienced by the palate. (A full-bodied wine makes the mouth literally feel full.) You'll also hear the word **mouthfeel** when tasters size up the texture of wine in their mouths.

Bordeaux blend. A red wine blended from varietals native to France's Bordeaux region—cabernet sauvignon, cabernet franc, Malbec, merlot, and Petit Verdot.

Corked. When a bottle's cork spoils and the wine inside takes on a musty flavor, the wine is corked.

Estate bottled. A wine entirely made by one winery at a single facility. The grapes must come from the winery's own vineyards within the same appellation (and this must be printed on the label).

Finish. The flavors that remain in the mouth after swallowing wine. A long finish is a good thing.

Flight. A few wines specially selected for tasting together.

Horizontal tasting. A tasting of several different wines of the same vintage.

Library wine. An older vintage that the winery has put aside to sell at a later date.

Oaky. A vanilla-woody flavor that develops when wine is aged in oak barrels. Leave a wine too long in a new oak barrel and that oaky taste overpowers the other flavors.

Reserve wine. Fuzzy term used by vintners to indicate that a wine is better in some way (through aging, source of the grapes, etc.) than others from their winery.

Rhône blend. A wine made from grapes hailing from France's Rhône Valley, such as Marsanne, Roussanne, Syrah, Cinsault, Mourvèdre, or Viognier.

Tannins. You can tell when they're there, but their origins are still a mystery. These natural grape compounds produce a sensation of drying or astringency in the mouth. Tannins settle out as wine ages; they're a big player in many red wines.

Terroir. French word that translates as "soil." Typically used to describe the unique environment (climate, soil, etc.) that influences the grapes and thus the wine.

Vertical tasting. A tasting of several wines of different vintages, generally starting with the youngest and proceeding to the oldest.

Vintage. The grape harvest of a given year, and the year in which the grapes are harvested (not the year in which the wine was bottled).

Oh, and that Brett effect? That's the funky flavor a certain yeast strain can cause in wine. Some like a mild Brett effect, but it's usually considered a fault in the wine.

well located for excursions to many big-name Napa wineries, especially those in the Stags Leap District, where big, bold cabernet sauvignons helped put the Napa Valley on the wine-making map.

In between bouts of eating and drinking, you might stop by **V Marketplace** (*✉6525 Washington St. ☎707/944–2451*). The vine-covered brick complex, which once housed a winery, livery stable, and distillery, contains a smattering of clothing boutiques, art galleries, and jewelry stores. NapaStyle, a large store, deli, and wine bar, sells cookbooks, luxury food items, and kitchen wares, as well as an assortment of prepared foods perfect for picnics. The complex's signature restaurant, Bottega, features the food of celebrity chef Michael Chiarello.

Across Highway 29 from downtown Yountville, in the Veterans Home, is the nifty **Napa Valley Museum** (*✉55 Presidents Circle ☎707/944–0500 🌐www.napavalleymuseum.org 🎫$4.50 ⏲Wed.–Mon. 10–5*). The interactive displays on wines and wine making are particularly engaging; for instance, you can test your knowledge of wine terms and food-and-wine pairings. The rotating shows upstairs, focusing on fine art and local history, are also worth a look.

French-owned **Domaine Chandon** claims one of Yountville's prime pieces of real estate, on a knoll west of downtown where whimsical sculptures sprout out of the lawn and ancient oaks shade the winery. Tours of the sleek, modern facilities are available for $12, but the highlight is a tasting (not included in the tour fee). The top-quality sparklers are made using the laborious *méthode champenoise*. To complete the decadent experience, you can order hors d'oeuvres to accompany the wines in the tasting room. Although they're best known for their bubblies, still wines like their unoaked chardonnay, pinot noir, and rosé of pinot noir are also worth a try. *✉1 California Dr., west of Rte. 29 ☎707/944–2280 🌐www.chandon.com 🎫Tasting $5.50–$16 by the glass, $16 by the flight ⏲Daily 10–6; tours Apr.–Oct., daily at 11, 1, 3, and 5; Nov.–Mar., daily at 11, 1, 3, and 4.*

It was the 1973 cabernet sauvignon produced by **Stag's Leap Wine Cellars** that put the winery—and the California wine industry—on the map by placing first in the famous Paris tasting of 1976. A visit to the winery is a no-frills affair; visitors in the small, spare tasting room are clearly serious about tasting wine and aren't interested in distractions like a gift shop. It costs $30 to taste the top-of-the-line wines, including their limited-production estate-grown cabernets, a few of which sell for well over $100. If you're interested in more modestly priced wines, try the $15 tasting, which usually includes a sauvignon blanc, chardonnay, merlot, and a cabernet. *✉5766 Silverado Trail ☎707/265–2441 🌐www.cask23.com 🎫Tasting $15–$30, tour $40 ⏲Daily 10–4:30; tour by appointment.*

Robert Sinskey Vineyards makes well-regarded pinot blanc and cabernet blends, from their all-organic, certified biodynamic vineyards, but is best known for its intense, brambly pinot noirs, grown in the cooler Carneros District, where the grape thrives. The influence of Robert's wife, Maria Helm Sinskey—a chef and cookbook author—is evident during the tastings, which come with a few bites of food paired with each wine.

But for the best sense of how Sinskey wines pair with food, reserve a spot on the culinary tour, which ends with local cheeses and charcuterie served with the wines. ✉*6320 Silverado Trail* ☎*707/944–9090* 🌐*www.robertsinskey.com* *Tasting $20, tours $30–$50* ⏲*Daily 10–4:30; 1-hr tours by appointment.*

WHERE TO EAT

$$$$ AMERICAN Fodor'sChoice ★ **Ad Hoc.** When superstar chef Thomas Keller opened this relatively casual spot in 2006, he meant to run it for only six months until he opened a burger joint in the same space—but locals were so charmed by the homey food that they clamored for the stopgap to stay. Now a single, seasonal fixed-price menu ($48) is served nightly, with a slightly less expensive menu but equally hearty meal served for Sunday brunch. The selection might include a juicy pork loin and buttery polenta, served family style, or a delicate panna cotta with a citrus glaze. The dining room is warmly low-key, with zinc-topped tables, wine served in tumblers, and rock and jazz on the stereo. If you just can't wait to know what's going be served before you visit, you can call a day in advance for the menu. ✉*6476 Washington St.* ☎*707/944–2487* *AE, MC, V* ⏲*No lunch Mon.–Sat.*

$$ FRENCH **Bistro Jeanty.** Chef Philippe Jeanty's French childhood provides the inspirations for the menu's classic cuisine. His traditional coq au vin will warm those nostalgic for France, and a hearty helping of the bistro classic *steak frites* might be served with a decadent béarnaise sauce. When the dining room is crowded, the kitchen can occasionally slip up, sending out an overcooked steak or a plate that's not composed as prettily as it should be, but most enjoy the friendly scene that's Gallic through and through (you're as likely to find French-speaking locals seated at the small bar as you are visitors from the Midwest). **TIP→The best seats are in the back room, near the fireplace.** ✉*6510 Washington St.* ☎*707/944–0103* *AE, MC, V.*

$$$ FRENCH **Bouchon.** The team that brought French Laundry to its current pinnacle is behind this place, where everything from the super-chic zinc bar to the elbow-to-elbow seating to the traditional French onion soup could have come straight from a Parisian bistro. *Boudin noir* (blood sausage) with potato puree and leg of lamb with white beans and *piquillo* peppers are among the hearty dishes served in the high-ceiling room. **TIP→Late-night meals from a limited menu are served until 12:30 AM—a rarity in the Wine Country, where it's often difficult to find a place to eat after 10 PM.** ✉*6534 Washington St.* ☎*707/944–8037* *AE, MC, V.*

$$$$ AMERICAN Fodor'sChoice ★ **French Laundry.** An old stone building laced with ivy houses the most acclaimed restaurant in Napa Valley—and, indeed, one of the most highly regarded in the country. The restaurant's two prix-fixe menus ($240), one of which is vegetarian, vary, but the "oysters and pearls," a silky sabayon of pearl tapioca with oysters and sevruga caviar, is a signature starter. Some courses rely on luxe ingredients like foie gras, while others take humble foods like fava beans and elevate them to art. Reservations at French Laundry are hard won, and not accepted more than two months in advance. **TIP→Call two months ahead to the day at 10 AM on the dot. Didn't get a reservation? Call on the day you'd like to dine here to be considered if there's a cancellation.** ✉*6640 Washington*

St. ☎*707/944–2380* ✍*Reservations essential, jacket required* ▭*AE, MC, V* ⊗*Closed 1st 2 wks in Jan. No lunch Mon.–Thurs.*

$$ AMERICAN ✕**Mustards Grill.** There's not an ounce of pretension at Cindy Pawlcyn's longtime Napa favorite, despite the fact that it's booked solid every day and night with fans of her hearty cuisine. The menu mixes updated renditions of traditional American dishes such as baby back pork ribs and lemon meringue pie with innovative choices such as sweet corn tamales with tomatillo-avocado salsa and pumpkin seeds. A black-and-white marble tile floor and upbeat artwork set a scene that one Fodors.com reader describes as "pure fun, if not fancy." ✉*7399 St. Helena Hwy./Rte. 29, 1 mi north of town* ☎*707/944–2424* ✍*Reservations essential* ▭*AE, D, DC, MC, V.*

WHERE TO STAY

$–$$ ★ **Maison Fleurie.** If you'd like to be within easy walking distance of most of Yountville's best restaurants, and possibly score a great bargain, look into this casual, comfortable inn. Rooms share a French country style (picture floral bedspreads and pastel trompe-l'oeil paintings) but vary dramatically in size and amenities. The largest have a private entrance, deck, fireplace, and spa bathtub. ■ **TIP→For a much lower rate you can get a tiny but well-kept room—and save for a French Laundry meal instead.** **Pros:** smallest rooms are some of the most affordable in town; free bike rental, refrigerator stocked with free soda. **Cons:** breakfast room can be crowded at peak times, bedding could be nicer. ✉*6529 Yount St.* ☎*800/788–0369* ⊕*www.maisonfleurienapa.com* *13 rooms* *In-room: refrigerator (some), DVD (some), no TV (some), Wi-Fi. In-hotel: pool, bicycles, no-smoking rooms* ▭*AE, D, DC, MC, V* *CP.*

$$$$ ★ **Villagio Inn & Spa.** The luxury here is quiet and refined, not flashy. Stroll past the fountains and clusters of low buildings to reach the pool, where automated misters cool the sunbathers. Streamlined furnishings, subdued color schemes, and high ceilings enhance a sense of spaciousness in the guest rooms. Each room also has a fireplace and, beyond louvered doors, a balcony or patio. A brand-new spa, completed in 2008, has huge "spa suites" big enough for small groups, as well as individual treatment rooms, spread out over 13,000 square feet. Rates include afternoon tea, a bottle of wine, and a generous buffet breakfast—and as the hotel's near the town center, you'll be right next to all those outstanding restaurants. **Pros:** decadent buffet breakfast; no charge for hotel guests to use the spa facilities; steps away from Yountville's best restaurants. **Cons:** can be bustling with large groups; some exterior rooms get highway noise. ✉*6481 Washington St.* ☎*707/944–8877 or 800/351–1133* ⊕*www.villagio.com* *86 rooms, 26 suites* *In-room: refrigerator, DVD, Wi-Fi. In-hotel: room service, tennis courts, pool, spa, bicycles, laundry service, no-smoking rooms* ▭*AE, D, DC, MC, V* *CP.*

$$$$ **Vintage Inn.** Rooms in this lavish inn are housed in two-story villas scattered around a lush, landscaped 3½-acre property. French fabrics and plump upholstered chairs outfit spacious, airy guest rooms with vaulted beamed ceilings, all of which have a private patio or balcony, a fireplace, and a whirlpool tub in the bathroom. Some private patios have vineyard views. You're treated to a bottle of wine, a buffet breakfast, and afternoon tea and scones. **Pros:** spacious bathrooms

with spa tubs; lavish breakfast buffet; luscious bedding. **Cons:** some exterior rooms get highway noise; pool area is smaller than the one at its sister property, the Villagio Inn & Spa. ✉ *6541 Washington St.* ☎ *707/944–1112 or 800/351–1133* 🖷 *707/944–1617* 🌐 *www.vintageinn.com* *68 rooms, 12 suites* *In-room: refrigerator, DVD, Wi-Fi. In-hotel: room service, bar, tennis courts, pool, bicycles, laundry service, some pets allowed, no-smoking rooms* ▭ *AE, D, DC, MC, V* 🍽 *CP.*

> **WORD OF MOUTH**
>
> "If you end up [in] Napa this summer be sure to check the Web site for the Mondavi winery—they have a great summer concert series every year!" —abhodges

OAKVILLE

2 mi west of Yountville on Rte. 29.

There are three reasons to visit the town of Oakville: its grocery store, its scenic mountain road, and its magnificent, highly exclusive wineries.

The **Oakville Grocery** (✉ *7856 St. Helena Hwy./Rte. 29* ☎ *707/944–8802*), built in 1881 as a general store, carries a surprisingly wide range of unusual and chichi groceries and prepared foods despite its tiny size. Unbearable crowds pack the narrow aisles on weekends, but it's still a fine place to sit on a bench out front and sip an espresso between winery visits.

Along the mountain range that divides Napa and Sonoma, the **Oakville Grade** (✉ *West of Rte. 29*) is a twisting half-hour route with breathtaking views of both valleys. Although the surface of the road is good, it can be difficult to negotiate at night, and the continual curves mean that it's not ideal for those who suffer from motion sickness.

The combined venture of the late California winemaker Robert Mondavi and the late French baron Philippe de Rothschild, **Opus One** produces only one wine: a big, inky Bordeaux blend that was the first of Napa's ultra-premium wines, fetching unheard-of prices before it was overtaken by cult wines like Screaming Eagle. The winery's futuristic limestone-clad structure, built into the hillside, seems to be pushing itself out of the earth. Although the tour, which focuses on why it costs so much to produce this exceptional wine, can come off as a bit "stuffy" in the words of one Fodors.com reader, the facilities are undoubtedly impressive, with gilded mirrors, exotic orchids, and a large semicircular cellar modeled on the Château Mouton Rothschild winery in France. You can also taste the current vintage without the tour ($30), as long as you've called ahead for a reservation. ■ **TIP→Take your glass up to the rooftop terrace if you want to appreciate the views out over the vineyards.** ✉ *7900 St. Helena Hwy./Rte. 29* ☎ *707/944–9442* 🌐 *www.opusonewinery.com* *Tour $35* ⏲ *Daily 10–4; tasting and tour by appointment.*

The arch at the center of the sprawling Mission-style building at **Robert Mondavi** perfectly frames the lawn and the vineyard behind, inviting a stroll under the lovely arcades. If you've never been on a winery tour before, the comprehensive 70- to 90-minute tour, followed by a seated

Far Niente's wine cellars have a touch of ballroom elegance.

tasting, is a good way to learn about oenology, as well as the late Robert Mondavi's role in California wine making. You can also head straight for one of the two tasting rooms. Serious wine lovers should definitely consider springing for the $30 reserve room tasting, where you can enjoy four tastes of Mondavi's top-of-the-line wines, including both the current vintage and several previous vintages of the reserve cabernet that cemented the winery's reputation. Concerts, mostly jazz and R&B, take place in summer on the lawn; call ahead for tickets. ✉ *7801 St. Helena Hwy./Rte. 29* ☎ *888/766–6328* 🌐 *www.robertmondaviwinery.com* 🎟 *Tasting $15–$30, tour $25* ⏲ *Daily 10–5; tours daily on the hr 10–4 (sometimes more often in high season, depending on the demand).*

Fodor's Choice ★

Though the fee for the combined tour and tasting is one of the higher ones in the valley, **Far Niente** is especially worth visiting if you're tired of elbowing your way through crowded tasting rooms and are looking for a more personal experience. Here you're welcomed by name and treated to a glimpse of one of the most beautiful Napa properties. Small groups are shepherded through the historic 1885 stone winery, including some of the 41,000 square feet of caves, for a lesson on the labor-intensive method for making Far Niente's two wines, one cabernet blend and one chardonnay. (The latter is made in the Burgundian style, without undergoing malolactic fermentation, so it doesn't have that buttery taste that's characteristic of many California chards.) The next stop is the Carriage House, where you can see the founder's gleaming collection of classic race cars. The tour ends with a seated tasting of wines and cheeses, capped by a sip of the spectacular Dolce, a late-harvest dessert wine made by Far Niente's sister winery. ✉ *1 Acacia Dr.* ☎ *707/944–2861* 🌐 *www.farniente.com* 🎟 *$50* ⏲ *Tasting and tour by appointment.*

RUTHERFORD

1 mi northwest of Oakville on Rte. 29.

From a fast-moving car, Rutherford is a quick blur of vineyards and a rustic barn or two, but don't speed by this tiny hamlet. With its singular microclimate and soil, this is an important viticultural center, with more big-name wineries than you can shake a corkscrew at. Cabernet sauvignon is king here. The well-drained, loamy soil is ideal for those vines, and since this part of the valley gets plenty of sun, the grapes develop exceptionally intense flavors. The late, great winemaker André Tchelistcheff's claimed that "it takes Rutherford dust to grow great cabernet."

But it's not all grapevines here—you can switch your fruit focus to olives ★ at **Round Pond.** This small farm grows five varieties of Italian olives and three types of Spanish olives. Within an hour of being handpicked, the olives are crushed in the mill on the property to produce pungent, peppery oils that are later blended and sold. Call at least 24 hours in advance to arrange a tour of the mill followed by an informative tasting, during which you can sample several types of oil, both alone and with Round Pond's own red-wine vinegars and other tasty foods. **■TIP→If you can arrange to visit between mid-November and the end of December, you might be lucky enough to see the mill in action.** ✉*877 Rutherford Rd.* ☎*877/963–9364* 🌐*www.roundpond.com* *Tour $25* ⏲*Tour by appointment.*

It's the house *The Godfather* built. Filmmaker Francis Ford Coppola began his wine-making career in 1975, when he bought part of the historic, renowned Inglenook estate. He eventually reunited the original Inglenook land and snagged the ivy-covered 19th-century château to boot. In 2006 he renamed the property **Rubicon Estate,** intending to focus on his premium wines, including the namesake cabernet sauvignon–based blend. (The less-expensive wines are showcased at Coppola's second winery, Rosso & Bianco in Sonoma County's Geyserville, which is currently undergoing renovations.) A visit here starts at a cool $25, but this price tag is tied to smooth orchestration. The fee covers valet parking, a tour of the château and discussion of the estate's history, and a tasting in the opulent, high-ceiling tasting room. Greeters explain the other offerings with additional fees, such as food-and-wine pairings and more in-depth tours. ✉*1991 St. Helena Hwy./Rte. 29* ☎*707/963–9099* 🌐*www.rubiconestate.com* *$25* ⏲*Daily 10–5; call for tour times.*

Your instinct may be to enter the beautifully restored 1882 Queen Anne Victorian at **St. Supéry** looking for the tasting room; actually the wines are being poured in the building behind it, a bland, unappealing, office-like structure. But you'll likely forgive the atmospheric lapse once you taste their fine sauvignon blancs, merlots, and chardonnays, as well as a couple of unusual wines that are made primarily of either cabernet franc or petit verdot, grapes usually used for blending with cabernet sauvignon. An excellent, free self-guided tour also allows you a peek at the barrel and fermentation rooms, as well as a gallery of rotating art exhibits. At the "Smell-a-Vision" station you can test your ability to identify different smells that might be present in wine. ✉*8440 St.*

Frog's Leap's picturesque country charm extends all the way to the white picket fence.

Helena Hwy. S/Rte. 29 ☎*707/963–4507* ⊕*www.stsupery.com* *Tasting $15–$25* ⏲*Daily 10–5.*

The cabernet sauvignon produced at ivy-covered **Beaulieu Vineyard** is a benchmark of the Napa Valley. The legendary André Tchelistcheff, who helped define the California style of wine making, worked his magic here from 1938 until his death in 1973. This helps explain why Beaulieu's flagship Georges de Latour Private Reserve Cabernet Sauvignon still garners high marks from major wine publications. The zinfandels, merlots, and chardonnays being poured in the main tasting room are notably good. Still, it's worth paying the few extra dollars to taste that special cabernet in the more luxe, less crowded reserve tasting room. ✉*1960 St. Helena Hwy./Rte. 29* ☎*707/967–5200* ⊕*www.bvwines.com* *Tasting $15–$30, tour $35* ⏲*Daily 10–5; tour by appointment.*

Fodor's Choice ★ **Frog's Leap** is the perfect place for wine novices to begin their education. The owners, the Williams family, maintain a goofy sense of humor about wine that translates into an entertaining yet informative experience. You'll also find some very fine zinfandel, cabernet sauvignon, merlot, chardonnay, sauvignon blanc, and a rosé called, simply enough, "Pink." The organization prides itself on the sustainability of their operation, and the tour guides can tell you about their organic farming and solar power techniques. The winery includes a red barn built in 1884, an eco-friendly visitor center, and, naturally, a frog pond topped with lily pads. ✉*8815 Conn Creek Rd.* ☎*707/963–4704* ⊕*www.frogsleap.com* *Tasting and tour free* ⏲*Mon.–Sat. 10–4; tastings and tour by appointment.*

Caymus Vineyards is run by wine master Chuck Wagner, who started making wine on the property in 1972. His family, however, had been farming in the valley since 1906. Though they make a fine zinfandel and sauvignon blanc, cabernet is the winery's claim to fame, a ripe, powerful wine that's known for its consistently high quality. ■ **TIP→There's no tour and you have to reserve to taste, but it's still worth planning ahead to visit because the low-key seated tasting (limited to 10 guests) is a great opportunity to learn about the valley's cabernet artistry.** ✉ *8700 Conn Creek Rd.* ☎ *707/967–3010* 🌐 *www.caymus.com* *Tasting $25* ⏲ *Sales daily 10–4; tastings by appointment.*

Mumm Napa Valley is one of California's best-known sparkling-wine producers. But enjoying the bubbly from the light-filled tasting room or on the terrace overlooking a vineyard—available in either single flutes ($7–$15) or by the flight ($15–$25)—isn't the only reason to visit. There's also an excellent photography gallery with 30 Ansel Adams prints and rotating exhibits. You can even take that glass of wonderfully crisp Brut Rosé with you as wander. ✉ *8445 Silverado Trail* ☎ *707/967–7700* 🌐 *www.mummnapavalley.com* *Tasting $7–$25, tour free* ⏲ *Daily 10–5; tour daily on the hr 10–3.*

Rutherford Hill Winery is a merlot lover's paradise in a cabernet sauvignon world. When the winery's founders were deciding what grapes to plant, they discovered that the climate and soil conditions of their vineyards resembled those of Pomerol, a region of Bordeaux where merlot is king. The wine caves here are some of the most extensive of any California winery—nearly a mile of tunnels and passageways. You can get a glimpse of the tunnels and the 8,000 barrels inside on the tours, then cap your visit with a picnic under their oak, olive, or madrone trees. With views over the valley from a perch high on a hill, the picnic grounds are far more charming than many others in Napa, which tend to be rather close to busy thoroughfares. ✉ *200 Rutherford Hill Rd., east of Silverado Trail* ☎ *707/963–1871* 🌐 *www.rutherfordhill.com* *Tasting $15–$30, tour $20* ⏲ *Daily 10–5; tour Mon.–Thurs. at 11:30, 1:30, and 3:30, Fri.–Sun. at 11:30, 12:30, 1:30, 2:30, and 3:30.*

WHERE TO STAY

$$$$ ★ **Auberge du Soleil.** Taking a cue from the olive-tree-studded landscape, this renowned hotel cultivates a Mediterranean look. It's luxury as simplicity: earth-tone tile floors, heavy wood furniture, and terra-cotta colors. This spare style is backed with lavish amenities, though, such as plasma TVs, private terraces, and truly grand bathrooms, many with whirlpool tubs and extra-large showers with multiple shower heads. However, some fodors.com users suggest that at these prices—some of the highest in all the Wine Country—service could be better. The Auberge du Soleil restaurant has an impressive wine list and serves a Mediterranean-inflected menu that relies largely on local produce. Be sure to ask for a table on the terrace in fair weather. The bar serves less expensive fare until 10 or 11 PM nightly. **Pros:** stunning views over the valley; spectacular pool and spa areas; the most expensive suites are fit for a superstar. **Cons:** prices are stratospheric; rooms in the main house get some noise from the bar and restaurant. ✉ *180 Rutherford Hill Rd., off Silverado Trail north of Rte. 128* ☎ *707/963–1211 or 800/348–5406*

www.aubergedusoleil.com 34 rooms, 18 suites In-room: safe, refrigerator, DVD, Wi-Fi. In-hotel: 2 restaurants, room service, bar, tennis court, pool, gym, spa, no-smoking rooms AE, D, DC, MC, V.

ST. HELENA

2 mi northwest of Oakville on Rte. 29.

Downtown St. Helena is a microcosm of the good life. Sycamore trees arch over Main Street (Route 29), a funnel of outstanding restaurants and tempting boutiques. At the north end of town looms the hulking stone building of the Culinary Institute of America. Weathered stone and brick buildings from the late 1800s give off that gratifying whiff of history.

By the time pioneer winemaker Charles Krug planted grapes in St. Helena around 1860, quite a few vineyards already existed in the area. Today the town is hemmed in by wineries, and you could easily spend days visiting vintners within a few miles. If you're looking for a break from sipping, drive 3 mi north of town, off Highway 29, to visit the **Bale Grist Mill State Historic Park,** where the 19th-century mill buildings are open daily and the water mill is in operation on weekends. Hiking trails lead from the mill through parkland.

6

Arguably the most beautiful winery in Napa Valley, the 1876 **Beringer Vineyards** is also the oldest continuously operating property. In 1884 Frederick and Jacob Beringer built the Rhine House Mansion to serve as Frederick's family home. Today it serves as the reserve tasting room, where you can sample four wines in a setting of Belgian art-nouveau hand-carved oak and walnut furniture and stained-glass windows, choosing from among such wines as a limited-release chardonnay, a few big but very drinkable cabernets, and a luscious white dessert wine named Nightingale. Another, less expensive tasting takes place in the less atmospheric but also historic original stone winery. Because of its big reputation and lovely grounds, the winery gets crowded in high season. **■ TIP→ If you're looking for an undiscovered gem, pass this one by, but first-time visitors to the valley will learn a lot about the history of wine making in the region on the introductory tour**. Longer tours, which might pass through a demonstration vineyard or end with a seated tasting in the wine-aging tunnels, are also offered a few times a day. *2000 Main St./Rte. 29 707/963–4812 www.beringer.com Tasting $10–$25, tours $15–$40 May 30–Oct. 23, daily 10–6; Oct. 24–May 29, daily 10–5; call for tour times.*

The first winery founded in the Napa Valley, **Charles Krug Winery,** opened in 1861 when Count Haraszthy lent Krug a small cider press. Today the Peter Mondavi family runs it. At this writing, tours have been suspended indefinitely because a major earthquake retrofit project is in the works, but you can still come for tastings. Though they are best known for their lush red Bordeaux blends, their zinfandel is also good—or go for something unusual with their New Zealand–style sauvignon blanc. Its zingy flavor of citrus and tropical fruit is rare in wines from this area. *2800 N. Main St. 707/963–5057 www.charleskrug.com Tasting $10–$20 Daily 10:30–5.*

The West Coast headquarters of the **Culinary Institute of America,** the country's leading school for chefs, are in the **Greystone Winery,** a national historic landmark and an imposingly large stone building. The campus consists of 30 acres of herb and vegetable gardens and a Mediterranean-inspired restaurant, which is open to the public. Also on the property is a well-stocked culinary store that tempts aspiring chefs with gleaming gadgets. One-hour cooking demonstrations take place two or three times a day Friday through Monday; call or check out their Web site for times and to reserve a spot. (You can also have dinner at the Wine Spectator Greystone restaurant. ⇨ *See details under Where to Eat and Stay.*) *⊠ 2555 Main St. ☎ 707/967–1100 🌐 www.ciachef.edu 🎟 Free, demonstrations $15 ⏲ Restaurant Sun.–Thurs. 11:30–9, Fri. and Sat. 11:30–10; store and museum daily 10–6.*

> **WORD OF MOUTH**
>
> "If your touring is limited to Highway 29 in Napa, everything will seem very busy and crowded, [but] if you take the time and trouble to research some alternatives and get off the beaten path, you will have some amazing experiences in Napa." —napamatt

WHERE TO EAT

$$$ SEAFOOD ★ ✕ **Go Fish.** Prolific restaurateur Cindy Pawlcyn and superstar chef Victor Scargle are the big names behind one of the few restaurants in the Wine Country to specialize in seafood. You can either sit at the long marble bar and watch the chefs whip up inventive sushi rolls and raw bar bites, or head into the dining room to study the mouthwatering menu. The large, lively space works a modern-chic look, with stainless-steel lamps and comfortable banquettes. You might try olive oil–poached haddock, clam chowder, or a rich crab-cake sandwich served on a brioche bun. *⊠ 641 Main St. ☎ 707/963–0700 ▭ AE, D, DC, MC, V.*

$$ AMERICAN ✕ **Market.** The fieldstone walls and friendly service would set a homey mood here even if the menu didn't present comfort food's greatest hits, from fried chicken with mashed potatoes to the signature macaroni and cheese. Locals know that it's a casual spot to socialize over oysters on the half shell at the full bar or a leisurely dinner of a slow-braised lamb shanks. *⊠ 1347 Main St. ☎ 707/963–3799 ▭ AE, MC, V.*

$$$$ AMERICAN ✕ **Martini House.** Beautiful and boisterous, St. Helena's most stylish restaurant fills a converted 1923 Craftsman-style home, where earthy colors are made even warmer by the glow of three fireplaces. Woodsy ingredients such as chanterelles or juniper berries might accompany braised veal sweetbreads or a hearty grilled loin of venison. Inventive salads and delicate desserts such as the blood-orange sorbet demonstrate chef-owner Todd Humphries' range. In warm weather, angle for a table on the patio, where lights sparkle in the trees. If you don't have a reservation, ask for a seat at the bar downstairs, where you can order from either the much less expensive bar menu or the full menu. *⊠ 1245 Spring St. ☎ 707/963–2233 ▭ AE, D, DC, MC, V ⏲ No lunch Mon.–Thurs.*

¢ AMERICAN ★ ✕ **Taylor's Automatic Refresher.** A slick 1950s-style outdoor hamburger stand goes upscale at this hugely popular spot, where locals are willing to brave long lines to order juicy burgers, root-beer floats, and garlic fries. There are also plenty of choices you wouldn't have found 50 years ago, such as the ahi tuna burger and chicken club with pesto mayo. Arrive early or late for lunch, or all the shaded picnic tables on the lawn might be filled with happy throngs. Lines are usually shorter at the Taylor's in downtown Napa's Oxbow Public Market, which opened in 2008. ⊠*933 Main St.* ☎*707/963–3486* ▭*AE, MC, V.*

$$$$ MEDITERRANEAN Fodor'sChoice ★ **Terra.** The look may be old-school romance, with candlelit tables in an 1884 fieldstone building, but the cooking is deliciously of the moment. Chef Hiro Sone tricks out Italian and southern French cuisine with unexpected twists, in dishes such as sweetbreads with braised endive, burdock, and black truffle sauce. A few, like the sake-marinated black cod in a shiso broth, draw on Sone's Japanese background. Inventive desserts, courtesy of Sone's wife, Lissa Doumani, might include a maple-sugar crème brûlée served in a baked apple. Servers gracefully and unobtrusively attend to every dropped fork or half-full water glass; they're head and shoulders above the enthusiastic but inexpert staff you can find at many other local restaurants. ⊠*1345 Railroad Ave.* ☎*707/963–8931* *Reservations essential* ▭*AE, DC, MC, V* *Closed Tues. and 1st 2 wks in Jan. No lunch.*

$$$ MEDITERRANEAN **Wine Spectator Greystone Restaurant.** The Culinary Institute of America runs this place in the handsome old Christian Brothers Winery. Century-old stone walls house a spacious restaurant that bustles at both lunch and dinner, with several cooking stations in full view. On busy nights you might find the hard-at-work chefs (who, incidentally, are full-fledged chefs rather than mere students) more entertaining than your dinner partner. But on fair days the tables on the terrace, shaded by red umbrellas, are away from the action but equally appealing. The menu has a Mediterranean spirit and emphasizes locally grown produce. Typical main courses include pan-seared scallops with a white-bean puree and winter-vegetable potpie. ⊠*2555 Main St.* ☎*707/967–1010* ▭*AE, D, DC, MC, V.*

6

WHERE TO STAY

¢–$ **El Bonita Motel.** Only in St. Helena would a basic room in a roadside motel cost around $200 a night in high season. Still, for budget-minded travelers the tidy rooms here are pleasant enough, and the landscaped grounds and picnic tables elevate the property over similar places. There's even a small sauna next to the hot tub and swimming pool, which is heated year-round. **TIP→Family-friendly pluses include roll-away beds and cribs for a modest charge. Its location right on Route 29 makes it convenient, but light sleepers should ask for rooms farthest from the road. Pros:** cheerful rooms; hot tub; microwaves and mini-refrigerators. **Cons:** road noise is a problem in some rooms. ⊠*195 Main St./Rte. 29* ☎*707/963–3216 or 800/541–3284* *707/963–8838* *www.elbonita.com* *38 rooms, 4 suites* *In-room: kitchen, refrigerator, Wi-Fi. In-hotel: pool, Internet terminal, some pets allowed, no-smoking rooms* ▭*AE, D, DC, MC, V* *CP.*

$$$$ Fodor'sChoice ★ **Meadowood Resort.** Everything at Meadowood seems to run seamlessly, starting with the gatehouse staff who alert the front desk to arrivals, so that a receptionist is ready for each guest. A rambling lodge and several bungalows are scattered across the sprawling property. Guest

rooms have views over these wooded grounds from expansive windows. The supremely comfortable beds defy you to get up and pursue the golf, tennis, hiking, or other activities on offer. In recent years the elegant but unstuffy dining room has won rave reviews, becoming a destination restaurant for its splurge dishes (think lobster and squab salad with zinfandel-onion marmalade) and expert service. **Pros:** site of one of Napa's best restaurants; lovely hiking trail on the property; serene atmosphere. **Cons:** very expensive; a five- to 10-minute drive from the restaurants and shops of downtown St. Helena. ✉ *900 Meadowood La.* ☎ *707/963–3646 or 800/458–8080* 📠 *707/963–5863* 🌐 *www.meadowood.com* *40 rooms, 45 suites* *In-room: refrigerator, DVD, Wi-Fi. In-hotel: 2 restaurants, room service, bar, golf course, tennis courts, pools, gym, children's programs (ages 6–12), no-smoking rooms* 💳 *AE, D, DC, MC, V.*

$$$–$$$$ **Wine Country Inn.** A pastoral landscape of hills surrounds this peaceful New England–style retreat. Rooms are comfortably done with homey furniture like four-poster beds topped with quilts, and many have a wood-burning or gas fireplace, a large jetted tub, or a patio or balcony overlooking the vineyards. A hearty breakfast is served buffet-style in the sun-splashed common room, and wine and appetizers are available in the afternoon next to the wood-burning cast-iron stove. Though it's not the most stylish lodging in the area, the thoughtful staff and the vineyard views from several rooms encourage many people to return year after year. **Pros:** free shuttle to selected restaurants (reserve early); lovely grounds; swimming pool is heated year-round. **Cons:** some rooms let in noise from neighboring rooms; some rooms could use updating. ✉ *1152 Lodi La., east of Rte. 29* ☎ *707/963–7077* 📠 *707/963–9018* 🌐 *www.winecountryinn.com* *24 rooms, 5 suites* *In-room: refrigerator (some), no TV, Wi-Fi. In-hotel: pool,no-smoking rooms* 💳 *MC, V* 🍽 *BP.*

SHOPPING

Dean & Deluca (✉ *607 St. Helena Hwy. S/Rte. 29* ☎ *707/967–9980*), a branch of the famous Manhattan store, is crammed with everything you need in the kitchen—including terrific produce and deli items—as well as a huge wine selection. Many of the cheeses sold here are produced locally. The airy **I. Wolk Gallery** (✉ *1354 Main St.* ☎ *707/963–8800*) has works by established and emerging American artists—everything from abstract and contemporary realist paintings to high-quality works on paper and sculpture. **Footcandy** (✉ *1239 Main St.* ☎ *707/963–2040*) will thrill foot fetishists with its provocative displays of precarious stilettos and high-heeled boots. The **Spice Islands Marketplace** (✉ *Culinary Institute of America, 2555 Main St.* ☎ *888/424–2433*) is the place to shop for all things related to preparing and cooking food, from cookbooks to copper bowls. Fine French table linens, custom-embroidered aprons, and other high-quality housewares fill **Jan de Luz** (✉ *1219 Main St.* ☎ *707/963–1550*). Chocolates handmade on the premises are displayed like miniature works of art at **Woodhouse Chocolate** (✉ *1367 Main St.* ☎ *707/963–8413*).

CALISTOGA

3 mi northwest of St. Helena on Rte. 29.

With false-fronted "Old West"–style shops, 19th-century hotels, and unpretentious cafés lining Lincoln Avenue, the town's main drag, Calistoga has a slightly rough-and-tumble feel that's unique in the Napa Valley. It comes across as down-to-earth, less showy or touristy than some of the polished towns to the south. And it's easier to find a bargain here, making it a handy home base for exploring the surrounding vineyards and backroads.

Ironically, Calistoga was developed as a swell, tourist-oriented getaway. In 1859 maverick entrepreneur Sam Brannan founded the Calistoga Hot Springs Resort, intending to use the area's natural hot springs as the basis of "the Saratoga of California." (He reputedly tripped up the pronunciation of the phrase at a formal banquet—it came out "Calistoga"—and the name stuck.) Brannan's gamble didn't pay off as he'd hoped, but the hotels and bathhouses won a local following. The slightly scruffy spas on the edges of town are still going strong, as visitors dip in the mud baths or indulge in massages.

6

Indian Springs has welcomed clients to mud baths, mineral pools, and steam rooms, all supplied with mineral water from its three geysers, since 1871. You can choose from the various spa treatments and volcanic-ash mud baths, or soak in the toasty Olympic-size mineral-water pool. If you're planning several sessions, you might want to overnight in one of the lodge rooms or bungalows ($–$$). Reservations are recommended for spa treatments. ✉*1712 Lincoln Ave./Rte. 29* ☎*707/942–4913* 🌐*www.indianspringscalistoga.com* ⏲*Daily 9–8.*

Fodor's Choice ★ **Schramsberg,** hidden on the hillside near Route 29, is one of Napa's oldest wineries; it produces a variety of bubblies made using the traditional *méthode champenoise* process (which means, among other things, that the bubbly undergoes a second fermentation in the bottle before the bottles are "riddled," or turned every few days over a period of weeks, to nudge the sediment into the neck of the bottle). If you want to taste, you must tour first, but what a tour: in addition to getting a glimpse of the winery's historic architecture, you get to tour the cellars dug in the late 19th century by Chinese laborers, where a mind-boggling 2.5 million bottles are stacked in gravity-defying configurations. The tour fee includes generous pours of four very different sparkling wines, as well as one still wine. ✉*1400 Schramsberg Rd.* ☎*707/942–4558* 🌐*www.schramsberg.com* 🎫*Tasting and tour $35* ⏲*Tastings and tours by appointment.*

The tasting room at **Dutch Henry Winery** isn't much more than a nook in the barrel room between towering American and French oak barrels full of their excellent cabernet sauvignon, merlot, and zinfandel. (Their chardonnay and a charming rosé also have fervent fans.) The winery produces about 6,000 cases annually—sold mostly on-site and through their wine club—which explains the simple facilities, but the wines are truly top-notch. Sometimes the tasting-room staffers can be playfully crotchety, but the absence of crowds and casual style make it a welcome change of pace from some of the winery's overly-serious neigh-

Floor-to-ceiling stacked bottles are no exaggeration in Schramsberg's cellars.

bors. ✉4310 Silverado Trail ☎707/942–5771 🌐www.dutchhenry.com 🎟Tasting $10 ⏲Daily 10–5.

The approach to **Sterling Vineyards**, perched on a hilltop about a mile south of Calistoga, is the most spectacular in the valley. Instead of driving up to their tasting room, you board an aerial tramway to reach the pristine, white buildings reminiscent the Greek islands (the winery's founder once lived on Mykonos). The views from the winery are superb, although the quality of the wines doesn't necessarily match the vista. ✉*1111 Dunaweal La., east of Rte. 29* ☎*707/942–3300* 🌐*www.sterlingvineyards.com* 🎟*$20–$25, including tramway, self-guided tour, and tasting* ⏲*Daily 10–4:30.*

★ Designed by postmodern architect Michael Graves, the **Clos Pegase** winery is a one-of-a-kind "temple to wine and art" packed with unusual art objects from the collection of owner and publishing entrepreneur Jan Shrem. After tasting the wines, which include a bright sauvignon blanc, fruity chardonnays, and mellow pinot noir, merlot, and cabernet (they're made in a fairly soft, approachable style and meant to be drunk somewhat young), be sure to check out the surrealist paintings near the main tasting room, which include a Jean Dubeffet painting you may have seen on one of their labels. Better yet, bring a picnic and have lunch in the courtyard, where a curvaceous Henry Moore sculpture is one of about two dozen works of art. ✉*1060 Dunaweal La., east of Rte. 29* ☎*707/942–4981* 🌐*www.clospegase.com* 🎟*Tasting $10, tour free* ⏲*Daily 10:30–5; tour daily at 11:30 and 2.*

Château Montelena is an architectural mash-up. The 19th-century, vine-covered building suggests France, but the lake below it is surrounded by Chinese-inspired gardens and dotted with islands topped by Chinese pavilions. For the best view of the quirky combination, take the pathway down to the lake. From here the château, with its little turrets and ornamental crenellations, looks like it's straight out of a fairy tale. In the tasting room, make a beeline for the bright chardonnay and the estate-grown cabernet sauvignon. ✉ *1429 Tubbs La.* ☎ *707/942–5105* 🌐 *www.montelena.com* 🎟 *Tasting $15–$40* 🕒 *Daily 9:30–4.*

Robert Louis Stevenson State Park encompasses the summit of **Mount St. Helena.** It was here, in the summer of 1880, in an abandoned bunkhouse of the Silverado Mine, that Stevenson and his bride, Fanny Osbourne, spent their honeymoon. This stay inspired the writer's travel memoir *The Silverado Squatters,* and Spyglass Hill in *Treasure Island* is thought to be a portrait of Mount St. Helena. The park's approximately 3,600 acres are mostly undeveloped except for a fire trail leading to the site of the bunkhouse—which is marked with a marble tablet—and to the summit beyond. ■ **TIP→If you're planning on attempting the hike to the top, bring plenty of water and dress appropriately: the trail is steep and lacks shade in spots, but the summit is often cool and breezy.** ✉ *Rte. 29, 7 mi north of Calistoga* ☎ *707/942–4575* 🌐 *www.parks.ca.gov* 🎟 *Free* 🕒 *Daily sunrise–sunset.*

6

★ Possibly the most astounding sight in Napa Valley is your first glimpse of the **Castello di Amorosa,** which looks for all the world like a medieval castle, complete with drawbridge and moat, a chapel, stables, and secret passageways. The brainchild of Daryl Sattui, who also owns several properties in Tuscany, it shows Sattui's passion for Italy and for medieval architecture down to the last obsessive detail: some of the 107 rooms contain replicas of 13th-century frescoes, and the dungeon has an actual iron maiden torture device from Nuremberg, Germany. Opened in 2007 after 14 years of construction, the winery immediately started attracting large crowds lured by the astonishing architecture (you must pay for a tour to get beyond the tasting room). The Italian-style wines, however, available at the winery only, are excellent as well. ■ **TIP→Prices for tastings and tours are $5 to $15 higher on Fridays and weekends (a rarity in the Wine Country), so schedule this stop for a weekday, if possible.** ✉ *4045 North St., Helena Hwy.* ☎ *707/967–6272* 🌐 *www.castellodiamorosa.com* 🎟 *Tasting $10–$25, tour $25–$50* 🕒 *Feb. 16–Nov., daily 9:30–6; Dec.–Feb. 15, daily 9:30–5; tours by appointment.*

The **Petrified Forest** contains the remains of the volcanic eruptions of Mount St. Helena 3.4 million years ago. The force of the explosion uprooted the gigantic redwoods, covered them with volcanic ash, and infiltrated the trees with silica and minerals, causing petrifaction. The 20-minute walk around the property, following signs explaining the process of petrifaction, is a good way to stretch your legs after a morning in the car, though the site isn't worth a long detour. For the best experience, call ahead to reserve a spot on a meadow hike, which leads through the woodland until you have a view of Mount St. Helena. ✉ *4100 Petrified Forest Rd., 5 mi west of Calistoga* ☎ *707/942–6667* 🌐 *www.petrifiedforest.org* 🎟 *$6* 🕒 *Memorial Day–Labor Day, daily 9–7; Labor Day–Memorial Day, daily 9–5.*

WHERE TO EAT

$$$ AMERICAN ✕**All Seasons Bistro.** Bistro cuisine takes a California spin in this sun-filled space, where tables topped with flowers sit upon a black-and-white checkerboard floor. The seasonal menu might include a spinach salad with bacon and a mustard vinaigrette, or seared Sonoma duck breast with a huckleberry-thyme glaze. Homey desserts include crème brûlée and rum raisin bread pudding. You can order reasonably priced wines from their extensive list, or buy a bottle at the attached wineshop and have it poured at your table. Attentive service contributes to the welcoming atmosphere. ✉*1400 Lincoln Ave.* ☎*707/942–9111* ▭*AE, D, MC, V* ⊙*Closed Mon.; no lunch Tues.–Thurs.*

$$ ITALIAN ✕**Bar Vino.** In 2006 Calistoga got a little more urbane with the addition of this Italian-inflected wine bar in the Mount View Hotel. With red-leather seats, stainless-steel light fixtures, and a marble bar indoors and café seating out, it's a stylish, modern spot for a glass of wine, with many from small producers you probably haven't heard of. Small plates that could come have straight from Tuscany—olives, mozzarella with an artichoke tapenade, risotto croquettes, a selection of *salumi*—are great for sharing. A handful of well-executed large plates, like the pappardelle with Italian sausage and sun-dried tomatoes and cumin-seared tuna, round out the menu. ✉*1457 Lincoln Ave.* ☎*707/942–9900* ▭*AE, MC, V* ⊙*No lunch.*

$$$ FRENCH ✕**Calistoga Inn Restaurant and Brewery.** On pleasant days this riverside restaurant and its sprawling, tree-shaded patio come into their own. At lunchtime, casual plates like a smoked turkey and Brie sandwich or a Chinese chicken salad are light enough to leave some energy for an afternoon of wine tasting. And at night, when there's often live music played on the patio during the warm months, you'll find heartier dishes such as flatiron steak or grilled Sonoma duck breast with a mushroom marsala sauce. Service can be a bit lackadaisical, so order one of the house-made brews and enjoy the atmosphere while you're waiting. ✉*1250 Lincoln Ave.* ☎*707/942–4101* ▭*AE, MC, V.*

WHERE TO STAY

¢–$ **Brannan Cottage Inn.** The pristine Victorian cottage with lacy white fretwork, large windows, and a shady porch is the only one of Sam Brannan's 1860 resort cottages still standing on its original site. Each room has individual touches such as a four-poster bed, a claw-foot tub, or a velvet settee. **Pros:** innkeepers go the extra mile; most rooms have fireplaces. **Cons:** owners' dog may be a problem for those with allergies; rooms look a bit worn. ✉*109 Wapoo Ave.* ☎*707/942–4200* 🌐*www.brannancottageinn.com* *6 rooms* *In-room: no phone, refrigerator, no TV (some), Wi-Fi. In-hotel: some pets allowed, no-smoking rooms* ▭*AE, MC, V* *BP.*

$$$$ ★ **Calistoga Ranch.** A sister property of Auberge du Soleil in Rutherford, this posh resort shares a similar wide-open feel. Spacious cedar-shingle bungalows throughout the wooded property have outdoor living areas, and even the restaurant, spa, and reception area have outdoor seating areas and fireplaces. Though the service is friendly and the lodges are luxurious, with sybaritic outdoor showers in every room, the overall result still has a casual ranchlike feel rather than the refined sheen

All it needs is a fair maiden: Castello di Amorosa's re-created castle.

of some similarly priced places. **Pros:** romantic outdoor showers for two; feels like an elegant country retreat; excellent spa. **Cons:** very expensive; innovative indoor/outdoor organization works better in fair weather than in rain or cold. ✉*580 Lommel Rd.* ☎*707/254–2800 or 800/942–4220* 🌐*www.calistogaranch.com* *46 rooms* *In-room: safe, refrigerator, DVD, Internet, Wi-Fi. In-hotel: restaurant, room service, bar, pool, gym, spa, bicycles, some pets allowed, no-smoking rooms* *AE, D, MC, V.*

$$$ **Cottage Grove Inn.** A long driveway lined with 16 freestanding cottages, each shaded by elm trees, looks a bit like Main Street USA, but inside the skylit buildings have all the perks you could want for a romantic weekend away. Each has overstuffed chairs in front of a wood-burning fireplace, flat-panel TVs, and an extra-deep two-person whirlpool tub. Each cottage also has its own variation on the overall comfy-rustic look, with telltale names like Fly Fishing Cottage and Provence. Spas and restaurants are within walking distance. Rates include afternoon wine and cheese. **Pros:** wicker chairs on each shady porch; freestanding cottages offer lots of privacy; bathtubs so big you could swim in them. **Cons:** no pool; decor may be a bit frumpy for some. ✉*1711 Lincoln Ave.* ☎*707/942–8400 or 800/799–2284* 🌐*www.cottagegrove.com* *16 rooms* *In-room: safe, refrigerator, DVD, Internet, Wi-Fi. In-hotel: bicycles, Internet, no-smoking rooms* *AE, D, DC, MC, V* *CP.*

$–$$ ★ **Indian Springs.** This old-time spa has welcomed clients to its mud baths, mineral pool, and steam room—all supplied with mineral water from its four geysers—since 1871. Rooms in the recently renovated lodge, though quite small, are beautifully done up a simple Zen style,

CLOSE UP

Best Wine Country Spas

Wine Country spas have a natural edge on the treatments you can find elsewhere in the country. First, there are the natural mud baths and mineral water sources, concentrated particularly in northern Napa Valley's Calistoga. Admittedly, being submerged in a thick, muddy paste isn't for everyone. A mud bath sometimes smells sulfurous or peaty, and it takes a minute to get used to the intense heat as you submerge yourself. Once you've lounged in it for several minutes, though, you may never want to leave, especially if an attendant has cooled your forehead with an icy wash cloth. Second, there are all those grapes, which are increasingly incorporated into treatments and products like grape-seed scrubs. Below are some of the best spas of the bunch.

■ **Dr. Wilkinson's.** The oldest spa in Calistoga. Although it's perhaps the least chic of the bunch, it's still well loved for its reasonable prices and its friendly, unpretentious vibe. Their mud baths are a mix of volcanic ash and peat moss. ✉ *1507 Lincoln Ave., Calistoga* ☎ *707/942–4102* 🌐 *www.drwilkinson.com.*

■ **Fairmont Sonoma Mission Inn & Spa.** The largest sybaritic destination in the Wine Country. The vast complex covers every amenity you could want in a spa, including several pools and Jacuzzis fed by local thermal mineral springs. ✉ *100 Boyes Blvd./Rte. 12, Boyes Hot Springs* ☎ *707/938–9000* 🌐 *www.fairmont.com/sonoma.*

■ **Health Spa Napa Valley.** Focuses on health and wellness, with personal trainers and an outdoor pool in addition to the usual spa fare. The grape-seed mud wrap, during which you're slathered with mud mixed with crushed Napa Valley grape seeds, is a more decadent alternative to a mud bath. ✉ *1030 Main St., St. Helena* ☎ *707/967–8800* 🌐 *www.napavalleyspa.com.*

■ **Kenwood Inn & Spa.** The prettiest spa setting in the Wine Country, thanks to the vineyards across the road and the Mediterranean style of the inn. It specializes in Caudalie's "vinotherapie" treatments, with massages, scrubs, and facials based on grape extracts. ✉ *10400 Sonoma Hwy./Rte. 12, Kenwood* ☎ *707/833–1293* 🌐 *www.kenwoodinn.com.*

■ **The Spa Hotel Healdsburg.** Larger hotel spas have more bells and whistles, but this intimate spot provides plush Frette robes, an outdoor Jacuzzi, and soothing minimalist decor, making it a tranquil choice for massages, body wraps, facials, and hand and foot treatments. ✉ *327 Healdsburg Ave., Healdsburg* ☎ *707/433–4747* 🌐 *www.hotelhealdsburg.com.*

■ **Spa at Villagio.** Opened in 2008, this 13,000-square-foot spa with fieldstone walls and a Mediterranean theme has all the latest gadgets, including men's and women's outdoor hot tubs and showers with an extravagant number of shower heads. Huge spa suites—complete with flat-panel TV screens and wet bars—are perfect for couples and groups. ✉ *6481 Washington St., Yountville* ☎ *707/948–5050.*

with Asian-inspired furnishings, Frette linens on the bed, and flat-panel televisions. The cottages dotted around the property have anything from a small kitchenette to a fully equipped kitchen, encouraging longer stays (book well in advance for these). A boccie ball court, shuffleboard, and croquet lawn outside your door provide entertainment when you're not indulging in various spa treatments and volcanic-ash mud baths, or soaking in the toasty Olympic-size mineral-water pool. **Pros:** lovely grounds with outdoor seating areas; stylish for the price; enormous mineral pool. **Cons:** lodge rooms are small; oddly uncomfortable pillows. ✉ *1712 Lincoln Ave.* ☎ *707/942–4913* 🌐 *www.indianspringscalistoga.com* *24 rooms, 17 suites* *In-room: no phone, Wi-Fi, kitchen (some), refrigerator (some). In-hotel: tennis court, pool, spa, no-smoking rooms* *D, MC, V.*

$–$$ Fodor'sChoice ★ **Meadowlark Country House.** Twenty hillside acres just north of downtown Calistoga surround this decidedly laid-back and sophisticated inn that's particularly popular with gay and lesbian travelers but welcoming to all. Each of the rooms in the main house and guest wing has its own charms: one has a deep whirlpool tub looking onto a green hillside, and others have a deck with a view of the mountains. Many rooms have fireplaces, and most have whirlpool tubs large enough for two. A spacious two-story guesthouse opens directly onto the clothing-optional pool, hot tub, and sauna area (open to all guests). Fodors.com readers point out that "Kurt and Richard are delightful, helpful hosts." **Pros:** sauna next to the pool and hot tub; welcoming vibe attracts diverse guests; some of the most gracious innkeepers in Napa. **Cons:** clothing-optional pool policy isn't for everyone. ✉ *601 Petrified Forest Rd.* ☎ *707/942–5651 or 800/942–5651* 🌐 *www.meadowlarkinn.com* *5 rooms, 5 suites* *In-room: no phone, kitchen (some), refrigerator (some), DVD (some), Wi-Fi. In-hotel: pool, some pets allowed, no-smoking rooms* *AE, MC, V* *BP.*

$$$$ **Solage.** A resort for sociable sorts who like to lounge at the bar overlooking the large pool or play a game of boccie after lunch at the indoor-outdoor restaurant, this Calistoga newcomer sprawls over 22 acres. The cottages don't look particularly luxurious from the outside, but inside they flaunt a Napa-Valley-barn-meets-San-Francisco-loft aesthetic, with high ceilings, polished concrete floors, recycled walnut furniture, and all-natural fabrics in soothing muted colors. Sports and fitness are a high priority here: in addition to a large, well-equipped spa and "mud bar" where you can indulge in decadent variation on the mud bath, there's a packed schedule of fitness activities, with everything from yoga to Pilates to biking and hiking excursions. **TIP→** If you want to be in the middle of the action, ask for a room facing the pool. For more seclusion, ask for one of the quieter rooms near the oak grove. **Pros:** great service; bike cruisers parked at every cottage for guests' use; separate pools for kids and adults. **Cons:** new landscaping looks a little bleak; some rooms don't have tubs. ✉ *755 Silverado Trail* ☎ *866/942–7442* 🌐 *www.solagecalistoga.com* *89 rooms* *In-room: safe, refrigerator, DVD, Wi-Fi. In-hotel: restaurant, room service, bar, pools, gym, spa, bicycles, laundry service, no-smoking rooms* *AE, D, DC, MC, V.*

6

SPORTS AND THE OUTDOORS

Calistoga Bikeshop (✉ *1318 Lincoln Ave.* ☎ *866/942–2453*) rents bicycles, including tandem bikes. Their Calistoga Cool Wine Tour package includes free tastings at a number of small wineries in the area. Best of all, they'll pick up any wine you purchase along the way if you've bought more than will fit in the handy bottle carrier on your bike.

SHOPPING

Enoteca Wine Shop (✉ *1348B Lincoln Ave.* ☎ *707/942–1117*), on Calistoga's main drag, conveniently displays almost all of its wines with extensive tasting notes, which makes it easier to choose from among their unusually fine collection, which includes both hard-to-find bottles from Napa and Sonoma and many French wines. Locally handcrafted beeswax candles are for sale at **Hurd Beeswax Candles** (✉ *1255 Lincoln Ave.* ☎ *707/963–7211*). Unusual tapers twisted into spiral shapes are a specialty. The **Wine Garage** (✉ *1020 Hwy. 29* ☎ *707/942–5332*) is the stop for bargain hunters, since each of their bottles goes for $25 or less. It's a great way to discover the work of smaller wineries producing undervalued wines, and the unusually helpful staffers are happy to share information on all the wines they stock.

THE SONOMA VALLEY

Although the Sonoma Valley may not have quite the cachet of the neighboring Napa Valley, wineries here entice with their unpretentious attitude and smaller crowds. The Napa-style glitzy tasting rooms with enormous gift shops and high tasting fees are the exception here. Sonoma's landscape seduces, too, its roads gently climbing and descending on their way to wineries hidden from the road by trees.

The scenic valley, bounded by the Mayacamas Mountains on the east and Sonoma Mountain on the west, extends north from San Pablo Bay nearly 20 mi to the eastern outskirts of Santa Rosa. The varied terrain, soils, and climate (cooler in the south because of the bay influence and hotter toward the north) allow grape growers to raise cool-weather varietals such as chardonnay and pinot noir as well as merlot, cabernet sauvignon, and other heat-seeking vines. The valley is home to dozens of wineries, many of them on or near Route 12, a California Scenic Highway that runs the length of the valley.

ESSENTIALS

Contacts **Sonoma County Tourism Bureau** (✉ *420 Aviation Blvd., Suite 106, Santa Rosa* ☎ *707/539–7282 or 800/576–6662* 🌐 *www.sonomacounty.com*). **Sonoma Valley Visitors Bureau** (✉ *453 1st St. E, Sonoma* ☎ *707/996–1090* 🌐 *www.sonomavalley.com*).

SONOMA

14 mi west of Napa on Rte. 12; 45 mi from San Francisco, north on U.S. 101, east on Rte. 37, and north on Rte. 121/12.

Founded in the early 1800s, Sonoma is the oldest town in the Wine Country, and one of the few where you can find some attractions not related to food and wine. The central **Sonoma Plaza** dates back to the mission era; surrounding it are 19th-century adobes, atmospheric hotels, and the swooping marquee of the 1930s Sebastiani Theatre. On summer days the plaza is a hive of activity, with children blowing off steam in the playground while their folks stock up on picnic supplies and browse the boutiques surrounding the square.

On your way into town from the south, you pass through the Carneros wine district, which straddles the southern sections of Sonoma and Napa counties.

A tree-lined driveway leads to **Lachryma Montis,** which General Mariano G. Vallejo, the last Mexican governor of California, built for his large family in 1852. The Victorian Gothic house, insulated with adobe, represents a blend of Mexican and American cultures. Opulent furnishings, including white-marble fireplaces and a French rosewood piano, are particularly noteworthy. Free tours are occasionally conducted by docents on the weekend. ✉ *W. Spain St., near 3rd St. W* ☎ *707/938–9559* 🎫 *$2, tour free* ⏲ *Daily 10–5.*

Reminiscent of a Tuscan villa, with its ocher-color buildings surrounded by olive trees, sprawling **Viansa** focuses on Italian varietals such as sangiovese, barbera, pinot grigio, and vernaccia. Fodor's readers are generally split when summing up the charms of the winery. Some love the market on the premises that sells sandwiches and deli foods to complement the Italian-style wines, as well as a large selection of dinnerware, cookbooks, and condiments. Others find the cavernous size of the market and the crowds that tend to congregate here off-putting. Regardless, the picnic area that overlooks the wetlands below is a fine place to enjoy a glass of wine while bird-watching (only food and wines sold on the premises are permitted). ✉ *25200 Arnold Dr.* ☎ *707/935–4700* 🌐 *www.viansa.com* 🎫 *Tasting $5–$20, tour $10 (tasting fee additional)* ⏲ *Daily 10–5; tour daily at 11, 2, and 3.*

The **Robledo Family Winery,** founded by Reynaldo Robledo Sr., a former migrant worker from Michoacán, Mexico, is truly a family affair. You're likely to encounter one of the charming Robledo sons in the tasting room, where he'll proudly tell you the story of the immigrant family while pouring tastes of their sauvignon blanc, pinot noir, pinot grigio, cabernet sauvignon, and other wines, including a chardonnay that comes from the vineyard right outside the tasting room's door. All seven Robledo sons and two Robledo daughters, as well as matriarch Maria, are involved in the winery operations. If you don't run into them on your visit to the winery, you can see their names and pictures on the bottles of wine, such as the "Dos Hermanas" late-harvest dessert wine, or the port dedicated to Maria Robledo. ✉ *21901 Bonness Rd.* ☎ *707/939–6903* 🌐 *www.robledofamilywinery.com* 🎫 *Tasting $5–$10* ⏲ *Tastings by appointment.*

Although **Cline Cellars** has planted vineyards here, most of their wines are Rhône varietals such as Syrah, Roussanne, and Viognier rather than the pinot noir and chardonnay grapes more common to the region (most of the grapes come from vines grown in Contra Costa Country, where zinfandel and heat-loving Marsanne, Mourvèdre, and Carignane thrive).

6

Be sure to taste the dark-red Carignane, but there are also Syrah and zinfandel for more traditional palates. The 1850s farmhouse that houses the tasting room has a pleasant wraparound porch for enjoying the weeping willow trees, ponds, fountains, and thousands of rose bushes on the property. Pack a picnic and plan to stay for a while, if you have the time. ✉*24737 Arnold Dr.* ☎*707/940–4030* 🌐*www.clinecellars.com* 🎟*Tasting free; $1 per reserve wine* ⏲*Daily 10–6.*

Buena Vista Carneros Estate is the oldest continually operating winery in California. It was here, in 1857, that Count Agoston Haraszthy de Mokcsa laid the basis for modern California wine making, bucking the conventional wisdom that vines should be planted on well-watered ground by instead planting on well-drained hillsides. Chinese laborers dug tunnels 100 feet into the hillside, and the limestone they extracted was used to build the main house, which is now surrounded by redwood and eucalyptus trees and a picnic area. If you're a bit peckish, consider paying a bit more ($20) for a tasting of five wines, which are paired with cheeses or other nibbles. ✉*18000 Old Winery Rd., off Napa Rd., follow signs from plaza* ☎*707/938–1266 or 800/678–8504* 🌐*buenavistacarneros.com* 🎟*Tasting $5–$10* ⏲*Daily 10–5.*

Ravenswood, whose tasting room is housed in a stone building covered in climbing fig vines, has a punchy three-word mission statement: "no wimpy wines." They generally succeed, especially with their signature big, bold zinfandels, which are sometimes blended with petite sirah, Carignane, or other varietals. Be sure to taste their Syrah and early-harvest Gewürztraminer, too. Tours include barrel tastings of wines in progress in the cellar. Reservations are recommended for their daily tour. ✉*18701 Gehricke Rd., off E. Spain St.* ☎*707/938–1960* 🌐*www.ravenswood-wine.com* 🎟*Tasting $10–$15, tour $15* ⏲*Daily 10–5; tour at 10:30.*

Gundlach-Bundschu may look like a grim bunker at first glance, but it's a lot of fun to visit. They let their hair down here, with pop or rock playing on the tasting room's sound system instead of the typical soft classical music; but they're serious about wine and craft some outstanding reds, like cabernet sauvignon, Tempranillo, Syrah, and zinfandel, all grown in the Rhinefarm Vineyard on the estate. One-hour tours include a visit to their wine cave, while the two-hour tour—offered during the growing season only—includes a ride through the vineyards; both culminate in a tasting. Climb up the hill from the tasting room and you can find a breathtaking valley view (and a perfect picnic spot). In summer, check their Web site for information about the musical and theatrical performances that take place on their outdoor stage. ✉*2000 Denmark St.* ☎*707/938–5277* 🌐*www.gunbun.com* 🎟*Tasting $5–$10, tours $20–$40* ⏲*Daily 11–4:30.*

WHERE TO EAT

$$ AMERICAN ✕**Cafe La Haye.** In a postage-stamp-size kitchen, skillful chefs turn out about half a dozen main courses that star on a small but worthwhile seasonal menu emphasizing local ingredients. Chicken, beef, pasta, and fish get deluxe treatment without fuss or fanfare. Mussels in an aromatic garlic and fennel broth frequently crop up, for instance, and the daily risotto

special is always good. The dining room matches the kitchen's stature, but it's balanced out with large, abstract paintings. ✉*140 E. Napa St.* ☎*707/935–5994* ▭*AE, MC, V* ⊙*Closed Sun. and Mon. No lunch.*

$ ITALIAN ✕**Della Santina's.** A longtime favorite with a charming brick patio out back serves the most authentic Italian food in town. (The Della Santina family, which has been running the restaurant since 1990, hails from Lucca, Italy.) Daily fish and veal specials join classic northern Italian pastas such as linguine with pesto and lasagna Bolognese. Of special note are the roasted meat dishes and, when available, petrale sole and sand dabs. ✉*133 E. Napa St.* ☎*707/935–0576* ▭*AE, D, MC, V.*

$$ FRENCH ✕**The Girl & the Fig.** Chef Sondra Bernstein has turned the historic barroom of the Sonoma Hotel into a hot spot for inventive French cooking. You can always find something with the signature figs in it here, whether it's a fig and arugula salad or an aperitif of sparkling wine with a fig liqueur. Also look for duck confit with French lentils, a burger with matchstick fries, or pastis-scented steamed mussels. The wine list is notable for its emphasis on Rhône varietals, and the *salon de fromage*—a counter in the bar area—sells artisanal cheese platters for eating here and cheese by the pound to go. Brunch is a Sunday exclusive, with rib-sticking dishes such as hanger steak and eggs and a goat cheese frittata. ✉*Sonoma Hotel, Sonoma Plaza, 110 W. Spain St.* ☎*707/938–3634* ▭*AE, D, MC, V.*

6

$$ AMERICAN ★ ✕**Harvest Moon Cafe.** It's easy to feel like one of the family at this little restaurant with the odd, zigzagging layout. Diners seated at one of the two tiny bars chat with the servers like old friends, but the husband-and-wife team in the kitchen are serious about the food. They're not exactly breaking new culinary ground here; the daily menu sticks to homey dishes like a fat grilled pork chop with cabbage and mashed potatoes, seared ahi tuna with sautéed swiss chard, and a chicory Caesar salad dusted generously with Parmesan. But everything is so perfectly executed and the vibe so genuinely warm, that a visit here is deeply satisfying. ✉*487 W. 1st St.* ☎*707/933–8160* ▭*AE, D, MC, V* ⊙*No lunch Mon–Sat.*

$$ MEXICAN ✕**La Casa.** Red-tile floors and ceramics on the walls evoke Old Mexico at this spot around the corner from Sonoma's plaza. There's bar seating, a patio, and large menu of traditional Mexican favorites, like enchiladas *suizas* (chicken enchiladas with a salsa verde), burritos, and fish tacos. Though the food is fairly standard, the casual, festive atmosphere and margaritas sold by the glass and the pitcher make it a popular stop. ✉*121 E. Spain St.* ☎*707/996–3406* ▭*AE, D, DC, MC, V.*

$$ PORTUGUESE ✕**LaSalette.** Chef-owner Manuel Azevedo, born in the Azores and raised in Sonoma, serves dishes inspired by his native Portugal in this warmly decorated spot a few steps off Sonoma's plaza. Boldly flavored dishes such as *porco à alentejana,* a traditional pork dish with clams and tomatoes, or one of the daily seafood specials might be followed by a dish of rice pudding with dried figs or a port from the varied list. ✉*452 E. 1st St.* ☎*707/938–1927* ▭*AE, MC, V.*

$$$$ AMERICAN ★ ✕**Santé.** Under the leadership of chef de cuisine Andrew Cain, this elegant dining room in the Sonoma Mission Inn has gained a reputation as a destination restaurant with its focus on seasonal- and locally sourced

Cloverdale
128
Cobb Mountain
175
Geyser Peak
Geysers Rd.
Balck Mountain
ALEXANDER VALLEY
Dutcher Creek Rd.
Lake Sonoma
101
26
25
Geyserville
Russian River
128
23
Pine Flat Rd
Lake Sonoma Recreation Area
West Dry Creek Rd.
Dry Creek Rd.
Lytton Springs Rd.
Lytton
KNIGHTS VALLEY
128
IDA Calyton Rd.
24
Dry Creek Rd.
Healdsburg Ave.
22
21
Chalk Hill Rd.
Healdsburg
Franz Valley Rd.
Mill Creek Rd.
Los Amigos Rd.
Austin Creek State Recreation Area
16
Westside Rd.
RUSSIAN RIVER VALLEY
Eastside Rd.
Sweetwater Springs Rd.
Armstrong Redwoods State Reserve
Windsor
Mark West Springs
17
Korbel Champagne Cellars
Rio Nido
Main St.
River Rd.
Guerneville
20
101
Russian River
Sonoma County Airport
Fulton
SONOMA COUNTY
116
19
Forestville
River Rd.
Martinelli Rd.
Olivet Rd.
Fulton Rd.
Piner Rd.
Monte Rio
18
116
Guerneville Rd.
Santa Rosa
Bohemian Hwy
Graton
Santa Rosa Creek
Hall Rd.
15
Willow Creek Rd.
Occidental Rd.
Bennett Valley
Graton Rd.
Sebastopol Hwy.
Occidental
12
Coleman Valley Rd.
Sebastopol
Taylor Mtn
Petaluma Hill Rd.
Bodega Hwy.
Freestone
Stony Point Rd.
Salmon Creek
Bodega Hwy.
Cunningham
Rohnert Park
Rd.
116
Bodega
1
Bodega Bay
Bloomfield
Valley Ford
Roblar Rd.
Cotati
Bay Hwy.
Valley Ford Cutoff
Bloomfield
101
Old Redwood Hwy.
Petaluma Hill Rd.
Petaluma Valley Ford Rd.
Bodega Bay
1
Fallon
Two Rock
Bodega Ave.
Dillon Beach
Tomales
MARIN COUNTY
0
4 mi
0
4 km
Laguna Lake
Point Reyes National Seashore
Tomales Bay

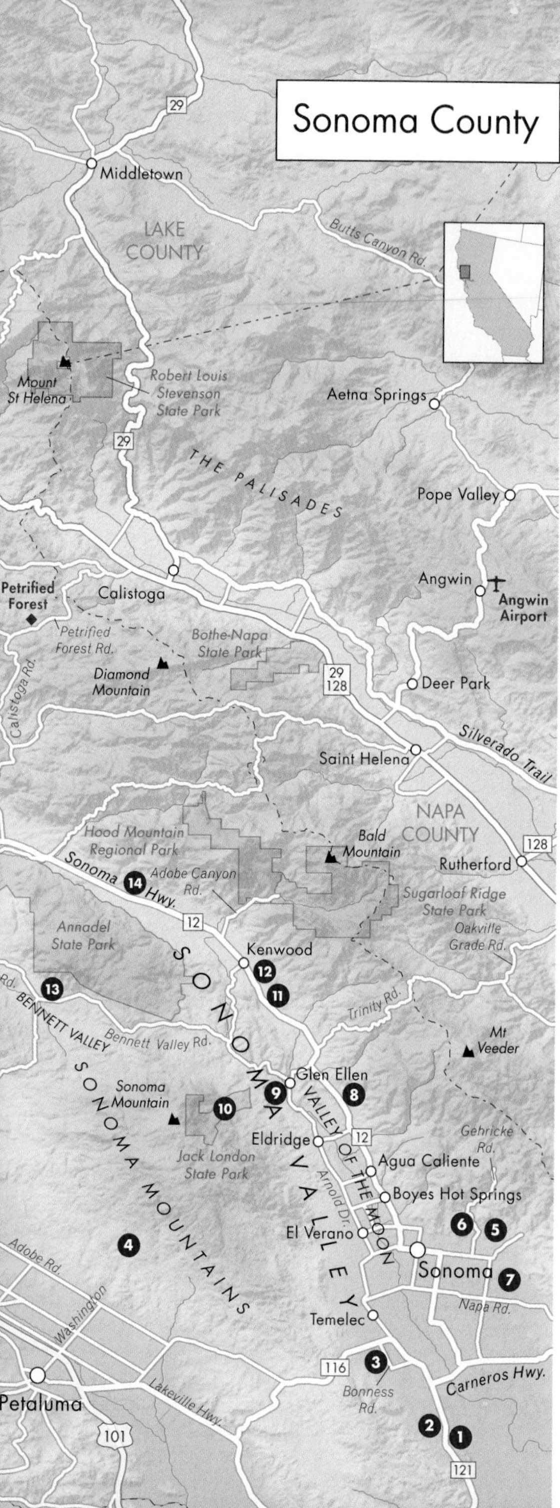

- Arrowood Vineyards & Winery 8
- Benziger Family Winery 9
- Buena Vista Carneros Estate 5
- Cline Cellars 2
- DeLoach Vineyards 4
- Dry Creek Vineyard 21
- Ferrari-Carano Winery 26
- Gary Farrell Winery 20
- Gundlach-Bundschu 7
- Hartford Family Winery 19
- Iron Horse Vineyards 18
- J Vineyards and Winery 16
- Jack London State Historic Park 10
- Kenwood Vineyards 12
- Kunde Estate Winery & Vineyards 11
- Ledson Winery & Vineyards 14
- Luther Burbank Home and Gardens 15
- Matanzas Creek Winery 13
- Michel-Schlumberger 24
- Preston Vineyards 25
- Quivira 22
- Ravenswood 6
- Robledo Family Winery 3
- Rochioli Vineyards and Winery 17
- Stryker- Sonoma 23
- Viansa 1

ingredients. The room is understated, with high-backed banquettes and matching drapes in rich earth tones and softly lit chandeliers—but the food is anything but. Dishes like the crispy pork belly with braised collard greens, endive marmalade, and mustard sauce are complex without being fussy; a starter of macaroni and cheese with chunks of lobster and a shaving of black truffles on top is pure decadence. A sumptuous brunch is served on Sundays and holidays. ✉*Fairmont Sonoma Mission Inn & Spa, 100 Boyes Blvd./Rte. 12, at Boyes Blvd., 2 mi north of Sonoma, Boyes Hot Springs* ☎*707/939–2415* ▭*AE, D, DC, MC, V* ⊗*No lunch.*

> **WORD OF MOUTH**
>
> "If you are starting your trip in San Francisco, it might be useful and amusing to visit a couple of wine bars in the city before striking out for the wine country. You could identify and sample some favorite wines and earmark [the California wineries] for visiting later in your trip." —dovima

WHERE TO STAY

$$$–$$$$ **The Fairmont Sonoma Mission Inn & Spa.** The real draw at this Mission-style resort is the extensive, swanky spa, easily the biggest in Sonoma. There's a vast array of massages and treatments, some using locally sourced grape and lavender products. The indoor and outdoor thermal soaking pools draw on the property's own mineral-water sources. (It's a co-ed spa, and there are several treatments designed for couples.) The focus on fitness and rejuvenation extends to a 7,087-yard golf course winding through trees and vineyards, a changing schedule of fitness classes, and guided hiking and biking excursions each morning. The guest rooms aren't terribly large, but are supremely comfortable; some have fireplaces and patios or balconies. The staff stays on top of every detail. **Pros:** enormous spa; excellent on-site restaurant; free shuttle to downtown. **Cons:** not as intimate as some similarly priced places; valet parking costs $20. ✉*100 Boyes Blvd./Rte. 12, 2 mi north of Sonoma, Boyes Hot Springs* ☎*707/938–9000* 📠*707/938–4250* 🌐*www.fairmont.com/sonoma* *168 rooms, 60 suites* *In-room: safe, refrigerator, Internet (some), Wi-Fi (some). In-hotel: 2 restaurants, room service, bars, golf course, tennis courts, pools, gym, spa, bicycles, laundry service, some pets allowed, no-smoking rooms* ▭*AE, D, DC, MC, V.*

$–$$ **Inn at Sonoma.** They don't skimp on the little luxuries here: wine and cheese is served every evening in the lobby, and the cheerfully painted rooms are equipped with Wi-Fi and warmed by gas fireplaces. In the closets you can find fluffy terry robes, which come in handy for trips to the hot tub on the inn's upper level. A teddy bear perched on each feather comforter–topped bed holds a remote control to a small TV. Though the inn is just off heavily trafficked Broadway, good soundproofing makes it quieter than many of the hotels on Sonoma Plaza. (The town square is a five-minute walk away.) Though rooms are not particularly large, you'd be hard-pressed to find this much charm for the price elsewhere in town. **Pros:** last-minute specials are a great deal; free soda in the lobby; lovely hot tub. **Cons:** staff is friendly but seems inexperienced; on a busy street rather than right on the plaza. ✉*630 Broadway* ☎*707/939–1340* 🌐*www.innatsonoma.com* *19 rooms*

CLOSE UP

Who's Who in the Grape World

Well over 50 different varieties of grapes are grown in the California Wine Country. Although you don't need to be on a first-name basis with them all, you'll see the following dozen again and again as you visit the wineries.

WHITES

■ **Chardonnay.** Now as firmly associated with California wine making as it is with Burgundy, its home. California chardonnays spent many years chasing big, buttery flavor, but the current trend is toward more restrained wines.

■ **Gewürztraminer.** Cooler California climes such as the Russian River Valley are great for growing this German-Alsatian grape, which is turned into a boldly perfumed, fruity wine.

■ **Riesling.** Can produce wines with brisk acidity and a lush floral or fruity bouquet. In California's Anderson and Alexander valleys, late-harvest dessert wines are often made with this cool-weather grape.

■ **Sauvignon Blanc.** Hails from Bordeaux and the Loire Valley. Wines made from this grape vary widely, from herbaceous to tropical-fruity.

■ **Viognier.** Until the early 1990s this was rarely planted outside France's Rhône Valley, but today it's one of the hottest white wine varietals in California. Usually made in a dry style, the best Viogniers have an intense fruity or floral bouquet.

REDS

■ **Cabernet Franc.** Though this Bordeaux grape is extremely important in California wine making, you'll rarely see it standing alone. A slightly softer, less tannic cousin of cabernet sauvignon, it's often blended with that grape to round out the rough edges.

■ **Cabernet Sauvignon.** The king of California red wine grapes; originally from Bordeaux. The best examples, like those from the Rutherford or Oakville AVAs, are big, bold, and often quite tannic, which means they usually require years in the cellar to reach their peak.

■ **Merlot.** A blue-black Bordeaux variety. In California it makes soft, fruity, full-bodied wine. Was well on its way to being the most popular red until anti-merlot jokes (popularized by the hit movie *Sideways*) damaged its rep . . . for now.

■ **Pinot Noir.** The darling of grape growers in cooler parts of Napa and Sonoma, such as the Carneros region and the Russian River Valley—but also called the "heartbreak grape" since it's hard to cultivate. At its best it has an addictively subtle earthy quality.

■ **Sangiovese.** Slow-ripening Tuscan grape that does well in warm areas. Because there are many different clones of this varietal, Sangioveses can vary from simple and light to complex and earthy.

■ **Syrah.** A big red from France's Rhône Valley. With good tannins it can become a full-bodied beauty, but without them it can be flabby and forgettable. Also known as Shiraz, particularly when it's grown in Australia.

■ **Zinfandel.** Often thought of as a quintessential California grape. Rich, jammy, and often spicy, zinfandel wines can be quite high in alcohol.

In-room: DVD, Wi-Fi. In-hotel: bicycles, no-smoking rooms AE, D, DC, MC, V CP.

$–$$ **Vineyard Inn.** Built as a roadside motor court in 1941, this inn with red-tile roofs brings a touch of Southwestern style to an otherwise lackluster and somewhat noisy location at the junction of two main highways. It's across from two vineyards and is the closest lodging to Infineon Raceway, a major racetrack. Though the rooms, which have queen- or king-size beds, are rather small, a friendly proprietor, continental breakfast in a pleasant tiled room, a convenient location, and a modest price make it a fine home base for those who'd rather spend their money elsewhere. **Pros:** attractive courtyard; friendly innkeepers. **Cons:** next to two busy highways; swimming pool is quite small. *23000 Arnold Dr., at junction of Rtes. 116 and 121 707/938–2350 or 800/359–4667 www.sonomavineyardinn.com 19 rooms, 2 suites In-room: DVD (some), refrigerator (some), Wi-Fi. In-hotel: pool, no-smoking rooms AE, MC, V CP.*

WORD OF MOUTH

"Napa was nice but much more crowded (a lot of tour groups) and we spent SO much more money in tasting fees. We've stayed in the towns of Sonoma and Healdsburg and really liked both. You can't go wrong either way." —raceloughren

NIGHTLIFE AND THE ARTS

The **Sebastiani Theatre** (*476 1st St. E 707/996–2020*), built on Sonoma's plaza in 1934 by Italian immigrant and entrepreneur Samuele Sebastiani, schedules first-run films, musical performances, and sometimes quirky theatrical performances.

Hit the **Swiss Hotel**'s bar (*18 W. Spain St. 707/938–2884*) to sip a Glariffee, a cold and potent cousin to Irish coffee that's unique to this 19th-century spot.

SHOPPING

Sonoma Plaza is the town's main shopping magnet, with tempting boutiques and specialty food purveyors facing the square or just a block or two away. **Sign of the Bear** (*Sonoma Plaza, 435 1st St. W 707/996–3722*) sells the latest and greatest in kitchenware and cookware, as well as a few Wine Country–theme items, like lazy Susans made from wine barrels. The **Sonoma Cheese Factory and Deli** (*Sonoma Plaza, 2 Spain St. 707/996–1931*), run by the same family for four generations, makes Sonoma Jack cheese and the tangy Sonoma Teleme. It has everything you could possibly need for a picnic.

GLEN ELLEN

7 mi north of Sonoma on Rte. 12.

Craggy Glen Ellen embodies the difference between the Napa and Sonoma valleys. In small Napa towns such as St. Helena well-groomed sidewalks are lined with upscale boutiques and restaurants; in Glen Ellen the crooked streets are shaded with stands of old oak trees and occasionally bisected by the Sonoma and Calabasas creeks.

Horseback riding tours loop around Jack London State Historic Park.

Jack London, who represents Glen Ellen's rugged spirit, lived in the area for many years; the town commemorates him with place-names and nostalgic establishments.

In the Jack London Village complex, **Figone's Olive Oil Co.** (✉*14301 Arnold Dr.* ☎*707/938–3164*) not only carries many local olive oils, serving bowls, books, and dining accessories but also presses fruit for a number of local growers, usually in the late fall. You can taste a selection of olive oils that have surprisingly different flavors.

Built in 1905, the **Jack London Saloon** (✉*13740 Arnold Dr.* ☎*707/996–3100* 🌐*www.jacklondonlodge.com*) is decorated with photos of London and other London memorabilia.

In the hills above Glen Ellen—known as the Valley of the Moon—lies **Jack London State Historic Park,** where you could easily spend the afternoon hiking along the edge of vineyards and through stands of oak trees. Several of the author's manuscripts and a handful of personal effects are on view at the House of Happy Walls museum, once the home of London's widow. The ruins of Wolf House—which London designed and which mysteriously burned down just before he was to move in—are a short hike away from the House of Happy Walls. Also restored and open to the public are a few farm outbuildings. London is buried on the property. ✉*2400 London Ranch Rd.* ☎*707/938–5216* *Parking $6* ⏲*Park Nov.–Mar., daily 9:30–5; Apr.–Oct., daily 9:30–7. Museum daily 10–5.*

Arrowood Vineyards & Winery is neither as old nor as famous as some of its neighbors, but winemakers and critics are quite familiar with the wines produced here by Richard Arrowood, especially the chardonnays,

Cloverdale
128
Cobb Mountain
175
Geyser Peak
ALEXANDER VALLEY
Dutcher Creek Rd.
Geysers Rd.
Balck Mountain
Lake Sonoma
101
Geyserville
Russian River
128
Pine Flat Rd
Clos du Bois
West Dry Creek Rd.
Dry Creek Rd.
Lake Sonoma Recreation Area
Lytton Springs Rd.
Lytton
KNIGHTS VALLEY
128
IDA Calyton Rd.
Healdsburg Ave.
Dry Creek Rd.
3 - 11
1
2
Healdsburg
Chalk Hill Rd.
Franz Valley Rd.
Mill Creek Rd.
Los Amigos Rd.
Austin Creek State Recreation Area
Westside Rd.
RUSSIAN RIVER VALLEY
Eastside Rd.
Sweetwater Springs Rd.
Armstrong Redwoods State Reserve
Windsor
Mark West Springs
Korbel Champagne Cellars
Rio Nido
River Rd.
Main St.
Guerneville
101
Russian River
12
Sonoma County Airport
Fulton
SONOMA COUNTY
13
116
Martinelli Rd.
Forestville
River Rd.
14
15
Olivet Rd.
Fulton Rd.
Piner Rd.
Monte Rio
116
Guerneville Rd.
Santa Rosa
Bohemian Hwy
Graton
Santa Rosa Creek
Hall Rd.
Occidental Rd.
Willow Creek Rd.
Graton Rd.
Bennett Valley
Sebastopol Hwy.
Occidental
12
Sebastopol
Coleman Valley Rd.
Petaluma Hill Rd.
Bodega Hwy.
Freestone
Stony Point Rd.
Bodega Hwy.
Cunningham
Rohnert Park
Salmon Creek
Rd.
116
Bodega Bay
1
Bodega
Bloomfield
Cotati
Petaluma Hill Rd.
Bay Hwy.
Valley Ford Cutoff
Roblar Rd.
Old Redwood Hwy.
Bloomfield
101
Petaluma Valley Ford Rd.
Bodega Bay
1
Fallon
Two Rock
Bodega Ave.
Dillon Beach
Tomales
MARIN COUNTY
0
4 mi
Laguna Lake
Point Reyes National Seashore
Tomales Bay
0
4 km

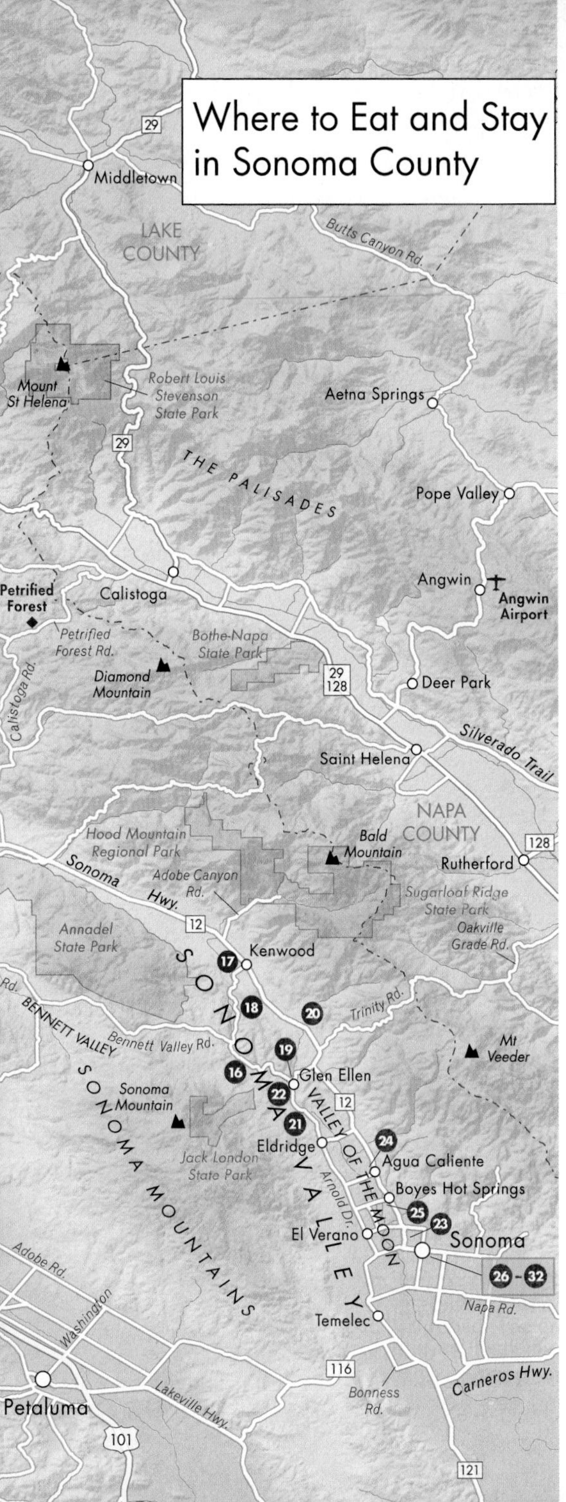

Restaurants ▼

- Barndiva **8**
- Bovolo **9**
- Café Citti **17**
- Cafe La Haye **29**
- Cyrus **10**
- Della Santina's **28**
- The Farmhouse Inn **12**
- The Fig Cafe **22**
- The Girl & the Fig **31**
- Harvest Moon Cafe **27**
- John Ash & Co. **15**
- La Casa **30**
- LaSalette **23**
- Olive & Vine Café **21**
- Santé **24**
- Scopa **6**
- Zin Restaurant and Wine Bar **7**

Hotels ▼

- Applewood Inn & Restaurant **13**
- Beltane Ranch **20**
- Best Western Dry Creek Inn **1**
- Camellia Inn **5**
- The Fairmont Sonoma Mission Inn & Spa **25**
- The Farmhouse Inn **12**
- Gaige House **19**
- Glenelly Inn and Cottages **16**
- The Honor Mansion **3**
- Hotel Healdsburg **4**
- Hôtel Les Mars **11**
- Inn at Sonoma **32**
- Kenwood Inn and Spa **18**
- Madrona Manor **2**
- Vineyard Inn **26**
- Vintners Inn **14**

cabernet sauvignons, and Syrahs. A wraparound porch with wicker chairs invites you to linger outside the tasting room, built to resemble a New England farmhouse. A stone fireplace in the tasting room makes this an especially enticing destination in winter. ■ **TIP→Call at least a week or so in advance if you'd like to take a tour; they're only offered twice a day, and they tend to fill up quickly.** ☒ *14347 Sonoma Hwy./Rte. 12* ☎ *707/935–2600* 🌐 *www.arrowoodvineyards.com* *Tasting $5–$10; tour $20–$30, includes tasting* ⏲ *Daily 10–4:30; tour by appointment.*

FARMERS' MARKET

The **Sonoma Farmers' Market** overflows with locally farmed produce, artisanal cheeses, and baked goods. It's held year-round at Depot Park, just north of the Sonoma Plaza, on Friday from 9 AM to noon. From April through October it gets extra play on Tuesday evenings from 5:30 PM to dusk at Sonoma Plaza.

★ One of the best-known local wineries is **Benziger Family Winery,** on a sprawling estate in a bowl with 360-degree sun exposure. Among the first wineries to identify certain vineyard blocks for particularly desirable flavors, Benziger is noted for its merlot, pinot blanc, chardonnay, and fumé blanc. The tram tours here are especially interesting (they're first come, first served). On a ride through the vineyards, guides explain the regional microclimates and geography and give you a glimpse of the extensive cave system. Tours depart several times a day, weather permitting, but are sometimes fully booked during the high season. Reservations are needed for smaller tours that conclude with a seated tasting ($40). ■ **TIP→Arrive before lunch for the best shot at joining a tour—and bring a picnic, since the grounds here are lovely.** ☒ *1883 London Ranch Rd.* ☎ *707/935–3000* 🌐 *www.benziger.com* *Tasting $10–$15, tours $15–$40* ⏲ *Daily 10–5.*

WHERE TO EAT AND STAY

$$ FRENCH ★ ✕ **The Fig Cafe.** Celadon booths, yellow walls, and a sloping high ceiling make this cozy, casual restaurant feel summery and airy even in the middle of winter. Artisanal cheese plates and fried calamari are popular appetizers, followed by comfort-food entrées such as braised pot roast and grilled hanger steak. Don't forget to look on the chalkboard for frequently changing desserts, such as chocolate and orange *pots de crème* and an apple and pear crisp. Brunch on Saturdays and Sundays features breakfast classics like French toast and eggs Florentine, in addition to some items from the regular dinner menu. ■ **TIP→The unusual no-corkage-fee policy makes it a great place to drink the wine you just discovered down the road.** ☒ *13690 Arnold Dr.* ☎ *707/938–2130* ▭ *AE, D, MC, V* *Reservations not accepted* ⏲ *No lunch weekdays.*

$ ITALIAN ✕ **Olive & Vine Café.** The selections change every day at this casual lunch-only café with wooden farmhouse tables. Take a look at the menu on the blackboard, which is likely to include panini like a barbecued pork sandwich with caramelized onions or inventive seasonal dishes like a refreshing watermelon gazpacho. But be sure to ask, too, about the items in the refrigerated case, like an updated three-bean salad or miniature pizzas with house-made tomato sauce. Though it's a good stop for picnic packers, you can eat in the dining room, a soaring barnlike space in the Jack London Village complex, or tote your dishes out to the deck, where tables overlook a creek. *⊠14301 Arnold Dr. ☎707/996–9150 Reservations not accepted ▭MC, V ⊗No dinner; closed Mon.–Tues.*

¢–$ ★ **Beltane Ranch.** On a slope of the Mayacamas range a few miles from Glen Ellen, this 1892 ranch house stands in the shade of magnificent oak trees. The charmingly old-fashioned rooms, each individually decorated with antiques, have separate entrances, and some open onto a wraparound balcony ideal for whiling away lazy afternoons. A detached cottage, once the gardener's quarters, has a small sitting room and a fireplace. **Pros:** bountiful breakfast; reasonably priced; beautiful grounds with ancient oak trees. **Cons:** downstairs rooms get some noise from upstairs rooms; credit cards are not accepted. *⊠11775 Sonoma Hwy./Rte. 12 ☎707/996–6501 ⊕www.beltaneranch.com 3 rooms, 3 suites In-room: no a/c, no phone, no TV, Wi-Fi. In-hotel: tennis court ▭No credit cards BP.*

$$$–$$$$ Fodor's Choice ★ **Gaige House.** Gorgeous orchids and Asian objets d'art are just a few of the little luxuries in this understated B&B. Rooms in the main house, an 1890 Queen Anne, are mostly done in pale colors and each has its advantages. One upstairs room has wraparound windows to let in floods of light, for instance, while the lavish creekside cottages have a pronounced Japanese influence, with massive granite soaking tubs overlooking private atriums. In addition to the main pool and hot tub, surrounded by magnolia trees, a second, private hot tub is available to those who sign up. Though the staffers are helpful, service never seems fussy, and there's a bottomless jar of cookies offered in the kitchen. **Pros:** beautiful lounge areas; cottages are very private. **Cons:** sound carries in the main house; the least expensive rooms are on the small side; breakfast is no longer included in the price. *⊠13540 Arnold Dr. ☎707/935–0237 or 800/935–0237 ⎙707/935–6411 ⊕www.gaige.com 12 rooms, 11 suites In-room: safe, refrigerator (some), DVD, Wi-Fi. In-hotel: pool, spa, no kids under 12, no-smoking rooms ▭AE, D, DC, MC, V.*

¢ **Glenelly Inn and Cottages.** On a quiet side street a few blocks from the town center, this sunny little establishment has a long history as a getaway. It was built as an inn in 1916, and the rooms, each individually decorated, tend toward a simple country style. Many have four-poster beds and touches such as a wood-burning stove or antique oak dresser; some have whirlpool tubs. All have puffy down comforters. Breakfast is served in front of the common room's fireplace, as are cookies or other snacks in the afternoon. ■ **TIP→Innkeeper Kristi Hallamore Jeppesen has two children of her own, so this is an unusually kid-friendly inn.** **Pros:** children are welcome; quiet location; hot tub in a pretty garden. **Cons:** some may not appreciate the presence of children; less-expensive rooms are on the small side. *⊠5131 Warm Springs Rd. ☎707/996–6720 ⊕www.glenelly.com 9 rooms, 2 suites In-room: no a/c (some), no phone (some), refrigerator (some), DVD, Wi-Fi. In-hotel: laundry facilities, some pets allowed, no-smoking rooms ▭AE, D, MC, V BP.*

6

KENWOOD

3 mi north of Glen Ellen on Rte. 12.

Blink and you might miss tiny Kenwood, which consists of little more than a few restaurants and shops and a historic train depot, now used for private events. But hidden in this pretty landscape of meadows and woods at the north end of Sonoma Valley are several good wineries, most just off the Sonoma Highway.

On your way in to **Kunde Estate Winery & Vineyards** you pass a terrace flanked with fountains, virtually coaxing you to stay for a picnic with views over the vineyard. The tour of the grounds includes its extensive caves, some of which stretch 175 feet below a Syrah vineyard. Kunde is perhaps best known for its chardonnays, which range from crisp ones aged in stainless-steel tanks to toastier ones that have spent time in French oak barrels. Tastings might include sauvignon blanc, cabernet sauvignon, and zinfandel as well. If you skip the tour, take a few minutes to wander around the demonstration vineyard outside the tasting room. In the months before crush (usually in September), you can taste the different grapes on the vines and see if you can taste the similarities between the grapes and wines you just tasted. ✉*9825 Sonoma Hwy./Rte. 12* ☎*707/833–5501* 🌐*www.kunde.com* 🎫*Tasting $10–$20, tour free* ⏲*Daily 10:30–4:30, tours Mon.–Thurs. at 11, Fri.–Sun. on the hr 11–3.*

Kenwood Vineyards makes some good value-priced red and white wines, as well as some showier cabernet sauvignons and zinfandels, many of which are poured in the tasting room housed in one of the original barns on the property. The best of these come from Jack London's old vineyard, in the Sonoma Mountain appellation, above the fog belt of the Sonoma Valley (Kenwood has an exclusive lease). But the crisp sauvignon blanc is what keeps wine connoisseurs coming back for more. **TIP→Free tastings are a boon to those discovering that all those $20 tasting fees are starting to add up.** ✉*9592 Sonoma Hwy./Rte. 12* ☎*707/833–5891* 🌐*www.kenwoodvineyards.com* 🎫*Tasting free–$5* ⏲*Daily 10–4:30.*

The outrageously ornate French Normandy castle visible from Route 12 might attract you even before you know that the **Ledson Winery & Vineyards** produces lovely wines, all of which are available only at the winery and a small number of restaurants. Although they produce only 30,000 cases a year, they make about 79 different, largely single-varietal wines, everything from California standbys like zinfandel to Rhone varietals like Syrah and Mourvèdre. The castle, intended as the Ledson family's opulent home when its construction began in 1989, is now a warren of tasting rooms, special event spaces, and a small market selling picnic supplies. ✉*7335 Sonoma Hwy./Rte. 12* ☎*707/537–3810* 🌐*www.ledson.com* 🎫*Tasting $10–$15, no tour* ⏲*Daily 10–5.*

WHERE TO EAT AND STAY

$ ITALIAN ✕**Café Citti.** Opera tunes in the background and a friendly staff (as well as a roaring fire when the weather's cold) keep this no-frills roadside café from feeling too spartan. Order dishes such as roast chicken and slabs of tiramisu from the counter and they're delivered to your table. An ample array of prepared salads and sandwiches means they do a brisk business in takeout for picnic packers, but you can also choose pasta made to order, mixing and matching linguine, penne, and other pastas with sauces like pesto or marinara. ✉ *9049 Sonoma Hwy./Rte. 12* ☎ *707/833–2690* ▭ *MC, V.*

$$$$ ★ **Kenwood Inn and Spa.** Buildings resembling graceful old haciendas and mature fruit trees shading the courtyards convey the sense that this inn has been here for more than a century. French doors opening onto terraces or balconies, fluffy featherbeds, and wood-burning fireplaces give the uncommonly spacious guest rooms, many with tile floors, a particularly romantic air. A swimming pool, Jacuzzis, and saunas pepper three atmospheric courtyards, and you could easily spend an afternoon padding from one to another in your robe and slippers. The intimate but well-equipped spa draws on the local preoccupation, using the Caudalie line of grape-derived products and treatments. **Pros:** large rooms; lavish furnishings; extremely romantic. **Cons:** expensive; restaurant isn't quite up to the level of the inn. ✉ *10400 Sonoma Hwy.* ☎ *707/833–1293* ⊕ *www.kenwoodinn.com* *29 rooms* *In-room: no TV, Wi-Fi. In-hotel: restaurant, bar, pool, spa, laundry service, Wi-Fi, no kids under 18, no-smoking rooms.*

6

ELSEWHERE IN SONOMA COUNTY

At nearly 1,598 square mi, there's much more to Sonoma County than the day-tripper favorites of Sonoma, Glen Ellen, and Kenwood. North of this trio of oenophile hotbeds is Healdsburg, a lovely small town with a rapidly rising buzz. The national media have latched onto it for its swank hotels and remarkable restaurants, and more and more Fodors.com readers recommend it as an ideal home base for wine tasting.

Within easy striking distance of Healdsburg are some of the Wine Country's most scenic vineyards, in the Alexander, Dry Creek, and Russian River valleys. And these lookers also happen to produce some of the country's best pinot noir, cabernet sauvignon, zinfandel, and sauvignon blanc. Though these regions are hardly unknown names, their quiet, narrow roads feel a world away from Highway 29 in Napa.

The western stretches of Sonoma county, which reach all the way to the Pacific Ocean, are sparsely populated in comparison to the above destinations, with only the occasional vineyard popping up in between isolated ranches. This chapter focuses on the wine-growing regions of Sonoma, but if you want to explore elsewhere in Sonoma (Bodega Bay to whale-watch, for example), contact the local visitor bureau for more information.

SANTA ROSA

8 mi northwest of Kenwood on Rte. 12.

Santa Rosa, the Wine Country's largest city, isn't likely to charm you with its office buildings, department stores, and almost perpetual snarl of traffic along U.S. 101. It is, however, home to a couple of interesting cultural offerings. Its chain motels and hotels are also handy if you're finding that everything else is booked up, especially since Santa Rosa is roughly equidistant from Sonoma, Healdsburg, and the Russian River Valley, three of the most popular wine-tasting destinations.

The **Luther Burbank Home and Gardens** commemorates the great botanist who lived and worked on these grounds and single-handedly developed the modern techniques of hybridization. The 1.6-acre garden and a greenhouse show the results of some of Burbank's experiments to develop spineless cacti, fruit trees, and flowers such as the Shasta daisy. In the music room of his house, a modified Greek Revival structure that was Burbank's home from 1884 to 1906, a dictionary lies open to a page on which the verb "burbank" is defined as "to modify and improve plant life." If you show up during the gift shop's open hours, it's worth the small fee ($5) to rent the interesting, self-guided audio tour. ✉ *Santa Rosa and Sonoma Aves.* ☎ *707/524–5445* 🌐 *www.lutherburbank.org* 🎫 *Gardens free, guided tour of house and greenhouse $5* ⏲ *Gardens daily 8–dusk; museum and gift shop Apr.–Oct., Tues.–Sun. 10–4; tour Apr.–Oct., Tues.–Sun. 10–3:30.*

Fodor'sChoice ★ The visitor center at beautiful **Matanzas Creek Winery** sets itself apart with an understated Japanese aesthetic, with a tranquil fountain and a koi pond. Best of all, huge windows overlook a vast field of lavender plants. ■ **TIP→The ideal time to visit is in June, when the lavender blooms and perfumes the air.** The winery specializes in three varietals—sauvignon blanc, merlot, and chardonnay—though in 2005 they also started producing a popular dry rosé. After you taste the wines, ask for the self-guided garden-tour book before taking a stroll. ✉ *6097 Bennett Valley Rd.* ☎ *707/528–6464 or 800/590–6464* 🌐 *www.matanzascreek.com* 🎫 *Tasting $5–$10, tour $10* ⏲ *Daily 10–4:30; tour weekdays at 10:30 and 2:30, Sat. at 10:30, by appointment.*

WHERE TO EAT AND STAY

$$$$ AMERICAN ✕ **John Ash & Co.** Patio seating, vaulted ceilings, and a cozy indoor fireplace make this spacious restaurant with vineyard views a good choice for romantics. The contemporary dishes draw from both Italian and French cuisine, but the ingredients are largely local (a few even come from gardens on the property). Hog Island oysters come from Tomales Bay and in season you might find local king salmon with a miso crust and shiitake mushrooms. The wine list is impressive even by Wine Country standards, and the bar opens early—at 4 PM, 3 PM Friday through Sunday—serving a smaller menu. ✉ *4330 Barnes Rd., River Rd. exit west from U.S. 101* ☎ *707/527–7687* ▭ *AE, D, DC, MC, V* ⏲ *No lunch.*

$$$ 🏨 **Vintners Inn.** On a property that includes about 80 acres of vineyards—the grapes are used by the inn's owners, who also own the winery Ferrari-Carano—this French provincial-style inn is notably calm and quiet, considering how close it is to U.S. 101 and downtown Santa Rosa. The spacious guest rooms, spread among three separate two-story buildings, all have a patio or balcony; many also have wood-burning fireplaces and views of the vineyards. An attractive event center designed to resemble a winery is a popular spot for weddings and meetings. **Pros:** comfortable king-size beds with feather mattress toppers; spacious rooms; jogging path through the vineyards. **Cons:** you can hear the freeway from the

hot tub; some of the furnishings are a bit dated. ✉*4350 Barnes Rd., River Rd. exit west from U.S. 101* ☎*707/575–7350 or 800/421–2584* 🖷*707/575–1426* 🌐*www.vintnersinn.com* *38 rooms, 6 suites* *In-room: safe, refrigerator, DVD, Wi-Fi. In-hotel: restaurant, room service, bar, gym, laundry service, Wi-Fi, no-smoking rooms* 💳*AE, D, DC, MC, V* *BP.*

RUSSIAN RIVER VALLEY

5 mi northwest of Santa Rosa.

The Russian River flows all the way from Mendocino to the Pacific Ocean, but in terms of wine making, the Russian River Valley is centered on a triangle with points at Healdsburg, Guerneville, and Sebastopol. Tall redwoods shade many of the two-lane roads that access this scenic area, where, thanks to the cooling marine influence, pinot noir and chardonnay are the king and queen of grapes.

ESSENTIALS

Contacts Russian River Wine Road (✉*Box 46, Healdsburg* ☎*707/433–4335 or 800/723–6336* 🌐*www.wineroad.com*).

6

Behind the bar in the tasting room, a dramatic steel sculpture studded with illuminated chunks of glass suggests a bottle of bubbly, cluing you in to the raison d'être of **J Vineyards and Winery** before your first sip. Their dry sparkling wines are made from pinot noir and chardonnay grapes planted in their Russian River vineyards. Still wines—made with the same varietals, as well as pinot gris and a few other grapes—are also good, if perhaps not as impressive as the sparklers, which have wonderfully complex fruit and floral aromas and good acidity. Although you can sample their wines on their own at the tasting bar, for a truly decadent experience make a reservation for the Bubble Room, where you can choose a flight of still or sparkling wines which are served with treats that might include caviar. Reservations aren't necessary to taste on the terrace, open May through October, where artisanal cheeses and charcuterie plates are served. ✉*11447 Old Redwood Hwy.* ☎*707/431–3646* *Tasting $10–$55* 🌐*www.jwine.com* *Daily 11–5; Bubble Room hours vary.*

★ Down a one-lane country road from Forestville, **Iron Horse Vineyards** makes a wide variety of sparkling wines, from the bright and austere to the rich and toasty, as well as estate chardonnays and pinot noirs. Three hundred acres of rolling, vine-covered hills, barnlike winery buildings, and a beautifully rustic outdoor tasting area with a view of Mount St. Helena set it apart from stuffier spots. (Instead of providing buckets for the wine you don't want to finish, they ask you to toss it into the grass behind you.) Tours are available by appointment on weekdays at 10 AM. ✉*9786 Ross Station Rd., near Sebastopol* ☎*707/887–1507* 🌐*www.ironhorsevineyards.com* *Tasting $10–$15, tour free* *Daily 10–3:30; tour by appointment.*

Rochioli Vineyards and Winery claims one of the prettiest picnic sites in the area, with tables overlooking vineyards, which are also visible from the airy little tasting room hung with modern artwork. Production is small—about 12,000 or 13,000 cases annually—and fans on the winery's mailing list snap up most of the bottles, but the wines are still worth a stop. Because of the cool growing conditions in the Russian River Valley, the flavors of their chardonnay and sauvignon blanc are intense and complex. It's their pinot, though, that is largely responsible for the winery's stellar reputation; it helped cement the Russian River's status as a pinot powerhouse. **TIP→Though they typically pour only a couple of wines for visitors, it's one of the few wineries of its stature that doesn't charge for a tasting.** *6192 Westside Rd. 707/433–2305 Tasting free Thurs.–Mon. 11–4, Tues.–Wed. by appointment; closed last two weeks of Dec. and first week of Jan.*

WORD OF MOUTH

"I like to purchase wine openers or other paraphernalia from the wineries I visit [as souvenirs]. They always have the winery name or logo and they are small [for easy packing]." —cabovacation

Fans of pinot noir will surely want to stop at **Hartford Family Winery,** a surprisingly opulent winery off a meandering country road in Forestville. Here grapes from the coolest areas of the Russian River Valley, Sonoma coast, Carneros, and other regions are turned into chardonnays, old-vine zinfandels, and pinots, many of which are single-vineyard wines. *8075 Martinelli Rd. 707/887–1756 www.hartfordwines.com Tasting $5–$15 Daily 10–4:30.*

Pass through an impressive metal gate and wind your way up a steep hill to reach **Gary Farrell Winery,** a spot with knockout views over the rolling hills and vineyards below. Though their mostly spicy, full-bodied zinfandels are all winners, the winery has built its reputation on pinot noir. They also makes a fine cabernet sauvignon, sauvignon blanc, and chardonnay. *10701 Westside Rd. 707/473–2900 www.garyfarrellwines.com Tasting $10–$15, tour $15–$25 Daily 11–4; tours by appointment.*

Just far enough off the beaten track to feel like a real find, **De Loach Vineyards** produces a variety of Russian River Valley sauvignon blancs, a rosé of pinot noir, merlots, and old-vine zinfandels but is best known for chardonnays and, especially, their pinot noir. Some of the pinot is made using open-top wood fermentation vats that are uncommon in Sonoma but have been used in France for centuries. (Some think that they intensify a wine's flavor.) Tours focus on the estate vineyards outside the tasting room door, where you can learn about the labor-intensive biodynamic and organic farming methods used here; they'll also take you through their culinary garden. *1791 Olivet Rd. 707/526–9111 www.deloachvineyards.com Tasting $10, tour free Daily 10–5; tours daily by appointment.*

OFF THE BEATEN PATH

Korbel Champagne Cellars. To be called Champagne, a wine must be made in the French region of Champagne—otherwise it's just sparkling wine. Whatever you call it, Korbel produces a tasty, reasonably priced bubbly and still wines, as well as its own brandy, which is distilled on the premises. The wine tour clearly explains the process of making sparkling wine and takes you through the winery's ivy-covered 19th-century buildings.

Annual barrel tasting along the Russian River Valley's wine road.

If you've already had the process of wine making explained to you one too many times, a tour of the rose garden, where there are more than 250 varieties of roses, may be a welcome break. Garden tours are given a few times daily Tuesday through Sunday, mid-April through mid-October. ✉ *13250 River Rd., Guerneville* ☎ *707/824–7000* 🌐 *www.korbel.com* *Tasting and tour free* ⏲ *Oct.–Apr., daily 9–4:30; May–Sept., daily 9–5; tour Oct.–Apr., daily on the hr 10–3; May–Sept., weekdays 10, 11, 12, 1, 2, 3, and 3:45, weekends at 10, 11, noon, 12:45, 1:30, 2:15, 3, and 3:45.*

WHERE TO EAT AND STAY

$$$$ FRENCH Fodor's Choice ★ ✕ **The Farmhouse Inn.** From the personable sommelier who arrives at the table to help you pick wines from the excellent list (one of only about a hundred Master Sommeliers working in the United States) to the maître d' who serves local and European cheeses from the cart with a flourish, the staff match the quality of the outstanding French-inspired cuisine. The signature dish, "rabbit, rabbit, rabbit," a rich trio of confit of leg, rabbit loin wrapped in applewood-smoked bacon, and roasted rack of rabbit with a mustard cream sauce, is typical of the dishes that are simultaneously rustic and refined. A hand-painted mural surrounds the tranquil, country-style dining room. ■ **TIP→ Dinner here is a particularly hot item, so reserve well in advance.** ✉ *7871 River Rd., Forestville* ☎ *707/887–3300 or 800/464–6642* *Reservations essential* *AE, D, DC, MC, V* ⏲ *Closed Tues. and Wed. No lunch.*

$–$$$ Fodor's Choice ★ **Applewood Inn & Restaurant.** On a knoll in the shelter of towering redwoods, this romantic inn has two distinct types of accommodations. Those in the original Belden House, where cozy chairs around a river-rock fireplace encourage loitering in the lounge area, are comfortable but modest in scale. Most of the 10 rooms in the newer buildings are larger and airier, decorated in sage green and terra-cotta tones. Readers rave about the accommodating service, soothing atmosphere, and the earthy Cal-Italian cuisine served in the restaurant ($$$) built to recall a French barn. In winter, up the romance factor by asking for a table near the fireplace. **Pros:** quiet, secluded location; decadent breakfast; eager-to-please staff. **Cons:** restaurant closed Sunday and Monday; guests arriving after 9 PM are charged for each hour they're late. ✉ *13555 Rte. 116, Guerneville* ☎ *707/869–9093 or 800/555–8509* 🌐 *www.applewoodinn.com* *19 rooms* *In-room: no a/c (some), Wi-Fi. In-hotel: restaurant, pool, spa, no-smoking rooms* 💳 *AE, MC, V* 🍽 *BP.*

$$–$$$$ ★ **The Farmhouse Inn.** This pale yellow 1873 farmhouse and adjacent cottages offer individually decorated rooms with comfortable touches such as down comforters, whirlpool tubs, and CD players. ■ **TIP→ Most rooms have wood-burning fireplaces and even their own private little saunas, which makes this place especially inviting during the rainy winter months.** It's worth leaving your supremely comfortable bed for the sumptuous breakfasts here. The inn's restaurant is one of the most highly regarded in the Wine Country (⇨ *see above*). Eight new large, even more luxurious rooms with indoor-outdoor gas-burning fireplaces are scheduled to open in May 2009 in a new building that is reminiscent of an old barn that was once on the property. **Pros:** saunas in many rooms; one of Sonoma's best restaurants is on-site. **Cons:** rooms closest to the street get a bit of road noise. ✉ *7871 River Rd., Forestville* ☎ *707/887–3300 or 800/464–6642* 📠 *707/887–3311* 🌐 *www.farmhouseinn.com* *8 rooms, 2 suites* *In-room: refrigerator, DVD, Wi-Fi. In-hotel: restaurant, pool, spa, no-smoking rooms* 💳 *AE, D, DC, MC, V* 🍽 *BP.*

SPORTS AND THE OUTDOORS

At **Burke's Canoe Trips** (✉ *River Rd. and Mirabel Rd., 1 mi north of Forestville* ☎ *707/887–1222*) you can rent a canoe for a leisurely paddle 10 mi downstream to Guerneville. A shuttle bus will return you to your car at the end of the day. May through October is the best time for boating.

HEALDSBURG

17 mi north of Santa Rosa on U.S. 101.

The buzz on Healdsburg is amplifying—especially among the platinum-card set who rave about relative newcomers like Cyrus and Hotel Les Mars. But you don't have to be a tycoon to stay here and enjoy the town, which locals—dismayed at recent developments—have been known to call Beverly Healdsburg. For every ritzy restaurant there's a great, low-key bakery or B&B. A whitewashed bandstand on the Healdsburg plaza hosts free summer concerts, where you might hear anything from bluegrass to Sousa marches. Add to that the fragrant magnolia trees shading the square and the bright flower beds, and the whole thing is as pretty as a Norman Rockwell painting.

The countryside around Healdsburg is a fantasy of pastoral bliss—beautifully overgrown and in constant repose. Alongside the relatively untrafficked roads, country stores offer just-plucked fruits and vine-ripened tomatoes. Wineries here are barely visible, tucked behind groves of eucalyptus or hidden high on fog-shrouded hills.

WORD OF MOUTH

"I would absolutely hands-down recommend a stay in Healdsburg and putter around the wineries here. There are few crowds, quiet bucolic country roads, much to recommend." —heatherfife

WHERE TO EAT

$$$ AMERICAN ✕ **Barndiva.** This hip joint trades in the homey vibe of so many Wine Country spots for an almost nightclub feel. Electronic music plays quietly in the background while hipster servers ferry inventive seasonal cocktails. The food is as stylish as the well-dressed couples cozying up next to one another on the banquette seats. Make a meal out of bar menu bites like the goat-cheese croquettes or pilsner-steamed mussels, or settle in for the evening with a crispy duck salad and shepherd's pie. During warm weather the beautiful patio is the place to be. ✉ *231 Center St.* ☎ *707/431–0100* ▭ *AE, MC, V* ⏲ *Closed Mon. and Tues.*

6

$ ITALIAN ✕ **Bovolo.** Husband and wife team John Stewart and Duskie Estes serve what they call "slow food . . . fast." Though you might pop into this casual café at the back of Copperfield's Books for a half hour, the staff will have spent hours curing the meats that star in the menu of salads, pizzas, pastas, and sandwiches. For instance, the Salumist's Salad mixes a variety of cured meats with greens, white beans, and a tangy vinaigrette, and a thin-crusted pizza might come topped with house-made Italian pork sausage and roasted peppers. House-made gelato served with Scharffen Berger chocolate sauce or biscotti is a simply perfect ending to a meal. ✉ *106 Matheson St.* ☎ *707/431–2962* ✍ *Reservations not accepted* ▭ *MC, V* ⏲ *Sun.–Thurs. 9–8, Fri.–Sat. 9–9.*

$$$$ AMERICAN Fodor'sChoice ★ ✕ **Cyrus.** Hailed as the best thing to hit the Wine Country since French Laundry when it opened in 2005, Cyrus has earned its stripes by racking up awards and the raves of guests. From the moment you're seated to the minute your dessert plates are whisked away, you'll be carefully tended by fleet servers and an expert sommelier. The formal dining room, with its vaulted Venetian-plaster ceiling, is a suitably plush setting for chef Douglas Keane's creative, subtle cuisine. Keane has a notably free hand with decadent ingredients like truffles. Three-, four-, and five-course tasting menus can be constructed any way you like—you can even order four desserts, the waiter enthuses. Most opt to work their way through savories first, such as a terrine of foie gras with curried apple compote and duck with tamarind-glazed eggplant, before finishing up with an espresso gelato with an almond dacquoise. If you've failed to make reservations, you can order any of their dishes à la carte at the bar. *29 North St.* ☎ *707/433–3311* ✍ *Reservations essential* ▭ *AE, DC, MC, V* ⏲ *No lunch. Closed 10 days in Jan.*

$$ ITALIAN ✕ **Scopa.** Scopa is a card game played in most parts of Italy, but at this tiny new Healdsburg eatery of the same name, food isn't a game—it's very serious business. Chef Ari Rosen cooks up northern Italian

specialties such as pillowy house-made gnocchi, tomato-braised chicken, and *Tonno del Chianti* (a marinated, shredded pork dish with greens and a fig balsamic marmellata). Simple thin-crust pizzas are worth ordering, too. Locals love the restaurant for its lack of pretension: wine is served in juice glasses, and the friendly hostess visits guests frequently to make sure all are satisfied. For the complete experience, book dinner on a Sunday and arrive early; the place opens at 1 PM to host a big game of—what else?—Scopa. ✉*109A Plaza St.* ☎*707/433–5282* ▭*AE, MC, V* ⊗*No lunch; closed Mon.*

$$ AMERICAN ✕ **Zin Restaurant and Wine Bar.** Concrete walls and floors and large canvases on the walls give the restaurant a casual, industrial, and slightly artsy feel. The American cuisine—such as smoked pork chop with homemade applesauce or the red beans and rice with andouille sausage—is hearty and highly seasoned. Portions are large, so consider sharing if you hope to save room for one of the decadent desserts, like the bread pudding with bourbon sauce. As you might have guessed, zinfandel is the drink of choice here: roughly half of the 100 or so bottles on the wine list are zins. ✉*344 Center St.* ☎*707/473–0946* ▭*AE, MC, V* ⊗*No lunch weekends.*

WHERE TO STAY

¢–$ **Camellia Inn.** In another of Healdsburg's 19th-century Victorians, this colorful B&B sits on a quiet residential street just a block from the town's main square. It's been run by the same family for more than 25 years. The parlors downstairs are chockablock with ceramics and other decorative items, while rooms are individually decorated with antiques, such as an impressive mid-19th-century tiger-maple bed from Scotland. **■ TIP→There's one cozy budget room with a private bath that's across the hallway.** **Pros:** reasonable rates for the neighborhood; a rare family-friendly inn; within easy walking distance of dozens of restaurants. **Cons:** some rooms feel a little tired; some may find the look too frilly. ✉*211 North St.* ☎*707/433–8182 or 800/727–8182* 📠*707/433–8130* 🌐*www.camelliainn.com* *8 rooms, 1 suite* *In-room: no TV. In-hotel: pool, no-smoking rooms* ▭*AE, D, MC, V* 🍽*BP.*

$–$$$ ★ **The Honor Mansion.** Each room is unique at this photogenic 1883 Italianate Victorian. Rooms in the main house preserve a sense of the building's heritage, while the larger suites out back are comparatively understated. Luxurious touches such as lovely antiques are found in every room, and suites have the added advantage of a deck; some even have private outdoor hot tubs. Fodors.com readers rave about the attentive staff, who "think of things you don't even know you want." **Pros:** beautiful, tranquil grounds; personable innkeepers; homemade sweets available at all hours. **Cons:** almost a mile from Healdsburg's plaza; on a moderately busy street. ✉*14891 Grove St.* ☎*707/433–4277 or 800/554–4667* 🌐*www.honormansion.com* *5 rooms, 8 suites* *In-room: refrigerator, DVD (some), Wi-Fi. In-hotel: tennis court, pool, no-smoking rooms* ▭*AE, MC, V* ⊗*Closed 1 wk around Christmas* 🍽*BP.*

$$$–$$$$ **Hotel Healdsburg.** Across the street from Healdsburg's tidy town plaza, this spare, sophisticated hotel caters to travelers with an urban sensibility. Unadorned olive-green walls, dark hardwood floors, and clean-lined

furniture fill the guest rooms; the beds are some of the most comfortable you can find anywhere. Spacious bathrooms continue the sleek style with monochromatic tiles and deep soaking tubs that are all right angles. The attached restaurant, Dry Creek Kitchen ($$$$), is one of the best in Healdsburg. Celebrity chef Charlie Palmer is the man behind seasonal dishes that largely rely on local ingredients, like a spice-crusted Sonoma duck breast or seared Sonoma foie gras, plus a wine list covering the best Sonoma vintners. **Pros:** several rooms overlook the town plaza; free valet parking; some of the most comfortable beds in all the Wine Country. **Cons:** least expensive rooms are on the small side; exterior rooms get some street noise. ✉*25 Matheson St.* ☎*707/431–2800 or 800/889–7188* 🌐*www.hotelhealdsburg.com* *45 rooms, 10 suites* *In-room: safe, refrigerator, DVD, Internet, Wi-Fi. In-hotel: restaurant, room service, bar, pool, gym, spa, laundry service, some pets allowed, no-smoking rooms* *AE, MC, V* *CP.*

FARMERS' MARKET

During two weekly **Healdsburg farmers' markets** you can buy locally made goat's cheese, fragrant lavender, and olive oil in addition to the usual produce. On Saturday the market takes place one block west of the town plaza, at the corner of North and Vine streets, from 9 AM to noon, May through November. The Tuesday market, run from June through October, takes place on the plaza itself from 4 to 6:30 PM.

6

$$$$ **Hotel Les Mars.** In 2005 posh Healdsburg got even more chichi with the opening of this opulent hotel. Guest rooms are spacious and elegant enough for French nobility, with 18th- and 19th-century antiques and reproductions and gas-burning fireplaces. Most of the gleaming, white marble bathrooms have spa tubs in addition to enormous showers. And when you return at night to a box of chocolate truffles and crawl into your canopy bed covered in pristine Italian linens you might wonder when you've ever had it so good. Rooms on the third floor have soaring ceilings that make them feel particularly large, while the second-floor rooms have a slightly more understated style. Wine and cheese are served every evening in the library, sumptuously paneled with hand-carved black walnut. **Pros:** large rooms; just off Healdsburg's plaza; impeccable service; Bulgari bath products. **Cons:** very expensive; no parking lot. ✉*27 North St.* ☎*707/433–4211* 🌐*www.lesmarshotel.com* *16 rooms* *In-room: safe, DVD, Wi-Fi. In-hotel: restaurant, bar, pool, gym, laundry service, no-smoking rooms* *AE, DC, MC, V* *CP.*

$$–$$$$ **Madrona Manor.** The oldest continuously operating inn in the area, this 1881 Victorian mansion surrounded by 8 acres of wooded and landscaped grounds is straight out of a storybook. Rooms in the three-story mansion, the carriage house, and the three separate cottages are splendidly ornate, with mirrors in gilt frames and paintings covering every wall. Much of the furniture is even original to the 19th-century home. Candlelight dinners are served in the formal dining rooms nightly except Monday and Tuesday. Chef Jesse Mallgren has earned much praise for his elaborate three-, four-, and five-course menus, where luxuries like Périgord truffle risotto might precede a bacon-wrapped rabbit loin and a warm chocolate soufflé. **TIP→For a ridiculously romantic**

experience, ask for Room 203 or 204. The most requested rooms at the inn, they both have huge balconies that overlook the hotel grounds and beyond. **Pros:** old-fashioned, romantic ambience; pretty veranda perfect for a cocktail. **Cons:** pool heated May through October only; decor might be too fussy for some. ✉ *1001 Westside Rd., central Healdsburg exit off U.S. 101, then left on Mill St.* ☎ *707/433–4231 or 800/258–4003* 🌐 *www.madronamanor.com* *17 rooms, 5 suites* *In-room: no TV, Wi-Fi. In-hotel: restaurant, bar, pool, no-smoking rooms* 💳 *AE, MC, V* *BP.*

SHOPPING

Oakville Grocery (✉ *124 Matheson St.* ☎ *707/433–3200*) has a bustling Healdsburg branch filled with wine, condiments, and deli items. A terrace with ample seating makes a good place for an impromptu picnic, but you might want to lunch early or late to avoid the worst crowds.

You'll find not only wine-related gadgets and gifts but also a wide selection of kitchenware and serving pieces at **Plaza Gourmet** (✉ *108 Matheson St.,* ☎ *707/433–7116*).

DRY CREEK AND ALEXANDER VALLEYS

On the west side of U.S. 101, Dry Creek Valley remains one of the least-developed appellations in Sonoma. Zinfandel grapes flourish on the benchlands, whereas the gravelly, well-drained soil of the valley floor is better known for chardonnay and, in the north, sauvignon blanc. The wineries in this region tend to be smaller, which makes them a good bet on summer weekends, when larger spots and those along the main thoroughfares tend to be filled to the gills with tourists.

The Alexander Valley, which lies east of Healdsburg, is similarly rustic, and you can see as many folks cycling along Highway 28 here as you can behind the wheel of a car.

Inside the tasting room at **Stryker Sonoma,** vaulted ceilings and seemingly endless walls of windows onto the vineyards suggest you've entered a cathedral to wine. The wines are almost as impressive as the architecture: most of their bottles are single varietals, such as chardonnay, pinot noir, merlot, zinfandel, and cabernet sauvignon. An exception, however, are a few Bordeaux-style blends, including the powerful E1K Red Blend, which, unfortunately, is not usually poured in the tasting room (though it never hurts to ask whether they have a bottle open). The picnic tables here are a particularly lovely way to enjoy the quiet countryside of the Alexander Valley. ✉ *5110 Hwy. 28* ☎ *707/433–1944* 🌐 *www.strykersonoma.com* *Tasting free–$10* ⏲ *Daily 10:30–5.*

Dry Creek Vineyard, where fumé blanc is the flagship wine, also makes well-regarded zinfandels, a zesty dry chenin blanc, a pinot noir, and a handful of cabernet sauvignon blends. Since many of their quality wines go for less than $20 or $30 a bottle, it's a popular shopping stop for those who want to stock their cellars for a reasonable price. After picking up a bottle, you might want to picnic on their lawn next to the flowering magnolia tree. Conveniently, a general store and deli with plenty of picnic fixings is just steps down the road. ✉ *3770 Lambert*

Bridge Rd. ☎*707/433–1000* 🌐*www.drycreekvineyard.com* 🎟*Tasting $5* ⏲*Daily 10:30–4:30.*

An unassuming winery in a modern wooden barn topped by solar panels, **Quivira** produces some of the most interesting wines in Dry Creek Valley. Though it's known for its dangerously drinkable reds—like a petite sirah, and a few different hearty zinfandel blends—the dry rosé made from grenache grapes and the crisp sauvignon blanc, which spends all its time in stainless-steel tanks rather than oak barrels, are also worth checking out. Redwood and olive trees shade the picnic area. ✉*4900 W. Dry Creek Rd.* ☎*707/431–8333* 🌐*www.quivirawine.com* 🎟*Tasting $5, tour $15* ⏲*Daily 11–5; tours by appointment.*

Fodor's Choice ★

Down a narrow road at the westernmost edge of the Dry Creek Valley, **Michel-Schlumberger** is one of Sonoma's finest producers of cabernet sauvignon, aptly described by the winery's tour guide as a "full, rich big mouthful of wine." The tour is unusually casual and friendly. Weather permitting, you'll wander up a hill on a gravel pathway to the edge of their lovely benchland vineyards before swinging through the barrel room in the California Mission–style building that once served as the home of the winery's founder, Jean-Jacques Michel. A tasting comes with a sampling of their coveted cabernet, plus some very fine chardonnay, Syrah, and pinot noir. ✉*4155 Wine Creek Rd.* ☎*707/433–7427 or 800/447–3060* 🌐*www.michelschlumberger.com* 🎟*Tasting $5, tour $15* ⏲*Tours at 11 and 2, by appointment.*

6

Known for its Disney-esque Italian villa, which has as many critics as it does fervent fans for its huge size and general over-the-topness, **Ferrari-Carano Winery** produces mostly chardonnays, fumé blancs, zinfandel, and cabernet sauvignons. Though whites have traditionally been the specialty here, the reds are now garnering more attention. Tours cover not only the wine-making facilities and underground cellar but also the manicured gardens, where you can see a cork tree and learn about how cork is harvested. ✉*8761 Dry Creek Rd., Dry Creek Valley* ☎*707/433–6700* 🌐*www.ferrari-carano.com* 🎟*Tasting $5–$15, tour free* ⏲*Daily 10–5; tour Mon.–Sat. at 10, by appointment.*

Fodor's Choice ★

Once you wind your way down **Preston Vineyards'** long driveway, flanked by vineyards and punctuated by the occasional olive tree, you'll be welcomed by the sight of a few farmhouses encircling a shady yard prowled by several friendly cats. In summer a small selection of organic produce grown in their gardens is sold from an impromptu stand on their front porch, and house-made bread and olive oil are available year-round. Their down-home style is particularly in evidence on Sundays, the only day of the week that tasting-room staffers sell a 3-liter bottle of Guadagni Red, a primarily zinfandel blend filled from the barrel right in front of you. Owners Lou and Susan Preston are committed to organic growing techniques and use only estate-grown grapes in their wines, which include a Viogner, a Rousanne, a Cinsault, and a Syrah–petite sirah blend, among several others. ✉*9282 West Dry Creek Rd.* ☎*707/433–3372* 🌐*www.prestonvineyards.com* 🎟*$5* ⏲*Daily 11–4:30.*

WHERE TO STAY

$-$$$ **Best Western Dry Creek Inn.** The lackluster location of this Spanish Mission–style motel near U.S. 101 nevertheless means quick access to downtown Healdsburg and other Wine Country hotspots. Deluxe rooms are slightly more spacious and muted in color than the standard rooms, but both types are kept spotless. The more expensive rooms in the Tuscan building, which opened in 2007, are considerably more upscale, with amenities like flat-panel TVs, spa tubs, and patios. A casual family restaurant is next door. **Pros:** free Wi-Fi; free laundry facilities; frequent discounts available on their Web site. **Cons:** thin walls; basic furnishings in standard rooms. ✉ *198 Dry Creek Rd., Healdsburg* ☎ *707/433–0300 or 800/222–5784* 🌐 *www.drycreekinn.com* *163 rooms* *In-room: refrigerator, DVD (some), Internet (some), Wi-Fi. In-hotel: restaurant, pool, gym, laundry facilities, some pets allowed, no-smoking rooms* 💳 *AE, D, DC, MC, V* *CP.*

7

The North Coast

FROM THE SONOMA COAST TO REDWOOD NATIONAL PARK

WORD OF MOUTH

"Steep stairs leads to a historic lighthouse at Point Reyes National Seashore. Whales are visible from this point a few months out of the year."

—photo by spirobulldog, Fodors.com member

WELCOME TO THE NORTH COAST

TOP REASONS TO GO

★ **Scenic coastal drives:** There's hardly a road here that *isn't* scenic.

★ **Wild beaches:** This stretch of California is one of nature's masterpieces. Revel in the unbridled, rugged coastline, without a building in sight.

★ **Dinnertime:** When you're done hiking the beach, refuel with delectable food; you'll find everything from burritos to bouillabaisse.

★ **Romance:** Here you can end almost every day with a perfect sunset.

★ **Wildlife:** Sea lions and otters and deer, oh my!

1 The Sonoma Coast. Heading up through northwestern Marin into Sonoma County, Highway 1 traverses gently rolling pastureland. North of Bodega Bay dramatic shoreline scenery takes over. The road snakes up, down, and around sheer cliffs and steep inclines—some without guardrails—where cows seem to cling precariously. Stunning vistas (or cottony fog) and hairpin turns make this one of the most exhilarating drives north of San Francisco.

2 The Mendocino Coast. The timber industry gave birth to most of the small towns strung along this stretch of the California coastline. Although tourism now drives the economy, the region has retained much of its old-fashioned charm. The beauty of the coastal landscape, of course, has not changed.

3 Redwood Country. There's a different state of mind in Humboldt County. Here, instead of spas, there are old-time hotels. Instead of wineries, there are breweries. The landscape is primarily thick redwood forest, which gets snow in winter and sizzles in summer while the coast sits covered in fog. Until as late as 1924, there was no road that went north of Willits; the coastal towns were reachable only by sea. That legacy is apparent in the communities here today: Eureka and Arcata are sizeable (both formerly ports), but otherwise towns are tiny and tucked away into the woods, and people have an independent spirit that recalls the original homesteaders. Coming from the south, Garberville is a good place to stop for picnic provisions and stretch your legs.

4 Redwood National Park. For a pristine encounter with giant redwoods, make the trek to this seldom-visited park where even casual visitors have easy access to the trees. (⇨ *See chapter 8, Redwood National Park*).

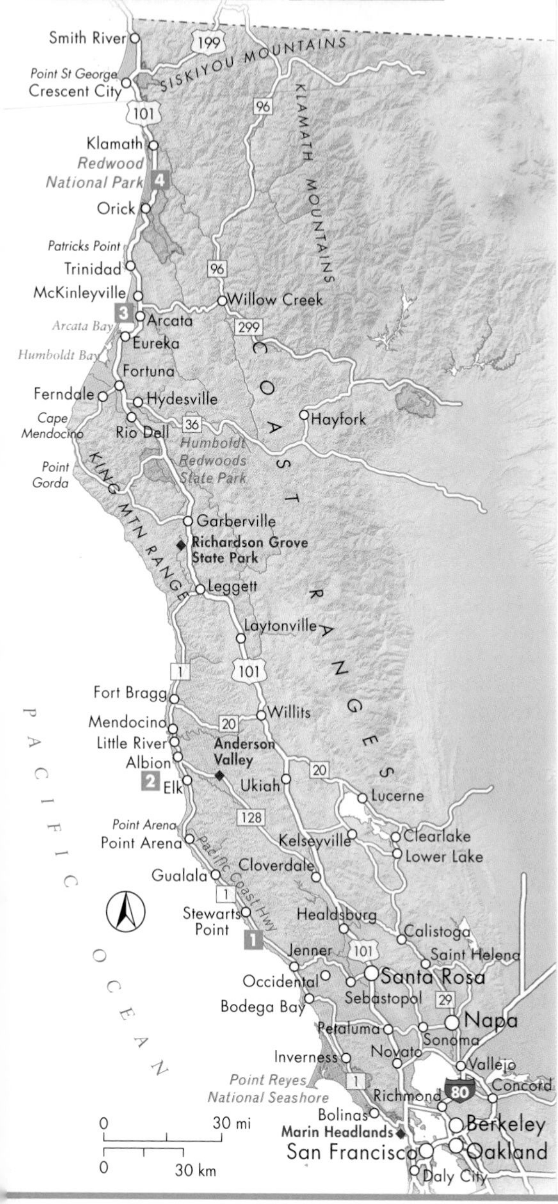

Smith River
199
SISKIYOU MOUNTAINS
Point St George
Crescent City
101
96
KLAMATH MOUNTAINS
Klamath
Redwood National Park
4
Orick
Patricks Point
Trinidad
96
McKinleyville
Willow Creek
3
Arcata
Arcata Bay
Eureka
299
Humboldt Bay
Fortuna
Ferndale
Hydesville
Cape Mendocino
Rio Dell
36
Hayfork
Humboldt Redwoods State Park
COAST RANGES
Point Gorda
KING MTN RANGE
Garberville
Richardson Grove State Park
Leggett
Laytonville
1
101
Fort Bragg
Willits
Mendocino
20
Little River
Anderson Valley
Albion
20
2
Elk
Ukiah
Lucerne
PACIFIC OCEAN
128
Point Arena
Point Arena
Kelseyville
Clearlake
Lower Lake
Pacific Coast Hwy
Cloverdale
Gualala
1
Stewarts Point
Healdsburg
1
Calistoga
Jenner
101
Saint Helena
Occidental
Santa Rosa
Sebastopol
29
Bodega Bay
Napa
Petaluma
Sonoma
Inverness
Novato
Vallejo
Point Reyes National Seashore
1
80
Concord
Richmond
Bolinas
Berkeley
Marin Headlands
San Francisco
Oakland
Daly City
0 30 mi
0 30 km

GETTING ORIENTED

It's all but impossible to explore the northern California coast without a car. Indeed, you wouldn't want to—driving here is half the fun. The main road is Highway 1, two lanes that twist and turn (sometimes 180 degrees) up cliffs and down through valleys. Towns appear every so often, but this is mostly a land of green pasture, dense forest, and natural, undeveloped coastline. Pace yourself: Most drivers stop frequently to appreciate the views (and you can't drive faster than 20–40 MPH on many portions of the highway), so don't plan to drive too far in one day.

THE NORTH COAST PLANNER

Getting Here and Around

Although there are excellent services along U.S. 101, long, lonesome stretches separate towns (with their gas stations and mechanics) along Highway 1, and services are even fewer and farther between on the smaller roads. **TIP→ If you're running low on fuel and see a gas station, stop for a refill.** Driving directly to Mendocino from San Francisco is quicker if, instead of driving up the coast on Highway 1, you take U.S. 101 north to Highway 128 west (from Cloverdale) to Highway 1 north. The quickest way to the far North Coast from the Bay Area is a straight shot up U.S. 101, which runs inland all way until Eureka. Weather sometimes forces closure of parts of Highway 1, but it's rare. For information on the condition of roads in northern California, call the Caltrans Highway Information Network's voice-activated system.

Road Conditions Caltrans Highway Information Network (☎ *800/427–7623* 🌐 *www.dot.ca.gov/hq/roadinfo*).

Restaurants

A few restaurants with national reputations, plus several more of regional note, entertain palates on the North Coast. Even the workaday local spots take advantage of the abundant fresh seafood and locally grown vegetables and herbs. Attire is usually informal, though at the pricier establishments dressy casual (somewhere between flip-flops and high heels) is the norm. As in many rural areas, plan to dine early: the majority of kitchens close at 8 or 8:30 and virtually no one serves past 9:30.

Hotels

Restored Victorians, rustic lodges, country inns, and vintage motels are among the accommodations available here. Hardly any have air-conditioning (the ocean breezes make it unnecessary), and many have no phones or TVs in the rooms. While several towns have only one or two places to spend the night, some of these lodgings are destinations in themselves. Budget accommodations are rare, but in winter you're likely to find reduced rates and nearly empty inns and B&Bs. In summer and on weekends, though, make bed-and-breakfast reservations as far ahead as possible—rooms at the best inns often sell out months in advance.

WHAT IT COSTS

	¢	$	$$	$$$	$$$$
Restaurants	under $10	$10–$15	$16–$22	$23–$30	over $30
Hotels	under $90	$90–$120	$121–$175	$176–$250	over $250

Restaurant prices are for a main course at dinner, excluding sales tax of 7.25% (depending on location). Hotel prices are for two people in a standard double room in high season, excluding service charges and 8%–10% tax.

Updated by Lisa M. Hamilton

The spectacular coastline between Marin County and the Oregon border defies what most people expect of California. The landscape is defined by the Pacific Ocean, but instead of boardwalks and bikinis there are ragged cliffs and pounding waves—and the sunbathers are mostly sea lions. Instead of strip malls and freeways, there are small towns that tuck in around sundown and a single-lane road that follows the fickle shoreline. And that's exactly why many Californians, especially those from the Bay Area, come here to escape daily life.

This stretch of Highway 1 is made up of numerous little worlds, each different from the next. From Point Reyes toward Bodega Bay the land spreads out into green, rolling pastures and sandy beaches. The road climbs higher and higher as it heads north through Sonoma County, where cows graze on precipitous cliffs and the ocean views are breathtaking. In Mendocino the coastline follows the ins and outs of lush valleys where rivers pour down from the forests and into the ocean. At Humboldt County the highway heads inland to the redwoods, then returns to the shoreline at the tidal flats surrounding the ports of Eureka and Arcata. Heading north to the Oregon border, the coast is increasingly wild and lined with redwood trees.

While the towns along the way vary from deluxe spa town to hippie hideaway, all are reliably sleepy. Most communities have fewer than 1,000 inhabitants, and most main streets are shuttered by 9 PM. Exceptions are Mendocino and Eureka, but even they are loved best by those who want to cozy up in bed rather than paint the town.

PLANNING

GETTING HERE AND AROUND

AIR TRAVEL

The only North Coast airport with commercial air service, Arcata/Eureka Airport (ACV) receives flights on United Express, Delta, and Horizon Airlines. The airport is in McKinleyville, which is 16 mi from Eureka. *See Air Travel in Travel Smart Northern California for airline phone numbers.*

A taxi to Eureka costs about $40 and takes roughly 20 minutes. Door to Door Airport Shuttle costs $19 to Arcata and Trinidad, $23 to Eureka, and $50 to Ferndale. All prices are for the first person, and go up only $5 total for each additional person.

Airport Contact **Arcata/Eureka Airport** (✉ *3561 Boeing Ave., McKinleyville* ☎ *707/839–5401*).

Shuttle Contact **Door to Door Airport Shuttle** (☎ *888/338–5497* 🌐 *www.doortodoorairporter.com*).

BUS TRAVEL

Greyhound buses travel along U.S. 101 from San Francisco to Seattle, with regular stops in Eureka and Arcata. Bus drivers will stop in other towns along the route if you specify your destination when you board. Humboldt Transit Authority connects Eureka, Arcata, and Trinidad.

Bus Contacts **Greyhound** (☎ *800/231–2222* 🌐 *www.greyhound.com*). **Humboldt Transit Authority** (☎ *707/443–0826* 🌐 *www.hta.org*).

CAR TRAVEL

Although there are excellent services along U.S. 101, long, lonesome stretches separate towns (with their gas stations and mechanics) along Highway 1, and services are even fewer and farther between on the smaller roads. ■ **TIP→If you're running low on fuel and see a gas station, stop for a refill.** Driving directly to Mendocino from San Francisco is quicker if, instead of driving up the coast on Highway 1, you take U.S. 101 north to Highway 128 west (from Cloverdale) to Highway 1 north. The quickest way to the far North Coast from the Bay Area is a straight shot up U.S. 101, which runs inland all way until Eureka. Weather sometimes forces closure of parts of Highway 1, but it's rare. For information on the condition of roads in northern California, call the Caltrans Highway Information Network's voice-activated system.

Road Conditions **Caltrans Highway Information Network** (☎ *800/427–7623* 🌐 *www.dot.ca.gov/hq/roadinfo*).

HEALTH AND SAFETY

In an emergency, dial 911. In state and national parks, park rangers serve as police officers and will help you in any emergency. Bigger towns along the coast have hospitals, but for major medical emergencies you will need to go to San Francisco. Note that cell phones don't work along large swaths of the North Coast.

Hospital Contacts **Santa Rosa Memorial Hospital** (✉ *1165 Montgomery Dr., Santa Rosa* ☎ *707/546–3201*). **Mendocino Coast District Hospital** (✉ *700*

River Dr., Fort Bragg ☎707/961–1234). **St. Joseph Hospital** (*✉2700 Dolbeer St., Eureka ☎707/445–8121).*

VISITOR INFORMATION

Information **Redwood Empire Association** (*☎415/292–5527 or 800/619–2125 🌐www.redwoodempire.com).* **Sonoma County Tourism Bureau** (*✉420 Aviation Blvd., Suite 106, Santa Rosa ☎707/522–5800 or 800/576–6662 🌐www.sonomacounty.com).* **Redwood Coast Chamber of Commerce** (*Box 199, Gualala 95445 ☎707/884–1080 or 800/778–5252 🌐www.redwoodcoastchamber.com).* **Mendocino County Alliance** (*✉525 S. Main St., Ukiah 95482 ☎707/462–7417 or 866/466–3636 🌐www.gomendo.com).* **Fort Bragg–Mendocino Coast Chamber of Commerce** (*✉332 N. Main St., Fort Bragg 95437 ☎707/961–6300 or 800/726–2780 🌐www.mendocinocoast.com).* **Humboldt County Convention and Visitors Bureau** (*✉1034 2nd St., Eureka 95501 ☎707/443–5097 or 800/346–3482 🌐www.redwoods.info).*

THE SONOMA COAST

BODEGA BAY

21 mi north of Marshall on Hwy. 1.

From the busy harbor here, commercial boats pursue fish and Dungeness crab. There's nothing cutesy about this working town without a center—it's just a string of businesses along several miles of Highway 1. But some tourists still come to see where Alfred Hitchcock shot *The Birds* in 1962. The buildings in the movie are gone, but in nearby Bodega you can find Potter Schoolhouse and the Tides Wharf complex, which was a major, if now unrecognizable, location for the movie.

WHERE TO EAT AND STAY

$$ SEAFOOD **Sandpiper Restaurant.** A local favorite for breakfast, this friendly café on the marina does a good job for a fair price. Peruse the board for the day's fresh catches or order a menu regular such as crab stew or wasabi tuna; clam chowder is the house specialty. There's often live jazz Friday and Saturday evenings. *✉1410 Bay Flat Rd. ☎707/875–2278 💳D, MC, V.*

$$$$ **Bodega Bay Lodge & Spa.** Looking out to the ocean across a wetland, a group of shingle-and-river-rock buildings houses Bodega Bay's finest accommodations. Capacious rooms are appointed with high-quality bedding, fireplaces, and patios or balconies; some have vaulted ceilings and jetted tubs. In the health complex, state-of-the-art fitness equipment sparkles and the spa provides a full roster of pampering treatments. The quiet Duck Club restaurant ($$–$$$$; no lunch), a notch or two above most places in town, hits more than it misses; try the Dungeness crab cakes with tomato-ginger chutney. **Pros:** pampering; ocean views. **Cons:** on the highway. *✉103 Hwy. 1, ☎707/875–3525 or 800/368–2468 🌐www.bodegabaylodge.com 79 rooms, 5 suites In-room: refrigerator, Wi-Fi. In-hotel: restaurant, room service, pool, gym, spa, laundry facilities, Internet terminal, Wi-Fi, no-smoking rooms 💳AE, D, DC, MC, V.*

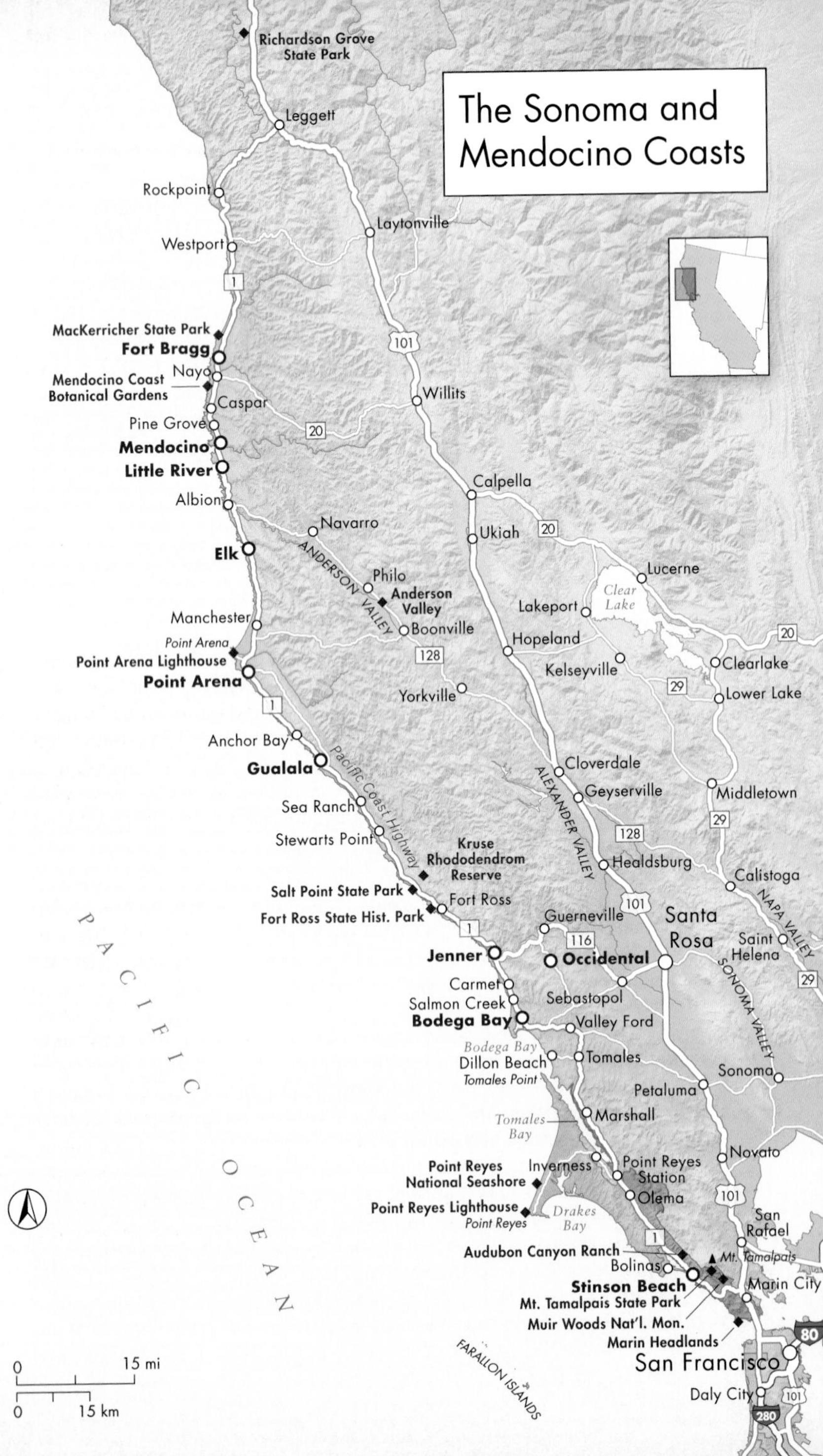

The Sonoma and Mendocino Coasts
Richardson Grove State Park
Leggett
Rockpoint
Laytonville
Westport
1
MacKerricher State Park
Fort Bragg
101
Nayo
Mendocino Coast Botanical Gardens
Willits
Caspar
Pine Grove
20
Mendocino
Little River
Calpella
Albion
Navarro
Ukiah
20
Elk
ANDERSON VALLEY
Philo
Anderson Valley
Lucerne
Clear Lake
Lakeport
Manchester
Boonville
Point Arena
Point Arena Lighthouse
Point Arena
128
Hopeland
20
Kelseyville
Clearlake
29
Lower Lake
Yorkville
1
Anchor Bay
Gualala
Pacific Coast Highway
Cloverdale
ALEXANDER VALLEY
Geyserville
Middletown
Sea Ranch
29
128
Stewarts Point
Kruse Rhododendrom Reserve
Healdsburg
Calistoga
Salt Point State Park
Fort Ross
Fort Ross State Hist. Park
101
NAPA VALLEY
Guerneville
Santa Rosa
1
116
Saint Helena
PACIFIC OCEAN
Jenner
Occidental
SONOMA VALLEY
29
Carmet
Salmon Creek
Sebastopol
Bodega Bay
Valley Ford
Bodega Bay
Dillon Beach
Tomales
Tomales Point
Sonoma
Petaluma
Marshall
Tomales Bay
Novato
Point Reyes National Seashore
Inverness
Point Reyes Station
Olema
Point Reyes Lighthouse
Point Reyes
Drakes Bay
101
San Rafael
1
Audubon Canyon Ranch
Mt. Tamalpais
Bolinas
Stinson Beach
Marin City
Mt. Tamalpais State Park
Muir Woods Nat'l. Mon.
80
Marin Headlands
FARALLON ISLANDS
San Francisco
0
15 mi
0
15 km
Daly City
101
280

SPORTS AND THE OUTDOORS

Bodega Bay Sportfishing (✉*Bay Flat Rd.* ☎*707/875–3344*) charters ocean-fishing boats and rents equipment. They also offer whale-watching trips in fall, winter, and spring. The operators of the 400-acre **Chanslor Guest Ranch** (✉*2660 Hwy. 1* ☎*707/875–3333* 🌐*www.chanslor.com*) lead guided horseback rides, some along the beach. At the incredibly scenic oceanfront **Links at Bodega Harbour** (✉*21301 Heron Dr.* ☎*707/875–3538 or 800/503–8158* 🌐*www.bodegaharbourgolf.com*) you can play an 18-hole Robert Trent Jones–designed course.

NORTH COAST WEATHER

The coastal climate is quite similar to San Francisco's, although with greater extremes: winter nights are colder than in the city, and in July and August thick fog can drop temperatures to the high 50s. If you do get caught in the summer fog, fear not! You need only drive inland (to Anderson Valley, in Mendocino, or to the redwoods of Humboldt County) to find temperatures that are often 20 degrees higher.

OCCIDENTAL

14 mi northeast of Bodega Bay on Bohemian Hwy.

A village surrounded by redwood forests, orchards, and vineyards, Occidental is a former logging hub with a bohemian feel. The 19th-century downtown offers a top-notch B&B, good food, and a handful of art galleries and boutiques. The neighboring town of Freestone offers much of the same, but on a smaller scale. To reach Occidental, take Highway 12 (Bodega Highway) east 5 mi from Highway 1. Take a left onto Bohemian Highway, where you'll find Freestone; another 3½ mi and you'll be in Occidental.

EXPLORING

A traditional Japanese detoxifying treatment awaits you at **Osmosis–The Enzyme Bath Spa,** the only such facility in America. Your bath is a deep redwood tub of damp cedar shavings and rice bran, naturally heated to 140°F by the action of enzymes. Serene attendants bury you up to the neck and during the 20-minute treatment bring you sips of water and place cool cloths on your forehead. After a shower, lie down and listen to brain-balancing music through headphones or have a massage, perhaps in one of the creek-side pagodas. A treatment and access to the gardens costs $85 per person (less for parties of two or more people); reservations are recommended. ✉*209 Bohemian Hwy., Freestone* ☎*707/823–8231* 🌐*www.osmosis.com* ▭*AE, MC, V* ⏲*Daily 9–9.*

Once a month, usually on Friday or Saturday evenings, chamber-music concerts featuring notable musicians from California and around the country are held at the Occidental Community Church. ✉*2nd and Church Sts.* ☎*707/874–1124* 🌐*www.redwoodarts.org* ▭*AE, MC, V.*

7

WHERE TO EAT AND STAY

¢ CAFÉ **Wild Flour Bread.** There are no appliances at this bakery, which occupies a renovated barn. Dough is kneaded by hand, and baked in a wood-fired oven. The result: delectable breads both savory and sweet (don't miss the sticky-bun bread). *140 Bohemian Hwy., Freestone 707/874–2938 No credit cards Closed Tues.–Thurs.*

$$$$ ★ **The Inn at Occidental.** Quilts, folk art, and original paintings and photographs fill this colorful and friendly inn. Some rooms—such as the Cirque du Sonoma Room, with a bright yellow-and-red color scheme—brim with personality and others are more sedate; all are comfortable and have fireplaces. Most guest rooms are spacious and have private decks and jetted tubs. An air of relaxed refinement prevails amid the whimsical antiques and fine Asian rugs in the ground-floor living room, where guests gather for evening hors d'oeuvres and wine. The two-bedroom Sonoma Cottage, which allows children under 10 (and pets for an additional fee), goes for $679 a night. **Pros:** colorful; luxurious; friendly. **Cons:** not for those with minimalist tastes; not for kids. *3657 Church St., Box 857, Occidental, 95465 707/874–1047 or 800/522–6324 www.innatoccidental.com 13 rooms, 3 suites, 1 cottage In-room: no a/c, refrigerator (some), TV (some), Wi-Fi. In-hotel: Wi-Fi, no kids under 10, no-smoking rooms AE, MC, V BP.*

SCENIC STOP

The gorgeous sandy coves of **Sonoma Coast State Beach** (*707/875–3483*) stretch along the shoreline from Bodega Head to a point several miles north of Jenner. Rock Point, Duncan's Landing, and Wright's Beach, clustered at about the halfway mark, have picnic areas. Wright's Beach and Bodega Dunes have developed campsites.

JENNER

10 mi north of Bodega Bay on Hwy. 1.

The broad, lazy Russian River empties into the Pacific Ocean at Jenner, a wide spot in the road where houses are sprinkled up a mountainside high above the sea. Facing south, the village looks across the river's mouth to **Goat Rock State Beach,** home to a colony of sea lions for most of the year; pupping season is March through June. The beach, accessed for free off Highway 1 a couple of miles south of town, is open daily from 8 AM to sunset. Bring binoculars and walk north from the parking lot to view the sea lions.

WHERE TO EAT

$$$–$$$$ NEW AMERICAN **River's End.** A magnificent ocean view makes lunch or an evening here memorable. Come for cocktails and Hog Island oysters on the half shell and hope for a splashy sunset. If you stay for dinner, choose from elaborate entrées such as grilled wild king salmon on cucumber noodles or elk with a red-wine-poached pear and Gorgonzola. The execution may not always justify the prices and the dining room is plain-Jane, but just look at that view. Open hours sometimes vary, so call to confirm. River's End also rents out a few ocean-view rooms and cabins ($–$$$).

Surfers check out the waves near Bodega Bay on the Sonoma Coast.

✉11048 Hwy. 1 ☎707/865–2484 🌐www.ilovesunsets.com ▭MC, V ⏲Closed mid-week fall through spring.

FORT ROSS STATE HISTORIC PARK

12 mi north of Jenner on Hwy. 1.

Fort Ross, established in 1812, became Russia's major outpost in California, meant to produce crops and other supplies for northerly fur-trading operations. The Russians brought Aleut sea-otter hunters down from Alaska. By 1841 the area was depleted of seals and otters, and the Russians sold their post to John Sutter, later of gold-rush fame. After a local Anglo rebellion against the Mexicans, the land fell under U.S. domain, becoming part of California in 1850. The state park service has reconstructed Fort Ross, including its Russian Orthodox chapel, a redwood stockade, the officers' barracks, and a blockhouse. The excellent museum here documents the history of the fort and this part of the North Coast. *✉19005 Hwy. 1 ☎707/847–3286 $7 per vehicle ⏲Daily 10–30 minutes after sunset ☞No dogs allowed past parking lot and picnic area.*

SALT POINT STATE PARK

6 mi north of Fort Ross on Hwy. 1.

For 5 mi, Highway 1 winds through this park, 6,000 acres of forest, meadows, and rocky shoreline. Heading north, the first park entrance (on the right) leads to forest hiking trails and several campgrounds. The next entrance—the park's main road—winds through meadows and along the wave-splashed coastline (a great place to stop so the kids can let off steam). This is also the route to the visitor center (open May to September, weekends 10–3) and Gerstle Cove, a favorite spot for divers and sunbathing seals. Next along the highway is Stump Beach Cove, with picnic tables, toilets, and a ¼-mile walk to the sandy beach. The park's final entrance is at Fisk Mill Cove, where centuries of wind and rain erosion have carved unusual honeycomb patterns in the sandstone called "tafonis." A five-minute walk uphill from the parking lot leads to a dramatic view of Sentinel Rock, an excellent spot for sunsets. Just up the highway, narrow, unpaved Kruse Ranch Road leads to the Kruse Rhododendron State Reserve (☎ *707/847–3221* *Free* *Daily sunrise–sunset*), where each May thousands of rhododendrons bloom within a quiet forest of redwoods and tan oaks. ✉ *20705 Hwy. 1* ☎ *707/847–3221* *$7 per vehicle* *Daily sunrise–sunset.*

THE MENDOCINO COAST

GUALALA

16 mi north of Salt Point State Park on Hwy. 1.

This former lumber port on the Gualala River has become a headquarters for exploring the coast. The busiest town between Bodega Bay and Mendocino, it has all the basic services plus a number of galleries and gift shops.

EXPLORING

Gualala Point Regional Park (✉ *1 mi south of Gualala on Hwy. 1* ☎ *707/785–2377* *Daily 8 AM–sunset*) has a long, sandy beach and picnic areas ($5 day-use fee), and is an excellent whale-watching spot December through April. Along the river, shaded by redwoods, are two dozen campsites.

WHERE TO EAT AND STAY

$$$–$$$$ NEW AMERICAN ✕ **Pangaea.** Some of Gualala's best food is prepared in the artsy jewel-color dining rooms of this little log cabin. The well-traveled chef serves imaginative dishes based on ingredients from local farms and fisheries, such as wild salmon with truffled golden beets, and lamb kebabs with blood oranges and asparagus. Cheeses from Sonoma County and throughout northern California are available for dessert. Intelligent and well priced, the wine list balances local and European selections. ✉ *39165 Hwy. 1* ☎ *707/884–9669* *www.pangaeacafe.com* *MC, V* *Closed Mon.–Thurs. No lunch.*

$$–$$$ **Mar Vista Cottages.** The dozen 1930s cottages at Mar Vista have been beautifully restored. Intentionally slim on modern gadgetry (no TV, phone, radio, or even a clock), the thoughtfully appointed and sparkling clean, one-story cottages are big on retro charm: windows are hung with embroidered drapes, coffee percolates on a white enamel stove in the full, if diminutive, kitchen, and straw sun hats hang from hooks. Outside, where benches overlook the blustery coastline, you can harvest greens, eggs, and flowers from the organic garden for your supper or take a path to Fish Rock Beach. Smoking is not allowed

anywhere on the property, and there's a two-night minimum stay. **Pros:** charming, peaceful retreat. **Cons:** no other businesses in walking distance. ✉*35101 S. Hwy 1, 5 mi north of Gualala* ☎*707/884–3522 or 877/855–3522* 🌐*www.marvistamendocino.com* *8 1-bedroom cottages, 4 2-bedroom cottages* *In-room: no a/c, no phone, kitchen, refrigerator, no TV, Wi-Fi. In-hotel: Wi-Fi, some pets allowed, no-smoking rooms* *MC, V.*

$$ **Seacliff on the Bluff.** Wedged behind a downtown shopping center, it's not much to look at. The interiors are motel standard, but you'll spend your time here staring at the Pacific panorama. Surprising extras ice the cake: take the binoculars out to your balcony or patio; stay in and watch the sunset from your jetted tub; snuggle into a robe and pop that complimentary champagne in front of your gas fireplace. Upstairs rooms have cathedral ceilings. **Pros:** budget choice; great views. **Cons:** less-than-scenic setting. ✉*39140 Hwy. 1* ☎*707/884–1213 or 800/400–5053* 🌐*www.seacliffmotel.com* *16 rooms* *In-room: refrigerator, Wi-Fi. In-hotel: Wi-Fi, no-smoking rooms* *MC, V.*

POINT ARENA

★ *14 mi north of Gualala on Hwy. 1.*

Occupied by an odd mixture of long-time locals and long-haired surfers, this former timber town is partly New Age, partly rowdy—and always sleepy. The one road going west out of downtown will lead you to the harbor, where fishing boats unload urchins and salmon and there's almost always someone riding the waves.

7

EXPLORING

For an outstanding view of the ocean and, in winter, migrating whales, take the marked road off Highway 1 north of town to the 115-foot **Point Arena Lighthouse.** The lighthouse is open for tours daily from 10 until 3:30; admission is $5. It's possible to stay out here, in one of four cottages ($$–$$$), all of which have full kitchens (on weekends there's a two-night minimum). ✉*6300 S. Hwy. 1* ☎*707/882–2777* 🌐*www.pointarenalighthouse.com.*

As you continue north on Highway 1 toward Elk, you'll pass several beaches. Most notable is the one at **Manchester State Park,** 3 mi north of Point Arena, which has 5 mi of sandy, usually empty shoreline and lots of trails through the dunes.

WHERE TO EAT AND STAY

¢ CAFÉ **Franny's Cup and Saucer.** Aided by her mother, Barbara, a former pastry chef at Chez Panisse, Franny turns out baked goods that are sophisticated and inventive. Take the coffee crunch cake: vanilla chiffon cake layered with coffee whipped cream, topped with chocolate ganache and puffs of coffee caramel "seafoam." More familiar options include berry tarts and strawberry-apricot crisp. ✉*213 Main St.* ☎*707/882–2500* *No credit cards* *Closed Sun.–Tues. No dinner.*

¢–$ CAFÉ **The Record.** Upscale sandwiches and excellent coffee are hallmarks of this café. Also noteworthy are homemade soups, like pork posole or carrot ginger. Picnickers can stock up in the front, where there's a top-notch gourmet/natural foods store. ✉265 Main St. ☎707/882–3663 ▭MC, V ⊗No dinner.

$$$–$$$$ ★ **Inn at Victorian Gardens.** Set amid 100 acres of meadows and trees, this Victorian is exquisite. The original house dates to 1904, but owner-architect Pauline Zamboni has updated and expanded it seamlessly over the past 17 years—skylights open up bathrooms with original hardwood floors, and peaked alcoves frame windows that look out onto lush gardens. Furnishings are crisp and tasteful—nothing knickknacky here—and multiple sitting rooms and patios offer plenty of room to spread out (indeed, many guests never leave the property during their stays). **Pros:** total relaxation; total quiet; total elegance. **Cons:** 6 mi from the nearest town. ✉*14409 S. Hwy. 1* ☎*707/882–3606* ⊕*www.innatvictoriangardens.com* *4 rooms* *In-room: no a/c, no phone, no TV. In-hotel: no kids under 12, no-smoking rooms* ▭*AE, MC, V* *BP.*

ELK

33 mi north of Gualala on Hwy. 1.

This quiet town is arranged on the cliff above Greenwood Cove, and just about every spot has a view of the rocky coastline and stunning Pacific sunsets. Beyond walking the beach there's little here for visitors, aside from a handful of restaurants and inns—and that's exactly why people come. Families don't tend to stay here, perhaps because it's such a romantic place.

WHERE TO EAT AND STAY

¢–$ AMERICAN **Queenie's Roadhouse Cafe.** The chrome and patent-leather diner-style chairs here are usually occupied by locals, as it's a good bet for big breakfasts (served all day) and casual lunches (the cheeseburgers are highly recommended). On sunny days, grab one of the two picnic tables out front. ✉*6061 S. Hwy. 1* ☎*707/877–3285* ▭*AE, MC, V* ⊗*Closed Tues. and Wed. No dinner.*

$$$–$$$$ **Elk Cove Inn & Spa.** Perched on a bluff above pounding surf and a driftwood-strewn beach, this property has stunning views from most rooms. The most romantic accommodations here are in the pretty, antiquey cottage buildings, where each room is unique but all have peaked ceilings and hardwood floors. A newer Arts-and-Crafts-style building houses suites ($345–$395) with a more modern feel (including Jacuzzi tubs). All rooms include a lavish breakfast in the main house as well as afternoon hors d'oeuvres with wine and cocktails. Spa treatments are offered one at a time in a private building with a view of the ocean. If you want a massage, book early; the calendar is often full. **Pros:** steps to the beach; gorgeous views; great breakfast. **Cons:** rooms in main house are smallish and within earshot of common TV. ✉*6300 S. Hwy. 1* ☎*707/877–3321 or 800/275–2967* ⊕*www.elkcoveinn.com* *7 rooms, 4 suites, 4 cottages* *In-room: no a/c, no phone, refrigerator (some), no TV, Wi-Fi. In-hotel: spa, beachfront, Wi-Fi* ▭*AE, D, MC, V* *BP.*

$$$$ **Harbor House.** Constructed in 1916, this redwood Craftsman-style house is as elegant as its location is rugged. Rooms in the main house are decorated with antiques and have gas fireplaces. The newer cottages

are luxurious; each has a fireplace and deck, and three have ocean-view claw-foot bathtubs. Room rates include breakfast and a four-course dinner (except on weeknights during January and February, when the rates drop drastically). The ocean-view restaurant ($$$$; reservations essential) serves California cuisine on a prix-fixe menu; seating for nonguests is limited. **Pros:** luxurious; romantic. **Cons:** not a place for kids. ✉ *5600 S. Hwy. 1* ☎ *707/877–3203 or 800/720–7474* 🌐 *www.theharborhouseinn.com* *6 rooms, 4 cottages* *In-room: no a/c, no phone, no TV, Wi-Fi. In-hotel: restaurant, laundry service, Wi-Fi, some pets allowed, no-smoking rooms* *AE, MC, V* *MAP.*

ANDERSON VALLEY

6 mi north of Elk on Hwy. 101, then 22 mi southeast on Hwy. 128.

At the town of Albion, Highway 128 leads southeast into the Anderson Valley, whose hot summer weather might lure those tired of coastal fog. Most of the first 13 mi wind through redwood forest along the Navarro River, then the road opens up to reveal farms and vineyards. While the community here is anchored in ranching, in the past few decades a progressive, gourmet-minded counterculture has taken root and that is what defines most visitors' experience. In the towns of Philo and Boonville you'll find B&Bs with classic Victorian style as well as small eateries.

Anderson Valley is best known to outsiders for its wineries. Tasting rooms here are more low-key than in Napa; most are in farmhouses and are more likely to play reggae than classical music. That said, Anderson Valley wineries produce world-class wines, particularly pinot noirs and Gewürztraminers, whose grapes thrive in the cool, coastal climate. All the wineries are along Highway 128, mostly in Philo with a few east of Boonville. The following are our favorites and are listed here from west to east.

7

EXPLORING

The valley's oldest winery, **Husch** (✉ *4400 Hwy. 128* ☎ *800/554–8724* ⏲ *Tasting room daily 10–5 winter, 10–6 summer*), has a cozy tasting room next to sheep pastures and picnic tables under a grapevine-covered arbor.

Roederer (✉ *4501 Hwy. 128* ☎ *707/895–2288* ⏲ *Tasting room daily 11–5*) pours its famed sparkling wines in a grand tasting room amid vineyards.

Look closely on the north side of Highway 128 for a rust-color sign reading LCV, and if the gate is open, drive the winding road through oak forest to **Lazy Creek Vineyards** (✉ *4741 Hwy. 128* ☎ *707/895–3623*). Gregarious owner and chef Josh Chandler offers unique wines, such as his Rosé of Pinot Noir, and has a bountiful rose garden where chickens run loose.

White Riesling is the specialty of **Greenwood Ridge Vineyards** (✉ *5501 Hwy. 128* ☎ *707/895–2002* ⏲ *Tasting room daily 10–5*), where awards line the walls and you can picnic at tables on a dock in the middle of a pond.

You'll find excellent vintages and great places to taste wine in the Anderson Valley—but it's much more laid-back than Napa.

★ Family-run **Navarro** (✉*5601 Hwy. 128* ☎*707/895–3686* ⏲*Tasting room daily 10–5 winter, 10–6 summer*) focuses on Alsatian varietals and offers a wide range of wines (pouring up to 15 at a time in the tasting room). The tasting room sells cheese and charcuterie for picnickers, and walking tours of the organic vineyard and winery are given daily at 10:30 AM (call in advance to make an appointment).

The aptly named **Navarro River Redwoods State Park** (✉*Hwy. 128, Navarro* ☎*707/937–5804*) is great for walks in the second-growth redwood forest and for swimming in the gentle Navarro River. There's also fishing and kayaking in the late winter and spring, when the river is higher. The two campgrounds (one on the river "beach") are quiet and clean. There's a $6 day-use fee.

WHERE TO EAT AND STAY

¢–$ CAFÉ ✕ **The Boonville General Store.** The café menu here is nothing surprising, but the exacting attention paid to ingredients elevates each dish above the ordinary. Sandwiches are served on fresh-baked bread, the beet salad comes with roasted pecans and local blue cheese. Even the macaroni and cheese—freshly made—is noteworthy. For breakfast there are granola and pastries, made in-house. ✉*14077A Hwy. 128, Boonville* ☎*707/895–9477* ▭*MC, V* ⏲ *No dinner.*

$$–$$$ **Boonville Hotel.** From the street it looks a little rusty, but inside this hotel's decor is straight out of Martha Stewart—artful linens, perfectly weathered tiles, walls painted tangerine and lime. Rooms upstairs are breezy and bright, and the luxurious bungalow in the garden includes a private porch with hammock. Equally of note is the restaurant ($$$; closed Tues. and Wed.; no lunch), where owner John Schmitt uses local

ingredients (including some from his kitchen garden, behind the hotel) to create simple, delicious dishes like braised oxtails with shiitake mushrooms and mashed potatoes, or strawberry-rhubarb shortcake. **Pros:** stylish; simple; building is the town's main hub. **Cons:** less-expensive rooms are small. ✉*Hwy. 128, Boonville* ☎*707/895–2210* 🌐*www.boonvillehotel.com* *8 rooms, 2 suites* *In-room: no a/c, no phone, refrigerator (some), no TV, Wi-Fi. In-hotel: restaurant, bar, Wi-Fi, some pets allowed, no-smoking rooms* ▭*MC, V.*

$$–$$$ **The Philo Apple Farm.** Set in an orchard of organic, heirloom apples, the three cottages and one guest room here are tasteful, spare, and inspired by the surrounding landscape. It all feels very Provençal, from the elegant country linens to the deep soaking tubs and dried flowers adorning the walls. On most weekends the cottages are reserved for people attending the highly respected cooking school here (two of the owners founded the renowned restaurant the French Laundry, in Napa), but midweek there is nearly always a room available. The farm stand, similarly refined, is also worth a stop. **Pros:** pretty; quiet; country feel. **Cons:** hard to get a reservation on weekends; occasionally hot in summer. ✉*18501 Greenwood Rd., Philo* ☎*707/895–2461* 🌐*www.philoapplefarm.com* *1 room, 3 cottages* *In-room: no a/c, no phone, no TV. In-hotel: no-smoking rooms* ▭*MC, V* *CP.*

7

LITTLE RIVER

14 mi north of Elk on Hwy. 1.

The town of Little River is not much more than a post office and a convenience store; Albion, its neighbor to the south, is even smaller. Along the winding road, though, you'll find numerous inns and restaurants, all of them quiet and focused on the breathtaking ocean.

EXPLORING

Van Damme State Park is best known for its beach and for being a prime abalone diving spot. Upland trails lead through lush riparian habitat and the bizarre **Pygmy Forest,** where acidic soil and poor drainage have produced mature cypress and pine trees that are no taller than a person. The visitor center has displays on ocean life and Native American history, and, oddly, Wi-Fi for travelers with laptops. There's a $6 day-use fee. ✉*Hwy. 1* ☎*707/937–4016 visitor center* 🌐*www.parks.ca.gov.*

WHERE TO EAT AND STAY

$$$–$$$$ FRENCH ★ ✕**Ledford House.** The only thing separating this bluff-top wood-and-glass restaurant from the Pacific Ocean is a great view. Entrées evoke the flavors of southern France and include hearty bistro dishes—stews, cassoulets, and pastas—and large portions of grilled meats and freshly caught fish (though it also is vegetarian-friendly). The long bar, with its unobstructed water view, is a scenic spot for a sunset aperitif. ✉*3000 N. Hwy. 1* ☎*707/937–0282* 🌐*www.ledfordhouse.com* ▭*AE, DC, MC, V* *Closed Mon. and Tues. No lunch.*

$$$–$$$$ **Albion River Inn.** Contemporary New England–style cottages at this inn overlook the dramatic bridge and seascape where the Albion River empties into the Pacific. All but two have decks facing the ocean, and one is wheelchair accessible. Six have spa tubs with ocean views; all

have fireplaces. The traditional, homey rooms are filled with antiques; at the glassed-in restaurant ($$–$$$)the grilled meats and fresh seafood are as captivating as the views. **Pros:** great views; great bathtubs. **Cons:** newer buildings aren't as quaint as they could be. ✉*3790 N. Hwy. 1* ☎*707/937–1919 or 800/479–7944* 🌐*www.albionriverinn.com* *18 rooms, 4 cottages* *In-room: refrigerator, no TV (some), Wi-Fi. In-hotel: restaurant, bar, Wi-Fi, no-smoking rooms* *AE, D, MC, V* *BP.*

$$$–$$$$ ★ **Glendeven Inn.** If Mendocino is the New England village of the West Coast, then Glendeven is the local country manor. The main house was built in 1867 and is surrounded by acres of gardens, complete with llamas and chickens. Inside are five guest rooms, three with fireplaces. A converted barn holds an art gallery and a wine bar that are open to the public daily. The 1986 Stevenscroft building, with its high gabled roof, contains four rooms with fireplaces. The carriage-house suite makes for a romantic retreat, and an additional two-story loft in the barn accommodates groups of up to six people (and children). The inn is on the road, so ask for a room on the far side of the property. **Pros:** picture-book pretty; elegant; romantic. **Cons:** not within walking distance of town; on the road. ✉*8205 N. Hwy. 1* ☎*707/937–0083 or 800/822–4536* 🌐*www.glendeven.com* *6 rooms, 4 suites* *In-room: no a/c, no phone (some), no TV (some), Wi-Fi. In-hotel: Wi-Fi, no kids under 17, no-smoking rooms* *AE, D, MC, V* *BP.*

MENDOCINO

3 mi north of Little River on Hwy. 1; 153 mi from San Francisco, north on U.S. 101, west on Hwy. 128, and north on Hwy. 1.

Many of Mendocino's original settlers came from the Northeast and built houses in the New England style. Thanks to the logging boom, the town flourished for most of the second half of the 19th century. As the timber industry declined, many residents left, but the town's setting was too beautiful to be ignored. Artists and craftspeople began flocking here in the 1950s, and Elia Kazan chose Mendocino as the backdrop for his 1955 film adaptation of John Steinbeck's *East of Eden,* starring James Dean. As the arts community thrived, restaurants, cafés, and inns started to open. Today the small downtown area consists almost entirely of places to eat and shop.

EXPLORING

The restored **Ford House,** built in 1854, serves as the visitor center for Mendocino Headlands State Park. The house has a scale model of Mendocino as it looked in 1890, when the town had 34 water towers and a 12-seat public outhouse. From the museum you can head out on a 3-mi trail across the spectacular seaside cliffs that border the town. ✉*Main St., west of Lansing St.* ☎*707/937–5397* *$2 suggested donation* *Daily 11–4.*

An 1861 structure holds the **Kelley House Museum,** whose artifacts include Victorian-era furniture and historical photographs of Mendocino's logging days. ✉*45007 Albion St.* ☎*707/937–5791* 🌐*mendocino* *history.org* $2 *June–Sept., Thurs.–Tues. 11–3; Oct.–May, Fri.–Mon. 11–3.*

The **Mendocino Art Center** (*45200 Little Lake St.* *707/937–5818* *www.mendocinoartcenter.org*), which has an extensive program of workshops, also mounts rotating exhibits in its galleries and is the home of the Mendocino Theatre Company.

WHERE TO EAT AND STAY

$$$–$$$$ AMERICAN **Cafe Beaujolais.** The Victorian cottage that houses this popular restaurant is surrounded by a garden of heirloom and exotic plantings. A commitment to the freshest possible organic, local, and hormone-free ingredients guides the chef here. The menu is eclectic and ever-evolving, but often includes free-range fowl, line-caught fish, and edible flowers. The bakery turns out several delicious varieties of bread from a wood-fired oven. *961 Ukiah St.* *707/937–5614* *www.cafebeaujolais.com* *AE, D, DC, MC, V* *No lunch Mon. and Tues.*

$$$$ ★ **Brewery Gulch Inn.** This tasteful inn gives a modern twist to the elegance of Mendocino. Furnishings are redwood and leather, beds are plush, and all rooms but two have whirlpool tubs with views. The luxury is in tune with the surrounding nature: Large windows frame views of the 10-acre property, bird-filled trees, and winding paths that lead through native plant gardens. Organic vegetable and herb gardens provide ingredients for the sumptuous breakfast menu. **Pros:** stylish; peaceful; intimate. **Cons:** must drive to town. *9401 Hwy. 1, 1 mi south of Mendocino,* *707/937–4752 or 800/578–4454* *www.brewerygulchinn.com* *10 rooms* *In-room: DVD, Wi-Fi. In-hotel: Internet terminal, Wi-Fi, no-smoking rooms* *AE, MC, V* *BP.*

$$$–$$$$ Fodor's Choice ★ **MacCallum House.** Set on two flower-filled acres in the middle of town, this inn is a perfect mix of Victorian charm and modern luxury. Rosebushes planted by the original owner in the late 1800s still bloom in the garden, but inside the rooms have private saunas and spa tubs. Rooms in the main house and renovated barn feel genteel and romantic, while the cottages are bright and honeymoon-y. The water tower is unforgettable—with a living room on the first floor, a sauna on the second, and a huge view of the ocean from the bed on the third. Don't miss the outstanding restaurant ($$$$), where the chef hand selects the best local ingredients—foraging for some of them himself—and everything from ice cream to mozzarella is prepared daily from scratch. **Pros:** best B&B around; excellent breakfast; great in-town location. **Cons:** new luxury suites on a separate property are less charming. *45020 Albion St.,* *707/937–0289 or 800/609–0492* *www.maccallumhouse.com* *10 rooms, 2 suites, 7 cottages* *In-room: refrigerator, DVD, Internet, Wi-Fi. In-hotel: restaurant, bar, bicycles, Internet terminal, Wi-Fi, some pets allowed, no-smoking rooms* *AE, D, MC, V* *BP.*

NIGHTLIFE AND THE ARTS

Mendocino Theatre Company (*Mendocino Art Center, 42500 Little Lake St.* *707/937–4477* *www.mcn.org/1/mtc*) has been around for nearly three decades. Their repertoire ranges all over the contemporary map, including works by David Mamet, Neil Simon, and local playwrights. Performances take place Thursday through Saturday evenings, with some Sunday matinees.

7

SPORTS & THE OUTDOORS

Catch-A-Canoe and Bicycles Too (✉ *Stanford Inn by the Sea, Comptche-Ukiah Rd., off Hwy. 1* ☎ *707/937–0273*) rents kayaks and regular and outrigger canoes as well as mountain and suspension bicycles.

FORT BRAGG

10 mi north of Mendocino on Hwy. 1.

The commercial center of Mendocino County, Fort Bragg is a working-class town that many feel is the most authentic place around; it's certainly less expensive across the board than towns to the south. The declining timber industry has been steadily replaced by booming tourism, but the city maintains a local feel since most people who work at the area hotels and restaurants live here, as do many local artists. A stroll down Franklin Street (one block east of Hwy. 1) takes you past numerous bookstores, antiques shops, and boutiques.

EXPLORING

★ The **Mendocino Coast Botanical Gardens** has something for nature lovers in every season. Even in winter, heather and camellias bloom. Along 2 mi of trails with ocean views and observation points for whale-watching is a splendid profusion of flowers. The rhododendrons are at their peak from April through June, and the dahlias are spectacular in August. ✉ *18220 N. Hwy. 1, 1 mi south of Fort Bragg* ☎ *707/964–4352* 🌐 *www.gardenbythesea.org* 🎟 *$10* ⏲ *Mar.–Oct., daily 9–5; Nov.–Feb., daily 9–4.*

Back in the 1920s a fume-spewing gas-powered train car shuttled passengers along a rail line dating from the logging days of the 1880s. Nicknamed the **Skunk Train,** it traversed redwood forests inaccessible to automobiles. The reproduction that you can ride today travels the same route, making a 3½-hour round-trip between Fort Bragg and the town of Northspur, 21 mi inland. The schedule varies depending on the season, and in summer includes evening barbecue excursions and wine parties. ✉ *Foot of Laurel St., west of Main St.* ☎ *707/964–6371 or 800/866–1690* 🌐 *www.skunktrain.com* 🎟 *$47–$70.*

MacKerricher State Park includes 9 mi of sandy beach and several square miles of dunes. The headland is a good place for whale-watching from December to mid-April. Fishing (at a freshwater lake stocked with trout), canoeing, hiking, jogging, bicycling, beachcombing, camping, and harbor seal–watching at Laguna Point are among the popular activities, many of which are accessible to the mobility-impaired. Rangers lead nature hikes in summer. ✉ *Hwy. 1, 3 mi north of Fort Bragg* ☎ *707/964–9112* 🎟 *Free.*

The ocean is not visible from most of Fort Bragg, but go three blocks west of Main Street and a flat, dirt path leads to wild coastline where you can walk for miles in either direction along the bluffs. The sandy coves in the area you first reach from the road are called **Glass Beach** (✉ *Elm St. and Glass Beach Dr.*) because this used to be the dumping ground for the city. That history is still apparent—in a good way. Look closely at the sand and you'll find the top layer is comprised

The North Coast is famous for its extremely fresh Dungeness crab; be sure to try some during your visit.

almost entirely of sea glass, likely more than you've ever seen in one place before.

An unexpected nod to Fort Bragg's rough-and-tumble past is the **Museum in the Triangle Tattoo Parlor** (*356-B N. Main St. 707/964–8814 Free Daily noon–6*). The two-room display shows a ramshackle collection of tattoo memorabilia, including pictures of astonishing tattoos from around the world, early 20th-century Burmese tattooing instruments, and a small shrine to sword-swallowing sideshow king, Captain Don Leslie.

WHERE TO EAT AND STAY

$–$$ ITALIAN **Piaci.** The seats are stools and your elbows might bang a neighbor's, but nobody seems to mind at this cozy little spot—this is hands down the most popular casual restaurant around. The food is simple, mostly pizza and calzones, but everything is given careful attention and comes out tasty. Alongside the selective list of wines is a distinctive beer list that has been given equal respect; noted are the origin, brewmaster, and alcohol content for each brew. Dogs and their owners are welcome at the tables outside. *120 W. Redwood Ave. 707/961–1133 MC, V No lunch weekends.*

$$$ FRENCH ★ **Rendezvous Inn.** Applying sophisticated European technique to fresh seasonal ingredients, chef Kim Badenhop turns out a northern California interpretation of country French cooking. To start, you might try Dungeness crab bisque finished with brandy, then follow with pheasant pot-au-feu with black chanterelles and glazed root vegetables. A sense of well-being prevails in the redwood-panel dining room, where service is never rushed. *647 N. Main St. 707/964–8142 or 800/491–8142*

www.rendezvousinn.com *D, MC, V* *Closed Mon. and Tues. No lunch.*

$$–$$$ **Weller House Inn.** It's hard to believe that when Ted and Eva Kidwell found this house in 1994 it was abandoned and slated for demolition. She is an artist and he a craftsman; together they have hammered and quilted this into the loveliest Victorian in Fort Bragg. Each of the nine guest rooms is colorful and tasteful, with hand-painted ceilings and deep, claw-foot tubs. Breakfast is served in a stunning redwood-panel ballroom, and the water tower—the tallest structure in town—offers ocean views from its second-floor hot tub and rooftop viewing deck. **Pros:** handcrafted details; homey; friendly innkeepers. **Cons:** some may find it too old-fashioned. *524 Stewart St.* *707/964–4415 or 877/893–5537* *www.wellerhouse.com* *10 rooms* *In-room: no a/c, no phone, refrigerator (some), no TV (some), Wi-Fi. In-hotel: bicycles, Wi-Fi, no-smoking rooms* *AE, D, DC, MC, V* *BP.*

SPORTS AND THE OUTDOORS

All Aboard Adventures (*32400 N. Harbor Dr.* *707/964–1881* *www.allaboardadventures.com*) operates whale-watching trips from December through mid-April, as well as fishing excursions all year. **Ricochet Ridge Ranch** (*24201 N. Hwy. 1* *707/964–7669 or 888/873–5777* *www.horse-vacation.com*) guides private and group trail rides through redwood forest and on the beach.

REDWOOD COUNTRY

HUMBOLDT REDWOODS STATE PARK

20 mi north of Garberville on U.S. 101.

The **Avenue of the Giants** *(Highway 254)* traverses the park south–north, branching off U.S. 101 about 7 mi north of Garberville and more or less paralleling that road for 33 mi north to Pepperwood. Some of the tallest trees on the planet tower over the stretch of two-lane blacktop that follows the south fork of the Eel River. At the **Humboldt Redwoods State Park Visitor Center** you can pick up information about the redwoods, waterways, and recreational activities in the 53,000-acre park. One brochure describes a self-guided auto tour of the park, with short and long hikes into redwood groves. *Ave. of the Giants, 2 mi south of Weott* *707/946–2263 visitor center* *www.humboldtredwoods.org* *Free; $6 day-use fee for parking and facilities in Williams Grove* *Park daily; visitor center Mar.–Oct., daily 9–5; Nov.–Feb., daily 10–4.*

Reached via a ½-mi trail off Avenue of the Giants is **Founders Grove** (*Hwy. 254, 4 mi north of Humboldt Redwoods State Park Visitor Center*). One of the most impressive trees here—the 362-foot-long Dyerville Giant—fell to the ground in 1991; its root base points skyward 35 feet. **Rockefeller Forest** (*Mattole Rd., 6 mi north of Humboldt Redwoods State Park Visitor Center*) is the largest remaining coastal redwood forest. It contains 40 of the 100 tallest trees in the world.

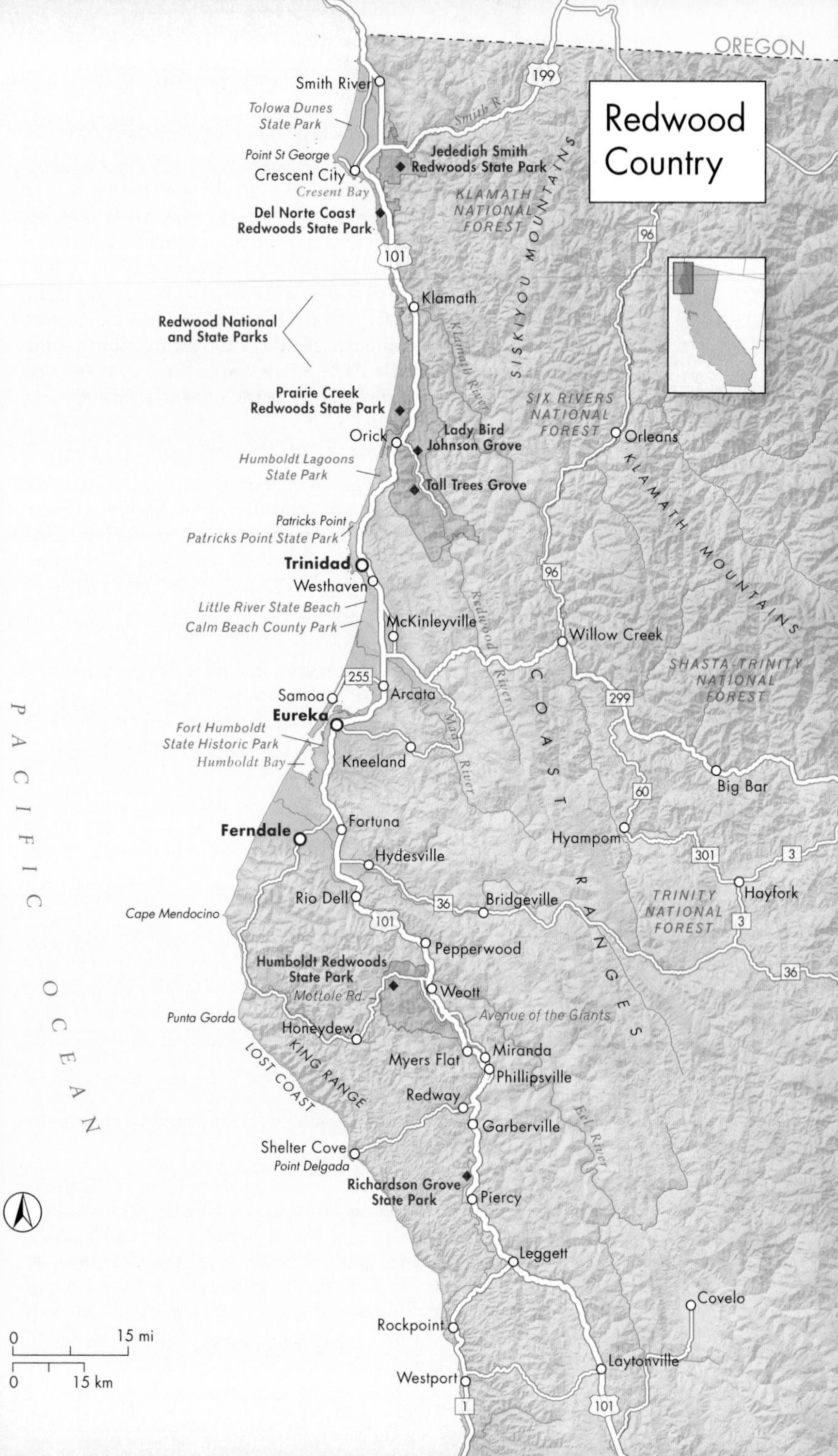

Redwood Country
OREGON
Smith River
Tolowa Dunes State Park
Point St George
Crescent City
Cresent Bay
Jedediah Smith Redwoods State Park
Del Norte Coast Redwoods State Park
KLAMATH NATIONAL FOREST
SISKIYOU MOUNTAINS
Smith R.
199
96
101
Klamath
Redwood National and State Parks
Klamath River
Prairie Creek Redwoods State Park
SIX RIVERS NATIONAL FOREST
Orick
Lady Bird Johnson Grove
Orleans
Humboldt Lagoons State Park
Tall Trees Grove
KLAMATH MOUNTAINS
Patricks Point
Patricks Point State Park
Trinidad
Westhaven
Little River State Beach
Calm Beach County Park
McKinleyville
Redwood River
Willow Creek
SHASTA-TRINITY NATIONAL FOREST
255
Samoa
Arcata
299
Eureka
Fort Humboldt State Historic Park
Humboldt Bay
Kneeland
Mad River
COAST RANGES
PACIFIC OCEAN
Big Bar
60
Fortuna
Ferndale
Hyampom
Hydesville
301
3
Hayfork
Rio Dell
36
Bridgeville
TRINITY NATIONAL FOREST
Cape Mendocino
101
Pepperwood
Humboldt Redwoods State Park
Weott
Mattole Rd.
Avenue of the Giants
Punta Gorda
Honeydew
Myers Flat
Miranda
LOST COAST
KING RANGE
Phillipsville
Redway
Garberville
Eel River
Shelter Cove
Point Delgada
Richardson Grove State Park
Piercy
Leggett
Covelo
0
15 mi
Rockpoint
Laytonville
0
15 km
Westport
1
101

FERNDALE

35 mi northwest of Weott, 57 mi northwest of Garberville via U.S. 101 north to Hwy. 211 west.

Gift shops and ice-cream stores make up a fair share of the businesses here, but at its core Ferndale miraculously remains a working small town. There's a butcher, a small grocery, and a local saloon (the westernmost in the contiguous United States), and descendants of the Portuguese and Scandinavian dairy farmers who settled this town continue to raise dairy cows on the pastures surrounding town. Ferndale is best known for its colorful Victorian architecture, the queen of which is the Gingerbread Mansion, built in 1899. Many shops carry a self-guided tour map that shows the town's most interesting historic buildings.

EXPLORING

The main building of the **Ferndale Museum** exhibits Victoriana and historical photographs and has a display of an old-style barbershop and another of Wiyot Indian baskets. In the annex are a horse-drawn buggy, a re-created blacksmith's shop, and antique farming, fishing, and dairy equipment. *✉515 Shaw Ave. ☎707/786–4466 ⊕www.ferndale-museum.org $1 ⊙June–Sept., Tues.–Sat. 11–4, Sun. 1–4; Oct.–Dec. and Feb.–May, Wed.–Sat. 11–4, Sun. 1–4.*

A walk through **Ferndale Historic Cemetery** on the east side of town gives interesting insight into the hard, often short lives of the European immigrants who cultivated this area of California in the mid-18th century. The gravestones are worn, lovely, and sometimes imaginative, one in the shape of a nubbly redwood log. The cemetery is rimmed by forest, and from the top of the hill here there's a nice view of town, the surrounding farms, and the ocean.

Memorial Day weekend's annual **Kinetic Sculpture Race** has artists and engineers (and plenty of hacks) building moving sculptures from used bicycle parts and other scraps, which they race from Arcata to the finish line in Ferndale. Contestants are judged as much on their creativity as their ability to cross the finish line, which makes for sculptures like the past Albino Rhino and a 93-foot-long fish. The **Ferndale Kinetic Museum** (*✉580 Main St. ☎No phone*) has a display of "vehicles, costumes, awards, and bribes" from past races. The museum is open 10–5 weekdays and 10–4 Sunday. Admission is free but donations are encouraged.

Eel River Delta Tours (*✉285 Morgan Slough Rd. ☎707/786–4902*) conducts two-hour boat trips that examine the wildlife and history of the Eel River's estuary and salt marsh.

WHERE TO STAY

$$–$$$ **Gingerbread Mansion.** This beautifully restored Victorian is dazzling enough to rival San Francisco's "painted ladies." The exterior has detailed spindle work, turrets, and gables; inside, the guest rooms are decorated in plush, flowery period splendor. Some rooms have views of the mansion's English garden; one has side-by-side bathtubs. One particularly posh suite is the Veneto, which has hand-painted scenes of Venice on the walls and ceiling as well as marble floors. Afternoon tea and

breakfast are both served with style. **Pros:** elegant; relaxing; friendly. **Cons:** some may find it a bit gaudy. *⊠400 Berding St., off Brown St. ☎707/786–4000 or 800/952–4136 ⊕www.gingerbread-mansion.com ⇨7 rooms, 4 suites ♨In-room: no a/c, no phone, Wi-Fi. In-hotel: water sports, bicycles, laundry service, Wi-Fi, no kids under 12, no-smoking rooms ▭AE, MC, V ⓘBP.*

EUREKA

18 mi north of Ferndale, 66 mi north of Garberville on U.S. 101.

With a population of 26,381, Eureka is the North Coast's largest city. Over the past century it has gone through several cycles of boom and bust—first with mining and later with timber and fishing—but these days, tourism is becoming a healthy industry. The town's nearly 100 Victorian buildings have caused some to dub it "the Williamsburg of the West." Shops draw people to the renovated downtown, and a walking pier reaches into the harbor.

EXPLORING

At the **Eureka Chamber of Commerce** you can pick up maps with self-guided driving tours of Eureka's Victorian architecture, and also learn about organized tours. *⊠2112 Broadway ☎707/442–3738 or 800/356–6381 ⊕www.eurekachamber.com ⊙May–Oct., weekdays 8:30–5, Sat. 10–4; Nov.–Apr., Mon.–Thurs. 8:30–5, Fri. 8:30–4.*

7

The Native American Wing of the **Clarke Memorial Museum** contains a beautiful collection of northwestern California basketry. Artifacts from Eureka's Victorian, logging, and maritime eras fill the rest of the museum. *⊠240 E St. ☎707/443–1947 ⊕www.clarkemuseum.org ⊡Donations accepted ⊙Tues.–Sat. 11–4.*

The structure that gave **Fort Humboldt State Historic Park** its name was built in response to conflicts between white settlers and Native Americans. It no longer stands, but on its grounds are some reconstructed buildings, fort and logging museums, and old logging locomotives. Demonstrators steam up the machines on the third Saturday of the month, April through September. The park is a good place for a picnic. *⊠3431 Fort Ave. ☎707/445–6567 ⊕www.parks.ca.gov ⊡Free ⊙Daily 8–5, museum and fort 8–4.*

Blue Ox Millworks is one of only a handful of woodshops in the country that specialize in Victorian-era architecture, but what makes it truly unique is that it uses antique tools to do the work. The most modern tool here is a 1948 band saw. Lucky for curious craftspeople and history buffs, the shop doubles as a dusty historical park. Visitors can watch craftsmen use printing presses, lathes, and even a mill that pares down whole redwood logs into the ornate fixtures for Victorians like those around town. The museum is less interesting on Saturday, when the craftspeople mostly take the day off. *⊠1 X St. ☎707/444–3437 or 800/248–4259 ⊕www.blueoxmill.com ⊡$7.50 ⊙Weekdays 9–5, Sat. 9–4.*

WHERE TO EAT AND STAY

> **A COLD ONE**
>
> **Lost Coast Brewery & Cafe** (✉*617 4th St.* ☎*707/445–4480*), a bustling microbrewery, is the best place in town to relax with a pint of ale or porter. Soups, salads, and light meals are served for lunch and dinner.

$$–$$$ Fodor's Choice ★ AMERICAN **Restaurant 301.** Eureka's most elegant restaurant, housed in the lovely Carter House, uses ingredients hand selected from the farmers' market, local cheese makers and ranchers, and the on-site gardens. Dishes are prepared with a delicate hand and a sensuous imagination—the ever-changing menu has featured sturgeon with house-made mushroom pasta, braised fennel, and white wine sauce. The extensive wine list has over 3,800 selections. ✉*301 L St.* ☎*707/444–8062 or 800/404–1390* *www.carterhouse.com* *AE, D, DC, MC, V* *No lunch.*

¢–$ AMERICAN **Samoa Cookhouse.** Originally a cafeteria that fed 500 local mill workers, the cookhouse became a public restaurant in the 1950s—though not much but the clientele has changed. Take a seat at one of the long, communal tables, and waiters will bring bottomless, family-style bowls of whatever is being served at that meal. For breakfast that means eggs, sausage, biscuits and gravy, and the like. Lunch and dinner usually feature soup, potatoes, salad, and pie, plus daily changing entrées such as pot roast and pork loin. A back room contains a museum of logging culture, but really the whole place is a tribute to the rough-and-tumble life and hard work that tamed this wild land. Dieters and vegetarians should look elsewhere for sustenance. ✉*Cookhouse Rd.; from U.S. 101 cross Samoa Bridge, turn left onto Samoa Rd., then left 1 block later onto Cookhouse Rd.* ☎*707/442–1659* *AE, MC, V.*

$$–$$$ **Abigail's Elegant Victorian Mansion.** Lodging at this 1890 Victorian mansion is not a passive experience. Innkeepers Doug and Lily Vieyra have devoted themselves to honoring this National Historic Landmark (once home to the town's millionaire real-estate sultan) by decorating it with authentic, Victorian-era opulence. It seems that every square inch is covered in brocade, antique wallpaper, or redwood paneling, and from every possible surface hangs a painting with gilt frame, or a historical costume. The Vieyras want their visitors not to just flop into bed, but to pretend they are the current inhabitants—drink tea in the parlor, play croquet on the lawn, select one of hundreds of period movies and watch it while the innkeepers wait on you in the sitting room. If you're ready, don your top hat or corset and embrace what Doug calls his "interactive living history museum." **Pros:** unique; lots of character; fun innkeepers. **Cons:** downtown is not within walking distance; bedrooms are a bit worn. ✉*1406 C St.* ☎*707/444–3144* *www.eureka-california.com* *4 rooms, 2 with shared bath* *In-hotel: tennis court, bicycles, laundry service, no-smoking rooms* *MC, V.*

$$$–$$$$ Fodor's Choice ★ **Carter House.** According to owner Mark Carter, his staff has been trained always to say yes. Whether it's breakfast in bed or an in-room massage, someone here will make sure you get what you want. Richly painted and aglow with wood detailing, rooms blend modern and antique furnishings in two main buildings and several cottages. **Pros:** elegant; every detail in place; excellent dining at Restaurant 301.

Cons: while kids are allowed, it's better for grown-ups. *301 L St. 707/444–8062 or 800/404–1390 www.carterhouse.com 32 rooms, 5 suites, 1 cottage In-room: kitchen (some), DVD, Wi-Fi. In-hotel: restaurant, bar, laundry service, Internet terminal, Wi-Fi, some pets allowed, no-smoking rooms AE, D, DC, MC, V No lunch BP.*

SPORTS AND THE OUTDOORS

Hum-Boats (*A Dock, Woodley Island Marina 707/443–5157 www.humboats.com*) provides kayak rental and lessons. They also offer a variety of group kayak tours, including popular whale-watching trips ($65, Dec.–June) that get you close enough to get good photos of migrating gray whales and resident humpback whales.

SHOPPING

Eureka has several art galleries and numerous antiques stores in the district running from C to I streets between 2nd and 3rd streets. Best for contemporary art is **First Street Gallery** (*422 1st St. 707/443–6363*), run by Humboldt State University, which showcases sophisticated work by local artists.

Eureka Books (*426 2nd St. 707/444–9593*) has an exceptional collection of used books on all topics.

TRINIDAD

7

21 mi north of Eureka on U.S. 101.

Trinidad got its name from the Spanish mariners who entered the bay on Trinity Sunday, June 9, 1775. The town became a principal trading post for the mining camps along the Klamath and Trinity rivers. Mining and whaling have faded from the scene, and now Trinidad is a quiet and genuinely charming community with enough sights and activities to entertain low-key visitors.

EXPLORING

On a forested plateau almost 200 feet above the surf, **Patrick's Point State Park** (*5 mi north of Trinidad on U.S. 101 707/677–3570 $6 per vehicle*) has stunning views of the Pacific, great whale- and sea lion–watching in season, picnic areas, bike paths, and hiking trails through old-growth spruce forest. There are also tidal pools at Agate Beach, a re-created Yurok Indian village, and a small museum with natural-history exhibits. Because the park is far from major tourist hubs, there are few visitors (most are local surfers), which leaves the land sublimely quiet. In spruce and alder forest above the ocean the park's three **campgrounds** (*800/444–7275 $20*) have all amenities except RV hookups. In summer it's best to reserve in advance.

Together, **Clam Beach County Park and Little River State Beach** (*6½ mi south of Trinidad, on Hwy. 1 707/445–7651 5 AM–midnight*) make a park that stretches from Trinidad to as far as one can see south. The sandy beach here is exceptionally wide, perfect for kids who need to get out of the car and burn off some energy. It's also the rare sort of beach where vehicles are allowed, so those with four-wheel-drive can drive to a perfect fishing spot or tailgate on the sand.

WHERE TO EAT AND STAY

¢–$ SEAFOOD ✕ **Katy's Smokehouse.** Purchase delectable picnic fixings at this tiny shop that has been doing things the same way since the 1940s, curing day-boat, line-caught fish with its original smokers. Salmon cured with brown sugar, albacore jerky, and smoked scallops are popular. Buy bread and drinks in town and walk to the waterside for alfresco snacking. Katy's closes at 6 PM. ✉ *740 Edwards St.* ☎ *707/677–0151* 🌐 *www.katyssmokehouse.com* 💳 *MC, V.*

$$–$$$ AMERICAN ✕ **Larrupin' Cafe.** Locals consider this restaurant one of the best places to eat on the North Coast. Set in a two-story house on a quiet country road north of town, it's often thronged with people enjoying fresh seafood, Cornish game hen, or mesquite-grilled ribs. While the garden setting and candlelight stir thoughts of romance, service is sometimes rather rushed. ✉ *1658 Patrick's Point Dr.* ☎ *707/677–0230* ✍ *Reservations essential* 💳 *No credit cards* ⏲ *Closed Tues. and Wed. No lunch.*

$$$ **Trinidad Bay Bed and Breakfast Inn.** Staying at this small Cape Cod–style inn perched above Trinidad Bay is like spending the weekend at a friend's vacation house. Every room has a downy, king-size bed and softly colored, beachy furnishings. There are as many windows as the walls will allow providing a view that starts at the harbor and stretches for miles south down the coastline. Since all rooms are roughly the same price, try to reserve the largest, Tidepool, which has overstuffed chairs in front of a gas fireplace, as well as two entire walls of windows. **Pros:** great location above bay; lots of light. **Cons:** if all rooms are full, the main house can feel a bit crowded. ✉ *560 Edwards St., Box 849* ☎ *707/677–0840* 🌐 *www.trinidadbaybnb.com* *4 rooms* *In-room: no a/c, refrigerator (some), no TV, Wi-Fi. In-hotel: Wi-Fi, no-smoking rooms* 💳 *AE, MC, V* *BP.*

$$$$ **Turtle Rocks Oceanfront Inn.** This comfortable inn has the best view in Trinidad, and the builders have made the most of it. Each room's private, glassed-in deck overlooks the ocean and rocks where sea lions lie sunning. Interiors are spare and contemporary, and all rooms have wonderfully comfortable king-size beds. The surrounding landscape has been left wild and natural; among the low bushes are sundecks for winter whale-watching and summer catnaps. Patrick's Point State Park is a short walk away. **Pros:** great ocean views; comfy king beds. **Cons:** no businesses within walking distance; not as deluxe as the price. ✉ *3392 Patrick's Point Dr., 4½ mi north of town* ☎ *707/677–3707* 🌐 *www.turtlerocksinn.com* *5 rooms, 1 suite* *In-room: no a/c, DVD (some), Wi-Fi. In-hotel: Wi-Fi, no-smoking rooms* 💳 *AE, D, MC, V* *BP.*

Redwood National Park

WORD OF MOUTH

"September is a great time for the redwoods and the coast. The 'best' weather of the year starts after Labor Day. At that time of the year, if the sky is clear, the groves are spectacular about an hour before sunset."

—GP

WELCOME TO REDWOOD NATIONAL PARK

TOP REASONS TO GO

★ **Giant trees:** These mature coastal redwoods are the tallest trees in the world.

★ **Hiking to the sea:** The park's trails wind between majestic redwood groves, and many connect to the Coastal Trail running along the western edge of the park.

★ **Step back in time:** Hike the Fern Canyon Trail, which weaves through a prehistoric scene of lush vegetation and giant ferns.

★ **Rare wildlife:** Mighty Roosevelt elk favor the park's flat prairie and open lands; seldom-seen black bears roam the backcountry; trout and salmon leap through streams, and Pacific gray whales swim along the coast during their biannual migrations.

★ **Cheeps, not beeps:** Amid the majestic redwoods you're out of range for cell-phone service—and in range for the soothing sounds of warblers and burbling creeks.

1 Del Norte Coast Redwoods State Park. In this long, mostly coastal area, the rugged terrain includes stretches of treacherous surf, steep cliffs, and forested ridges. On a clear day it's postcard-perfect; with fog, it's mysterious and mesmerizing.

2 Jedediah Smith Redwoods State Park. Gargantuan old growth redwoods dominate the scenery in this northernmost section of the park. The Smith River cuts through canyons and splits across boulders, carrying salmon to the inland creeks where they spawn.

3 Prairie Creek Redwoods State Park. The forests here give way to spacious, grassy plains where abundant wildlife thrives. Roosevelt elk are a common sight in the meadows and down to Gold Bluffs Beach.

4 Orick Area. The highlight of the southern portion of Redwood National Park is the Tall Trees Grove. It's difficult to reach and requires a special pass, but definitely worth the hassle—this section has the tallest coast redwood trees, with a new record-holder discovered in 2006.

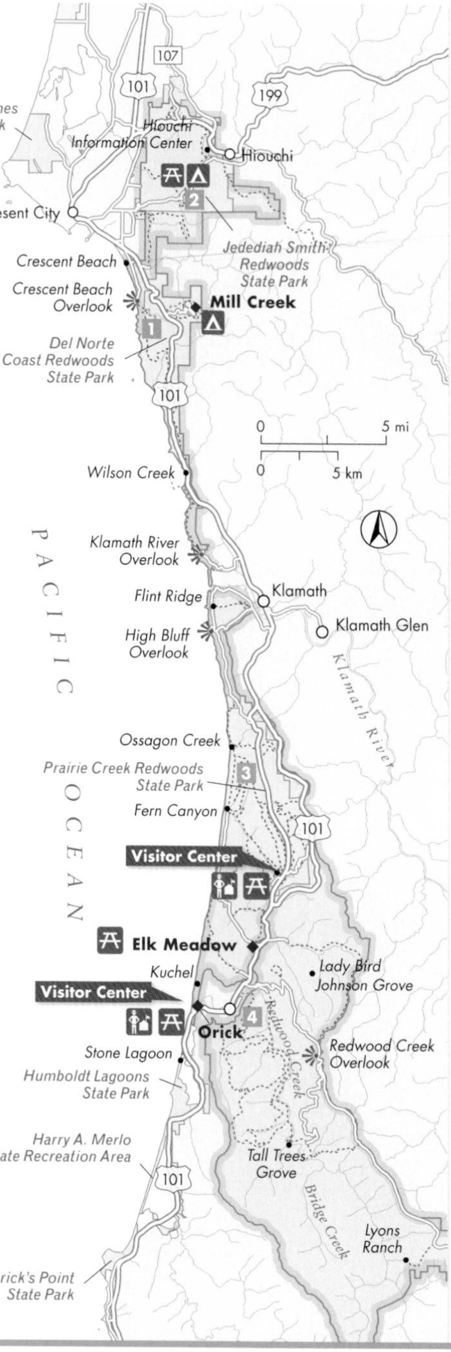

GETTING ORIENTED

What many refer to as Redwoods National Park is in fact one national park and three state parks, all conjoined along the coast of far northwest California. The majority of the national park's acreage lies east of Highway 101; by the time the highway enters the park, at Orick, drivers have already "passed" much of it. A minor road leads south to access the national park, while the highway continues north, slipping in and out of state parkland nearly all the way to the Oregon border. The graveled Coastal Drive curves along ocean vistas and dips down to the Klamath River in the park's central section. Kuchel Visitor Center, Prairie Creek Redwoods State Park and Visitor Center, Tall Trees Grove, Fern Canyon, and Lady Bird Johnson Grove are all in the national park. To the north you'll find Mill Creek Trail, Enderts Beach, and Crescent Beach Overlook in Del Norte Coast Redwoods State Park, as well as Jedediah Smith Redwoods State Park, Stout Grove, Little Bald Hills, and Simpson-Reed Grove.

REDWOOD NATIONAL PARK PLANNER

Getting There and Around

U.S. 101 runs north–south along the park, and Highway 199 cuts east–west through its northern portion. Access routes off 101 include Bald Hills Road, Davison Road, Newton B. Drury Scenic Parkway, Coastal Drive, Requa Road, and Enderts Beach Road. From 199 take South Fork Road to Howland Hill Road. Many of the park's roads aren't paved, and winter rains can turn them into obstacle courses; sometimes they're closed completely. RVs and trailers aren't permitted on some routes or beyond certain points on others.

When to Go

Campers and hikers flock to the park from mid-June to early September. In winter the crowds disappear, but the tradeoff for solitude is frequent rains and nasty potholes. Temperatures fluctuate widely throughout the park: during summer the foggy coastal lowland is much cooler than the higher-altitude interior. The average annual rainfall here is 90 to 100 inches.

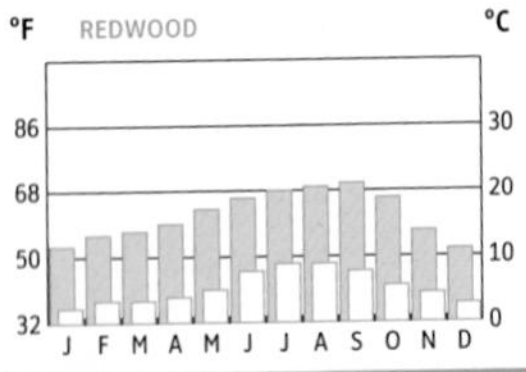

Flora and Fauna

A healthy redwood forest is diverse and includes Douglas firs, Western hemlocks, tan oaks, and madrone trees.

In the park's backcountry, you might spot mountain lions, black bears, black-tailed deer, river otters, beavers, and minks. Roosevelt elk roam the flatlands, and the rivers and streams teem with salmon and trout. Gray whales, seals, and sea lions cavort near the coastline. More than four hundred species of birds have been sighted here.

About the Campgrounds

Within a 30-minute drive of Redwood National and State parks there are nearly 60 public and private camping facilities. None of the four primitive areas in Redwood—DeMartin, Flint Ridge, Little Bald Hills, and Nickel Creek—is a drive-in site. Although you don't need a permit at these four hike-in sites, stop at a ranger station to inquire about availability. Camping along Redwood Creek in the backcountry does require a permit. At all these sites you must bring your own water.

If you'd rather drive than hike in, Redwood has four developed campgrounds—Elk Prairie, Gold Bluffs Beach, Jedediah Smith, and Mill Creek—that are within the state park boundaries. None has RV hookups, and some length restrictions apply. Fees are $20 in state park campgrounds. For details and reservations, call ☎ *800/444–7275* or check 🌐 *www.reserveamerica.com.*

WHAT IT COSTS

	¢	$	$$	$$$	$$$$
Hotels	under $70	$70–$120	$121–$175	$176–$250	over $250
Camping	under $10	$10–$17	$18–$35	$36–$50	over $50

Camping prices are for a standard (no hookups, pit toilets, fire grates, picnic tables) campsite per night.

Updated by Lisa M. Hamilton

Soaring to more than 300 feet, the coastal redwoods that give this park its name are miracles of efficiency—many have survived several centuries, and some more than 2,000 years. The world's tallest trees (a new record holder, topping out at 379 feet, was found within the park in 2006), they thrive in an environment that exists in only a few hundred coastal miles along the Pacific Ocean.

The trees commonly live 600 years—though some have been around for 2,000 years. Of the original 3,125 square mi (2 million acres) in the Redwoods Historic Range, only 4% remain following logging that began in 1850.

8

PLANNING

ADMISSION FEES

Admission to the national park portion of Redwood National and State parks is free. There's a $6 day-use fee to enter one or all of the state parks.

ADMISSION HOURS

The park is open year-round, 24 hours a day.

PERMITS

To visit Tall Trees Grove you must get a free permit at the Kuchel Information Center in Orick. Permits are also needed to camp in Redwood Creek backcountry.

VISITOR INFORMATION

Contacts Redwood National Park (✉ *1111 2nd St., Crescent City* ☎ *707/465–7306* 🌐 *www.nps.gov/redw*).

SCENIC DRIVES

★ **Coastal Drive.** This 8-mi, partially paved road on the northern side of Prairie Creek Redwoods state park is closed to trailers and RVs; in a standard auto it takes about 45 minutes to drive one way. The slow pace alongside stands of redwoods offers close-up views of the Klamath River and expansive panoramas of the Pacific. From here you'll find access to the Flint Ridge section of the Coastal Trail.

WHAT TO SEE

SCENIC STOPS

★ **Tall Trees Grove.** From the Kuchel Visitor Center you can get a free permit to make the drive up the steep 17-mi Tall Trees Access Road (the last 6 mi are gravel) to the grove's trailhead (trailers and RVs not allowed). Access to the popular grove is first-come, first-served, and a maximum of 50 permits is handed out each day. ✉ *Access road is 10 mi drive east of Kuchel Visitor Center, via U.S. 101 and Bald Hills Rd.*

Lady Bird Johnson Grove. This section of the park was dedicated by, and named for, the former first lady. A 1-mi, wheelchair-accessible nature loop follows an old logging road through a mature redwood forest. Allow 45 minutes to complete the trail. ✉ *5 mi east of Kuchel Visitor Center, along U.S. 101 and Bald Hills Rd.*

Fern Canyon. Enter another world and be surrounded by 60-foot canyon walls covered with sword, maidenhair, and five-finger ferns. Allow an hour to explore the ¼-mi-long vertical garden along a 1½-mi round-trip trail. From the north end of Gold Bluffs Beach it's an easy walk, although you'll have to wade across a small stream several times (in addition to driving across streams on the way to the parking area). ✉ *10 mi northwest of Prairie Creek Visitor Center, via Newton B. Drury Scenic Pkwy. (U.S. 101) and Davison Rd.*

Yurok Loop Trail. Beginning at the Lagoon Creek picnic area, this 1-mi round-trip trail has good bird-watching opportunities. Visit in spring to enjoy a riot of wildflowers. You'll need 45 minutes to follow the trail. ✉ *Just off Hwy. 101, 5 mi north of Klamath.*

Crescent Beach Overlook. The scenery here includes ocean views and, in the distance, Crescent City and its working harbor; this is a good place for a picnic. The overlook is known as a good spot to see gray whales that migrate November through December and March through April. ✉ *2 mi south of Crescent City off Enderts Beach Rd.*

VISITOR CENTERS

At the **Thomas H. Kuchel Visitor Center** (✉ *Off U.S. 101, Orick* ☎ *707/465–7765* 🌐 *www.nps.gov/redw*), open March–October, daily 9–5, and November–February, daily 9–4, you can get brochures, advice, and a free permit to drive up the access road to Tall Trees Grove. Whale-watchers will find the deck of the visitor center an excellent observation point, and bird-watchers will enjoy the nearby Freshwater Lagoon, a popular layover for migrating waterfowl.

Prairie Creek Visitor Center (✉ *Off southern end of Newton B. Drury Scenic Pkwy., Orick* ☎ *707/465–7354* 🌐 *www.parks.ca.gov*), open March–October, daily 9–5, and Wednesday–Sunday 9–5 the rest of the year, is housed in a redwood lodge with a massive stone fireplace built in 1933. Stretch your legs with an easy stroll along Revelation Trail, a short loop behind the lodge.

Crescent City Information Center (✉ *Off U.S. 101 at 2nd and K Sts., Crescent City* ☎ *707/465–7306* 🌐 *www.nps.gov/redw*), open March–October, daily 9–5, and November–February, daily 9–4, is the park's headquarters. It's the main information stop if you're approaching the redwoods from the north.

Jedediah Smith Visitor Center (✉ *Off Hwy. 199, Hiouchi* ☎ *707/458–3496* 🌐 *www.parks.ca.gov*), open late May–September, daily 9–5, and Friday–Sunday 10–6 the rest of the year, has information about ranger-led walks and evening campfire programs held in summer in Jedediah Smith Redwoods State Park.

The **Hiouchi Information Center** (✉ *Hiouchi Information Center, Hwy. 199, Hiouchi* ☎ *707/458–3294* 🌐 *www.nps.gov/redw*) is open daily, 9–5, mid-June to mid-September, in Jedediah Smith Redwoods State Park. The park is 2 mi west of Hiouchi and 9 mi east of Crescent City off Highway 199.

OUTFITTERS

Coast True Value. This hardware store sells fishing gear, bait, tackle, and licenses (good for both river and ocean fishing). ✉ *900 Northcrest Dr., Crescent City* ☎ *707/464–3535.*

Lunker's. You can rent inflatable and hard-shell kayaks for $25–$65 a day; another $10–$100 gets you transportation to and from various put-in points on the Smith River (make reservations a day or two in advance). They also sell bait, rent fishing gear, and can arrange for fishing guides ($175). ✉ *2095 Hwy. 199, Hiouchi* ☎ *707/458–4704 or 800/248–4704* ⏲ *Early Sept.–late May, daily 8–5.*

8

SPORTS AND THE OUTDOORS

FISHING

Both deep-sea and freshwater fishing are popular sports here. Anglers often stake out sections of the Klamath and Smith rivers in their search for salmon and trout. (A single fishing license covers both ocean and river fishing.) Less serious anglers can go crabbing or clamming on the coast, but check the tides carefully. ⇨ *For information on equipment, see Outfitters box.*

HIKING

★ **Coastal Trail.** Although this trail runs along most of the park's length, smaller sections—of varying degrees of difficulty—are accessible via frequent, well-marked trailheads. The somewhat difficult DeMartin section leads past 5 mi of mature redwoods and through prairie. If you're up for a real workout, you'll be well rewarded with the brutal but stunning Flint Ridge section, a 4½-mi stretch of steep grades and numerous switchbacks that leads past redwoods and Marshall Pond. The 4-mi-long Hidden Beach section connects the Lagoon Creek picnic area with Klamath Overlook and provides coastal views and whale-watching opportunities. ✉ *Flint Ridge trailhead: Douglas Bridge parking area, north end of Coastal Dr.*

KAYAKING

With many miles of often shallow rivers and streams in the area, kayaking is a popular pastime in the park. ⇨ *For information on equipment, see Outfitters box.*

WHALE-WATCHING

Good vantage points for whale-watching include Crescent Beach Overlook, the Kuchel Visitor Center in Orick, points along the Coastal Drive, and the Klamath River Overlook. Late November through January are the best months to see their southward migrations; February through April they return and generally pass closer to shore.

WHERE TO STAY

¢ **Hostels International–Redwood.** Travelers of all ages are welcome at this vintage 1908 Edwardian-style hostel. Perks include an enthusiastic staff and a location across the highway from the ocean. There are three dorm rooms and three private rooms; linens are included. A wood-burning stove warms the common room, and kitchen and laundry facilities are available. ✉ *14480 U.S. 101, Klamath* ☎ *707/482–8265 or 800/295–1905* 🌐 *www.norcalhostels.org/redwoods* *30 beds* ▭ *AE, D, MC, V* ⊙ *Mar.–Nov. daily; Dec.–Feb. weekends daily*

CAMPGROUNDS

$$ **Jedediah Smith Campground.** This is one of the few places to camp—in tents or RVs—within groves of old-growth redwood forest. The length limit on RVs and trailers is 35 feet. ✉ *8 mi northeast of Crescent City on Hwy. 199* ☎ *800/444–7275* *89 RV or tent sites* *Flush toilets, dump station, drinking water, bear boxes, fire pits, picnic tables, public telephone, play area, ranger station, swimming (river)* ▭ *AE, D, MC, V.*

$$ **Mill Creek Campground.** Mill Creek is the largest of the state park campgrounds. ✉ *West of U.S. 101, 7 mi southeast of Crescent City* ☎ *800/444–7275* *145 tent or RV sites* *Flush toilets, dump station, drinking water, showers, bear boxes, fire pits, picnic tables* ▭ *AE, D, MC, V* ⊙ *Daily.*

$$ Fodor's Choice ★ **Gold Bluffs Beach Campground.** You can camp in tents or RVs right on the beach at this Prairie Creek Redwoods State Park campground near Fern Canyon. Keep your eyes open for Roosevelt elk. Note that RVs must be less than 24 feet long and 8 feet wide, and trailers aren't allowed on the access road. ✉ *At end of Davison Rd., 5 mi north of Redwood Information Center off U.S. 101* ☎ *800/444–7275* *29 tent and 25 RV sites* *Flush toilets, drinking water, showers, fire pits, picnic tables* ▭ *AE, D, MC, V.*

The Southern Sierra

AROUND SEQUOIA, KINGS CANYON, AND YOSEMITE NATIONAL PARKS

WORD OF MOUTH

"Sitting on the edge of Sierra Nevada Mountains, Mono Lake is an ancient saline lake. It is home to trillions of brine shrimp and alkali flies. You can see many limestone formations known as Tufa Towers, such as this, rising from the water's surface. Mono Lake is visited by millions of migratory birds each year."

—photo by Randall Pugh, Fodors.com member

WELCOME TO THE SOUTHERN SIERRA

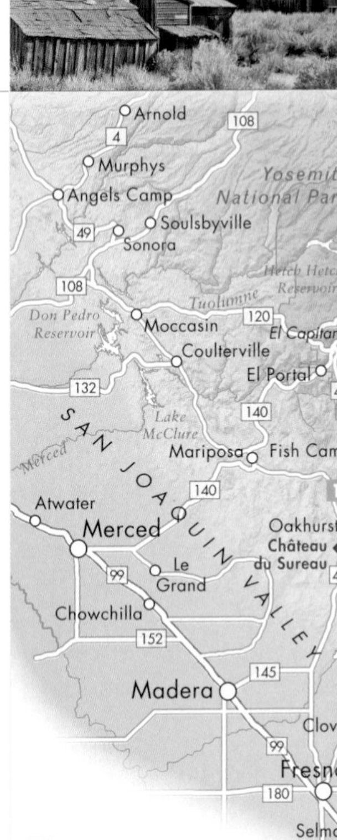

TOP REASONS TO GO

★ **Take a Hike:** Whether you walk the paved loops in the national parks (⇨ *Chapter 10, Yosemite National Park, and Chapter 11, Sequoia and Kings Canyon National Parks*) or head off the beaten path into the backcountry, a hike through groves and meadows or alongside streams and waterfalls will allow you to see, smell, and feel nature up close.

★ **Hit the Slopes:** Famous for its incredible snowpack—some of the deepest in the North American continent—the Sierra Nevada has something for every winter-sports fan.

★ **Mammoth fun:** Mammoth Lakes is eastern California's most exciting resort area.

★ **Old World charm:** Tucked in the hills south of Oakhurst, the elegant Château du Sureau will make you feel as if you've stepped into a fairy tale.

★ **Go with the flow:** Three Rivers, the gateway to Sequoia National Park, is the launching pad for white-water trips down the Kaweah River.

1 South of Yosemite National Park. Several gateway towns to the south and west of Yosemite National Park (⇨ *Chapter 10*), most within an hour's drive of Yosemite Valley, have food, lodging, and other services.

2 Mammoth Area. A jewel in the vast eastern Sierra Nevada, the Mammoth Lakes area lies just east of the Sierra crest, on the back side of Yosemite and the Ansel Adams Wilderness. It's a place of rugged beauty, where giant sawtooth mountains drop into the vast deserts of the Great Basin. In winter, 11,053-foot-high Mammoth Mountain provides the finest skiing and snowboarding in California—sometimes as late as June or even July. Once the snows melt, Mammoth transforms itself into a warm-weather playground, with fishing, mountain biking, golfing, hiking, and horseback riding. Nine deep-blue lakes are spread through the Mammoth Lakes Basin, and another 100 lakes dot the surrounding countryside.

3 East of Yosemite National Park. The area to the east of Yosemite National Park (⇨ *Chapter 10*) includes some ruggedly handsome, albeit desolate, terrain, most notably around Mono Lake. The area is best visited by car, as distances are great and public transportation is negligible. U.S. 395 is the main north–south road on the eastern side of the Sierra Nevada, at the western edge of the Great Basin. It's one of California's most beautiful highways; plan to snap pictures at roadside pullouts.

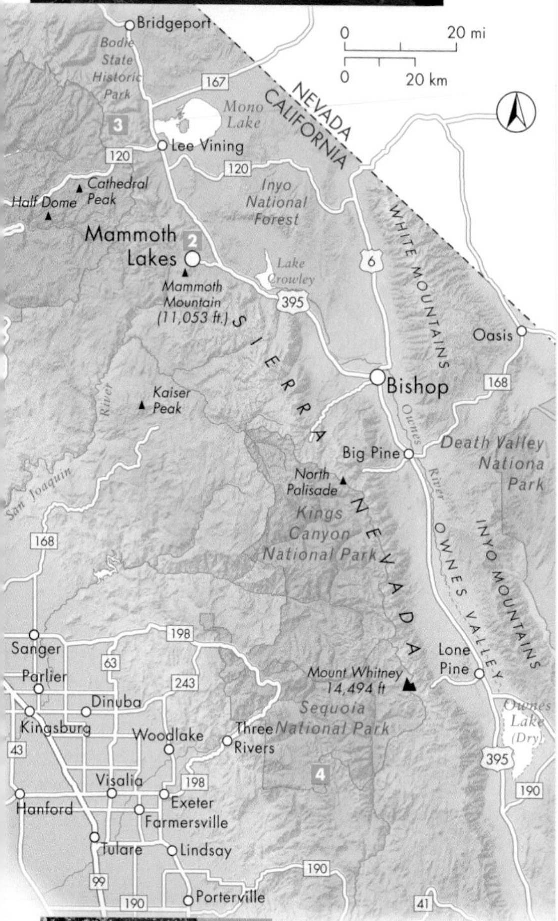

Bridgeport
Bodie State Historic Park
167
Mono Lake
NEVADA
CALIFORNIA
3
Lee Vining
120
120
Cathedral Peak
Half Dome
Inyo National Forest
Mammoth Lakes
2
Lake Crowley
Mammoth Mountain (11,053 ft.)
6
395
WHITE MOUNTAINS
SIERRA NEVADA
Oasis
Bishop
168
Kaiser Peak
River
San Joaquin
Owens
Big Pine
Death Valley National Park
North Palisade
Kings Canyon National Park
River
OWENS VALLEY
INYO MOUNTAINS
168
198
Sanger
63
Parlier
243
Dinuba
Kingsburg
Woodlake
43
Three Rivers
Mount Whitney 14,494 ft
Sequoia National Park
Lone Pine
Owens Lake (Dry)
395
4
Visalia
198
Exeter
Hanford
Farmersville
190
Tulare
Lindsay
190
99
190
Porterville
41
0 20 mi
0 20 km

GETTING ORIENTED

The transition between the Central Valley and the rugged Southern Sierra may be the most dramatic in California sightseeing; as you head into the mountains your temptation to stop the car and gawk will increase with every foot gained in elevation. While you should spend most of your time here in the national parks (⇨ *Chapter 10, Yosemite National Park, and chapter 11, Sequoia and Kings Canyon National Parks)*, be sure to check out some of the mountain towns on the parks' fringes—in addition to being great places to stock up on supplies, they have a variety of worthy attractions, restaurants, and lodging options.

4 South of Sequoia and Kings Canyon National Parks. Tiny Three Rivers is the main gateway for Sequoia and Kings Canyon National Parks (⇨ *Chapter 11*).

THE SOUTHERN SIERRA PLANNER

Getting Here and Around

Fresno Yosemite International Airport (FYI) is the nearest airport to the national parks; Reno–Tahoe is the closest major airport to Mammoth Lakes.

Airport Contacts Fresno Yosemite International Airport (✉ *5175 E. Clinton Ave., Fresno* ☎ *559/621–4500 or 559/498–4095* 🌐 *www.flyfresno.org*). **Reno–Tahoe International Airport** (✉ *U.S. 395, Exit 65B, Reno, NV* ☎ *775/328–6400* 🌐 *www.renoairport.com*).

From San Francisco, Interstate 80 and Interstate 580 are the fastest routes toward the central Sierra Nevada. Through the Central Valley, Interstate 5 and Highway 99 are the fastest north–south routes, but the latter is narrower and has heavy farm-truck traffic.

To get to Mammoth Lakes in summer and early fall (or whenever snows aren't blocking Tioga Road), you can travel via Highway 120 (to U.S. 395 south) through the Yosemite high country; the quickest route in winter is Interstate 80 to U.S. 50 to Highway 207 (Kingsbury Grade) to U.S. 395 south; either route takes about seven hours.

Contacts California Road Conditions (☎ *800/427–7623* 🌐 *www.dot.ca.gov/hq/roadinfo*).

About the Restaurants

Most small towns in the Sierra Nevada have at least one restaurant; with few exceptions, dress is casual. You'll most likely be spending a lot of time in the car while you're exploring the area, so pick up snacks and drinks to keep with you. With picnic supplies on hand, you'll be able to enjoy an impromptu meal under giant trees.

About the Hotels

If you're planning to stay on the Sierra's western side, book your hotel in advance—especially in summer. Otherwise, you may end up driving pretty far to find a place to sleep. Thanks to the surge in hotel development in Mammoth Lakes, making an advance reservation is not as critical on the Sierra's less-traveled eastern side. Wherever you visit, however, be prepared for sticker shock—rural and rustic does not mean inexpensive here.

Booking a Room

If you'd like assistance booking your lodgings, try the following agencies: **Mammoth Lakes Visitors Bureau Lodging Referral** (☎ *760/934–2712 or 888/466–2666* 🌐 *www.visitmammoth.com*). **Mammoth Reservations** (☎ *800/223–3032* 🌐 *www.mammothreservations.com*). **Three Rivers Reservation Center** (☎ *866/561–0410 or 559/561–0410* 🌐 *www.rescentre.com*).

WHAT IT COSTS

	¢	$	$$	$$$	$$$$
Restaurants	under $10	$10–$15	$16–$22	$23–$30	over $30
Hotels	under $90	$90–$120	$121–$175	$176–$250	over $250

Restaurant prices are for a main course at dinner, excluding sales tax of 7.25%–7.75% (depending on location). Hotel prices are for two people in a standard double room in high season, excluding service charges and 9%–10% tax.

Updated by Reed Parsell

Vast granite peaks and giant sequoias are among the mind-boggling natural wonders of the Southern Sierra, many of which are protected in three national parks (⇨ *Chapter 10, Yosemite National Park, and Chapter 11, Sequoia and Kings Canyon National Parks*).

Outside the parks, pristine lakes, superb skiing, rolling hills, and small towns complete the picture of the Southern Sierra. Heading up Highway 395, on the Sierra's eastern side, you'll be rewarded with outstanding vistas of dramatic mountain peaks, including Mt. Whitney, the highest point in the contiguous United States, and Mono Lake, a vast but slowly vanishing expanse of deep blue—one of the most-photographed natural attractions in California.

9

SOUTH OF YOSEMITE NATIONAL PARK

OAKHURST

40 mi north of Fresno and 23 mi south of Yosemite National Park's south entrance on Hwy. 41.

Motels, restaurants, gas stations, and small businesses line both sides of Highway 41 as it cuts through Oakhurst. This is the last sizeable community before Yosemite (⇨ *Chapter 10*) and a good spot to find provisions. There are two major grocery stores near the intersection of highways 41 and 49. Three miles north of town, then 6 mi east, honky-tonky Bass Lake is a popular spot in summer with motorboaters, jet skiers, and families looking to cool off in the reservoir.

ESSENTIALS

Visitor Information **Yosemite Sierra Visitors Bureau** (*41969 Hwy. 41, Box 1998, Oakhurst 93644 ☎ 559/683–4636 www.yosemitethisyear.com*).

WHERE TO EAT AND STAY

$$$$ CONTINENTAL Fodor'sChoice ★ **Erna's Elderberry House.** Austrian-born Erna Kubin-Clanin, the grande dame of Château du Sureau, has created a culinary oasis, stunning for its elegance, gorgeous setting, and impeccable service. Crimson walls and dark beams accent the dining room's high ceilings, and arched windows reflect the glow of candles. The seasonal six-course prix-fixe dinner can be paired with superb wines, a must-do for oenophiles. When the waitstaff places all the plates on the table in perfect synchronicity, you know this will be a meal to remember. Pre-meal drinks are served in the former wine cellar. *48688 Victoria La. 559/683–6800 www.elderberryhouse.com Reservations essential AE, D, MC, V No lunch Mon.–Sat.*

DRIVING TIPS

Keep your tank full. Distances between gas stations can be long. If you're traveling from October through April, rain on the coast can mean heavy snow in the mountains. Carry tire chains, know how to put them on (on Interstate 80 and U.S. 50 you can pay a chain installer $20 to do it for you, but on other routes you'll have to do it yourself), and always check road conditions before you leave. Traffic in national parks in summer can be heavy, and there are sometimes travel restrictions.

$ AMERICAN **Yosemite Fork Mountain House.** Bypass Oakhurst's greasy spoons and instead head to this family restaurant 3 mi north of the Highway 49/Highway 41 intersection, with an open-beam ceiling and a canoe in the rafters. Portions are huge. Expect standard American fare: bacon and eggs at breakfast, sandwiches at lunch, and pastas and steaks at dinner. *Hwy. 41, at Bass Lake turnoff 559/683–5191 Reservations not accepted D, MC, V.*

$$$$ Fodor'sChoice ★ **Château du Sureau.** This romantic inn, adjacent to Erna's Elderberry House, is straight out of one of the Grimms' fairy tales. From the moment you drive through the wrought-iron gates and up to the enchanting castle, you feel pampered. Every room is impeccably styled with European antiques, sumptuous fabrics, fresh-cut flowers, and oversize soaking tubs. Fall asleep by the glow of a crackling fire amid feather-light goose-down pillows and Italian linens, awaken to a hearty European breakfast in the dining room, then relax with a game of chess in the grand salon beneath an exquisite mural—or play chess on the giant board amid tall pine trees off the impeccably landscaped garden trail. Cable TV is available by request only. In 2006 the Château added a stunning spa. **Pros:** luxurious; spectacular property. **Cons:** you'll need to take out a second mortgage to stay here. *48688 Victoria La. 559/683–6860 www.elderberryhouse.com 10 rooms, 1 villa In-room: Internet, Wi-Fi. In-hotel: restaurant, bar, pool, spa, laundry service, no kids under 8, no-smoking rooms AE, MC, V BP.*

FISH CAMP

57 mi north of Fresno and 4 mi south of Yosemite National Park's south entrance.

As you climb in elevation along Highway 41 northbound, you see nothing but trees until you get to the small settlement of Fish Camp, where there's a post office and general store, but no gasoline (for gas, head 10 mi north to Wawona, in the park, or 17 mi south to Oakhurst).

The **Yosemite Mountain Sugar Pine Railroad** has a narrow-gauge steam train that chugs through the forest. It follows 4 mi of the route the Madera Sugar Pine Lumber Company cut through the forest in 1899 to harvest timber. The steam train, as well as Jenny railcars, run year-round on fluctuating schedules; call for details. On Saturday (and Wednesday in summer), the Moonlight Special dinner excursion (reservations essential) includes a picnic with toe-tappin' music by the Sugar Pine Singers, followed by a sunset steam-train ride. ✉*56001 Hwy. 41* ☎*559/683–7273* 🌐*www.ymsprr.com* *$17.50 steam train; Jenny railcar $13.50; Moonlight Special $46* ⌚*Mar.–Oct., daily.*

WHERE TO STAY

$$–$$$ ★ **Narrow Gauge Inn.** All the rooms at this well-tended, family-owned property have balconies (some shared) and great views of the surrounding woods and mountains. For maximum atmosphere, book a room overlooking the brook; for quiet, choose a lower-level room on the edge of the forest. The recently renovated rooms are comfortably furnished with old-fashioned accents. Reserve way ahead. The restaurant ($$–$$$$; open Apr.–Oct., Wed.–Sun.), which is festooned with moose, bison, and other wildlife trophies, specializes in steaks and American fare, and merits a special trip. **Pros:** close to Yosemite's south entrance; well-appointed; wonderful balconies. **Cons:** rooms can feel a bit dark; dining options are limited (especially for vegetarians). ✉*48571 Hwy. 41* ☎*559/683–7720 or 888/644–9050* 🌐*www.narrowgaugeinn.com* *26 rooms, 1 suite* *In-room: no a/c (some), Internet, Wi-Fi (some). In-hotel: restaurant, bar, pool, some pets allowed, no-smoking rooms* *D, MC, V* *CP.*

$$$$ ★ **Tenaya Lodge.** One of the region's largest hotels, the Tenaya Lodge is ideal for people who enjoy wilderness treks by day but prefer creature comforts at night. The hulking prefab buildings and giant parking lot look out of place in the woods, but inside, the rooms have all the amenities of a modern, full-service hotel. The ample regular rooms are decorated in pleasant earth tones, deluxe rooms have minibars and other extras, and the suites have balconies. Off-season rates can be as low as $100. The Sierra Restaurant ($$–$$$$), with its high ceilings and giant fireplace, serves continental cuisine. The more casual Jackalopes Bar and Grill ($–$$) has burgers, salads, and sandwiches. **Pros:** rustic setting with modern comforts; good off-season deals. **Cons:** so big it can seem impersonal; pricey during summer; few dining options. ✉*1122 Hwy. 41* *Box 159, 93623* ☎*559/683–6555 or 888/514–2167* 🌐*www.tenayalodge.com* *244 rooms, 6 suites* *In-room: refrigerator, Internet, Wi-Fi. In-hotel: 2 restaurants, room service, bar, pool, gym, bicycles,*

children's programs (ages 5–12), laundry service, no-smoking rooms ▭AE, D, DC, MC, V.

EL PORTAL

14 mi west of Yosemite Valley on Hwy. 140.

The market in town is a good place to pick up provisions before you get to Yosemite (⇨*Chapter 10*). There's also a post office and a gas station, but not much else.

WHERE TO STAY

$$–$$$ **Yosemite View Lodge.** The Yosemite View Lodge's motel-like design aesthetic is ameliorated by its location right on the banks of the boulder-strewn Merced River and its proximity to the park entrance 2 mi east. Many rooms have whirlpool baths, fireplaces, kitchenettes, and balconies or decks. The motel complex is on the public bus route to the park, near fishing and river rafting. Ask for a river-view room. The lodge's sister property, the Cedar Lodge, sits 6 mi farther west and has similar-looking, less expensive rooms without river views. **Pros:** huge spa baths; great views; friendly service. **Cons:** air-conditioning is inconsistent; restaurant can get crowded; can be pricey. ✉*11136 Hwy. 140* ☎*209/379–2681 or 888/742–4371* 🌐*www.yosemiteresorts.us* *335 rooms* *In-room: kitchen (some). In-hotel: restaurant, bar, pools, laundry facilities, some pets allowed, no-smoking rooms* ▭*AE, MC, V.*

MAMMOTH AREA

MAMMOTH LAKES

30 mi south of eastern edge of Yosemite National Park on U.S. 395.

Much of the architecture in Mammoth Lakes (elevation 7,800 feet) is of the faux-alpine variety. You'll find increasingly sophisticated dining and lodging options here. International real-estate developers joined forces with Mammoth Mountain Ski Area and have worked hard to transform the once sleepy town into a chic ski destination. The Mammoth Mountain Village *(below)* is the epicenter of all the recent development. Winter is high season at Mammoth; in summer room rates plummet. Highway 203 heads west from U.S. 395, becoming Main Street as it passes through the town of Mammoth Lakes, and later Minaret Road (which makes a right turn) as it continues west to the Mammoth Mountain ski area and Devils Postpile National Monument.

ESSENTIALS

Visitor Information Mammoth Lakes Visitors Bureau (✉*Along Hwy. 203, Main St., near Sawmill Cutoff Rd., Box 48, Mammoth Lakes* ☎*760/934–2712 or 888/466–2666* 🌐*www.visitmammoth.com*).

The lakes of the **Mammoth Lakes Basin,** reached by Lake Mary Road off Highway 203 southwest of town, are popular for fishing and boating in summer. First comes Twin Lakes, at the far end of which is Twin Falls, where water cascades 300 feet over a shelf of volcanic rock. Also popular

Twin Lakes, in the Mammoth Lakes region, is a great place to unwind.

are Lake Mary, the largest lake in the basin; Lake Mamie; and Lake George. Horseshoe Lake is the only lake in which you can swim.

The glacier-carved sawtooth spires of the Minarets, the remains of an ancient lava flow, are best viewed from the **Minaret Vista,** off Highway 203 west of Mammoth Lakes.

Fodor's Choice ★ Even if you don't ski, ride the **Panorama Gondola** to see Mammoth Mountain, the aptly named dormant volcano that gives Mammoth Lakes its name. Gondolas serve skiers in winter and mountain bikers and sightseers in summer. The high-speed, eight-passenger gondolas whisk you from the chalet to the summit, where you can read about the area's volcanic history and take in top-of-the-world views. Standing high above the tree line atop this dormant volcano, you can look west 150 mi across the state to the Coastal Range; to the east are the highest peaks of Nevada and the Great Basin beyond. You won't find a better view of the Sierra High Country without climbing. Remember, though, that the air is thin at the 11,053-foot summit; carry water, and don't overexert yourself. The boarding area is at the Main Lodge. *Off Hwy. 203 760/934–2571 Ext. 2400 information, Ext. 3850 gondola station $18 in summer July 4–Oct., daily 9–4:30; Nov.–July 3, daily 8:30–4.*

The overwhelming popularity of Mammoth Mountain has generated a real-estate boom, and a huge new complex of shops, restaurants, and luxury accommodations, called the **Village at Mammoth,** has become the town's tourist center. Parking can be tricky. There's a lot across the street on Minaret Road; pay attention to time limits.

WHERE TO EAT

$$$ AMERICAN

Petra's Bistro & Wine Bar. Other restaurateurs speak highly of Petra's as the most convivial restaurant in town. Its lovely ambience—quiet, dark, and warm—complements the carefully prepared meat main dishes and seasonal sides, and the more than two dozen California wines from behind the bar. The service is top-notch. Downstairs, the Clocktower Cellar bar provides a late-night, rowdy alternative—or chaser. *6080 Minaret Rd. 760/934–3500 Reservations essential AE, D, DC, MC, V No lunch.*

$$$–$$$$ AMERICAN ★

Restaurant at Convict Lake. Tucked in a tiny valley ringed by mile-high peaks, Convict Lake is one of the most spectacular spots in the eastern Sierra. Thank heaven the food lives up to the view. The chef's specialties include beef Wellington, rack of lamb, and pan-seared local trout, all beautifully prepared. The woodsy room has a vaulted knotty-pine ceiling and a copper-chimney fireplace that roars on cold nights. Natural light abounds there in the daytime, but if it's summer, opt instead for outdoor dining under the white-barked aspens. Service is so good that if you forget your glasses, the waiter will provide a pair. The wine list is exceptional for its reasonably priced European and California varietals. *2 mi off U.S. 395, 4 mi south of Mammoth Lakes 760/934–3803 Reservations essential AE, D, MC, V No lunch early Sept.–July 4.*

$$$–$$$$ AMERICAN ★

Restaurant LuLu. LuLu imports the sunny, sensual, and assertive flavors of Provençal cooking—think olive tapenade, aioli, and lemony vinaigrettes—to Mammoth Lakes. At this outpost of the famous San Francisco restaurant, the formula remains the same: small plates of southern French cooking served family-style in a spare, modern, and sexy dining room. Standouts include rotisserie meats, succulent roasted mussels, homemade gnocchi, and a fantastic wine list, with 50 vintages available in 2-ounce pours. Outside, the sidewalk café includes a fire pit where kids will love do-it-themselves s'mores. LuLu's only drawback is price, but if you can swing it, it's worth every penny. The waiters wear jeans, so you can, too. *Village at Mammoth, 1111 Forest Trail, Unit 201 760/924–8781 Reservations essential AE, D, MC, V.*

¢–$ CAFÉ

Side Door Café. Half wine bar, half café, this is a laid-back spot for an easy lunch or a long, lingering afternoon. The café serves grilled panini sandwiches, sweet and savory crepes, and espresso. At the wine bar, order cheese plates and charcuterie platters, designed to pair with the 25 wines (fewer in summertime) available by the glass. If you're lucky, a winemaker will show up and hold court at the bar. *Village at Mammoth, 1111 Forest Trail, Unit 229 760/934–5200 AE, D, MC, V.*

$–$$ AMERICAN

The Stove. A longtime family favorite for down-to-earth, folksy cooking, the Stove is the kind of place you take the family to fill up before a long car ride. The omelets, pancakes, huevos rancheros, and meat loaf won't win any awards, but they're tasty. The room is cute, with gingham curtains and pinewood booths, and service is friendly. Breakfast and lunch are the best bets here. *644 Old Mammoth Rd. 760/934–2821 Reservations not accepted AE, MC, V.*

WHERE TO STAY

$-$$ **Alpenhof Lodge.** The owners of the Alpenhof lucked out when developers built the fancy-schmancy Village at Mammoth right across the street from their mom-and-pop motel. The place remains a simple, mid-budget motel, with basic comforts and a few niceties like attractive pine furniture. Rooms are dark and the foam pillows thin, but the damask bedspreads are pretty and the low-pile carpeting clean, and best of all you can walk to restaurants and shops. Downstairs there's a lively, fun pub; if you want quiet, request a room that's not above it. Some rooms have fireplaces and kitchens. In winter the Village Gondola is across the street, a major plus for skiers. **Pros:** convenient for skiers; good price. **Cons:** could use an update; rooms above the pub can be noisy. ⊠*6080 Minaret Rd., Box 1157* ☎*760/934–6330 or 800/828–0371* 🌐*www.alpenhof-lodge.com* *54 rooms, 3 cabins* *In-room: no a/c, kitchen (some), refrigerator (some). In-hotel: restaurant, bar, pool, laundry facilities, no-smoking rooms* ▭*AE, D, MC, V.*

$$$-$$$$ **Double Eagle Resort and Spa.** You won't find a better spa retreat in the eastern Sierra than the Double Eagle. Dwarfed by towering, craggy peaks, the resort is in a spectacularly beautiful spot along a creek, near June Lake, 20 minutes north of Mammoth Lakes. Accommodations are in comfortable knotty-pine two-bedroom cabins that sleep up to six or in cabin suites with efficiency kitchens; all come fully equipped with modern amenities. If you don't want to cook, the Eagles Landing Restaurant serves three meals a day, but the quality is erratic. Spa services and treatments are available for nonguests by reservation. The small, uncrowded June Mountain Ski Area is 1½ mi away. **Pros:** pretty setting; generous breakfast; good for families. **Cons:** expensive. ⊠*5587 Hwy. 158, Box 736, June Lake* ☎*760/648–7004 or 877/648–7004* 🌐*www.doubleeagleresort.com* *16 2-bedroom cabins, 16 cabin suites, 1 3-bedroom cabin* *In-room: no a/c, kitchen (some), refrigerator, Internet. In-hotel: restaurant, bar, pool, gym, spa, some pets allowed, no-smoking rooms* ▭*AE, D, MC, V.*

$$$-$$$$ **Juniper Springs Lodge.** Tops for slope-side comfort, these condominium-style units have full kitchens and ski-in ski-out access to the mountain. Extras include gas fireplaces, balconies, and stereos with CD players; the heated outdoor pool—surrounded by a heated deck—is open year-round. If you like to be near nightlife, you'll do better at the Village, but if you don't mind having to drive to go out for the evening, this is a great spot. In summer fewer people stay here, although package deals and lower prices provide incentive. Skiers: the lifts on this side of the mountain close in mid-April; for springtime ski-in, ski-out access, stay at the Mammoth Mountain Inn. **Pros:** bargain during summer; direct access to the slopes; good views. **Cons:** no nightlife within walking distance; no a/c; some complaints about service. ⊠*4000 Meridian Blvd.* *Box 2129, 93546* ☎*760/924–1102 or 800/626–6684* 🌐*www.mammothmountain.com* *10 studios, 99 1-bedrooms, 92 2-bedrooms, 3 3-bedrooms* *In-room: no a/c, kitchen, refrigerator, Internet. In-hotel: restaurant, room service, bar, golf course, pool, bicycles, laundry facilities, no-smoking rooms* ▭*AE, MC, V.*

9

$$$–$$$$ **Mammoth Mountain Inn.** If you want to be within walking distance of the Mammoth Mountain Main Lodge, this is the place. In summer the proximity to the gondola means you can hike and mountain bike to your heart's delight. The accommodations, which vary in size, include standard hotel rooms and condo units. The inn, ski lodge, and other summit facilities are likely to be razed and rebuilt within a decade, bringing more of a 21st-century ski-resort feel to what's been a quaint 1950s-born resort. Meanwhile, the inn has done a respectable job with continual refurbishing. **Pros:** great location; big rooms; a traditional place to stay. **Cons:** can be crowded in ski season; won't be around for many more years. *Minaret Rd., 4 mi west of Mammoth Lakes Box 353, 93546 760/934–2581 or 800/626–6684 www.mammothmountain.com 124 rooms, 91 condos In-room: no a/c, kitchen (some), refrigerator (some), Internet. In-hotel: Wi-Fi, 2 restaurants, bar, pool, laundry facilities, no-smoking rooms AE, MC, V.*

$$–$$$$ Fodor's Choice ★ **Tamarack Lodge Resort & Lakefront Restaurant.** On the edge of the John Muir Wilderness Area, where cross-country ski trails loop through the woods, this original 1924 lodge looks like something out of a snow globe, and the lake it borders is serenely beautiful. Rooms in the charming main lodge have spartan furnishings, and in old-fashioned style some share a bathroom. For more privacy, opt for one of the cabins, which range from rustic to downright cushy; many have fireplaces, kitchens, or wood-burning stoves. In warm months, fishing, canoeing, hiking, and mountain biking are right outside. The small and romantic Lakefront Restaurant ($$$) serves outstanding contemporary French-inspired dinners, with an emphasis on game, in a candlelit dining room. Reservations are essential. **Pros:** rustic but not run-down; tons of nearby outdoor activities. **Cons:** thin walls; some main lodge rooms have shared bathrooms. *Lake Mary Rd., off Hwy. 203 Box 69, 93546 760/934–2442 or 800/626–6684 www.tamaracklodge.com 11 rooms, 35 cabins In-room: no a/c, kitchen (some), no TV. In-hotel: restaurant, bar, Wi-Fi, no-smoking rooms AE, MC, V.*

$$$$ **Village at Mammoth.** At the epicenter of Mammoth's burgeoning dining and nightlife scene, this cluster of four-story timber-and-stone condo buildings nods to Alpine style, with exposed timbers and peaked roofs. Units have gas fireplaces, kitchens or kitchenettes, daily maid service, high-speed Internet access, DVD players, slate-tile bathroom floors, and comfortable furnishings. The decor is a bit sterile, but there are high-end details like granite counters. And you won't have to drive anywhere: the buildings are connected by a ground-floor pedestrian mall, with shops, restaurants, bars, and—best of all—a gondola (November through mid-April only) that whisks you right from the Village to the mountain. **Pros:** central location; clean; big rooms; lots of good restaurants nearby. **Cons:** pricey; can be noisy outside. *100 Canyon Blvd. Box 3459, 93546 760/934–1982 or 800/626–6684 www.mammothmountain.com 277 units In-room: no a/c, kitchen (some), Internet. In-hotel: pool, gym, laundry facilities, parking (free), no-smoking rooms AE, MC, V.*

SPORTS AND THE OUTDOORS

For information on winter conditions around Mammoth, call the **Snow Report** (☎*760/934–7669 or 888/766–9778*). The **U.S. Forest Service ranger station** (☎*760/924–5500*) can provide general information year-round.

MAMMOTH MUSIC

The summertime **Mammoth Lakes Jazz Jubilee** (☎*760/934–2478 or 877/686–5299* 🌐*www.mammothjazz.org*) takes place in 10 venues, most with dance floors. For one long weekend every summer, Mammoth Lakes holds **Bluesapalooza and Festival of Beers** (☎*760/934–0606 or 800/367–6572* 🌐*www.mammothbluesbrewsfest.com/*), a blues-and-beer festival—with emphasis on the beer. Concerts occur throughout the year on Mammoth Mountain; contact **Mammoth Mountain Music** (☎*760/934–0606* 🌐*www.mammothevents.com*) for listings.

BICYCLING **Mammoth Mountain Bike Park** (✉*Mammoth Mountain Ski Area* ☎*760/934–3706* 🌐*www.mammothmountain.com*) opens when the snow melts, usually by July, with 70-plus mi of single-track trails—from mellow to super-challenging. Chairlifts and shuttles provide trail access, and rentals are available. Various shops around town also rent bikes and provide trail maps, if you don't want to ascend the mountain.

FISHING Crowley Lake is the top trout-fishing spot in the area; Convict Lake, June Lake, and the lakes of the Mammoth Basin are other prime spots. One of the best trout rivers is the San Joaquin, near Devils Postpile. Hot Creek, a designated Wild Trout Stream, is renowned for fly-fishing (catch-and-release only). The fishing season runs from the last Saturday in April until the end of October. To maximize your time on the water, get tips from local anglers, or better yet, book a guided fishing trip with **Sierra Drifters Guide Service** (☎*760/935–4250* 🌐*www.sierradrifters.com*).

Kittredge Sports (✉*3218 Main St., at Forest Trail* ☎*760/934–7566* 🌐*www.kittredgesports.com*) rents rods and reels and also conducts guided trips.

HIKING Hiking in Mammoth is stellar, especially along the trails that wind through the pristine alpine scenery around the Lakes Basin. Carry lots of water; and remember, you're above 8,000-foot elevation, and the air is thin. Stop at the **U.S. Forest Service ranger station** (✉*Hwy. 203* ☎*760/924–5500* 🌐*www.fs.fed.us/r5/inyo*), on your right just before the town of Mammoth Lakes, for a Mammoth area trail map and permits for backpacking in wilderness areas.

HORSEBACK RIDING Stables around Mammoth are typically open from June through September. **Mammoth Lakes Pack Outfit** (✉*Lake Mary Rd., between Twin Lakes and Lake Mary* ☎*760/934–2434 or 888/475–8747* 🌐*www.mammothpack.com*) runs day and overnight horseback trips, or will shuttle you to the high country. **McGee Creek Pack Station** (☎*760/935–4324 or 800/854–7407* 🌐*www.mcgeecreekpackstation.com*) customizes pack trips or will shuttle you to camp alone. Operated by the folks at McGee Creek, **Sierra Meadows Ranch** (✉*Sherwin Creek Rd., off Old Mammoth*

Rd. ☎*760/934–6161*) conducts horseback and wagon rides that range from one-hour to all-day excursions.

HOT-AIR BALLOONING The balloons of **Mammoth Balloon Adventures** (☎*760/937–8787* ⊕*www.mammothballoonadventures.com*) glide over the countryside in the morning from spring until fall, weather permitting.

SKIING **June Mountain Ski Area.** In their rush to Mammoth Mountain, most people overlook June Mountain, a compact, low-key resort 20 mi north of Mammoth. Snowboarders especially dig it. Two freestyle terrain areas are for both skiers and boarders, including a huge 16-foot-wall super pipe. Best of all, there's rarely a line for the lifts—if you want to avoid the crowds but must ski on a weekend, this is the place. And in a storm June is better protected from wind and blowing snow than Mammoth Mountain. (If it starts to storm, you can use your Mammoth ticket at June.) Expect all the usual services, including a rental-and-repair shop, ski school, and sports shop, but the food quality is better at Mammoth. Lift tickets run $64, with discounts for multiple days. ✉*3819 Hwy. 158, off June Lake Loop, June Lake* ☎*760/648–7733 or 888/586–3686* ⊕*www.junemountain.com* ☞*35 trails on 500 acres, rated 35% beginner, 45% intermediate, 20% advanced. Longest run 2½ mi, base 7,510 feet, summit 10,174 feet. Lifts: 7.*

Fodor's Choice ★ **Mammoth Mountain Ski Area.** If you ski only one mountain in California, make it Mammoth. One of the West's largest and best ski areas, Mammoth has more than 3,500 acres of skiable terrain and a 3,100-foot vertical drop. The views from the 11,053-foot summit are some of the most stunning in the Sierra. Below, you'll find a 6½-mi-wide swath of groomed boulevards and canyons, as well as pockets of tree-skiing and a dozen vast bowls. Snowboarders are everywhere on the slopes; there are three outstanding freestyle terrain parks of varying technical difficulty, with jumps, rails, tabletops, and giant super pipes (this is the location of several international snowboarding competitions). Mammoth's season begins in November and often lingers into May. Lift tickets cost $65. Lessons and equipment are available, and there's a children's ski and snowboard school. Mammoth runs free shuttle-bus routes around town and to the ski area, and the Village Gondola runs from the Village complex to Canyon Lodge. However, only overnight guests are allowed to park at the Village for more than a few hours. Warning: The main lodge is dark and dated, unsuited in most every way for the crush of ski season. Within a decade, it's likely to be replaced. ✉*Minaret Rd., west of Mammoth Lakes* ☎*760/934–2571, 800/626–6684, 760/934–0687 shuttle* ☞*150 trails on 3,500 acres, rated 30% beginner, 40% intermediate, 30% advanced. Longest run 3 mi, base 7,953 feet, summit 11,053 feet. Lifts: 27, including 9 high-speed and 2 gondolas.*

Trails at **Tamarack Cross Country Ski Center** (✉*Lake Mary Rd., off Hwy. 203* ☎*760/934–5293 or 760/934–2442* ⊕*www.tamaracklodge.com*), adjacent to Tamarack Lodge, meander around several lakes. Rentals are available.

Mammoth Sporting Goods (✉*1 Sierra Center Mall, Old Mammoth Rd.* ☎*760/934–3239* ⊕*www.mammothsportinggoods.com*) rents good skis for intermediates, and sells equipment, clothing, and accessories.

Advanced skiers should rent from **Kittredge Sports** (✉*3218 Main St.* ☎*760/934–7566* 🌐*www.kittredgesports.com*).

★ When the U.S. Ski Team visits Mammoth and needs boots adjusted, they head to **Footloose** (✉*3043 Main St.* ☎*760/934–2400* 🌐*www.footloosesports.com*), the best place in town—and possibly all California—for ski-boot rentals and sales, as well as custom insoles (ask for Kevin or Corty).

EAST OF YOSEMITE NATIONAL PARK

LEE VINING

20 mi east of Tuolumne Meadows via Hwy. 120 to U.S. 395; 30 mi north of Mammoth Lakes on U.S. 395.

Tiny Lee Vining is known primarily as the eastern gateway to Yosemite National Park (summer only; ⇨*Chapter 10*) and the location of vast and desolate Mono Lake. Pick up supplies at the general store year-round, or stop here for lunch or dinner before or after a drive through the high country. In winter the town is all but deserted, except for the ice climbers who come to scale frozen waterfalls. You can meet these hearty souls at Nicely's restaurant, where the climbers congregate for breakfast around 8 on winter mornings.

ESSENTIALS

Visitor Information **Lee Vining Chamber of Commerce** (*Box 130, Lee Vining 93541* ☎*760/647–6629* 🌐*www.leevining.com/*). **Mono Lake** (*Box 49, Lee Vining 93541* ☎*760/647–3044* 🌐*www.monolake.org*).

If you want to try your hand at the ice climbing, contact **Sierra Mountain Guides** (☎*760/648–1122 or 877/423–2546* 🌐*www.themountainguide.com*).

9

★ Eerie tufa towers—calcium carbonate formations that often resemble castle turrets—rise from impressive **Mono Lake.** Since the 1940s the city of Los Angeles has diverted water from streams that feed the lake, lowering its water level and exposing the tufa. Court victories by environmentalists in the 1990s forced a reduction of the diversions, and the lake has since risen about 9 feet. From April through August millions of migratory birds nest in and around Mono Lake. The best place to view the tufa is at the south end of the lake along the mile-long **South Tufa Trail.** To reach it, drive 5 mi south from Lee Vining on U.S. 395, then 5 mi east on Highway 120. There's a $3 fee. You can swim (or float) in the salty water at Navy Beach near the South Tufa Trail or take a kayak or canoe trip for close-up views of the tufa (check with rangers for boating restrictions during bird-nesting season). You can rent kayaks in Mammoth Lakes. The sensational **Scenic Area Visitor Center** (✉*U.S. 395* ☎*760/647–3044*) is open daily from June through September (Sunday–Thursday 8–5, Friday and Saturday 8–7), and the rest of the year Thursday–Monday 9–4. Its hilltop, sweeping views of Mono Lake, along with its interactive exhibits inside, make this one of California's best visitor centers. Rangers and naturalists lead walking tours of

WORD OF MOUTH

"Bodie is in a state of 'arrested decay'; many buildings are intact, complete with furniture and dishes left behind when the residents left. There is much to see and it is a fascinating piece of history." –elnap29

the tufa daily in summer and on weekends (sometimes on cross-country skis) in winter. In town, the Mono Lake Committee Information Center & Bookstore (✉ *U.S. 395 and Third St.* ☎ *760/647–6595* 🌐 *www.monolake.org*) has more information about this beautiful area.

WHERE TO EAT AND STAY

$–$$ DELI ★ ✕ **Tioga Gas Mart & Whoa Nelli Deli.** Near the eastern entrance to Yosemite, Whoa Nelli serves some of Mono County's best food, including lobster taquitos, pizzas, and enormous slices of multilayered cakes. But what makes it special is that it's in a gas station—possibly the only one in America where you can order cocktails (a pitcher of mango margaritas, anyone?)—and outside there's a full-size trapeze where you can take lessons (by reservation).This wacky spot is well off the noisy road, and has plenty of shaded outdoor tables with views of Mono Lake; bands play here on summer evenings, and locals love it, too. ✉ *Hwy. 120 and U.S. 395* ☎ *760/647–1088* 💳 *AE, MC, V* ⏲ *Closed mid-Nov.–mid-Apr.*

$ **Lake View Lodge.** Lovely landscaping, which includes several inviting and shaded places to sit, is what sets this clean motel apart from its handful of competitors in town. It's also up and off the highway by a few hundred feet, which means it's peaceful as well as pretty. Open morning and early afternoon, a stand-alone coffee shop adds to the appeal. The cottages lack the main building's lake views; some have kitchens and can sleep up to six. **Pros:** attractive; clean; friendly staff. **Cons:** could use updating. ✉ *51285 U.S. 395* ☎ *760/647–6543 or 800/990–6614* 🌐 *www.lakeviewlodgeyosemite.com* *76 rooms, 12 cottages* *In-room: no a/c, kitchen (some), refrigerator (some), Wi-Fi. In-hotel: no-smoking rooms* 💳 *AE, D, MC, V.*

BODIE STATE HISTORIC PARK

23 mi northeast of Lee Vining via U.S. 395 to Hwy. 270 (last 3 mi are unpaved).

Old shacks and shops, abandoned mine shafts, a Methodist church, the mining village of Rattlesnake Gulch, and the remains of a small Chinatown are among the sights at fascinating **Bodie Ghost Town.** The town, at an elevation of 8,200 feet, boomed from about 1878 to 1881, as gold prospectors, having worked the best of the western Sierra mines, headed to the high desert on the eastern slopes. Bodie was a mean place—the booze flowed freely, shootings were commonplace, and licentiousness reigned. Evidence of the town's wild past survives today at an excellent museum, and you can tour an old stamp mill and a ridge that contains many mine sites. Bodie, unlike Calico in Southern California near Barstow, is a genuine ghost town, its status proudly stated as "arrested decay." No food, drink, or lodging is available in Bodie. Though the park stays open in winter, snow may close Highway 270. Still, it's a fantastic time to visit: rent cross-country skis in Mammoth Lakes, drive north, ski in, and have the park to yourself. ✉ *Museum: Main and Green Sts.* ☎ *760/647–6445* 🌐 *www.bodie.net* *Park $3, museum free* ⏲ *Park: late May–early Sept., daily 8–7; early Sept.–late May, daily 8–4. Museum: late May–early Sept., daily 9–6; early Sept.–late May, hrs vary.*

Fodor's Choice ★

9

SOUTH OF SEQUOIA AND KINGS CANYON NATIONAL PARKS

THREE RIVERS

200 mi north of Los Angeles via I–5 to Hwy. 99 to Hwy. 198; 8 mi south of Ash Mountain/Foothills entrance to Sequoia National Park on Hwy. 198.

In the foothills of the Sierra along the Kaweah River, this sparsely populated, serpentine hamlet serves as the main gateway town to Sequoia and Kings Canyon national parks (⇨ *Chapter 11, Sequoia and Kings Canyon National Parks*). Its livelihood depends largely on tourism from the parks, courtesy of two markets, a few service stations, banks, a post office, and several lodgings, which are good spots to find a room when park accommodations are full.

WHERE TO EAT AND STAY

¢ ECLECTIC ✕ **We Three Bakery.** This friendly, popular-with-the-locals spot packs lunches for trips into the nearby national parks; they're also open for breakfast. ✉ *43688 Sierra Dr.* 🌐 *www.wethreerestaurant.com* ☎ *559/561–4761* ▭ *MC, V.*

$–$$ **Buckeye Tree Lodge.** Every room at this two-story motel has a patio facing a sun-dappled grassy lawn, right on the banks of the Kaweah River. Accommodations are simple and well kept, and the lodge sits a mere quarter mile from the park gate. Book well in advance for the summer. The jointly owned Sequoia Village Inn, across the highway, was extensively renovated in 2006 and is another good option (☎ *559/561–3652*); accommodation options there are cottages, cabins, and chalets. **Pros:** scenic setting; clean; popular. **Cons:** could use an update. ✉ *46000 Sierra Dr., Hwy. 198,* ☎ *559/561–5900* 🌐 *www.buckeyetree.com* *11 rooms, 1 cottage* *In-room: Wi-Fi. In-hotel: pool, some pets allowed, no-smoking rooms* ▭ *AE, D, DC, MC, V* *CP.*

SPORTS AND THE OUTDOORS

Kaweah White Water Adventures (☎ *559/561–1000 or 800/229–8658* 🌐 *www.kaweah-whitewater.com*) guides two-hour and full-day rafting trips in spring and early summer, with some Class III rapids; longer trips may include some Class IV.

For hourly horseback rides or riding lessons, contact **Wood 'n' Horse Training Stables** (✉ *42846 N. Fork Dr.* ☎ *559/561–4268*).

Yosemite National Park

10

WORD OF MOUTH

"I tried cross country skiing for the first time in Yosemite. An avid downhill skier, I quickly learned that cross country is more physically demanding, slower going, but scenically spectacular. I chose to use the time to find the perfect shot of Half Dome."

—photo by Sarah Corley, Fodors.com member

WELCOME TO YOSEMITE NATIONAL PARK

TOP REASONS TO GO

★ **Feel the earth move:** An easy stroll brings you to the base of Yosemite Falls, America's highest, where thundering springtime waters shake the ground.

★ **Tunnel to heaven:** Winding down into Yosemite Valley, Wawona Road passes through a mountainside and emerges before one of the park's most heart-stopping vistas.

★ **Touch the sky:** Watch clouds scudding across the bright blue dome that arches above the High Sierra's Tuolumne Meadows, a wide-open alpine valley ringed by 10,000-foot granite peaks.

★ **Walk away from it all:** Early or late in the day, leave the crowds behind and take a forest hike on a few of Yosemite's 800 mi of trails.

★ **Powder your nose:** Winter's hush floats into Yosemite on snowflakes. Wade into a fluffy drift, lift your face to the sky, and listen to the trees.

1 Yosemite Valley. In the southern third of the park, east of the High Sierra, beats Yosemite's heart. This is where you'll find the park's most famous sights and biggest crowds.

2 Wawona. The park's southeastern tip holds Wawona, with its grand old hotel and pioneer history center, and the Mariposa Grove of Big Trees, filled with giant sequoias. These are closest to the South Entrance, 35 mi (a 1½-hour drive) south of Yosemite Village.

3 Tuolumne Meadows. The highlight of east-central Yosemite is this wildflower-strewn valley with hiking trails, nestled between sharp, rocky peaks. It's a two-hour drive northeast of Yosemite Valley along Tioga Road (closed November–May).

4 Hetch Hetchy. The most remote, least-visited part of Yosemite accessible by automobile, this glacial valley is dominated by a reservoir and veined with wilderness trails. It's near the park's western boundary, about half an hour's drive north of Big Oak Flat Entrance.

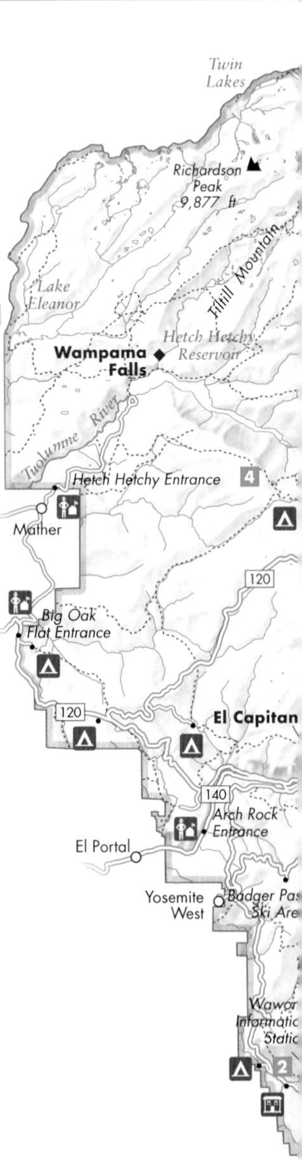

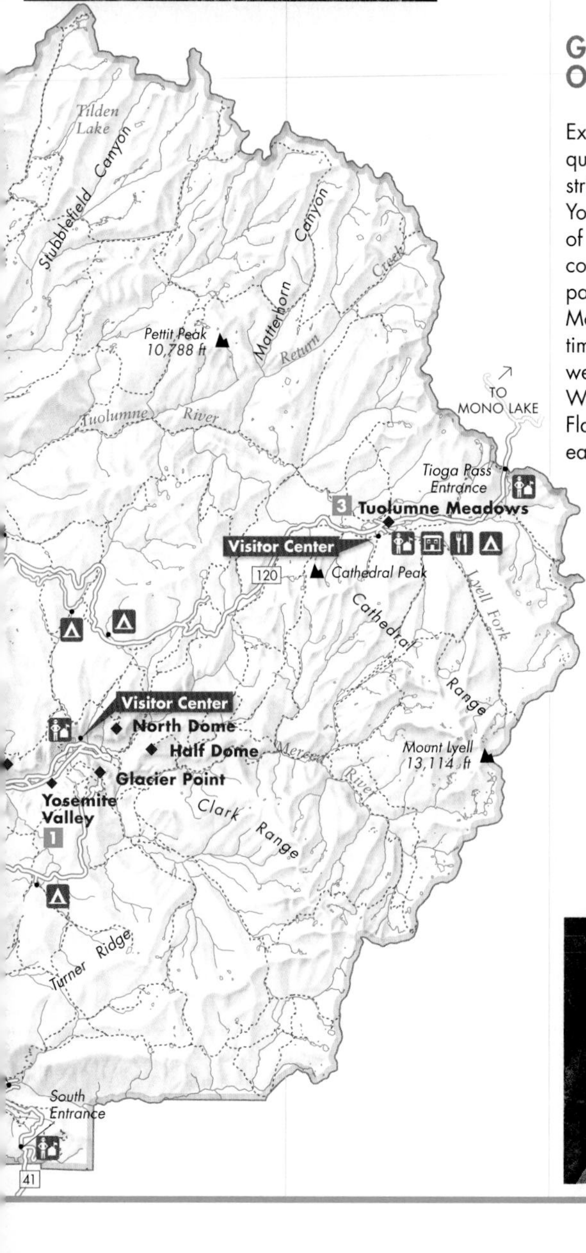

GETTING ORIENTED

Except for its southwestern quadrant and a narrow strip across its midsection, Yosemite—a park the size of Rhode Island—is wild country seen only by backpackers and horse-packers. Most visitors spend their time along the park's southwestern border, between Wawona and Big Oak Flat Entrance; a bit farther east in Yosemite Valley and Badger Pass Ski Area; and along the east–west corridor of Tioga Road, which spans the park north of Yosemite Valley and bisects Tuolumne Meadows.

Tilden Lake
Stubblefield Canyon
Matterhorn Canyon
Return Creek
Pettit Peak 10,788 ft
Tuolumne River
TO MONO LAKE
Tioga Pass Entrance
3 Tuolumne Meadows
Visitor Center
120
Cathedral Peak
Cathedral Range
Lyell Fork
Visitor Center
North Dome
Half Dome
Glacier Point
Yosemite Valley
1
Merced River
Mount Lyell 13,114 ft
Clark Range
Turner Ridge
South Entrance
41

YOSEMITE NATIONAL PARK PLANNER

When to Go

Yosemite National Park has different appeals depending on the time of year. For a potential "winter wonderland" feel, make reservations to stay in the Valley sometime between Thanksgiving and late March. If you want to see waterfalls at their fullest, visit in late spring or early summer. If you want to stroll about Tuolumne Meadow and take hikes off Tioga Road—and if you want access to all the park's amenities and ranger programs—go in the summer.

Make lodging and campground reservations for Yosemite Valley as far in advance as you can.

Yosemite receives most of its precipitation, which averages 37 inches a year, from November through April. Summer rainfall is rare. The average high and low temperatures in the Valley are 49 and 26 in January, 65 and 35 in April, 90 and 54 in July, and 74 and 39 in October.

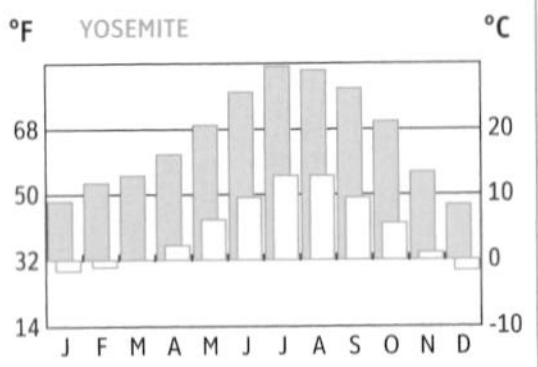

Flora and Fauna

Dense stands of incense cedar and Douglas fir—as well as ponderosa, Jeffrey, lodgepole, and sugar pines—cover much of the park, but the stellar standout, quite literally, is the *Sequoia sempervirens,* the giant sequoia. Sequoias grow only along the west slope of the Sierra Nevada between 4,500 and 7,000 feet in elevation. Starting from a seed the size of a rolled-oat flake, each of these ancient monuments assumes remarkable proportions in adulthood; you can see them in the Mariposa Grove of Big Trees. In late May the Valley's dogwood trees bloom with white, star-like flowers. Wildflowers, such as black-eyed Susan, bull thistle, cow parsnip, lupine, and meadow goldenrod, peak in June in the Valley and in July at higher elevations.

The most visible animals in the park are the mule deer, the only kind of deer in Yosemite. Though sightings of bighorn sheep are infrequent in the park itself, you can sometimes see them on the eastern side of the Sierra Crest, just off Route 120 in Lee Vining Canyon. The American black bear, which often has a brown, cinnamon, or blond coat, is the only species of bear in Yosemite (the California grizzlies were hunted to extinction in the 1920s), though few people ever see them. Watch for the blue Steller's jay along trails, in campgrounds, and around public buildings. Golden eagles are sometimes seen soaring above the Valley.

Getting There and Around

To get to Yosemite, take Route 120 east to the Big Oak Flat entrance or west to the Tioga Pass entrance (summer to late fall only); Route 140 east to the Arch Rock entrance; or Route 41 to the South entrance. Yosemite Valley is about 200 mi from San Francisco; the park is about 300 mi from Reno or Los Angeles, and about 500 mi from Las Vegas.

When it's especially crowded, some roads are closed to private vehicles; the road to Happy Isles and the Mist Trail are only accessible by shuttle. You can avoid traffic jams, save time, and take in more of the scenery by leaving your car at any of the designated lots and taking the free hybrid diesel-electric shuttle bus. Shuttles serve eastern Yosemite Valley between Camp 4 and Happy Isles year-round, every day. From May to September shuttles run from 7 AM to 10 PM; the rest of the year shuttles run from 9 AM to 10 PM. In summer shuttles also operate between the visitor center and El Capitan, between Wawona and the Mariposa Grove, and between the Tioga Pass entrance and Olmstead Point. In winter a shuttle runs between Yosemite Valley and Badger Pass Ski Area. For more information on shuttles within the park, visit *www.nps.gov/yose/trip/shuttle.htm* or call *209/372–1240.*

There are few gas stations within Yosemite (near the entrances), so fuel up before you reach the park. From late fall until early spring the weather is unpredictable, and driving can be treacherous. You should carry chains; they are often mandatory on Sierra roads in snowstorms. Pick chains up before you arrive—if you buy them in the Valley, you'll pay twice the normal price. For information about road conditions, call *800/427–7623 or 209/372–0200* from within California or go to *www.dot.ca.gov.*

WHAT IT COSTS

	¢	$	$$	$$$	$$$$
Restaurants	under $8	$8–$12	$13–$20	$21–$30	over $30
Hotels	under $70	$70–$120	$121–$175	$176–$250	over $250
Camping	under $8	$8–$14	$15–$20	$21–$25	over $25

Restaurant prices are per person for a main course at dinner. Hotel prices are per night for two people in a standard double room in high season, excluding taxes and service charges. Camping prices are for a standard (no hookups, pit toilets, fire grates, picnic tables) campsite per night.

Bears

The Sierra Nevada is home to thousands of bears, and you should take all necessary precautions to keep yourself—and the bears—safe. Bears that acquire a taste for human food can become very aggressive and destructive, and often must be destroyed by rangers. The national parks' campgrounds and some campgrounds outside the parks provide food-storage boxes that can keep bears from pilfering your edibles (portable canisters for backpackers can be rented in most park stores). It's imperative that you move all food, coolers, and articles with a scent (including toiletries, toothpaste, chewing gum, and air fresheners) from your car (including the trunk) to the storage box at your campsite; day-trippers should lock food in bear boxes provided at parking lots. If you don't, a bear may break into your car by literally peeling off the door or ripping open the trunk, or it may ransack your tent. The familiar tactic of hanging your food from high tree limbs is not an effective deterrent, as bears can easily scale trees.

By Reed Parsell

You can lose your perspective in Yosemite. This is a land where everything is big. Really big. There are big rocks, big trees, and big waterfalls.

The park has been so extravagantly praised and so beautifully photographed that some people wonder if the reality can possibly measure up. For almost everyone it does: here, you will remember what *breathtaking* really means.

With 1,189 square mi of parkland—94.5% of it undeveloped wilderness accessible only to the backpacker and horseback rider—Yosemite is a nature lover's wonderland. The western boundary dips as low as 2,000 feet in the chaparral-covered foothills; the eastern boundary rises to 13,000 feet at points along the Sierra Crest. Yosemite Valley has many of the park's most famous sites and is easy to reach, but take the time to explore the high country above the Valley and you'll see a different side of the park; the fragile and unique alpine terrain is arresting. Wander through this world of wind-warped trees, scurrying animals, and bighorn sheep, and you'll come away with a distinct sense of peace and solitude.

PLANNING

ADMISSION FEES

For Yosemite, vehicle admission fee is $20 per car and is valid for seven days. Visitors arriving by bus, or on foot, bicycle, motorcycle, or horseback pay $10 for a seven-day pass.

A one-year pass for Yosemite is $40. A 12-month "America the Beautiful—National Parks and Federal Recreational Lands Pass" is $80 and gets you (and your family) into all federal recreation sites that charge entrance fees. Seniors (ages 62 and older) can purchase the annual pass for $10. People with lifetime disabilities are entitled to an "Access Pass," which is free.

ADMISSION HOURS

Yosemite is open daily, 24 hours a day. All entrances are open at all hours, except for Hetch Hetchy Entrance, open roughly dawn to dusk.

The park is in the Pacific time zone.

DID YOU KNOW?

Abraham Lincoln established Yosemite Valley and the Mariposa Grove of Giant Sequoias as public land in 1864, deeding the areas to the state of California. The grant was the first of its kind in America, and it laid the foundation for the establishment of national and state parks.

EMERGENCIES

In an emergency, call 911 from any park phone.

In Yosemite you call the Yosemite Medical Clinic, which provides 24-hour emergency care.

Contact a ranger station or visitor center for police matters. For non-emergencies, call the parks' main number.

Emergency Services **Emergency services** (☎ *911*). **Yosemite Medical Clinic** (✉ *Yosemite Village, Yosemite National Park* ☎ *209/372–4637*).

PERMITS

If you plan to camp in the Yosemite backcountry, you must have a wilderness permit. Availability of permits, which are free, depends upon trailhead quotas. It's best to make a reservation, especially if you will be visiting from May through September. You can reserve two days to 24 weeks in advance by phone, mail, or e-mail; a $5 per person processing fee is charged if and when your reservations are confirmed. In your request, include your name, address, daytime phone, the number of people in your party, trip date, alternative dates, starting and ending trailheads, and a brief itinerary. Without a reservation, you may still get a free permit on a first-come, first-served basis at wilderness permit offices at Big Oak Flat, Hetch Hetchy, Tuolumne, Wawona, the Wilderness Center, and Yosemite Valley in summer; fall through spring, visit the Valley Visitor Center.

Yosemite Contacts **Wilderness Permits** (*Box 545, Yosemite 95389* ☎ *209/372–0740* *www.nps.gov/yose/wilderness/permits.htm*).

VISITOR INFORMATION

Contacts **Delaware North Companies Parks & Resorts** (☎ *559/565–4070 or 888/252–5757* *www.visitsequoia.com*) operates the lodgings and visitor services in Sequoia, and some in Kings Canyon. **Yosemite National Park** (☎ *209/372–0200* *www.nps.gov/yose*).

EXPLORING YOSEMITE NATIONAL PARK

YOSEMITE VALLEY

The Yosemite Valley Visitor Center is 11 mi from the Arch Rock entrance on Rte. 140, 25 mi from the Big Oak Flat entrance on Rte. 120, 35 mi from the south entrance on Rte. 41, and 62 mi from east entrance on Tioga Rd.

So many attractions are packed into this 7-mi-long, 1-mi-wide valley that you might have difficulty deciding what to do. Start by parking at either the Curry Village or, better yet, Yosemite Village daily lot. From the latter, stroll over to the Yosemite Visitor Center and get your bearings. After that, the free shuttle buses (which operate on low emissions, have 21 stops, running every 10 minutes or so from 9 AM to 6 PM) can take you to, or very near, most of the Valley's most popular sights. If you do insist on driving about the Valley, be aware that roadside parking is limited, and the Southside Drive/Northside Drive loop is one-way.

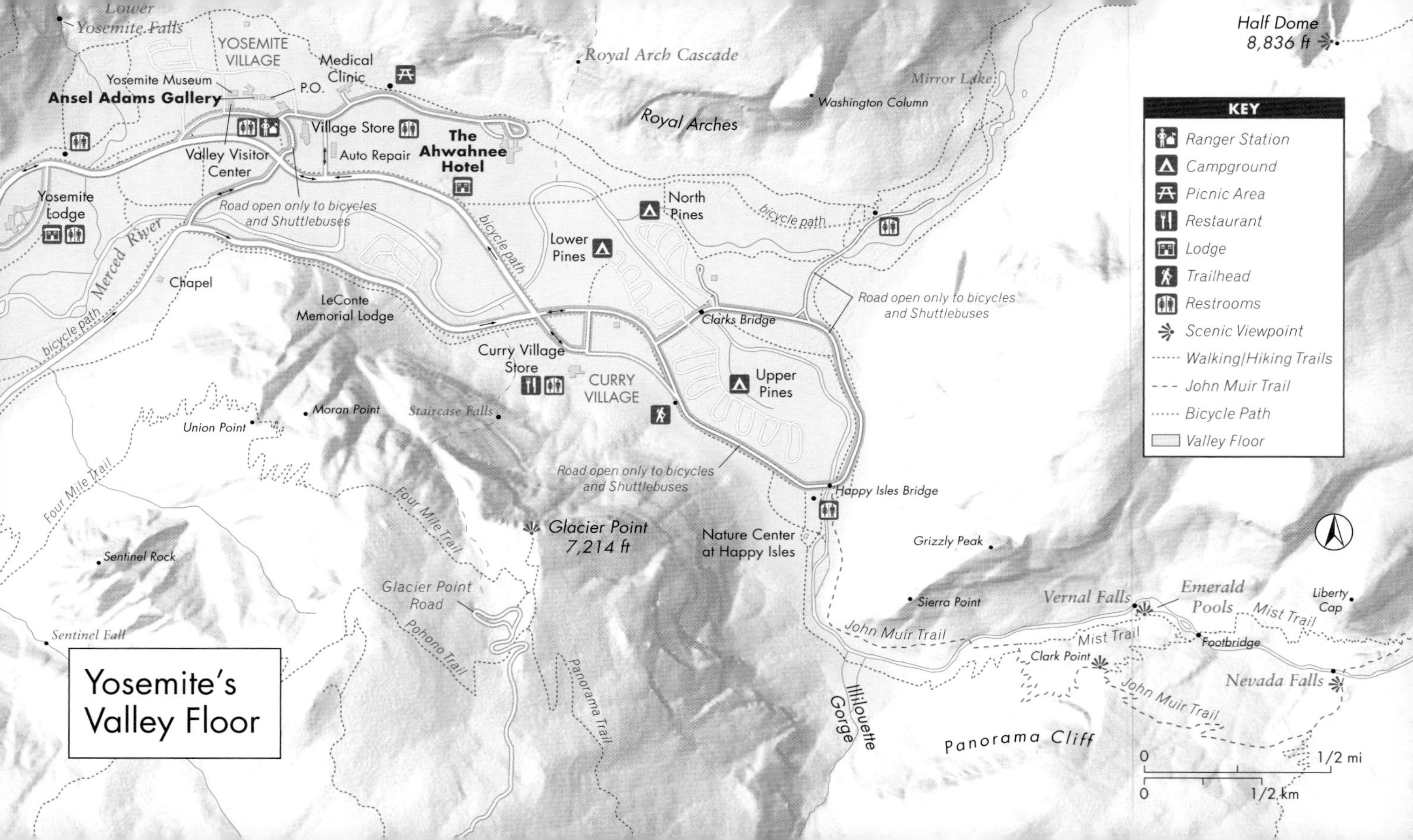

Yosemite's Valley Floor
KEY
Ranger Station
Campground
Picnic Area
Restaurant
Lodge
Trailhead
Restrooms
Scenic Viewpoint
Walking/Hiking Trails
John Muir Trail
Bicycle Path
Valley Floor
Lower Yosemite Falls
YOSEMITE VILLAGE
Yosemite Museum
Ansel Adams Gallery
P.O.
Medical Clinic
Village Store
Auto Repair
Valley Visitor Center
The Ahwahnee Hotel
Yosemite Lodge
Road open only to bicycles and Shuttlebuses
Merced River
bicycle path
Chapel
LeConte Memorial Lodge
Royal Arch Cascade
Royal Arches
Washington Column
Mirror Lake
North Pines
Lower Pines
Clarks Bridge
Upper Pines
Curry Village Store
CURRY VILLAGE
Happy Isles Bridge
Nature Center at Happy Isles
Half Dome 8,836 ft
Moran Point
Union Point
Staircase Falls
Four Mile Trail
Glacier Point 7,214 ft
Sentinel Rock
Sentinel Fall
Glacier Point Road
Pohono Trail
Panorama Trail
Illilouette Gorge
Grizzly Peak
Sierra Point
John Muir Trail
Vernal Falls
Emerald Pools
Mist Trail
Liberty Cap
Footbridge
Clark Point
Nevada Falls
Panorama Cliff
0 1/2 mi
0 1/2 km

Lots of people tour the Valley via bicycle; Curry Village and Yosemite Lodge have rentals.

VISITOR CENTERS

Le Conte Memorial Lodge. Step inside to see this visitor center's cathedral-like interior, which contains a library and environmental exhibits. Le Conte Memorial Lodge (relocated from Camp Curry in 1919) is across from Housekeeping Camp. ✉ *9002 Southside Dr., about ½ mi west of Curry Village, Curry Village* 🎫 *Free* ⏲ *May–Oct., Wed.–Sun. 10–4.*

Nature Center at Happy Isles. Designed for children, this small museum could use some updating. In addition to exhibits and dioramas, it's also home to one of the better kid-oriented gift shops, with coloring books, T-shirts, and water bottles. ✉ *Center of Curry Village Loop, about ¾ mi east of Curry Village, Curry Village* 🎫 *Free* ⏲ *Mid-May–Oct., daily 10–noon and 12:30–4.*

Valley Visitor Center. Exhibits at this visitor center focus on how Yosemite Valley was formed and about its vegetation, animals, and human inhabitants over the past thousands of years; it was thoroughly overhauled in 2007. In the lobby, rangers and volunteers can answer most any question you have about Yosemite and provide pamphlets and maps; a pool-table–size relief map of the Valley will help with your bearings. Don't leave the area without watching the superb "Spirit of Yosemite," a 23-minute introductory film that runs every half-hour in the theater behind the visitor center. ✉ *Center of Curry Village Loop, Yosemite Village* ☎ *209/372–0299* 🌐 *www.yosemitepark.com* 🎫 *Free* ⏲ *Memorial Day–Labor Day, daily 8–6; Labor Day–Memorial Day, daily 9–5.*

Yosemite Valley Wilderness Center. Backpackers come here for free wilderness permits, which are mandatory for overnight trips into the mountains. They also can purchase maps, check on current weather conditions and campsite availability, rent bear canisters to store their food, and tap into the expertise of the staff members. ✉ *9039 Village Dr., between the Ansel Adams Gallery and the post office, Yosemite Village* ⏲ *Memorial Day–Labor Day, daily 7:30–6.*

HISTORIC SITES

Ahwahnee Hotel. Built in 1927, this stately lodge of granite and concrete beams stained to look like redwood is a perfect man-made complement to Yosemite's natural majesty. The Great Lounge, 77 feet long with magnificent 24-foot ceilings and all manner of Indian artwork on display, is the most special interior space in Yosemite by a long shot. You can stay here, for $450 a night, or simply explore the first-floor shops and perhaps have breakfast or lunch in the lovely Dining Room. Its windows soar from the floor 34 feet on up to the ceiling, which has interlaced sugar-pine beams. Dinner here is a more formal, and much more expensive, proposition than anywhere else in the park, but if you have the money it's worth a splurge. ✉ *1 Ahwahnee Rd., about ¾ mi east of Yosemite Valley Visitor Center, Yosemite Village* ☎ *209/372–1489.*

Indian Village of Ahwahnee. The Southern Sierra Miwok tribe inhabited what's now known as Yosemite Valley for thousands of years. The Valley's last few Indian homes were razed in 1969; this solemn smattering of re-created structures, accessed by a short loop trail, is an imagination

Views don't get much better than the vista from atop Glacier Point.

of what Indian life might have resembled here in the 1870s. ✉ *Northside Dr., behind the visitor center, Yosemite Village* 🎟 *Free* ⏲ *Daily sunrise–sunset.*

Ansel Adams Gallery. Here you can purchase gorgeous prints by the famous nature photographer, as well as works by contemporary photographers and American Indian jewelry and handicrafts. The gallery's elegant camera shop conducts photography workshops and sometimes holds private showings of fine prints on Saturday. ✉ *9031 Village Dr., between the visitor center and Wilderness Center, Yosemite Village* ☎ *209/372–4413 or 888/361–7622* 🌐 *www.anseladams.com* 🎟 *Free* ⏲ *Apr.–Oct., daily 9–6; Nov.–Mar., daily 9–5.*

Curry Village. A couple of school teachers from Indiana, Jenny and David Curry, founded Camp Curry in 1899. Their idea was to make staying overnight in Yosemite Valley affordable for people of modest means, a tradition that continues today. Curry's 628 lodging options, most of them tent cabins, are spread over a large chunk of the Valley's southeastern side. The central dining area does boffo business for its breakfast and dinner buffets, and on warm summer days the pool practically overflows with kids. In wintertime, you can ice-skate here. ✉ *Southside Dr., about ½ mi east of Yosemite Village, Curry Village.*

Yosemite Museum. In this small museum, which consists of a permanent exhibit room and an adjacent gallery that promotes contemporary Yosemite art, an American Indian sometimes is on hand to demonstrate the ancient techniques of beadwork and basket weaving, as well as answer your questions. ✉ *9039 Village Dr., Yosemite Village* ☎ *209/372–0299* 🎟 *Free* ⏲ *Daily 9–noon and 1–4:30.*

DID YOU KNOW?

Yosemite National Park is one of the world's premier climbing destinations, and El Capitan (or "El Cap") is its most famous—and difficult—ascent.

SCENIC STOPS

★ **El Capitan.** You almost certainly will do a double-take the first time you see "El Cap," the largest exposed-granite monolith in the world, more than twice as tall as the Rock of Gibraltar. The free El Capitan Shuttle, which connects to the Valley's year-round shuttle loop and goes to the El Capitan Picnic Area, operates from mid-June into early September. ⊠*Off Northside Dr., about 4 mi west of the Valley Visitor Center.*

Fodor'sChoice ★ **Glacier Point.** If you lack the time, desire, or stamina to hike more than 3,200 feet up to Glacier Point from the Yosemite Valley floor, you can drive here for a bird's-eye view. If you get here via the morning guided-tour bus ($25 one way, $41 round-trip), consider a return trip via the 8-mi Panorama Trail, one of the most visually stunning hikes in the state, if not the world. The shuttle bus runs whenever Glacier Point Road is open, which tends to be from late May through early November. During the winter the road is plowed only to the Badger Ski Area, from which hearty souls can snowshoe or cross-country ski on up to Glacier Point. ⊠*Glacier Point Rd., 16 mi northeast of Rte. 41, Glacier Point.*

Half Dome. When visiting Yosemite National Park, people's eyes are continually drawn to this remarkable granite formation that tops out more than 4,700 feet above the Valley floor. It is the park's premier attraction. You can hike to the top of Half Dome, as thousands do every summer, on an 8.5-mi (one-way) trail whose last 400 feet must be ascended by holding tightly onto a steel cable. ⚠ **Beware that people have died on this hike, whether by falling off the edge or being struck by lightning.** ⊠*Trailhead is off Happy Isles, near Curry Village (the first 3.5 mi of the hike are along the Mist Trail to Nevada Fall).*

WATERFALLS

Yosemite's waterfalls are at their most spectacular in May and June. By summer's end some falls, including the mighty Yosemite Falls, dry up. They begin flowing again in late fall, and in winter they may be hung dramatically with ice.

Bridalveil Fall. A filmy fall of 620 feet, which is often diverted as much as 20 feet one way or the other by the breeze, is the first marvelous view of Yosemite Valley you will see if you come in via Route 41. ⊠*4 mi west of Yosemite Lodge, at the junction of Southside Dr. and Wawona Rd.*

Nevada Fall. Climb Mist Trail from Happy Isles for an up-close view of 594-foot Nevada Fall, the first major fall as the Merced River plunges out of the high country toward the eastern end of Yosemite Valley. Along the way you will pass Vernal Fall, which is a sensible place to turn around for those hikers who are (justifiably) leery of the strenuous stepping needed to reach Nevada Fall. ■ **TIP→ If you don't want to hike, you can see both falls—distantly—from Glacier Point.** ⊠*South of Curry Village and Upper Pines Campground, just past Happy Isles; Shuttle Stop 16.*

Ribbon Fall. At 1,612 feet, Ribbon Fall is the highest single waterfall in North America (Yosemite Falls is actually the highest, but it's not a single waterfall). It's also the first Valley waterfall to dry up in summer; the rainwater and melted snow that create the slender fall evaporate quickly at this height. Look just west of El Capitan from the Valley floor for the best view of the fall from the base of Bridalveil Fall. ✣ *For the best view of the waterfall, park off Southside Dr., a few hundred yards east of the Rte. 41 junction and Bridalveil Fall lot.*

Vernal Fall. Fern-covered black rocks frame 317-foot Vernal Fall, and rainbows play in the spray at its base. Take Mist Trail from Happy Isles to see it—or, if you'd rather not hike, go to Glacier Point for a distant view. ☒*3-mi from the trailhed just off Happy Isles to the top of the waterfall*

Fodor's Choice ★ **Yosemite Falls.** The park's namesake waterfall is actually composed of three falls, and together they constitute the highest waterfall in North America and the fifth-highest in the world. The water from the top descends a total of 2,425 feet, and when the falls run hard you can hear them thunder all across the Valley. When they dry up, as often happens in late summer, the Valley seems naked without the wavering tower of spray. ■TIP→ **To view the falls up close, head to their base on the trail from Camp 4.** ☒*About halfway between Valley Visitor Center and Yosemite Village off Northside Drive; Shuttle Stop 6.*

WAWONA

Wawona Hotel is approximately 7 mi north of park's south entrance, and 27 mi southwest of Yosemite Valley Visitor Center.

Way back in 1864, President Abraham Lincoln acknowledged the special nature of Mariposa Grove when he bundled it with Yosemite Valley as a public trust granted to the young state of California. More than 140 years later, the grove of some 500 Sequoias represents the biggest tourist attraction in the park's southwestern section. If you are unable to visit Giant Forest in Sequoia National Park or Grant Grove in Kings Canyon National, Mariposa Grove is the next best thing.

VISITOR CENTERS

Wawona Information Station. Find out more about this region of the park by talking with rangers here in what's also known as Hill's Studio. Born in England in 1829, Thomas Hill was a teenager when his family immigrated to the United States. He made a lot of money—up to $10,000 per painting—selling his landscapes that depicted Yosemite Valley, and in his later years he operated a gallery and studio here next to the Wawona Hotel. Today some of Hill's works are exhibited in the information center. You can purchase maps and guidebooks, as well as secure free wilderness permits and rent bear canisters. ☒*Forest Dr., off Rte. 41, Wawona* ☎*209/375–9531* 🎫 *Free* ⏲*Apr.–Nov., Sun.–Thurs. 8–5, Fri. and Sat. 8–6.*

HISTORIC SITES

★ **Wawona Hotel.** You might blink when you first come across this 19th-century hotel, because there is something about it that suggests not just another time, but another place. Its architecture, sometimes referred to as "Victorian resort," has a certain elegance. One can imagine an older Mark Twain relaxing in a rocking chair on one of the broad verandas. There is history here, all right, but it appears time has passed without great incident. Across the road is a somewhat odd sight: Yosemite's golf course, which claims to be the first golf course in the Sierra Nevada, and one of the few links in the world that does not employ fertilizers or other chemicals. The Wawona is an excellent place to stay or to stop for lunch when making the drive from the South entrance to the Valley, but be aware that the hotel is closed in January. ✉*Rte. 41, Wawona* ☎*209/375–1425.*

SCENIC STOPS

★ **Mariposa Grove of Big Trees.** Of Yosemite National Park's three sequoia groves—the others being Merced and Tuolumne, both near Crane Flat well to the north—Mariposa is by far the largest and easiest to navigate on foot. Actually, you can take quite an extended hike here, if you are so inclined, but many of the so-called "big trees" are near the correspondingly massive parking lot. **Grizzly Giant,** whose base measures 96 feet around, has been estimated to be the world's 25th-largest tree by volume. Perhaps more astoundingly, it's about 2,700 years old. On up the hill, find many more sequoias, a small museum, and fewer people. Summer weekends are especially crowded here. During those or any other occasions, instead of driving here you may be better off taking the free shuttle from Wawona; it operates daily from 9 to 6; the trip takes about 15 minutes each way. The access road to the grove may be closed by snow for extended periods from November to mid-May; you can still usually walk, snowshoe, or ski in. ✉*Rte. 41, 2 mi north of the South entrance station, Wawona.*

TUOLUMNE MEADOWS

Approximately 7 mi west of the east entrance on Tioga Rd., 39 mi east of Crane Flat, and 55 mi northeast of the Yosemite Valley Visitor Center.

Most park visitors do not have the time, and in some cases the inclination, to make the 56-mi drive here from Yosemite Valley. The setting is not as dramatic, admittedly, but Tuolumne Meadows is intriguing in its own way. You are confronted, practically out of the blue, with an almost perfectly flat basin, about 2.5 mi long, that in July is resplendent with wildflowers. Backpackers love to launch their journeys into remoteness here, and active day-trippers can work up a sweat on several scenic trails, mostly notably the one that mounts Lembert Dome, which offers breathtaking views of the basin below. Driving here from Lee Vining, on the eastern portion of Tioga Road, is a scenic experience that would not soon be forgotten. Do not count on the high-altitude road's being open, however, sooner than June or later than mid-October.

VISITOR CENTERS

Tuolumne Meadows Visitor Center. The standard services are available here at Yosemite's highest and easternmost visitor center: you can get free wilderness permits, rent bear canisters, or shop for various maps, books, and limited souvenirs. Rangers can fill you in on the area's many trails, which vary from an easy stroll about the meadow to a very long day's trek down the Pacific Coast Trail to Mammoth Lakes, to a multiday backpacking adventure past Waterwheel Falls into the Grand Canyon of the Tuolumne River. Nearby there's also a mountaineering school and sport shop, as well as a little gem of a grocery store. ✉ *Rte. 120, approximately 55 mi from the Yosemite Valley Visitor Center, Tuolumne Meadows* ☎ *209/372–0263* 🎫 *Free* ⏲ *Early June–late Sept., daily 9–5.*

SCENIC STOPS

★ **Tuolumne Meadows.** Nowhere in the Sierra Nevada mountain range will you find a larger subalpine meadow. At an elevation of 8,600 feet, Tuolumne is a place where the air is very crisp and thin, which is something to keep in mind if you are contemplating any form of exercise. Your heart is pounding not because you are suddenly out of shape, but because there is not as much oxygen to breathe. The area's two most popular day hikes are the 1-mi Soda Springs/Parson's Lodge Trail, a flat and easy path that cuts through the meadow north of the road, and the considerably more strenuous, 4-mi round-trip to the top of Lembert Dome. Rangers conduct walks and talks throughout the summer, including three-hour bird-watching hikes. Campfire programs are held nightly at the Tuolumne Meadows Campground. ✉ *Tioga Rd. (Rte. 120), about 8 mi west of the Tioga Pass entrance station, Tuolumne Meadows.*

HETCH HETCHY

Hetch Hetchy parking lot is 12 mi north of the Big Oak entrance on Rte. 120 and 37 mi northwest of the Yosemite Valley Visitor Center.

If you think that by visiting the Valley, the Wawona area, and Tuolumne Meadows you have seen all the good parts of Yosemite National Park, you are missing out on what John Muir described as "a great landscape garden, one of nature's most precious mountain temples." He was referring to Hetch Hetchy, a 38-mi drive from the Valley that is reached via a 9-mi paved road off Route 120, just outside the Big Oak Flat entrance. Until the early 1920s Hetch Hetchy was a valley whose scenery rivaled that of Yosemite Valley, what with its flat, meadow floor, long waterfalls, and looming granite formations, most notably Kolana Rock. For the past 86 years, however, Hetch Hetchy has been underwater. The O'Shaughnessy Dam first plugged the Tuolumne River here in 1923, and it was expanded in 1938. Many preservationists and others who long for the Hetch Hatchy Valley of old continue to lobby hard for the dam's relocation farther downstream. Meanwhile, hikers can get an idea of the area's charms by taking the mildly strenuous, 5-mi round-trip Wapama Falls Trail.

Backpacking is the only way to see the rest of Yosemite National Park—and there is a lot more to see. Of the park's 1,169 square mi, more than 94% is designated as wilderness.

SCENIC STOPS

Hetch Hetchy Reservoir. When Congress gave O'Shaughnessy Dam the green light here in 1913, pragmatism triumphed over aestheticism. Some 2.4 million residents of the San Francisco Bay Area continue to get their water from this 117-billion-gallon reservoir, although spirited efforts are being made to move the dam farther down the Tuolumne

River so that the Hetch Hetchy Valley can be restored to its former, pristine glory. Eight miles long, the reservoir is Yosemite's largest body of water, and one that can be seen up close from several trails that begin at the backpackers camp, a 9-mi paved drive off Route 120. ✉ *Hetch Hetchy Rd., about 12 mi northeast of the Big Oak Flat entrance station, Hetch Hetchy.*

SPORTS AND THE OUTDOORS

HIKING

The staff at the **Wilderness Center** (✉ *Yosemite Village, next to the post office* ✆ *Yosemite Wilderness Reservations, Box 545, Yosemite Village,* ☎ *209/372–0740* 🌐 *www.nps.gov/yose*) provides free wilderness permits, which are required for overnight camping (advance camping reservations are available for $5 and are highly recommended for popular trailheads from May through September and on weekends). It also provides maps and advice to hikers heading into the backcountry.

Yosemite Mountaineering School & Guide Service (✉ *Yosemite Mountain Shop, Curry Village* ☎ *209/372–8344* 🌐 *www.yosemitepark.com*) can take you on guided two-hour to full-day treks from April through November.

YOSEMITE VALLEY

Most visitors, especially first-timers, take the Lower Yosemite Falls Trail. It's easy enough for everyone and, except when the falls are reduced to a drip in late summer, visually thrilling. Otherwise, the Valley offers a number of varied hiking possibilities, including a leisurely day spent traversing the flat paths over bridges and through meadows, among the buildings and picnic areas. Park at the Valley Visitor Center or Curry Village, apply sunscreen, and grab a water bottle, camera and binoculars, and you're set. If you get weary of walking or sapped by the sun, hop on the free, air-conditioned shuttle bus. Food and bathrooms are never far away.

WAWONA

The most popular hikes in this southern portion of Yosemite are in the Mariposa Grove of Giant Sequoias, not quite 7 mi from the Wawona Hotel. Pick up a small map and guide for 50¢ so you can plot your stroll within the network of interconnected trails, most of which begin at the large parking lot.

TUOLUMNE MEADOWS

Many backpacking adventures begin at Tuolumne Meadows, the hiking-boot gateway to wilderness areas in Yosemite's northern, eastern, and central regions. This is also a popular day-hike destination for people who have been to Yosemite Valley and perhaps have grown weary of the crowds there.

Bicycling the park's many miles of paved paths is a great way to enjoy Yosemite's natural wonders.

HETCH HETCHY

Hetch Hetchy is an hour's drive from Yosemite Valley and lacks amenities other than a few flush toilets just before you get to the loop parking lot. Its remoteness comes with a big silver lining, however: few visitors. Also, this is Yosemite's lowest elevation, which means pleasant temperatures in the spring and fall.

BICYCLING

There may be no more enjoyable way to see Yosemite Valley than riding a bike in the shadow of its lofty granite monoliths. The eastern valley has 12 mi of paved, flat bicycle paths across meadows and through woods, with bike racks at convenient stopping points. For a greater challenge you can ride on 196 mi of paved park roads—but bicycles are not allowed on hiking trails or in the backcountry. Kids younger than 18 must wear a helmet.

Yosemite Bike Rentals (✉ *Yosemite Lodge, Yosemite Village* ☎ *209/372–1208* ✉ *Curry Village* 🌐 *www.yosemitepark.com*) rents bikes by the hour ($9.50) or by day ($25.50) from either its Yosemite Lodge or Curry Village bike stand, both of which are open from April through October. Bikes with child trailers, baby-jogger strollers, and wheelchairs also are available.

BIRD-WATCHING

Nearly 250 bird species have been spotted in the park, including the sage sparrow, pygmy owl, blue grouse, and mountain bluebird. Park rangers lead free bird-watching walks in Yosemite Valley one day a week in summer; check at a visitor center or information station for times and locations. Binoculars are sometimes available for loan.

Birding Seminars (☎ *209/379–2321* 🌐 *www.yosemite.org*) are sponsored by the Yosemite Association, which offers one- to four-day seminars for beginner and intermediate birders from April through August. Expect to pay between $82 and $254.

HORSEBACK RIDING

For overnight saddle trips, which use mules, you will need to make reservations for remote lodging. To do so, call the **Delaware North Corporation** (☎ *801/559–5000, option 4*) on or after September 15 to request a lottery application for the following year.

Tuolumne Meadows Stables (✉ *Off Tioga Rd., about 2 mi east of Tuolumne Meadows Visitor Center, Toulomne Meadows* ☎ *209/372–8427* 🌐 *www.yosemitepark.com*) runs two-, four-, and eight-hour trips—and High Sierra four- to six-day camping treks on mules, which begin at $625. Reservations are essential.

Wawona Stables (✉ *Rte. 41, Wawona* ☎ *209/375–6502*) offers rides for $59 (two hours), $79 (four hours), and $119 (eight hours) in the Wawona area. Reserve in advance.

Yosemite Valley Stables (✉ *At entrance to North Pines Campground, 100 yards northeast of Curry Village, Curry Village* ☎ *209/372–8348* 🌐 *www.yosemitepark.com*) offers rides in Yosemite Valley for $59 (two-hour), $79 (four-hour), and $119 (eight-hour). Reserve in advance.

RAFTING

For no charge, you can drop your inflatable on the Merced River between Stoneman Bridge (near Curry Village) and Sentinel Beach Picnic Area. Restrictions apply: Rafting is allowed only between 10 AM and 6 PM, the river level must not be measured above 6½ feet at Sentinel Bridge, and the combined total of the air and water temperatures must exceed 100 degrees. You can also go rafting on the South Fork of the Merced River, in Wawona.

The per-person rental fee at **Curry Village Raft Stand** (✉ *South side of Southside Dr., Curry Village* ☎ *209/372–8319* 🌐 *www.yosemitepark.com*) covers the raft (4- to 6-person), two paddles, and life jackets, plus a shuttle to the launch point on Sentinel Beach. You'll pay $20.50 to ride the river back to Curry Village; rafting happens between late May and July, weather and river conditions permitting.

DID YOU KNOW?
There are myriad climbing options in Yosemite for all skill levels—from beginner to expert.

ROCK CLIMBING

Fodor'sChoice ★ The one-day basic lesson at **Yosemite Mountaineering School & Guide Service** (✉ *Yosemite Mountain Shop, Curry Village* ☎ *209/372–8344* 🌐 *www.yosemitepark.com*) includes some bouldering and rappelling, and three or four 60-foot climbs. Guided hikes and backpacking adventures are available, too. Climbers must be at least 10 (kids under 12 must be accompanied by a parent or guardian) and in reasonably good physical condition. Intermediate and advanced classes include instruction in belays, self-rescue, summer snow climbing, and free climbing. Expect to pay $117 to $317, depending on what kind of adventure you choose; the school is generally open from April through November.

ICE-SKATING

Winter visitors have skated at the outdoor **Curry Village Ice-Skating Rink** (✉ *South side of Southside Dr., Curry Village* ☎ *209/372–8319*) for decades, and there's no mystery why: it's a kick to glide across the ice while soaking up views of Half Dome and Glacier Point. The cost is $8 to skate for up to 2½ hours; skates can be rented for $3. The rink is open from mid-November through mid-March, with daily sessions in the afternoon and evening, as well as morning sessions on weekends.

SKIING AND SNOWSHOEING

California's first ski resort, **Badger Pass Ski Area** (✉ *Badger Pass Rd., off Glacier Point Rd., 18 mi from Yosemite Valley, Glacier Point* ☎ *209/372–8430* 🌐 *www.yosemitepark.com*) has 10 downhill runs, 90 mi of groomed cross-country trails, and two excellent ski schools. Free shuttle buses from Yosemite Valley operate during ski season (December–early April, weather permitting). Lift tickets are $38, downhill equipment rents for $24, and snowboard rental with boots is $35. The mix is about 35% beginners, 50% intermediate skiers, and 15% advanced skiers; the longest run is 0.3 mi. The base is at 7,200 feet, and the summit at 8,000 feet.

The gentle slopes of Badger Pass make **Yosemite Ski School** (☎ *209/372–8430*) an ideal spot for children and beginners to learn downhill skiing or snowboarding for as little as $28 for a group lesson.

The highlight of Yosemite's cross-country skiing center is a 21-mi loop from Badger Pass to Glacier Point. You can rent cross-country skis for $21.50 per day at the **Cross-Country Ski School** (☎ *209/372–8444*), which also rents snowshoes ($19.50 per day), telemarking equipment ($29), and skate-skis ($24).

Yosemite Mountaineering School (✉ *Badger Pass Rd., off Glacier Point Rd., 18 mi from Yosemite Valley, Glacier Point* ☎ *209/372–8344* 🌐 *www.yosemitepark.com*) conducts snowshoeing, cross-country skiing, telemarking, and skate-skiing classes starting at $30.

EDUCATIONAL PROGRAMS

CLASSES AND SEMINARS

Free **Art Workshops** (✉ *Art Activity Center, Yosemite Village* ☎ *209/372–1442* 🌐 *www.yosemite.org*) are conducted by professional artists in watercolor, drawing, and other mediums from early April through late November; most are on Monday through Saturday from 10 to 2. Bring your own materials, or purchase the basics at the Art Activity Center, which is next to the Village Store in Yosemite Village.

Yosemite Outdoor Adventures (☎ *209/379–2321* 🌐 *www.yosemite.org*) offers educational outings on topics ranging from woodpeckers to fire management to pastel painting. Naturalists, scientists, and park rangers lead the outings, which can run from several hours to several days and cost from $82 to $465.

RANGER PROGRAMS

Junior Ranger Programs (✉ *Valley Visitor Center or the Nature Center at Happy Isles, Yosemite Village* ☎ *209/372–0299*) are offered for children ages 3 through 13. Kids can participate in the informal, self-guided Little Cub and Junior Ranger programs. A park activity handbook ($6) is available at the Valley Visitor Center or the Nature Center at Happy Isles; once your child has completed the book, a ranger will present him or her with a certificate and a badge.

Ranger-Led Programs include walks and hikes as well as informative and entertaining talks on a range of topics at different locations in the park several times a day from spring through fall. In the evening at Yosemite Lodge and Curry Village lectures by rangers, slide shows, and documentary films present unique perspectives on Yosemite. On summer weekends Camp Curry and Tuolumne Meadows Campground host sing-along campfire programs. There's usually at least one ranger-led activity every night in the Valley; schedules and locations are posted on bulletin boards throughout the park and published in *Yosemite Today.*

TOURS

★ **Ansel Adams Camera Walks** (☎ *209/372–4413 for Ansel Adams Gallery* 🌐 *www.yosemitepark.com*) are a must for photography enthusiasts. These free two-hour guided camera walks are usually offered several mornings a week by professional photographers.

DNC Parks & Resorts (☎ *209/372–1240* 🌐 *www.yosemitepark.com*), the main concessionaire at Yosemite National Park, operates several guided tours and programs throughout the park, including the **Big Trees Tram Tour** of the Mariposa Grove of Big Trees, the **Glacier Point Tour,** the **Grand Tour** (both Mariposa Grove and Glacier Point), the **Moonlight Tour** of Yosemite Valley, the **Tuolumne Meadows Tour,** and the **Valley Floor Tour.**

WHERE TO EAT

RESTAURANTS

$$$–$$$$ CONTINENTAL Fodor'sChoice ★ ✕**Ahwahnee Hotel Dining Room.** Raves about the dining room's architecture are fully justified—floor-to-ceiling windows, a 34-foot-high ceiling with interlaced sugar pine beams, massive chandeliers, all in an elegant, refined yet rustic setting. The Sunday brunch ($40) is consistently praised. The dinner menu includes duck breast, pork shoulder, and the like, as well as a vegetarian dish or two for those who want to honor the environmental spirit of the national parks. The seasonal vegetable tagine, for example, consists of chickpeas, Moroccan spices, and dried fruit. Reservations are always advised, and for dinner, guests are asked to dress "resort casual"—collared shirts and long pants for men, dresses or skirts—or a blouse and slacks—for women. ✉*Ahwahnee Hotel, 1 Ahwahnee Rd., about ¾ mi east of Yosemite Valley Visitor Center, Yosemite Village* ☎*209/372–1489* ✍*Reservations essential* ▭*AE, D, DC, MC, V.*

$$$ AMERICAN ★ ✕**Mountain Room.** Though good, the food becomes secondary when you see Yosemite Falls through this dining room's wall of windows—almost every table has a view. The chef makes a point of using locally sourced, organic ingredients, so you can be assured of fresh greens and veggies here. Grilled trout and salmon, steak, pasta, and several children's dishes are also on the menu. The Mountain Room Lounge, a few strides away in the Yosemite Lodge complex, has a broad bar with about 10 beers on tap. You also can order chips and salsa, hot sandwiches, or even something more substantial, such as vegetarian lasagna. The tall windows and comparatively small, usually uncrowded setting will make you want to linger. ✉*Yosemite Lodge, Northside Dr., about ¾ mi west of the visitor center, Yosemite Village* ☎*209/372–1281* ✍*Reservations essential* ▭*AE, D, DC, MC, V* ⊙*No lunch.*

$$ AMERICAN ✕**Tuolumne Lodge Restaurant.** At the back of a small building that contains the lodge's front desk and small gift shop, this restaurant serves hearty American fare at breakfast and dinner. Let the front desk know in advance if you have any dietary restrictions, and the cooks will not let you down. ■ **TIP→ Box lunches can be ordered the night before.** ✉*Tioga Rd. (Rte. 120), Toulomne Meadows* ☎*209/372–8413* ✍*Reservations essential* ▭*AE, D, DC, MC, V* ⊙*No lunch. Closed late Sept.–Memorial Day.*

$$–$$$ AMERICAN ✕**Wawona Hotel Dining Room.** Watch deer graze on the meadow while you dine in the romantic, candlelit dining room of the whitewashed Wawona Hotel, which dates from the late 1800s. The American-style cuisine favors fresh California ingredients and flavors; trout is a menu staple. Steak, pork, chicken, and turkey entrées also are on the dinner menu, while vegetarians are likely to be pleased with the eggplant Parmesan. Salads are made from organic greens, and the wine slection is decently varied. There is a Sunday brunch offered from Easter through Thanksgiving, as well as a barbeque on the lawn every Saturday evening in the summer. For men, a jacket is required at dinner. ✉*Wawona*

Hotel, Rte. 41, Wawona ☎*209/375–1425* *Reservations essential* *AE, D, DC, MC, V* *Closed Jan. and Feb.*

PICNIC AREAS

Ready-made picnic lunches are available at Ahwahnee and Wawona with advance notice. Otherwise, stop at the Food Court at Yosemite Lodge for a pre-packaged salad or sandwich, or at grocery stores in the village to pick up supplies. There are 13 designated picnic areas around the park; restrooms and grills or fire grates are available only at those in the valley. Outside the valley, there are picnic areas at Cascades Falls, Glacier Point, Lembert Dome, Mariposa Grove, Wawona, Tenaya Lake, and Yosemite Creek.

WHERE TO STAY

Almost all reservations for lodging in Yosemite (Redwood Guest Cottages is the exception) are made through the concessionaire, **Delaware North Corporation** (☎*801/559–4884* *www.yosemitepark.com*). Within an hour or two of reservations becoming available—and remember, you can start reserving one year and one day in advance of your proposed stay—the Ahwahnee Hotel, Yosemite Lodge, and Wawona Hotel sometimes are fully booked for weekends, holiday periods, and all days between Memorial Day and Labor Day.

$$$$ Fodor'sChoice ★ **Ahwahnee Hotel.** From its shiny wood-plank floor, on which stand many comfortable chairs, up past the big windows with magnificent views and walls that contain marvelous artwork, all the way to its lovely crossed-beam ceiling, decorated with colorful Indian designs, the Ahwahnee's Great Lounge is one of California's best interiors. A National Historic Landmark, the hotel is constructed primarily of concrete and sugar-pine logs. Guest rooms have Native American design motifs; public spaces are decorated with art-deco detailing, oriental rugs, and elaborate iron- and woodwork. Some luxury hotel amenities, including turndown service and guest bathrobes, are standard here. The Dining Room is by far the most impressive restaurant in the park and one of the most beautiful rooms in California. If you stay in a cottage room, be aware that each cottage has multiple guest rooms, though all have an en suite bath. If you cannot afford to stay here, take the time to stroll about the main floor. **Pros:** best lodge in Yosemite, if not all of California. **Cons:** expensive; some reports that service has slipped in recent years. ✉*1 Ahwahnee Rd., about ¾ mi east of Yosemite Valley Visitor Center, Yosemite Village* ☎*209/372–1407 front desk, 801/559–4884 reservations* *www.yosemitepark.com* *95 lodge rooms, 4 suites, 24 cottage rooms* *In-room: no a/c (some), refrigerator, Wi-Fi. In-hotel: restaurant, room service, bar, tennis court, pool* *EP* *AE, D, DC, MC, V.*

$–$$ **Curry Village.** Low on charm but comparatively good on value, Curry Village is the favored place for families on a budget. In summer, expect to be absorbed in a swarm of happy kids and their sometimes harried parents trying to keep the peace. Opened in 1899 as a place where travelers could enjoy the beauty of Yosemite for a modest price, Curry Village has plain accommodations: standard motel rooms, cabins, and tent cabins, which have rough wood frames, canvas walls, and roofs. The tent cabins are a step up from camping, with linens and blankets provided (maid service upon request). Some have heat. Most of the cabins share shower and toilet facilities. Dining options abound here, the breakfast and dinner buffets drawing big crowds. At this writing, renovations to Curry's guest registration, lounge, and ampitheater were expected to be completed by mid-May 2009. Happy Isles and the popular Mist Trail are a few minutes' walk away. Reserve far in advance, especially for summer and holiday stays. **Pros:** comparatively economical; family-friendly atmosphere. **Cons:** can be crowded and, for the great outdoors, a bit noisy. ✉*910 Curry Village Dr., Curry Village* ☎*209/372–8333 front desk, 801/559–4884 reservations* 🌐*www.yosemitepark.com* *18 rooms, 390 cabins (most are tent cabins, some have baths)* *In-room: no a/c, no phone, no TV. In-hotel: 3 restaurants, bar, pool, bicycles, no-smoking rooms* *EP* *AE, D, DC, MC, V.*

$ **Tuolumne Meadows Lodge.** Day hikers and backpackers are served well here at Yosemite National Park's highest (elevation: 8,775 feet) formal accommodations. The tent cabins, sprinkled not too densely on the gentle hills of this spacious property, come equipped with beds, linens, woodstoves, and candles; there's no electricity. You can have breakfast and dinner in the lodge's inviting dining room, although you need to let the friendly front-desk staff know in advance. Box lunches are available, too. Vegetarians and vegans eat well here. **Pros:** convenient for hikers; comparatively inexpensive; friendly. **Cons:** a bit rustic; reservations must be made far in advance. ✉*Tioga Rd., Toulomne Meadows* ☎*209/372–8413 front desk, 801/559–4884 reservations* 🌐*www.yosemitepark.com* *69 tent cabins* *EP* *AE, D, DC, MC, V* *Closed mid-Sept.–early June.*

$$–$$$ **Wawona Hotel.** This 1879 National Historic Landmark sits at Yosemite's southern end, a 15-minute drive (or free shuttle bus ride) from the Mariposa Grove of Giant Sequoias. It's an old-fashioned New England-style estate, with whitewashed buildings, wraparound verandas, and pleasant, no-frills rooms decorated with period furnishings. About half the rooms share bathrooms; those that do come equipped with robes. The romantic, candlelit dining room lies across the lobby from the cozy Victorian parlor, which has a fireplace, board games, and a piano, where a pianist plays ragtime most evenings. **Pros:** lovely, peaceful atmosphere; close to Mariposa Grove. **Cons:** few modern in-room amenities. ✉*8308 Wawona Rd. (Hwy. 41), Wawona* ☎*209/375–6556 front desk, 801/559–4884 reservations* 🌐*www.yosemitepark.com* *104 rooms, 50 with bath* *In-room: no a/c, no phone, no TV. In-hotel: restaurant, bar, golf course, tennis court, pool* *EP* *AE, D, DC, MC, V* *Closed Jan. and Feb.*

$–$$ **White Wolf Lodge.** Set in a subalpine meadow at the end of a slim road that heads north 1 mi from Route 120, White Wolf offers rustic accommodations in tent cabins that share nearby baths or in wooden cabins with baths. This is an excellent base camp for hiking the backcountry. Breakfast and dinner are served home-style in the snug, white

10

main building. Keep in mind that you will be seated in one of four time slots, so you might eat earlier or later than you would prefer if you do not reserve well in advance. **Pros:** quiet; convenient for hikers; good restaurant. **Cons:** far from the Valley; not much to do other than hiking. ✉*Off Tioga Rd. (Rte. 120), 45 minutes west of Tuolumne Meadows and 30 minutes east of Crane Flat* ☎*801/559–4884 (reservations), no phone at hotel* *24 tent cabins, 4 cabins* *In-room: no a/c, no phone, no TV. In-hotel: restaurant* *EP* *AE, D, DC, MC, V* *Closed mid-Sept.–early June.*

$$–$$$ **Yosemite Lodge at the Falls.** This lodge near Yosemite Falls, which dates from 1915, looks like a 1960s motel-resort complex, with numerous brown, two-story buildings tucked beneath the trees around large parking lots. Motel-style rooms have two double beds; the larger rooms also have dressing areas and patios or balconies. A few have views of the falls. Of the lodge's eateries, the Mountain Room Restaurant is the most formal. The cafeteria-style Food Court also serves three meals a day. Many park tours depart from the main building. **Pros:** centrally located; dependably clean rooms; lots of tours leave from out front. **Cons:** can feel impersonal; appearance is little dated. ✉*Northside Dr. about ¾ mi west of the visitor center, Yosemite Village* ☎ *209/372–1274 front desk, 801/559–4884 reservations* *www.yosemitepark.com* *245 rooms* *In-room: no a/c, no phone, Wi-Fi. In-hotel: restaurant, bar, pool, bicycles, no-smoking rooms* *EP* *AE, D, DC, MC, V.*

CAMPING

All Yosemite National Park campground reservations (except those for Housekeeping Camp) are now are handled through a central system that is not NPS-operated called Recreation One-Stop (☎*877/444–6777* *www.recreation.gov* *D, MC, V*).

Delaware North Corporation (☎*801/559–4909* *www.yosemitepark.com*) operates five High Sierra Camps with comfortable, furnished tent cabins in the remote reaches of Yosemite; rates include breakfast and dinner service. The park concessionaire books the extremely popular backcountry camps by lottery; applications are due by late November for the following summer season. Phone for more information, or check for current availability by navigating through the Web site to the High Sierra Camps pages.

The **Yosemite Association** (*Box 545, Yosemite, CA 95389* ☎*209/372–0740* *www.yosemite.org/visitor*) manages wilderness permit reservation requests. You can make reservations up to 24 weeks in advance. First, visit the National Park Service Web site (*www.nps.gov/yose/planyourvisit/wildpermits.htm*) and check on availability for your trailhead. For a $5 nonrefundable fee you can make reservations by phone or by mail (make checks payable to YOSEMITE ASSOCIATION). You might be able to make reservations online, although that Web site is not always available.

Sequoia and Kings Canyon National Parks

WORD OF MOUTH

"My wife and I just returned from a trip out west that included Sequoia National Park. Wow!! . . . We took the shuttle up to Moro Rock from the museum and the views from Moro Rock were incredible. Then we hiked 2.4 miles back to the museum where we had parked. The hike was through a grove of giant sequoia trees. Un-freekin-believable!! Best hike ever."

—emv0816

WELCOME TO SEQUOIA AND KINGS CANYON NATIONAL PARKS

TOP REASONS TO GO

★ **Gentle giants:** You'll feel small—in a good way—walking among some of the world's largest living things in Sequoia's Giant Forest and Kings Canyon's Grant Grove.

★ **Because it's there:** You can't even glimpse it from the main part of Sequoia, but the sight of majestic Mt. Whitney is worth the trek to the eastern face of the High Sierra.

★ **Underground exploration:** Far older even than the giant sequoias, the gleaming limestone formations in Crystal Cave will draw you along dark, marble passages.

★ **A grander-than-Grand Canyon:** Drive the twisting Kings Canyon Scenic Byway down into the jagged, granite Kings River Canyon, deeper in parts than the Grand Canyon.

★ **Regal solitude:** To spend a day or two hiking in a subalpine world of your own, pick one of the 11 trailheads at Mineral King.

1 Giant Forest. The most heavily visited area of Sequoia lies at the base of the "thumb" portion of Kings Canyon National Park and contains major sights such as Giant Forest, General Sherman Tree, Crystal Cave, and Moro Rock.

2 Grant Grove. The "thumb" of Kings Canyon National Park is its busiest section, where Grant Grove, General Grant Tree, Panoramic Point, and Big Stump are the main attractions.

3 Cedar Grove. Most visitors to the huge, high-country portion of Kings Canyon National Park don't go farther than Roads End, a few miles east of Cedar Grove on the canyon floor. Here, the river runs through Zumwalt Meadow, surrounded by magnificent granite formations.

4 Mineral King. In the southeast section of Sequoia, the highest road-accessible part of the park is a good place to hike, camp, and soak up the unspoiled grandeur of the Sierra Nevada.

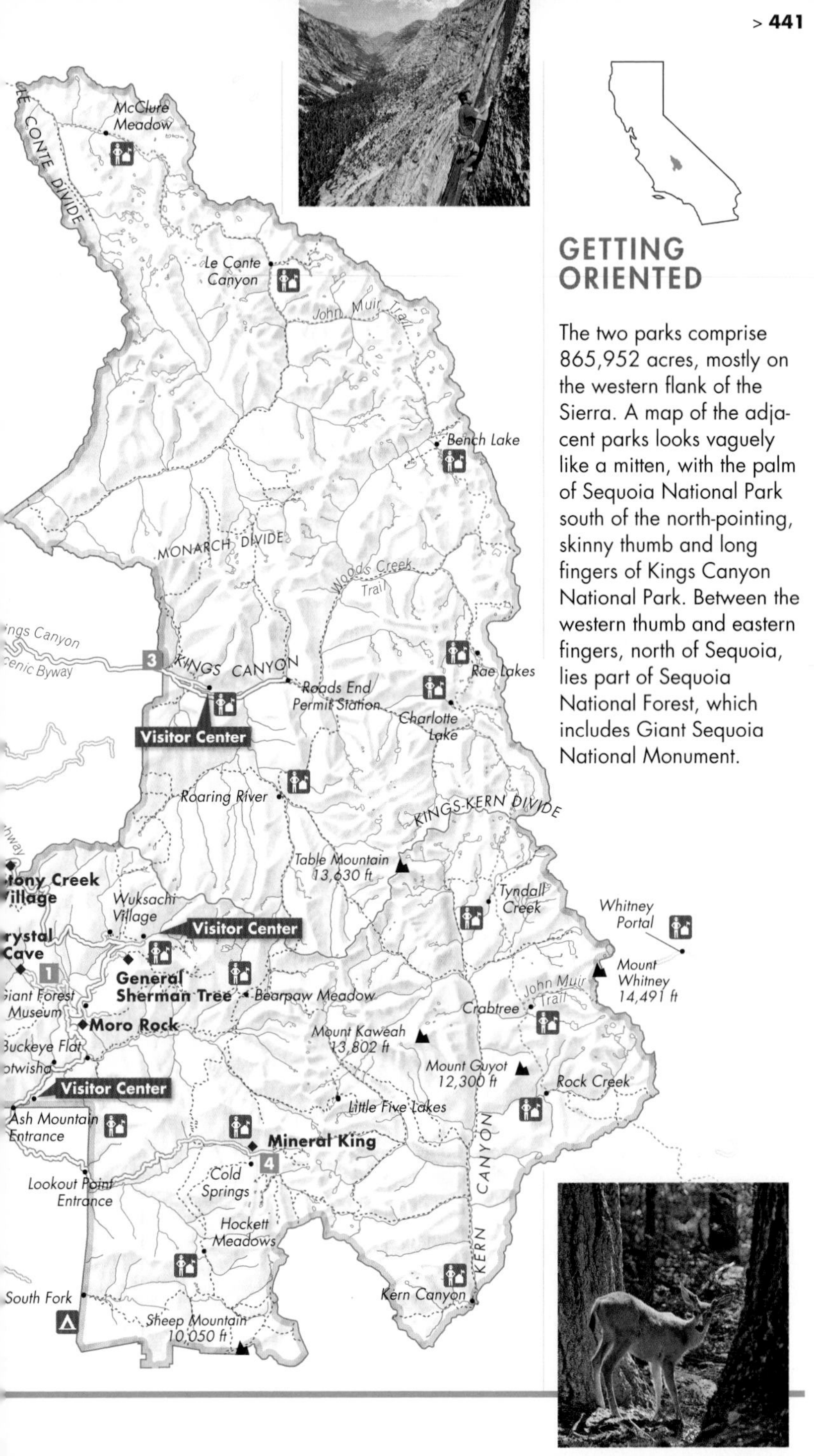

GETTING ORIENTED

The two parks comprise 865,952 acres, mostly on the western flank of the Sierra. A map of the adjacent parks looks vaguely like a mitten, with the palm of Sequoia National Park south of the north-pointing, skinny thumb and long fingers of Kings Canyon National Park. Between the western thumb and eastern fingers, north of Sequoia, lies part of Sequoia National Forest, which includes Giant Sequoia National Monument.

SEQUOIA AND KINGS CANYON NATIONAL PARKS PLANNER

When to Go

Most people visit Sequoia and Kings Canyon National Parks in the summer, when everything is open and accessible. Generals Highway (Rte. 198), which connects the two parks, is open year-round, but may impose chain requirements during snowstorms and their aftermath. The parks' two significant secondary roads (Kings Canyon Scenic Byway [Rte. 180 between Grant Grove Village and Cedar Grove Village] and Mineral King Road [which branches off Rte. 198 at Three Rivers]), both about 30 mi long, are closed from mid- to late October through May, typically, due to snow accumulation and rockslide dangers.

Make lodging and campground reservations for Sequoia National Park's Giant Forest area as far in advance as you can.

Like Yosemite, the parks receive most of their precipitation from November through April. Summer rainfall is rare.

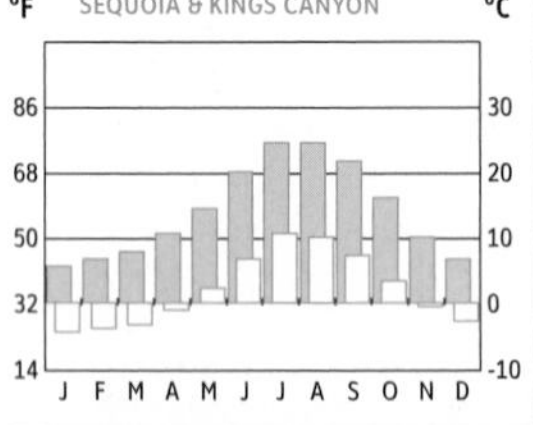

Getting There and Around

Sequoia is 36 mi east of Visalia on Route 198; Kings Canyon is 53 mi east of Fresno on Route 180. There is no automobile entrance on the eastern side of the Sierra. Routes 180 and 198 are connected by Generals Highway, a paved two-lane road that's open year-round. Ongoing improvements to Generals Highway can cause delays of up to an hour at peak times, and the road is extremely narrow and steep from Route 198 to Giant Forest.

Do not travel beyond Potwisha Campground with an RV longer than 22 feet on Route 198; take straighter, easier Route 180 instead. Maximum vehicle length on Generals Highway is 40 feet, or 50 feet combined length for vehicles with trailers.

Snowstorms are common late October–April. Unless you have four-wheel drive with snow tires, always carry chains and know how to apply them to the tires on the drive axle. Generals Highway between Lodgepole and Grant Grove is sometimes closed by snow. The Mineral King Road from Route 198 into southern Sequoia National Park is closed 2 mi below Atwell Mill either on November 1 or after the first heavy snow. The Buckeye Flat–Middle Fork Trailhead Road is closed mid-October–mid-April when the Buckeye Flat Campground closes. The lower Crystal Cave Road is closed when the cave closes in November. Its upper 2 mi, as well as the Panoramic Point and Moro Rock–Crescent Meadow roads, are closed with the first heavy snow. Because of the danger of rockfall, the portion of Kings Canyon Scenic Byway east of Grant Grove closes in winter.

WHAT IT COSTS

	¢	$	$$	$$$	$$$$
Restaurants	under $8	$8–$12	$13–$20	$21–$30	over $30
Hotels	under $70	$70–$120	$121–$175	$176–$250	over $250
Camping	under $8	$8–$14	$15–$20	$21–$25	over $25

Restaurant prices are per person for a main course at dinner. Hotel prices are per night for two people in a standard double room in high season, excluding taxes and service charges. Camping prices are for a standard (no hookups, pit toilets, fire grates, picnic tables) campsite per night.

Updated by Reed Parsell

The silent giants of Sequoia and Kings Canyon, surrounded by vast granite canyons and towering snowcapped peaks, strike awe in most everyone who sees them. No less than famed naturalist John Muir proclaimed the sequoia tree "the most beautiful and majestic on earth."

The largest living things on the planet, *Sequoiadendron giganteum* trees are not as tall as the coast redwoods (*Sequoia sempervirens*), but they're more massive and, on average, older. Exhibits at the visitor centers explain why they can live so long and grow so big, as well as the special relationship between these trees and fire (their thick, fibrous bark helps protect them from flames and insects, and their seeds can't germinate until they first explode out of a burning pinecone).

Sequoia and Kings Canyon share a boundary and are administered together. They encompass 1,353 square mi, rivaled only by Yosemite in rugged Sierra beauty. The topography ranges from the western foothills at an elevation of 1,500 feet to the towering peaks of the Great Western Divide and the Sierra Crest. The Kings River cuts a swath through the backcountry, and over the years has formed a granite canyon that, in places, descends nearly 4,000 feet from the rim. From Junction Overlook, on the drive to Cedar Grove, you can see the 8,200-foot drop from Spanish Mountain to the Kings River, as well as the confluence of the Middle and South forks of the Kings River.

PLANNING

ADMISSION FEES

For the combination of Sequoia and Kings Canyon, the vehicle admission fee is $20 per car and is valid for seven days. For either park, visitors arriving by bus, or on foot, bicycle, motorcycle, or horseback pay $10 for a seven-day pass.

A one-year pass for Sequoia and Kings Canyon is $30. A 12-month "America the Beautiful—National Parks and Federal Recreational Lands Pass" is $80 and gets you (and your family) into all federal recreation sites that charge entrance fees. Seniors (ages 62 and older) can purchase the annual pass for $10. People with lifetime disabilities are entitled to an "Access Pass," which is free.

ADMISSION HOURS

The parks are open daily 24 hours. Sequoia and Kings Canyon National Parks are in the Pacific time zone.

EMERGENCIES

In an emergency, call 911 from any park phone.

In Sequoia/Kings Canyon, there is no medical clinic, but rangers at the Cedar Grove, Foothills, Grant Grove, and Lodgepole visitor centers and the Mineral King ranger station are trained in first aid.

PERMITS

If you plan to camp in the Sequoia or Kings Canyon backcountry, your group must have a backcountry camping permit, which costs $15 for hikers or $30 for stock users (horseback riders, etc.). One permit covers the entire group. Availability of permits depends upon trailhead quotas. Advance reservations are accepted by mail, fax, or e-mail for a $15 processing fee, beginning March 1, and must be made at least three weeks in advance. Without a reservation you may still get a permit on a first-come, first-served basis starting at 1 PM the day before you plan to hike. For more information on backcountry camping or travel with pack animals (horses, mules, burros, or llamas), contact Sequoia and Kings Canyon's Wilderness Permit Office.

Sequoia and Kings Canyon Contacts **Wilderness Permit Office** (☎ *530/565-3761*). **Wilderness Permit Reservations** (*HCR 89 Box 60, Three Rivers 93271* ☎ *559/575-3766* *559/565-4239* *www.nps.gov/seki/planyourvisit/wilderness_permits.htm*).

VISITOR INFORMATION

Contacts **Delaware North Companies Parks & Resorts** (☎ *559/565-4070 or 888/252-5757* *www.visitsequoia.com*) operates the lodgings and visitor services in Sequoia, and some in Kings Canyon. **Kings Canyon Park Services** (☎ *559/335-5500 or 888/564-7775* *www.sequoia-kingscanyon.com*) operates some park services, including lodging. **Sequoia and Kings Canyon National Parks** (☎ *559/565-3341 or 559/565-3134* *www.nps.gov/seki*). **Sequoia Natural History Association** (☎ *559/565-3759* *www.sequoiahistory.org*) operates Crystal Cave and the Pear Lake Ski Hut, and provides educational materials and programs.

EXPLORING SEQUOIA AND KINGS CANYON NATIONAL PARKS

GIANT FOREST

16 mi north of Ash Mountain entrance and 25 mi southeast of the Big Stump entrance on Generals Hwy.

Only Redwood Mountain Grove has a few more sequoias, but Giant Forest is where you will find the world's biggest tree and many of Sequoia National Park's other must-see sights. Step into the Giant

Forest Museum, open year-round weather permitting, to learn all you care to about the Sierra redwoods. The nearby Big Trees and Congress Trails are two of the most spectacular showcases of mature sequoias, and both are short and paved. Hop on the shuttle to Moro Rock, where you can climb its amazing stone staircase for sweeping views of the Middle Fork Canyon, and then on to Crescent Meadow, reportedly John Muir's favorite place in the Sierra Nevada outside Yosemite. Retreat to the Lodgepole complex and Wuksachi Village for diverse food and lodging options.

Giant Forest merits at least a half-day visit, but spend a full day here if you can. ■ **TIP→ And remember that if you intend to tour Crystal Cave, you must purchase tickets at either the Lodgepole or Foothills Visitor Center.**

VISITOR CENTERS

Beetle Rock Family Nature Center. Across the road from Giant Forest Museum and a few strides south of the multi-tiered parking lot, the Sequoia Natural History Association operates a nature center with interactive exhibits and a children's bookstore with science-oriented books, games, and toys. "Beetle Rock Rollick," a ranger-led family program, is conducted at 2 PM daily. On the massive rock children have lots of room to run around and climb on smooth and gentle slopes that should ease parents' anxieties. ✉ *Generals Hwy. (Rte. 198), 4 mi south of Lodgepole Visitor Center, Giant Forest* ☎ *559/565–4251* *Free* *Early July–late Aug., conditions permitting; daily 10–4.*

Foothills Visitor Center. Learn about foothills resource issues such as drought and fire in this small center at the southern end of Generals Highway. You also can pick up books, maps, and a list of ranger-led walks, and get wilderness permits. Buy tickets here if you plan to see Crystal Cave before you get to Lodgepole Visitor Center, the only other place they are sold. ✉ *Generals Hwy. (Rte. 198), 1 mi north of the Ash Mountain entrance,Giant Forest* ☎ *559/565–3135* *Oct.–mid-May, daily 8–4:30; mid-May–Sept., daily 8–6.*

★ **Giant Forest Museum.** Well-imagined and interactive displays give you the basics about sequoias, of which there are 2,161 with diameters exceeding 10 feet in the 2,115-acre Giant Forest. ✉ *Generals Hwy., 4 mi south of Lodgepole Visitor Center, 18 mi north of Ash Mountain entrance Giant Forest* ☎ *559/565–4480* *Free* *Daily 8–5.*

Lodgepole Visitor Center. Along with exhibits on the area's geologic history, wildlife, and longtime American Indian inhabitants, the center screens an outstanding 22-minute film about bears. Books, maps, and souvenirs are sold here, as are tickets to Crystal Cave. ✉ *Generals Hwy. (Rte. 198), 4 mi north of Giant Forest Museum, 22 mi north of Ash Mountain entrance, Giant Forest* ☎ *559/565–4436* *June–Oct., daily 7–6; Nov.–May, weekends 7–6.*

Walter Fry Nature Center. The hands-on nature exhibits here are designed primarily for children, but the center is open only afternoons for a few short weeks in the summer. ✉ *Lodgepole Campground, ½ mi east of Lodgepole Visitor Center, Giant Forest* ☎ *559/565–4436* *Free* *July–mid-Aug., weekends noon–5.*

SCENIC STOPS

Crescent Meadow. John Muir called this the "gem of the Sierra." Take an hour or two to walk around it, and see if you agree. Wildflowers bloom throughout the summer. ✉ *End of Moro Rock–Crescent Meadow Rd., 2.6 mi east off Generals Hwy., Giant Forest.*

Crystal Cave. One of more than 200 caves in the two parks, Crystal is unusual in that it's composed largely of marble, the result of limestone being hardened under heat and pressure. It contains several impressive formations that will be more clearly seen once an environmentally sensitive relighting project is completed in the next few years. The standard tour allows 45 minutes inside the cave. ■ **TIP→ Spend more time, with fewer people, on the Discovery Tour ($19). All tickets must be bought at least 90 minutes in advance at either the Foothills or Lodgepole Visitor Centers.** ✉ *Crystal Cave Rd., 6 mi west off Generals Hwy., Giant Forest* ☎ *559/565–3759* 🌐 *www.sequoiahistory.org* 🎫 *$11* ⏲ *Early May—late Oct.; call for schedule..*

★ **General Sherman Tree.** Neither the world's tallest nor oldest sequoia, General Sherman is nevertheless tops in volume—and it is still putting on weight, adding the equivalent of a 60-foot-tall tree every year to its 2.7 million–pound bulk. ✉ *Generals Hwy. (Rte. 198), 2 mi south of Lodgepole Visitor Center, Giant Forest.*

★ **Moro Rock.** Sequoia National Park's best non-tree attraction, Moro Rock offers panoramic views to those fit and determined enough to mount its 350-ish steps. The rock's 6,725-foot summit overlooks the Middle Fork Canyon, sculpted by the Kaweah River and approaching the depth of Arizona's Grand Canyon. ✉ *Moro Rock–Crescent Meadow Rd., 1½ mi east off Generals Hwy. (Rte. 198) to parking area, Giant Forest.*

Tunnel Log. This 275-foot tree fell in 1937, and soon a 17-foot-wide, 8-foot-high hole was cut through it for vehicular passage that continues today. ✉ *Moro Rock–Crescent Meadow Rd., 2 mi east of Generals Hwy. (Rte. 198), Giant Forest.*

GRANT GROVE

3 mi northeast of the Big Stump entrance and 45 mi north of the Ash Mountain entrance on Rte. 180.

What in 1890 was created as the 4-square-mi Grant Grove National Park is now the hub of Kings Canyon National Park's western, smaller portion. Grant Grove Village, 55 mi due east of Fresno via Route 180, has year-round services that include a general store, John Muir Lodge, and even a campground. If you devote two or three days to see both national parks, this is a good place to spend the night: You'll be roughly the same driving distance from the main attractions of Sequoia (General Sherman Tree, Giant Forest, Moro Rock) as you are from those of eastern Kings Canyon (Kings River Canyon, Cedar Grove, Zumwalt Meadow).

DID YOU KNOW?

Sequoias once grew throughout the Northern Hemisphere, until they were almost wiped out by glaciers. In fact, some of the fossils in Arizona's Petrified Forest National Park are extinct Sequoia species.

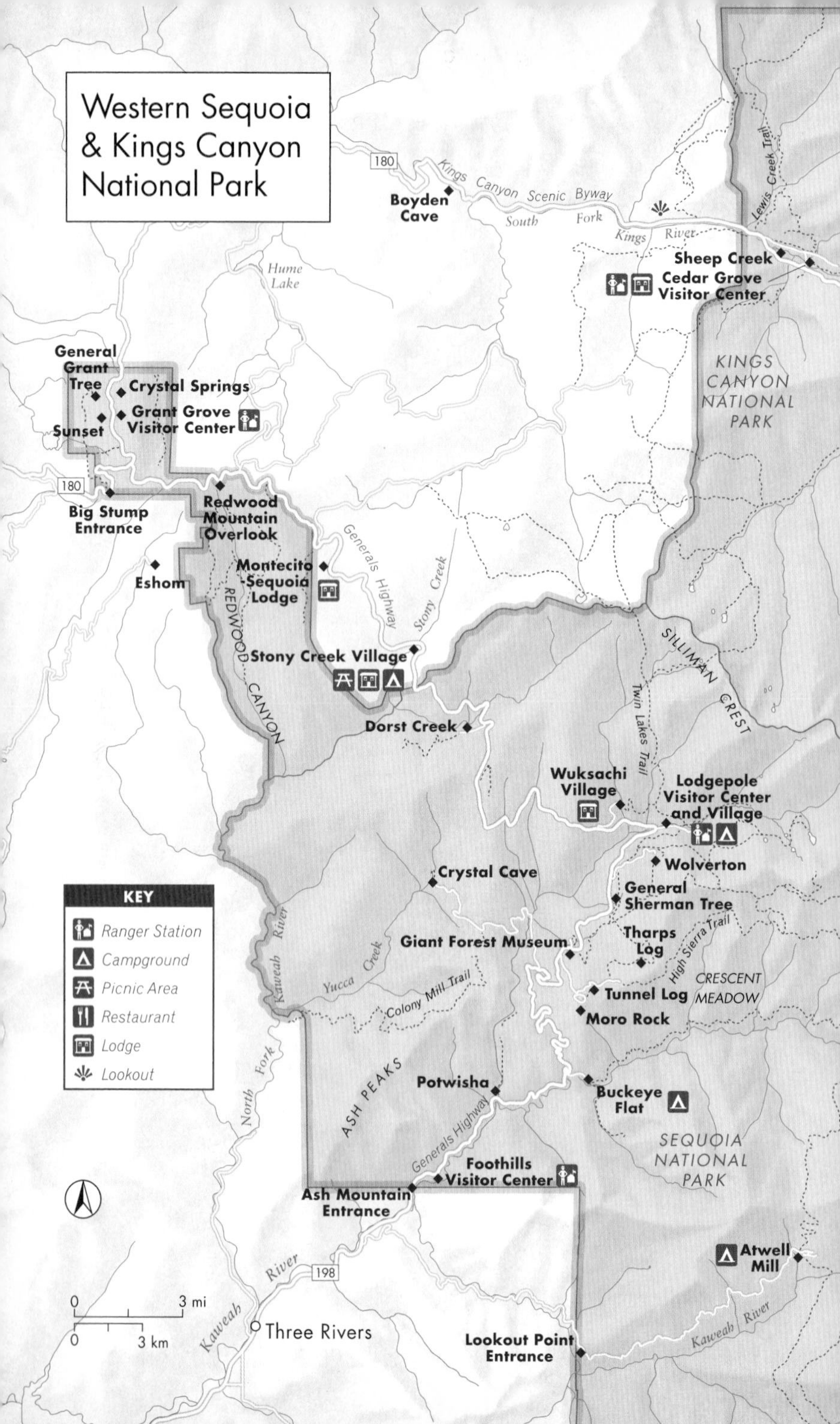

Western Sequoia & Kings Canyon National Park
180
Kings Canyon Scenic Byway
Boyden Cave
South Fork Kings River
Lewis Creek Trail
Sheep Creek
Cedar Grove Visitor Center
Hume Lake
KINGS CANYON NATIONAL PARK
General Grant Tree
Crystal Springs
Grant Grove Visitor Center
Sunset
180
Big Stump Entrance
Redwood Mountain Overlook
Generals Highway
Stony Creek
Montecito -Sequoia Lodge
Eshom
REDWOOD CANYON
Stony Creek Village
SILLIMAN CREST
Twin Lakes Trail
Dorst Creek
Wuksachi Village
Lodgepole Visitor Center and Village
Wolverton
Crystal Cave
General Sherman Tree
Tharps Log
High Sierra Trail
Giant Forest Museum
Kaweah River
Yucca Creek
Colony Mill Trail
Tunnel Log
CRESCENT MEADOW
Moro Rock
KEY
Ranger Station
Campground
Picnic Area
Restaurant
Lodge
Lookout
North Fork
ASH PEAKS
Potwisha
Buckeye Flat
Generals Highway
SEQUOIA NATIONAL PARK
Foothills Visitor Center
Ash Mountain Entrance
Atwell Mill
River
198
0
3 mi
0
3 km
Three Rivers
Kaweah
Lookout Point Entrance
Kaweah River

VISITOR CENTERS

Kings Canyon Visitor Center. Acquaint yourself with the varied charms of this two-section national park by watching a 15-minute film and perusing the center's exhibits on the canyon, sequoias, and human history. Books, maps, and free wilderness permits are available, as are updates on the parks' weather and air-quality conditions. ✉ *Generals Hwy. (Rte. 198), 3 mi northeast of Rte. 180, Big Stump entrance, Grant Grove* ☎ *559/565–4307* ⏲ *Summer, daily 8–6; spring and fall, daily 9–4:30; winter, daily 9:30–4:30.*

HISTORIC SITES

★ **Fallen Monarch.** This sequoia's hollow base was used in the second half of the 19th century as a home for settlers, a saloon, and even a stable for U.S. Cavalry horses. As you walk through it (assuming entry is permitted, which has not always been the case in recent years), check out how little the wood has decayed. ✉ *Trailhead 1 mi north of Grant Grove Visitor Center, Grant Grove.*

SCENIC STOPS

General Grant Tree. President Coolidge proclaimed this to be "the nation's Christmas tree," and 30 years later President Eisenhower designated it as a living shrine to all those Americans who have died in wars. Bigger at its base than the General Sherman Tree, it tapers rather quickly and is estimated to be the world's second- or third-largest sequoia by volume. ✉ *Trailhead 1 mi north of Grant Grove Visitor Center, Grant Grove.*

★ **Redwood Mountain Grove.** If you are serious about sequoias, you should consider visiting this, the world's largest big-tree grove. Within its 2,078 acres are 2,172 sequoias whose diameters exceed 10 feet. Your options range from the distant (pulling off the Generals Highway onto an overlook) to the intimate (taking a 6- to 10-mi hike down into its richest regions, which include two of the world's 25 heaviest trees). To reach the trailhead, you must take a poorly maintained, summer-only dirt road that tumbles down from Generals Highway on the southern edge of Kings Canyon National Park's western portion. ✥ *Drive 5 mi south of Grant Grove on Generals Hwy. (Rte. 198), then turn right at Quail Flat; follow it 1½ mi to the Redwood Canyon trailhead, Grant Grove.*

CEDAR GROVE

30 mi east of Grant Grove Village and 33 mi east of the Big Stump Entrance on Kings Canyon Scenic Byway (Rte. 180).

The gateway to Kings Canyon National Park's large eastern portion and to the pristine wilderness that beckons beyond, Cedar Grove is a popular launching pad for many backpacking trips. In summertime, the Road's End parking lot is crowded with cars whose occupants have disappeared into the High Sierra, sometimes for weeks.

Day-trip opportunities abound here, too, for those who either have seen all the big trees they want or are just ready for a different type of outing. The seasonal, 30-mi road to Cedar Grove Village and to the trailheads beyond has been designated as Kings Canyon Scenic Byway. As you drive through Sequoia National Forest on your way

DID YOU KNOW?

President Calvin Coolidge ordained King Canyon's General Grant Tree as the nation's Christmas tree in 1926. It's also the world's third-largest tree.

to the park, you will pass through the canyon's deepest point. Be sure to pause at an overlook or two along the way, and once you're in the Cedar Grove area, walk around Zumwalt Meadow and take the short trail to Roaring River Falls. Admire the natural, gray beauty of North Dome and Grand Sentinel that loom above the canyon. Grab a meal from the Cedar Grove snack bar and take it out onto a deck that overlooks the South Fork of the Kings River, which is a mighty force when mountain snowmelt is at its peak.

MOUNT WHITNEY

At 14,494 feet, Mount Whitney is the highest point in the contiguous United States and stands on Sequoia National Park's wild eastern side. From the west side of the park the peak is hidden behind the Great Western Divide. To see it, you must either undertake an extended backpacking trip or drive hundreds of miles around the Sierra Nevada range, via Yosemite National Park's Tioga Pass to the north or around Isabella Lake (and the small resort town of Kernville) to the south. The best vantage point is at the end of 13-mi Whitney Portal Road (closed in the winter) off memorably scenic Highway 395.

VISITOR CENTERS

Cedar Grove Visitor Center. Off the main road and behind the Sentinel campground, this small ranger station has books and maps, plus information about hikes and other things to do in the area. ✉*Kings Canyon Scenic Byway, 30 mi east of park entrance, Cedar Grove* ☎*559/565–3793* ⏲*Apr.–Oct., daily 9–5.*

Road's End Permit Station. If you're planning to hike the backcountry, you can pick up a permit and information on the backcountry here. You can also rent or buy bear canisters, a must for campers. When the station is closed, you can still complete a self-service permit form. ✉*6 mi east of Cedar Grove Visitor Center, at the end of Kings Canyon Scenic Byway, Cedar Grove* ☎*No phone* ⏲*Late May–late Sept., daily 7–3:30.*

SCENIC STOPS

Canyon View. There are many places along the scenic byway to pull over for sightseeing, but this spot is special in that it showcases evidence of the canyon's glacial history. Here, maybe more than anywhere else, you can understand why John Muir compared Kings Canyon vistas with those in Yosemite. ✉*Kings Canyon Scenic Byway (Rte. 180), 1 mi east of the Cedar Grove turnoff, Cedar Grove.*

MINERAL KING

25 mi east of Three Rivers and 26 mi from Sequoia National Park's Ash Mountain entrance via Mineral King Rd.

People who come to this remote section at the southern end of Sequoia National Park sometimes make it an annual habit. They love the remoteness and the crisp, light air of 7,800 feet. They enjoy gazing up at Sawtooth Peak, 12,343 high and with a series of sharp granite bumps that do indeed resemble a saw. They venture onto the 11 trails, up mountainsides, past abandoned mine shafts, to gorgeous lakes. And

CLOSE UP

Flora and Fauna

The parks can be divided into three distinct zones. In the west (1,500–4,500 feet) are the rolling, lower-elevation foothills, covered with shrubby chaparral vegetation or golden grasslands dotted with oaks. Chamise, red-barked manzanita, and the occasional yucca plant grow here. Fields of white popcorn flower cover the hillsides in spring, and the yellow fiddleneck flourishes. In summer intense heat and absence of rain cause the hills to turn golden brown. Wildlife includes the California ground squirrel, noisy blue-and-gray scrub jay, black bears, coyotes, skunks, and gray fox.

At middle elevation (5,000–9,000 feet), where the giant sequoia belt resides, rock formations mix with meadows and huge stands of evergreens—red and white fir, incense cedar, and ponderosa pines to name a few. Wildflowers, including yellow blazing star and red Indian paintbrush, bloom in spring and summer. Golden-mantled ground squirrels, Steller's jays, mule deer, and black bears (most active in fall) inhabit the area, as does the Douglas squirrel, or chickaree.

The high alpine section of the parks is extremely rugged, with a string of rocky peaks reaching above 13,000 feet to Mt. Whitney's 14,494 feet. Fierce weather and scarcity of soil make vegetation and wildlife sparse. Foxtail and whitebark pines have gnarled and twisted trunks, the result of high wind, heavy snowfall, and freezing temperatures. In summer you can see yellow-bellied marmots, pikas, weasels, mountain chickadees, and Clark's nutcrackers. Leopard lilies and shooting stars grow near streams and meadows.

secretly, they pray that 25-mi Mineral King Road—which branches here off Route 198 at Three Rivers—remains in crummy condition. Otherwise, more people would come spoil the quiet fun.

Mineral King is the highest spot you can drive to in Sequoia National Park, and the road is open only from late May through October. If you plan to make a day-trip here from Three Rivers, get going very early, pack a picnic lunch, and be prepared to be shaken in your car seat during the drive in and out.

VISITOR CENTERS

Mineral King Ranger Station. On your way to hiking at the end of Mineral King Road, consider stopping here to ask rangers for suggestions and insights. You also can buy maps, books, and wilderness permits. ✉ *Near the end of Mineral King Rd., 24 mi east of East Fork entrance, Mineral King* ☎ *559/565–3768* ⏲ *Late May–late Sept., daily 8–4.*

SCENIC STOPS

Mineral King. Silver was discovered here at 7,800 feet in the early 1870s. Subsequent attempts to extract the mineral were commercial flops. A road had been probed into the remoteness, however, and the lovely sub-alpine valley lured loggers, hydro-electric power developers, tourists, and people who built mountain cabins as summer retreats from the Central Valley or Los Angeles. **■ TIP→ If you're hiking very far into the backcountry, be aware that there are abandoned, open mines capable**

of ruining your day. ✉*End of Mineral King Rd., 25 mi east of Generals Hwy. (Rte. 198), east of Three Rivers, Mineral King.*

SPORTS AND THE OUTDOORS

HIKING

Both Kings Canyon and Sequoia National Park contain several easy hikes that will allow you to closely examine their rust-barked skyscrapers without taking too much of your time. The best short trails (Big Trees, Congress, Grant Grove, General Sherman Tree) are paved, and parts of them are even wheelchair-accessible.

If you're an ambitious hiker, choose from among many intriguing options, including more than a dozen half- and full-day trails that you might have to yourself. With a wilderness permit, you can venture deep into the High Sierra, trekking for days on trails that pass by lakes and meadows and are shared by other mammals.

Free general park maps are available at the entrance stations and visitor centers that probably will serve your purposes unless you are going on a backpacking adventure. Montecito-Sequoia Lodge, in Sequoia National Forest, has a bank of free information sheets about several hikes in its lobby. You can purchase detailed maps at the visitor centers or in most park stores.

SUMMER SPORTS AND ACTIVITIES

BIRD-WATCHING

More than 200 species of birds inhabit the two national parks. Not seen in most parts of the United States, the white-headed woodpecker and the pileated woodpecker are common in most mid-elevation areas here. There are also many hawks and owls, including the renowned spotted owl. Species are diverse in both parks due to the changes in elevation, and range from warblers, kingbirds, thrushes, and sparrows in the foothills to goshawk, blue grouse, red-breasted nuthatch, and brown creeper at the highest elevations. Ranger-led bird-watching tours are held on a sporadic basis. Call the park's main information number to find out more about these tours.

HORSEBACK RIDING

Scheduled trips take you through redwood forests, flowering meadows, across the Sierra, or even up to Mount Whitney. One-day destinations by horseback out of Cedar Grove include Mist Falls and Upper Bubb's Creek. In the backcountry, many equestrians head for Volcanic Lakes or Granite Basin, ascending trails that reach elevations of 10,000 feet.

From May through October you can take a one-day or overnight trip along the Kings River Canyon from **Cedar Grove Pack Station** (✉*Kings Canyon Scenic Byway, 1 mi east of Cedar Grove Village, Cedar Grove* ☎*559/565–3464 in summer, 559/337–2314 off-season*).

DID YOU KNOW?

Trail rides—like this one from Cedar Grove to Mist Falls—are available in both Sequoia and Kings Canyon National Parks.

A one- or two-hour trip from **Grant Grove Stables** (✉ *Rte. 180, ½ mi north of Grant Grove Visitor Center, near Grant Grove Village, Grant Grove* ☎ *559/335–9292 mid-June–Sept., 559/337–2314 Oct.–mid-June*) is a good way to get a taste of horseback riding in Kings Canyon.

From May through September, hourly, half-day, full-day, or overnight trips through Sequoia are available from **Horse Corral Pack Station** (✉ *Off Big Meadows Rd., 10 mi east of Generals Hwy. [Rte. 198] between Sequoia and Kings Canyon national parks, Sequoia National Forest* ☎ *559/565–3404 in summer, 559/564–6429 in winter* 🌐 *www.horsecorralpackers.com*) for beginning and advanced riders, who must be at least 7 years old.

Day and overnight tours in the high-mountain area around Mineral King are available from July through late September at **Mineral King Pack Station** (✉ *End of Mineral King Rd., 25 mi east of East Fork entrance, Mineral King* ☎ *559/561–3039 in summer, 520/855–5885 in winter* 🌐 *mineralking.tripod.com*).

WINTER SPORTS AND ACTIVITIES

CROSS-COUNTRY SKIING

Grant Grove Ski Touring Center (✉ *Grant Grove Market, Generals Hwy. [Rte. 198], 3 mi northeast of Rte. 180, Big Stump entrance, Grant Grove* ☎ *559/335–2665*) is set up in the Grant Grove Market in the winter, and you can rent cross-country skis here. The shop is open daily from 9 to 6, and the cost to rent skis runs from $6 to $11 per day. This is a good starting point for a number of marked trails, including the Panoramic Point Trail and the General Grant Tree Trail.

In the backcountry, **Pear Lake Ski Hut** (✉ *Trailhead at end of Wolverton Rd., 1½ mi northeast off Generals Hwy. [Rte. 198], Giant Forest* ☎ *559/565–3759*) offers primitive lodging during the winter ski season. The hut is reached by a steep and extremely difficult 7-mi trail from Wolverton. Only expert skiers should attempt this trek. Space is limited; make reservations well in advance. You'll pay $30 to $38 per night, and the hut is generally available from mid-December through mid-April.

Wuksachi Lodge (✉ *Off Generals Hwy. [Rte. 198], 2 mi north of Lodgepole, Giant Forest* ☎ *559/565–4070*) rents skis ($15 to $20 per day) daily from 9 to 4 in the winter season (usually November through May, unless there is no snow). Depending on snowfall amounts, there may also be instruction available. Reservations are strongly recommended if you want to stay at the lodge. Marked trails cut through Giant Forest, which sits 5 mi south of the lodge.

SNOWSHOEING

Snowshoeing is good around Grant Grove, which along with Wuksachi has naturalist-guided snowshoe walks Saturdays and holidays from mid-December through mid-March as conditions permit.

Snowshoers may stay at the Pear Lake Ski Hut (*see* ⇨ Cross-country Skiing, *above*). You can rent snowshoes for $15 to $20 at the Giant Forest Museum or Wuksachi Lodge. Make reservations and check schedules at both sites.

Grant Grove Market (✉ *Generals Hwy. [Rte. 198], 3 mi northeast of Rte. 180, Big Stump entrance, Grant Grove* ☎ *559/335–2665*) rents snowshoes in the winter if you prefer to take a self-guided walk. It's open daily from 9 to 6.

Grant Grove Visitor Center (✉ *Generals Hwy. [Rte. 198], 3 mi northeast of Rte. 180, Big Stump entrance, Grant Grove* ☎ *559/565–4307*) rents out snowshoes for the ranger-led walks for a $1 donation. Call ahead to check on the schedule; walks are usually on Saturdays and holidays.

EDUCATIONAL PROGRAMS

All visitor centers have maps for self-guided tours of Sequoia National Park. Ranger-led walks and programs take place throughout the year in Lodgepole Village and Wuksachi Lodge. Forest Service campgrounds have activities from Memorial Day to Labor Day. Schedules for activities are posted on bulletin boards and at visitor centers.

There are no regularly scheduled guided tours of Kings Canyon. Grant Grove Visitor Center has maps of self-guided park tours. Ranger-led programs take place throughout the year in Grant Grove. Cedar Grove and Forest Service campgrounds have activities from Memorial Day to Labor Day. Check bulletin boards or visitor centers for schedules.

Sequoia Sightseeing Tours (☎ *559/561–4189* 🌐 *www.sequoiatours.com*) is the only licensed tour operator in either park. The company offers daily interpretive sightseeing tours in a 10-passenger van with a friendly, knowledgeable guide. Full-day tours ($88) depart from the town of Three Rivers, and half-day tours ($59) begin at Wuksachi Lodge. Reservations are essential.

CLASSES AND SEMINARS

Evening Programs (☎ *559/565–3341*) during the summer may include documentary films and slide shows, as well as evening lectures. Locations and times vary; pick up a schedule at any visitor center or check bulletin boards near ranger stations.

★ **Seminars** (☎ *559/565–4251 or 559/565–3759* 🌐 *www.sequoiahistory.org*) led by expert naturalists cover a range of topics, including birds, wildflowers, geology, botany, photography, park history, backpacking, caving, and pathfinding. For information and prices, pick up a course catalogue at any visitor center or from Sequoia Natural History Association.

RANGER PROGRAMS

Free Nature Programs are offered on almost every summer day. Ranging in length from ½ to 1½ hours, ranger talks and walks explore subjects such as the life of the sequoia, the geology of the park, and the habits of bears. Check bulletin boards throughout the parks for that week's schedule.

Rangers conduct daily **Ranger Walks** to General Grant Tree, the General Sherman Tree, and in various Kings River Canyon locales daily in summer, less often at other times of year. The larger campgrounds typically have some sort of campfire program nightly in summer. Check bulletin boards throughout the park for the week's schedule.

The **Junior Ranger Program** (☎ *559/565–3341* ⊕ *www.nps.gov/webrangers*), a free, self-guided program, is offered year-round for children ages 5 and older. Pick up a Junior Ranger booklet at any of the visitor centers. When your child finishes an activity, a ranger signs the booklet. Kids earn a patch upon completion.

WHERE TO EAT

Treat yourself (or the family) to a high-quality meal in a wonderful setting in the Wuksachi Dining Room, if you would like, but otherwise keep your expectations modest and embrace outdoor eating whenever possible. Grab bread, spreads, drinks, and fresh produce at one of several small grocery stores. Alternatively, you can get take-out food from the Grant Grove Restaurant or Cedar Grove Snack Bar, or from one of the two small Lodgepole eateries. The nightly Wolverton Barbecue is a hybrid experience between dining in and picnicking out; the all-you-can-eat feast is staged on a patio that overlooks a sublime meadow. Between the parks and just off Generals Highway, the Montecito Sequoia Lodge has a year-round buffet.

$ ✕ **Cedar Grove Snack Bar.** For what looks to be a small operation, the menu is surprisingly extensive, with dinner entrées such as pasta, pork chops, and steak. For breakfast, try the biscuits and gravy, French toast, pancakes, or cold cereal. Burgers (including vegetarian patties) and hot dogs dominate the lunch choices. Outside, a patio dining area overlooks the Kings River. ✉ *Cedar Grove Village, Cedar Grove* ☎ *559/565–0100* 💳 *AE, D, MC, V* ⏲ *Closed Oct.–May.*

$$$ ✕ **Grant Grove Village Restaurant.** In a no-frills, open room, order basic American fare such as pancakes for breakfast or hot sandwiches and chicken for later meals. You can put a $37 dent in your wallet by ordering veal, but why? The kitchen's old-fashioned idea of a healthy plate is a hamburger with cottage cheese; vegetarians and vegans will have to content themselves with a simple salad. Take-out service is available. ✉ *Grant Grove Village, Grant Grove* ☎ *559/335–5500* 💳 *AE, D, MC, V.*

¢ ✕ **Lodgepole Market, Deli & Snack Bar.** The choices here run the gamut from simple to very simple, with the three counters only a few strides apart in a central eating complex. For hot food, venture into the snack bar, where the usual burgers and fries are amended with chicken-tender and pizza-slice options. The deli sells prepackaged sandwiches along with ice cream scooped from tubs. Find more prepackaged foods, along with picnic supplies, in the market. ✉ *Next to Lodgepole Visitor Center, Giant Forest* ☎ *559/565–3301* 💳 *AE, D, DC, MC, V* ⏲ *Closed early Sept.–mid-Apr.*

$$ ✕ **Wolverton Barbecue.** The view is bound to be more memorable than the food, no matter how much you enjoy the all-you-can-eat buffet.

Weather permitting, diners congregate on a wooden porch that looks directly out onto a small but strikingly verdant meadow. In addition to the predictable meats such as ribs and chicken, the menu has sides that include baked beans, corn on the cob, and potato salad. Following the meal, listen to a ranger talk and clear your throat for a campfire sing-along. Purchase tickets at Lodgepole Market, Wuksachi Lodge, or Wolverton Recreation Area's office. ✉ *Wolverton Rd., 1½ mi northeast off Generals Hwy. (Rte. 198), Giant Forest* ☎ *559/565–4070 or 559/565–3301* ▭ *AE, D, DC, MC, V* ⏲ *No lunch. Closed early Sept.–mid-June.*

> **PICNICKING**
>
> Why not enjoy a leisurely lunch in the shade of some of the world's tallest trees? Just take special care to dispose of your food scraps properly.

$$$ ✕ **Wuksachi Village Dining Room.** Huge windows run the length of the high-ceilinged dining room, and a large fireplace on the far wall warms body and soul. The diverse dinner menu—by far the best in the two parks—includes filet mignon, rainbow trout, and vegetarian pasta, in addition to the inescapable burgers. Wines are from California only, which isn't such a bad thing. Try the peach cobbler for dessert. The children's menu is economically priced. Breakfast and lunch are also served. ✉ *Wuksachi Village, Giant Forest* ☎ *559/565–4070* ✍ *Reservations essential* ▭ *AE, D, DC, MC, V.*

WHERE TO STAY

HOTELS

$$ **Cedar Grove Lodge.** Backpackers like to stay here on the eve of their long treks into the High Sierra wilderness, so bedtimes tend to be early and quiet. The lodge is not attractive, aside from the natural beauty that surrounds it, but it is the only indoor accommodation in this part of Kings Canyon National Park. Each room has two queen-size beds, and three have kitchenettes and patios. You can order trout, hamburgers, hot dogs, and sandwiches at the snack bar (¢–$) and take them to one of the picnic tables along the river's edge. **Pros:** a definite step up from camping in terms of comfort. **Cons:** impersonal; not everybody agrees it's clean enough. ✉ *Kings Canyon Scenic Byway, 30 mi east of Grant Grove Village, Cedar Grove* ☎ *559/565–0100 front desk, 866/522–6966 reservations* 🌐 *www.sequoia-kingscanyon.com* *21 rooms* *In-room: no phone, kitchen (some), no TV. In-hotel: laundry facilities, no-smoking rooms, Wi-Fi* ▭ *AE, D, MC, V* ⏲ *Closed mid-Oct.–mid-May* *EP.*

$$$ **John Muir Lodge.** This modern, timber-sided lodge is nestled in a wooded area in the hills above Grant Grove Village and offers year-round accommodations. The rooms and suites all have queen-size beds and private baths, and there is a comfortable common room where you can play cards and board games, or read a loaner book. Look above the stone fireplace at a giant painting of Muir himself, shown relaxing on a rock by a meadow. The inexpensive, family-style Grant Grove

Restaurant is a three-minute walk away. This is a good motel in a beautiful forest setting. **Pros:** common room stays warm; it's far enough from the main road to be quiet. **Cons:** check-in is down in the village. ✉ *Kings Canyon Scenic Byway, ¼ mi north of Grant Grove Village, Grant Grove* ☎ *559/335–5500 front desk, 866/522–6966 reservations* 🌐 *www.sequoia-kingscanyon.com* *24 rooms, 6 suites* *In-room: no a/c, no TV. In-hotel: Wi-Fi* *AE, D, MC, V* *EP.*

$$$–$$$$ Fodor's Choice ★ **Wuksachi Lodge.** The striking cedar-and-stone main building is a fine example of how a man-made structure can blend effectively with lovely mountain scenery. The lobby is small but offers a comfy setting—it has sort of a Ralph Lauren–esque rustic appeal. Guest rooms, which have modern amenities, are in three buildings up the hill a bit from the main lodge. Many of the rooms have spectacular views of the surrounding mountains. You can usually see deer roaming around the spacious and hilly grounds, which are 7,200 feet above sea level. The front desk can help you arrange any number of outdoor activities, including ski and snowshoe rental. Wi-Fi is available in the main lodge but not in guest rooms. **Pros:** best place to stay in the parks; wildlife much in evidence. **Cons:** rooms can be small; the main lodge is a few minutes' walk away from guest rooms. ✉ *Wuksachi Village, 2 mi north of the Lodgepole Visitor Center and 23 mi southeast of the Big Stump entrance, Giant Forest Box 89, Wuksachi Village, Sequoia National Park* ☎ *559/565–4070 front desk, 559/253–2199, 888/252–5757 reservations* 🌐 *www.visitsequoia.com* *102 rooms* *In-room: no a/c, refrigerator, dial-up. In-hotel: restaurant, bar, no-smoking rooms, Wi-Fi* *AE, D, DC, MC, V* *EP.*

CAMPING

Campgrounds in Sequoia and Kings Canyon are in wonderful settings, with lots of shade and nearby hiking possibilities. But beware that party-loving "locals" from Fresno and other Central Valley cities swarm up here on Friday and Saturday nights. Their boisterous banter and loud music can detract from the back-to-nature experience. Only the Dorst and Lodgepole campgrounds accept reservations (up to five months in advance), and none has RV hookups. Those around Lodgepole and Grant Grove get quite busy in summer with vacationing families. Permits are required for backcountry camping.

Sacramento and the Gold Country

WORD OF MOUTH

"[Instead of] Rafting, how about repelling in Moaning Caverns! My Hubby and I did that together and will never forget the experience! What an exciting, fun, Happy Day!.And the cave is so magnificent!"

—bodi

WELCOME TO SACRAMENTO AND THE GOLD COUNTRY

TOP REASONS TO GO

★ **Golden opportunities:** Marshall Gold Discovery State Park and Hangtown's Gold Bug & Mine conjure up California's mid-19th century boom.

★ **Capital connections:** The old saying "Sacramento is a nice place to live, but you wouldn't want to visit here" seems rather snarky now, with the city's downtown and midtown resurgence.

★ **That festive feeling:** Sacramento is home to the California State Fair in August and many ethnic food festivals. Nevada City and environs are known for summer mountain music festivals and Victorian and Cornish winter holiday celebrations.

★ **The next Napa:** With bucolic scenery and friendly tasting rooms, the Shenandoah Valley is like Napa, without the traffic.

★ **Back to nature:** Moaning Cavern's main chamber is big enough to hold the Statue of Liberty, and Calaveras Big Trees State Park is filled with giant sequoias.

1 Sacramento and Vicinity. The gateway to the Gold Country, the seat of state government (headed by Governor Arnold Schwarzenegger), and an agricultural hub, Sacramento plays many important contemporary roles. About 2 million people live in the metropolitan area, and the continuing influx of newcomers seeking opportunity, sunshine, and lower housing costs than in coastal California made it one of the nation's fastest-growing regions in the first half of this decade.

2 The Gold Country—South. South of its junction with U.S. 50, Highway 49 traces in asphalt the famed Mother Lode. The sleepy former gold-rush towns strung along the road have for the most part been restored and made presentable to visitors with an interest in one of the most frenzied episodes of American history.

3 The Gold Country—North. Highway 49 north of Placerville links the towns of Coloma, Auburn, Grass Valley, and Nevada City. Most are gentrified versions of once-rowdy mining camps, vestiges of which remain in roadside museums, old mining structures, and restored homes now serving as inns.

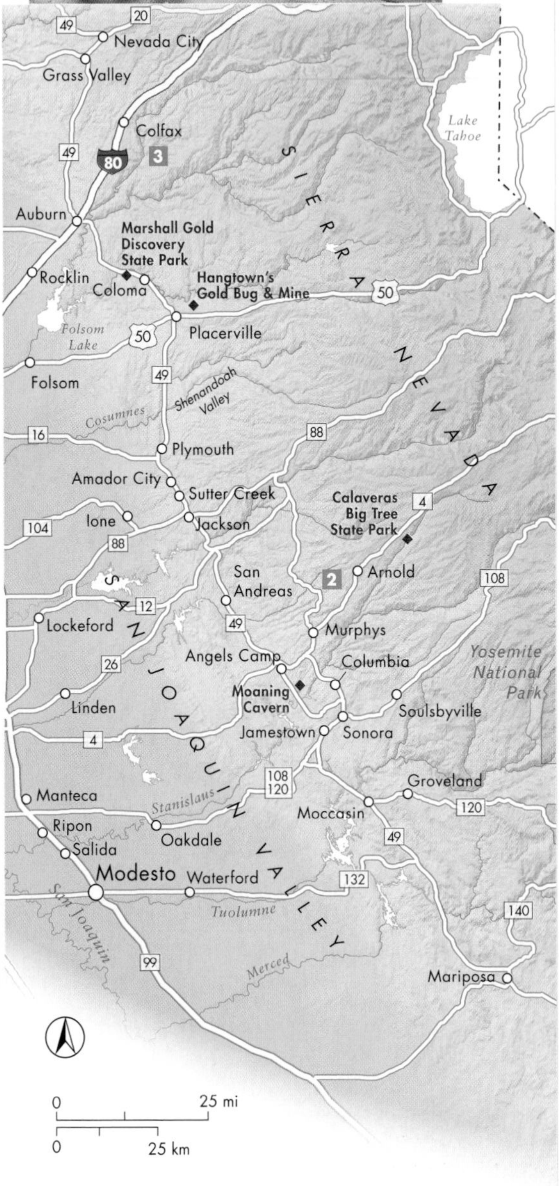

GETTING ORIENTED

The Gold Country is a largely laid-back and lower-tech destination for those seeking to escape glitzy Southern California and the Bay Area. Sacramento, Davis, and Woodland are in an enormous valley bordered to the east by the Sierra Nevada mountain range. Foothill communities Nevada City, Placerville, and Sutter Creek were products of the gold rush.

SACRAMENTO AND THE GOLD COUNTRY PLANNER

Exploring the Gold Country

Visiting Old Sacramento's museums is a good way to immerse yourself in history, but the Gold Country's heart lies along Highway 49, which winds the 325-mi north–south length of the historic mining area. The highway, often a twisting, hilly, two-lane road, begs for a convertible with the top down.

Timing

The Gold Country is most pleasant in spring, when the wildflowers are in bloom, and in fall. Summers are hot: temperatures of 100°F are fairly common. Sacramento winters tend to be cool with occasionally foggy and/or rainy days; many Sacramentans drive to the foothills to escape the winter weather. Throughout the year Gold Country towns stage community and ethnic celebrations. In December many towns are decked out for Christmas.

Tours

Gold Prospecting Adventures, LLC (☎ *209/984–4653 or 800/596–0009* 🌐 *www.goldprospecting.com*), based in Jamestown, arranges gold-panning trips.

Getting There and Around

Traveling by car is the only way to explore the Gold Country. From Sacramento three highways fan out toward the east, all intersecting with Highway 49: I–80 heads 34 mi northeast to Auburn; U.S. 50 goes east 40 mi to Placerville; and Highway 16 angles southeast 45 mi to Plymouth. Highway 49 is an excellent two-lane road that winds and climbs through the foothills and valleys, linking the principal Gold Country towns.

About the Restaurants

American, Italian, and Mexican are common Gold Country fare, but chefs also prepare ambitious continental, French, and California cuisine. Grass Valley's meat- and vegetable-stuffed *pasties,* introduced by 19th-century gold miners from Cornwall, are one of the region's more unusual treats.

About the Hotels

Full-service hotels, budget motels, and small inns can all be found in Sacramento. Larger towns along Highway 49—among them Placerville, Nevada City, Auburn, and Mariposa—have chain motels and inns. Many Gold Country bed-and-breakfasts occupy former mansions, miners' cabins, and other historic buildings.

WHAT IT COSTS

	¢	$	$$	$$$	$$$$
Restaurants	under $10	$10–$15	$16–$22	$23–$30	over $30
Hotels	under $90	$90–$120	$121–$175	$176–$250	over $250

Restaurant prices are for a main course at dinner, excluding sales tax of 7%–8% (depending on location). Hotel prices are for two people in a standard double room in high season, excluding service charges and 7%–8% tax.

12

Updated by Reed Parsell

A new era dawned for California when James Marshall turned up a gold nugget in the tailrace of a sawmill he was constructing along the American River. Before January 24, 1848, Mexico and the United States were still wrestling for ownership of what would become the Golden State. With Marshall's discovery the United States tightened its grip on the region, and prospectors from all over the world came to seek their fortunes in the Mother Lode.

The gold rush boom lasted scarcely 20 years, but it changed California forever. It produced 546 mining towns, of which fewer than 250 remain. The hills of the Gold Country were alive, not only with prospecting and mining but also with business, the arts, gambling, and a fair share of crime. Opera houses went up alongside brothels, and the California State Capitol, in Sacramento, was built with the gold dug out of the hills.

Today the Gold Country is one of California's less expensive destinations, a region of the Sierra Nevada foothills that is filled with natural and cultural pleasures. Visitors come to Nevada City, Auburn, Coloma, Sutter Creek, and Columbia not only to relive the past but also to explore art galleries, to shop for antiques, and to stay at inns full of character. Spring brings wildflowers, and in fall the hills are colored by bright red berries and changing leaves. Because it offers a mix of indoor and outdoor activities, the Gold Country is a good place to take the kids.

PLANNING

GETTING HERE AND AROUND

BY AIR

Sacramento International Airport is served by Alaska, American, Continental, Delta, Frontier, Hawaiian, Horizon Air, JetBlue, Mexicana, Northwest, Southwest, United, and US Airways/America West. *See Air*

Travel in Travel Smart Northern California for airline phone numbers. A private taxi from the airport to downtown Sacramento is about $30. The cost of the Super Shuttle from the airport to downtown Sacramento is $20. Call in advance to arrange transportation from your hotel to the airport.

Contacts **Sacramento International Airport** (*✉ 6900 Airport Blvd., 12 mi northwest of downtown off I–5, Sacramento ☎ 916/874–0700 🌐 www.sacairports.org*). **Super Shuttle** (*☎ 800/258–3826*).

BY BOAT

Sacramento's riverfront location enables you to sightsee while getting around by boat. Channel Star Excursions operates the *Spirit of Sacramento,* a riverboat that takes passengers on happy-hour, dinner, lunch, and champagne-brunch cruises in addition to one-hour narrated tours.

Contacts **Channel Star Excursions** (*✉ 110 L St. ☎ 916/552–2933 or 800/433–0263*).

BY BUS

Getting to and from SIA can be accomplished via taxi, the Super Shuttle (F By Air), or by Yolo County Public Bus 42, which operates a circular service around SIA, downtown Sacramento, West Sacramento, Davis, and Woodland. Other Gold Country destinations are best reached by private car.

Greyhound serves Sacramento, Davis, Auburn, and Placerville. It's a two-hour trip from San Francisco's Transbay Terminal, at 1st and Mission streets, to the Sacramento station, at 7th and L streets.

Sacramento Regional Transit buses and light-rail vehicles transport passengers in Sacramento. Most buses run from 6 AM to 10 PM, most trains from 5 AM to midnight. A DASH (Downtown Area Shuttle) bus and the No. 30 city bus link Old Sacramento, midtown, and Sutter's Fort. The fare is 50¢ within this area.

Contacts **Greyhound** (*☎ 800/231–2222 🌐 www.greyhound.com*). **Sacramento Regional Transit** (*☎ 916/321–2877 🌐 www.sacrt.com*). **Yolo County Bus** (*☎ 530/666–2837 🌐 www.yolobus.com*).

BY TRAIN

Several trains operated by Amtrak stop in Sacramento and Davis. Trains making the 2½-hour trip from Jack London Square, in Oakland, stop in Emeryville (across the bay from San Francisco), Richmond, Martinez, and Davis before reaching Sacramento; some stop in Berkeley and Suisun-Fairfield as well; a few venture as far south as San Jose and as far north as Auburn.

Contact **Amtrak** (*☎ 800/872–7245 🌐 www.amtrakcalifornia.com*).

HEALTH AND SAFETY

In an emergency, dial 911. Each of the following medical facilities has an emergency room open 24 hours a day.

Hospitals **Mercy Hospital of Sacramento** (*✉ 4001 J St., Sacramento ☎ 916/453–4424*). **Sutter General Hospital** (*✉ 2801 L St., Sacramento*

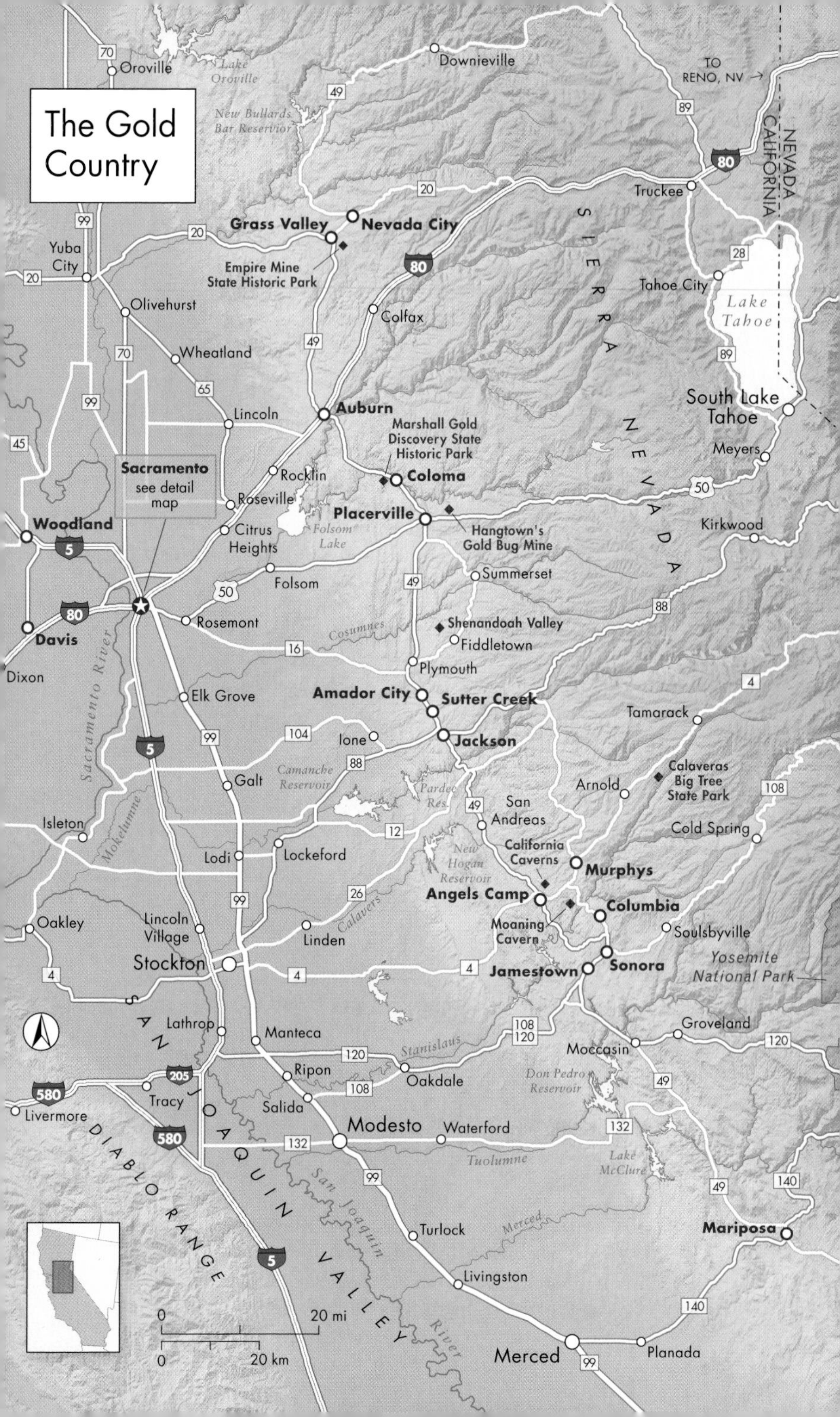

The Gold Country
Oroville
Lake Oroville
Downieville
New Bullards Bar Reservoir
TO RENO, NV
NEVADA
CALIFORNIA
Truckee
Grass Valley
Nevada City
SIERRA NEVADA
Yuba City
Empire Mine State Historic Park
Tahoe City
Lake Tahoe
Olivehurst
Colfax
Wheatland
South Lake Tahoe
Lincoln
Auburn
Marshall Gold Discovery State Historic Park
Meyers
Sacramento
see detail map
Rocklin
Coloma
Roseville
Placerville
Woodland
Citrus Heights
Folsom Lake
Hangtown's Gold Bug Mine
Kirkwood
Summerset
Folsom
Davis
Rosemont
Shenandoah Valley
Cosumnes
Fiddletown
Dixon
Sacramento River
Plymouth
Amador City
Sutter Creek
Elk Grove
Tamarack
Ione
Jackson
Camanche Reservoir
Pardee Res.
Galt
Arnold
Calaveras Big Tree State Park
San Andreas
Isleton
Mokelumne
Cold Spring
Lodi
Lockeford
New Hogan Reservoir
California Caverns
Murphys
Angels Camp
Columbia
Calavers
Oakley
Lincoln Village
Moaning Cavern
Soulsbyville
Linden
Stockton
Jamestown
Sonora
Yosemite National Park
SAN JOAQUIN VALLEY
Lathrop
Manteca
Groveland
Moccasin
Stanislaus
Ripon
Oakdale
Don Pedro Reservoir
Tracy
Salida
Livermore
DIABLO RANGE
Modesto
Waterford
Tuolumne
Lake McClure
San Joaquin River
Merced
Turlock
Mariposa
Livingston
0
20 mi
0
20 km
Merced
Planada

916/733-8900). **Sutter Memorial Hospital** (*52nd and F Sts., Sacramento* *916/733-1000*).

LODGING

A number of organizations can supply information about Gold Country B&Bs and other accommodations.

Contacts **Amador County Innkeepers Association** (*209/267-1710 or 800/726-4667*). **Gold Country Inns of Tuolumne County** (*209/533-1845*). **Historic Bed & Breakfast Inns of Grass Valley & Nevada City** (*530/477-6634 or 800/250-5808*).

VISITOR INFORMATION

Contacts **Amador County Chamber of Commerce & Visitors Bureau** (*571 S. Hwy. 49, Jackson* *209/223-0350* *www.amadorcountychamber.com*). **El Dorado County Chamber of Commerce** (*542 Main St., Placerville* *530/621-5885 or 800/457-6279* *www.eldoradocounty.org*). **Grass Valley/Nevada County Chamber of Commerce** (*248 Mill St., Grass Valley* *530/273-4667 or 800/655-4667* *www.grassvalleychamber.com*). **Mariposa County Visitors Bureau** (*5158 Hwy. 140, Mariposa* *209/966-7081 or 866/425-3366* *www.homeofyosemite.com*). **Tuolumne County Visitors Bureau** (*542 W. Stockton Rd., Sonora* *209/533-4420 or 800/446-1333* *www.thegreatunfenced.com*).

SACRAMENTO AND VICINITY

EXPLORING SACRAMENTO

Driving 87 mi northeast of San Francisco (I–80 to Highway 99 or I–5) brings you to the Golden State's seat of government and to echoes of the gold-rush days. Wooden sidewalks and horse-drawn carriages on cobblestone streets lend a 19th-century feel to Old Sacramento, a 28-acre district along the Sacramento River waterfront. The museums at the north end hold artifacts of state and national significance, and historic buildings house shops and restaurants. River cruises and train rides are fun family diversions for an hour or two.

The midtown area, just east of downtown between 15th Street and the Capital City Freeway, contains many of the city's best restaurants and trendy boutiques. Midtown is a vibrant mix of genteel Victorian edifices, ultramodern lofts, and—at least until the recession hit—a rapidly growing number of innovative restaurants and cozy wine bars. It really springs to life the second Saturday evening of every month, when art galleries hold open houses and the sidewalks are packed. A couple of intersections are lively most evenings when the weather's good; they include the corner of 20th and L streets in what's known as Lavender Heights, the center of the city's gay and lesbian community. Overall, midtown is a safe and interesting place in which to take a walk, and is the city's most interesting neighborhood.

Call the **Old Sacramento Events Hotline** (*916/558-3912*) for information about living-history re-creations and merchant hours.

ESSENTIALS

Visitor Information **Sacramento Convention and Visitors Bureau** (✉ *1608 I St., Suite 600, Sacramento* ☎ *916/808–7777* 🌐 *www.sacramentocvb.org*).

WHAT TO SEE

6 **California Museum for History, Women, and the Arts.** California's first lady, Maria Shriver, has taken an active role in having this museum stress women's issues. Though many exhibits use modern technology, there are also scores of archival drawers that you can pull out to see the real artifacts of history and culture—from the California State Constitution to surfing magazines. Board a 1949 cross-country bus to view a video on immigration, visit a Chinese herb shop maintained by a holographic proprietor, or find familiar names inducted into the California Hall of Fame. There's also a café that's open weekdays until 2:30 PM. ✉ *1020 O St.* ☎ *916/653–7524* 🌐 *www.californiamuseum.org* 🎫 *$8.50* ⏲ *Mon.–Sat. 10–5, Sun. noon–5.*

9 **California State Indian Museum.** Among the interesting displays at this well-organized museum a few strides from Sutter's Fort is one devoted to Ishi, the last Yahi Indian to emerge from the mountains, in 1911. Ishi provided scientists with insight into the traditions and culture of this group of Native Americans. Arts-and-crafts exhibits, a demonstration village, and an evocative 10-minute video bring to life the

The California State Railroad Museum is North America's most popular railroad museum.

multifaceted past and present of California's native peoples. ✉ *2618 K St.* ☎ *916/324–0971* 🌐 *www.parks.ca.gov* 🎟 *$2* 🕙 *Daily 10–5.*

1 **California State Railroad Museum.** Near what was once the terminus of the transcontinental and Sacramento Valley railroads (the actual terminus was at Front and K streets), this 100,000-square-foot museum—the best of its kind in the region, if not the country—has 21 locomotives and railroad cars on display along with dozens of other exhibits. You can walk through a post-office car and peer into cubbyholes and canvas mailbags, enter a sleeping car that simulates the swaying on the roadbed and the flashing lights of a passing town at night, or glimpse the inside of the first-class dining car. One thousand vintage toy trains constitute a much-heralded permanent exhibit, and the recently introduced "Lost Spike" is compelling. ✉ *125 I St.* ☎ *916/445–6645* 🌐 *www.csrmf.org* 🎟 *$8* 🕙 *Daily 10–5.*

Fodor's Choice ★

7 ★ **Capitol.** The lacy plasterwork of the Capitol's 120-foot-high rotunda has the complexity and colors of a Fabergé egg. Underneath the gilded dome are marble floors, glittering chandeliers, monumental staircases, reproductions of 19th-century state offices, and legislative chambers decorated in the style of the 1890s (the Capitol was built in 1869). Guides conduct tours of the building and the 40-acre Capitol Park, which contains a rose garden, an impressive display of camellias (Sacramento's city flower), and the California Vietnam Veterans Memorial. ✉ *Capitol Mall and 10th St.* ☎ *916/324–0333* 🌐 *www.statecapitolmuseum.com* 🎟 *Free* 🕙 *Daily 9–5; tours hourly 9–4.*

2 **Central Pacific Passenger Depot.** At this reconstructed 1876 station there's rolling stock to admire, a typical waiting room, and a small restaurant.

A steam-powered train ($8) departs hourly on weekends April through September, and for special occasions October through December from the freight depot, south of the passenger depot, making a 40-minute out-and-back trip along the Sacramento riverfront. *930 Front St. 916/445–6645 $3, free with same-day ticket from California State Railroad Museum Daily 10–4.*

4 **Crocker Art Museum.** The oldest art museum in the American West has a collection of art from Europe, Asia, and California, including *Sunday Morning in the Mines* (1872), a large canvas by Charles Christian Nahl depicting aspects of the original mining industry, and the magnificent *Great Canyon of the Sierra, Yosemite* (1871), by Thomas Hill. In 2010 the museum plans to open a modern addition that will triple the facility's size. *216 O St. 916/264–5423 www.crockerartmuseum.org $6, free Sun. 10–1 Tues.–Sun. 10–5, first and third Thurs. 10–9.*

8 ★ **Governor's Mansion.** This 15-room house was built in 1877 and used by the state's chief executives from the early 1900s until 1967, when Ronald Reagan vacated it in favor of a newly built home in the more upscale suburbs. Many of the Italianate mansion's interior decorations were ordered from the Huntington, Hopkins & Co. hardware store, one of whose partners, Albert Gallatin, was the original occupant. Each of the seven marble fireplaces has a petticoat mirror that ladies strolled past to see if their slips were showing. Extensive renovation work to the exterior was completed in 2008. *1526 H St. 916/323–3047 $4 Daily 10–5; tours hourly, last one at 4.*

NEED A BREAK?

The River City Brewing Co. (*Downtown Plaza* 916/447–2739) is the best of several breweries that have cropped up in the capital city. The brewery is at the west end of the K Street Mall, between the Capitol and Old Sacramento.

3 **Old Sacramento Visitor Information Center.** Find brochures about nearby attractions, check local restaurant menus, and get advice from the helpful staff here. *1004 2nd St., at K St. 916/442–7644 www.oldsacramento.com Daily 10–5.*

10 ★ **Sutter's Fort.** German-born Swiss immigrant John Augustus Sutter founded Sacramento's earliest Euro–American settlement in 1839. Audio speakers give information at each stop along a self-guided tour that includes a blacksmith's shop, bakery, prison, living quarters, and livestock areas. Costumed docents sometimes reenact fort life, demonstrating crafts, food preparation, and firearms maintenance. *2701 L St. 916/445–4422 www.parks.ca.gov $4 Daily 10–5.*

5 **Towe Auto Museum.** With more than 150 vintage automobiles on display, and exhibits ranging from the Hall of Technology to Dreams of Speed and Dreams of Cool, this museum explores automotive history and car culture. A 1920s roadside café and garage exhibit re-creates the early days of motoring. Friendly docents are ready to explain everything. The gift shop sells vintage-car magazines, model kits, and other car-related items. The museum is near downtown and Old Sacramento, with ample free parking. *2200 Front St., 1 block off Broadway 916/442–6802 www.toweautomuseum.org $7 Daily 10–6.*

WHERE TO EAT

$$–$$$ ITALIAN Fodor's Choice ★ ✕**Biba.** Owner Biba Caggiano is a nationally recognized authority on Italian cuisine. The Capitol crowd flocks here for homemade ravioli, osso buco, grilled pork loin, and veal and rabbit specials. A pianist adds to the upscale ambience nightly. ✉*2801 Capitol Ave.* ☎*916/455–2422* 🌐*www.biba-restaurant.com* *Reservations essential* 💳*AE, DC, MC, V* ⏲*Closed Sun. No lunch Sat.*

¢–$ MEXICAN ✕**Ernesto's Mexican Food.** Customers wait up to an hour for a table on Friday and Saturday evenings at this popular midtown restaurant. Fresh ingredients are stressed in the wide selection of entrées, and the margaritas are especially refreshing. **Zocalo** (✉*1801 Capitol Ave.* ☎*916/441–0303*), launched in 2004 under Ernesto's ownership, has a striking indoor-outdoor atmosphere and is a popular launching spot for nights out on the town. Its menu differs slightly from Ernesto's. ✉*16th and S Sts.* ☎*916/441–5850* 🌐*www.ernestosmexicanfood.com* 💳*AE, D, DC, MC, V.*

$$–$$$$ CONTINENTAL Fodor's Choice ★ ✕**The Firehouse.** Consistently ranked by local publications as one of the city's top 10 restaurants, this formal and historic restaurant has a full bar, courtyard seating (its signature attraction), and creative American cooking, such as char-grilled spring rack of lamb with baby-artichoke and fava-bean succotash, served with roasted French fingerling potatoes. Visitors who can afford to treat themselves to a fine and leisurely meal can do no better in Old Sacramento. ✉*1112 2nd St.* ☎*916/442–4772* 🌐*www.firehouseoldsac.com* 💳*AE, MC, V* ⏲*No lunch Sat.*

$–$$$ SEAFOOD ✕**The Park Downtown.** Atmosphere is what it's all about at this complex of cutting-edge eateries across from Capitol Park. The upscale Mason's Restaurant specializes in seasonal California cuisine; Ma Jong's Asian Diner has less-expensive fare, some suitable for vegetarians; the indoor-outdoor Park Lounge is a supermodern bar and dance club; and the Park To Go puts a classy spin on breakfasts and lunches for people to take away. ✉*1116 15th St.* ☎*916/492–1960* 🌐*www.theparkdowntown.com* 💳*AE, DC, MC, V.*

WHERE TO STAY

$$–$$$$ ★ **Amber House Bed & Breakfast Inn.** This B&B about a mile from the Capitol encompasses two homes. The original house is a Craftsman-style home with five bedrooms, and the second is an 1897 Dutch Colonial Revival home. Baths are tiled in Italian marble; some rooms have skylights, fireplaces, patios, and two-person spa tubs, or a combination of some of those features. Amber House's location has become increasingly desirable as its midtown neighborhood has blossomed this decade with distinctive new shops and restaurants, many within 15-minutes' walking distance. **Pros:** midtown location; attentive service. **Cons:** no nearby freeway access. ✉*1315 22nd St. 95816* ☎*916/444–8085 or 800/755–6526* 🌐*www.amberhouse.com* *10 rooms* *In-room: Internet, Wi-Fi. In-hotel: no-smoking rooms* 💳*AE, D, DC, MC, V* *BP.*

$$–$$$$ **Citizen Hotel.** Billed as Sacramento's first luxury boutique hotel, the Citizen opened in 2008 downtown in the 1926 Cal Western Life building. Overnight it's become a power hub for politicians, business leaders, and deep-pocketed tourists. **Pros:** all the modern amenities with older-world charms; within easy walking distance of the Capitol and other

downtown attractions. **Cons:** pricey; still working out a few kinks. *926 J St. 916/447–2700 www.jdvhotels.com 175 rooms, 23 suites In-room: Wi-Fi. In-hotel: restaurant, room service, bar, gym, no-smoking rooms AE, D, DC, MC, V BP.*

$$–$$$$ ★ **Hyatt Regency Sacramento.** With a marble-and-glass lobby and luxurious rooms, this hotel across from the Capitol and adjacent to the convention center is arguably Sacramento's finest. The multitiered, glass-dominated hotel has a striking Mediterranean design. The best rooms have Capitol Park views. The service and attention to detail are outstanding. **Pros:** "important" people stay here (although Governor Schwarzenegger now commutes from Southern California); beautiful Capitol Park is across the street. **Cons:** downtown streets can be dodgy at night; somewhat impersonal. *1209 L St. 95814 916/443–1234 or 800/633–7313 www.hyatt.com 500 rooms, 24 suites In-hotel: 2 restaurants, bar, pool, gym, laundry service, parking (paid) AE, D, DC, MC, V.*

NIGHTLIFE AND THE ARTS

Downtown Events Hotline (*916/442–2500 www.downtownsac.org*) has recorded information about seasonal events in the downtown area.

WOODLAND

20 mi northwest of Sacramento on I–5.

Woodland's downtown lies frozen in a quaint and genteel past. In its heyday it was one of the wealthiest cities in California, established in 1861 by gold seekers and entrepreneurs. Once the boom was over, attention turned to the rich surrounding land, and the area became an agricultural gold mine. The legacy of the old land barons lives on in the Victorian homes that line Woodland's wide streets. Many of the houses have been restored and are surrounded by lavish gardens.

ESSENTIALS

Visitor Information **Woodland Chamber of Commerce** (*307 1st St., Woodland 530/662–7327 or 888/843–2636 www.woodlandchamber.org*).

More than 300 touring companies, including John Philip Sousa's marching band and Frank Kirk, the Acrobatic Tramp, appeared at the **Woodland Opera House,** built in 1885 (and rebuilt after it burned in 1892). Now restored, the building is the site of concerts and, September through July, a season of musical theater. Free guided tours feature old-fashioned stage technology. *Main and 2nd Sts. 530/666–9617 www.wohtheatre.org Weekdays 10–5, weekends noon–5, tours Tues. noon–4.*

This 10-room neoclassical home of settler William Byas Gibson was purchased by volunteers and restored as the **Yolo County Historical Museum.** You can see collections of furnishings and artifacts from the 1850s to 1930s. Old trees and an impressive lawn cover the 2½-acre site off Highway 113. *512 Gibson Rd. 530/666–1045 www.yolo.net/ychm/index.html $2 Mon. and Tues. 10–4, Sat. noon–4.*

Old trucks and farm machinery seem to rumble to life within the shed-like **Heidrick Ag History Center,** where you can see the world's largest collection of antique agricultural equipment. Also here are multimedia exhibits and a gift shop. ✉ *1962 Hays La.* ☎ *530/666–9700* 🌐 *www.aghistory.org* 🎟 *$7* ⏲ *Weekdays 10–5, Sat. 10–6, Sun. 10–4.*

DAVIS

10 mi west of Sacramento on I–80.

Though it began as—and still is—a rich agricultural area, Davis doesn't feel like a cow town. It's home to the University of California at Davis, whose students hang at the cafés and bookstores in the central business district, making the city feel a little more cosmopolitan. Downtown is compact and walkable; bicyclists are everywhere (and are treated with respect by drivers) throughout town. The city has long enjoyed a progressive, liberal reputation (it's been called "the People's Republic of Davis"), but a rash of 1990s-built yuppie-stocked subdivisions reflect how Davis is becoming more of a mainstream commuter community, whether residents admit it or not.

ESSENTIALS

Visitor Information **Davis Chamber of Commerce** (✉ *130 G St., Davis* ☎ *530/756–5160* 🌐 *www.davischamber.com*).

The center of action in town is the **Davis Campus of the University of California,** which often ranks among the top 25 research universities in the United States. You can take tours of the campus, which depart from Buehler Alumni and Visitors Center. The **Mondavi Center for the Performing Arts,** a strikingly modern glass structure off I–80, offers a busy and varied schedule of performances by top-tier musical, dance and other artists. ✉ *1 Shields Ave.* ☎ *530/752–8111* 🌐 *www.ucdavis.edu* ⏲ *Tours weekends at 11:30, weekdays by appointment.*

THE GOLD COUNTRY—SOUTH

PLACERVILLE

10 mi south of Coloma on Hwy. 49; 44 mi east of Sacramento on U.S. 50.

It's hard to imagine now, but in 1849 about 4,000 miners staked out every gully and hillside in Placerville, turning the town into a rip-roaring camp of log cabins, tents, and clapboard houses. The area was then known as Hangtown, a graphic allusion to the nature of frontier justice. It took on the name Placerville in 1854 and became an important supply center for the miners. Mark Hopkins, Philip Armour, and John Studebaker were among the industrialists who got their starts here.

★ **Hangtown's Gold Bug Park & Mine,** owned by the City of Placerville, centers on a fully lighted mine shaft open for self-guided touring. ■ **TIP→ The self-guided audio tour is well worth the expense ($1).** A shaded stream runs through the park, and there are picnic facilities. ✉ *North on Bedford Ave., 1 mi off U.S. 50* ☎ *530/642–5207* 🌐 *www.goldbugpark.org* 🎟 *$4* ⏲ *Tours mid-Apr.–Oct., daily 10–4; Nov.–mid-Apr., weekends noon–4. Gift shop Mar.–Nov., daily 10–4.*

Continued on page 480

EUREKA! CALIFORNIA'S GOLD RUSH

When James W. Marshall burst into John Sutter's Mill on January 24, 1848, carrying flecks of gold in his hat, the millwright unleashed the glittering California Gold Rush with these immortal words:

"Boys, I believe I've found a gold mine!" 

Before it was over, drowsy San Francisco had become the boomtown of the Golden West, Columbia's mines alone yielded $87,000,000, and California's Mother Lode—a vein of gold-bearing quartz that stretched 150 miles across the Sierra Nevada foothills—had been nearly tapped dry. Even though the Gold Rush soon became the gold bust, today you can still strike it rich by visiting the historic sites where it all happened.

Journey down the Gold Country Highway—a serpentine, nearly 300-mi-long two-lane route appropriately numbered 49—to find pure vacation treasure: fascinating mother lode towns, rip-roaring mining camps, and historic strike sites. In fact, in Placerville—as the former Hangtown, this spot saw so much new money and crime that outlaws were hanged in pairs—you can still pan the streams. And after you've seen the sights, the prospects remain just as golden: the entire region is a trove of gorgeous wineries, fun eateries, and Victorian-era hotels.

by: Reed Parsell and Robert I.C. Fisher

ALL THAT GLITTERED: '49ER FEVER

From imagination springs adventure, and perhaps no event in the 19th century provoked more wild adventures than the California Gold Rush of 1848 to 1855.

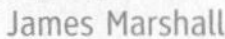

James Marshall

1856 U.S. quarter

John Sutter

GOLD IN THEM THAR HILLS California's golden lava was discovered purely by accident. Upon finding his cattle ranch had gone to ruin while he was away fighting in the Mexican-American War, New Jersey native James W. Marshall decided to build a sawmill, with John Sutter, outside the town of Coloma, 40 miles upstream of Sutter's Fort on the American River. To better power the mill, he had a wider siphon created to divert the river water and, one morning, spotted golden flakes in the trench. Rich fur magnate Sutter tried to keep the mother strike quiet, but his own staff soon decamped to pan the streams and the secret was out. The Gold Rush's impact was so profound that, practically overnight, it catapulted San Francisco into one of the nation's—and the world's—wealthiest cities.

BROTHER, CAN YOU SPARE AN INGOT? After John Marshall, 37 at the time, saw his fledgling sawmill abandoned by workers who went to pan the streams, he left Coloma for almost a decade. During the 1860s he made some money as a vintner there—a dicey profession for a reported alcoholic. Eventually Marshall's wine business dried up, and he returned to prospecting, co-owning a gold mine in Kesley (near Coloma) in the 1870s. Before long, that venture failed, too. For six years starting in 1872, the state Legislature gave him a small pension as an acknowledgment of his Gold Rush importance, but for the last years of his life he was practically penniless. He died on Aug. 10, 1885, at age 74.

THE GOLD CRUSH Before the Gold Rush ended, in 1855, it is estimated that it drew 300,000 people—Americans, Europeans, and Chinese—to the Sierra Nevada foothills to seek their fortune. Sadly, accidents, disease, and skirmishes with Indians took their toll. In addition, the gold lust of '49er fever left more than a thousand murders in its wake (not counting the infamous "suspended" sentences meted out at Hangtown).

BOOM TO BUST

Jan. 24, 1848: James W. Marshall spies specks of bright rock in the streambed at his sawmill's site; Sutter certifies they are gold.
May, 1848: California's coastal communities empty out as prospectors flock to the hills to join the "forty-eighters."
Aug. 19, 1848: The *New York Herald* is the first East Coast newspaper to report a gold rush in California.
Oct. 13, 1849: California's state constitution is approved in Monterey. The state's new motto becomes "Eureka!"
1855: The California Gold Rush effectively ends, as digging for the precious mineral becomes increasingly difficult, and large corporations monopolize mining operations.

DID YOU KNOW?

You can still pan the streams, but any shiny stuff will usually be worthless iron pyrite. Here a young prospector tries his hand at Marshall Gold Discovery State Park.

GOING FOR THE GOLD

Marshall Gold Discovery State Park

If you want to go prospecting for the best sightseeing treasures in Gold Country, just follow this map.

Coloma

Empire Mine State Historic Park, Grass Valley: During the century that it was operating, Empire Mine produced some 5.6 million ounces of gold. More than 350 miles of tunnels were dug, most under water. Operations ceased in 1956, but today visitors to the 800-acre park can go on 50-minute guided tours of the mines and enjoy great hiking trails and picnic spots.

Marshall Gold Discovery State Historic Park, Coloma: Here's where it all began—a can't-miss Gold Rush site. See the stone cairn that marks the spot of James Marshall's discovery, the huge statue of him that rests on his grave site, and visit—together with crowds of schoolchildren—the updated museum, and more.

Hangtown's Gold Bug Park & Mine, Placerville: Put on a hardhat and step into the 19th century at Gold Bug, located a few miles south of Marshall's jackpot site. Take a self-guided audio tour of a mine that opened in 1888, or a special tour of a mine opened in the 1850s, and do some "placering" (panning for gold) yourself, outside the gift shop. "Fool's gold" (used for billiard tables and chalkboards) was mostly found here before digging stopped in 1942.

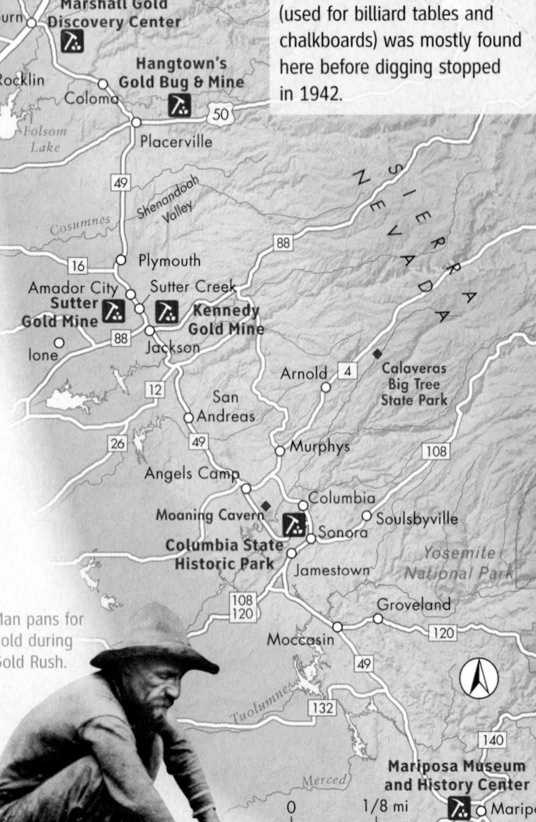

Man pans for gold during Gold Rush.

Empire Mine State Historic Park

Gold sifting pan

Columbia State Historic Park

Sutter Gold Mine: Between Amador City and Sutter Creek off Highway 49, this is the place to see how the so-called "Forty-Niner" individual prospectors were succeeded by large, deep-pocket mining companies. One-hour tours, offered daily April through most of October, take visitors deep into a hard-rock mine, where they can see ore veins that contain gold and learn the basics of hydraulic extraction.

Kennedy Gold Mine, Jackson: At 5,912 feet below ground, this is one of the world's deepest mines. Its head frame is one of the most dominant man-made sights along Highway 49's 295 miles. In operation from 1880 until World War II, the mine produced tens of millions of dollars of gold. One-hour tours, offered weekends and holidays from March through October, include a look inside the stately Mine Office.

Columbia State Historic Park

Columbia State Historic Park. Just north of Sonora, this is the best extant example of a Gold Rush-era town as it appeared in the mid-19th century. During its "golden" years, Columbia yielded more than $85 million in gold. Since World War II, the town has been restored. Fandango halls, Wells Fargo stage coaches, and a costumed staff bring a working 1850's mining town to life again.

Gold dollars

Mariposa Museum and History Center, Mariposa: Find all sorts of mining equipment, including a five-stamp ore mill, at this modest museum in the Gold Rush region's southernmost area. Also here is the fascinating California State Mining and Mineral Museum, home to a famous 13-pound golden nugget.

A PROSPECTING PRIMER

Grab any non-Teflon-coated pan with sloping sides and head up to "them thar hills." Find a stream—preferably one containing black sand—you can stoop beside, and then:

- Scoop out sediment to fill your pan.
- Add water, then gently shake the pan sideways, back and forth. This allows any gold to settle at the bottom.
- Pick out and toss away any larger rocks.
- Keep adding water, keep shaking the pan, and slowly pour the loosened waste gravel over the rim of the pan, making sure not to upend the pan while doing so.
- If you're left with gold, yell "Eureka!" then put it in a glass container. Your findings may not make you rich, but will entitle you to bragging rights for as long as you keep the gold handy to show friends.

TIP→ If you'd rather not pan on your own, plenty of attractions and museums in the Gold Country will let you try your hand at prospecting. See listings in this chapter for more details on these historic sites.

WHERE TO EAT AND STAY

¢ VEGETARIAN ★ ✕ **The Cozmic Cafe.** Crowds convene here at any time of day for healthful wraps, burritos, sandwiches, salads, and the like, plus breakfasts (served anytime), smoothies, and coffee drinks; vegetarians are well served here. The portions are big, prices are low, and the ambience is among the most distinctive in Placerville. The eatery is in the 1859 Pearson's Soda Works Building, and extends back into the side of a mountain, into what used to be a mineshaft. Live music here is among the best in the foothills, and an upstairs pub beckons with local wines and microbrews; unwind with yoga classes there before the evening's libations. ✉ *594 Main St.* ☎ *530/642–8481* 🌐 *www.thecozmiccafe.com* ▭ *MC, V.*

APPLE HILL

This roadside stand sells fresh produce from more than 50 family farms in this area. During the fall harvest season (from September through December), members of the Apple Hill Growers Association open their orchards and vineyards for apple and berry picking, picnicking, and wine and cider tasting. Many sell baked items and picnic food. ✉ *About 5 mi east of Hwy. 49; take Camino exit from U.S. 50* ☎ *530/644–7692.*

$–$$ **Seasons Bed & Breakfast.** A 10-minute walk from downtown, one of Placerville's oldest homes has been transformed into a lovely and relaxing oasis. The main house, cottages, and gardens are filled with paintings and sculptures. Privacy is treasured here. A suite with a sitting room and stained-glass windows occupies the main house's top floor. One cottage has a little white-picket fence around its own mini-garden; another has a two-person shower. **Pros:** quiet setting; attentive hosts; great breakfasts. **Cons:** nothing really—as long as you can afford it. ✉ *2934 Bedford Ave. 95667* ☎ *530/626–4420* 🌐 *www.theseasons.net* *4 rooms, 1 suite* *In-hotel: no-smoking rooms* ▭ *MC, V* *BP.*

SHENANDOAH VALLEY

20 mi south of Placerville on Shenandoah Rd., east of Hwy. 49.

The most concentrated Gold Country wine-touring area lies in the hills of the Shenandoah Valley, east of Plymouth. ■ **TIP→ This region is gaining steam as a less-congested alternative to overrun Napa Valley.** Robust zinfandel is the primary grape grown here, but vineyards also produce other varietals. Most wineries are open on weekend afternoons; several have shaded picnic areas, gift shops, and galleries or museums; all have tasting rooms.

At **Charles Spinetta Winery** (✉ *12557 Steiner Rd., Plymouth* ☎ *209/245–3384* 🌐 *www.charlesspinettawinery.com* ⊙ *Mon., Thurs., and Fri. 8–4, weekends 9–5*) you can see a wildlife art gallery in addition to tasting the wine.

The gallery at the Sobon-affiliated **Shenandoah Vineyards** (✉ *12300 Steiner Rd., Plymouth* ☎ *209/245–4455* 🌐 *www.sobonwine.com* ⊙ *Daily 10–5*) displays contemporary art and sells pottery, framed photographs, and souvenirs.

Sobon Estate (✉*14430 Shenandoah Rd., Plymouth* ☎*209/245–6554* 🌐*www.sobonwine.com* ⏲*Daily, 9:30–5*) operates the Shenandoah Valley Museum, illustrating pioneer life and wine making in the valley.

AMADOR CITY

6 mi south of Plymouth on Hwy. 49.

The history of tiny Amador City mirrors the boom-bust-boom cycle of many Gold Country towns. With an output of $42 million in gold, its Keystone Mine was one of the most productive in the Mother Lode. After all the gold was extracted, the miners cleared out, and the area suffered. Amador City now derives its wealth from tourists, who come to browse through its antiques and specialty shops, many of them on or just off Highway 49.

WHERE TO STAY

$–$$$ AMERICAN ★ **Imperial Hotel.** The whimsically decorated mock-Victorian rooms at this 1879 hotel give a modern twist to the excesses of the era. Antique furnishings include iron-and-brass beds, gingerbread flourishes, and, in one room, art-deco appointments. The two front rooms, which can be noisy, have balconies. The menu at the hotel's fine restaurant ($$–$$$$) changes quarterly and ranges from country hearty to contemporary eclectic. The Imperial recently added a hilltop cottage with three suites; prices are higher, but good views, lower noise levels, and Jacuzzis help compensate. **Pros:** comfortable; good restaurant and bar; small-town charm. **Cons:** lots of noise from bordering Highway 49. ✉*Hwy. 49,* ☎*209/267–9172* 🌐*www.imperialamador.com* *6 rooms, 3 suites* *In-room: no phone, no TV. In-hotel: restaurant, bar, no-smoking rooms* *AE, MC, V* *BP.*

SUTTER CREEK

★ *2 mi south of Amador City on Hwy. 49.*

Sutter Creek is a charming conglomeration of balconied buildings, Victorian homes, and neo–New England structures. The stores on suddenly more peaceful Main Street (formerly part of busy Highway 49, which thankfully has been rerouted around town) are worth visiting for works by the many local artists and craftspeople.

Seek out the **Monteverde Store Museum** (✉*3 Randolph St.*), a typical turn-of-the-20th-century emporium with vintage goods on display (but not for sale), an elaborate antique scale, and a chair-encircled potbellied stove in the corner. The store is open Thursday–Monday provided there are volunteers available. The **Sutter Creek Visitor Center** (✉*11A Randolph St.* ☎*209/267–1344 or 800/400–0305* 🌐*www.suttercreek.org*) has similar hours and a helpful Web site.

WHERE TO EAT AND STAY

$$–$$$$ AMERICAN **Caffe Via d'Oro.** Tables can be hard to secure at this upscale restaurant, where short ribs, grilled duck breast and pan-seared rainbow trout—all accompanied by seasonal vegetables—are highly recommended by the loyal local patrons. The brick structure dates from the 1860s. ✉*36*

Main St. ☎*209/267–0535* 🌐*www.caffeviadoro.com* ▭*AE, D, MC, V* ⏲*Closed Mon. and Tues.*

¢–$ AMERICAN ✕ **Chatterbox Café.** Don't miss this classic 1940s luncheonette with an attitude. It has only six tables and 10 counter stools, but a new room next door was added in 2007. Read a vintage newspaper or examine the jazz instruments and World War II–era memorabilia on the shelves while you wait for your chicken-fried steak, burger, homemade pie, or handmade chocolate malt (with the tin). The menu is as big as the Chatterbox is small. ✉*39 Main St.* ☎*209/267–5935* ▭*AE, D, MC, V* ⏲*No dinner Wed.–Sun.*

$$ ★ **Eureka Street Inn.** Original redwood paneling, wainscoting, beams, and cabinets as well as leaded- and stained-glass windows lend the Eureka Street Inn a certain coziness. The Craftsman-style bungalow was built in 1914 as a family home. Most rooms have gas-log fireplaces, and wireless Internet is available. **Pros:** quiet location; lovely porch; engaging owners. **Cons:** only four rooms. ✉*55 Eureka St.,* ☎*209/267–5500 or 800/399–2389* 🌐*www.eurekastreetinn.com* *4 rooms* *In-room: no TV, Wi-Fi.* ▭*AE, D, MC, V* *BP.*

$$$–$$$$ ★ **The Foxes Inn of Sutter Creek.** The rooms in this 1857 white-clapboard house are handsome, with high ceilings, antique beds, and armoires. Five have gas fireplaces. Breakfast is cooked to order and delivered on a silver service to your room or to the gazebo in the garden. **Pros:** lovely inside and out; friendly owners. **Cons:** pricey; distracting road noise. ✉*77 Main St.,* ☎*209/267–5882 or 800/987–3344* 🌐*www.foxesinn.com* *5 rooms, 2 suites* *In-room: DVD, Wi-Fi (some). In-hotel: no-smoking rooms* ▭*AE, D, MC, V* *BP.*

JACKSON

8 mi south of Sutter Creek on Hwy. 49.

Jackson wasn't the Gold Country's rowdiest town, but the party lasted longer here than most anywhere else: "girls' dormitories" (brothels) and nickel slot machines flourished until the mid-1950s. Jackson also had the world's deepest and richest gold mines, the Kennedy and the Argonaut, which together produced $70 million in gold. These were deep-rock mines with tunnels extending as much as a mile underground. Most of the miners who worked the lode were of Serbian or Italian origin, and they gave the town a European character that persists to this day. Jackson has pioneer cemeteries whose headstones tell the stories of local Serbian and Italian families.

The terraced cemetery on the grounds of the handsome **St. Sava Serbian Orthodox Church** (✉*724 N. Main St.*) is the town's most impressive burial ground.

The heart of Jackson's historic section is the **National Hotel** (✉*2 Water St.* ☎*209/233–0500*), which operates an old-time saloon in the lobby. The hotel is especially active on weekends, when people come from miles around to participate in Saturday-night sing-alongs.

The **Amador County Museum**, built in the late 1850s as a private home, provides a colorful take on gold-rush life. Displays include a kitchen with a woodstove, the Amador County bicentennial quilt, and a classroom. A time line recounts the county's checkered past. The museum conducts hourly tours of large-scale working models of the nearby Kennedy Mine. ✉225 *Church St.* ☎*209/223–6386* *Museum free; mine tours $1* ⏲*Wed.–Sun. 10–4.*

12

WHERE TO EAT

¢ AMERICAN **Rosebud's Classic Café.** Art-deco accents and music from the 1930s and 1940s set the mood at this homey café. Charbroiled burgers, freshly baked pies, and espresso drinks round out the lunch menu; Rosebud's pies receive rave reviews. Omelets, hotcakes, and many other items are served for breakfast. ✉*26 Main St.* ☎*209/223–1035* *MC, V* ⏲*Closed Tues. No dinner.*

ANGELS CAMP

20 mi south of Jackson on Hwy. 49.

Angels Camp is famed chiefly for its May jumping-frog contest, based on Mark Twain's short story "The Celebrated Jumping Frog of Calaveras County." The writer reputedly heard the story of the jumping frog from Ross Coon, proprietor of Angels Hotel, which has been in operation since 1856.

Angels Camp Museum houses gold-rush relics, including photos, rocks, petrified wood, old blacksmith and mining equipment, and a horse-drawn hearse. The carriage house out back holds 31 carriages and an impressive display of mineral specimens. ✉*753 S. Main St.* ☎*209/736–2963* *$2* ⏲*Jan. and Feb., weekends 10–3; Mar.–Dec., daily 10–3.*

California Cavern. A ½-mi subterranean trail winds through large chambers and past underground streams and lakes. There aren't many steps to climb, but it's a strenuous walk with some narrow passageways and steep spots. The caverns, at a constant 53°F, contain crystalline formations not found elsewhere, and the 80-minute guided tour explains local history and geology. ✉*9 mi east of San Andreas on Mountain Ranch Rd., then about 3 mi on Cave City Rd., follow signs* ☎*209/736–2708* *www.caverntours.com* *$14.25* ⏲*May–Oct., daily 10–5; Nov.–Apr., weekdays 11–4, weekends 10–4.*

Fodor's Choice ★ **Moaning Cavern.** A 235-step spiral staircase leads into this vast cavern. More adventurous sorts can rappel into the chamber—ropes and instruction are provided. Otherwise, the only way inside is via the 45-minute tour, during which you'll see giant (and still growing) stalactites and stalagmites and an archaeological site that holds some of the oldest human remains yet found in America (an unlucky person has fallen into the cavern about once every 130 years for the last 13,000 years). ✉*5350 Moaning Cave Rd., off Parrots Ferry Rd., about 2 mi south of Vallecito* ☎*209/736–2708* *www.caverntours.com* *$14.25* ⏲*May–Oct., daily 9–6; Nov.–Apr., weekdays 10–5, weekends 9–5.*

DID YOU KNOW?

Calaveras Big Trees State Park protects the northernmost grove of giant sequoias known to exist.

MURPHYS

10 mi northeast of Angels Camp on Hwy. 4.

Murphys is a well-preserved town of white-picket fences, Victorian houses, and interesting shops that exhibits an upscale vibe, with its nearby wineries and free-spending Bay Area visitors. Horatio Alger and Ulysses S. Grant came through here, staying at Murphys Historic Hotel & Lodge when they, along with many other 19th-century tourists, came to see the giant sequoia groves in nearby Calaveras Big Trees State Park.

TIP→ Ironstone Vineyards is worth a visit even if you don't drink wine. Tours take you through the spectacular gardens and into underground tunnels cooled by a waterfall from a natural spring, and include a performance on a massive automated pipe organ. The winery schedules concerts during summer in its huge outdoor amphitheater, plus art shows and other events on weekends. On display is a 44-pound specimen of crystalline gold. Visit the deli for lunch. ✉ *1894 6 Mile Rd.* ☎ *209/728–1251* 🌐 *www.ironstonevineyards.com* ⏲ *Daily 10–5; open until 6 in summer.*

CALAVERAS BIG TREE STATE PARK

This state park protects hundreds of the largest and rarest living things on the planet—magnificent giant sequoia redwood trees. Some are 3,000 years old, 90 feet around at the base, and 250 feet tall. There are campgrounds and picnic areas; swimming, wading, fishing, and sunbathing on the Stanislaus River are popular in summer. For wintertime visits, expect to walk in slushy snow. ✉ *Off Hwy. 4, 15 mi northeast of Murphys, 4 mi northeast of Arnold* ☎ *209/795–2334* 🎟 *$6 per vehicle, day use; campsites $20* ⏲ *Park daily sunrise–sunset, day use; visitor center May–Oct., daily 11–3; Nov.–Apr., weekends 11–3.*

WHERE TO EAT AND STAY

¢–$$ AMERICAN **Grounds.** Light entrées, grilled vegetables, chicken, seafood, and steak are the specialties at this bistro and coffee shop. Sandwiches, salads, and homemade soups are served for lunch. The crowd is friendly and the service attentive. ✉ *402 Main St.* ☎ *209/728–8663* 💳 *MC, V* ⏲ *No dinner Mon. and Tues.*

¢–$$ **Murphys Historic Hotel & Lodge.** This 1855 stone hotel, whose register has seen the signatures of Mark Twain and the bandit Black Bart, figured in Bret Harte's short story "A Night at Wingdam." Accommodations are in the hotel and a modern motel-style addition. The older rooms are furnished with antiques, many of them large and hand carved. The hotel has a convivial old-time restaurant ($–$$$) and dark saloon, which can be noisy into the wee hours. **Pros:** loads of historical ambience; great bar; smack in the middle of downtown. **Cons:** dated; creaky. ✉ *457 Main St. 95247* ☎ *209/728–3444 or 800/532–7684* 🌐 *www.murphyshotel.com* *29 rooms, 20 with bath* *In-hotel: restaurant, bar* 💳 *AE, D, DC, MC, V.*

COLUMBIA

14 mi south of Angels Camp via Hwy. 49 to Parrots Ferry Rd.

Columbia is the gateway for Columbia State Historic Park, which is one of the Gold Country's most-visited sites.

Fodor'sChoice ★ **Columbia State Historic Park,** known as the Gem of the Southern Mines, comes as close to a gold-rush town in its heyday as any site in the Gold Country. You can ride a stagecoach, pan for gold, and watch a blacksmith working at an anvil. Street musicians perform in summer. Restored or reconstructed buildings include a Wells Fargo Express office, a Masonic temple, stores, saloons, two hotels, a firehouse, churches, a school, and a newspaper office. At times all are staffed to simulate a working 1850s town. The park also includes the **Historic Fallon House Theater,** where a full schedule of entertainment is presented. ✉ *11175 Washington St.* ☎ *209/532–0150* 🌐 *www.parks.ca.gov* *Free* ⏲ *Daily 9–5.*

WHERE TO STAY

$–$$ **City Hotel.** The rooms in this restored 1856 hostelry are furnished with period antiques. Two have balconies overlooking Main Street, and six rooms open onto a second-floor parlor. All the accommodations have private half baths, with showers nearby; robes and slippers are provided. The restaurant ($$–$$$; closed Monday), one of the Gold Country's best, serves French-accented California cuisine complemented by a large selection of the state's respected wines. The What Cheer Saloon is right out of a Western movie. Combined lodging, dinner, and theater packages are available. **Pros:** quiet; good bar. **Cons:** can feel remote. ✉ *22768 Main St. 95310* ☎ *209/532–1479 or 800/532–1479* 🌐 *www.cityhotel.com* *10 rooms* *In-hotel: restaurant, bar* *AE, D, MC, V* *CP.*

SONORA

4 mi south of Columbia via Parrots Ferry Rd. to Hwy. 49.

Miners from Mexico founded Sonora and made it the biggest town in the Mother Lode. Following a period of racial and ethnic strife, the Mexican settlers moved on, and Yankees built the commercial city that is visible today. Sonora's historic downtown section sits atop the Big Bonanza Mine, one of the richest in the state. Another mine, on the site of nearby Sonora High School, yielded 990 pounds of gold in a single week in 1879. Reminders of the gold rush are everywhere in Sonora, in prim Victorian houses, typical Sierra-stone storefronts, and awning-shaded sidewalks. Reality intrudes beyond the town's historic heart, with strip malls, shopping centers, and modern motels. Downtown gridlock on Highway 49 is unlikely to ease until gas prices get much, much higher.

The **Tuolumne County Museum and History Center** occupies a gold rush–era building that served as a jail until 1951. Listed on the National Register of Historic Places, it houses a museum with vintage firearms and paraphernalia, a case with gold specimens, a cute exhibit on soapbox derby racing in hilly Sonora, and the historical society's and genealogical society's libraries. ✉ *158 W. Bradford St.* ☎ *209/532–1317* 🌐 *www.tchistory.org* *Free* ⏲ *Daily 10–4.*

WHERE TO EAT AND STAY

¢ MEXICAN **Garcia's Taqueria.** This casual, inexpensive eatery—named for and decorated in the spirit of Grateful Dead legend Jerry Garcia—serves Mexican and Southwestern fare. Vegetarians and vegans are well served here. *145 S. Washington St. 209/588–1915 No credit cards Closed Sun.*

$–$$$ **Barretta Gardens Bed and Breakfast Inn.** This inn is perfect for a romantic getaway. Its elegant Victorian rooms vary in size, but all are furnished with period pieces. The three antiques-filled parlors carry on the Victorian theme. The breakfast porch overlooks a fountain and mature gardens. **Pros:** lovely grounds; yummy breakfasts; romantic. **Cons:** only five rooms. *700 S. Barretta St. 95370 209/532–6039 or 800/206–3333 www.barrettagardens.com 5 rooms AE, MC, V CP.*

A LIVING BACKDROP

If the countryside surrounding Sonora seems familiar, that's because it has been the backdrop for many movies over the years. Scenes from *High Noon, For Whom the Bell Tolls, The Virginian, Back to the Future III,* and *Unforgiven* were filmed here.

JAMESTOWN

4 mi south of Sonora on Hwy. 49.

Compact Jamestown supplies a touristy, superficial view of gold rush–era life. Shops in brightly colored buildings along Main Street sell antiques and gift items.

The California State Railroad Museum operates **Railtown 1897** at what were the headquarters and general shops of the Sierra Railway from 1897 to 1955. The railroad has appeared in more than 200 movies and television productions, including *Petticoat Junction, The Virginian, High Noon,* and *Unforgiven*. You can view the roundhouse, an air-operated 60-foot turntable, shop rooms, and old locomotives and coaches. Six-mile, 40-minute steam-train rides through the countryside are offered weekends in warm months and on some holiday weekends. *5th Ave. and Reservoir Rd., off Hwy. 49 209/984–3953 www.csrmf.org Roundhouse tour $2; train ride $6 Apr.–Oct., daily 9:30–4:30, Nov.–Mar., daily 10–3. Train rides Apr.–Oct., weekends 11–3.*

WHERE TO STAY

$$ **National Hotel.** The National has been in business since 1859, and the furnishings—brass beds, regal comforters, and lace curtains—are authentic but not overly embellished. The saloon, which still has its original redwood bar, is a great place to linger. The popular restaurant ($–$$$) serves special sandwiches and a variety of salads and pastas for lunch. Dinners feature more upscale continental cuisine (reservations essential). **Pros:** wonderful historic feel; great brunches—especially the crepes. **Cons:** only nine rooms. *18183 Main St. 209/984–3446, 800/894–3446 in CA www.national-hotel.com 9 rooms In-room: Internet. In-hotel: restaurant, bar AE, D, DC, MC, V CP.*

MARIPOSA

50 mi south of Jamestown on Hwy. 49.

Mariposa marks the southern end of the Mother Lode. Much of the land in this area was part of a 44,000-acre land grant Colonel John C. Fremont acquired from Mexico before gold was discovered and California became a state.

At the **California State Mining and Mineral Museum** a glittering 13-pound chunk of crystallized gold makes it clear what the rush was about. Displays include a reproduction of a typical tunnel dug by hard-rock miners, a miniature stamp mill, and a panning and sluicing exhibit. ✉*Mariposa County Fairgrounds, Hwy. 49* ☎*209/742–7625* *$3* *May–Sept., daily 10–6; Oct.–Apr., Wed.–Mon. 10–4.*

WHERE TO EAT AND STAY

$$–$$$$ AMERICAN ✕ **Charles Street Dinner House.** Ever since Ed Uebner moved here from Chicago to become the owner-chef in 1980, Charles Street has been firmly established as the classiest dinner joint in town—plus, it's centrally located. The extensive menu includes beef, chicken, pork, lamb, duck, and lobster; recently a few vegetarian options were added. ✉*Hwy. 140, at 7th St.* ☎*209/966–2366* *www.charlesstreetdinnerhouse.com* *D, MC, V* *No lunch.*

$–$$ **Little Valley Inn.** Historical photos and old mining tools recall Mariposa's heritage at this modern B&B. A suite that sleeps five people includes a full kitchen. All rooms have private entrances, baths, and decks. The large grounds include a creek where you can pan for gold. **Pros:** quiet; comfortable; about halfway between Yosemite's western entrances. **Cons:** still about 40 minutes outside the park. ✉*3483 Brooks Rd., off Hwy. 49* ☎*209/742–6204 or 800/889–5444* *www.littlevalley.com* *4 rooms, 1 suite, 1 cabin* *In-room: refrigerator. In-hotel: no-smoking rooms* *AE, MC, V* *BP.*

THE GOLD COUNTRY—NORTH

COLOMA

8 mi northwest of Placerville on Hwy. 49.

The California gold rush started in Coloma. "My eye was caught with the glimpse of something shining in the bottom of the ditch," James Marshall recalled. Marshall himself never found any more "color," as gold came to be called.

★ Most of Coloma lies within **Marshall Gold Discovery State Historic Park.** Though crowded with tourists in summer, Coloma hardly resembles the mob scene it was in 1849, when 2,000 prospectors staked out claims along the streambed. The town's population grew to 4,000, supporting seven hotels, three banks, and many stores and businesses. But when reserves of the precious metal dwindled, prospectors left as quickly as they had come. A working reproduction of an 1840s mill lies near the spot where James Marshall first saw gold. A trail leads to a sign marking his discovery. **TIP→ The museum is not as interesting as the outdoor** exhibits. ✉Hwy. 49 ☎530/622–3470 🌐www.parks.ca.gov 🎟$5 per vehicle, day use ⏲Park daily 8–sunset. Museum daily 10–3.

WHERE TO STAY

$$–$$$ **Coloma Country Inn.** Four of the rooms at this B&B on 2½ acres in the state historic park are inside an 1850s farmhouse (extensively updated in 2007). Two suites with kitchenettes are in the carriage house. Appointments include charming decor, private bathrooms, and welcoming grounds. At breakfast the owners can direct you to tour operators leading rafting trips on the American River. ✉*345 High St. 95613* ☎*530/622–6919* 🌐*www.colomacountryinn.com* *4 rooms, 2 suites* *In-room: kitchen, Wi-Fi* *MC, V* *BP.*

AUBURN

18 mi northwest of Coloma on Hwy. 49; 34 mi northeast of Sacramento on I–80.

Auburn is the Gold Country town most accessible to travelers on I–80. An important transportation center during the gold rush, Auburn has a small Old Town district with narrow climbing streets, cobblestone lanes, wooden sidewalks, and many original buildings. ■ **TIP→ Fresh produce, flowers, baked goods, and gifts are for sale at the farmers' market, held Saturday morning year-round.**

Auburn's standout structure is the **Placer County Courthouse.** The classic gold-dome building houses the Placer County Museum, which documents the area's history—Native American, railroad, agricultural, and mining—from the early 1700s to 1900. ✉*101 Maple St.* ☎*530/889–6500* 🎟*Free* ⏲*Daily 10–4.*

The **Bernhard Museum Complex,** whose centerpiece is the former Traveler's Rest Hotel, was built in 1851. A residence and adjacent winery buildings reflect family life in the late Victorian era. The carriage house contains period conveyances. ✉*291 Auburn–Folsom Rd.* ☎*530/889–6500* 🎟*Free* ⏲*Tues.–Sun. 11–4.*

The **Gold Country Museum** surveys life in the mines. Exhibits include a walk-through mine tunnel, a gold-panning stream, and a reproduction saloon. ✉*1273 High St., off Auburn–Folsom Rd.* ☎*530/889–6500* 🎟*Free* ⏲*Tues.–Sun. 11–4.*

WHERE TO EAT

$$ ECLECTIC ★ **Latitudes.** Delicious multicultural cuisine is served in an 1870 Victorian. The menu (with monthly specials from diverse geographical regions) includes seafood, chicken, beef, and turkey entrées prepared with the appropriate Mexican spices, curries, cheeses, or teriyaki sauce. Vegetarians and vegans have several inventive choices, too. Sunday brunch is deservedly popular. ✉*130 Maple St.* ☎*530/885–9535* 🌐*www.latitudesrestaurant.com* *AE, D, MC, V* ⏲*Closed Mon. and Tues.*

Almost 6 million ounces of gold were extracted from the Empire Mine.

GRASS VALLEY

24 mi north of Auburn on Hwy. 49.

More than half of California's total gold production was extracted from mines around Grass Valley, including the Empire Mine, which, along with the North Star Mining Museum, is among the Gold Country's most fascinating attractions. Unlike neighboring Nevada City, urban sprawl surrounds Grass Valley's historic downtown.

In the center of town, on the site of the original, stands a reproduction of the **Lola Montez House** (✉*248 Mill St.* ☎*530/273–4667, 800/655–4667 in CA*), home of the notorious dancer, singer, and courtesan. Montez, who arrived in Grass Valley in the early 1850s, was no great talent—her popularity among miners derived from her suggestive "spider dance"—but her loves, who reportedly included composer Franz Liszt, were legendary. According to one account, she arrived in California after having been "permanently retired from her job as Bavarian king Ludwig's mistress," literary muse, and political adviser. She apparently pushed too hard for democracy, which contributed to his overthrow and her banishment as a witch—or so the story goes. The Grass Valley/Nevada County Chamber of Commerce is headquartered here.

The landmark **Holbrooke Hotel** (✉*212 W. Main St.* ☎*530/273–1353 or 800/933–7077*), built in 1851, was host to Lola Montez and Mark Twain as well as Ulysses S. Grant and a stream of other U.S. presidents. Its restaurant-saloon is one of the oldest operating west of the Mississippi.

12

★ The hard-rock gold mine at **Empire Mine State Historic Park** was one of California's richest. An estimated 5.8 million ounces were extracted from its 367 mi of underground passages between 1850 and 1956. On the 50-minute tours you can walk into a mine shaft, peer into the mine's deeper recesses, and view the owner's "cottage," which has exquisite woodwork. With its shaded picnic areas and gentle hiking trails, this is a pleasant place for families. ✉*10791 E. Empire St., south of Empire St. exit of Hwy. 49* ☎*530/273–8522* 🌐*www.parks.ca.gov* *$3* *May–Aug., daily 9–6; Sept.–Apr., daily 10–5. Tours May–Aug., daily on the hr 11–4; Sept.–Apr., weekends at 1 (cottage only) and 2 (mine yard only), weather permitting.*

Housed in the former North Star powerhouse, the **North Star Mining Museum** displays the 32-foot-high enclosed Pelton Water Wheel, said to be the largest ever built. It was used to power mining operations and was a forerunner of the modern turbines that generate hydroelectricity. Hands-on displays are geared to children. There's a picnic area nearby. ✉*Empire and McCourtney Sts., north of Empire St. exit of Hwy. 49* ☎*530/273–4255* *Donation requested* *May–mid-Oct., daily 10–5.*

WHERE TO EAT AND STAY

¢ BRITISH ★ **Cousin Jack Pasties.** Meat- and vegetable-stuffed pasties are a taste of the region's history, having come across the Atlantic with Cornish miners and their families in the mid-19th century. The flaky crusts practically melt in your mouth. A simple food stand, which sometimes closes early on dreary winter days, Jack's is nonetheless a local landmark and dear to its loyal clientele. ✉*Auburn and Main Sts.* ☎*530/272–9230* *No credit cards.*

NEVADA CITY

4 mi north of Grass Valley on Hwy. 49.

Nevada City, once known as the Queen City of the Northern Mines, is the most appealing of the northern Mother Lode towns. The iron-shutter brick buildings that line the narrow downtown streets contain antiques shops, galleries, bookstores, boutiques, B&Bs, restaurants, and a winery. Horse-drawn carriage tours add to the romance, as do gas streetlamps. At one point in the 1850s Nevada City had a population of nearly 10,000, enough to support much cultural activity.

ESSENTIALS

Visitor Information **Nevada City Chamber of Commerce** (✉*132 Main St., Nevada City* ☎*530/265–2692* 🌐*www.nevadacitychamber.com*).

With its gingerbread-trim bell tower, **Firehouse No. 1** is one of the Gold Country's most distinctive buildings. A museum, it houses gold-rush artifacts and a Chinese joss house (temple). ✉*214 Main St.* ☎*530/265–5468* *Donation requested* *Apr.–Nov., daily 11–4; Dec.–Mar., Thurs.–Sun. 11:30–4.*

The redbrick **Nevada Theatre,** constructed in 1865, is California's oldest theater building. Mark Twain, Emma Nevada, and many other notable people appeared on its stage. Housed in the theater, the **Foothill Theatre**

Company (☎530/265–8587 or 888/730–8587 ⊕*www.nevadatheatre.com*) holds theatrical and musical events. Old films are screened here, too. ✉*401 Broad St.* ☎*530/265–6161, 530/274–3456 for film showtimes.*

The **Miners Foundry,** erected in 1856, produced machines for gold mining and logging. The Pelton Water Wheel, a source of power for the mines (the wheel also jump-started the hydroelectric power industry), was invented here. A cavernous building, the foundry is the site of plays, concerts, weddings, receptions, and other events; call for a schedule. ✉*325 Spring St.* ☎*530/265–5040* ⊕*www.minersfoundry.org.*

You can watch wine being created while you sip at the **Nevada City Winery,** where the tasting room overlooks the production area. ✉*Miners Foundry Garage, 321 Spring St.* ☎*530/265–9463 or 800/203–9463* ⊕*www.ncwinery.com* *Free* *Tastings Mon.–Sat. 11–5, Sun. noon–5.*

WHERE TO EAT AND STAY

$–$$$ AMERICAN ✕**South Pine Cafe.** Locals flock here, especially for brunch. Although lobster and beef are on the menu, the real attention-grabbers are vegetarian entrées and side dishes, such as breakfast potatoes and apple-ginger muffins. This place is starting to take off regionally; it recently opened branches in Grass Valley and Auburn. ✉*110 S. Pine St.* ☎*530/265–0260* ⊕*www.southpinecafe.com* *MC, V* *Daily 8–3.*

$–$$ **Northern Queen Inn.** Most accommodations at this bright creek-side inn are typical motel units, but there are eight two-story chalets and eight rustic cottages with efficiency kitchens and gas-log fireplaces in a secluded wooded area. For a fee, you can ride on the hotel's narrow-gauge railroad, which offers excursions through Maidu Indian homelands and a Chinese cemetery from gold-rush days. **Pros:** one of this charming town's less-expensive options; secluded cabins: **Cons:** some furniture seems worn. ✉*400 Railroad Ave., Sacramento St. exit off Hwy. 49* ☎*530/265–5824 or 800/226–3090* ⊕*www.northernqueeninn.com* *70 rooms, 16 suites* *In-room: kitchen (some), refrigerator. In-hotel: restaurant, pool* *AE, D, DC, MC, V.*

$$–$$$ Fodor'sChoice ★ **Red Castle Historic Lodgings.** A state landmark, this 1857 Gothic Revival mansion stands on a forested hillside overlooking Nevada City, and is a special place for those who appreciate the finer points of Victorian interior design. Its brick exterior is trimmed with white-icicle woodwork. A steep private pathway leads down through the terraced gardens into town; there's also a well-lighted set of city stairs. Handsome antique furnishings and Oriental rugs decorate the rooms. **TIP→ Red Castle features a delightful afternoon tea, by request, and morning breakfast buffet that is unparalleled among Gold Country B&Bs.** **Pros:** friendly owners; spectacular food; fascinating architecture. **Cons:** you'll get a built-in workout walking up the hill from downtown—although many would consider that a good thing. ✉*109 Prospect St. 95959* ☎*530/265–5135 or 800/761–4766* ⊕*www.historic-lodgings.com* *4 rooms, 3 suites* *MC, V* *BP.*

Lake Tahoe

WITH RENO, NEVADA

WORD OF MOUTH

"Our family spent a long weekend at Zephyr Cove resort several years ago and really liked it . . . they have cabins and a lodge right on the lake, a nice beach, and a dock where you can rent small boats, take a cruise on a paddlewheeler, etc."

—november_moon

WELCOME TO LAKE TAHOE

TOP REASONS TO GO

★ **The lake:** Blue, deep, and alpine-pure, Lake Tahoe is far and away the main reason to visit this high Sierra paradise.

★ **Snow, snow, snow:** Daring black-diamond runs or baby bunny bumps—whether you're an expert, a beginner, or somewhere in between, there are many slopes to suit your skills at the numerous Tahoe area ski parks.

★ **The great outdoors:** A ring of national forests and recreation areas and miles of trails make Tahoe a nature lover's paradise.

★ **Dinner with a view:** You can picnic lakeside at state parks or dine in restaurants perched along the shore.

★ **A date with lady luck:** Whether you want to roll dice, play the slots, or hope the blackjack dealer goes bust before you do, you'll find round-the-clock gambling at the casinos in Reno and on the Nevada side of the lake.

1 California Side. With the exception of Stateline, Nevada—which, aside from its casino-hotel towers, seems almost indistinguishable from South Lake Tahoe, California—the California side is more developed than the Nevada side. Here you can find both commercial enterprises—restaurants, motels, lodges, resorts, residential subdivisions—and public-access facilities, such as historic sites, parks, campgrounds, marinas, and beaches.

2 Nevada Side. You don't need a highway sign to know when you've crossed from California into Nevada: the flashing lights and elaborate marquees of casinos announce legal gambling in garish hues. But you'll find more here than tables and slot machines. Reno, the Biggest Little City in the World, has a vibrant art scene and a serene downtown RiverWalk. And when you really need to get away from the chip-toting crowds, you can hike through pristine wilderness at Lake Tahoe–Nevada State Park, or hit the slopes at Incline Village.

GETTING ORIENTED

Situated in the northern section of the Sierra Nevada mountain range, the Lake Tahoe area covers portions of five national forests, several state parks, and rugged wilderness areas with names like Desolation and Granite Chief. Lake Tahoe, the star attraction, straddles California and Nevada and is one of the world's largest, clearest, and deepest alpine lakes. The region's proximity to the Bay Area and Sacramento to the west and Reno to the east draws hordes of thrill-seekers during ski season and summer, when water sports, camping, and hiking are the dominant activities.

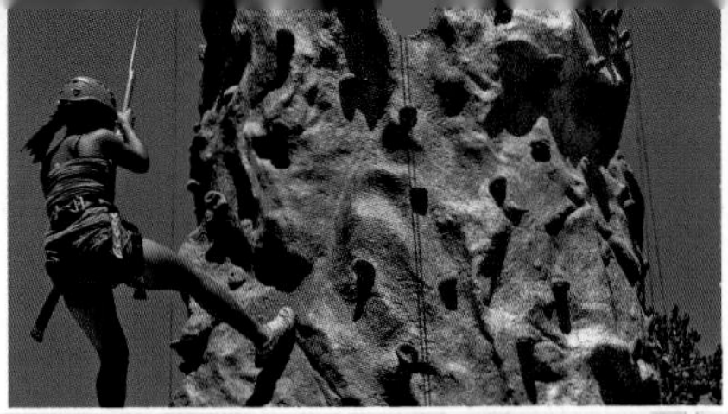

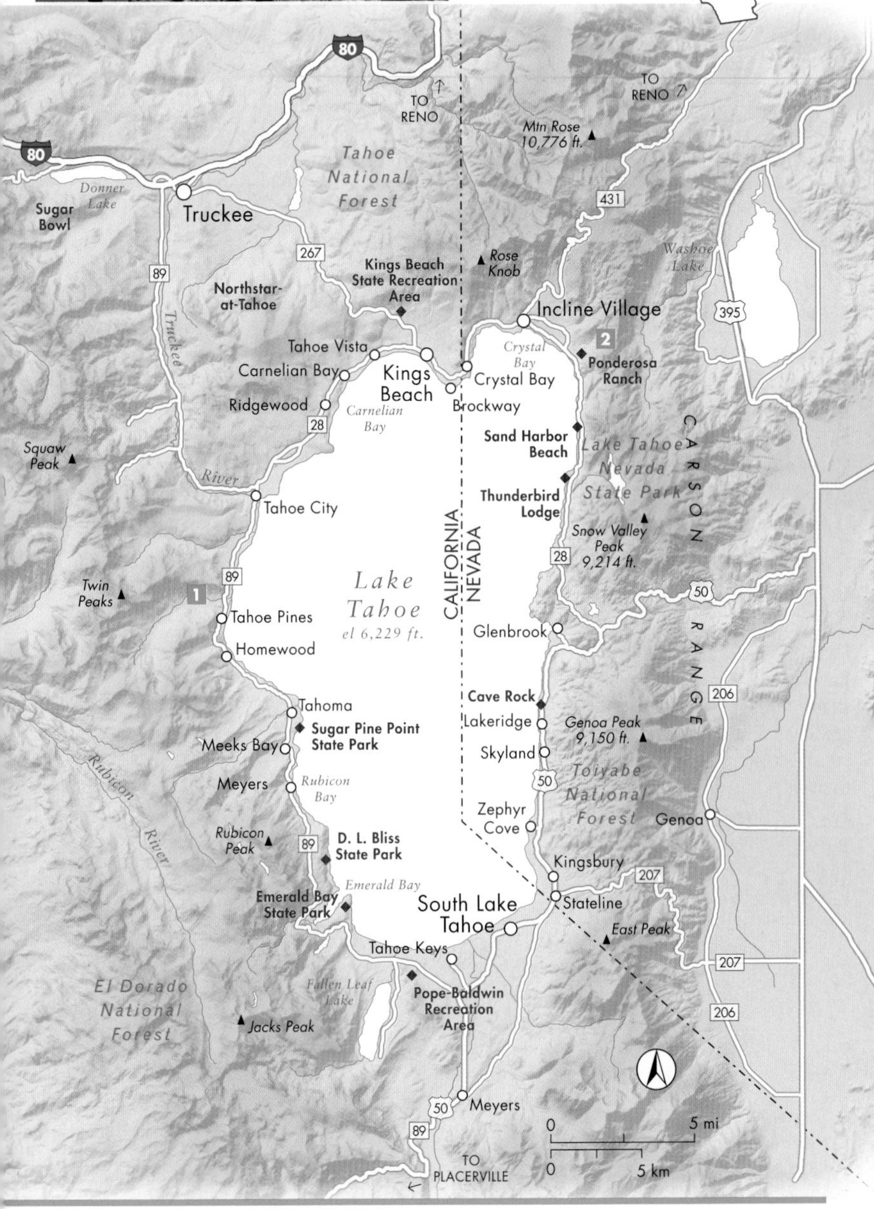

80
TO RENO
TO RENO
Mtn Rose 10,776 ft.
Tahoe National Forest
Donner Lake
Sugar Bowl
Truckee
431
267
89
Kings Beach State Recreation Area
Rose Knob
Washoe Lake
Northstar-at-Tahoe
Truckee
Incline Village
395
2
Crystal Bay
Tahoe Vista
Ponderosa Ranch
Carnelian Bay
Kings Beach
Crystal Bay
Brockway
Ridgewood
Carnelian Bay
28
Sand Harbor Beach
Lake Tahoe Nevada State Park
CARSON RANGE
Squaw Peak
River
Thunderbird Lodge
Tahoe City
CALIFORNIA
NEVADA
Snow Valley Peak 9,214 ft.
28
89
Lake Tahoe el 6,229 ft.
Twin Peaks
1
50
Tahoe Pines
Glenbrook
Homewood
206
Cave Rock
Tahoma
Lakeridge
Genoa Peak 9,150 ft.
Sugar Pine Point State Park
Meeks Bay
Skyland
Rubicon
50
Toiyabe National Forest
Meyers
Rubicon Bay
Zephyr Cove
Genoa
Rubicon Peak
River
89
D. L. Bliss State Park
Kingsbury
207
Emerald Bay
Emerald Bay State Park
South Lake Tahoe
Stateline
East Peak
Tahoe Keys
207
El Dorado National Forest
Fallen Leaf Lake
Pope-Baldwin Recreation Area
206
Jacks Peak
50
Meyers
89
0 5 mi
0 5 km
TO PLACERVILLE

LAKE TAHOE PLANNER

Getting There

The closest airport to Lake Tahoe is Reno, served by nearly a dozen airlines and all the major car-rental agencies. If you're also visiting the Bay Area or California's northern towns, fly into San Francisco, Oakland, or Sacramento airport.

Truckee, the north Tahoe resorts, and Reno are all accessible via I–80. For South Lake Tahoe, take Hwy. 50 from I–80 (in Sacramento). Try to travel midweek: both routes are jammed on weekends in summer and winter.

Exploring the Lake

The typical way to explore the Lake Tahoe area is to drive the 72-mi road that follows the shore through wooded flatlands and past beaches, climbing to vistas on the rugged southwest side of the lake and passing through busy commercial developments and casinos on its northeastern and southeastern edges. Another option is to actually go out *on* the lake on a sightseeing cruise or kayaking trip.

When to Go

A sapphire-blue lake shimmering deep in the center of an ice-white wonderland—that's Tahoe in winter. But those blankets of snow mean lots of storms that often close roads and force chain requirements on the interstate. In summer the roads are open, but the lake and lodgings are clogged with visitors seeking respite from valley heat. If you don't ski, the best times to visit are early fall and late spring. The crowds thin, prices dip, and you can count on Tahoe's being beautiful year-round.

Most Lake Tahoe accommodations, restaurants, and even a handful of parks are open year-round, but many visitor centers, mansions, state parks, and beaches are closed from November through May. During those months, multitudes of skiers and other winter-sports enthusiasts are attracted to Tahoe's downhill resorts and cross-country centers, North America's largest concentration of skiing facilities. Ski resorts try to open by Thanksgiving, if only with machine-made snow, and can operate through May or later. During the ski season Tahoe's population swells on the weekends. If you're able to come midweek, you'll have the resorts and neighboring towns almost to yourself.

Unless you want to ski, you'll find that Tahoe is most fun in summer, when it's cooler here than in the scorched Sierra Nevada foothills, the clean mountain air is bracingly crisp, and the surface temperature of Lake Tahoe is an invigorating 65°F to 70°F (compared with 40°F to 50°F in winter). This is also the time, however, when it may seem as if every tourist at the lake—100,000 on peak weekends—is in a car on the main road circling the 72-mi shoreline (especially on Highway 89, just south of Tahoe City; on Highway 28, east of Tahoe City; and on U.S. 50 in South Lake). The crowds increase as the day wears on, so the best strategy for avoiding the crush is to do as much as you can early in the day. The parking lots of the Lake Tahoe Visitor Center, Vikingsholm, and Emerald Bay State Park can be jammed at any time, and the lake's beaches can be packed. September and October, when the throngs have dispersed but the weather is still pleasant, are among the most satisfying—and cheapest—months to visit Lake Tahoe. Christmas week and July 4 are the busiest times, and prices go through the roof; plan accordingly.

About the Restaurants

On weekends and in high season, expect a long wait in the more popular restaurants. And expect to pay resort prices almost everywhere. Remember, restaurants see business only six out of 12 months. During the "shoulder seasons" (April to May and September to November), some places may close temporarily or limit their hours, so call ahead. Also, check local papers for deals and discounts during this time, especially two-for-one coupons. Many casinos use their restaurants to attract gamblers. Marquees often tout "$8.99 prime rib dinners" or "$1.99 breakfast specials." Some of these meals are downright lousy and they are usually available only in the coffee shops and buffets, but at those prices, it's hard to complain. The finer restaurants in casinos deliver pricier food, as well as reasonable service and a bit of atmosphere. Unless otherwise noted, even the most expensive area restaurants welcome customers in casual clothes.

About the Hotels

Quiet inns on the water, suburban-style strip motels, casino hotels, slope-side ski lodges, and house and condo rentals throughout the area constitute the lodging choices at Tahoe. The crowds come in summer and during ski season; reserve as far in advance as possible, especially for holiday periods, when prices skyrocket. Spring and fall give you a little more leeway and lower—sometimes significantly lower—rates. Check hotel Web sites for the best deals.

WHAT IT COSTS

	¢	$	$$	$$$	$$$$
Restaurants	under $10	$10–$15	$16–$22	$23–$30	over $30
Hotels	under $90	$90–$120	$121–$175	$176–$250	over $250
Camping	under $8	$8–$14	$15–$20	$21–$25	over $25

Restaurant prices are for a main course at dinner, excluding sales tax of 7.25%–7.50% (depending on location). Hotel prices are for two people in a standard double room in high season, excluding service charges and 10%–14% tax.

Skiing and Snowboarding

The mountains around Lake Tahoe are bombarded by blizzards throughout most winters and sometimes in fall and spring; 10- to 12-foot bases are common. Indeed, the Sierra often has the deepest snowpack on the continent, but because of the relatively mild temperatures over the Pacific, falling snow can be very heavy and wet—it's nicknamed Sierra Cement for a reason. The upside is that you can sometimes ski and board as late as July (snowboarding is permitted at all Tahoe ski areas). Note that the major resorts get extremely crowded on weekends. If you're going to ski on a Saturday, arrive early and quit early. Avoid moving with the masses: eat at 11 AM or 1:30 PM, not noon. Also consider visiting the ski areas with few high-speed lifts or limited lodging and real estate at their bases: Alpine Meadows, Sugar Bowl, Homewood, Mt. Rose, Sierra-at-Tahoe, Diamond Peak, and Kirkwood. And to find out the true ski conditions, talk to waiters and bartenders—most of whom are ski bums.

The Lake Tahoe area is also a great destination for Nordic skiers. "Skinny" (i.e., cross-country) skiing at the resorts can be costly, but you get the benefits of machine grooming and trail preparation. If it's bargain Nordic you're after, take advantage of thousands of acres of public forest and parkland trails.

Updated by Christine Vovakes

Stunning cobalt-blue Lake Tahoe is the largest alpine lake in North America, famous for its clarity, deep blue water, and surrounding snowcapped peaks. Straddling the state line between California and Nevada, it lies 6,225 feet above sea level in the Sierra Nevada.

The border gives this popular resort region a split personality. About half its visitors are intent on low-key sightseeing, hiking, fishing, camping, and boating. The rest head directly for the Nevada side, where bargain dining, big-name entertainment, and the lure of a jackpot draw them into the glittering casinos.

The lake and the communities around it are the region's main draw, but other nearby destinations are gaining in popularity. Truckee, with an Old West feel and hot new restaurants, lures visitors looking for a relaxed pace and easy access to Tahoe's north shore and Olympic Valley ski parks. And today Reno, once known only for its casinos, is also drawing tourists with its buzzing arts scene, revitalized downtown riverfront, and campus attractions at the University of Nevada.

Though Lake Tahoe possesses abundant natural beauty and accessible wilderness, nearby towns are highly developed, and roads around the lake are often congested with traffic. If you prefer solitude, you can escape to the many state parks, national forests, and protected tracts of wilderness that ring the 22-mi-long, 12-mi-wide lake.

PLANNING

GETTING HERE AND AROUND

AIR TRAVEL

Reno–Tahoe International Airport, in Reno, 35 mi northeast of the closest point on the lake, is served by Alaska, American, Delta, Horizon, Southwest, United, and US Airways. *See Air Travel in Travel Smart Northern California for airline phone numbers.*

Airport Contact Reno–Tahoe International Airport (✉ *U.S. 395, Exit 65B, Reno, NV* ☎ *775/328–6400* 🌐 *www.renoairport.com*).

BUS TRAVEL

Greyhound stops in Sacramento, Truckee, and Reno, Nevada. Blue Go runs along U.S. 50 and through the neighborhoods of South Lake Tahoe daily from morning to evening (times vary; check schedules); it also operates a 24-hour door-to-door van service to most addresses in South Lake Tahoe and Stateline for $6 per person (reservations essential). Tahoe Area Regional Transit (TART) operates buses along Lake Tahoe's northern and western shores between Tahoma and Incline Village daily, plus five shuttles daily to Truckee. All local buses cost $1.50. In summer TART buses have bike racks; in winter they have ski racks. Shuttle buses run between the casinos, major ski resorts, and motels of South Lake Tahoe. Tahoe Casino Express runs 11 daily buses between Reno–Tahoe Airport and hotels in Stateline. Reserve online or by telephone. A nonrefundable adult ticket is $26 one-way, $46.50 round-trip.

Bus Contacts Greyhound (☎ *800/231–2222* 🌐 *www.greyhound.com*). **Blue Go** (☎ *530/541–7149* 🌐 *www.bluego.org*). **Tahoe Area Regional Transit (TART)** (☎ *530/550–1212 or 800/736–6365* 🌐 *www.laketahoetransit.com*). **Tahoe Casino Express** (☎ *775/325–8944 or 866/898–2463* 🌐 *www.southtahoeexpress.com*).

CAR TRAVEL

Lake Tahoe is 198 mi northeast of San Francisco, a drive of less than four hours in good weather. Avoid the heavy traffic leaving the San Francisco area for Tahoe on Friday afternoon and returning on Sunday afternoon. The major route is I–80, which cuts through the Sierra Nevada about 14 mi north of the lake. From there Highway 89 and Highway 267 reach the west and north shores, respectively. U.S. 50 is the more direct route to the south shore, taking about two hours from Sacramento. From Reno you can get to the north shore by heading south on U.S. 395 for 10 mi, then west on Highway 431 for 25 mi. For the south shore, head south on U.S. 395 through Carson City, and then turn west on U.S. 50 (50 mi total).

The scenic 72-mi highway around the lake is marked Highway 89 on the southwest and west shores, Highway 28 on the north and northeast shores, and U.S. 50 on the east and southeast. Sections of Highway 89 sometimes close during snowy periods in winter, usually at Emerald Bay because of avalanche danger, which makes it impossible to complete the circular drive around the lake. Interstate 80, U.S. 50, and U.S. 395 are all-weather highways, but there may be delays as snow is cleared during major storms. (Note that I–80 is a four-lane freeway; a large part of U.S. 50 is only two lanes with no center divider.) Carry tire chains from October through May, or rent a four-wheel-drive vehicle (most rental agencies do not allow tire chains to be used on their vehicles; ask when you book).

Contacts California Highway Patrol (☎ *530/577–1001 South Lake Tahoe* 🌐 *www.chp.ca.gov*). **Cal-Trans Highway Information Line** (☎ *800/427–7623* 🌐 *www.dot.ca.gov/hq/roadinfo*). **Nevada Department of Transportation Road Information** (☎ *877/687–6237* 🌐 *www.nevadadot.com/traveler/roads*). **Nevada Highway Patrol** (☎ *775/687–5300* 🌐 *nhp.nv.gov*).

TRAIN TRAVEL

Amtrak's cross-country rail service makes stops in Truckee and Reno. The *California Zephyr* stops in both towns once daily eastbound (Salt Lake, Denver, and Chicago) and once daily westbound (Sacramento and Oakland). Amtrak also operates several buses daily between Reno and Sacramento to connect with the *Coast Starlight,* which runs south to Southern California and north to Oregon and Washington.

Train Contact Amtrak (☎ *775/329–8638 or 800/872–7245* ⊕ *www.amtrak california.com*).

HEALTH AND SAFETY

In an emergency, dial 911.

Hospital Contacts Barton Memorial Hospital (✉ *2170 South Ave., South Lake Tahoe* ☎ *530/541–3420*). **St. Mary's Regional Medical Center** (✉ *235 W. 6th St., Reno, NV* ☎ *775/770–3000 general information, 775/770–3188 emergency room*). **Tahoe Forest Hospital** (✉ *10121 Pine Ave., Truckee* ☎ *530/587–6011*).

TOUR OPTIONS

The 350-passenger *Tahoe Queen,* a glass-bottom paddle wheeler, departs from South Lake Tahoe daily for 2½-hour sightseeing cruises year-round by reservation and 3-hour dinner–dance cruises daily from late spring to early fall (weekly the rest of the year). Fares range from $46 to $81. In winter the boat becomes the only waterborne ski shuttle in the world: $114 covers hotel transfers, a bus transfer from South Lake Tahoe or Stateline to Squaw Valley, lift ticket, and boat transportation back across the lake to South Lake. There's a full bar on board, live music, and an optional dinner. The *Sierra Cloud,* a large 50-passenger catamaran owned by the Hyatt Hotel, cruises the north shore area morning and afternoon, May through September. The fare is $50. The 570-passenger MS *Dixie II,* a stern-wheeler, sails year-round from Zephyr Cove to Emerald Bay on sightseeing, lunch, and dinner cruises. Fares range from $41 to $71.

Also in Zephyr Cove, the *Woodwind II,* a 50-passenger catamaran, sails on regular and champagne cruises April through October. Fares range from $32 to $42. For the same price the *Woodwind I,* a 30-passenger trimaran, sails from Camp Richardson April through October. Woodwind Cruises also operates half-day round-the-lake cruises aboard the *Safari Rose,* an 80-foot-long wooden motor yacht; $95 includes lunch.

Lake Tahoe Balloons conducts excursions over the lake May through October and over the Carson Valley December through April; the hour-long flights cost $250 (the entire experience takes four hours total). Soar Minden offers glider rides and instruction over the lake and the Great Basin. Flights cost $155 to $295 and depart from Minden–Tahoe Airport, a municipal facility in Minden, Nevada.

Tour Contacts Lake Tahoe Balloons (☎ *530/544–1221 or 800/872–9294* ⊕ *www.laketahoeballoons.com*). **MS Dixie II** (✉ *Zephyr Cove Marina, Zephyr Cove* ☎ *775/589–4906 or 800/238–2463* ⊕ *www.laketahoecruises.com*). **Sierra Cloud** (✉ *Hyatt Regency Lake Tahoe, Incline Village* ☎ *775/832–1234*). **Soar Minden** (☎ *775/782–7627 or 800/345–7627* ⊕ *www.soarminden.com*). **Tahoe**

Queen (✉ *Ski Run Marina, off U.S. 50, South Lake Tahoe* ☎ *775/589–4906 or 800/238–2463* 🌐 *www.laketahoecruises.com*). **Woodwind Cruises** (✉ *Zephyr Cove Resort, U.S. 50, Zephyr Cove* ☎ *775/588–3000 or 888/867–6394* 🌐 *www.tahoeboatcruises.com*).

VISITOR INFORMATION

Contacts **Lake Tahoe Visitors Authority** (✉ *3066 Lake Tahoe Blvd., South Lake Tahoe* ☎ *530/544–5050 or 800/288–2463* 🌐 *www.bluelaketahoe.com*). **U.S. Forest Service** (☎ *530/587–2158 backcountry recording* 🌐 *www.fs.fed.us/r5*).

CALIFORNIA SIDE

SOUTH LAKE TAHOE

50 mi south of Reno on U.S. 395 and U.S. 50; 198 mi northeast of San Francisco on I–80 and U.S. 50.

The city of South Lake Tahoe's raison d'être is tourism: the casinos of adjacent Stateline, Nevada; the ski slopes at Heavenly Mountain; the beaches, docks, bike trails, and campgrounds all around the south shore; and the backcountry of Eldorado National Forest and Desolation Wilderness. The town itself, however, is disappointingly unattractive, with its mix of cheap motels, strip malls, and low-rise prefab-looking buildings that line both sides of U.S. 50. Though there are lots and lots of places to stay, we haven't recommended many because they're not cream-of-the-crop choices. The small city's saving grace is its convenient location and bevy of services, as well as its gorgeous lake views.

ESSENTIALS

Visitor Information **Lake Tahoe Visitors Authority** (✉ *3066 Lake Tahoe Blvd., South Lake Tahoe* ☎ *530/544–5050 or 800/288–2463* 🌐 *www.bluelaketahoe.com*).

EXPLORING

Fodor's Choice ★ Whether you ski or not, you'll appreciate the impressive view of Lake Tahoe from the **Heavenly Gondola.** Its 138 eight-passenger cars travel from the middle of town 2½ mi up the mountain in 15 minutes. When the weather's fine, you can take one of three hikes around the mountaintop and then have lunch at Adventure Peak Grill. Heavenly also offers day care for children. ✉ *Downtown* ☎ *775/586–7000 or 800/432–8365* 🌐 *www.skiheavenly.com* 💲 *$30* ⏲ *Hrs vary; summer, daily 10–5; winter, daily 9–4.*

At the base of the gondola the **Heavenly Village** is the centerpiece of South Lake Tahoe's efforts to reinvent itself and provide a focal point for tourism. Essentially a pedestrian mall, it includes some good shopping, a cinema, an arcade for kids, and the Heavenly Village Outdoor Ice Rink.

WHERE TO EAT

¢–$$ ECLECTIC ✕ **Blue Angel Café.** A favorite of locals, who fill the dozen or so wooden tables, the Blue Angel serves everything from frittatas, Benedicts, and house-made granola at breakfast to Mama's meatloaf, paella, and fresh fish and pasta dishes at lunch and dinner—and best of all, the prices are extremely reasonable. This cozy café has Wi-Fi and is open all day, 8 AM to 8 PM. ✉ *1132 Ski Run Blvd.* ☎ *530/544–6544* ⊙ *Call for hrs in May and Nov.* ▭ *AE, D, MC, V.*

$–$$ MEXICAN ✕ **The Cantina.** The Cantina serves generous portions of traditional Mexican dishes, such as burritos, enchiladas, and tamales, as well as more stylized Southwestern cooking, including smoked chicken polenta with grilled vegetables, and crab cakes in jalapeño cream sauce. The bar makes great margaritas and serves 30 different kinds of beer. ✉ *765 Emerald Bay Rd.* ☎ *530/544–1233* ✍ *Reservations not accepted* ▭ *AE, D, MC, V.*

$$$–$$$$ ECLECTIC ★ ✕ **Evan's.** The top choice for high-end dining in South Lake, Evan's serves creative American cuisine including such specialties as seared foie gras with grilled pineapple and curried ice cream; and veal loin with prosciutto, smoked mozzarella, and sage served with mushroom risotto. While some might find the tables a tad close to each other, the 40-seat dining room in the converted Tahoe cabin is intimate. The excellent service and food merit a special trip. ✉ *536 Emerald Bay Rd.* ☎ *530/542–1990* ▭ *AE, D, MC, V* ⊙ *No lunch.*

$$–$$$$ ASIAN ✕ **Kalani's.** Fresh-off-the-plane seafood gets flown directly from the Honolulu fish market to Heavenly Village's sexiest (and priciest) restaurant. The sleek, white-tablecloth dining room is decked out with carved bamboo, a burnt-orange color palette, and a modern-glass sculpture, all of which complement contemporary Pacific Rim specialties such as melt-from-the-bone baby back pork ribs with sesame-garlic soy sauce. Sushi selections with inventive rolls and sashimi combos, plus less expensive vegetarian dishes, add depth to the menu. ✉ *1001 Heavenly Village Way, #26* ☎ *530/544–6100* ▭ *AE, D, MC, V.*

¢ AMERICAN ✕ **Red Hut Café.** A vintage-1959 Tahoe diner, all chrome and red plastic, the Red Hut is a tiny place with a wildly popular breakfast menu: huge omelets; banana, pecan, and coconut waffles; and other tasty vittles. There's another branch in Stateline, too. ✉ *2749 U.S. 50* ☎ *530/541–9024* ✍ *Reservations not accepted* ▭ *No credit cards* ⊙ *No dinner* ✉ *227 Kingsbury Grade, Stateline, NV* ☎ *775/588–7488.*

$–$$$ ITALIAN ✕ **Scusa!** The kitchen here turns out big plates of linguine with clam sauce, veal scallopine, and chicken piccata. There's nothing fancy about the menu, just straightforward Italian-American food—and lots of it. ✉ *1142 Ski Run Blvd.* ☎ *530/542–0100* ▭ *AE, D, MC, V* ⊙ *No lunch.*

WHERE TO STAY

$$$–$$$$ Fodor'sChoice ★ **Black Bear Inn Bed and Breakfast.** South Lake Tahoe's most luxurious inn feels like one of the grand old lodges of the Adirondacks. Its great room has rough-hewn beams, plank floors, cathedral ceilings, Persian rugs, and even an elk's head over the giant river-rock fireplace. Built in the 1990s with meticulous attention to detail, the five inn rooms and three cabins feature 19th-century American antiques, fine art, and fireplaces; cabins also have kitchenettes. Never intrusive, the affable innkeepers provide a sumptuous breakfast in the morning and wine and cheese in the afternoon. **Pros:** intimate; within walking distance of several good restaurants; massive stone fireplace in great room. **Cons:** not appropriate for children under 16; pricey. ✉ *1202 Ski Run Blvd. 96150* ☎ *530/544–4451 or*

Continued on page 510

TAHOE A LAKE FOR ALL SEASONS

by Christine Vovakes

Best known for its excellent skiing, Lake Tahoe is a year-round resort and outdoor sports destination. All kinds of activities are available, from snowboarding some of the best runs in North America and gliding silently along the lakeshore on cross-country skis in winter, to mountain biking through lush forests and puttering around the alpine lake in a classic yacht in summer. Whatever you do—and whenever you visit—the sapphire lake is at the center of it all, pulling you out of your posh resort or rustic cabin rental like a giant blue magnet. There are many ways to enjoy and experience Lake Tahoe, but here are some of our favorites.

(top) Heavenly Mountain Resort, (bottom) Sand Harbor Beach.

WINTER WONDERLAND

Home to a host of world-famous Sierra resorts, Tahoe is a premier ski destination. Add sledding, ice skating, cross-country skiing, and jingly sleigh rides under the stars to the mix, and you begin to get a glimpse of Tahoe's cold-weather potential.

DOWNHILL SKIING AND SNOWBOARDING

Even if you've never made it off the bunny hill before, you should definitely hit the slopes here at least once. The Lake Tahoe region has the deepest snowpack in North America, and you can ski from Thanksgiving until it melts—which is sometimes July.

One of the top-rated resorts in the country, Olympic Valley's **Squaw Valley USA** hosted the 1960 Winter Olympics that put Tahoe on the map. A great classic resort is **Sugar Bowl,** where you can revel in a bit of Disney nostalgia while you swoop down the slopes. Walt helped start the resort, which opened in 1939 and had Tahoe's first chair lift.

Even if you're not hitting the slopes at South Lake Tahoe's **Heavenly Mountain,** be sure to take a ride on their **Heavenly Gondola** so you can take in awe-inspiring views of the frozen circle of white ice that rings the brilliant lake.

(top) Skiing in Lake Tahoe,. (above left) Cross-country skiing, (above right) Snow boarding at Heavenly Mountain.

SKI RESORT	LOCATION	TRAILS	ACRES	BEGIN.	INTER.	ADV./ EXP.
CALIFORNIA						
Alpine Meadows	Tahoe City	100	2,400	25%	40%	35%
Heavenly Mountain	South Lake Tahoe	95	4,800	20%	45%	35%
Homewood Mountain	Tahoma	60	1,260	15%	50%	35%
Kirkwood	South Lake Tahoe	65	2,300	15%	50%	35%
Northstar-at-Tahoe	Truckee	89	2,904	13%	60%	27%
Sierra-at-Tahoe	South Lake Tahoe	46	2,000	25%	50%	25%
Squaw Valley USA	Olympic Valley	170	4,000	25%	45%	30%
Sugar Bowl	Truckee	84	1,500	17%	45%	38%
NEVADA						
Diamond Peak	Incline Village	30	655	18%	46%	36%
Mt. Rose Ski Tahoe	Incline Village	61	1,200	20%	30%	50%

CROSS-COUNTRY SKIING

Downhill skiing may get all the glory here, but Lake Tahoe is also a premier cross-country (or Nordic) skiing destination. "Skinny" skiers basically have two options: pony up the cash to ski the groomed trails at a resort, or hit the more rugged (but cheaper—or free) public forest and parkland trails.

Beautiful **Royal Gorge** is the country's largest cross-country ski resort. Other resorts with good skinny skiing include **Kirkwood, Squaw Valley USA, Tahoe Donner,** and **Northstar-at-Tahoe.** Private operators **Spooner Lake Cross Country** and **Hope Valley Cross Country** will also have you shushing through pristine powder in no time.

For bargain Nordic on public trails, head to **Sugar Pine Point State Park.** Other good low-cost cross-country skiing locations include **Donner Memorial State Park, Lake Tahoe—Nevada State Park,** and **Tahoe Meadows** near Incline Village.

CAUTION⚠ Cross-country skiing is relaxing and provides a great cardiovascular workout—but it's also quite strenuous. If it's your first time out or you're not in great shape, start out slow.

SLEDDING AND TUBING

Kirkwood, Squaw Valley USA, Boreal, Soda Springs, and many other Tahoe resorts have areas where you can barrel down hills in sleds and inflatable tubes. Some good non-resort sledding spots are **Tahoe National Forest** and **Tahoe Meadows,** near Incline Village.

ICE SKATING

Want to work on your triple lutz? You can skate seasonally at **Heavenly Village Outdoor Ice Rink,** or year-round at the **South Tahoe Ice Arena.** Other great gliding spots include **Kirkwood** and **Squaw Valley USA's Olympic Ice Pavilion.**

WARMING UP

To defrost your ski-stiff limbs, take a dip in a resort's heated pool, de-stress in a hotel spa . . . or enjoy a brandy by the fire at a cozy restaurant. Our favorite places to warm up and imbibe include Tahoe City's Christy Hill, Graham's of Squaw Valley, and Soule Domain, near Crystal Bay.

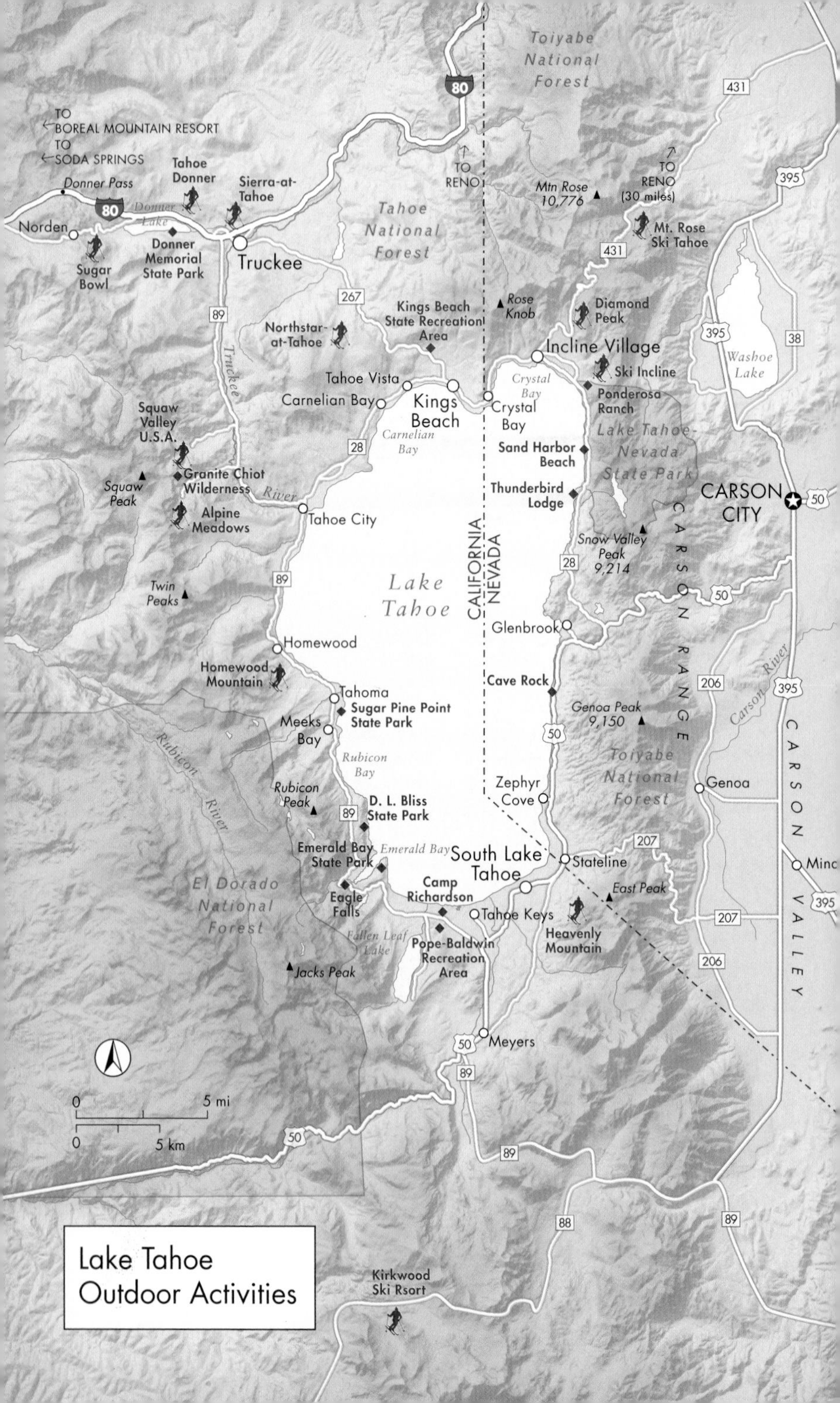

Lake Tahoe
Outdoor Activities
Toiyabe National Forest
TO BOREAL MOUNTAIN RESORT
TO SODA SPRINGS
Donner Pass
Norden
Sugar Bowl
Donner Lake
Tahoe Donner
Sierra-at-Tahoe
Donner Memorial State Park
Truckee
TO RENO
TO RENO (30 miles)
Mtn Rose 10,776
Mt. Rose Ski Tahoe
Tahoe National Forest
Kings Beach State Recreation Area
Rose Knob
Diamond Peak
Northstar-at-Tahoe
Incline Village
Ski Incline
Ponderosa Ranch
Washoe Lake
Tahoe Vista
Carnelian Bay
Kings Beach
Crystal Bay
Lake Tahoe-Nevada State Park
Sand Harbor Beach
Thunderbird Lodge
CARSON CITY
Squaw Valley U.S.A.
Granite Chiot Wilderness
Squaw Peak
Alpine Meadows
Truckee River
Tahoe City
Snow Valley Peak 9,214
CARSON RANGE
Twin Peaks
Lake Tahoe
CALIFORNIA
NEVADA
Glenbrook
Homewood
Homewood Mountain
Cave Rock
Tahoma
Sugar Pine Point State Park
Meeks Bay
Genoa Peak 9,150
Carson River
Rubicon River
Rubicon Bay
Toiyabe National Forest
Zephyr Cove
Genoa
CARSON VALLEY
Rubicon Peak
D. L. Bliss State Park
Emerald Bay State Park
Emerald Bay
South Lake Tahoe
Stateline
Minden
El Dorado National Forest
Eagle Falls
Camp Richardson
East Peak
Tahoe Keys
Heavenly Mountain
Fallen Leaf Lake
Pope-Baldwin Recreation Area
Jacks Peak
Meyers
0 5 mi
0 5 km
Kirkwood Ski Rsort
80
431
395
267
89
38
28
50
206
207
88

FROSTY CATCH

Too cold to fish? Nonsense. South Lake's Tahoe Sport Fishing runs charters year-round with crews that will clean and package your catch.

IN THE WARM CALIFORNIA SUN

Summer in Tahoe means diving into pure alpine waters, hiking a mountain trail with stunning lake views, or kayaking on glorious Emerald Bay. From tennis to golf to fishing, you can fill every waking moment with outdoor activity—or just stretch out on a sunny lakeside beach with a good book and a cool drink.

HIKING

The lake is surrounded by protected parkland, offering countless opportunities to take jaunts through the woods or rambles along lakeside trails.

One of the most unique hiking experiences in Tahoe is at Heavenly Mountain Resorts, where the **Heavenly Gondola** runs up to three nice trails. When you're done enjoying sky-high views of the lake, grab lunch at the nearby Adventure Peak Grill.

Another out-of-the-ordinary option is a romantic moonlit trek. **Camp Richardson** has lots of trails and a long curve of lake to catch the moonlight.

In **Eldorado National Forest and Desolation Wilderness,** you can hike a small portion of the famous Pacific Crest Trail and branch off to discover beautiful backcountry lakes. Nearby **Eagle Falls** has stunning views of Emerald Bay.

One of Tahoe's best hikes is a 4½-mi trail at **D.L. Bliss State Park;** it has lovely views of the lake and leads to bizarre **Vikingsholm** (*see box on next page*).

Other great places to hike in Lake Tahoe include **Sugar Pines Point State Park, Olympic Valley's Granite Chief Wilderness, Squaw Valley USA's High Camp, Donner Memorial State Park,** and **Lake Tahoe—Nevada State Park.**

You can pick up hiking maps at the **U.S. Forest Service** office at the **Lake Tahoe Visitor Center.**

HIT THE BEACH

Lake Tahoe has some gorgeous lakeside sunbathing terrain; get to perennial favorite **Kings Beach State Recreation Area** early to snag a choice spot. Or, if you never want to be far from the water, reserve one of the prime beachside spots at **D.L. Bliss State Park Campground.**

(left) Fannette Island in Emerald Bay. (right) A young man leaps off a cliff into Lake Tahoe.

MOUNTAIN BIKING AND CYCLING

You don't need to be preparing for the Tour de France to join the biking fun. While there are myriad rugged mountain biking trails to choose from, the region is also blessed with many flat trails.

Truly intrepid cyclists take the lift up **Northstar-at-Tahoe** and hit the resort's 100 mi of trails. Another good option is **Sugar Pine Point State Park,** where you can hop on a 10-mi trail to Tahoe City.

Tahoe Sports in South Lake Tahoe is a good place for bike rentals and tips for planning your trip. **Cyclepath Mountain Bikes Adventures** in Tahoe City leads guided mountain biking tours, and **Flume Trail Bikes** in Incline Village rents bikes and operates a bike shuttle to popular trails.

LAKE TOURS AND KAYAKING

One of the best ways to experience the lake is by getting out on the water.

The ***Tahoe Queen*** is a huge glass-bottomed paddle-wheel boat that offers sightseeing cruises and dinner-dance cruises; in winter, it's the only waterborne ski shuttle in the world. The ***Sierra Cloud, MS Dixie II,*** and ***Woodwind I and II*** also ply the lake, offering a variety of enjoyable cruises. *(See Tour Options in the Planning section at the beginning of this chapter for contact info.)*

Another enjoyable option is taking a throwback wooden cruiser from Tahoe Keys Marina in South Lake Tahoe to tour **Thunderbird Lodge,** the meticulously crafted stone mansion built in 1936 by socialite George Whittell.

For a more personal experience, rent a kayak and glide across **Emerald Bay. Kayak Tahoe** in South Lake Tahoe will have you paddling in no time.

VIKINGS?

As you kayak around Tahoe, you'll see many natural wonders . . . and a few manmade ones as well. One of the most impressive and strangest is **Vikingsholm**, a grand 1929 estate that looks like an ancient Viking castle. You can see it from **Emerald Bay** (which, appropriately, resembles a fjord), or hike to it via a steep one-mile trail.

(left top) Biking along the shore. (left bottom) Kayaking. (right) Steamboat cruise.

877/232–7466 ⊕www.tahoeblackbear.com ⇆5 rooms, 3 cabins ☆In-room: kitchen (some), DVD, Wi-Fi. In-hotel: Wi-Fi, no kids under 16, no-smoking rooms ▭AE, D, MC, V ¶⊙¶BP.

> **WORD OF MOUTH**
>
> "Bike trails are wonderful from Camp Richardson (near South Shore). It's like hiking in the middle of the woods, but on a bicycle. You can bike from beach to beach. Take a picnic lunch." —elnap29

$–$$$ **Camp Richardson.** An old-fashioned family resort, Camp Richardson is built around a 1920s lodge, with a few dozen cabins and a small inn, all beneath giant pine trees on 80 acres of lakefront land on the southwest shore of Lake Tahoe. The rustic log cabin–style lodge has simple, straightforward accommodations. The cabins (one-week minimum in summer) have lots of space, fireplaces or woodstoves, and full kitchens; some units sleep eight. The Beachside Inn has more modern amenities and sits right on the lake, but its rooms feel like those of an ordinary motel. Best of all, the resort sits well off the road and there's tons of space; kids have a blast here. Rates drop significantly in winter, plus you can snowshoe and zip along cross-country ski trails on the property. **Pros:** wide choice of accommodations; beautiful lakeside location. **Cons:** no phones or TVs in some rooms. *✉1900 Jameson Beach Rd. 96158 ☎530/541–1801 or 800/544–1801 ⊕www.camprichardson.com ⇆28 lodge rooms, 40 cabins, 7 inn rooms, 300 campsites ☆In-room: no a/c, no phone (some), kitchen (some), no TV (some). In-hotel: restaurant, beachfront, bicycles, Wi-Fi (paid), no-smoking rooms ▭AE, D, MC, V.*

$$–$$$ ★ **Inn by the Lake.** Of all the mid-range lodgings in South Lake, this one is probably the best. Across the road from a beach, the "inn" is essentially a high-end motel, with spacious, spotless rooms and suites decorated in soft, slightly dated color schemes. All rooms have balconies; pricier rooms have lake views (across the road), wet bars, and kitchens. In the afternoon the staff sets out cookies and cider. **Pros:** great value; stellar service; just a short drive from Heavenly Mountain. **Cons:** sits on Lake Tahoe Boulevard; the busy main route into town. *✉3300 Lake Tahoe Blvd. 96150 ☎530/542–0330 or 800/877–1466 ⊕www.innbythelake.com ⇆93 rooms, 7 suites ☆In-room: kitchen (some), refrigerator, Wi-Fi. In-hotel: room service, pool, gym, bicycles, laundry facilities, laundry service, Wi-Fi, no-smoking rooms ▭AE, D, DC, MC, V ¶⊙¶CP.*

$$$–$$$$ ★ **Marriott's Grand Residence and Timber Lodge.** You can't beat the location of these two gigantic, modern condominium complexes right at the base of Heavenly Gondola, smack in the center of town. Though both are extremely comfortable, Timber Lodge feels more like a family vacation resort; Grand Residence is geared to upper-end travelers. Units vary in size from studios to three bedrooms, and some have amenities such as stereos, fireplaces, daily maid service, and full kitchens. Ask about vacation packages. **Pros:** central location; great for families; within walking distance of excellent restaurants. **Cons:** can be jam-packed on weekends. *✉1001 Park Ave. ☎530/542–8400 or 800/627–7468 ⊕www.marriott.com ⇆431 condos ☆In-room: kitchen (some), Wi-Fi. In-hotel: pool,*

gym, laundry facilities, laundry service, parking (paid), Wi-Fi, no-smoking rooms ▭*AE, D, MC, V.*

$$–$$$$ **Sorensen's Resort.** Escape civilization by staying in a log cabin at this woodsy 165-acre resort within the Eldorado National Forest, 20 minutes south of town. You can lie on a hammock beneath the aspens or sit in a rocker on your own front porch. All but three of the cabins have a kitchen and wood-burning stove or fireplace. Some cabins are close together, and the furnishings aren't fancy (think futons as sofas), but there's a wonderful summer-camp charm about the place that makes it special. There are also five modern homes that sleep six. The resort sits on the edge of the highway, which allows it to stay open in winter—a boon for skiers—but in summer, request a cabin away from the road. **Pros:** gorgeous, rustic setting. **Cons:** nearest nightlife is 20 mi away in South Lake Tahoe. ✉*14255 Hwy. 88, Hope Valley* ☎*530/694–2203 or 800/423–9949* ⊕*www.sorensensresort.com* *2 rooms with shared bath, 35 cabins, 5 houses* *In-room: no a/c, no phone, kitchen (some), no TV, Wi-Fi. In-hotel: restaurant, children's programs (ages 3–18), Wi-Fi, some pets allowed, no-smoking rooms* ▭*AE, D, DC, MC, V.*

13

$$$–$$$$ **Tahoe Seasons Resort.** It's a 150-yard walk to California Lodge of Heavenly Mountain Resort from this all-suites time-share hotel, where every room has a two-person sunken hot tub. Most units have gas fireplaces, and some can sleep up to six people. Beautifully renovated, the resort is situated in a more residential part of town. It has a seasonal restaurant and offers shuttle service to nearby casinos. **Pros:** steps away from ski resort; a less touristy location. **Cons:** no restaurants or casinos within walking distance. ✉*3901 Saddle Rd.* ☎*530/541–6700 front desk, 800/540–4874 reservations* ⊕*www.tahoeseasons.com* *160 suites* *In-room: kitchen, refrigerator, DVD, Internet. In-hotel: bar, tennis courts, pool, no-smoking rooms* ▭*AE, D, MC, V.*

SPORTS AND THE OUTDOORS

FISHING **Tahoe Sport Fishing** (✉*Ski Run Marina* ☎*530/541–5448, 800/696–7797 in CA* ⊕*www.tahoesportfishing.com*) is one of the largest and oldest fishing-charter services on the lake. Morning trips cost $95, afternoon trips $85. Year-round outings include all necessary gear and bait, and the crew cleans and packages your catch.

GOLF The 18-hole, par-71 **Lake Tahoe Golf Course** (✉*U.S. 50, between Lake Tahoe Airport and Meyers* ☎*530/577–0788* ⊕*www.laketahoegc.com*) has a driving range. Greens fees start at $55; a cart (mandatory Friday to Sunday) costs $25. Twilight rates drop as low as $25.

HIKING The south shore is a great jumping-off point for day treks into nearby Eldorado National Forest and Desolation Wilderness. Hike a couple of miles on the **Pacific Crest Trail** (✉*Echo Summit, about 12 mi southwest of South Lake Tahoe off U.S. 50* ☎*916/349–2109 or 888/728–7245* ⊕*www.pcta.org*). The Pacific Crest Trail leads into **Desolation Wilderness** (✉*El Dorado National Forest Information Center* ☎*530/644–6048* ⊕*www.fs.fed.us/r5/eldorado*), where you can pick up trails to gorgeous backcountry lakes and mountain peaks (bring a proper topographic map and compass, and carry water and food). Late May through early September the easiest way to access Desolation Wilderness is via boat taxi ($10 one way) across Echo Lake from **Echo Chalet**

(✉Echo Lakes Rd. off U.S. 50 near Echo Summit ☎530/659–7207 🌐www.echochalet.com).

ICE-SKATING If you're here in winter, practice your jumps and turns at the **Heavenly Village Outdoor Ice Rink.** It's between the gondola and the cinema. ☎530/542–4230 *$20, includes skate rentals* ⏲*Nov.–Mar., daily 10–10, weather permitting.*

For year-round fun, head to the city-operated **South Tahoe Ice Arena.** You can rent equipment and sign up for lessons at this NHL regulation size indoor rink. Call ahead to check on the irregular hours. ✉*1176 Rufus Allen Blvd.* ☎*530/542–6262* 🌐*www.recreationintahoe.com/ice_arena* *$9, plus $3 skate rental* ⏲*Daily.*

KAYAKING **Kayak Tahoe** (✉*Timber Cove Marina; 3411 Lake Tahoe Blvd., behind Best Western Timber Cove Lodge* ☎*530/544–2011* 🌐*www.kayaktahoe.com*) has long been teaching people to kayak on Lake Tahoe and the Truckee River. Lessons and excursions (to the south shore, Emerald Bay, and Sand Harbor) are offered May through September. You can also rent a kayak and paddle solo.

MOUNTAIN BIKING With so much national forest land surrounding Lake Tahoe, you may want to try mountain biking. You can rent both road and mountain bikes and get tips on where to ride from the friendly staff at **Tahoe Sports Ltd.** (✉*4000 Lake Tahoe Blvd.* ☎*530/542–4000* 🌐*www.tahoesportsltd.com*).

SKIING Fodor'sChoice ★ Straddling two states, vast **Heavenly Mountain Resort**—composed of nine peaks, two valleys, and four base-lodge areas, along with the largest snowmaking system in the western United States—has terrain for every skier. Beginners can choose wide, well-groomed trails, accessed from the California Lodge or the gondola from downtown South Lake Tahoe; kids have short and gentle runs in the Enchanted Forest area all to themselves. The Sky Express high-speed quad chair whisks intermediate and advanced skiers to the summit for wide cruisers or steep tree-skiing. Mott and Killebrew canyons draw experts to the Nevada side for steep chutes and thick-timber slopes. For snowboarders and tricksters, there are four terrain parks, including an enormous 22-foot super-pipe. True thrill-seekers will hop into the harness of the mountain's newest addition, the Heavenly Flyer, a 3,100-foot zip line with a plunging vertical drop of 525 feet. (Minors need a parent's signature on consent form.) The ski school is big, and offers everything from learn-to-ski packages to canyon-adventure tours. Call about ski and boarding camps. Skiing lessons are available for children ages four and up; there's day care for infants older than six weeks. ✉*Ski Run Blvd., off Hwy. 89, U.S. 50, Stateline, NV* ☎*775/586–7000 or 800/432–8365* 🌐*www.skiheavenly.com* ☞*95 trails on 4,800 acres, rated 20% beginner, 45% intermediate, 35% expert. Longest run 5½ mi, base 6,540 feet, summit 10,067 feet. Lifts: 30, including 1 aerial tram, 1 gondola, 2 high-speed 6-passenger lifts, and 7 high-speed quads.*

★ Thirty-six miles south of Lake Tahoe, **Kirkwood Ski Resort** is the hardcore skiers' and boarders' favorite south-shore mountain, known for its craggy gulp-and-go chutes, sweeping cornices, steep-aspect glade skiing, and high base elevation. But there's also fantastic terrain for newbies and intermediates down wide-open bowls, through wooded gullies, and along rolling tree-lined trails. Tricksters can show off in the Stomping Grounds terrain park on jumps, wall rides, rails, and a half-pipe, all visible from the base area. The mountain gets hammered with more than 500 inches of snow annually, and often has the most in all of North America. If you're into out-of-bounds skiing, check out Expedition Kirkwood, a backcountry-skills program that teaches basic safety awareness. Kirkwood is also the only Tahoe resort to offer Cat-skiing. If you're into cross-country, the resort has 80 km (50 mi) of superb groomed-track skiing, with skating lanes, instruction, and rentals. Nonskiers can snowshoe, snow-skate, ice-skate, and go dogsledding or snow-tubing. The children's ski school has programs for ages four to 12, and there's day care for children two to six years old. ✉*Hwy. 88, 14 mi west of Hwy. 89* ☎*209/258–6000 downhill, 209/258–7248 cross-country, 209/258–7293 lodging information, 209/258–3000 snow phone* 🌐*www.kirkwood.com* ☞*65 trails on 2,300 acres, rated 15% beginner, 50% intermediate, 20% advanced, 15% expert. Longest run 2½ mi, base 7,800 feet, summit 9,800 feet. Lifts: 12, including 2 high-speed quads.*

Often overlooked by skiers and boarders rushing to Heavenly or Kirkwood, **Sierra-at-Tahoe** has meticulously groomed intermediate slopes, some of the best tree-skiing in California, and gated backcountry access. Extremely popular with local snowboarders, Sierra also has six terrain parks, including a super-pipe with 17-foot walls. For nonskiers there's a snow-tubing hill. Sierra has a low-key atmosphere that's great for families. Kids and beginners take the slow routes in the Mellow Yellow Zone. ✉*12 mi from South Lake Tahoe off U.S. 50, near Echo Summit* ☎*530/659–7453* 🌐*www.sierraattahoe.com* ☞*46 trails on 2,000 acres, rated 25% beginner, 50% intermediate, 25% advanced. Longest run 2½ mi, base 6,640 ft, summit 8,852 ft. Lifts: 12, including 3 high-speed quads.*

Operating from a yurt at Pickett's Junction, **Hope Valley Cross Country** (✉*Hwy. 88, at Hwy. 89, Hope Valley* ☎*530/694–2266* 🌐*www.hopevalleyoutdoors.com*) provides lessons and equipment rentals to prepare you for cross-country skiing and snowshoeing. The outfit has 50 mi of trails through Humboldt–Toiyabe National Forest, 10 of which are groomed.

If you don't want to pay the high cost of rental equipment at the resorts, you'll find reasonable prices and expert advice at **Tahoe Sports Ltd.** (✉*Downhill: 4000 Lake Tahoe Blvd.* ☎*530/542–4000* 🌐*www.tahoesportsltd.com* ✉*Cross-Country and telemark: South Y Center, Hwy. 89 and U.S. 50* ☎*530/544–2284*).

POPE-BALDWIN RECREATION AREA

5 mi west of South Lake Tahoe on Hwy. 89.

To the west of downtown South Lake Tahoe, U.S. 50 and Highway 89 come together, forming an intersection nicknamed "the Y." If you head northwest on Highway 89 and follow the lakefront, commercial development gives way to national forests and state parks. One of these is Pope-Baldwin Recreation Area.

EXPLORING

Stroll or picnic lakeside at **Tallac Historic Site**. Then explore **Pope House,** the magnificently restored 1894 mansion of George S. Pope, who made his money in shipping and lumber and played host to the business and cultural elite of 1920s America. There are two other estates here. One belonged to entrepreneur "Lucky" Baldwin; today it houses the **Baldwin Museum,** a collection of family memorabilia and Washoe Indian artifacts. The **Valhalla** (*www.valhallatahoe.com*), with a spectacular floor-to-ceiling stone fireplace, belonged to Walter Heller. Its Grand Hall and a lakeside boathouse, refurbished as a theater, host summertime concerts, plays, and cultural activities. Docents conduct tours of the Pope House in summer; call for tour times. In winter you can cross-country ski around the site. *Hwy. 89 530/541–5227 www.tahoeheritage.org Free; Pope House tour $5 Grounds daily sunrise–sunset. Pope House and Baldwin Museum late May–mid-June, weekends 11–3; mid-June–early Sept., daily 11–4.*

At **Taylor Creek Visitor Center,** operated by the U.S. Forest Service, you can visit the site of a Washoe Indian settlement; walk self-guided trails through meadow, marsh, and forest; and inspect the Stream Profile Chamber, an underground display with windows right into Taylor Creek (in fall you may see spawning kokanee salmon digging their nests). In summer U.S. Forest Service naturalists organize discovery walks and evening programs (call ahead). *Hwy. 89, 3 mi north of junction with U.S. 50 530/543–2674 June–Oct., 530/543–2600 year-round www.fs.fed.us/r5/ltbmu/recreation/summer-index.shtml Free Mid-June–late Sept., daily 8–5:30; Memorial Day–mid-June weekends, and in Oct., daily 8–4:30.*

EMERALD BAY STATE PARK

Fodor's Choice ★ *4 mi west of Pope-Baldwin Recreation Area on Hwy. 89.*

Emerald Bay, a 3-mi-long and 1-mi-wide fjordlike inlet on Lake Tahoe's shore, was carved by a massive glacier millions of years ago. Famed for its jewel-like shape and colors, it surrounds Fannette, Tahoe's only island. Highway 89 curves high above the lake through Emerald Bay State Park; from the Emerald Bay lookout, the centerpiece of the park, you can survey the whole scene. This is one of the don't-miss views of Lake Tahoe. Come before the sun drops below the mountains to the west; the light is best in mid- to late mornings, when the bay's colors really pop.

EXPLORING

A steep 1-mi-long trail from the lookout leads down to **Vikingsholm,** a 38-room estate completed in 1929. The original owner, Lora Knight, had this precise copy of a 1,200-year-old Viking castle built out of materials native to the area. She furnished it with Scandinavian antiques and hired artisans to build period reproductions. The sod roof sprouts wildflowers each spring. There are picnic tables nearby and a gray-sand

Fjordlike Emerald Bay is quite possibly the prettiest part of Lake Tahoe.

beach for strolling. The hike back up is hard (especially if you're not yet acclimated to the elevation), but there are benches and stone culverts to rest on. At the 150-foot peak of Fannette Island are the ruins of a stone structure known as the Tea House, built in 1928 so that Knight's guests could have a place to enjoy afternoon refreshments after a motorboat ride. The island is off-limits from February through June to protect nesting Canada geese. The rest of the year it's open for day use. ✉ *Hwy. 89* ☎ *530/541–6498 summer, 530/525–7277 year-round* 🌐 *www.vikingsholm.com* 🎫 *Day-use parking fee $6, mansion tour $5* ⏲ *Late May–mid-June, weekends, call for hrs; mid-June–Sept., daily 10–4.*

SPORTS AND THE OUTDOORS

HIKING Leave your car in the parking lot for Eagle Falls picnic area (near Vikingsholm; arrive early for a good spot), and head to **Eagle Falls,** a short but fairly steep walk-up canyon. You'll have a brilliant panorama of Emerald Bay from this spot, near the boundary of Desolation Wilderness. If you want a full-day's hike and you're in good shape, continue 5 mi, past Eagle Lake, to Upper and Middle Velma Lakes. You can pick up trail maps from the U.S. Forest Service at their Lake Tahoe Visitor Center in summer or at park headquarters in South Lake Tahoe year-round.

D.L. BLISS STATE PARK

3 mi north of Emerald Bay State Park on Hwy. 89.

D.L. Bliss State Park takes its name from Duane LeRoy Bliss, a 19th-century lumber magnate. At one time Bliss owned nearly 75% of Tahoe's lakefront, along with local steamboats, railroads, and banks. The park shares 6 mi of shoreline with Emerald Bay State Park; combined the two parks cover 1,830 acres, 744 of which were donated to the state by the Bliss family in 1929. At the north end of Bliss is Rubicon Point, which overlooks one of the lake's deepest spots. Short trails lead to an old lighthouse and Balancing Rock, which weighs 250,000 pounds and balances on a fist of granite. A 4.25-mi trail—one of Tahoe's premier hikes—leads to Vikingsholm and provides stunning lake views. Two white-sand beaches front some of Tahoe's warmest water. ☒*Hwy. 89* ☎*530/525–7277* *$6 per vehicle, day use* ⏲*Late May–Sept., daily sunrise–sunset.*

CAMPING

$$$–$$$$ **D.L. Bliss State Park Campground.** In one of California's most beautiful spots, quiet, wooded hills make for blissful family camping near the lake. The campground is open June to September, and reservations are accepted up to seven months in advance. It's expensive for a campground, but the location can't be beat, especially at the beach campsites. Book early. Trailers and RVs longer than 18 feet are not allowed. ☒*Off Hwy. 89, 17 mi south of Tahoe City on lake side* ☎*916/638–5883 or 800/444–7275* *www.reserveamerica.com* *168 sites* *Flush toilets, drinking water, showers, bear boxes, fire pits, grills, picnic tables, public telephone, swimming (beach).*

SUGAR PINE POINT STATE PARK

★ *8 mi north of D. L. Bliss State Park on Hwy. 89.*

The main attraction at Sugar Pine Point State Park is **Ehrman Mansion,** a 1903 stone-and-shingle summer home furnished in period style. In its day it was the height of modernity, with a refrigerator, an elevator, and an electric stove (tours leave hourly). Also in the park are a trapper's log cabin from the mid-19th century, a nature preserve with wildlife exhibits, a lighthouse, the start of the 10-mi-long biking trail to Tahoe City, and an extensive system of hiking and cross-country skiing trails. If you're feeling less ambitious, you can relax on the sun-dappled lawn behind the mansion and gaze out at the lake. ☒*Hwy. 89* ☎*530/525–7982 mansion in season, 530/525–7232 year-round* *$6 per vehicle, day use; mansion tour $5* ⏲*Mansion Memorial Day–Labor Day, daily 11–4.*

CAMPING

$$$ **Sugar Pine Point State Park Campground/General Creek Campground.** This beautiful and homey campground on the mountain side of Highway 89 is one of the few public ones to remain open in winter, when it's popular with cross-country skiers. There are no hookups here, and the showers operate from late May to early September only. ☒*Hwy. 89, 1 mi south of Tahoma* ☎*916/638–5883 or 800/444–7275* *www.reserveamerica.com* *175 sites* *Flush toilets, drinking water, showers, bear boxes, fire pits, grills, public telephone.*

13

TAHOMA

1 mi north of Sugar Pine Point State Park on Hwy. 89; 23 mi south of Truckee on Hwy. 89.

Tahoma exemplifies life on the lake in its early days, with rustic waterfront vacation cottages that are far from the blinking lights of South Shore's casinos. In 1960 Tahoma was host to the Olympic Nordic skiing competitions. Today there's little to do here except stroll by the lake and listen to the wind in the trees, making it a favorite home base for mellow families and nature buffs.

WHERE TO STAY

$$–$$$ ★ **Tahoma Meadows B&B Cottages.** It's hard to beat Tahoma Meadows for atmosphere and woodsy charm; it's a great retreat for families and couples. Fifteen individually decorated little red cottages sit tucked beneath towering pine trees. Inside, they're cheerful, with fun details like model ships on the shelf and a stuffed bear on the bed; some have claw-foot tubs and fireplaces. Cottages without kitchens include breakfast in the cozy, gable-roof lodge. Down-to-earth and simple, this is one of Tahoe's best hideaways. **Pros:** lovely setting; good choice for families. **Cons:** far from the casinos. ✉*6821 W. Lake Blvd.,* ☎*530/525–1553 or 866/525–1553* 🌐*www.tahomameadows.com* *15 cabins* *In-room: no a/c, no phone, kitchen (some), Wi-Fi. In-hotel: Wi-Fi, some pets allowed, no-smoking rooms* *AE, D, MC, V* *BP.*

SPORTS AND THE OUTDOORS

You'll feel as though you're going to ski into the lake when you schuss down the face of **Homewood Mountain Resort**—and you could if you really wanted to, because the mountain rises right off the shoreline. This is the favorite area of locals on a fresh-snow day, because you can find lots of untracked powder. It's also the most protected and least windy Tahoe ski area during a storm; when every other resort's lifts are on wind hold, you can almost always count on Homewood's to be open. There's only one high-speed chairlift, but there are rarely any lines, and the ticket prices are some of the cheapest around—kids five to 12 ski for $10 while those four and under are free. It may look small as you drive by, but most of the resort is not visible from the road. ✉*Hwy. 89, 6 mi south of Tahoe City* ☎*530/525–2992* 🌐*www.skihomewood.com* ☞*60 trails on 1,260 acres, rated 15% beginner, 50% intermediate, and 35% advanced. Longest run 2 mi, base 6,230 feet, summit 7,880 feet. Lifts: 4 chairlifts, 3 surface lifts.*

TAHOE CITY

★ *10 mi north of Sugar Pine Point State Park on Hwy. 89; 14 mi south of Truckee on Hwy. 89.*

Tahoe City is the only lakeside town with a compact downtown area good for strolling and window-shopping. Of the larger towns ringing the lake, it has the most bona-fide charm. Stores and restaurants are all within walking distance of the Outlet Gates, enormous Lake Tahoe's only outlet, where water is spilled into the Truckee River to control the surface level of the lake. You can spot giant trout in the river from

Fanny Bridge, so-called for the views of the backsides of sightseers leaning over the railing.

ESSENTIALS

Visitor Information **North Lake Tahoe Resort Association** (*Box 1757, Tahoe City 96145 530/583–3494 www.puretahoenorth.com*).

EXPLORING

★ The **Gatekeeper's Cabin Museum** preserves a little-known part of the region's history. Between 1910 and 1968 the gatekeeper who lived on this site was responsible for monitoring the level of the lake, using a hand-turned winch system to keep the water at the correct level. That winch system is still used today. The site is also home to a fantastic Native American basket museum that displays 800 baskets from 85 tribes and is reason enough to visit. *130 W. Lake Blvd. 530/583–1762 www.northtahoemuseums.org $3 May–mid-June and Sept., Wed.–Sun. 11–5; mid-June–Aug., daily 11–5; Oct.–Apr., weekends 11–3.*

In the middle of town the **Watson Cabin Living Museum,** a 1909 log cabin built by Robert M. Watson and his son, is filled with some century-old furnishings and many reproductions. Docents are available to answer questions and will lead tours with advance arrangements. *560 N. Lake Blvd. 530/583–8717 or 530/583–1762 www.northtahoemuseums.org $2 donation suggested Late May–June, weekends noon–4; July–early Sept., Wed.–Mon. noon–4.*

WHERE TO EAT

$$–$$$$ AMERICAN **Christy Hill.** Sit near the fireplace in the sparsely decorated, whitewashed dining room or outside on the deck, and take in mesmerizing lake views while dining on solid Euro–Cal preparations of fresh seafood, filet mignon, or vegetarian selections. An extensive wine list and exceptionally good desserts earn accolades, as do the gracious service and casual vibe. And oh, those lake views. Come early to see the sunset—and you'll understand why the entrée prices are so high. *Lakehouse Mall, 115 Grove St. 530/583–8551 Reservations essential AE, MC, V Closed Mon. No lunch.*

$$–$$$ ITALIAN **Fiamma.** Join the hip young singles at the little wine bar, or settle into one of the comfy booths at this modern mom-and-pop trattoria that specializes in roasted and grilled meats, homemade pastas, and pizzas from the wood-fired oven. Prices run a bit high, but this is generally a good bet for a casual, easy dinner. And everything from soup stock to gelato is made from scratch. For a sure bet, stick to the crispy, delicious pizzas. *521 N. Lake Blvd. 530/581–1416 AE, MC, V No lunch.*

¢–$ AMERICAN ★ **Fire Sign Café.** Watch the road carefully or you'll miss this great little diner 2 mi south of Tahoe City on Highway 89. There's often a wait at the west shore's best spot for breakfast and lunch, but it's worth it. The pastries are made from scratch, the salmon is smoked in-house, the salsa is hand cut, and there's real maple syrup for the many flavors of pancakes and waffles. The eggs Benedict are delicious. *1785 W. Lake Blvd. 530/583–0871 Reservations not accepted AE, MC, V No dinner.*

$$$–$$$$ ECLECTIC ★ **Wolfdale's.** Going strong since 1978, Wolfdale's offers consistent, inspired cuisine that makes it one of the top restaurants on the lake. Seafood is the specialty on the changing menu; the imaginative entrées merge Asian and European cooking (drawing on the chef-owner's training in Japan) and trend toward light and healthful, rather than heavy and overdone. And everything from teriyaki glaze to smoked fish is made in-house. Request a window table, and book early enough to see the lake view from the elegantly sparse dining room. *640 N. Lake Blvd. 530/583–5700 Reservations essential MC, V Closed Tues. and Wed. No lunch.*

WHERE TO STAY

$$–$$$$ **Cottage Inn.** Avoid the crowds by staying just south of town in one of these charming circa-1938 log cottages under the towering pines on the lake's west shore. Cute as a button, with knotty-pine paneling, rustic pine furniture, and a gas-flame stone fireplace, each unit is decorated in old-Tahoe style while embracing you with up-to-date comfort. If you're exceptionally tall, you may find some of the sloped ceilings in the upstairs rooms a bit low (ask for a downstairs room when you book). There's also a private beach and Wi-Fi in the lobby. **Pros:** romantic, woodsy setting; each room has a fireplace. **Cons:** no kids under 12. *1690 W. Lake Blvd., Box 66 530/581–4073 or 800/581–4073 www.thecottageinn.com 23 rooms In-room: no a/c, no phone, DVD (some). In-hotel: beachfront, Wi-Fi, no kids under 12, no-smoking rooms MC, V BP.*

$$–$$$ **River Ranch Lodge.** In a bend of the Truckee River, this intimate lodge is a short distance from major ski resorts and the town center. Each of the rooms has rustic pine furnishings and comfy bedding; most overlook the river. In summer you can watch rafts skim the rapids while enjoying the daily barbecue lunch on the patio. Fuel up for a day on the slopes with a complimentary continental breakfast. **Pros:** beautiful site on the Truckee River; great lounge with a gorgeous curved wall of windows. **Cons:** rooms fill quickly. *Hwy. 89, at Alpine Meadows Rd., Tahoe City 530/583–4264 or 866/991–9912 www.riverranchlodge.com 19 rooms In-room: no a/c, Wi-Fi. In-hotel: restaurant, bar, Wi-Fi AE, MC, V CP.*

$$$–$$$$ ★ **Sunnyside Steakhouse and Lodge.** The views are superb at this pretty little lodge right on the lake, 3 mi south of Tahoe City. All but four rooms have balconies and locally crafted furnishings; some have river-rock fireplaces and wet bars, and some have pull-out sofas. While the lodge is great for couples, families also favor it because of its proximity to kid-friendly Homewood Mountain Resort in winter and water sports and hiking in summer. The inviting Sunnyside Steakhouse ($$$–$$$$) echoes the design of old mahogany Chris Craft speedboats. The pricey steak, seafood, and pasta menu will thin out your wallet a bit; the Mountain Grill is a less expensive option, a good choice for those with kids in tow. Be forewarned: this is *not* a quiet place on summer weekends. The bar is a blast, and gets packed with boaters and Bacchanalian revelers. **Pros:** complimentary continental breakfast and afternoon tea; most rooms have balconies overlooking the lake. **Cons:** can be pricey for families. *1850 W. Lake Blvd., Box 5969 530/583–7200 or*

800/822–2754 ⊕www.sunnysideresort.com ⇨18 rooms, 5 suites ☝In-room: no a/c, Wi-Fi. In-hotel: restaurant, room service, bar, beachfront, Wi-Fi, no-smoking rooms ▭AE, D, MC, V ⓘCP.

SPORTS AND THE OUTDOORS

GOLF Golfers use pull carts or caddies at the 9-hole **Tahoe City Golf Course** (✉*252 N. Lake Blvd.* ☎*530/583–1516*), which opened in 1917. ■ **TIP→ All greens break toward the lake.**

Though rates vary by season, the maximum greens fees are $45 for 9 holes, $75 for 18; a power cart costs $18 to $30.

MOUNTAIN BIKING **Cyclepaths Mountain Bike Adventures** (✉*1785 W. Lake Blvd.* ☎*530/581–1171* ⊕*www.cyclepaths.com*) is a combination full-service bike shop and bike-adventure outfitter. It offers instruction in mountain biking, guided tours (from half-day to weeklong excursions), tips for self-guided bike touring, bike repairs, and books and maps on the area.

RIVER RAFTING In summer you can take a self-guided raft trip down a gentle 5-mi stretch of the Truckee River through **Truckee River Rafting** (☎*530/583–7238 or 888/584–7238* ⊕*www.truckeeriverrafting.com*). They will shuttle you back to Tahoe City at the end of your two- to four-hour trip. On a warm day, this makes a great family outing.

SKIING ★ The locals' favorite place to ski on the north shore, **Alpine Meadows Ski Area** is also the unofficial telemarking hub of the Sierra. With 495 inches of snow annually, Alpine has some of Tahoe's most reliable conditions. It's usually one of the first areas to open in November and one of the last to close in May or June. Alpine isn't the place for arrogant show-offs; instead, you'll find down-to-earth alpine fetishists. The two peaks here are well suited to intermediate skiers, with a number of runs for experts only. Snowboarders and hot-dog skiers will find a terrain park with a half-pipe, super-pipe, rails, and tabletops, as well as a boarder-cross course. Alpine is a great place to learn to ski, and the Tahoe Adaptive Ski School here teaches and coaches those with physical and mental disabilities. There's also an area for overnight RV parking. On Saturday, because of the limited parking, there's more acreage per person than at other resorts. ✉*2600 Alpine Meadows Rd., off Hwy. 89, 6 mi northwest of Tahoe City and 13 mi south of I–80* ☎*530/583–4232, 800/441–4423, 530/581–8374 snow phone* ⊕*www.skialpine.com* ☞*100 trails on 2,400 acres, rated 25% beginner, 40% intermediate, 35% advanced. Longest run 2½ mi, base 6,835 feet, summit 8,637 feet. Lifts: 14, including 1 high-speed 6-passenger lift and 2 high-speed quads.*

You can rent skis, boards, and snowshoes at **Tahoe Dave's Skis and Boards** (✉*590 N. Lake Blvd.* ☎*530/583–0400*), which has the area's best selection of downhill rental equipment. If you plan to ski or board the backcountry, you'll find everything from crampons to transceivers at **The BackCountry** (✉*690 N. Lake Blvd.* ☎*530/582–0909, 888/625–8444* ⊕*www.thebackcountry.net*).

TAHOE SPORTS TIPS

If you're planning to spend any time outdoors around Lake Tahoe, whether hiking, climbing, or camping, be aware that weather conditions can change quickly in the Sierra. To avoid a life-threatening case of hypothermia, always bring a pocket-size, fold-up rain poncho (available in all sporting-goods stores) to keep you dry. Wear long pants and a hat. Carry plenty of water. Because you'll likely be walking on granite, wear sturdy, closed-toe hiking boots, with soles that grip rock. If you're going into the backcountry, bring a signaling device (such as a mirror), emergency whistle, compass, map, energy bars, and water purifier. When heading out alone, tell someone where you're going and when you're coming back.

If you plan to ski, be aware of resort elevations. In the event of a winter storm, determine the snow level before you choose the resort you'll ski. Often the level can be as high as 7,000 feet, which means rain at some resorts' base areas but snow at others. For storm information, check the **National Weather Service's Web page** (🌐 *www.wrh.noaa.gov/rev*). If you plan to do any backcountry skiing, check with the **U.S. Forest Service** (☎ *530/587-2158 backcountry recording*) for conditions. A shop called the **Backcountry** (☎ *530/581-5861 Tahoe City, 530/582-0909 Truckee* 🌐 *www.thebackcountry.net*), with branches in Tahoe City and Truckee, operates an excellent Web site with current information about how and where to (and where not to) ski, mountain bike, and hike in the backcountry around Tahoe.

If you plan to camp in the backcountry, you'll need to purchase a wilderness permit, which you can pick up at the **Lake Tahoe Visitor Center** (✉ *Hwy. 89* ☎ *530/543-2600* 🌐 *www.fs.fed.us/r5/ltbmu*) or at a ranger station at the entrance to any of the national forests. For reservations at campgrounds in California state parks, contact **Reserve America** (☎ *800/444-7275* 🌐 *www.reserveamerica.com*).

OLYMPIC VALLEY

7 mi north of Tahoe City via Hwy. 89 to Squaw Valley Rd.; 8½ mi south of Truckee via Hwy. 89 to Squaw Valley Rd.

Olympic Valley got its name in 1960, when Squaw Valley USA, the ski resort here, hosted the winter Olympics. Snow sports remain the primary activity, but once summer comes you can hike into the adjacent Granite Chief Wilderness, explore wildflower-studded alpine meadows, or lie by a swimming pool in one of the Sierra's prettiest valleys.

EXPLORING

The centerpiece of Olympic Valley is the **Village at Squaw Valley** (☎ *530/584-1000, 530/584-6205, 888/805-5022 condo reservations* 🌐 *www.thevillageatsquaw.com*), a pedestrian mall at the base of several four-story ersatz Bavarian stone-and-timber buildings, where you'll find restaurants, high-end condo rentals, boutiques, and cafés. The village often holds events and festivals.

Squaw Valley USA has runs for skiers of all ability levels—from beginner trails to cliff drops for experts.

You can ride the Squaw Valley cable car to **High Camp,** which at 8,200 feet commands superb views of Lake Tahoe and the surrounding mountains. In summer, go for a hike, sit by the pool at the High Camp Bath and Tennis Club, or have a cocktail and watch the sunset. In winter you can ski, ice-skate, or snow-tube. There's also a restaurant, lounge, and small Olympics museum. ✉ *Cable Car Bldg., Squaw Valley* ☎ *530/581–7278 High Camp, 530/583–6985 cable car* 🌐 *www.squaw.com* *Cable car $22; special packages include swimming or skating* ⏲ *Daily; call for hrs.*

WHERE TO EAT

$$–$$$$ ECLECTIC ✕ **Graham's of Squaw Valley.** Sit by a floor-to-ceiling river-rock hearth under a knotty-pine peaked ceiling in the intimate dining room in the Christy Inn Lodge. The southern European–inspired menu changes often, but expect hearty entrées such as fillet of beef and venison with lingonberry demi-glace, along with lighter-fare small plates like grilled quail or sea scallops. You can also stop in at the fireside bar for appetizers and wine from Graham's huge and highly regarded wine list. ✉ *1650 Squaw Valley Rd.* ☎ *530/581–0454* *Reservations essential* ▭ *AE, MC, V* ⏲ *Closed Mon. No lunch.*

$$–$$$ JAPANESE ✕ **Mamasake.** The hip and happening spot for sushi at Squaw serves stylized presentations in an industrial-warehouse-like room. In the evening, sit at the bar and watch extreme ski movies, many of which were filmed right outside the window. Or drop in from 3 PM to 5 PM to enjoy the incredibly inexpensive afternoon special: a spicy-tuna or salmon hand roll and a can of Bud for five bucks. ✉ *The Village at Squaw Valley* ☎ *530/584–0110* ▭ *AE, MC, V.*

$$$–$$$$ AMERICAN Fodor'sChoice ★ **PlumpJack Café.** The best restaurant at Olympic Valley is also the finest in the entire Tahoe Basin, the epitome of discreet chic and a must-visit for all serious foodies. The menu changes seasonally, but look for Dungeness crab cones with cashews and tangerine dressing, crispy veal sweetbreads, stuffed venison loin with fig jam, or grass-fed beef tenderloin. Rather than complicated, heavy sauces, the chef uses simple reductions to complement a dish. The result: clean, dynamic, bright flavors. The wine list is exceptional for its variety and surprisingly low prices. If not for the view of the craggy mountains through the windows lining the cushy, 60-seat dining room, you might swear you were in San Francisco. A less expensive but equally adventurous menu is served at the bar. *1920 Squaw Valley Rd., Olympic Valley 530/583–1578 or 800/323–7666 Reservations essential AE, D, MC, V.*

13

WHERE TO STAY

$$$–$$$$ Fodor'sChoice ★ **PlumpJack Squaw Valley Inn.** If style and luxury are a must, make PlumpJack your first choice. The two-story, cedar-sided inn near the cable car has a snappy, sophisticated look and laid-back sensibility, perfect for the Bay Area cognoscenti who flock here on weekends. All rooms have sumptuous beds with down comforters, high-end bath amenities, and hooded terry robes to wear on your way to the outdoor hot tubs. The bar is a happening après-ski destination, and the namesake restaurant *(⇨above)* superb. PlumpJack may not have the bells and whistles of big luxury hotels, but the service—personable and attentive—can't be beat. Not all rooms have tubs: if it matters, request one. A complimentary buffet breakfast for two is included. **Pros:** small; intimate; lots of attention to details. **Cons:** not the best choice for families with small children. *1920 Squaw Valley Rd., Olympic Valley 530/583–1576 or 800/323–7666 www.plumpjack.com 56 rooms, 5 suites In-room: no a/c (some), refrigerator, DVD, Wi-Fi. In-hotel: restaurant, room service, bar, pool, gym, bicycles, Wi-Fi, parking (free), no-smoking rooms AE, D, MC, V BP.*

$$$–$$$$ **Resort at Squaw Creek.** Completely redesigned and refurbished in 2005, the rooms at this vast 650-acre resort-within-a-resort are done up in warm earth tones, with attractive wooden furnishings and rich fabrics. The resort has been converted into a condo hotel, and about half the units are fireplace suites with kitchens. The black-glass-and-concrete architecture may look more like Scottsdale than the Sierra, but the extensive facilities have all the amenities and services you could possibly want in the Tahoe area, making it good for large groups and families year-round. In winter the resort operates its own chairlift to the mountain. **Pros:** every conceivable amenity; private chairlift. **Cons:** very large; very pricey. *400 Squaw Creek Rd. 96146 530/583–6300 or 800/327–3353 www.squawcreek.com 203 rooms, 200 suites In-room: kitchen (some), refrigerator, Wi-Fi. In-hotel: 4 restaurants, room service, bar, golf course, tennis courts, pools, gym, spa, children's programs (ages 4–12), laundry service, Wi-Fi, parking (free), no-smoking rooms AE, D, DC, MC, V.*

$$$–$$$$ **The Village at Squaw Valley USA.** Right at the base of the slopes at the center point of Olympic Valley, the Village's studios and one-, two-, or three-bedroom condominiums were built in 2000 and still look fresh.

Each unit comes complete with gas fireplace, daily maid service, and heated slate-tile bathroom floors. The individually owned units are uniformly decorated with granite counters, wood cabinets, and comfortable furnishings. They're especially appealing to families, since each condo can sleep at least four people. **Pros:** family-friendly; near Village restaurants and shops. **Cons:** claustrophobia-inducing crowds. ✉*1750 Village East Rd. 96146* ☎*530/584–1000 or 866/818–6963* 🌐*www.thevillageatsquaw.com* *290 suites* *In-room: no a/c, kitchen, DVD, Internet. In-hotel: laundry facilities, Wi-Fi, parking (free), no-smoking rooms* *AE, D, DC, MC, V.*

SPORTS AND THE OUTDOORS

GOLF The **Resort at Squaw Creek Golf Course** (✉*400 Squaw Creek Rd.* ☎*530/583–6300* 🌐*www.squawcreek.com*), an 18-hole championship course, was designed by Robert Trent Jones Jr. Greens fees range from $60 for afternoon play to $115 for prime time, and include the use of a cart.

HIKING The Granite Chief Wilderness and the high peaks surrounding Olympic Valley are accessible by foot, but save yourself a 2,000-foot elevation gain by riding the Squaw Valley cable car to **High Camp** (☎*530/583–6985* 🌐*www.squaw.com*), the starting point for a variety of hikes. Pick up trail maps at the cable-car building. In late summer, High Camp offers full-moon and sunset hikes.

ICE-SKATING Ice-skate from November to late September at the **Olympic Ice Pavilion** (✉*High Camp, Squaw Valley* ☎*530/583–6985 or 530/581–7246* 🌐*www.squaw.com*). A ride up the mountain and a skating pass cost $27, including skate rental; pay $5 extra to end your outing in the hot tub. Prices drop after 5 PM in winter.

ROCK CLIMBING Before you rappel down a granite monolith, hone your skills at the **Headwall Climbing Wall** (✉*Near Village at Squaw Valley* ☎*530/583–7673*), at the base of the cable car.

★ Next to the Olympic Village Lodge, on the far side of the creek, the **Squaw Valley Adventure Center** (☎*530/583–7673*) has a ropes course, a 50-foot tower, an 18-hole miniature golf course, a giant swing, and sometimes a bungee-trampoline, a blast for kids.

SKIING Fodor'sChoice ★ Known for some of the toughest skiing in the Tahoe area, **Squaw Valley USA** was the centerpiece of the 1960 winter Olympics. Today it's the definitive North Tahoe ski resort and among the top-three megaresorts in California (the other two are Heavenly and Mammoth). Although Squaw has changed significantly since the Olympics, the skiing is still world-class and extends across vast bowls stretched between six peaks. Experts often head directly to the untamed terrain of the infamous KT-22 face, which has bumps, cliffs, and gulp-and-go chutes, or to the nearly vertical Palisades, where many famous Warren Miller extreme-skiing films have been shot. Fret not, beginners and intermediates: you have plenty of wide-open, groomed trails at High Camp (which sits at the *top* of the mountain) and around the more challenging Snow King Peak. Snowboarders and show-off skiers can tear up the three fantastic terrain parks, which include a giant super-pipe. Lift prices include night skiing until 9 PM. Tickets for skiers 12 and under cost only $10. ✉*1960 Squaw Valley Rd., off Hwy. 89, Olympic Valley, 7 mi northwest of Tahoe City* ☎*530/583–6985, 800/545–4350 lodging reservations, 530/583–6955 snow phone* 🌐*www.squaw.com* ☞*170 trails on 4,000 acres, rated 25% beginner, 45% intermediate, 30% advanced. Longest run 3.2 mi, base 6,200 feet, summit 9,050 feet. Lifts: 34, including a gondola-style funitel, a cable car, 7 high-speed chairs, and 18 fixed-grip chairs.*

If you don't want to pay resort prices, you can rent and tune downhill skis and snowboards at **Tahoe Dave's Skis and Boards** (✉*Squaw Valley Rd., at Hwy. 89* ☎*530/583–5665* 🌐*www.tahoedaves.com*).

Cross-country skiers will enjoy looping through the valley's giant alpine meadow. The **Resort at Squaw Creek** (✉*400 Squaw Creek Rd.* ☎*530/583–6300* 🌐*www.squawcreek.com*) rents cross-country equipment and provides trail maps.

TRUCKEE

13 mi northwest of Kings Beach on Hwy. 267; 14 mi north of Tahoe City on Hwy. 89.

Formerly a decrepit railroad town in the mountains, Truckee is now the trendy first stop for many Tahoe visitors. Around 1863 the town was officially established; by 1868 it had gone from a stagecoach station to a major stopover for trains bound for the Pacific via the new transcontinental railroad. Freight trains and Amtrak's California Zephyr still stop every day at the depot right in the middle of town. Across from the station, where Old West facades line the main drag, you'll find galleries, gift shops, boutiques, old-fashioned diners, and several remarkably good restaurants. Look for outlet stores, strip malls, and discount skiwear shops along Donner Pass Road, north of the freeway. Because of its location on I–80, Truckee is a favorite stopover for people traveling from the San Francisco Bay Area to the north shore of Lake Tahoe, Reno, and points east.

ESSENTIALS

Visitor Information **Truckee Donner Chamber of Commerce** (✉*10065 Donner Pass Rd., Truckee, CA* ☎*530/587–8808* 🌐*www.truckee.com*).

EXPLORING

Stop by the downtown **information booth** (✉*Railroad St., at Commercial Rd.*) in the Amtrak depot for a walking-tour map of historic Truckee.

Donner Memorial State Park and Emigrant Trail Museum commemorates the Donner Party, a group of 89 westward-bound pioneers who were trapped in the Sierra in the winter of 1846–47 in snow 22 feet deep. The top of the stone pedestal beneath the monument marks the snow level that year. Only 49 pioneers survived, some by resorting to cannibalism, though none consumed his own kin. (For the full story, pick up a copy of *Ordeal by Hunger*, by George R. Stewart.) The museum's hourly slide show details the Donner Party's plight. Other displays and dioramas relate the history of railroad development through the Sierra.

In the park you can picnic, hike, camp, and go boating, fishing, and waterskiing in summer; winter brings cross-country skiing and snowshoeing on groomed trails. The day-use parking fee includes admission to the museum. ✉ *Donner Pass Rd., off I–80, 2 mi west of Truckee* ☎ *530/582–7892 museum, 800/444–7275 camping reservations* 🌐 *www.parks.ca.gov* 🎫 *$6 parking, day use* 🕐 *Museum daily 9–4.*

OFF THE BEATEN PATH

Tahoe National Forest. Draped along the Sierra Nevada Crest above Lake Tahoe, the national forest offers abundant outdoor recreation: picnicking and camping in summer, and in winter, snowshoeing, skiing, and sledding over some of the deepest snowpack in the West. The **Big Bend Visitor Center** occupies a state historic landmark within the forest, 10 mi west of Donner Summit. Exhibits in the visitor center explore the area's transportation history. Take the Rainbow–Big Bend exit off I–80. ✉ *U.S. 40, Soda Springs* ☎ *530/426–3609 or 530/265–4531* 🌐 *www.fs.fed.us/r5/tahoe/recreation* 🎫 *Free* 🕐 *Hrs vary; call ahead.*

WHERE TO EAT

$$–$$$$ ECLECTIC

✕ **Cottonwood.** Perched above town on the site of North America's first chairlift, the Cottonwood restaurant is a veritable institution. The bar is decked out with old wooden skis, sleds, skates, and photos of Truckee's early days. The dining area serves an ambitious menu—everything from grilled New York strip steak to Thai red curry prawns, plus fresh-baked breads and desserts—but people come here mainly for the atmosphere and hilltop views. There's live music on weekends. ✉ *Old Brockway Rd., off Hwy. 267, ¼ mi south of downtown* ☎ *530/587–5711* 💳 *D, MC, V* 🕐 *No lunch.*

$$–$$$$ ASIAN ★

✕ **Dragonfly.** Flavors are bold and zingy at this old-town, Cal-Asian spot, where every dish is artfully prepared and stylishly presented—and most importantly, well executed. The bright tones of Southeast Asian cooking inspire most dishes on the changing menu, which you can savor in the bright, contemporary dining rooms—one for sushi—or an outdoor terrace overlooking Main Street and the train depot. Lunch is a bargain, and there are lots of choices for vegetarians. Look for the staircase: the restaurant is on the second floor, not street level. ✉ *10118 Donner Pass Rd.* ☎ *530/587–0557* 💳 *D, MC, V.*

$–$$$ AMERICAN

✕ **FiftyFifty Brewing Company.** In this Truckee brewpub warm red tones and comfy booths, plus a pint of their Donner Party Porter, will take the nip out of a cold day on the slopes. The menu includes salads, pasta, burgers, and the house specialty, a pulled pork sandwich. After 5 PM you can tuck into entrées like barbecued ribs, steak, and caramelized yellowfin tuna. There's a full bar along with the brews, and lots of après-ski action. ✉ *11197 Brockway Rd.* ☎ *530/587–2337* 💳 *AE, D, MC, V.*

$$–$$$$ ECLECTIC ★

✕ **Moody's.** Head here for contemporary-Cal cuisine in a sexy dining room with pumpkin-color walls, burgundy velvet banquettes, and art-deco fixtures. The chef-owner's earthy, sure-handed cooking features organically grown ingredients: look for ahi tuna "four ways," house-made charcuterie samplings, pan-roasted wild game, fresh seafood, and Niman Ranch steak. Lunch fare is lighter. In summer, dine alfresco surrounded by flowers. Wednesday through Saturday there's live music in the borderline-raucous bar that gets packed with Truckee's bon vivants. ✉*10007 Bridge St.* ☎*530/587–8688* ▭*AE, D, MC, V.*

WHERE TO STAY

$$$–$$$$ **Cedar House Sport Hotel.** Built in 2006, Cedar House ups the ante for lodging at Tahoe. Outside, the clean, spare lines of the wooden exterior evoke a modern European feel. Inside, energy-saving heating, cooling, and lighting systems, countertops made from recycled paper, and other green features emphasize the owners' commitment to sustainability. Rooms in the three two-story satellite buildings are understatedly sexy with merlot-and-camel color schemes and mod-Italian overtones (think chrome and leather). Although not all rooms have tubs, heated-tile bathroom floors, goose-down duvets, and comfy cotton robes are luxurious extras. Ask about outdoor-sports trips when you book. **Pros:** an environmentally friendly facility that's also comfortable and hip. **Cons:** some bathrooms are on the small side. ✉*10918 Brockway Rd.,* ☎*530/582–5655* or *866/582–5655* 🌐*www.cedarhousesporthotel.com* *42 rooms* *In-room: safe, refrigerator, Wi-Fi. In-hotel: bar, Wi-Fi, parking (free), no-smoking rooms* ▭*AE, D, DC, MC, V* *CP.*

$$$–$$$$ **Northstar-at-Tahoe Resort.** The area's most complete destination resort is perfect for families, thanks to its many sports activities—from golf and tennis to skiing and snowshoeing—and its concentration of restaurants, shops, recreation facilities, and accommodations (the Village Mall). Lodgings range from hotel rooms to condos to private houses, some with ski-in, ski-out access. The list continues to grow: Northstar has been building lots of new condos, plus a new Ritz-Carlton. Lodging options often include free lift tickets, on-site shuttle transportation, and complimentary access to the Swim and Racquet Club's pools, outdoor hot tubs, and fitness center. TC's Pub ($$–$$$, open winter only) serves contemporary American fare. **Pros:** vast array of lodging types; on-site shuttle. **Cons:** family accommodations are very pricey. ✉*Hwy. 267, 6 mi southeast of Truckee, Box 129* ☎*530/562–1010 or 800/466–6784* 🌐*www.northstarattahoe.com* *240 units* *In-room: no a/c (some), kitchen (some), DVD, Internet (some). In-hotel: 3 restaurants, golf course, tennis courts, pool, gym, bicycles, children's programs (ages 2–6), laundry facilities, no-smoking rooms* ▭*AE, D, MC, V.*

$$ **River Street Inn.** On the banks of the Truckee River, this 1885 wood-and-stone inn was at times a boardinghouse and a brothel. Now completely modernized, the uncluttered, comfortable rooms are simply decorated, with attractive, country-style wooden furniture and extras like flat-screen TVs. The cushy beds have top-quality mattresses, down comforters, and high-thread-count sheets. Bathrooms have claw-foot tubs. The affable off-site proprietors are there when you need them. **Pros:** nice rooms; good value. **Cons:** parking is a half-block from inn. ✉*10009 E. River St.* ☎*530/550–9290* 🌐*www.riverstreetinntruckee.com* *11 rooms* *In-room: no a/c, no phone, Wi-Fi. In-hotel: Wi-Fi, no-smoking rooms* ▭*MC, V* *CP.*

SPORTS AND THE OUTDOORS

GOLF The **Coyote Moon Golf Course** (✉*10685 Northwoods Blvd.* ☎*530/587–0886* 🌐*www.coyotemoongolf.com*) is both challenging and beautiful, with no houses to spoil the view. Fees range from $100 to $160, including cart.

Northstar (✉ *Hwy. 267* ☎ *530/562–3290*) has open links–style play and tight, tree-lined fairways, including water hazards. Fees range from $40 to $80, including cart. At **Old Greenwood** (✉ *12915 Fairway Dr., off the Overland Trail exit—Exit 190—from I–80; call for specific directions* ☎ *530/550–7010* 🌐 *www.oldgreenwood.com*), north Lake Tahoe's only Jack Nicklaus signature course, the water hazards are trout streams where you can actually fish. The $100–$185 fee includes a cart.

MOUNTAIN BIKING

In summer you can rent a bike and ride the lifts up the mountain at **Northstar-at-Tahoe** (✉ *Hwy. 267, at Northstar Dr.* ☎ *530/562–2268* 🌐 *www.northstarattahoe.com*) for 100 mi of challenging terrain. A ride to the mountain-biking park on the lift is $49 for ages 13 and above; $29 for ages 9–12. The season extends from July through September with varying hours; call for times.

SKIING

Several smaller resorts around Truckee give you access to the Sierra's slopes for less than half the price of the big resorts. Though you'll sacrifice vertical rise, acreage, and high-speed lifts, you can ski or ride and still have money left over for room and board. These are great places for first-timers and families with kids learning to ski.

Boreal (✉ *Boreal/Castle Peak exit off I–80* ☎ *530/426–3666* 🌐 *www.borealski.com*) has 380 acres and 500 vertical feet of terrain visible from the freeway; there's also lift-served snow-tubing and night skiing until 9. **Donner Ski Ranch** (✉ *19320 Donner Pass Rd., Norden* ☎ *530/426–3635* 🌐 *www.donnerskiranch.com*) has 460 acres and 750 vertical feet and sits across from the more challenging Sugar Bowl (*⇨ below*). **Soda Springs** (✉ *Soda Springs exit off 1–80, Soda Springs* ☎ *530/426–3901* 🌐 *www.skisodasprings.com*) has 200 acres and 652 vertical feet and lift-served snow-tubing. **Tahoe Donner** (✉ *11603 Slalom Way* ☎ *530/587–9444* 🌐 *www.tahoedonner.com*) is just north of Truckee and covers 120 acres and 560 vertical feet; the cross-country center includes 51 trails on 114 km (71 mi) of groomed tracks on 4,800 acres, with night skiing on Wednesdays January and February.

Northstar-at-Tahoe may be the best all-around family ski resort at Tahoe. With two tree-lined, northeast-facing, wind-protected bowls, it's the ideal place to ski in a storm. Hotshot experts unfairly call the mountain "Flatstar," but the meticulous grooming and long cruisers make it an intermediate skier's paradise. Boarders are especially welcome, with awesome terrain parks, including a 420-foot-long super-pipe, a half-pipe, rails and boxes, and lots of kickers. Experts can ski the steeps and bumps off Lookout Mountain, where there's rarely a line for the high-speed quad. Northstar-at-Tahoe's cross-country center has 40 km (25 mi) of groomed trails, including double-set tracks and skating lanes. The school has programs for skiers ages four and up, and day care is available for tots two and older. The mountain gets packed on busy weekends but when there's room on the slopes Northstar is loads of fun. (*See "Skiing and Snowboarding" at the beginning of this chapter for alternatives on busy days.*) ✉ *Hwy. 267, 6 mi southeast of Truckee* ☎ *530/562–1010 or 800/466–6784, 530/562–1330 snow phone* 🌐 *www.northstarattahoe.com* ☞ *89 trails on 2,904 acres, rated 13% beginner, 60% intermediate, 27% advanced. Longest run 1.4 mi, base*

6,330 feet, summit 8,610 feet. Lifts: 18, including a gondola and 6 high-speed quads.

Opened in 1939 by Walt Disney, **Sugar Bowl** is the oldest—and one of the best—resort at Tahoe. Atop Donner Summit, it receives an incredible 500 inches of snowfall annually. Four peaks are connected by 1,500 acres of skiable terrain, with everything from gentle groomed corduroy to wide-open bowls to vertical rocky chutes and outstanding tree skiing. Snowboarders can hit two terrain parks and a 20-foot-high by 450-foot-long super-pipe. Because it's more compact than some of the area's megaresorts, there's a certain gentility here that distinguishes Sugar Bowl from its competitors, making this a great place for families and a low-pressure, low-key place to learn to ski. It's not huge, but there's some very challenging terrain (experts: head to the Palisades). There's limited lodging at the base area. This is the closest resort to San Francisco (three hours via I–80). ☒*Donner Pass Rd., 3 mi east of Soda Springs/Norden exit off I–80, 10 mi west of Truckee* ☎*530/426–9000 information and lodging reservations, 530/426–1111 snow phone, 866/843–2695 lodging referral* 🌐*www.sugarbowl.com* ☞*84 trails on 1,500 acres, rated 17% beginner, 45% intermediate, 38% advanced. Longest run 3 mi, base 6,883 feet, summit 8,383 feet. Lifts: 12, including 5 high-speed quads.*

13

For the ultimate in groomed conditions, head to the nation's largest ★ cross-country ski resort, **Royal Gorge** (☒*Soda Springs/Norden exit off I–80, Soda Springs* ☎*530/426–3871* 🌐*www.royalgorge.com*). It has 308 km (191 mi) of 18-foot-wide track for all abilities, 90 trails on a whopping 9,172 acres, two ski schools, and eight warming huts. Three trailside cafés, two lodges, and a hot tub and sauna round out the facilities. Since it's right on the Sierra Crest, the views are drop-dead gorgeous, and the resort feels like it goes on forever. If you love to cross-country, don't miss Royal Gorge.

You can save money by renting skis and boards at **Tahoe Dave's** (☒*10200 Donner Pass Rd.* ☎*530/582–0900*), which has the area's best selection and also repairs and tunes equipment.

CARNELIAN BAY TO KINGS BEACH

5–10 mi northeast of Tahoe City on Hwy. 28.

The small lakeside commercial districts of Carnelian Bay and Tahoe Vista service the thousand or so locals who live in the area year-round and the thousands more who have summer residences or launch their boats here. Kings Beach, the last town heading east on Highway 28 before the Nevada border, is to Crystal Bay what South Lake Tahoe is to Stateline: a bustling California town full of basic motels and rental condos, restaurants, and shops, used by the hordes of hopefuls who pass through on their way to the casinos.

The 28-acre **Kings Beach State Recreation Area,** one of the largest such areas on the lake, is open year-round. The 700-foot-long sandy beach gets very crowded with people swimming, sunbathing, jet skiing, riding in paddleboats, spiking volleyballs, and tossing Frisbees. If you're going to spend the day, come early enough to snag a table in the picnic area; there's also a good playground. ✉*N. Lake Blvd., Kings Beach* ☎*530/546–7248* *Free* ⏲*Daily.*

> **WORD OF MOUTH**
>
> "Here's my kayaking hint for Lake Tahoe: DON'T FALL IN! Because that water is COLD—even in July!!" —k2rider

WHERE TO EAT AND STAY

$$–$$$$ ECLECTIC ✕ **Gar Woods Grill and Pier.** The view's the thing at this lakeside stalwart, where you can watch the sun shimmer on the water through the dining room's plate-glass windows or from the heated outdoor deck. Grilled steak and fish are menu mainstays, but be sure to try Southwestern specialties like crab chilies rellenos and mahimahi fish tacos. At all hours in season the bar gets packed with boaters who pull up to the restaurant's private pier. ✉*5000 N. Lake Blvd., Carnelian Bay* ☎*530/546–3366* ▭*AE, D, MC, V.*

$$–$$$ AMERICAN ✕ **Spindleshanks.** This handsome roadhouse, decorated with floor-to-ceiling knotty pine, serves mostly classic American cooking—ribs, steaks, and seafood updated with adventurous sauces—as well as house-made ravioli. On cold nights request seating near the crackling fireplace and enjoy a drink from the full bar or the extensive wine list. ✉*6873 N. Lake Blvd, Tahoe Vista* ☎*530/546–2191* *Reservations essential* ▭*AE, MC, V* ⏲*No lunch.*

$–$$$ **Ferrari's Crown Resort.** One of the few remaining family-owned and -operated motels in Kings Beach, Ferrari's has straightforward motel rooms in a resort setting, great for families with kids. Comprised of two formerly separate vintage-1950s motels sitting side-by-side on the lake, Ferrari's is impeccably kept. It's not a fancy-pants place by any stretch, just a plain-old motel, but some of the rooms have awesome views, and for value you can't beat it. Kids love the two pools; adults enjoy the hot tubs. There are also kayak rentals on-site. **Pros:** family-friendly; lakeside location. **Cons:** older facility. ✉*8200 N. Lake Blvd., Kings Beach* ☎*530/546–3388 or 800/645–2260* ⊕*www.tahoecrown.com* *71 rooms* *In-room: no a/c (some), kitchen (some), refrigerator, Internet, Wi-Fi. In-hotel: pools, beachfront, no-smoking rooms* ▭*AE, D, MC, V* *CP.*

$$$–$$$$ ★ **Shore House.** Every room has a gas fireplace, down comforter, and featherbed at this lakefront B&B in Tahoe Vista. The lovingly tended, knotty-pine-paneled guest rooms beautifully and simply capture the woodsy spirit of Tahoe, but without overdoing the pinecone motif. All have private entrances and extra touches such as bathrobes, stereo CD players, down comforters, and rubber duckies in the bathtubs; many have great views of the water. There's also a private beach. Yes, it's pricey, but at how many places can you sip morning coffee while gazing out at the mist rising off the lake? **Pros:** waterfront honeymoon cottage; massage appointments available. **Cons:** pricey (even off-season). ✉*7170 N. Lake Blvd., Tahoe Vista* ☎*530/546–7270 or 800/207–5160* ⊕*www.shorehouselaketahoe.com* *8 rooms, 1 cottage* *In-room: no a/c, no phone, refrigerator, Wi-Fi (some). In-hotel: beachfront, Wi-Fi, no-smoking rooms* ▭*D, MC, V* *BP.*

NEVADA SIDE

CRYSTAL BAY

1 mi east of Kings Beach on Hwy. 28; 30 mi north of South Lake Tahoe via U.S. 50 to Hwy. 28.

Right at the Nevada border, Crystal Bay has a cluster of casinos that look essentially the same, but have a few minor differences. These casinos tend toward the tacky, and most of the lodging is pretty lackluster.

13

EXPLORING

The **Cal-Neva Lodge** (✉ *2 Stateline Rd.* ☎ *800/225–6382* 🌐 *www.calnevaresort.com*) is bisected by the state line. Opened in 1927, this joint has weathered many scandals, the largest involving former owner Frank Sinatra (he lost his gaming license in the 1960s for alleged mob connections). The secret tunnel that Frank built so that he could steal away unnoticed to Marilyn Monroe's cabin is definitely worth a look; call for tour times.

The **Tahoe Biltmore** (✉ *Hwy. 28, at Stateline Rd.* ☎ *800/245–8667* 🌐 *www.tahoebiltmore.com*) has live bands with dancing on weekends.

Jim Kelley's Tahoe Nugget (✉ *Hwy. 28, at Stateline Rd.* ☎ *775/831–0455*) serves nearly 100 kinds of beer.

The **Crystal Bay Club** (✉ *Hwy. 28, at Stateline Rd.* 🌐 *www.crystalbaycasino.com* ☎ *775/833–6333*) has a restaurant with a towering open-truss ceiling that looks like a wooden ship's hull.

WHERE TO STAY

$$–$$$ ECLECTIC ★ ✕ **Soule Domain.** Rough-hewn wood beams and a vaulted wood ceiling lend high romance to this cozy 1927 pine-log cabin beneath tall trees next to the Tahoe Biltmore. On the eclectic menu, chef-owner Charles Soule's specialties include curried cashew chicken, lamb ravioli, fresh sea scallops poached in champagne with kiwi and mango cream sauce, and a vegan sauté with ginger and jalapeños, but you'll find the chef's current passion in the always-great roster of nightly specials. Some find it a little pricey, but if you're looking for someplace with a solid menu and where you can hold hands by candlelight, this is it. In winter request a table near the crackling fireplace. ✉ *9983 Cove Ave., ½ block up Stateline Rd. from Hwy. 28, Kings Beach* ☎ *530/546–7529* ✍ *Reservations essential* 💳 *AE, D, MC, V* ⊙ *No lunch.*

INCLINE VILLAGE

3 mi east of Crystal Bay on Hwy. 28.

Incline Village, Nevada's only privately owned town, dates to the early 1960s, when an Oklahoma developer bought 10,000 acres north of Lake Tahoe. His idea was to sketch out a plan for a town without a central commercial district, hoping to prevent congestion and to preserve the area's natural beauty. One-acre lakeshore lots originally fetched $12,000 to $15,000; today you couldn't buy even the land for less than several million.

ESSENTIALS

Visitor Information **Lake Tahoe Incline Village/Crystal Bay Visitors Bureau** (*⊠969 Tahoe Blvd., Incline Village ☎775/832–1606 or 800/468–2463 ⊕www.gotahoenorth.com*).

EXPLORING

Check out **Lakeshore Drive,** along which you'll see some of the most expensive real estate in Nevada. The drive is discreetly marked: to find it, start at the Hyatt Hotel and drive westward along the lake.

Fodor's Choice ★

George Whittell, a San Francisco socialite who once owned 40,000 acres of property along the lake, built the **Thunderbird Lodge** in 1936. You can tour the mansion and the grounds by reservation only, and though it's pricey, it provides a rare glimpse back to a time when only the very wealthy had homes at Tahoe. The lodge is accessible via a bus from the Incline Village Visitors Bureau, a catamaran from the Hyatt in Incline Village, or a 1950 wooden cruiser from Tahoe Keys Marina in South Lake Tahoe (which includes lunch). *⊠5000 Hwy. 28 ☎775/832–8750 lodge; 800/468–2463 reservations; 775/588–1881 or 888/867–6394 Tahoe Keys boat; 775/832–1234 or 800/553–3288 Hyatt Incline Village boat ⊕www.thunderbirdlodge.org $39 bus tour, $110 boat tour ⊙May–Oct., call for tour times.*

OFF THE BEATEN PATH

Lake Tahoe–Nevada State Park. Protecting much of the lake's eastern shore from development, Lake Tahoe–Nevada State Park comprises several sections that stretch from Incline Village to Zephyr Cove. Beaches and trails provide access to a wilder side of the lake, whether you're into cross-country skiing, hiking, or just relaxing at a picnic. The east shore gets less snow and more sun than the west shore, making it a good early- or late-season outdoor destination. One of the most likable areas is **Sand Harbor Beach** (*⊠Hwy. 28, 3 mi south of Incline Village ☎775/831–0494 ⊕parks.nv.gov/lt.htm*). It's so popular that it's sometimes filled to capacity by 11 AM on summer weekends. Stroll the boardwalk and read the information signs for a good lesson in the local ecology. Pets are not allowed.

WHERE TO EAT AND STAY

$$$ ECLECTIC

✕**Frederick's.** Copper-top tables lend a chic look to the small dining room at this intimate bistro. The menu consists of a mélange of European and Asian cooking, mostly prepared using organic produce and free-range meats. Try the braised short ribs, sea bass with pineapple-ginger beurre blanc, duck confit with huckleberry, or the deliciously fresh sushi rolls. Ask for a table by the fire. *⊠907 Tahoe Blvd. ☎775/832–3007 Reservations essential ▭AE, MC, V ⊙Closed Sun. and Mon. No lunch.*

$$ FRENCH ★

✕**Le Bistro.** Incline Village's hidden gem, Le Bistro serves expertly prepared French-country cuisine in a relaxed, cozy, romantic dining room. The chef-owner makes everything himself, using organically grown ingredients, and changes the menu almost daily. Expect such dishes as pâté de campagne, baked tomato bisque en croute, escargots, and herb-crusted roast lamb loin. Try the five-course prix-fixe menu ($45), which can be paired with their award-winning wine selections. Service is gracious and attentive. Be sure to ask directions when you book, since the restaurant is hard to find. *⊠120 Country Club Dr.,*

Get to Sand Harbor Beach in Lake Tahoe–Nevada State Park early; the park sometimes fills to capacity before lunchtime in summer.

#29 ☎*775/831–0800* ▭*AE, D, MC, V* ⏲*Closed Sun. and Mon. No lunch.*

¢ SOUTHERN ✕ **T's Rotisserie.** There's nothing fancy about T's (it looks like a small snack bar), but the mesquite-grilled chicken and tri-tip steaks are delicious and inexpensive—a rare combination in pricey Incline Village. It's mainly a take-out spot; seating is limited. ✉*901 Tahoe Blvd.* ☎*775/831–2832* ▭*No credit cards.*

$$$–$$$$ **Hyatt Regency Lake Tahoe.** Once a dowdy casino hotel, the Hyatt underwent a $60 million renovation between 2001 and 2003 and is now a smart-looking, upmarket, full-service destination resort. On 26 acres of prime lakefront property, the resort has a nice range of luxurious accommodations, from tower-hotel rooms to lakeside cottages. The Lone Eagle Grille ($$$–$$$$) serves steaks and seafood in one of the north shore's handsomest lake-view dining rooms. There's also a state-of-the-art spa and fitness center. Standard rates are very high, but look for midweek or off-season discounts. **Pros:** incredible views; first-class spa. **Cons:** pricey (especially for families). ✉*Lakeshore and Country Club Drs.* ☎*775/832–1234 or 888/899–5019* 🌐*www.laketahoe.hyatt.com* *422 rooms, 28 suites* *In-room: safe, kitchen (some), refrigerator, Internet, Wi-Fi. In-hotel: 4 restaurants, room service, bars, pool, spa, beachfront, bicycles, children's programs (ages 3–12), laundry service, Wi-Fi, no-smoking rooms* ▭*AE, D, DC, MC, V.*

SPORTS AND THE OUTDOORS

GOLF **Incline Championship** (✉*955 Fairway Blvd.* ☎*866/925–4653* 🌐*www.inclinegolf.com*) is an 18-hole, par-72 Robert Trent Jones Sr. course with a driving range, both completely renovated between 2002 and

2004. The $174 greens fee includes an optional cart. **Incline Mountain** (✉*690 Wilson Way* ☎*866/925–4653* 🌐*www.inclinegolf.com*) is an executive (shorter) 18-hole course; par is 64. Greens fees start at $56, including optional cart.

MOUNTAIN BIKING You can rent bikes and get helpful tips from **Flume Trail Bikes** (✉*Spooner Summit, Hwy. 28, ¾ mi north of U.S. 50, Glenbrook* ☎*775/749–5349* 🌐*www.theflumetrail.com*), which also operates a bike shuttle to popular trailheads. Ask about the secluded backcountry rental cabins for overnight rides.

SKIING A fun family mood prevails at **Diamond Peak,** which has many special programs and affordable rates. Snowmaking covers 75% of the mountain, and runs are groomed nightly. The ride up the 1-mi Crystal chair rewards you with some of the best views of the lake from any ski area. Diamond Peak is less crowded than the larger areas and provides free shuttles to nearby lodging. It's a great place for beginners and intermediates, and it's appropriately priced for families. However, though there are some steep-aspect black-diamond runs, advanced skiers may find the acreage too limited. For snowboarders there's a half-pipe and super-pipe. ✉*1210 Ski Way, Incline Village* ☎*775/832–1177* 🌐*www.diamondpeak.com* ☞*30 trails on 655 acres, rated 18% beginner, 46% intermediate, 36% advanced. Longest run 2½ mi, base 6,700 feet, summit 8,540 feet. Lifts: 6, including 2 high-speed quads.*

Ski some of the highest slopes at Tahoe, and take in bird's-eye views of Reno and the Carson Valley at **Mt. Rose Ski Tahoe.** Though more compact than the bigger Tahoe resorts, Mt. Rose has the area's highest base elevation and consequently the driest snow. The mountain has a wide variety of terrain. The most challenging is the Chutes, 200 acres of gulp-and-go advanced-to-expert vertical. Intermediates can choose steep groomers or mellow, wide-open boulevards. Beginners have their own corner of the mountain, with gentle, nonthreatening, wide slopes. Boarders and tricksters have three terrain parks to choose from, on opposite sides of the mountain, allowing them to follow the sun as it tracks across the resort. Because of its elevation, the mountain gets hit hard in storms; check conditions before heading up during inclement weather or on a windy day. ✉*Hwy. 431, 11 mi north of Incline Village* ☎*775/849–0704 or 800/754–7673* 🌐*www.skirose.com* ☞*61 trails on 1,200 acres, rated 20% beginner, 30% intermediate, 40% advanced, 10% expert. Longest run 2½ mi, base 7,900 feet, summit 9,700 feet. Lifts: 8, including 2 high-speed 6-passenger lifts.*

On the way to Mt. Rose from Incline Village, **Tahoe Meadows** (✉*Hwy. 431*) is the most popular area near the north shore for noncommercial cross-country skiing, sledding, tubing, snowshoeing, and snowmobiling.

You'll find superbly groomed tracks and fabulous views of Lake Tahoe at **Spooner Lake Cross-Country** (✉*Spooner Summit, Hwy. 28, ½ mi north of U.S. 50, Glenbrook* ☎*775/749–5349* 🌐*www.spoonerlake.com*). It has more than 50 mi of trails on more than 9,000 acres, and two rustic, secluded cabins are available for rent for overnight treks.

ZEPHYR COVE

22 mi south of Incline Village via Hwy. 28 to U.S. 50.

The largest settlement between Incline Village and the Stateline area is Zephyr Cove, a tiny resort. It has a beach, marina, campground, picnic area, coffee shop in a log lodge, rustic cabins, and nearby riding stables.

TAHOE TESSIE

Local lore claims that this huge sea monster slithers around Lake Tahoe. Skeptics laugh, but true believers keep their eyes peeled for surprise sightings.

13

EXPLORING

★ Nearby **Cave Rock** (✉ *U.S. 50, 4 mi north of Zephyr Cove* ☎ *775/831–0494*), 75 feet of solid stone at the southern end of Lake Tahoe–Nevada State Park, is the throat of an extinct volcano. Tahoe Tessie, the lake's version of the Loch Ness monster, is reputed to live in a cavern below the impressive outcropping. Cave Rock towers over a parking lot, a lakefront picnic ground, and a boat launch. The views are some of the best on the lake; this is a good spot to stop and take a picture. However, this area is a sacred burial site for the Washoe Indians, and climbing up to the cave, or through it, is prohibited.

WHERE TO EAT AND STAY

¢ **Zephyr Cove Resort.** Beneath towering pines at the lake's edge stand 28 cozy, modern vacation cabins ($$–$$$$) with peaked knotty-pine ceilings. While not fancy, they come in a variety of sizes, some perfect for families. Across U.S. 50, a sprawling year-round campground is geared toward RVers, but with drive-in and walk-in tent sites, too. The resort has horseback riding, snowmobiling facilities, and a marina with boat and WaveRunner rentals, all of which contribute to the summer-camp atmosphere. **Pros:** family-friendly. **Cons:** lodge rooms are very basic; can be noisy. ✉ *U.S. 50, 4 mi north of Stateline* ☎ *775/589–4907 or 888/896–3830* 🌐 *www.zephyrcove.com* *150 tent and RV sites, 28 cabins* *In-room: no a/c, kitchen (some), Internet (some). In-hotel: restaurant, beachfront, laundry facilities, flush toilets, full hookups, partial hookups, dump station, drinking water, showers, fire pits, grills, picnic tables, general store, some pets allowed, no-smoking rooms* *AE, D, MC, V.*

STATELINE

5 mi south of Zephyr Cove on U.S. 50.

Stateline is the archetypal Nevada border town. Its four high-rise casinos are as vertical and contained as the commercial district of South Lake Tahoe, on the California side, is horizontal and sprawling. And Stateline is as relentlessly indoors oriented as the rest of the lake is focused on the outdoors. This strip is where you'll find the most concentrated action at Lake Tahoe: restaurants (including typical casino buffets), showrooms with famous headliners and razzle-dazzle revues, tower-hotel rooms and suites, and 24-hour casinos.

WHERE TO EAT AND STAY

$$–$$$ FRENCH ★ **Mirabelle.** Don't be put off by this restaurant's nondescript exterior. Inside there's a lovely, airy dining room with creamy yellow walls and white tablecloths—and some of the most delectable dishes you'll find in the Tahoe area. Enticing scents drift from the kitchen where the French Alsatian–born chef-owner personally prepares everything from puff pastry to meringues to homemade bread. Specialties include venison loin with red-wine lingonberry sauce, garlicky escargots, and rack of lamb Provençale. There's always a vegetarian entrée, and on some evenings a fixed-price menu is available for $33.50 per person. *290 Kingsbury Grade 775/586–1007 AE, MC, V Closed Mon. No lunch.*

$$$–$$$$ **Harrah's Tahoe Hotel/Casino.** Harrah's major selling point is that every room has two full bathrooms, each with a television and telephone, a boon if you're traveling with family. The South Shore Room hosts first-rate entertainment. Among the restaurants, the top-floor Friday's Station Steak & Seafood Grill ($$$$), with good views from every table, is a standout (but an expensive one); there's also a buffet on the 18th floor. A tunnel runs under U.S. 50 to Harveys, which Harrah's now owns. Upper-floor rooms have views of the lake or mountains, but if you really want the view, stay at Harveys instead. Cheaper rates are available midweek. **Pros:** central location; great midweek values. **Cons:** can get noisy. *U.S. 50 at Stateline Ave. 775/588–6611 or 800/427–7247 www.harrahstahoe.com 470 rooms, 62 suites In-room: Internet, Wi-Fi. In-hotel: 7 restaurants, room service, pool, gym, spa, laundry service AE, D, DC, MC, V.*

$$–$$$$ **Harveys Resort Hotel/Casino.** Harveys began as a cabin in 1944, and now it's Tahoe's largest casino-hotel. Premium rooms have custom furnishings, oversize marble baths, minibars, and good lake views. Although it was acquired by Harrah's and has lost some of its cachet, Harveys remains a fine property. At Cabo Wabo ($–$$), an always-hopping Baja-style cantina owned by Sammy Hagar, sip agave-style tequila while munching on tapas and shouting across the table at your date. Harveys Cabaret is the hotel's showroom. **Pros:** hip entertainment; just a few blocks south of the Heavenly Gondola. **Cons:** can get loud at night. *U.S. 50, at Stateline Ave. 775/588–2411 or 800/648–3361 www.harrahs.com 705 rooms, 38 suites In-room: Internet, Wi-Fi. In-hotel: 7 restaurants, room service, pool, gym, spa AE, D, DC, MC, V.*

$$–$$$$ **MontBleu.** Formerly Caesar's Tahoe, MontBleu opened in summer 2006, and the tired Roman theme is gone. In its place you'll find a less garish—though still slightly kitschy—contemporary style. All guest rooms have luxurious bedding with down comforters; most have oversize tubs, king-size beds, two telephones, and a view of Lake Tahoe and the surrounding mountains (avoid those that overlook the parking lot's glaring lights). Famous entertainers sometimes perform in the 1,600-seat MontBleu Theater (formerly Circus Maximus). **Pros:** indoor pool; first-class spa. **Cons:** can get noisy. *55 U.S. 50, Box 5800 775/588–3515 or 800/648–3353 www.montbleuresort.com 328 rooms, 109 suites In-room: Internet, Wi-Fi. In-hotel: 4 restaurants, room service, pool, gym, spa, Wi-Fi AE, D, DC, MC, V.*

NIGHTLIFE

Each of the major casinos has its own showroom, including Harrah's **South Shore Room** (☎*775/588–6611*). They feature everything from comedy to magic acts to sexy floor shows to Broadway musicals. If you want to dance to DJ grooves and live bands, check out the scene at MontBleu's **Blu** (✉*55 U.S. 50* ☎*775/588–3515*). At Harrah's, you can dance at **Vex** (✉*U.S. 50, at state line* ☎*775/588–6611*). **Harveys Outdoor Summer Concert Series** (☎*800/427–7247* 🌐*www.harrahs.com*) presents outdoor concerts on weekends in summer with headliners such as the Eagles, Toby Keith, Stevie Wonder, Beyoncé, and James Taylor.

SPORTS AND THE OUTDOORS

One of the south shore's best, **Nevada Beach** (✉*Elk Point Rd., 3 mi north of Stateline via U.S. 50* ☎*530/543–2600*) has a superwide sandy beach that's great for swimming (most Tahoe beaches are rocky). There are also picnic tables, restrooms, barbecue grills, and a campground beneath towering pines. This is the best place to watch the July 4 or Labor Day fireworks. The beach is open Memorial Day weekend through October.

On the lake, **Edgewood Tahoe** (✉*U.S. 50 and Lake Pkwy., behind Horizon Casino* ☎*775/588–3566 or 888/881–8659* 🌐*www.edgewood-tahoe.com*) is an 18-hole, par-72 course with a driving range. Fees range from $140–$220, depending on the month, and include a cart (though you can walk if you wish). You can have breakfast or lunch in the bar, but the best meal at Edgewood is at the lake-view restaurant inside the clubhouse ($$$-$$$$; dinner only).

RENO

32 mi east of Truckee on I–80; 38 mi northeast of Incline Village via Hwy. 431 and U.S. 395.

Established in 1859 as a trading station at a bridge over the Truckee River, Reno grew along with the silver mines of nearby Virginia City and the transcontinental railroad that chugged through town. Train officials named it in 1868, but gambling—legalized in 1931—put Reno on the map.

Today a sign over the upper end of Virginia Street proclaims Reno THE BIGGEST LITTLE CITY IN THE WORLD. This is still a gambling town, with most of the casinos crowded into five square blocks downtown. The city has lost significant business to California's Indian casinos over the past few years, which has resulted in cheaper rooms, but mediocre upkeep; there just isn't the money coming into town that there once was.

Though parts of downtown are sketchy, things are changing. Several defunct casinos are being converted into condominiums, and downtown is undergoing an urban renewal, sparked by the development of the riverfront, with new shops, boutiques, and nongaming, family-friendly activities like kayaking on the Truckee River. Excellent restaurants have shown up outside the hotels. Temperatures year-round in this high-mountain-desert climate are warmer than at Tahoe, though it rarely gets as hot here as in Sacramento and the Central Valley, making strolling around town a pleasure.

ESSENTIALS

Visitor Information Reno-Sparks Convention and Visitors Authority (✉ *4001 S. Virginia St., Reno, NV* ☎ *775/827–7600 or 800/367–7366* 🌐 *www.visitrenotahoe.com*).

RENO'S RIVERWALK

Stroll along the Truckee River and check out the art galleries, cinema, specialty shops, theater, and restaurants that line this lively refurbished section of town near Reno's casino district.

EXPLORING

Families with kids in tow head for **Circus Circus** (✉ *500 N. Sierra St.* ☎ *775/329–0711 or 800/648–5010* 🌐 *www.circusreno.com*). A midway above the casino floor has clowns, games, fun-house mirrors, and circus acts.

★ A few miles from downtown, the **Peppermill** (✉ *2707 S. Virginia St.* ☎ *775/826–2121 or 800/648–6992* 🌐 *www.peppermillreno.com*) is known for its excellent restaurants and neon-bright gambling areas. For cocktails, the Fireside Lounge is a blast.

Eldorado (✉ *345 N. Virginia St.* ☎ *775/786–5700 or 800/648–5966* 🌐 *www.eldoradoreno.com*) is action packed, with tons of slots, popular bar-top video poker, and good coffee-shop and food-court fare.

Harrah's (✉ *219 N. Center St.* ☎ *775/786–3232 or 800/648–3773* 🌐 *www.harrahs.com*) occupies two city blocks, with a sprawling casino and an outdoor promenade.

Silver Legacy (✉ *407 N. Virginia St.* ☎ *775/329–4777 or 800/687–8733* 🌐 *www.silverlegacy.com*) has a Victorian-theme casino, a 120-foot-tall mining rig, and video poker games that draw in the gamblers.

The **Downtown RiverWalk** (✉ *S. Virginia St. and the Truckee River* 🌐 *www.renoriver.org*) has gentrified the Reno waterfront district, replacing a seedy atmosphere with street performers, art exhibits, shops, a lovely park, and good strolling. The 2,600-foot-long Truckee River white-water kayaking course runs right through downtown and has become a major attraction for water-sports enthusiasts. On the third Saturday of each month, from 2 to 5, local merchants host a **Wine Walk.** The cost is $20; stop inside the RiverWalk's shops, galleries, and boutiques, and they'll refill your wine glass. In July look for stellar outdoor art, opera, dance, and kids' performances as part of the month-long **Artown festival** (🌐 *www.renoisartown.com*), presented mostly in Wingfield Park, along the river.

On the University of Nevada campus, the sleekly designed **Fleischmann Planetarium** has films and astronomy shows, providing a great alternative to the glittering lights of the casinos. ✉ *1650 N. Virginia St.* ☎ *775/784–4811* 🌐 *www.planetarium.unr.nevada.edu* 🎟 *Exhibits free, films and star shows $6* ⏲ *Sun.–Thurs. 10:30–7, Fri. and Sat. 10:30–8.*

★ The **Nevada Museum of Art** has changing exhibits in a dramatic modern building; it's a must-see for art aficionados. ✉ *160 W. Liberty St.* ☎ *775/329–3333* 🌐 *www.nevadaart.org* 🎟 *$10* ⏲ *Tues., Wed., and Fri.–Sun. 10–5, Thurs. 10–8.*

More than 220 antique and classic automobiles, including an Elvis Presley Cadillac and a 1949 Mercury coupe driven by James Dean in the movie *Rebel Without a Cause,* are on display at the **National Automobile Museum.** ✉*Mill and Lake Sts.* ☎*775/333–9300* 🌐*www.automuseum.org* *$10* *Mon.–Sat. 9:30–5:30, Sun. 10–4.*

WHERE TO EAT

¢–$ THAI **Bangkok Cuisine.** If you want to eat well in a pretty dining room but don't want to break the bank, come to this cute little Thai restaurant where delicious soups, salads, stir-fries, and curries are prepared by a Thai national. ✉*55 Mt. Rose St.* ☎*775/322–0299* *AE, D, MC, V.* *No lunch Sun.*

$$$–$$$$ FRENCH **Beaujolais Bistro.** Consistently spot-on Beaujolais serves earthy, country-style French food with zero pretension. The understated chef-owner is known for classics like beef bourguignon, roast duck, escargots, and steak frites, all lovingly prepared and seasoned just right. For dessert, try the profiteroles, made with homemade ice cream. They're perfect. The comfortable, airy dining room has exposed brick walls, a parquet floor, and an inviting, casual vibe, making it a good choice for an unfussy meal a short walk from the casinos. ✉*130 West St.* ☎*775/323–2227* *AE, D, MC, V* *Closed Mon. No lunch weekends.*

¢–$$ CAFÉ **Chocolate Bar.** If you love chocolate, don't miss this place. Part café, part cocktail bar, this hip little joint a mile from downtown makes killer truffles, chocolate fondue, fabulous fruity cocktails, gourmet appetizers and small-plate selections—and, of course, stellar hot chocolate, served at a small bar or at a dozen or so tables. It's open 4:30 PM to midnight and gets crowded on weekend evenings with twenty- and thirtysomethings. ✉*475 S. Arlington St.* ☎*775/337–1122* *AE, MC, V.* *Closed Mon.*

$$$$ AMERICAN **White Orchid.** When high rollers win big, they head straight for the White Orchid, northern Nevada's fanciest restaurant. Signature dishes on the seasonal French–California menu include veal fillet with Dungeness crab legs and Arctic char with a wild mushroom lobster risotto. Yes, the frilly rose-pattern upholstered ceiling and fake flowering vines might be a bit much, but the oversize ivory-color armchairs are wonderfully comfortable, and the solicitous waiters in white dinner jackets make you feel as if you're eating in the first-class dining room aboard a great ocean liner. And you won't find a better wine list anywhere in town. Period. ✉*2707 S. Virginia St., inside Peppermill Casino* ☎*775/826–2121* *AE, D, MC, V* *Closed Mon. and Tues. No lunch.*

WHERE TO STAY

$–$$$ **Harrah's.** Of the big-name casino hotels in downtown Reno, double-towered Harrah's does a good job, with no surprises. The large guest rooms, decorated in blues and mauves, overlook downtown and the entire mountain-ringed valley. The dark and romantic dining room at Harrah's Steak House ($$$–$$$$; reservations essential, no lunch weekends) serves excellent prime steaks and seafood that merit a special trip by meat lovers; try the Caesar salad and steak Diane, both prepared table-side by a tuxedoed waiter. **Pros:** Harrah's sets the standard for downtown Reno; great midweek rates. **Cons:** huge property. ✉*219 N. Center St. 89501* ☎*775/786–3232 or 800/648–3773* 🌐*www.harrahs.*

com ⇒*876 rooms, 52 suites* *In-room: safe, refrigerator (some), Internet (some), Wi-Fi. In-hotel: 8 restaurants, room service, bars, pool, gym, laundry service, no-smoking rooms* ▭*AE, D, DC, MC, V.*

$–$$$ ★ **Peppermill.** A few miles removed from downtown Reno's flashy main drag, the Peppermill generates its own glitz with a neon-filled casino that's as dazzling as any. Setting a new standard for luxury in Reno, the 600 baroque suites in the Tuscan Tower that opened in 2008 have plush king-size beds, marble bathrooms, and European soaking tubs. The casino's superior dining options include the White Orchid *(⇨above)*; Oceana ($–$$$), an over-the-top seafood restaurant that feels like you're eating inside an aquarium; and Romanza ($$–$$$$), with fabulous place settings of Versace china and a planetarium star show. **Pros:** casino decor is worth a special trip; good (and inexpensive) coffee shop. **Cons:** some may find the amount of neon a bit over the top. ✉*2707 S. Virginia St.* ☎*775/826–2121 or 800/648–6992* 🌐*www.peppermillreno.com* ⇒*915 rooms, 720 suites* *In-room: refrigerator (some), Wi-Fi. In-hotel: 10 restaurants, room service, bars, pool, gym, spa, no-smoking rooms* ▭*AE, D, MC, V.*

$–$$$ **Siena Hotel Spa Casino.** When it opened with a bang in 2001, the Siena was Reno's most luxurious hotel, breaking the floral-print mold with blond-wood furnishings and top-of-the-line beds dressed with white Egyptian-cotton linens. And you won't have to navigate past miles of slots to find the front desk, because the casino is in a self-contained room. The spa merits a special trip, as does Lexie's ($$–$$$$; dinner only), which serves terrific steaks and seafood in a sleek, river-view dining room. **Pros:** beautiful rooms; smaller-scale facility; helpful staff. **Cons:** located a few blocks from the town center. ✉*1 S. Lake St. 89501* ☎*775/337–6260 or 877/743–6233* 🌐*www.sienareno.com* ⇒*193 rooms, 21 suites* *In-room: refrigerator, Internet, Wi-Fi. In-hotel: 3 restaurants, room service, bar, pool, gym, spa, laundry service, Wi-Fi* ▭*AE, D, MC, V.*

The Far North

WITH LAKE SHASTA, MT. SHASTA, AND LASSEN VOLCANIC NATIONAL PARK

WORD OF MOUTH

"We were in Lassen on June 29th and there was still a very thick layer of snow throughout the park. Many of the picnic areas and trails were closed due to the snow. It was lovely to drive, through . . . Burney Falls is a lovely area as are the roads along the Russian River and the little town of Paradise. Shasta Lake is also beautiful."

—BJinHolland

WELCOME TO THE FAR NORTH

TOP REASONS TO GO

★ **Mother nature's wonders:** California's far north has more rivers, streams, lakes, forests, and mountains than you'll ever have time to explore.

★ **Rock and roll:** With two volcanoes to entice you—Lassen and Shasta—you can learn firsthand what happens when a mountain blows its top.

★ **Fantastic fishing:** Whether you like casting from a riverbank or letting your line bob beside a boat, you'll find fabulous fishing in all the northern counties.

★ **Cool hops:** On a hot day there's nothing quite as inviting as a visit to Chico's world-famous Sierra Nevada Brewery. Take the tour and then savor a chilled glass on tap at the adjacent brewpub.

★ **Shasta:** Wonderful in all its forms: lake, dam, river, mountain, forest, and town.

1 From Chico to Mt. Shasta. The far north is bisected, south to north, by I-5, which passes through several historic towns and state parks, as well as miles of mountainous terrain. Halfway to the Oregon border is Lake Shasta, a favorite recreation destination, and farther north stands the spectacular snowy peak of Mt. Shasta.

2 The Backcountry. East of I-5, the far north's main corridor, dozens of scenic two-lane roads crisscross the wilderness, leading to dramatic mountain peaks and fascinating natural wonders. Small towns settled in the second half of the 19th century seem frozen in time, except that they are well equipped with tourist amenities.

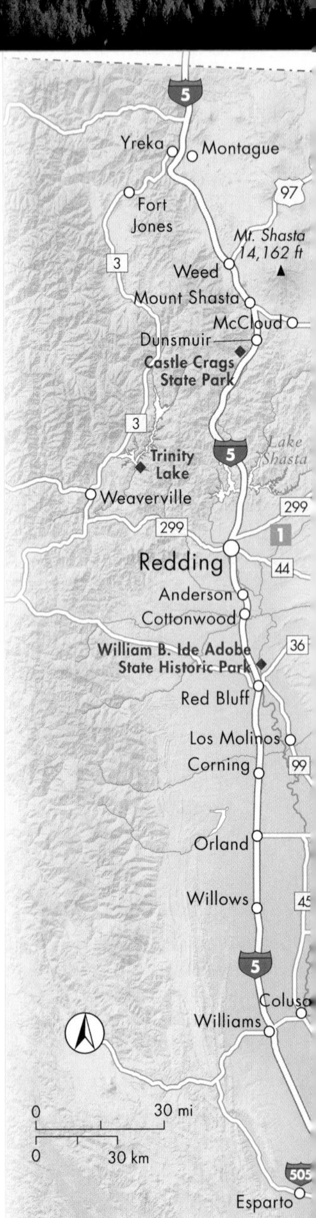

OREGON
Dorris
Tulelake
Lava Beds National Monument
Clear Lake
Goose Lake
139
395
Canby
Alturas
299
89
Adin
Burney
2
139
44
395
Old Station
Shingletown
Lassen Volcanic National Park
Mt. Lassen
Susanville
NEVADA
Chester
36
Westwood
Honey Lake (Dry)
SIERRA NEVADA
Greenville
395
32
70
Quincy
70
Portola
Chico
Loyalton
Reno
Oroville
99
Gridley
Nevada City
80
Truckee
Live Oak
70
20
Grass Valley
Yuba City
Olivehurst
49
Colfax
Lake Tahoe
70
Wheatland
65
Auburn
Rocklin
Woodland
Citrus Heights
Sacramento
50

GETTING ORIENTED

The far north is a vast area that stretches from the upper reaches of the Sacramento Valley north to the Oregon border and east to Nevada. The region includes all or part of seven counties with sparsely populated rural farming and mountain communities, as well as thriving small cities in the valley. Much of the landscape was shaped by two volcanoes—Mt. Shasta and Mt. Lassen—that draw amateur geologists, weekend hikers, and avid mountain climbers to their rugged terrain. An intricate network of high-mountain watersheds feeds lakes large and small, plus streams and rivers that course through several forests.

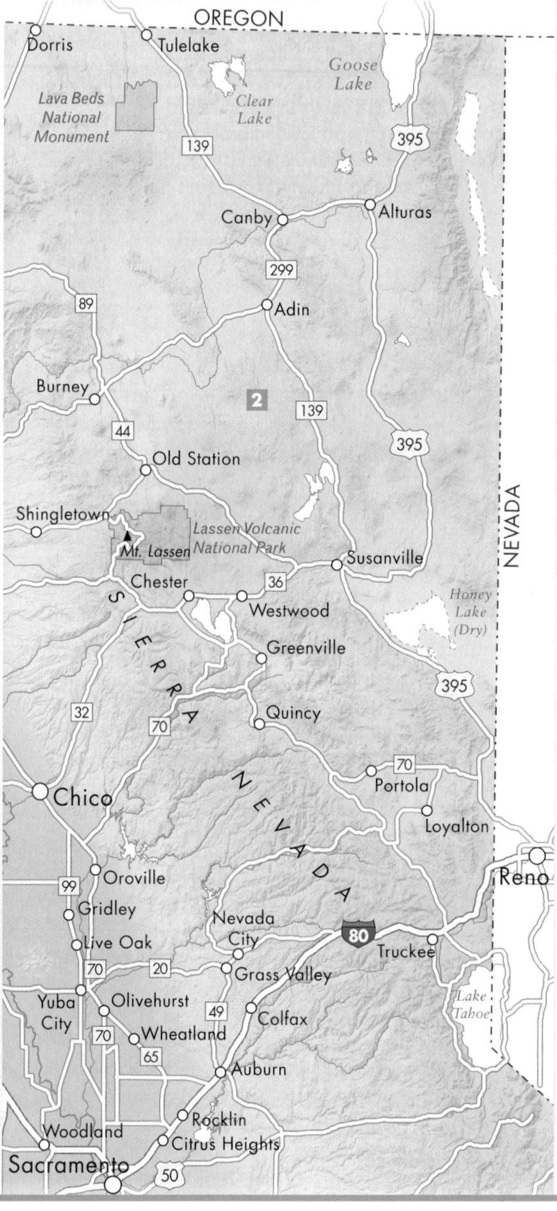

THE FAR NORTH PLANNER

Getting Here and Around

Both Chico and Redding have small regional airports, but for the cheapest fares, fly into Sacramento airport and rent a car for your northern explorations.

Interstate 5 runs up the center of California through Red Bluff and Redding; the other main roads here are good two-lane highways that are, with few exceptions, open year-round. Check weather reports and carry detailed maps, warm clothing, and tire chains whenever you head into mountainous terrain in winter.

Contacts Caltrans Highway Information Network (☎ *800/427-7623*).

When to Go

Heat scorches the valley in summer. Temperatures above 110°F are common, but the mountains provide cool respite. Fall throughout the far north is beautiful, rivaled only by the spring months when wildflowers bloom and snowmelt sends mountain creeks splashing through forests. Winter is usually temperate in the valley, but cold and snowy in high country. A few favorite tourist attractions are closed in winter.

About the Restaurants

Redding, the urban center of the far north, and college-town Chico have the greatest selection of restaurants. Cafés and simple eateries are the rule in the smaller towns, though trendy, innovative restaurants have been popping up. Dress is always informal.

About the Hotels

The far north—especially the mountainous backcountry—is gaining popularity as a tourist destination. For summer holiday weekends in towns at higher elevations that escape the valley heat, such as Mt. Shasta, Dunsmuir, and Chester, and at camping sites within state or national parks, make lodging reservations well in advance.

Rooms in Redding, Chico, and Red Bluff are usually booked solid only when local events jam motels. Aside from the large chain hotels and motels in Redding and Chico, most accommodations in the far north blend rusticity, simplicity, and coziness. Wilderness resorts close in fall and reopen after the snow season ends in May.

The Web site of the **California Association of Bed & Breakfast Inns** (🌐 *www.cabbi.com*) lists numerous bed-and-breakfasts in the far north region.

WHAT IT COSTS

	¢	$	$$	$$$	$$$$
Restaurants	under $10	$10–$15	$16–$22	$23–$30	over $30
Hotels	under $90	$90–$120	$121–$175	$176–$250	over $250
Camping	under $8	$8–$14	$15–$20	$21–$25	over $25

Restaurant prices are for a main course at dinner, excluding sales tax of 7.75%. Hotel prices are for two people in a standard double room in high season, excluding service charges and 7.25%–10% tax.

14

Updated by Christine Vovakes

The Wondrous Landscape of California's northeastern corner, relatively unmarred by development, congestion, and traffic, is the product of volcanic activity. At the southern end of the Cascade Range, Lassen Volcanic National Park is the best place to witness the far north's fascinating geology. Beyond the sulfur vents and bubbling mud pots, the park owes much of its beauty to 10,457-foot Mt. Lassen and 50 wilderness lakes.

The most enduring image of the region, though, is Mt. Shasta, whose 14,162-foot snowcapped peak beckons outdoor adventurers of all kinds. There are many versions of Shasta to enjoy—the mountain, the lake, the river, the town, the dam, and the forest—all named after the Native Americans known as the Shatasla, or Sastise, who once inhabited the region. Its soaring mountain peaks, wild rivers teeming with trout, and almost unlimited recreational possibilities make the far north the perfect destination for sports lovers. You won't find many hot nightspots or cultural enclaves, but you'll find some of the best hiking and fishing in the state.

PLANNING

GETTING HERE AND AROUND

AIR TRAVEL

Chico Municipal Airport and Redding Municipal Airport are served by United Express. Horizon Air also uses the airport in Redding. *See Air Travel in Travel Smart Northern California for airline phone numbers.* There's no shuttle service from either airport, but taxis can be ordered. The approximate cost from the airport to downtown Redding is $28 to $30, and it's $18 from the Chico airport to downtown.

Air Contacts **Chico Municipal Airport** (*✉150 Airpark Blvd., off Cohasset Rd., Chico ☎530/896–7200*). **Redding Municipal Airport** (*✉Airport*

Rd., Redding ☎ *530/224–4320*). **Taxi Service, Chico** (☎ *530/893–4444 or 530/342–2929*). **Taxi Service, Redding** (☎ *530/246–0577 or 530/222–1234*).

BUS TRAVEL

Greyhound buses travel I–5 and interior highways, serving Burney, Chico, Red Bluff, Redding, and Susanville. Butte County Transit serves Chico, Oroville, and elsewhere. Chico Area Transit System provides bus service within Chico. The vehicles of the Redding Area Bus Authority operate daily except Sunday within Redding, Anderson, and Shasta Lake. STAGE buses serve Siskiyou County, on weekdays only, from Yreka to Dunsmuir, stopping in Mt. Shasta and other towns, and provide service in Scott Valley, Happy Camp, Hornbrook, Lake Shastina, and the Klamath River area. Lassen Rural Bus serves the Susanville, northeast Lake Almanor, and south and east Lassen County areas, running weekdays except holidays. Lassen Rural Bus connects with Plumas County Transit, which serves the Quincy area, and with Modoc County Sage Stage, which serves the Alturas area.

Bus Contacts **Butte County Transit/Chico Area Transit System** (☎ *530/342–0221 or 800/822–8145* 🌐 *www.bcag.org/transit/index.html*). **Greyhound** (☎ *800/229–9424* 🌐 *www.greyhound.com*). **Lassen Rural Bus** (☎ *530/252–7433*). **Modoc County Sage Stage** (☎ *530/233–3883 or 233–6410*). **Plumas County Transit** (☎ *530/283–2538* 🌐 *www.susanvillestuff.com/bus.html*). **Redding Area Bus Authority** (☎ *530/241–2877* 🌐 *www.ci.redding.ca.us*). **STAGE** (☎ *530/842–8295* 🌐 *www.co.siskiyou.ca.us*).

CAMPING

Some campgrounds in California's far north get booked as much as a year in advance for the Fourth of July. Although that's not the norm, it's still a good idea to make summer reservations two to three months in advance. You can reserve a site at many of the region's campgrounds through **ReserveAmerica** (☎ *800/444–7275* 🌐 *www.reserveamerica.com*) and, for federal recreation reservations, **Recreation.gov** (☎ *877/444–6777* 🌐 *www.recreation.gov*).

CAR TRAVEL

Chico is east of I–5 on Highway 32. Lassen Volcanic National Park can be reached by Highway 36 from Red Bluff or (except in winter) Highway 44 from Redding. Highway 299 connects Redding and Alturas. Highway 139 leads from Susanville to Lava Beds National Monument. Highway 89 will take you from Mt. Shasta to Quincy. Highway 36 links Chester and Susanville.

Road Conditions **Caltrans Highway Information Network** (☎ *800/427–7623*).

TRAIN TRAVEL

Amtrak has stations in Chico, Redding, and Dunsmuir, and operates buses that connect to Greyhound service through Redding, Red Bluff, and Chico.

Train Contacts **Amtrak** (✉ *W. 5th and Orange Sts., Chico* ✉ *1620 Yuba St. (for Amtrak's Coach Starlight) or 1650 Yuba St. (Amtrak motor coach connections to Sacramento), Redding* ✉ *5750 Sacramento Ave., Dunsmuir* ☎ *800/872–7245* 🌐 *www.amtrakcalifornia.com*).

HEALTH AND SAFETY

In an emergency, dial 911.

Hospitals **Banner-Lassen Medical Center** (✉ *1800 Spring Ridge Dr., Susanville* ☎ *530/252–2000*). **Enloe Medical Center** (✉ *1531 Esplanade, Chico* ☎ *530/891–7300*). **Mercy Medical Center** (✉ *2175 Rosaline Ave., Redding* ☎ *530/225–6000*).

VISITOR INFORMATION

Contacts **Lassen County Chamber of Commerce** (✉ *601 Richmond Rd., Susanville* ☎ *530/257–4323* 🌐 *lassencountychamber.org*). **Shasta Cascade Wonderland Association** (✉ *1699 Hwy. 273, Anderson* ☎ *530/365–7500 or 800/474–2782* 🌐 *www.shastacascade.org*). **Siskiyou County Visitors Bureau** (✉ *300 Pine St., Mt. Shasta* ☎ *530/926–3850 or 800/926–4865* 🌐 *www.visitsiskiyou.org*).

FROM CHICO TO MT. SHASTA

CHICO

180 mi from San Francisco, east on I–80, north on I–505 to I–5, and east on Hwy. 32; 86 mi north of Sacramento on Hwy. 99.

Chico (Spanish for "small") sits just west of Paradise in the Sacramento Valley, and offers a welcome break from the monotony of Interstate 5. The Chico campus of California State University, the scores of local artisans, and the area's agriculture (primarily almond orchards) all influence the culture here. Chico's true claim to fame, however, is the popular Sierra Nevada Brewery, which keeps locals and beer drinkers across the country happy with its distinctive microbrews.

ESSENTIALS

Visitor Information **Chico Chamber of Commerce** (✉ *300 Salem St., Chico* ☎ *530/891–5556 or 800/852–8570* 🌐 *www.chicochamber.com*).

EXPLORING

★ The sprawling 3,670-acre **Bidwell Park** (✉ *River Rd. south of Sacramento St.* ☎ *530/896–7800*) is a community green space straddling Big Chico Creek, where scenes from *Gone With the Wind* and the 1938 version of *Robin Hood* (starring Errol Flynn) were filmed. The region's recreational hub, it includes a golf course, swimming areas, and paved biking, hiking, and in-line skating trails. One of the largest city-run parks in the country, Bidwell starts as a slender strip downtown and expands eastward 11 mi toward the Sierra foothills.

★ The renowned **Sierra Nevada Brewing Company,** one of the pioneers of the microbrewery movement, still has a hands-on approach to beer making. Tour the brew house and see how the beer is produced—from the sorting of hops through fermentation and bottling. You can also visit the gift shop and enjoy a hearty lunch or dinner in the brewpub (it's closed Monday), where tastings are available (for a fee). ✉ *1075 E. 20th St.* ☎ *530/345–2739* 🌐 *www.sierranevada.com* *Free* ⏲ *Tours Sun.–Fri. 2:30, Sat. noon–3 on the ½ hr.*

★ In **Bidwell Mansion State Historic Park** you can take a one-hour tour of most of the mansion's 26 rooms. Built between 1865 and 1868 by General John Bidwell, the founder of Chico, the home was designed by Henry W. Cleaveland, a San Francisco architect. Bidwell and his wife welcomed many distinguished guests to the distinctive pink Italianate mansion, including President Rutherford B. Hayes, naturalist John Muir, suffragist Susan B. Anthony, and General William T. Sherman. ✉*525 The Esplanade* ☎*530/895–6144* *$4* ⏲*Tues.–Fri. noon–5, weekends 10–5, last tour at 4.*

WHERE TO EAT AND STAY

$$–$$$$ STEAK ✕ **5th Street Steakhouse.** Hand-cut steak is the star in this refurbished early 1900s building, the place to come when you're craving red meat and a huge baked potato. Exposed redbrick walls warm the small dining area. A long mahogany bar catches the overflow crowds that jam the place on weekends. No reservations are accepted on Fridays and Saturdays, but it's worth the wait. ✉*345 W. 5th St.* ☎*530/891–6328* *Reservations essential* *AE, MC, V* ⏲*No lunch.*

$–$$$ AMERICAN ✕ **The Black Crow Grill & Taproom.** Large windows and a long, polished bar in one room, and redbrick walls in the other, create a warm atmosphere that draws big lunch and dinner crowds to this popular downtown restaurant. Reading the list of wildly inventive "crowtails" will amuse you even if you don't imbibe. Hearty salads, like the classic Fuji apple with crumbled blue cheese and candied walnuts, are favorites. Steaks and chops share star billing with salmon and chicken entrées. ✉*209 Salem St.* ☎*530/892–1392* *AE, MC, V* ⏲*No lunch Sat; no dinner Sun.*

$$–$$$$ ★ **Hotel Diamond.** Crystal chandeliers and gleaming wood floors and banisters elegantly welcome guests into the foyer of this restored gem in downtown Chico near the university. Some rooms are furnished with antiques that reflect the town's historic past. Johnnie's ($$–$$$$), the hotel's restaurant and bar, provides room service, and is open for lunch and dinner. **Pros:** refined; great location. **Cons:** pricey; not a good choice for families. ✉*220 W. 4th St. 95928* ☎*530/893–3100 or 866/993–3100* *www.hoteldiamondchico.com* *39 rooms, 4 suites* *In-room: Internet. In-hotel: restaurant, room service, Wi-Fi* *AE, D, MC, V* *CP.*

$–$$ **Johnson's Country Inn.** Nestled in an almond orchard five minutes from downtown, this Victorian-style farmhouse with a wraparound veranda is a welcome change from motel row. It's full of antique furnishings and modern conveniences. **Pros:** rural setting; beautifully maintained; serene walks. **Cons:** a car is essential. ✉*3935 Morehead Ave. 95928* ☎*530/345–7829 or 866/872–7780* *www.chico.com/johnsonsinn* *4 rooms* *In-room: no TV, Wi-Fi. In-hotel: Wi-Fi, no-smoking rooms* *AE, MC, V* *BP.*

RED BLUFF

41 mi north of Chico on Hwy 99.

Historic Red Bluff is a gateway to Lassen Volcanic National Park. Established in the mid-19th century as a shipping center and named for the color of its soil, the town is filled with dozens of restored Victorians.

It's a great home base for outdoor adventures in the area.

ESSENTIALS

Visitor Information **Red Bluff–Tehama County Chamber of Commerce** (✉*100 Main St., Red Bluff* ☎*530/527-6220* 🌐*www.redbluffchamberofcommerce.com*).

RED BLUFF ROUND-UP

Check out old-time rodeo at its best during the Red Bluff Round-Up. Held the third weekend of April, this annual event attracts some of the best cowboys in the country. For more information, visit www.redbluffroundup.com.

EXPLORING

★ **William B. Ide Adobe State Historic Park,** on an oak-lined bank of the Sacramento River, is named for the first and only president of the short-lived California Republic of 1846. The Bear Flag Party proclaimed California a sovereign nation, separate from Mexican rule, and the republic existed for 22 days before it was taken over by the United States. The republic's flag has survived, with only minor refinements, as California's state flag. The park's main attraction is an adobe home built in the 1850s and outfitted with period furnishings; tours are available on request. There's also a carriage shed, a blacksmith shop, and a small visitor center. ✉*21659 Adobe Rd.* ☎*530/529–8599* 🌐*www.parks.ca.gov* *$4 per vehicle* *Park and picnic facilities daily sunrise–sunset.*

14

WHERE TO EAT AND STAY

¢–$ AMERICAN **Feedbag Grill.** Locals gather at this friendly diner that serves meals from early morning until late evening. Try the "Trail Boss"—three eggs, a hefty side of sausage, and hash browns—for breakfast, the barbecued pork ribs for dinner, and the house-made pie any time. ✉*259 S. Main St.* ☎*530/528–8777* *Reservations not accepted* *MC, V* *No dinner Sun.*

$–$$$ STEAK **Green Barn Steakhouse.** You're likely to find cowboys sporting Stetsons and spurs and feasting on sizzling porterhouse, baby back ribs, and filet mignon at Red Bluff's premier steak house. For lighter fare, there's garlicky scampi or fettuccine primavera, along with fresh fish specials. As a sweet indulgence, don't miss the bread pudding with rum sauce. The lounge is usually hopping, especially when there's an event at the nearby rodeo grounds. ✉*5 Chestnut Ave.* ☎*530/527–3161* *AE, D, MC, V* *Closed Sun.*

$–$$ **The Jeter Victorian Inn.** On sunny days breakfast is served in the garden pavilion outside this 1881 Victorian home. The four guest rooms are elegantly decorated with antiques and period furnishings; two have private baths, and the Imperial Room has a Jacuzzi. A separate cottage is also available. **Pros:** quiet residential area; within walking distance of restaurants. **Cons:** no Internet access. ✉*1107 Jefferson St. 96080* ☎*530/527–7574* 🌐*www.jetervictorianinn.com* *4 rooms, 2 with bath; 1 cottage* *In-room: no phone, no TV (some). In-hotel: no-smoking rooms* *MC, V* *BP.*

Fisherman under Santiago Calatrava's striking Sundial Bridge in Turtle Bay Exploration Park.

REDDING

32 mi north of Red Bluff on I–5.

As the largest city in the far north, Redding is an ideal headquarters for exploring the surrounding countryside.

ESSENTIALS

Visitor Information **Redding Convention and Visitors Bureau** (✉ *777 Auditorium Dr., Redding* ☎ *530/225–4100* 🌐 *www.visitredding.org*).

EXPLORING

Fodor's Choice ★

Curving along the Sacramento River, **Turtle Bay Exploration Park** has a museum, an arboretum with walking trails, and lots of interactive exhibits for children, including a miniature dam, a gold-panning area, and a seasonal Butterfly House where monarchs emerge from their cocoons. The main draw at the park, however, is the stunning **Sundial Bridge,** a modernist pedestrian footbridge designed by world-renowned Spanish architect Santiago Calatrava. The bridge's architecture consists of a translucent, illuminated span that stretches across the river, and—most strikingly—a soaring white 217-foot needle that casts a slender moving shadow, like a sundial's, over the water and surrounding trees. Watching the sun set over the river from this bridge is a magical experience. The bridge links to the Sacramento River Trail and the park's arboretum and botanical gardens. Access to the bridge and arboretum is free; a fee admits you to both the museum and the botanical gardens. ✉ *840 Auditorium Dr.* ☎ *530/243–8850 or 800/887–8532* 🌐 *www.turtlebay.org* *$13* *Closed Tues. Nov.–Feb.*

WHERE TO EAT AND STAY

¢–$$ SEAFOOD **Buz's Crab.** This casual restaurant in central Redding shares space with a bustling seafood market where locals snap up ocean-fresh Dungeness crab in season. The fish-and-chips is a favorite; seafood combos, including Cajun-style selections are also noteworthy. Try the wild salmon or trout charbroiled over mesquite wood. *2159 East St. 530/243–2120 D, MC, V.*

$–$$$ STEAK **Jack's Grill.** Famous for its 16-ounce steaks, this popular bar and steak house also serves shrimp and chicken. A town favorite, the place is usually jam-packed and noisy. *1743 California St. 530/241–9705 AE, D, MC, V Closed Sun. No lunch.*

$$ ★ **The Red Lion.** Adjacent to I–5, and close to Redding's convention center and regional recreation sites, this hotel is a top choice for both business and vacation travelers. Rooms are spacious and comfortable; a large patio surrounded by landscaped grounds is a relaxing spot to enjoy an outdoor meal or snack. Rooms have irons, ironing boards, and hair dryers, and there's a gym near the pool. The hotel's restaurant, 3-Shastas Bar and Grill ($–$$$), is a popular place for locals. **Pros:** family-friendly; close to a major shopping area. **Cons:** busy area. *1830 Hilltop Dr., Hwy. 44/299 exit off I–5 530/221–8700 or 800/733–5466 www.redlion.com 192 rooms, 2 suites In-room: Wi-Fi. In-hotel: restaurant, room service, bar, pool, gym, Wi-Fi AE, D, DC, MC, V.*

SPORTS AND THE OUTDOORS

The **Fly Shop** (*4140 Churn Creek Rd. 530/222–3555*) sells fishing licenses and has information about guides, conditions, and fishing packages.

WEAVERVILLE

46 mi west of Redding on Hwy. 299, called Main St. in town.

A man known only as Weaver struck gold here in 1849, and the fledgling community at the base of the Trinity Alps was named after him. With its impressive downtown historic district, today Weaverville is a popular headquarters for family vacations and biking, hiking, fishing, and gold-panning excursions.

EXPLORING

Fodor's Choice ★ Weaverville's main attraction is the **Weaverville Joss House,** a Taoist temple built in 1874 and called Won Lim Miao ("the temple of the forest beneath the clouds") by Chinese miners. The oldest continuously used Chinese temple in California, it attracts worshippers from around the world. With its golden altar, antique weaponry, and carved wooden canopies, the Joss House is a piece of California history that can best be appreciated on a guided 30-minute tour. The original temple building and many of its furnishings—some of which came from China—were lost to fire in 1873, but members of the local Chinese community soon rebuilt it. *Oregon and Main Sts. 530/623–5284 Museum free; guided tour $3 Wed.–Sun. 10–5; last tour at 4.*

Trinity County Courthouse (✉ *Court and Main Sts.*), built in 1856 as a store, office building, and hotel, was converted to county use in 1865. The Apollo Saloon, in the basement, became the county jail. It's the oldest courthouse still in use in California.

★ **Trinity County Historical Park** houses the **Jake Jackson Memorial Museum,** which has a blacksmith shop, a stamp mill (where ore is crushed) from the 1890s that is still in use, and the original jail cells of the Trinity County Courthouse. ✉ *508 Main St.* ☎ *530/623–5211* ⏲ *Late Apr.–Oct., daily 10–5; Nov. and Dec., daily noon–4; Jan.–late Apr., Tues. and Sat. noon–4.*

WHERE TO EAT AND STAY

$–$$$ AMERICAN **La Grange Café.** In two brick buildings dating from the 1850s (they're among the oldest edifices in town), this eatery serves buffalo and other game meats, pasta, fresh fish, and farmers' market vegetables when they're available. There's a full premium bar, and an extensive wine list. ✉ *520 Main St.* ☎ *530/623–5325* ▭ *AE, D, MC, V* ⏲ *No lunch Sun.*

¢ **Red Hill Motel.** This 1940s-era property is popular with anglers, who appreciate the outdoor fish-cleaning area on the premises. The separate wooden lodgings, painted red and surrounded by pine trees, encircle a grassy knoll. One cozy cabin with full kitchen is good for families; two others have kitchenettes, and three have mini-refrigerators and microwaves. **Pros:** close to popular bass fishing sites; inexpensive. **Cons:** older facility. ✉ *Red Hill Rd.* ☎ *530/623–4331* *4 rooms, 6 cabins, 2 duplexes* *In-room: kitchen (some), refrigerator (some)* ▭ *AE, D, MC, V.*

SPORTS AND THE OUTDOORS

Below the Lewiston Dam, east of Weaverville on Highway 299, is the **Fly Stretch** of the Trinity River, an excellent fly-fishing area. The **Pine Cove Boat Ramp,** on Lewiston Lake, provides fishing access for anglers with disabilities—decks here are built over prime trout-fishing waters. Contact the **Weaverville Ranger Station** (✉ *210 Main St.* ☎ *530/623–2121*) for maps and information about hiking trails in the Trinity Alps Wilderness.

LAKE SHASTA AREA

★ *12 mi north of Redding on I–5.*

Twenty-one types of fish inhabit **Lake Shasta,** including rainbow trout and salmon. The lake region also has the largest nesting population of bald eagles in California. You can rent fishing boats, ski boats, sailboats, canoes, paddleboats, Jet Skis, and windsurfing boards at one of the many marinas and resorts along the 370-mi shoreline.

ESSENTIALS

Visitor Information **Shasta Cascade Wonderland Association** (✉ *1699 Hwy. 273, Anderson* ☎ *530/365–7500 or 800/474–2782* 🌐 *www.shastacascade.org*).

EXPLORING

Stalagmites, stalactites, flowstone deposits, and crystals entice people of all ages to the **Lake Shasta Caverns.** To see this impressive spectacle you must take the two-hour tour, which includes a catamaran ride across the

McCloud arm of Lake Shasta and a bus ride up Grey Rock Mountain to the cavern entrance. The caverns are 58°F year-round, making them a cool retreat on a hot summer day. The most awe-inspiring of the limestone rock formations is the glistening Cathedral Room, which appears to be gilded. During peak summer months (June through August) tours depart every half hour; in April, May, and September it's every hour. A gift shop is open from 8 to 4:30. ✉*Shasta Caverns Rd. exit off I–5* ☎*530/238–2341 or 800/795–2283* 🌐*www.lakeshastacaverns.com* *$21* ⏲*June–Aug., daily 9–4 with departures every ½ hr; Apr., May, and Sept., daily 9–3 with departures every hr; Oct.–Mar., daily 10–2 with departures every 2 hrs.*

★ **Shasta Dam** is the second-largest concrete dam in the United States (only Grand Coulee in Washington is bigger). On clear days snowcapped Mt. Shasta glimmers on the horizon above the still waters of its namesake lake. The visitor center has computerized photographic tours of the dam construction, video presentations, fact sheets, and historical displays. Hour-long guided tours take visitors inside the dam and its powerhouse. ✉*16349 Shasta Dam Blvd.* ☎*530/275–4463* 🌐*www.usbr.gov/mp/ncao* ⏲*Visitor center daily 8–5; call for tour times.*

14

WHERE TO EAT

$–$$$ SEAFOOD ✕**Tail o' the Whale.** As its name suggests, this restaurant has a nautical theme. You can enjoy a panoramic view of Lake Shasta here while you savor house specials like prawns with fettuccine in a garlic cream sauce, or prime rib with tempura shrimp. This is a favorite spot for boaters, who anchor at a courtesy dock while they're dining. ✉*10300 Bridge Bay Rd., Bridge Bay exit off I–5* ☎*530/275–3021* ▭*D, MC, V.*

SPORTS AND THE OUTDOORS

FISHING **The Fishin' Hole** (✉*3844 Shasta Dam Blvd., Shasta Lake City* ☎*530/275–4123*) is a bait-and-tackle shop a couple of miles from the lake. It sells fishing licenses and provides information about conditions.

HOUSEBOATING Houseboats here come in all sizes except small. As a rule, rentals are outfitted with cooking utensils, dishes, and most of the equipment you'll need—all you supply are the food and the linens. When you rent a houseboat, you receive a short course in how to maneuver your launch before you set out. You can fish, swim, sunbathe on the flat roof, or sit on the deck and watch the world go by. The shoreline of Lake Shasta is beautifully ragged, with countless inlets; it's not hard to find privacy. Expect to spend a minimum of $350 a day for a craft that sleeps six. A three-day, two-night minimum is customary. Prices are often lower during the off-season (September through May). The **Shasta Cascade Wonderland Association** (✉*1699 Hwy. 273, Anderson* ☎*530/365–7500 or 800/474–2782* 🌐*www.shastacascade.com*) provides names of rental companies and prices for Lake Shasta houseboating. **Bridge Bay Resort** (✉*10300 Bridge Bay Rd., Redding* ☎*800/752–9669*) rents houseboats, fishing boats, and patio boats.

DUNSMUIR

10 mi south of Mt. Shasta on I–5.

Castle Crags State Park surrounds the town of Dunsmuir, which was named for a 19th-century Scottish coal baron who offered to build a fountain if the town was renamed in his honor. The town's other major attraction is the Railroad Park Resort, where you can spend the night in restored railcars.

> **FINE FISHING**
>
> The upper Sacramento River near Dunsmuir is consistently rated one of the best fishing spots in the country. Check with the chamber of commerce for local fishing guides.

EXPLORING

★ Named for its 6,000-foot glacier-polished crags, which tower over the Sacramento River, **Castle Crags State Park** offers fishing in Castle Creek, hiking in the backcountry, and a view of Mt. Shasta. The crags draw climbers and hikers from around the world. The 4,350-acre park has 28 mi of hiking trails, including a 2.75-mi access trail to **Castle Crags Wilderness,** part of the **Shasta-Trinity National Forest.** There are excellent trails at lower altitudes, along with picnic areas, restrooms, showers, and campsites. ⌧*6 mi south of Dunsmuir, Castella/Castle Crags exit off I–5; follow for ¼ mi* ☎*530/235–2684* *$6 per vehicle, day use.*

WHERE TO EAT AND STAY

$–$$$ MEDITERRANEAN **Café Maddalena.** Café Maddalena serves an adventurous Mediterranean menu with a French influence that draws in diners from nearby mountain communities and as far away as Redding. Selections change seasonally but always feature a vegetarian offering along with fresh fish and meat entrées like crispy cod in a chickpea crust, and lamb chops with Moroccan stuffed eggplant and spiced tomato sauce. Wines from Spain, Italy, and France complement the meals. ⌧*5801 Sacramento Ave.* ☎*530/235–2725* *AE, D, MC, V* *Closed Mon.–Wed. and Jan. No lunch.*

$–$$ **Railroad Park Resort.** The antique cabooses here were collected over more than three decades and have been converted into cozy motel rooms in honor of Dunsmuir's railroad legacy. The resort has a vaguely *Orient Express*–style dining room and a lounge fashioned from vintage railcars. A creek runs next to the landscaped grounds, where you'll find a huge steam engine, a restored water tower, and a spectacular view of Castle Crags. There's also an RV park and campground. **Pros:** gorgeous setting; kitschy fun. **Cons:** cabooses can feel cramped; restaurant open mid-April through September. ⌧*100 Railroad Park Rd.* ☎*530/235–4440 or 800/974–7245* *www.rrpark.com* *23 cabooses, 4 cabins* *In-room: kitchen (some), refrigerator. In-hotel: restaurant, pool, some pets allowed* *MC, V.*

MT. SHASTA

34 mi north of Lake Shasta on I–5.

The crown jewel of the 2.5-million-acre Shasta-Trinity National Forest, Mt. Shasta, a 14,162-foot-high dormant volcano, is a mecca for day hikers. It's especially enticing in spring, when fragrant Shasta lilies and other flowers adorn the rocky slopes. The paved road reaches only as far as the timberline; the final 6,000 feet are a tough climb of rubble, ice, and snow (the summit is perpetually ice packed). Only a hardy few are qualified to make the trek to the top.

The town of Mt. Shasta has real character and some fine restaurants. Lovers of the outdoors and backcountry skiers abound, and they are more than willing to offer advice on the most beautiful spots in the region, which include out-of-the-way swimming holes, dozens of high mountain lakes, and a challenging 18-hole golf course with 360 degrees of spectacular views.

ESSENTIALS

Visitor Information **Siskiyou County Visitors Bureau** (*⊠300 Pine St., Mt. Shasta ☎530/926–3850 or 800/926–4865 ⊕www.visitsiskiyou.org*).

WHERE TO EAT AND STAY

$$–$$$ ECLECTIC ✕**Lilys.** This restaurant in a white-clapboard home, framed by a picket fence and arched trellis, serves everything from steaks and pastas to Mexican and vegetarian dishes. Daily specials include prime rib and a fresh fish entrée. For innovative vegetarian fare try a roasted eggplant hoagie with three cheeses, or a dhal burger made with walnuts, fresh veggies, garbanzo beans, and rice. *⊠1013 S. Mt. Shasta Blvd. ☎530/926–3372 ▭AE, D, MC, V.*

¢ CAFÉ ✕**Seven Suns Coffee and Cafe.** A favorite gathering spot for locals, this small coffee shop serves specialty wraps for breakfast and lunch, plus soup and salad selections. Pastries, made daily, include muffins and scones, and blackberry fruit bars in season. If the weather's nice, grab a seat on the patio. *⊠1011 S. Mt. Shasta Blvd. ☎530/926–9701 ▭AE, MC, V.*

$$–$$$ ★ **Mount Shasta Resort.** Private chalets are nestled among tall pine trees along the shore of Lake Siskiyou, all with gas-log fireplaces and full kitchens. The resort's Highland House Restaurant, above the clubhouse of a spectacular 18-hole golf course, has uninterrupted views of Mt. Shasta. Large steaks and prawn dishes are menu highlights at the restaurant. Take the Central Mount Shasta exit west from I–5, then go south on Old Stage Road. **Pros:** incredible views; romantic woodsy setting. **Cons:** kids may get bored. *⊠1000 Siskiyou Lake Blvd. 96067 ☎530/926–3030 or 800/958–3363 ⊕www.mountshastaresort.com ⇆65 units ♿In-room: kitchen (some), refrigerator (some). In-hotel: restaurant, bar, golf course, spa ▭AE, MC, V.*

SPORTS AND THE OUTDOORS

HIKING The **Forest Service Ranger Station** (*☎530/926–4511 or 530/926–9613*) keeps tabs on trail conditions and gives avalanche reports.

MOUNTAIN CLIMBING **Fifth Season Mountaineering Shop** (*⊠300 N. Mt. Shasta Blvd. ☎530/926–3606 or 530/926–5555*) rents skiing and climbing equipment and operates a recorded 24-hour climber-skier report. **Shasta Mountain Guides** (*☎530/926–3117 ⊕www.shastaguides.com*) leads hiking, climbing, and ski-touring groups to the summit of Mt. Shasta.

SKIING On the southeast flank of Mt. Shasta, **Mt. Shasta Board & Ski Park** has three triple-chair lifts and one surface lift on 425 skiable acres. It's a great place for novices because three-quarters of the trails are for beginning or intermediate skiers. The area's vertical drop is 1,390 feet, with a top elevation of 6,600 feet. The longest of the 32 trails is 1.75 mi. A package for beginners, available through the ski school, includes a lift ticket, ski rental, and a lesson. The school also runs ski and snowboard programs for children. There's night skiing for those who want to see the moon rise as they schuss. The base lodge has a simple café, a ski shop, and a ski-snowboard rental shop. The **Mt. Shasta Nordic Center,** with 25 km (15 mi) of groomed cross-country trails, is on the same road. ✉ *Hwy. 89 exit east from I–5, south of Mt. Shasta* ☎ *530/926–8610 or 800/754–7427, 530/926–2142 Mt. Shasta Nordic Center* 🌐 *www.skipark.com; www.mtshastanordic.org* ⏲ *Winter ski season schedule: Sun.–Tues. 9–4, Wed.–Sat. 9–9.*

THE BACKCOUNTRY

MCARTHUR–BURNEY FALLS MEMORIAL STATE PARK

Fodor'sChoice ★

Hwy. 89, 52 mi southeast of Mt. Shasta and 41 mi north of Lassen Volcanic National Park.

Just inside the park's southern boundary, Burney Creek wells up from the ground and divides into two falls that cascade over a 129-foot cliff into a pool below. Countless ribbonlike streams pour from hidden moss-covered crevices; resident bald eagles are frequently seen soaring overhead. You can walk a self-guided nature trail that descends to the foot of the falls, which Theodore Roosevelt—according to legend—called "the eighth wonder of the world." You can also swim at Lake Britton; lounge on the beach; rent motorboats, paddleboats, and canoes; or relax at one of the campsites or picnic areas. The camp store is open from early May to the end of October. ✉ *24898 Hwy. 89, Burney* ☎ *530/335–2777* 🎟 *$6 per vehicle, day use.*

ALTURAS

86 mi northeast of McArthur–Burney Falls Memorial State Park on Hwy. 299.

Alturas is the county seat and largest town in northeastern California's Modoc County. The Dorris family arrived in the area in 1874, built Dorris Bridge over the Pit River, and later opened a small wayside stop for travelers. Today the Alturas area is a land of few people but much rugged natural beauty. Travelers come to see eagles and other wildlife, the Modoc National Forest, and active geothermal areas.

ESSENTIALS

Visitor Information **Alturas Chamber of Commerce** (✉ *522 S. Main St., Alturas* ☎ *530/233–4434* 🌐 *www.alturaschamber.org*).

DID YOU KNOW?

President Theodore Roosevelt supposedly called McArthur–Burney Falls "the eighth wonder of the world."

EXPLORING

Modoc National Forest encompasses 1.6 million acres and protects 300 species of wildlife, including Rocky Mountain elk, wild horses, mule deer, and pronghorn antelope. In spring and fall, watch for migratory waterfowl as they make their way along the Pacific Flyway above the forest. Hiking trails lead to Petroglyph Point, one of the largest panels of rock art in the United States. ✉*800 W. 12th St.* ☎*530/233–5811.*

Established to protect migratory waterfowl, the 6,280-acre **Modoc National Wildlife Refuge** gives refuge to Canada geese, sandhill cranes, mallards, teal, wigeon, pintail, white pelicans, cormorants, and snowy egrets. The refuge is open for hiking, bird-watching, and photography, but one area is set aside for hunters. Regulations vary according to season. ✉*1½ mi south of Alturas on Hwy. 395* ☎*530/233–3572* *Free* *Daily dawn–dusk.*

WHERE TO EAT

$$ SPANISH **Brass Rail.** This authentic Basque restaurant offers hearty dinners at fixed prices that include wine, homemade bread, soup, salad, side dishes, coffee, and ice cream. Steak, lamb chops, fried chicken, shrimp, and scallops are among the best entrée selections. A full bar and lounge adjoin the dining area. ✉*395 Lakeview Hwy.* ☎*530/233–2906* *MC, V* *Closed Mon. No lunch Sat.*

SUSANVILLE

104 mi south of Alturas via Rte. 395; 65 mi east of Lassen Volcanic National Park via Hwy. 36.

Susanville tells the tale of its rich history through murals painted on buildings in the historic uptown area. Established as a trading post in 1854, it's the second-oldest town in the western Great Basin. You can take a self-guided tour around the original buildings and stop for a bite at one of the restaurants now housed within them; or, if you'd rather work up a sweat, you can hit the Bizz Johnson Trail and Eagle Lake recreation areas just outside of town.

ESSENTIALS

Visitor Information Lassen County Chamber of Commerce (✉*601 Richmond Rd., Susanville* ☎*530/257–4323* *lassencountychamber.org*).

EXPLORING

Bizz Johnson Trail follows a defunct line of the Southern Pacific Railroad for 25 mi. Known to locals as the Bizz, the trail is open for hikers, walkers, mountain bikers, horseback riders, and cross-country skiers. It skirts the Susan River through a scenic landscape of canyons, bridges, and forests abundant with wildlife. ✉*Trailhead: 601 Richmond Rd.* ☎*530/257–0456* *www.blm.gov/ca/eaglelake/bizztrail.html* *Free.*

Anglers travel great distances to fish the waters of **Eagle Lake**, the second largest freshwater lake wholly in California. The Eagle Lake rainbow trout is prized for its size and fighting ability. Surrounded by high desert to the north and alpine forests to the south, the lake is also popular for picnicking, hiking, boating, waterskiing and windsurfing, and bird-watching—ospreys, pelicans, western grebes, and many other waterfowl visit the lake. On land you might see mule deer, small mammals, and even pronghorn antelope—and be sure to watch for bald eagle nesting sites. ✉*20 mi north of Susanville on Eagle Lake Rd.* ☎*530/257–0456 for Eagle Lake Recreation Area, 530/825–3454 for Eagle Lake Marina* 🌐*www.blm.gov/ca/eaglelake*

WHERE TO EAT AND STAY

¢–$ MEXICAN ✕ **Mazatlan Grill.** The sauces and tortillas are prepared on-site in this friendly, family-run restaurant and lounge, which serves lunch and dinner daily. The dining room is simple and tidy, with comfortable upholstered booths. The extensive menu offers authentic, inexpensive Mexican fare ranging from fajitas and enchiladas to a vegetarian burrito. ✉*1535 Main St.* ☎*530/257–1800* ▭*D, MC, V.*

¢–$ **High Country Inn.** Rooms are spacious in this two-story, colonial-style motel on the east edge of town. Complimentary continental breakfast is provided; more extensive dining is available next door at the Sage Hen restaurant. **Pros:** great mountain views; continental breakfast. **Cons:** must drive to town's historic center. ✉*3015 Riverside Dr. 96130* ☎*530/257–3450* 🌐*www.high-country-inn.com* *66 rooms* *In-room: refrigerator, Internet (some), Wi-Fi. In-hotel: pool, gym, Wi-Fi, no-smoking rooms* ▭*AE, D, MC, V* *CP.*

14

LASSEN VOLCANIC NATIONAL PARK

Fodor'sChoice ★ *45 mi east of Redding on Hwy. 44; 48 mi east of Red Bluff on Hwy. 36.*

A dormant plug dome, Lassen Peak is the focus of Lassen Volcanic National Park's 165.6 square mi of distinctive landscape. The peak began erupting in May 1914, sending pumice, rock, and snow thundering down the mountain and gas and hot ash billowing into the atmosphere. Lassen's most spectacular outburst occurred in 1915, when it blew a cloud of ash some 7 mi into the stratosphere. The resulting mudflow destroyed vegetation for miles in some directions; the evidence is still visible today, especially in Devastated Area. The volcano finally came to rest in 1921. Now fumaroles, mud pots, lakes, and bubbling hot springs create a fascinating but dangerous landscape that can be viewed throughout the park, especially via a hiked descent into Bumpass Hell. Because of its significance as a volcanic landscape, Lassen became a national park in 1916. Several volcanoes—the largest of which is now Lassen Peak—have been active in the area for roughly 600,000 years. The four types of volcanoes found in the world are represented in the park, including shield (Prospect Peak), plug dome (Lassen Peak), cinder cone (Cinder Cone), and composite (Brokeoff Volcano). Lassen Park Road (the continuation of Highway 89 within the park) and 150 mi of hiking trails provide access to many of these volcanic wonders. Caution is key here: signs warn visitors to stay on the trails and railed boardwalks to avoid falling into boiling water or through dangerous thin-crusted areas of the park. Although the park is closed to cars in winter, it's usually open to intrepid cross-country skiers and snowshoers. The Kohm Yah-mah-nee Visitor Center, at the southwest entrance to the park, is open year-round.

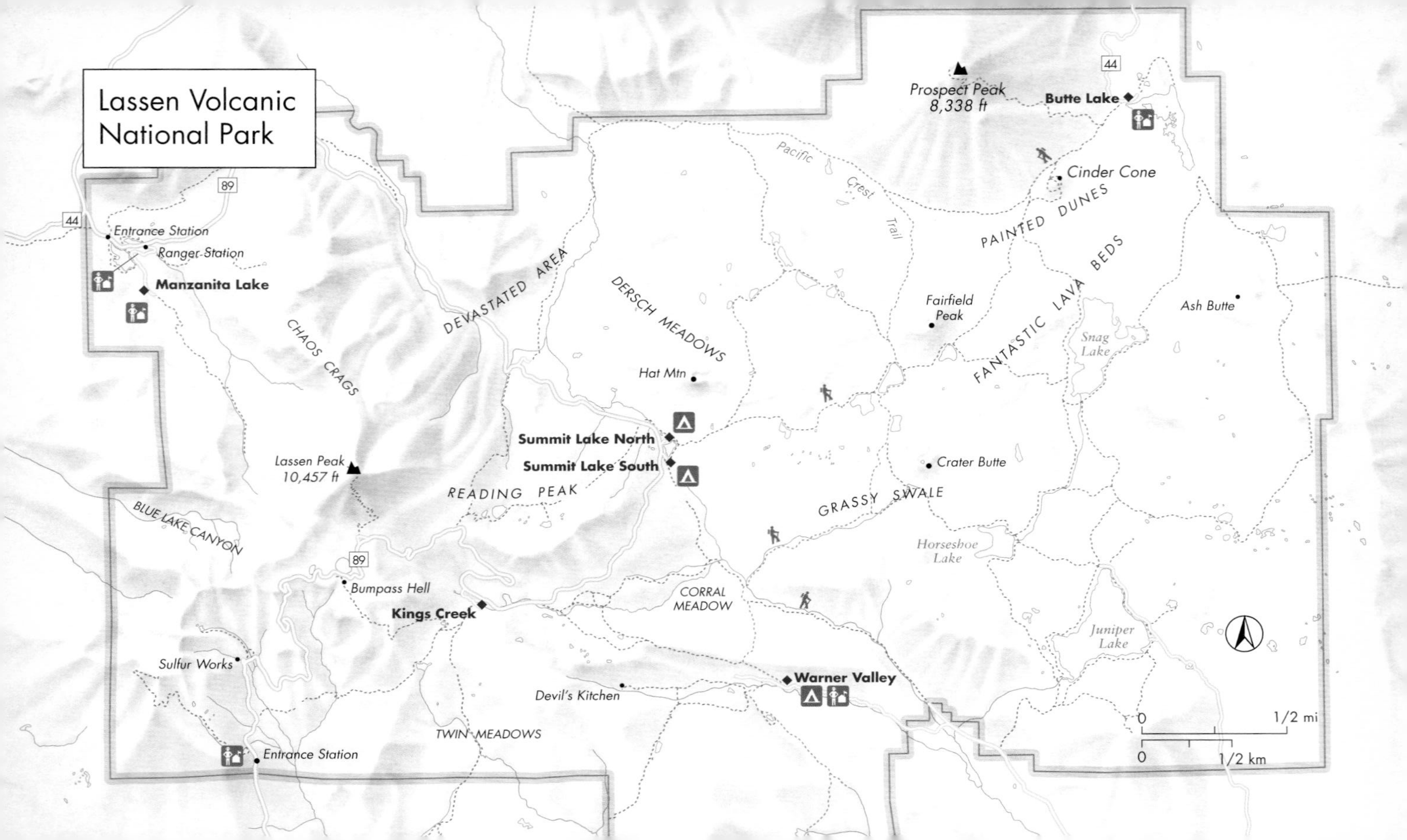
Lassen Volcanic National Park
89
44
Entrance Station
Ranger Station
Manzanita Lake
CHAOS CRAGS
DEVASTATED AREA
DERSCH MEADOWS
Hat Mtn
Summit Lake North
Summit Lake South
Lassen Peak
10,457 ft
READING PEAK
BLUE LAKE CANYON
89
Bumpass Hell
Kings Creek
CORRAL MEADOW
Sulfur Works
Devil's Kitchen
Warner Valley
TWIN MEADOWS
Entrance Station
Prospect Peak
8,338 ft
44
Butte Lake
Cinder Cone
Pacific Crest Trail
PAINTED DUNES
FANTASTIC LAVA BEDS
Fairfield Peak
Ash Butte
Snag Lake
Crater Butte
GRASSY SWALE
Horseshoe Lake
Juniper Lake
0
1/2 mi
0
1/2 km

EXPLORING

Sulphur Works Thermal Area. Proof of Lassen Peak's volatility becomes evident shortly after you enter the park at the southwest entrance. Boardwalks take you over bubbling mud and boiling springs and through sulfur-emitting steam vents. ✉ *Lassen Park Rd., 1 mi from the* Kohm Yah-mah-nee Visitor Center.

Lassen Peak Hike. This trail winds 2½ mi to the mountaintop. It's a tough climb—2,000 feet uphill on a steady, steep grade—but the reward is a spectacular view. At the peak you can see into the rim and view the entire park (and much of the far north). Bring sunscreen, water, and a jacket, since it's often windy and much cooler at the summit. ✉ *Lassen Park Rd., 7 mi north of the southwest entrance station.*

14

Lassen Scenic Byway. Beginning in Chester, this 185-mi scenic drive loops through the forests, volcanic peaks, geothermal springs, and lava fields of Lassen National Forest and Lassen National Park. It's an all-day excursion into dramatic wilderness; the road goes through the park and Lassen National Forest, veers southeast toward Susanville, then cuts west to make a loop around Lake Almanor before ending in Chester. The road is partially inaccessible in winter; call the Almanor Ranger District headquarters or Caltrans for current road conditions. From Chester, take Route 36 west to Route 89 north through the park (subject to closures due to snow), then Route 44 east to Route 36 west. Optionally, at Route 147, cut south to loop around Lake Almanor, and return to Route 89 north; at Route 36, turn east to return to Chester. ☎ *530/258–2141 Almanor Ranger District, 800/427–7623 Caltrans.*

Bumpass Hell Trail. Boiling springs, steam vents, and mud pots are featured on this 3½-mi round-trip hike. There's an overall descent of 700 feet from the parking lot to the base of the area. Expect to spend about three hours to do the loop. ✉ *Lassen Park Rd., 6 mi from the southwest entrance station.*

Hot Rock. This 400-ton boulder tumbled down from the summit during the volcano's active period and was still hot to the touch when locals discovered it nearly two days later. Although it's cool now, it's still an impressive sight. ✉ *Lassen Park Rd., 7 mi south of northwest entrance station.*

Chaos Jumbles. More than 350 years ago an avalanche from the Chaos Crags lava domes scattered hundreds of thousands of rocks—many of them 2 to 3 feet in diameter—over a couple of square miles. ✉ *Lassen Park Rd., 2 mi north of the northwest entrance station.*

WHERE TO STAY

$$$$ **Drakesbad Guest Ranch.** Situated at an elevation of 5,700 feet, this guest ranch is near Lassen Volcanic National Park's southern border. (It can't be reached from within the park; however, it's accessible only by a partially paved road leading out of the town of Chester.) Everything about this more-than-100-year-old property is rustic, from the comfortable furnishings to the propane furnaces, to the kerosene lamps in lieu of electricity. Meals, casual during the day and rather elegant in the evening, are included in the room rate. The ranch begins taking reservations in mid-February for the summer season. **Pros:** a true back-to-nature experience; great for family adventures. **Cons:** difficult to get a

Lassen Volcanic National Park's King Creek Falls Hike, which takes you through forests and meadows dotted with wildflowers, is a good hike for nature photographers.

reservation; no Internet access. ✉ *Chester–Warner Valley Rd., north from Hwy. 36* *Booking office: 2150 N. Main St., Suite 5, Red Bluff 96080* ☎ *530/529–1512* 🌐 *www.drakesbad.com* *19 rooms* *In-hotel: restaurant, pool* *D, MC, V* *Closed early Oct.–early June* *FAP.*

$$ **Manzanita Lake Campground.** The largest of Lassen Volcanic National Park's eight campgrounds is near the northern entrance. This family-friendly site has showers and a camp store, and can accommodate vehicles up to 35 feet. Most ranger programs begin here or at nearby Loomis Museum. A trail near the campground leads east to a crater that now holds Crags Lake. Summer reservations for group campgrounds can be made up to seven months in advance. There is no running water from the end of September until snow closes the campground. ✉ *Off Lassen Park Rd., 2 mi east of junction of Hwys. 44 and 89* ☎ *530/595–4444* 🌐 *www.recreation.gov* *148 tent/RV sites, no hookups; 31 tent sites* *Flush toilets, dump station, drinking water, showers, fire pits, picnic tables* *D, MC, V* *Mid-May–late Oct., depending on snowfall.*

CHESTER

36 mi west of Susanville on Hwy 36.

The population of this small town on Lake Almanor swells from 2,500 to nearly 5,000 in summer as tourists come to visit. It serves as a gateway to Lassen Volcanic National Park.

ESSENTIALS

Visitor Information **Chester–Lake Almanor Chamber of Commerce** (✉ *529 Main St., Chester* ☎ *530/258–2426 or 800/350–4838* 🌐 *www.chester-lakealmanor.com*).

EXPLORING

Lake Almanor's 52 mi of shoreline lie in the shadow of Mt. Lassen, and are popular with campers, swimmers, water-skiers, and anglers. At an elevation of 4,500 feet, the lake warms to above 70°F for about eight weeks in summer. Information is available at the Chester–Lake Almanor Chamber of Commerce. ✉ *900 W. Hwy. 36* ☎ *530/258–2426* ⏲ *Mid-May–mid-Oct.*

WHERE TO EAT AND STAY

¢–$$ AMERICAN ✕ **Kopper Kettle Cafe.** Locals return again and again to this coffee shop–style restaurant that serves savory home-cooked lunch and dinner, and breakfast whenever you've got a hankering for eggs with biscuits and gravy or other morning fare. A junior-senior menu and beer and wine are available. The patio is open in summer. ✉ *243 Main St.* ☎ *530/258–2698* ▭ *MC, V.*

¢–$ MEXICAN ✕ **Maria and Walker's Mexican Restaurant.** A festive atmosphere prevails in this family-friendly restaurant and lounge, where traditional south-of-the-border fare is served. Lunch specials and children's plates are available. It's one of the few restaurants in the area with a full bar, a great place to enjoy a margarita at the end of a long day spent hiking. ✉ *159 Main St.* ☎ *530/258–2262* ▭ *D, MC, V*

$–$$ **Best Western Rose Quartz Inn.** Down the road from Lake Almanor and close to Lassen Volcanic National Park, this small-town inn with its modern, wired rooms lets you venture into the wilderness and stay in touch with cyberspace. A large parking area accommodates motor homes and fishing boats. **Pros:** near Lake Almanor and Lassen Park; modern conveniences in a rural setting. **Cons:** on the pricey side. ✉ *306 Main St., Chester* ☎ *530/258–2002 or 888/571–4885* ⊕ *www.bestwesterncalifornia.com* *50 rooms* *In-room: Internet. In-hotel: gym, Internet terminal, no-smoking rooms* ▭ *AE, D, MC, V* *CP.*

¢–$$ ★ **Bidwell House.** This 1901 ranch house sits on 2 acres of cottonwood-studded lawns and gardens, and has views of Lake Almanor and Mt. Lassen. Chairs and swings make the front porch inviting, and there are plenty of puzzles and games in the sunroom. Some rooms have wood-burning stoves, claw-foot or Jacuzzi tubs, hardwood floors, and antiques. A separate cottage, which sleeps six, has a kitchen. The inn's three-course gourmet breakfast features blueberry-walnut pancakes. **Pros:** unique decor in each room; standout breakfast. **Cons:** not ideal for kids. ✉ *1 Main St. 96020* ☎ *530/258–3338* ⊕ *www.bidwellhouse.com* *14 rooms, 2 with shared bath* *In-room: no a/c, no phone (some), Wi-Fi. In-hotel: Wi-Fi, no-smoking rooms* ▭ *MC, V* *BP.*

QUINCY

67 mi southwest of Susanville via Hwys. 36 and 89.

A center for mining and logging in the 1850s, Quincy is nestled against the western slope of the Sierra Nevada. The county seat and largest community in Plumas County, the town is rich in historic buildings that have been the focus of preservation and restoration efforts. The four-story courthouse on Main Street, one of several stops on a self-guided tour, was built in 1921 with marble posts and staircases. The arts are thriving in Quincy, too: catch one of the plays or bluegrass performances at the Town Hall Theatre.

ESSENTIALS

Visitor Information **Plumas County Visitors Bureau** (✉550 Crescent St., Quincy ☎530/283–6345 or 800/326–2247 🌐www.plumascounty.org). **Quincy Chamber of Commerce** (✉464 Main St., Quincy ☎530/283–0188 🌐www.quincychamber.com).

EXPLORING

The main recreational attraction in central Plumas County, **Bucks Lake Recreation Area** is 17 mi southwest of Quincy at 5,200 feet. During warm months the lake's 17-mi shoreline, two marinas, and eight campgrounds attract anglers and water-sports enthusiasts. Trails through the tall pines beckon hikers and horseback riders. In winter much of the area remains open for snowmobiling and cross-country skiing. *✉Bucks Lake Rd. ☎800/326–2247 🌐www.plumascounty.org.*

Plumas County is known for its wide-open spaces, and the 1.2-million-acre **Plumas National Forest,** with its high alpine lakes and crystal-clear woodland streams, is a beautiful example. Hundreds of campsites are maintained in the forest, and picnic areas and hiking trails abound. You can enter the forest from numerous sites along highways 70 and 89. *✉159 Lawrence St. ☎530/283–2050 ⊙U.S. Forest Service office weekdays 8–4:30.*

The cultural, home arts, and industrial history displays at the **Plumas County Museum** contain artifacts dating to the 1850s. Highlights include collections of Maidu Indian basketry, pioneer weapons, and rooms depicting life in the early days of Plumas County. There are a blacksmith shop and gold-mining cabin, equipment from the early days of logging, a restored buggy, and railroad and mining exhibits. *✉500 Jackson St. ☎530/283–6320 $2 ⊙Tues.–Sat. 8–5.*

WHERE TO EAT AND STAY

$–$$$ ITALIAN ✕**Moon's.** This restored 1930 building houses a restaurant that serves such delights as honey-almond chicken, eggplant parmigiana, calamari, and Tuscan pasta. Sauces, salad dressings, pastas, breads, and desserts are all made from scratch. A verdant garden patio adds to Moon's allure. *✉497 Lawrence St. ☎530/283–0765 ▭AE, MC, V ⊙Closed Mon. No lunch.*

$–$$ ★ **Ada's Place.** This place is actually four cottages, secluded on a quiet street one block from the county courthouse and downtown Quincy. Each is decorated with a different motif—Ruth's Garden has floral accents, while the serene Hop Sing's (which has lovely wood floors) has Oriental-art details—and each has a private yard or deck and a full kitchen. **Pros:** on-site owners' meticulous upkeep. **Cons:** a bit pricey. *✉562 Jackson St. 95971 ☎530/283–1954 or 877/234–2327 🌐www.adasplace.com 4 cottages In-room: no a/c (some), kitchen, Wi-Fi. In-hotel: no-smoking rooms ▭MC, V.*

Travel Smart Northern California

WORD OF MOUTH

"If you are driving from SF to LA, or vice versa, consider that you will be on the coastal side of the beach route down HWY 1 if you go north to south. If you drive south to north, your car will be on the inside lane. Just a consideration for good views."

–traveldawg

www.fodors.com/community

GETTING HERE AND AROUND

Wherever you plan to go in California, getting there will likely involve driving (even if you fly). Major airports are usually far from main attractions. (In San Francisco, it's a 30-minute-plus trip between any Bay Area airport and downtown.) California's major airport hubs are LAX in Los Angeles and SFO in San Francisco, but satellite airports can be found around most major cities. When booking flights, it pays to check these locations, as you may find cheaper flights, more convenient times, and a better location in relation to your hotel. Most small cities have their own commercial airports, with connecting flights to larger cities—but service may be extremely limited, and it may be cheaper to rent a car and drive from L.A. or San Francisco.

There are two basic north–south routes in California: I–5, an interstate highway, runs inland most of the way from the Oregon border to the Mexican border; and Highway 101 hugs the coast for part of the route from Oregon to Mexico. (A slower but much more scenic option is to take California State Route 1, also referred to as Highway 1 and the Pacific Coast Highway, which winds along much of the California coast and provides an occasionally hair-raising, but breathtaking, ride.) From north to south, the state's east–west interstates are I–80, I–15, I–10, and I–8. Much of California is mountainous, and you may encounter very winding roads, frequently cliff-side, and steep mountain grades. In winter, roads crossing the Sierra east to west may close at any time due to weather, and chains may be required on these roads when they are open. Also in winter, I–5 north of Los Angeles closes during snowstorms. The flying and driving times in the following charts are best-case-scenario estimates, but know that the infamous California traffic jam can occur at any time.

FROM SAN FRANCISCO TO:	BY AIR	BY CAR
San Jose		1 hour 20 minutes
Monterey	40 minutes	2 hours 30 minutes
Los Angeles	1 hour 30 minutes	6 hours
Portland, OR	1 hour 45 minutes	10 hours
Mendocino		3 hours
Yosemite NP/ Fresno	45 minutes	4 hours
Lake Tahoe/ Reno	1 hour and 10 minutes	4 hours

AIR TRAVEL

Flying time to California is less than six hours from New York and four hours from Chicago. Travel from London to San Francisco is 11 hours and from Sydney approximately 14. Flying between San Francisco and Los Angeles takes about 90 minutes.

AIRPORTS

California's gateways are Los Angeles International Airport (LAX), San Francisco International Airport (SFO), San Diego International Airport (SAN), Sacramento International Airport (SMF), and San Jose International Airport (SJC). Oakland International Airport (OAK) is another option in the Bay Area.

Airport Information **Los Angeles International Airport** (☎ *310/646–5252* 🌐 *www.lawa.org/lax*). **Oakland International Airport** (☎ *510/563–3300* 🌐 *www.flyoakland.com*). **Sacramento International Airport** (☎ *916/929–5411* 🌐 *www.sacairports.org/int*). **San Diego International Airport** (☎ *619/400–2404* 🌐 *www.san.org*). **San Francisco International Airport** (☎ *650/761–0800* 🌐 *www.flysfo.com*). **San**

Jose International Airport (☎ *408/277-4759* 🌐 *www.sjc.org*).

FLIGHTS

United, with hubs in San Francisco and Los Angeles, has the greatest number of flights into and within California. But most national and many international airlines fly here. Southwest Airlines connects smaller cities within California, often from satellite airports near major cities.

Airline Contacts Air Canada (☎ *888/247-2262* 🌐 *www.aircanada.com*). **Alaska Airlines** (☎ *800/252-7522 or 206/433-3100* 🌐 *www.alaskaair.com*). **American Airlines** (☎ *800/433-7300* 🌐 *www.aa.com*). **ATA** (☎ *800/435-9282 or 317/282-8308* 🌐 *www.ata.com*). **British Airways** (☎ *800/247-9297* 🌐 *www.britishairways.com*). **Cathay Pacific** (☎ *800/233-2742* 🌐 *www.cathaypacific.com*). **Continental Airlines** (☎ *800/523-3273 for U.S. and Mexico reservations, 800/231-0856 for international reservations* 🌐 *www.continental.com*). **Delta Airlines** (☎ *800/221-1212 for U.S. reservations, 800/241-4141 for international reservations* 🌐 *www.delta.com*). **Japan Air Lines** (☎ *800/525-3663* 🌐 *www.japanair.com*). **JetBlue** (☎ *800/538-2583* 🌐 *www.jetblue.com*). **Midwest Airlines** (☎ *800/452-2022* 🌐 *www.midwestairlines.com*). **Northwest Airlines** (☎ *800/225-2525* 🌐 *www.nwa.com*). **Qantas** (☎ *800/227-4500* 🌐 *www.qantas.com*). **Southwest Airlines** (☎ *800/435-9792* 🌐 *www.southwest.com*). **Spirit Airlines** (☎ *800/772-7117 or 586/791-7300* 🌐 *www.spiritair.com*). **United Airlines** (☎ *800/864-8331 for U.S. reservations, 800/538-2929 for international reservations* 🌐 *www.united.com*). **US Airways** (☎ *800/428-4322 for U.S. and Canada reservations, 800/622-1015 for international reservations* 🌐 *www.usairways.com*).

BOAT TRAVEL

CRUISES

A number of major cruise lines offer trips that begin or end in California. Most voyages sail north along the Pacific Coast to Alaska or south to Mexico. One line, Cruise West, will take you from San Francisco through the Sacramento Delta and Napa Valley wine country. California cruise ports include Los Angeles, San Diego, and San Francisco.

Cruise Lines Carnival Cruise Line (☎ *305/599-2600 or 800/227-6482* 🌐 *www.carnival.com*). **Celebrity Cruises** (☎ *305/539-6000 or 800/437-3111* 🌐 *www.celebrity.com*). **Cruise West** (☎ *888/851-8133* 🌐 *www.cruisewest.com*). **Crystal Cruises** (☎ *310/785-9300 or 800/446-6620* 🌐 *www.crystalcruises.com*). **Holland America Line** (☎ *206/281-3535 or 877/932-4259* 🌐 *www.hollandamerica.com*). **Norwegian Cruise Line** (☎ *305/436-4000 or 800/327-7030* 🌐 *www.ncl.com*). **Princess Cruises** (☎ *661/753-0000 or 800/774-6237* 🌐 *www.princess.com*). **Regent Seven Seas Cruises** (☎ *954/776-6123 or 800/477-7500* 🌐 *www.rssc.com*). **Royal Caribbean International** (☎ *305/539-6000 or 800/327-6700* 🌐 *www.royalcaribbean.com*). **Silversea Cruises** (☎ *954/522-4477 or 800/722-9955* 🌐 *www.silversea.com*).

BUS TRAVEL

Greyhound is the major bus carrier in California. Regional bus service is available in metropolitan areas.

Bus Information Greyhound (☎ *800/231-2222* 🌐 *www.greyhound.com*).

CAR TRAVEL

Three major highways—I–5, U.S. 101, and Highway 1—run north–south through California. The main east–west route in Northern California is I–80.

GASOLINE

Gasoline prices in California vary widely, depending on location, oil company, and whether you buy it at a full-serve or self-serve pump. It's less expensive to buy fuel in the southern part of the state than in the north. If you're planning to travel near Nevada, you can save a bit by purchasing gas over the border. Gas stations are plentiful throughout the state. Most stay open late (24 hours along major highways and in big cities), except in rural areas, where Sunday hours are limited and where you may drive long stretches without a chance to refuel.

ROAD CONDITIONS

Rainy weather can make driving along the coast or in the mountains treacherous. Some of the smaller routes over mountain ranges and in the deserts are prone to flash flooding. When the rains are severe, coastal Highway 1 can quickly become a slippery nightmare, buffeted by strong winds and obstructed by falling debris from the cliffs above. When the weather is particularly bad, Highway 1 may be closed due to mud and rock slides.

FROM SAN FRANCISCO	TO	RTE./ DISTANCE
San Jose	Hwy. 101	50 mi
Monterey	Hwy. 101 to Hwy. 156	120 mi
Los Angeles	Hwy. 101 to Hwy. 156 to I-5	403 mi
Portland, OR	I-80 to I-505 to I-5	635 mi
Mendocino	Hwy. 1	174 mi
Yosemite NP	I-80 to I-580 to I-205 to Hwy. 120 east	184 mi
Lake Tahoe/ Reno	I-80	250 mi

Many smaller roads over the Sierra Nevada are closed in winter, and if it's snowing, tire chains may be required on routes that are open, most notably those to Yosemite and Lake Tahoe. From October through April, if it's raining along the coast, it's usually snowing at higher elevations. Consider renting a four-wheel-drive vehicle, or purchase chains before you get to the mountains. (Chains or cables generally cost $30 to $70, depending on tire size; cables are easier to apply than chains, but chains are more durable.) If you delay and purchase them in the vicinity of the chain-control area, the cost may double. Be aware that most rental-car companies prohibit chain installation on their vehicles. If you choose to risk it and do not tighten them properly, they may snap—your insurance likely will not cover any resulting damage. Uniformed chain installers on I–80 and U.S. 50 will apply them at the checkpoint for $30 or take them off for less than that. (Chain installers are independent businesspeople, not highway employees, and set their own fees. They are not allowed to sell or rent chains.) On smaller roads, you're on your own. Always carry extra clothing, blankets, water, and food when driving to the mountains in the winter, and keep your gas tank full to prevent the fuel line from freezing.

Road Conditions **Statewide Hotline** (*800/GAS-ROAD or 916/445-1534 www.dot.ca.gov/hq/roadinfo*).

Weather Conditions **National Weather Service** (*707/443-6484 northernmost California, 831/656-1725 San Francisco Bay area and central California, 775/673-8100 Reno, Lake Tahoe, and northern Sierra www.weather.gov*).

ROADSIDE EMERGENCIES

Dial 911 to report accidents on the road and to reach the police, the California Highway Patrol (CHP), or the fire department. On some rural highways and on most interstates, look for emergency phones on the side of the road.

RULES OF THE ROAD

Children under age 6 or weighing less than 60 pounds must be secured in a federally approved child passenger restraint system and ride in the back seat. Seat belts are required at all times and children must wear them regardless of where they're seated (studies show that children are safest in the rear seats). Unless otherwise indicated, right turns are allowed at red lights after you've come to a full stop. Left turns between two one-way streets are allowed at red lights after you've come to a full stop. Drivers with a blood-alcohol level higher than 0.08 who are stopped by police are subject to arrest, and police officers can detain those with a level of 0.05 if they appear impaired. California's drunk-driving laws are extremely tough—violators may have their licenses immediately suspended, pay hefty fines, and spend the night in jail. The speed limit on many interstate highways is 70 MPH; unlimited-access roads are usually 55 MPH. In cities, freeway speed limits are between 55 MPH and 65 MPH. Many city routes have commuter lanes during rush hour.

Effective July 2008, drivers 18 and older must use a hands-free device for their mobile phones while driving, while teenagers under 18 are not allowed to use mobile phones or wireless devices while driving. Smoking in a vehicle where a minor is present is an infraction. For more information refer to the Department of Motor Vehicles driver's handbook at *www.dmv.ca.gov/dmv.htm*.

CAR RENTAL

When you reserve a car, ask about cancellation penalties, taxes, drop-off charges (if you're planning to pick up the car in one city and leave it in another), and surcharges (for being under or over a certain age, for additional drivers, or for driving across state or country borders or beyond a specific distance from your point of rental). All these things can add substantially to your costs. Request car seats and extras such as GPS when you book.

Rates are sometimes—but not always—better if you book in advance or reserve through a rental agency's Web site. There are other reasons to book ahead, though: for popular destinations, during busy times of the year, or to ensure that you get certain types of cars (vans, SUVs, exotic sports cars).

TIP→ Make sure that a confirmed reservation guarantees you a car. Agencies sometimes overbook, particularly for busy weekends and holiday periods.

A car is essential in most parts of California, but in compact San Francisco it's better to use public transportation to avoid parking headaches.

Rates statewide for the least expensive vehicle begin at around $73 a day and $120 a week (though they increase rapidly from here). This does not include additional fees or tax on car rentals, which is 8.25% in San Francisco. Be sure to shop around—you can get a decent deal by carefully shopping the major car-rental companies' Web sites. Also, compare prices by city before you book, and ask about "drop charges" if you plan to return the car in a city other than the one where you rented the vehicle. If you pick up at an airport, there may also be a facility charge of as much as $12 per rental; ask when you book. When you're returning your rental, be aware that gas stations can be few and far between near airports.

In California you must have a valid driver's license and be 21 to rent a car; rates may be higher if you're under 25. Some agencies will not rent to drivers under 25; check when you book. Non-U.S. residents must have a license with text that is in the Roman alphabet that is valid for the entire rental period. Though it need not be entirely written in English, it must have English letters that clearly identify it as a driver's license. An international license is recommended but not required.

Specialty Car Agencies In San Francisco **Specialty Rentals** (*800/400-8412 www.specialtyrentals.com*)

Major Rental Agencies **Alamo** (*800/462-5266 www.alamo.com*). **Avis** (*800/331-1212 www.avis.com*). **Budget** (*800/527-0700 www.budget.com*). **Hertz** (*800/654-3131 www.hertz.com*). **National Car Rental** (*800/227-7368 www.nationalcar.com*).

TRAIN TRAVEL

One of the most beautiful train trips in the country is along the Pacific Coast from Los Angeles to Oakland via Amtrak's *Coast Starlight*, which hugs the waterfront before it turns inland at San Luis Obispo for the rest of its journey to Seattle. (Be aware that this train is frequently late arriving at and departing from Central Coast stations.) The *California Zephyr* travels from Chicago to Oakland via Denver; the *Pacific Surfliner* connects San Diego and San Luis Obispo via Los Angeles and Santa Barbara with multiple departures daily; and the *Sunset Limited* runs from Los Angeles to New Orleans via Arizona, New Mexico, and Texas.

Information **Amtrak** (☎ *800/872-7245* 🌐 *www.amtrak.com*).

ESSENTIALS

ACCOMMODATIONS

The lodgings we list are the cream of the crop in each price category. We always list the facilities that are available, but we don't specify whether they cost extra; when pricing accommodations, always ask what's included and what costs extra. ⇨ *For price information, see the planner in each chapter.*

Most hotels require you to give your credit-card details before they will confirm your reservation. If you don't feel comfortable e-mailing this information, ask if you can fax it (some places even prefer faxes). However you book, get confirmation in writing and have a copy of it handy when you check in.

■ **TIP→** Assume that hotels operate on the European Plan (EP, no meals) unless we specify that they use the Breakfast Plan (BP, with full breakfast), Continental Plan (CP, Continental breakfast), Full American Plan (FAP, all meals), or Modified American Plan (MAP, breakfast and dinner), or are all-inclusive (AI, all meals and most activities).

BED AND BREAKFASTS

California has more than 1,000 bed-and-breakfasts. You'll find everything from simple homestays to lavish luxury lodgings, many in historic hotels and homes. The California Association of Bed and Breakfast Inns has about 300 member properties that you can locate and book through their Web site.

Reservation Services **Bed & Breakfast.com** (☎ *512/322–2710 or 800/462–2632* 🌐 *www.bedandbreakfast.com*) also sends out an online newsletter. **Bed & Breakfast Inns Online** (☎ *310/280–4363 or 800/215–7365* 🌐 *www.bbonline.com*). **BnB Finder.com** (☎ *646/205–8016 or 888/547–8226* 🌐 *www.bnbfinder.com*). **California Association of Bed and Breakfast Inns** (☎ *800/373–9251* 🌐 *www.cabbi.com*).

COMMUNICATIONS

INTERNET

Internet access is widely available in California's urban areas, but it's usually more difficult to get online in the state's rural areas. Most hotels offer some kind of connection—dial-up, broadband, or Wi-Fi (which is becoming much more common). Most hotels charge a daily fee (about $10) for Internet access. Cybercafés are also located throughout California.

Contacts **Cybercafes** (🌐 *www.cybercafes.com*) lists more than 4,000 Internet cafés worldwide.

EATING OUT

California has led the pack in bringing natural and organic foods to the forefront of American cooking. Though rooted in European cuisine, California cooking sometimes has strong Asian and Latin influences. Wherever you go, you're likely to find that dishes are made with fresh produce and other local ingredients.

The restaurants we list are the cream of the crop in each price category. ⇨ *For price information, see the planner in each chapter.*

For information on food-related health issues, see Health below.

CUTTING COSTS

If you're on a budget, take advantage of the "small plates" craze sweeping California by ordering several appetizer-size portions and having a glass of wine at the bar, rather than having a full meal. Also, better grocery and specialty-food stores have grab-and-go sections, with prepared foods on par with restaurant cooking, perfect for picnicking (remember, it rarely rains between May and October). At resort areas in the off-season (such as Lake Tahoe in October and May), you can often find two-for-one dinner specials at upper-end restaurants; check local papers or with visitor bureaus.

RESERVATIONS AND DRESS

Regardless of where you are, it's a good idea to make a reservation if you can. We only mention them specifically when reservations are essential (there's no other way you'll ever get a table) or when they are not accepted. For popular restaurants, book as far ahead as you can (often 30 days), and reconfirm as soon as you arrive. (Large parties should always call ahead to check the reservations policy.) We mention dress only when men are required to wear a jacket or a jacket and tie.

Online reservation services make it easy to book a table before you even leave home. OpenTable covers most states, including 20 major cities, and has limited listings in Canada, Mexico, the United Kingdom, and elsewhere. DinnerBroker has restaurants throughout the United States as well as a few in Canada.

Contacts OpenTable (*www.opentable.com*). **DinnerBroker** (*www.dinnerbroker.com*).

WINES, BEER, AND SPIRITS

If you like wine, your trip to California won't be complete unless you sample a few of the local vintages. Throughout the state, most famously in the Napa and Sonoma valleys, you can visit wineries, many of which have tasting rooms and offer tours. Microbreweries are an emerging trend in the state's cities and in some rural areas in northern California. The legal drinking age is 21.

HEALTH

Do not fly within 24 hours of scuba diving.

Smoking is illegal in all California bars and restaurants, except on outdoor patios or in smoking rooms. This law is typically not well enforced and some restaurants and bars do not comply, so take your cues from the locals. Hotels and motels are also decreasing their inventory of smoking rooms; inquire at the time you book your reservation if any are available. In addition, a tax is added to cigarettes sold in California, and prices can be as high as $6 per pack. You might want to bring a carton from home.

MEDICAL INSURANCE AND ASSISTANCE

Consider buying trip insurance with medical-only coverage. Neither Medicare nor some private insurers cover medical expenses anywhere outside of the United States. Medical-only policies typically reimburse you for medical care (excluding that related to pre-existing conditions) and hospitalization abroad, and provide for evacuation. You still have to pay the bills and await reimbursement from the insurer, though.

Another option is to sign up with a medical-evacuation assistance company. A membership in one of these companies gets you doctor referrals, emergency evacuation or repatriation, 24-hour hotlines for medical consultation, and other assistance. International SOS Assistance Emergency and AirMed International provide evacuation services and medical referrals. MedjetAssist offers medical evacuation.

Medical Assistance Companies AirMed International (*www.airmed.com*). **International SOS Assistance Emergency** (*www.intsos.com*). **MedjetAssist** (*www.medjetassist.com*).

Medical-Only Insurers International Medical Group (*800/628–4664* *www.imglobal.com*). **International SOS** (*www.internationalsos.com*). **Wallach & Company** (*800/237–6615 or 540/687–3166* *www.wallach.com*).

HOURS OF OPERATION

Banks in California are typically open weekdays from 9 to 6 and Saturday morning; most are closed on Sunday and most holidays. Smaller shops usually operate from 10 to 6, with larger stores remaining open until 8 or later. Hours vary for museums and historical sites, and many are closed one or more days a week, or for extended periods during off-season months. It's a good idea to check before you visit a tourist site.

MONEY

San Francisco tends to be an expensive city to visit, and rates at coastal and desert resorts are almost as high. A day's admission to a major theme park can run upward of $65 a head, hotel rates average $150 to $250 a night (though you can find cheaper places), and dinners at even moderately priced restaurants often cost $20 to $40 per person. Costs in the Gold Country and the Far North are considerably less—many fine Gold Country bed-and-breakfasts charge around $100 a night, and some motels in the Far North charge $70 to $90.

Prices throughout this guide are given for adults. Reduced fees are almost always available for children, students, and senior citizens.

CREDIT CARDS

Throughout this guide, the following abbreviations are used: **AE,** American Express; **D,** Discover; **DC,** Diners Club; **MC,** MasterCard; and **V,** Visa.

It's a good idea to inform your credit-card company before you travel, especially if you're going abroad and don't travel internationally very often. Otherwise, the credit-card company might put a hold on your card owing to unusual activity—not a good thing halfway through your trip. Record all your credit-card numbers—as well as the phone numbers to call if your cards are lost or stolen—in a safe place, so you're prepared should something go wrong. Both MasterCard and Visa have general numbers you can call (collect if you're abroad) if your card is lost, but you're better off calling the number of your issuing bank, since MasterCard and Visa normally just transfer you to your bank; your bank's number is usually printed on your card.

Reporting Lost Cards American Express (*☎800/992–3404 in the U.S. or 336/393–1111 collect from abroad* *www.americanexpress.com*). **Discover** (*☎800/347–2683 in the U.S. or 801/902–3100 collect from abroad* *www.discovercard.com*). **Diners Club** (*☎800/234–6377 in the U.S. or 303/799–1504 collect from abroad* *www.dinersclub.com*). **MasterCard** (*☎800/622–7747 in the U.S. or 636/722–7111 collect from abroad* *www.mastercard.com*). **Visa** (*☎800/847–2911 in the U.S. or 410/581–9994 collect from abroad* *www.visa.com*).

SAFETY

California is a safe place to visit, as long as you take the usual precautions. In large cities ask the concierge or desk clerk to point out areas on your map that you should avoid. Lock valuables in a hotel safe when you're not using them. (Some hotels have in-room safes large enough to hold a laptop computer.) Keep an eye on your handbag when you're out in public. Security is high (but mostly invisible) at theme parks and resorts.

TIP→ Distribute your cash, credit cards, IDs, and other valuables between a deep front pocket, an inside jacket or vest pocket, and a hidden money pouch. Don't reach for the money pouch once you're in public.

TAXES

Sales tax in California varies from about 7.25% to 8.5% and applies to all purchases except for food purchased in a grocery store; food consumed in a restaurant is taxed, but take-out food purchases are not. Hotel taxes vary widely by region, from 10% to 15%.

TIME

California is in the Pacific time zone. Pacific daylight time (PDT) is in effect from early March through early November; the rest of the year the clock is set to Pacific standard time (PST).

TIPPING

Most service workers in California are fairly well paid compared to those in the rest of the country, and extravagant tipping is not the rule here. Exceptions include wealthy enclaves such as Beverly Hills, La Jolla, and San Francisco as well as the most expensive resort areas.

TIPPING GUIDELINES FOR CALIFORNIA	
Bartender	\$1–\$5 per round of drinks, depending on the number of drinks
Bellhop	\$1–\$5 per bag, depending on the level of the hotel
Hotel Concierge	\$5 or more, if he/she performs a service for you
Hotel Doorman	\$1–\$2 if he/she helps you get a cab
Valet Parking Attendant	\$1–\$2 when you get your car
Hotel Maid	\$1–\$2 per person, per day
Waiter	15%–20% (20% is standard in upscale restaurants); nothing additional if a service charge is added to the bill
Skycap at Airport	\$1–\$3 per bag
Hotel Room-Service Waiter	\$1–\$2 per delivery, even if a service charge has been added
Taxi Driver	15%–20%, but round up the fare to the next dollar amount
Tour Guide	10% of the cost of the tour

TOURS

Guided tours are a good option when you don't want to do it all yourself. You travel along with a group (sometimes large, sometimes small), stay in prebooked hotels, eat with your fellow travelers (the cost of meals sometimes included in the price of your tour, sometimes not), and follow a schedule.

But not all guided tours are an if-it's-Tuesday-this-must-be-Belgium experience. A knowledgeable guide can take you places that you might never discover on your own, and you may be pushed to see more than you would have otherwise. Tours aren't for everyone, but they can be just the thing for trips to places where making travel arrangements is difficult or time-consuming (particularly when you don't speak the language).

Whenever you book a guided tour, find out what's included and what isn't. A "land-only" tour includes all your travel (by bus, in most cases) in the destination, but not necessarily your flights to and from or even within it. Also, in most cases prices in tour brochures don't include fees and taxes. And remember that you'll be expected to tip your guide (in cash) at the end of the tour.

SPECIAL-INTEREST TOURS

BIKING

Bicycling is a popular way to see the California countryside, and commercial tours are available throughout the state. Most three- to five-day trips are all-inclusive—you'll stay in delightful country inns, dine at good regional restaurants, and follow experienced guides. The Northern California Wine Country, with its flat valley roads, is one of the most popular destinations. When booking, ask about level of difficulty, as nearly every trip will involve some hill work. Tours fill up early, so book well in advance.

TIP→ Most airlines accommodate bikes as luggage, provided they're dismantled and boxed.

Contacts **Napa and Sonoma Valley Bike Tours** (✉ *6488 Washington St., Yountville* ☎ *800/707–2453* 🌐 *www.napavalleybiketours.com*). **Bicycle Adventures** (✉ *Box 11219, Olympia, WA* ☎ *800/443–6060* 🌐 *www.bicycleadventures.com*).

INDEX

N

Photo Credits: 1, Yuen Kwan, Fodors.com member. Bryan Brazil/Shutterstock. 5, Heavenly Mountain Resort. Chapter 1: Experience California: 8-9, Jay Anderson, Fodors.com member. 11, Helio San Miguel. 12 (top), Clinton Steeds/Flickr. 12 (bottom), Jose Vigano, Fodors.com member. 13, comfortablynirm, Fodors.com member. 14, Helio San Miguel. 15, vathomp, Fodors.com member. 16, Robert Holmes. 17 (left), sd_foodies, Fodors.com member. 17 (right), Lisa M. Hamilton. 18, Warren H. White. 19, Thomas Kranzel/Venture Media. 20 (left), Christophe Testi/iStockphoto. 20 (top right), Corbis. 20 (bottom right), Warren H. White. 21 (top left), Alan A. Tobey/iStockphoto. 21 (bottom left), Janet Fullwood. 21 (right), Aaron Kohr/iStockphoto. 23, Andrew Zarivny/iStockphoto. 25, Robert Holmes. 26, yummyporky/Flickr. 27 (top and bottom), Lisa M. Hamilton. 28, John Elk III/Alamy. 29 (top), Janine Bolliger/iStockphoto. 29 (bottom), Lise Gagne/iStockphoto. 30, iStockphoto. **Chapter 2: The Central Coast:** 31, TweetieV, Fodors.com member. 32, Stephen Walls/iStockphoto. 33 (top), Bart Everett/iStockphoto. 33 (bottom), Robert Holmes. 35, David M. Schrader/Shutterstock. 36 (top right) Evan Meyer/iStock-photo. 36 (center right) Kyle Maass/iStockphoto. 36 (left) iStockphoto. 36 (bottom right) Lise Gagne/iStockpohoto. 37, Tom Baker/Shutterstock. 48, S. Greg Panosian/iStockphoto. 49, Nancy Nehring/iStockphoto. 50 (top), Richard Wong/www.rwongphoto.com/Alamy. 50 (bottom), Mats Lund/iStockphoto. 51 (top left), Witold Skrypczak/Alamy. 51 (top right), S. Greg Panosian/iStockphoto. 51 (bottom), Janet Fullwood. 52 (top left), GIPhotoStock Z/Alamy. 52 (top right), Craig Lovell/Eagle Visions Photography/Alamy. 52 (bottom) and 53 (top), S. Greg Panosian/iStockphoto. 53 (bottom), Eugene Zelenko/wikipedia.org. 57, David M. Schrader/Shutterstock. 65, Doreen Miller, Fodors.com member. 78, Robert Holmes. 92-93, Valhalla | Design & Conquer, Fodors.com member. **Chapter 3: The Monterey Bay Area:** 97, mellifluous, Fodors.com member. 98, Janet Fullwood. 99 (top), vittorio sciosia/age fotostock. 99 (bottom), Jeff Greenberg/age fotostock. 101, Brent Reeves/Shutterstock. 102 (left), SuperStock/age fotostock.102 (top right), CURAphotography/Shutterstock. 102 (bottom right), Michael Almond/iStockphoto. 103 (top), iStockphoto. 103 (bottom), Lise Gagne/iStockphoto. 108, Robert Holmes. 119, Holger Mette/iStockphoto. 125, laurel stewart/iStockphoto. **Chapter 4: San Francisco:** 143-147, Brett Shoaf/Artistic Visuals Photography. 148 (left), TebNad/Shutterstock. 148 (top right), Ross Stapleton-Gray/iStockphoto. 148 (bottom right), Jay Spooner/iStockphoto. 149 (top), Jay Spooner/iStockphoto. 149 (bottom), Lise Gagne/iStockphoto. 157, Robert Holmes. 159, Brett Shoaf/Artistic Visuals Photography. 160 (top), Arnold Genthe. 160 (bottom), Library of Congress Prints and Photographs Division. 161 (left), Sandor Balatoni/SFCVB. 161 (right), Detroit Publishing Company Collection, Photography Collection, Miriam and Ira D. Wallach Division of Art, Prints and Photographs, The New York Public Library, Astor, Lenox and Tilden Foundation. 162, Brett Shoaf/Artistic Visuals Photography. 163 (top), Gary Soup/Flickr. 163 (bottom), Albert Cheng/Shutterstock. 164 (top), Sheryl Schindler/SFCVB. 164 (center), Ronen/Shutterstock. 164 (bottom), Robert Holmes. 167, Walter Bibikow/age fotostock. 173, travelstock44/Alamy. 175, Brett Shoaf/Artistic Visuals Photography. 176, San Francisco Municipal Railway Historical Archives. 181, Lewis Sommer/SFCVB. 189, Robert Holmes. 198, aprillilacs, Fodors.com member. 203, Rafael Ramirez Lee/iStockphoto. 220, Queen Anne Hotel. 226 (top), George Apostolidis/Mandarin Oriental Hotel Group. 226 (center left), David Phelps/Argonaut Hotel. 226 (center right), Joie de Vivre Hospitality. 226 (bottom left), Starwood Hotels & Resorts. 226 (bottom right), Cris Ford/Union Street Inn. 227 (top), Rien van Rijthoven/InterContinental Hotels & Resorts. 227 (center left), Orchard Hotel. 227 (center right), Hotel Nikko San Francisco. 227 (bottom), The Ritz-Carlton, San Francisco. 234, Rough Guides/Alamy. 239, Robert Holmes. **Chapter 5: The Bay Area:** 241 and 242, Robert Holmes. 243, Jyeshern Cheng/iStockphoto. 245, Brett Shoaf/Artistic Visuals Photography. 249, Robert Holmes. 254, Mark Rasmussen/iStockphoto. 257, Robert Holmes. 261, S. Greg Panosian/iStockphoto. 269 and 277, Robert Holmes. **Chapter 6: The Wine Country:** 287, Robert Holmes. 288, iStockphoto. 289 and 290, Robert Holmes. 292, Warren H. White. 296, Robert Holmes. 297 (top), kevin miller/iStockphoto. 297 (bottom), Far Niente+Dolce+Nickel & Nickel. 298 (top and bottom) and 299 (top), Robert Holmes. 299 (bottom), star5112/Flickr. 300 (top left), Rubicon Estate. 300 (top right and bottom) and 301 (top and bottom), Robert Holmes. 302 (top), Philippe Roy/Alamy. 302 (center), Agence Images/Alamy. 302 (bottom), Cephas Picture Library/Alamy. 303 (top), Napa Valley Conference Bureau. 303 (second and third from top), Wild Horse Winery (Forrest L. Doud). 303 (fourth from top), Napa Valley Conference Bureau. 303 (fifth from top), Panther Creek Cellars (Ron Kaplan). 303 (sixth from top), Clos du Val (Marvin Collins). 303 (seventh from top), Panther Creek Cellars (Ron Kaplan). 303 (bottom), Warren H. White. 304 and 307, Robert Holmes. 317, Far Niente+Dolce+Nickel & Nickel. 319, Terry Joanis/Frog's Leap. 326, Chuck Honek/Schramsberg Vineyard. 329, Castello di Amorosa. 341 and 351, Robert Holmes. **Chapter 7: The North Coast:** 359, John Redwine, Fodors.com member. 360 (all), Robert Holmes. 361 (top), Russ Bishop/age fotostock. 361 (bottom), Robert Holmes. 363, Janet Fullwood. 369, 374, and 379, Robert Holmes. **Chapter 8: Redwood National Park:** 387, iStockphoto. 388 (top), Michael Schweppe/wikipedia.org.

388 (center), Agnieszka Szymczak/iStockphoto. 388 (bottom), Natalia Bratslavsky/Shutterstock. 391, WellyWelly/Shutterstock. **Chapter 9: The Southern Sierra:** 395, Randall Pugh, Fodors.com member. 396, Craig Cozart/iStockphoto. 397 (top), David T Gomez/iStockphoto. 397 (bottom left and bottom right), Robert Holmes. 399, christinea78, Fodors.com member. 403, moonjazz/Flickr. 410, Douglas Atmore/iStockphoto. **Chapter 10: Yosemite National Park:** 413, Sarah P. Corley, Fodors.com member. 414, Yosemite Concession Services. 415 (top), Andy Z./Shutterstock. 415 (bottom), Greg Epperson/age fotostock. 416, Thomas Barrat/Shutterstock. 417, Nicholas Roemmelt/iStockphoto. 418, Doug Lemke/ Shutterstock. 419, Paul Erickson/iStockphoto. 423, .Bala/Flickr. 424, David Safanda/iStockphoto. 430, tibchris/Flickr. 432, Eric Foltz/iStockphoto. **Chapter 11: Sequoia and Kings Canyon National Parks:** 439 and 440, Robert Holmes. 441 (top), Greg Epperson/age fotostock. 441 (bottom) and 443-455, Robert Holmes. **Chapter 12: Sacramento and the Gold Country:** 461 and 463 (top and bottom), Robert Holmes. 465, Andy Z./Shutterstock. 470, Marcin Wichary/Flickr. 475, Image Asset Management/age fotostock. 476 (left) and 476 (right), wikipedia.org. 476 (center), Charles Danek. 477, Ambient Images Inc./Alamy. 478 (top), Trailmix.Net/Flickr. 478 (center), oger jones/Flickr. 478 (bottom), L. C. McClure/ wikipedia.org. 479 (top left), Russ Bishop/age fotostock. 479 (top center), vera bogaerts/iStockphoto. 479 (top right and bottom left), Walter Bibikow/age fotostock. 479 (bottom right), Charles Danek. 484, Janet Fullwood. 490, RickC/Flickr. **Chapter 13: Lake Tahoe:** 493, Tom Zikas/North Lake Tahoe. 494 (top), Rafael Ramirez Lee/iStockphoto. 494 (bottom) and 495, Janet Fullwood. 498, Jay Spooner/ iStockphoto. 503 (top), Heavenly Mountain Resort. 503 (bottom), Jake Foster/iStockphoto. 504 (top), Lake Tahoe Visitors Authority. 504 (bottom left), iStockphoto. 504 (bottom right), Heavenly Mountain Resort. 507 and 508 (left), Andrew Zarivny/iStockphoto. 508 (right), Harry Thomas/iStockphoto. 509 (top left), Joy Strotz/Shutterstock. 509 (bottom left), iStockphoto. 509 (right), Jennifer Stone/Shutterstock. 515, Jay Spooner/iStockphoto. 522, Tom O'Neill. 533, Christopher Russell/iStockphoto. **Chapter 14: The Far North:** 541, NPS. 542 (top and bottom), Robert Holmes. 543 (top), Andy Z./ Shutterstock. 543 (bottom), NPS. 545, ThreadedThoughts/Flickr. 550, Robert Holmes. 557, kathycsus/ Flickr. 562, NPS.

ABOUT OUR WRITERS

Native Californian Cheryl Crabtree—who updated the Central Coast and Monterey Bay Area chapters and wrote On a Mission and The Ultimate Road Trip: California's Legendary Highway 1 for this edition—has worked as a freelance writer since 1987. She has contributed to *Fodor's California* since the 2003 and has also written for *Fodor's Complete Guide to the National Parks of the West*. Cheryl is editor of *Montecito Magazine*. She currently lives in Santa Barbara with her husband, two sons, and Jack Russell terrier.

Lisa M. Hamilton is a writer and photographer who focuses on food, farming, and travel. She lives in the Bay Area but would pretty much always rather be on a rocky beach somewhere along the North Coast. She updated our Bay Area, North Coast, and Redwood National Park coverage for this edition.

A Northern California resident for 15 years, Reed Parsell has traveled extensively throughout the region and written hundreds of newspaper travel stories based on his experiences. A part-time copy editor and travel writer for the *Sacramento Bee*, Parsell also writes a "going green" column for *Sacramento* magazine and was the primary writer for *Fodor's InFocus Yosemite, Sequoia and Kings Canyon National Parks*. He updated our Southern Sierra, Yosemite National Park, Sequoia and Kings Canyon National Parks, and Sacramento and the Gold Country coverage and wrote Eureka! California's Gold Rush.

Freelance writer Christine Vovakes—who updated the Far North, Lake Tahoe, and Travel Smart Northern California chapters and wrote Tahoe: A Lake for all Seasons for this edition—has also contributed to *Fodor's National Parks of the West* and *Essential USA*. Her travel articles and photographs have also appeared in many other publications, including *The Washington Post, The Christian Science Monitor, The Sacramento Bee* and the *San Francisco Chronicle*.

Bobbi Zane—who updated the Experience Northern California chapter for this edition—grew up in Southern California, watching the region grow from its mostly rural roots into one of the most exciting places in the world. Her articles on Palm Springs have appeared in the *Orange County Register* and *Westways* magazine. She recently contributed to *Fodor's Complete Guide to the National Parks of the West, Fodor's San Diego*, and *Escape to Nature Without Roughing It*. A lifelong Californian, Bobbi has visited every corner of the state on behalf of Fodor's.